Flea PRICE GUIDE TO Market Treasures

3RD EDITION

HARRY L. RINKER JR.

Wallace-Homestead Book Company
Radnor, Pennsylvania

Copyright © 1995 by Rinker Enterprises, Inc.

Third Edition   All Rights Reserved

Published in Radnor, Pennsylvania 19089, by Wallace-Homestead,
a division of Chilton Book Company

No part of this book may be reproduced, transmitted or stored
in any form or by any means, electronic or mechanical,
without prior written permission from the publisher

Designed by Anthony Jacobson
Manufactured in the United States of America

Library of Congress Cataloging in Publication Data

Rinker, Harry L., Jr.
     Price guide to flea market treasures / Harry L. Rinker, Jr.—3rd ed.
        p.   cm.
     Includes index.
     ISBN 0-87069-719-6 (pbk.)
     1. Flea markets—United States—Directories.   2. Collectibles—
Prices—United States.   3. Americana—Catalogs.   I. Title.
HF5482.M54   1995
381′.192′0296—dc20   94-40881
                                                              CIP

1 2 3 4 5 6 7 8 9 0   4 3 2 1 0 9 8 7 6 5

Contents

6 The Flea Market Scene Today   27

PART TWO: FLEA MARKET TREASURES

PART THREE: REFERENCE SOURCES

Foreword

This is the last Foreword that I plan to write for Harry Jr.'s *Price Guide to Flea Market Treasures.* Time to cut Harry Jr. loose and let him fend for himself. He has learned to swim. I no longer am concerned that he will sink, albeit, I confess that I have been tempted to drown him on more than one occasion over the years.

Harry Jr.'s pride in *Price Guide to Flea Market Treasures* continues to grow. It should. When a competitor recently published a flea market book featuring full color illustrations, Harry Jr. was ready to charge down to Radnor and demand (isn't it wonderful how the minds of the young work) that *his* book have color illustrations as well. Although I explained that the contract for the third edition called for black and white photographs, Harry Jr. did not care. He wanted color—would settle for nothing less.

Well, as you will see, Harry Jr. did not get the color that he wanted. Part of growing up is learning that you do not get everything you want, especially immediately. The positive, as far as I was concerned, is Harry Jr.'s pride in his product and his desire that it be the best, even though he focused his emphasis incorrectly.

What Harry Jr. needed to understand, and hopefully he now does, is that "best" in respect to a general price guide means quality of information, not whether or not the illustrations are in black and white or color. There is no doubt in my mind, proud father aside, that the information that you find in Harry Jr.'s *Price Guide to Flea Market Treasures* is significantly better than in any rival publication.

The information is solid and thorough. It is fresh, not stolen (like the products of some other publishers who will remain nameless) from other titles in the line. If objects are repeated, it is because they are extremely common and provide a means for those individuals with an interest in tracking market trends to do so.

Most importantly, *Price Guide to Flea Market Treasures* is geared to the market that it serves. You will find many categories in Harry Jr.'s book that do not exist in other general price guides in the market. This is because there are generally two types of goods sold at a flea market: (1) items of interest to collectors and decorators and (2) items bought for the primary purpose of reuse. A good flea market price guide includes material from both groups. Harry Jr.'s book is the only one that does.

I have attended more garage sales and flea markets in the past six months than I did during the past two years. The reason is simple. Without realizing it, I was spending so much time writing, lecturing, and teaching about the middle and high end of the market that I lost touch with my market's base and the large number of individuals involved in it.

This is a common problem with anyone involved with antiques and collectibles for an extended period of time. While a few individuals may be content to remain on the same plane, most move up as they become more advanced and sophisticated. They often forget the base on which they built. It is easy to look down and ignore. Trust me, I know.

The entire issue struck home in late March 1994 when I spent two days appraising antiques and collectibles at the Red River Valley Home and Garden Show in Fargo, North Dakota. KFGO-Radio of Fargo–Moorhead is home base for *Whatcha Got,* my weekly radio show. I was making a guest appearance on behalf of the station and the home and garden show.

While at the show, I also sold books. Along with several cases of my own books, I had a case of the second edition of *Price Guide to Flea Market Treasures.* Harry Jr.'s book sold better than mine, even though I made it quite clear to the buyers who I was and that I did not edit the book. The reason it did so well was that the buyers were from the general public, not specialized collectors and dealers. When they compared *Price Guide to Flea Market Treasures* with *Warman's Antiques and Collectibles Price Guide* and *Warman's Americana and Collectibles,* they identified more with Harry Jr.'s flea market book than they did with my price guides.

The point of the story is that the flea market and garage sale markets are huge, far larger than the collector, dealer, and decorator markets to which over ninety percent of the books about antiques and collectibles cater. Look for Harry Jr., myself, and Rinker Enterprises, Inc., to become much more active in this sector in the years ahead. *Price Guide to Flea Market Treasures* will be the keystone in a series of publications and products designed to serve this market.

This edition of *Price Guide to Flea Market Treasures* represents a first for Rinker Enterprises, Inc. Harry Jr., the staff, and I are looking forward to our first 8½-by-11-inch format book. It will be fun to see our efforts in larger type and pictures of sufficient size to show objects in detail.

The dimensions of the book are not the only major change. Harry Jr. exercised far more control over the selection of the categories for this edition than he did in the past. As mentioned in previous Forewords, any book from Rinker Enterprises, Inc., is a joint staff effort. Everyone loves working on the flea market book because of the fun that results from so much category flexibility. By their very nature, Warman titles are patterned and rigid in approach. Anything goes and does with the flea market book.

Harry Jr. has worked at Rinker Enterprises, Inc., for three years. His primary contributions remain in the area of photography. Over a dozen books, numerous newspaper and magazine articles, and several CD-ROM discs contain his images. His next big challenge is to move Rinker Enterprises, Inc., deeper into the computer age.

The rediscovery of the flea-market and garage-sale base of our market has not been my only awakening over the past few months. Harry Jr. and others have convinced me that if Rinker Enterprises, Inc., is going to serve the next generation of collectors, dealers, and other individuals interested in antiques and collectibles, Rinker Enterprises, Inc., must become involved in electronic publishing, imaging, and information services. It will.

Rinker Enterprises, Inc., already is producing products for the information highway ranging from weekly radio and television shows to educational videos and cassette tapes. For an organization that did its first three editions of *Warman's Antiques and Their Prices* by collecting information on 50,000 3-by-5-inch cards, ordering it, and retyping it on IBM Selectric machines, the changes are mind boggling. The key is that the transition is being made, thanks, in part, to pressure from Harry Jr. to keep current and stay tuned-in.

The future of the antiques and collectibles field rests on the shoulders of Harry Jr. and the generations that will follow him. These are the individuals who are cutting their collecting teeth at garage sales, flea markets, and specialized collectibles shows. It is the group Rinker Enterprises, Inc., most wants to serve.

Hopefully, Harry Jr. will continue to edit *Price Guide to Flea Market Treasures* for decades to come. If he does, he will avoid the risk of losing touch with our market's base and having to rediscover it as I did. I learned my lesson. Let's see if the son can learn from his father after all.

Harry L. Rinker
Vera Cruz, PA
February 1995

Preface

Now that my father has finished his babbling on the preceding pages, it is time to introduce myself—Harry L. Rinker Jr. Let's get one thing straight from the beginning, I am not my Dad—do not want to be, have no desire to be. Assume "Jr." stands for the new improved version.

I am at the point where I stand and fall on my own efforts, not those of my Dad. When you judge the quality and usefulness of *Price Guide to Flea Market Treasures,* you are judging me. Hopefully, I will pass the test.

This is not to say that I have not learned from Dad nor exhibit some of his characteristics. I like to think I am a little looser, a bit more humorous and easy going than Dad—aspects you will find reflected throughout the book. He keeps telling me that these attributes are due to my lack of maturity. If this is the case, I never want to grow up.

One characteristic I did inherit from Dad is a passionate belief that what I have done is right. This passion often creates a few testy moments at the office when Dad and I are not in agreement over a point. Arrogant, opinionated, Type-A personality—Hank Williams, Jr., said it best when he sang: "It's a family tradition."

Those who have read the Forewords and Prefaces in previous editions of this book know that Dad and I agreed to work together on a two-year trial basis. The period ended in January 1994; and, yes, I am still working for Rinker Enterprises, Inc.

I know of few professional fields that provide so much allowance for individual freedom as does the an-tiques and collectibles trade. It is a field composed of independent, high-spirited, aggressive individuals, most of whom refuse to fit into a predetermined societal or corporate norm. If one is looking for an analogy, think of life on the western frontier.

There is both order and chaos in the antiques and collectibles field. Not every transaction is equivalent to a gunfight at the OK Corral, but such gunfights do occasionally happen. It takes skill and wit to survive. Each day offers new and different challenges. I could not ask for more.

The reason there is a third edition of *Price Guide to Flea Market Treasures* is that the first two editions sold well. Thanks to everyone who purchased one or both of these editions. Further, my appreciation to those of you who are experiencing this book for the first time. It is my wish that it become a useful companion and friend.

Like all books at Rinker Enterprises, Inc., *Price Guide to Flea Markets* is a team effort. Dad's team is known as The Rinkettes, a group of rock 'n' rollers who prefer to write and perform their own music rather than copy from someone else. While all have titles, everyone shares equally in the load. The research staff of Nancy Butt, Dana Morykan, Ellen Schroy, and Terese Yeakel is supported by Jocelyn Mousley, Richard Schmeltzle, and numerous members of the Morykan, Schroy, and Oswald-Yeakel clans.

One of the greatest joys of being part of the antiques and collectibles field is that "yes" is heard far more often than "no" when someone asks for help. Thanks to the numerous flea market promoters, managers, workers, dealers, and buyers who responded positively when asked for assistance during the past two years. May you all enjoy nothing but success in the years ahead.

The editorial and sales staff at Chilton Books, parent company of Wallace-Homestead, matched and often exceeded my expectations for the second edition of this book. I sincerely appreciate the talents and efforts they bring to this ongoing project.

One thing about Harry L. Rinker, my Dad, is that, no matter how good his intentions, he eventually gets involved with everything. Everyone knows he is a control freak. His fingers are in this flea market pie. I slapped them a few times, but missed on more occasions than I care to think about. Having said all this, I do want him to know that I appreciate the freedom that he has given me to do the job as I felt it should be done. Now, if I can only get him to recognize my talents and release me from the 1990s indentured servitude under which I have labored for the past three years.

This book is not perfect, as much as I would like it to be. To achieve perfection, I need your help and suggestions. Send any comments and/or criticisms you may have to: Harry L. Rinker Jr., *Price Guide to Flea Market Treasures,* 5093 Vera Cruz Road, Emmaus, PA 18049.

Harry L. Rinker Jr.
Vera Cruz, PA
February 1995

Introduction

GOOOOD MORNNNNNING-GGG, Flea Marketeers. Welcome to *Price Guide to Flea Market Treasures*. Today's specials are the very best goodies, tidbits, and knick-knacks found in every flea market throughout the good old U.S. of A. It's all here—neatly printed and organized for your use and reading pleasure.

Sound a bit like a carnival barker? It should. Going to a good flea market will produce as much fun, enjoyment, treasures, and memories as a visit to any carnival. Flea marketeering is a grand adventure. You have an idea of what to expect, but you know there will be a number of surprises. If you are lucky, you will grab a brass ring.

This edition of *Price Guide to Flea Market Treasures* is the famous third edition Dad always keeps talking about—the one that you would have liked to be the first edition if you had had all the time in the world to write it. He's right. The categories, listings, and prices have been tweaked and fine-tuned. I'm not certain you will notice the changes, but they are there.

It is impossible to resist the analogy of a boy growing into a man. This new volume is a handful. It will take some getting used to. It's big in many ways—not only in size but in the amount and quality of information that it contains.

Price Guide to Flea Market Treasures, third edition, also provides a first look at many new potential collecting categories. Col-

lectibility is tested at the flea market level. Dealers are continually offering material not seen previously. The successful sale of new groups of items immediately attracts the attention of other dealers. Their enthusiasm spreads. Before long, a new collecting category enters the established market as reflected in the publications edited and authored by my Dad.

Not all efforts to establish a new collecting category succeed. This is why some categories that appeared in the first and/or second edition of *Price Guide to Flea Market Treasures* have been dropped from this edition. A few others have become so pricey that they now belong in *Warman's Americana & Collectibles* rather than this book.

The success of the second edition of this book exceeded the first. I am pleased, but not surprised. Following the premise that when you have a winner, stay with it, I have chosen not to tamper with the overall approach of this book, which is to combine basic information about flea marketeering with price listings by category. Those familiar with the first and/or second edition will renew acquaintances with an old friend. Those discovering this book for the first time have an opportunity to make a friend for life.

Price Guide to Flea Market Treasures is divided into three principal parts.

The first part is a guide for flea marketeers. It helps you identify a "true" flea market, tells you how to

find and evaluate flea markets, provides a list of the top twenty-five flea markets nationwide, gives tips for surviving the flea market experience and honing your shopping skills, and provides in-depth analysis of the current flea market scene.

Much of the information is a repeat of that which appeared in the first and second editions. You will find minor changes in the sections dealing with general guides to flea market locations, trade papers, and top twenty-five flea markets. Chapter 6, "The Flea Market Scene Today," has been totally rewritten to reflect changes within the flea market scene over the past two years.

In talking with many of the individuals who purchased earlier editions of this book, I was surprised to learn how many "experienced" flea marketeers had skipped this first part. They made a mistake. Even the most experienced flea marketeer will find something of value. One of the worst mistakes you can make in the antiques and collectibles field is to assume that you know all you need to know.

The second part of the book is devoted to price listings by category. Previous users are advised to thumb through the categories and not rely on the assumption that they know what the book contains. This third edition of *Price Guide to Flea Market Treasures* contains over 30 new categories.

You will make a serious mistake if you assume this book is just another general antiques and collectibles price guide. Not true. This book was prepared using the premise that everything imaginable turns up at a flea market—from the finest antiques to good reusable secondhand items. "Dearly Departed" and "Secondhand Roses" categories are not found in any other antiques or collectibles price guides.

In a few categories you will not find specific priced items. Instead you are provided with general information that allows a broad understanding of the category. Occasionally, you are referred to specialized books on the subject.

One of the great joys about working on the categories in this book is that so many are supported with collectors' clubs, newsletters, and periodicals. You will find full addresses for these listed in the appropriate category before the price listings.

Just like Dad, I am one of those "wild and crazy guys." Unlike Dad, whose books tend toward the conventional, my book allows me to express this aspect of my character. As a result, you will find that the category introductions range from serious to humorous to sublime. If the key to a great flea market is that it evokes these emotions and more within you, why should this book do any less?

Although I am not certain why, the third part of this book, which contains reference material for flea marketeers, including the "Flea Marketeer's Annotated Reference Library" and a list of "Antiques and Collectibles Trade Papers," was used least by those who bought the first and second editions of this book. I strongly recommend that you become familiar with this section. The information not only helps you become highly proficient as a flea marketeer but also serves as your introduction to the other wonderful areas of the antiques and collectibles field.

It is time to honor the cry of the Circus ringmaster: "On with the show." Take a moment and read the program (the first section) before you watch the acts in the center ring (the second section) and then relive the memories (the third section). Most of all, don't forget—the entire purpose of the performance is for you to have fun.

PART ONE

A Flea Market Education

CHAPTER ONE

What Is a Flea Market?

It is difficult to explain the sense of excitement and anticipation felt by collectors and dealers as they get ready to shop a flea market. They are about to undertake a grand adventure, a journey into the unknown. Flea markets turn the average individual into an explorer in search of buried treasure. The search is not without adversity—conditions ranging from a hostile climate to intense competition as one waits with other collectors and dealers for the gates to open may be encountered. Victory is measured in "steals" and bargains and in stories that can be shared at the end of the day over dinner with friendly rivals.

Flea markets provide the opportunity for prospective collectors to get their feet wet in the exciting world of antiques and collectibles and for novice dealers to test their merchandise and selling skills at minimal expense. Many first contacts, some of which last a lifetime, are made between and among collectors and dealers there. More than any other aspect of the antiques and collectibles trade, the flea market is the one forum where everyone is on equal footing.

Before you learn how to find, evaluate, and survive flea markets, it is important that you understand *exactly* what a flea market is, how it fits into the antiques and collectibles market, and the many variations of it that exist. This is the first step to identifying the flea markets that are most likely to provide the greatest opportunities for you.

Defining a Flea Market

Few terms in the antiques and collectibles field are as difficult to define as *flea market*. If you visit the Rose Bowl Flea Market in Pasadena, California, you will find discontinued and knock-off merchandise, handmade crafts, clothing (from tube socks to dresses), home-care items, plants of all types, and specialty foods more in evidence than antiques and collectibles. On the other hand, if you visit the Ann Arbor Antiques Market in Michigan, you will find primarily middle- and upper-level antiques and collectibles. Both are flea markets, yet they are light-years apart from one another.

The flea market concept is generations old. As it spread throughout the world, each country changed and adapted the form to meet its own particular needs. Regional differences developed. In New England, the Mid-Atlantic states, and throughout the Midwest, the term generally is used to describe a place where antiques and collectibles are sold. In the South and Southwest, the term is more loosely interpreted, with the emphasis on secondhand and discounted goods.

It is not hard to see where the confusion originates. Check the dictionary definition for *flea market*. *Webster's Ninth New Collegiate Dictionary* (Springfield, MA: Merriam-Webster, Inc., 1984) defines a flea market as "a usually open-air market for secondhand articles and antiques." Individuals involved with antiques and collectibles make a big distinction between secondhand (recycled or reusable) goods and antiques and collectibles. Although the dictionary may lump them together, collectors and dealers clearly differentiate one from the other. The flea markets described in this book fit a much more narrow definition than the dictionary definition.

When collectors use the term *flea market,* they mean *a regularly scheduled market, held either indoors or outdoors, in which the primary goods offered for sale are those defined by the trade as antiques or collectibles.* Occasionally, you will find some handcrafted products and secondhand goods among the offerings, especially in the seasonal and roadside flea markets, where professional flea market dealers mix with individuals selling on a one-shot basis.

The problem with trying to define *flea market,* even when limited to the antiques and collectibles perspective, is that a multiplicity of flea market types exist. There are the great seasonal flea markets such as Renninger's Extravaganza (Kutztown, Pennsylvania) and Brimfield's (Brimfield, Massachusetts), the monthlies such as the Metrolina Expo (Charlotte, North Carolina), and numerous weeklies scattered across the country. Personally, I feel that Atlantique City, held in Atlantic City, New Jersey, in March each year, is really a flea market rather than the "show" it purports to be.

One of the best ways to understand what an antiques and collectibles flea market encompasses is to discuss how it differs from three other closely related institutions in the antiques and collectibles trade: the mall, the garage sale, and the show. While the differences may appear subtle, they are significant to collectors and dealers.

Prior to the arrival of the mall, there was a clearly defined ladder of quality within the antiques and collectibles community which progressed from garage sale or country auction to flea market to small show to major show or shop. This is how most goods moved through the market. This is the route many dealers used to establish themselves in the trade. Two things changed the equation: (1) collectors recognized the role flea markets played as the initial source of goods and actively participated in flea markets in order to eliminate the "middleman" and (2) the antiques and collectibles mall came into existence.

The 1980s was the decade of the antiques and collectibles mall. Malls resulted because many flea market and weekend dealers wanted a means of doing business on a daily basis without the overhead of their own shop. They also needed an indoor environment free from the vagaries of weather. Additionally, the buying public wanted to find as many sellers as possible in one location when shopping for antiques and collectibles. Antiques and collectibles malls bring together a number of dealers—from ten to hundreds—in one location. Malls differ from flea markets in that they are open for business on a daily basis (a minimum of five and often seven days a week), the display and sales process is often handled by a manager or other representative of the owner of the items, a more formal business procedure is used, and the quality of material is

somewhat higher than that found at flea markets. The main drawbacks are that the buyer generally has no contact with the owner of the merchandise and price negotiation is difficult.

Garage sales are usually one-time events, often conducted by people with no pretensions of being antiques or collectibles dealers—they are merely attempting to get rid of used or damaged goods that they no longer find useful. While it is true that some antiques and collectibles enter the market through this source, most individuals conducting garage sales have enough good sense to realize that this is the worst way to sell these items. Emphasis in a garage sale is on secondhand merchandise, often in heavily used and partially damaged condition.

A recent development in the garage sale area is the annual or semi-annual community garage sale. A promoter rents a large hall or auditorium and sells space to any individual wishing to set up. Usually there is a rule that no established antiques and collectibles dealers are allowed to take part. However, many dealers sneak in with friends or simply use a different name to rent a space in order to "pick" the merchandise during the setup period. Although community garage sales fit the dictionary definition of a flea market, the large volume of secondhand merchandise distinguishes them from the flea markets discussed in this book.

An antiques or collectibles show consists of a number of professional dealers (weekend, full-time, or a combination of both) who meet in a fixed location on a regular basis, usually two to three times each year, to offer quality antiques and collectibles primarily to collectors, interior decorators, and others. Once an antique or collectible reaches the show circuit, the general assumption is that it is priced close to book value. Flea markets thrive on the concept that merchandise priced for sale is

significantly below book value. While this concept is more myth than reality in the 1990s, it still prevails.

Confusion arises because a number of monthly flea markets have dropped the term *flea market* from their titles. They call themselves *shows* or *markets*. They do not use *flea* because of a growing list of problems, ranging from unscrupulous dealers to an abundance of unmarked reproductions, that plague flea markets in the 1990s. Calling yourself something else does not change what you really are. Most monthly markets and shows are nothing more than flea markets in disguise.

Seasonal Flea Markets

Seasonal flea markets are those held a maximum of three times a year. Theoretically, they are held outdoors. However, many sites now provide either indoor or pavilion shelters for participants, especially those whose merchandise is expensive or suspectible to damage by weather. Most have clearly established dates. For example, Renninger's Extravaganza is held the last weekend in April, June, and September.

If there is a Mecca in the flea market world, it is Brimfield. The name is magic. You are not an accomplished flea marketeer until you have been there. Actually, Brimfield is not a flea market, it is an event. For the first full week in May, July, and September over fifteen separate flea markets open and close. On Fridays the dealer count exceeds 1,500. Area motel rooms are booked over a year in advance. Traffic jams last hours.

For the past several years Renninger's has been promoting seasonal markets during the winter months at its Mount Dora, Florida, location. They are an important stop on the Southern winter circuit. Although there are a few seasonal markets in the Midwest, none are on a par with the Renninger's Extravaganzas and the Brimfield weeks.

Monthly Flea Markets

The monthly flea market's strength rests on a steady dealer clientele supplemented by other dealers passing through the area, a frequency that allows dealers enough time to find new merchandise, and a setting that is usually superior to the seasonal and weekly flea markets. The monthlies range from the upscale Ann Arbor Antiques Market to the mid-range antiques and collectibles show copycat (for example, the Fairgrounds Antiques Market in Phoenix, Arizona) to the something-for-everybody flea market (like the Kane County Flea Market in St. Charles, Illinois).

Most of the monthly flea markets have some outdoor spaces. The Kentucky Flea Market in Louisville, Kentucky, and the Fairgrounds Antiques Market in Phoenix, Arizona, are two exceptions. Flea markets with outdoor space operate only during warm weather months, generally April through November. A few of the larger operations (e.g., the Springfield Antiques Show & Flea Market in Springfield, Ohio) operate year-round. Double-check the schedule of any flea market you plan to visit between November and April, with the possible exception of those located in the Deep South or the Southwest.

Another strength of the monthly flea markets rests in the fact that they attract a large number of dealers who appear on a regular basis; hence collectors and dealers have time to cul-

tivate good working relationships. A level of buying trust is created because the collector knows that he or she will be able to find the seller again if questions develop.

Weekly Flea Markets

The weekly flea markets break down into two types: those held on a weekday and those held on a weekend. The weekday markets are primarily for dealers in the trade. Monday flea markets at Perkiomenville, Pennsylvania, and Wednesday flea markets at Shipshewana, Indiana, are legends. These markets begin in the predawn hours. The best buys are found by flashlight as participants check merchandise as it is being unpacked. Most selling ends by 9:00 A.M. These markets are designed primarily for individuals actively involved in the resale of antiques and collectibles. Most collectors prefer something a bit more civilized.

Renninger's #1 in Adamstown, Pennsylvania, shows the staying power of the weekend flea market. Within driving distance of several major population centers, yet far enough in the country to make the day an outing, Renninger's combines an ever-changing outdoor section with an indoor facility featuring primarily permanent dealers. Renninger's #1 has survived for years by opening only on Sundays, except for Extravaganza weekends. However, because buyers like to shop for antiques and collectibles on Saturdays as well, Renninger's Promotions created Renninger's #2 in Kutztown, Pennsylvania.

Weekend flea markets are now a fixture across the country and constitute the largest segment of the flea market community. It is not unusual to find several in one location as

each tries to capitalize on the success of the other. However, their quality varies tremendously.

The biggest problem with weekend flea markets is merchandise staleness. Many dealers add only a few new items each week. Most collectors shop them on a four- to eight-week cycle. The way to avoid missing a shot at a major new piece is to maintain a close working relationship with the dealers at the flea markets who specialize in the category of items you collect. Most weekend flea market dealers do get to shop the market. They can be your eyes when you are not there.

As with the monthly flea markets, you can buy from indoor dealers knowing that you are likely to find them if a problem develops later. You must be much more careful when purchasing from the transient outside dealers. The key is to get a valid name, address, and phone number from anyone from whom you make a purchase at a flea market.

One of the things I like best about large weekend flea markets is that they feature one or more book dealers who specialize in antiques and collectibles books. I always stop at these booths to check on the latest titles included in the large stock of privately published titles carried by these dealers. In some cases, I find a book I never saw advertised in the trade papers. Some of the dealers offer search services for out-of-print titles. Spending time getting to know these book dealers is something I never regret.

Roadside Flea Markets

I have ignored roadside flea markets up to this point because the merchandise they offer is more often than not secondhand and of garage sale quality. This is not to say that I have not experienced some great finds at roadside markets at which I have stopped. However, when I consider the amount of time that I spend finding these few precious jewels, I quickly realize I can do much better at one of the more traditional flea markets.

Chances are that you collect one or two specific categories. If so, not every type of flea market is right for you. How do you find the best markets? What type of evaluation can you do in advance to save the frustration of coming home empty-handed? These questions and more are answered in the next chapter.

CHAPTER TWO

Finding and Evaluating Flea Markets

In order to attend a flea market, you have to locate one. It is not as easy as it sounds. In order to thoroughly research the available markets in any given area, you will have to consult a variety of sources. Even when you have finished, you are still likely to spot a flea market that you missed in your research along the way. I told you there was a strong sense of adventure in flea marketeering.

Flea Market Guides

There are four national guides to United States flea markets: *The Original Clark's Flea Market U.S.A.: A National Directory of Flea Markets and Swap Meets* (Clark Publications, 419 Garcon Point Road, Milton, FL 32583), *The Great Americana Flea Market Directory* (21st Century Marketing, PO Box 702, Palmyra, NJ 08065), *The Official Directory to U.S. Flea Markets, Fourth Edition,* edited by Kitty Werner (House of Collectibles, Division of Random House, 201 East 50th Street, New York, NY 10022), and *The Confident Collector: U.S. Flea Market Directory,* edited by Albert LaFarge (The Confident Collector, Division of Avon Books, 1350 Avenue of the Americas, New York, NY 10019). Buy them all.

Clark's, issued quarterly, lists over 2,000 flea markets and swap meets. The guide is organized alpha-

betically by state. The secondary organization is city or town closest to the flea market within the state. You will find information on name, address, days and occasionally hours of operation, and telephone number. Information provided about each market varies greatly. Completely missing are directions for hard-to-find markets. Do not be fooled by the fact that this guide appears to be produced using an old manual typewriter. The information is helpful. I buy an issue every year or two as a safety check against my regular sources. A one-year subscription is $25.00. Single copies are available from the publisher at $7.50, a price that includes postage and handling.

The *Great Americana* guide, published twice a year, lists approximately 2,500 markets using the same format as *Clark's.* 21st Century Marketing, the current publisher, has revised the format and made some improvements in the listings. However, the listings still are weak when compared to the *Official Directory.* A single issue is available from 21st Century Marketing for $12.45, a price that includes postage and handling.

The *Official Directory* experienced a transformation between its third and fourth edition. Credit Kitty Werner, its editor, with making the best even better. The book now covers over 800 flea markets in the United States and Canada. Yes, Canada—it's time someone paid attention to our northern neighbor. The *Official Directory's* strength rests in the quality information that it pro-

vides about each flea market. Detailed comments about merchandise and operating practices are extremely helpful. You can purchase a copy of this guide in most larger bookstores. It is a bargain at $6.00.

U.S. Flea Market is the newest arrival on the block and a welcome addition. Designed to compete with the *Official Directory,* it provides detailed information that includes maps and travel directions, days and times, number of dealers, description of goods sold, dealer information, and other useful tidbits for approximately 850 flea markets nationwide. As one might expect, LaFarge covers many of the same flea markets that are found in the *Official Directory.* However, there are more than enough differences to make both books a must buy. *The Confident Collector: U.S. Flea Market Directory* retails for $6.00 and is available at most bookstores.

Antiques and collectibles flea markets are not unique to the United States. In fact, the modern antiques and collectibles flea market originated in Paris. Flea markets play a vital role throughout Europe, especially in France, Great Britain, and Germany. Accordingly, Travel Keys (PO Box 160691, Sacramento, CA 95816) has published a separate flea market price guide for each country. Peter B. Manston is editor of *Manston's Flea Markets of Britain, Manston's Flea Markets of France,* and *Manston's Flea Markets of Germany.* Read the introductory material carefully, especially the section on export laws and regulations. This is information you will not find anywhere else. The books are dated, so be sure to confirm the vital information before visiting any of the markets listed. I continue to recommend the books because many of the markets they describe have existed for decades.

Regional Shop Guides

A number of specialized regional guides for locating antiques and collectibles flea markets, malls, and shops exist. Most are published by trade papers. A few are done privately. None focus solely on the flea market scene.

The *Antique Week Mid-Central Antique Shop Guide* (Antique Week, PO Box 90, Knightstown, IN 46148) is typical. Organization is by state, region, and alphabetically by city and town within a region. Brief listings for each business are supplemented by display advertising. The Mid-Central edition (there is also an Eastern edition) covers more than 3,000 flea markets, malls, shops, and shows. One of the features I like most about the guide is that it designates businesses selling new gift and reproduction items. The principal problem with the guide is that you have to pay a fee in order to be listed. As a result, coverage is limited to those willing to pay. It is a great starting point for the region it covers, but it is not all-encompassing.

David Maloney, Jr.'s *1994–1995 Maloney's Antiques and Collectibles Resource Directory* contains category listings for "Antique Shop Directories" and "Flea Market Directories." The listings include address and telephone number. Hopefully, you own a copy of Maloney's book. If you do not, you should. Make a resolution—right now—to buy a copy the next time you visit a

bookstore or the stand of an antiques and collectibles bookseller at a flea market. Dad thinks it is the best investment anyone in the trade can make. For once, we agree.

When planning to visit a new area, contact some of the trade papers that serve the region and ask if they publish a regional guide or know of such a guide. Regional guides are inexpensive, ranging from $4.00 to $10.00. Many of the businesses listed in the guide sell it across the counter. I always pick up a copy. The floor behind the front seat of my car is littered with road maps and regional guides, most of which show signs of heavy use.

Trade Newspapers

The best source of flea market information is advertisements in trade newspapers. Some papers put all the flea market advertisements in one location, while others place them in their appropriate regional section. Most trade papers' events calendars include flea markets with the show listings.

Once again, the problem rests with the fact that all advertising is paid advertising. Not all flea markets advertise in every issue of a trade paper. Some advertise in papers outside their home area because the locals know where and when to find them. Flea markets that operate between April and September usually do not advertise in December and January. The only way to conduct a complete search is to obtain a four- to six-month run of a regional paper and carefully scan each issue. When doing this, keep your eyes open for reports and features about flea markets. As advertisers, flea markets expect to get written up at least once a year.

The following is a list of national and regional trade papers that I rec-

ommend you consult for flea market information. You will find their full addresses and phone numbers (when known) in the listing of trade newspapers at the back of this book.

National Trade Papers

American Collector, Southfield, MI
American Collector's Journal, Kewanee, IL
Antique Trader Weekly, Dubuque, IA
Antique Week, Knightstown, IN
Antiques & the Arts Weekly, Newtown, CT
Collector News, Grundy Center, IA
Maine Antique Digest, Waldoboro, ME

Regional Trade Papers

NEW ENGLAND
Antiques & Collectibles and the Long Island Arts Review Magazine, Westbury, NY
Cape Cod Antiques & Arts, Yarmouth Port, MA
The Hudson Valley Antiquer, Rhinebeck, NY
MassBay Antiques, Danvers, MA
New England Antiques Journal, Ware, MA
Unravel The Gavel, Ctr. Barnstead, NH

MIDDLE ATLANTIC STATES
Antique Country, Berryville, VA
Antiquer's Guide to the Susquehanna Region, Sidney, NY
Antiques & Auction News, Mount Joy, PA
Eastern Seaboard Antique Monthly, Burtonsville, MD
The New York Antique Almanac of Art, Antiques, Investments & Yesteryear, Lawrence, NY
New York–Pennsylvania Collector, Fishers, NY
Renninger's Antique Guide, Lafayette Hill, PA
Treasure Chest, New York, NY

SOUTH
The Antique Press, Tampa, FL
The Antique Shoppe, Bradenton, FL
Antiques & Crafts Gazette, Cumming, GA
Carolina Antique News, Charlotte, NC
Cotton & Quail Antique Trail, Monticello, FL
MidAtlantic Antiques Magazine, Henderson, NC
The Old News Is Good News Antiques Gazette, Baton Rouge, LA
Southern Antiques, Decatur, GA

MIDWEST
The Antique Collector and Auction Guide, Salem, OH
Antique Gazette, Nashville, TN
Antique Review, Worthington, OH
Buckeye Marketeer, Westerville, OH
Collectors Journal, Vinton, IA
Indiana Antique Buyers News, Silver Lake, IN
Michigan Antiques Trading Post, Williamstown, MI
Midwest Illinois Antiques Gazette, Winchester, IL
Old Times, Minneapolis, MN
Yesteryear, Princeton, WI

SOUTHWEST
Antique & Collector's Guide, Beaumont, TX
Antique Traveler, Mineola, TX
Arizona Antique News and Southwest Antiques Journal, Phoenix, AZ

ROCKY MOUNTAIN STATES
Mountain States Collector, Evergreen, CO

WEST COAST
Antique & Collectables, El Cajon, CA
Antique & Collectible Marketplace, Huntington Beach, CA
Antiques Today, Carson City, NV
Antiques West, San Francisco, CA
Art, Antiques & Collectibles, Petaluma, CA
Collector, Pomona, CA

Flea Market Shoppers Guide, Maywood, CA
Old Stuff, McMinnville, OR
West Coast Peddler, Whittier, CA

This list is by no means complete. I am certain that I have missed a few regional papers. However, these papers provide a starting point. Do not be foolish and go flea marketeering without consulting them.

Which Flea Market Is Right for You?

The best flea market is the one at which you find plenty to buy at good to great prices. This means that most flea markets are not right for you. Is it necessary to attend each one to make your determination? I do not think so.

I am a great believer in using the telephone. If long distance rates jump dramatically as a result of the publication of this book, I plan to approach AT&T and ask for a piece of the action. It is a lot cheaper to call than to pay for transportation, lodging, and meals—not to mention the value of your time. Do not hesitate to call promoters and ask them about their flea markets.

What type of information should you request? First, check the number of dealers. If the number falls below one hundred, think twice. Ask for a ratio of local dealers to transient dealers. A good mix is 75% local and 25% transient for monthly and weekly markets. Second, inquire about the type of merchandise being offered for sale. Make a point not to tell the promoter what you collect. If you do, you can be certain that the flea market has a number of dealers who offer the material. Do not forget to ask about the quality of the merchandise. Third,

ask about the facilities. The more indoor space available, the higher the level of merchandise is likely to be. What happens if it rains? Finally, ask yourself this question: Do you trust what the promoter has told you?

When you are done talking to the promoter, call the editor of one of the regional trade papers and ask his or her opinion about the market. If they have published an article or review of the market recently, request that a copy be sent to you. If you know someone who has attended, talk to that person. If you still have not made up your mind, try the local daily newspaper or chamber of commerce.

Do not be swayed by the size of a flea market's advertisement in a trade paper. The Kane County advertisement is often less than a sixteenth of a page. A recent full-page advertisement for Brimfield flea markets failed to include J & J Promotions or May's Antique Market, two of the major players on the scene. This points out the strong regional competition between flea markets. Be suspicious of what one promoter tells you about another promoter's market.

Evaluating a Flea Market

After you have attended a flea market, it is time to decide if you will attend it again, and if so, how frequently. Answer the nineteen questions on page 11 yes or no. In this test, "no" is the right answer. If more than half the questions are yes, forget about going back. There are plenty of flea markets from which to choose. If twelve or more are answered no, give it another chance in a few months. If seventeen or more answers are no, plan another visit soon. What are you doing next week?

Flea Market Quick Quiz

YES NO

___ ___ Was the flea market hard to find?

___ ___ Did you have a difficult time moving between the flea market and your car in the parking area?

___ ___ Did you have to pay a parking fee in addition to an admission fee?

___ ___ Did the manager fail to provide a map of the market?

___ ___ Was a majority of the market in an open, outdoor environment?

___ ___ Were indoor facilities poorly lighted and ventilated?

___ ___ Was there a problem with the number of toilet facilities or with the facilities' cleanliness?

YES NO

___ ___ Was your overall impression of the market one of chaos?

___ ___ Did collectibles outnumber antiques?

___ ___ Did secondhand goods and new merchandise outnumber collectibles?

___ ___ Were reproductions, copycats, fantasy items, and fakes in abundance? (See Chapter 5.)

___ ___ Was there a large representation of home crafts and/or discontinued merchandise?

___ ___ Were the vast majority of antiques and collectibles that you saw in fair condition or worse?

YES NO

___ ___ Were individuals that you expected to encounter at the market absent?

___ ___ Did you pass out fewer than five lists of your "wants"?

___ ___ Did you buy fewer than five new items for your collection?

___ ___ Were more than half the items that you bought priced near or at book value?

___ ___ Was there a lack of good restaurants and/or lodging within easy access of the flea market?

___ ___ Would you tell a friend never to attend the market?

There are some flea markets that scored well for me, and I would like to share them with you. They are listed in the next chapter.

CHAPTER THREE

Top Twenty-five U.S. Flea Markets

The first two editions of *Price Guide to Flea Market Treasures* contained a list of the top twenty U.S. Flea Markets. Deciding which markets would and would not be on the list was not an easy task. There are thousands of flea markets throughout the United States.

In each edition there were four to six markets that I excluded simply because of the arbitrary number that I selected. Over the past four years Dad's and my travels have provided us with the opportunity to visit many flea markets that we knew previously only by reputation. When making the final selection for this book, we could not narrow the list to twenty, hence the "Top Twenty-five U.S. Flea Markets."

Adding five more flea markets to the list will not silence all our critics. Everyone has regional favorites that failed to make the cut. I wish I could list them all, but that is not the purpose of this price guide.

In making my choices, I have used the following criteria. First, I wanted to provide a representative sample from the major flea market groups—seasonal, monthly, and weekly. Since this price guide is designed for the national market, I made certain that the selections covered the entire United States. Finally, I selected flea markets that I feel will "turn on" a prospective or novice collector. Nothing is more fun than getting off to a great start.

This list is only a starting point. Almost every flea market has a table containing promotional literature for other flea markets in the area. Follow up on the ones of interest. Continue to check trade paper listings. There are always new flea markets being started.

Finally, not every flea market is able to maintain its past glories. Are there flea markets that you think should be on this list? Have you visited some of the listed flea markets and found them to be unsatisfactory? As each edition of this guide is prepared, this list will be evaluated. Send any thoughts and comments that you may have to: Harry L. Rinker Jr., Rinker Enterprises, Inc., 5093 Vera Cruz Road, Emmaus, PA 18049.

Name of Flea Market

Location

Frequency and general admission times

Type of goods sold and general comments

Number of dealers, indoor and/or outdoor, and special features

1995 Admission Fee

Address and phone number (if known) of manager or promoter

Seasonal Flea Markets

America's Largest Antique and Collectible Sale

Portland Expo Center, Portland, OR. Exit 306B off I-5.

Saturday and Sunday, March, July, and October, usually mid-month.

Antiques and collectibles.

Over 1,250 dealers in March and October; over 1,500 dealers in July. Indoors.

1995 Admission: $5.00 per person. Parking costs an additional $4.00.

Palmer/Wirfs & Associates, 4001 NE Halsey, Portland, OR 97232. (503) 282-0877.

Cow Palace, San Francisco, CA. Exit off Highway 101.

Saturday and Sunday, February, May, and August, usually mid-month, Saturday 8:00 A.M. to 7:00 P.M.; Sunday 9:00 A.M. to 5:00 P.M.

Antiques and collectibles.

Over 350 dealers. Indoors.

1995 Admission: $5.00 per person. Parking costs an additional $3.00.

Palmer/Wirfs & Associates, 4001 NE Halsey, Portland, OR 97232. (503) 282-0877.

Brimfield

Route 20, Brimfield, MA 01010.

Six days, starting on the Tuesday before the second full weekend in May, July, and September and ending on that Sunday.

Antiques, collectibles, and second-hand goods.

Over 3,000 dealers. Indoor and outdoor. 22 separate fields.

1995 Admission: Varies according to field, ranging from free admission to $3.00. Average parking fee: $3.00.

More than ten different promoters: Brimfield Acres North/The Last Hurrah, PO Box 397, Holden, MA 01520, (508) 754-4185; Central Park Antiques Shows, PO Box 224, Brimfield, MA 01010, (413) 596-9257; The Dealers' Choice, PO Box 28, Fiskdale, MA 01518, (508) 347-3929; Faxon's Treasure Chest/Midway Shows, PO Box 28, Fiskdale, MA 01518, (508) 347-3929; Heart-O-The-Mart, PO Box 26, Brimfield, MA 01010, (413) 245-9556; J & J Promotions, Route 20, Brimfield, MA 01010, (413) 245-3436 or (508) 597-8155; May's Antique Market, PO Box 416, Brimfield, MA 01010, (413) 245-9271; New England Motel Antiques Market, Inc., PO Box 139, Sturbridge, MA 01010, (413) 245-9427; Shelton Antique Shows, PO Box 124, Brimfield, MA 01010, (413) 245-3591.

You can subscribe to the *Brimfield Antique Guide* from Brimfield Publications, PO Box 442, Brimfield, MA 01010. Phone: (413) 245-9329. Three issues for $9.95, first class mail.

Renninger's Extravaganza

Noble Street, Kutztown, PA 19530.
Thursday, Friday, and Saturday of last full weekend of April, June, and September. Thursday opens 10:00 A.M. for pre-admission only ($40.00 per car carrying one to four people). Friday and Saturday, 7:00 A.M. to 5:00 P.M.
Antiques and collectibles.
Over 1,200 dealers. Indoor and outdoor.
1995 Admission: $4.00 on Friday, $2.00 on Saturday.
Renninger's Promotions, 27 Bensinger Drive, Schuylkill Haven, PA 17972. Monday through Friday (717) 385-0104, Saturday (610) 683-6848, and Sunday (717) 336-2177.

Monthly Flea Markets

Allegan Antiques Market

Allegan Fairgrounds, Allegan, MI 49010.
Last Sunday of the month, April through September, 7:30 A.M. to 4:30 P.M.
Antiques and collectibles.
Over 170 dealers indoors, 200 dealers outdoors.
1995 Admission: $3.00.
Larry L. Wood and Morie Faulkerson, 2030 Blueberry Drive N.W., Grand Rapids, MI 49504, (616) 453-8780 or (616) 887-7677.

Ann Arbor Antiques Market

5055 Ann Arbor–Saline Road, Ann Arbor, MI 48103.
Third Sunday of the month, April through October, 5:00 A.M. to 4:00 P.M. November market usually occurs second Sunday of month.
Antiques and select collectibles. The most upscale flea market in the trade.
Over 350 dealers. All under cover. Locator service for specialties and dealers.
1995 Admission: $5.00.
M. Brusher, Manager, PO Box 1512, Ann Arbor, MI 48106.

Birmingham Fairgrounds Flea Market

Birmingham Fairgrounds, Birmingham, AL 35208. Exit 120 off I-20/59, follow signs for Alabama State Fair Complex.
First weekend of every month, year round, plus second and third weekends in December. Friday, 3:00 P.M. to 9:00 P.M.; Saturday and Sunday, 7:00 A.M. to 6:00 P.M.

Antiques, collectibles, and new merchandise. Somewhat swap meetish.
Over 600 dealer spaces. Indoors and outdoors.
1995 Admission: Free.
The Flea Market, PO Box 39063, Birmingham, AL 35208. 1-800-362-7538.

Burlington Antiques Show

Boone County Fairgrounds, Burlington, KY 41005.
Third Sunday of the month, April through October, 8:00 A.M. to 3:00 P.M.
Antiques and collectibles.
Outdoor.
1995 Admission: $2.00. Early buyers 5:00 A.M. to 8:00 A.M.: $5.00.
Paul Kohls, PO Box 58367, Cincinnati, OH 45258, (513) 922-5265.

Caravan Antiques Market

The Fairgrounds, State Route 86, Centreville, MI 49032.
One Sunday per month, May through October, excluding September, 7:00 A.M. to 4:00 P.M.
Antiques and collectibles. All merchandise guaranteed.
Over 600 dealers.
1995 Admission: $3.00.
Humberstone Management, 1510 N. Hoyne, Chicago, IL 60622, (312) 227-4464.

Don Scott Antiques Market

Ohio State Fairgrounds, Columbus, OH.
Saturday 9:00 A.M. to 6:00 P.M. and Sunday 10:00 A.M. to 5:00 P.M., November through July. Weekend dates vary. Check Scott advertisements in the trade papers.
Antiques and collectibles.
1,500 booths. Indoor and outdoor.
1995 Admission: Free.

Don Scott, PO Box 60, Bremen, OH 43107, (614) 569-4912.

Note: Don Scott conducts a second monthly flea market: The Don Scott Antique Market, Atlanta Exposition Center (I-285 to Exit 40 at Jonesboro Road, two miles east of Atlanta airport), second weekend of every month.

Fairgrounds Antiques Market

Arizona State Fairgrounds, 19th Avenue & McDowell, Phoenix, AZ 85009.

Third weekend of the month, year-round, except March (second weekend) and December (first weekend). No show in October. Saturday 9:00 A.M. to 5:00 P.M. and Sunday 10:00 A.M. to 4:00 P.M.

Antiques, collectibles, and crafts. Antique glass and clock repairs.

Approximately 200 dealers. All indoor.

1995 Admission: $2.00.

Jack Black Shows, PO Box 61172, Phoenix, AZ 85082-1172, (800) 678-9987 or (602) 943-1766.

Gordyville USA Flea Market & Auction

Rantoul, IL 61866. On Route 136, 7½ miles east of I-57.

Second weekend (Friday, Saturday, Sunday) of each month. First weekend in December. Friday 4:00 P.M. to 9:00 P.M., Saturday 9:00 A.M. to 6:00 P.M., and Sunday 9:00 A.M. to 4:00 P.M.

Antiques, collectibles, vintage items, arts, crafts, and other unique items.

Indoor and outdoor.

1995 Admission: Free.

Gordon Hannagan Auction Company, PO Box 490, Gifford, IL 61847, (217) 568-7117.

(Kane County) Antiques Flea Markets

Kane County Fairgrounds, Randall Road, St. Charles, IL 60175.

First Sunday of every month and preceding Saturday, except New Year's and Easter. Year-round. Saturday 1:00 P.M. to 5:00 P.M. and Sunday 7:00 A.M. to 4:00 P.M.

Antiques, collectibles, and some crafts. A favorite in the Midwest, especially with the Chicago crowd.

Combination indoor and outdoor. Country breakfast served.

1995 Admission: $4.00.

Mrs. J. L. Robinson, Mgr., PO Box 549, St. Charles, IL 60174, (708) 377-2252.

Kentucky Flea Market

Kentucky Fair and Exposition Center (take Exit 12B off Interstate 264), Louisville, KY.

Three- or four-day show. Dates vary. Check trade papers. Friday Noon to 8:00 P.M., Saturday 10:00 A.M. to 8:00 P.M., and Sunday 11:00 A.M. to 5:00 P.M.

Antiques, collectibles, arts and crafts, and new merchandise.

Approximately 1,000 booths. Indoor, climate-controlled.

1995 Admission: Free.

Stewart Promotions, 2950 Breckinridge Lane, Suite 4A, Louisville, KY 40220, (502) 456-2244.

Long Beach Outdoor Antiques & Collectibles Market

Veterans Stadium, Long Beach, CA.

Third Sunday of each month, 8:00 A.M. to 3:00 P.M.

Antiques and collectibles including: vintage clothing, pottery, quilts, primitives, advertising, etc.

Over 700 dealers.

1995 Admission: $3.50. No early admission charge; stalwarts can get in at 6:30 A.M.

Americana Enterprises, Inc., PO Box 69219, Los Angeles, CA 90069, (213) 655-5703.

Metrolina Expo

7100 North Statesville Road, Charlotte, NC.

First and third Saturday of every month, year-round. Friday, Saturday, and Sunday first weekend; Saturday, Sunday third weekend; 8:00 A.M. to 5:00 P.M.

Antiques and collectibles.

Indoor and outdoor. First weekend approximately 1,500 dealers; third weekend between 800 and 1,000 dealers. Metrolina hosts two Spectaculars yearly—April and November—which feature more than 2,000 dealers.

1995 Admission: First weekend $2.50 per day, third weekend $1.50 per day, and spectaculars $5.00 per day. Early buyer's fee and sneak preview fee are available.

Metrolina EXPO Center, PO Box 26652, Charlotte, NC 18221, (704) 596-4643.

Sandwich Antiques Market

The Fairgrounds, State Route 34, Sandwich, IL 60548.

One Sunday per month, May through October, 8:00 A.M. to 4:00 P.M.

Antiques and collectibles.

Over 600 dealers.

1995 Admission: $3.00.

Sandwich Antiques Market, 1510 N. Hoyne, Chicago, IL 60622, (312) 227-4464.

Springfield Antiques Show & Flea Market

Clark County Fairgrounds, Springfield, OH.

Third weekend of the month, year-round, excluding July. December market is held the second weekend of the month. Saturday 8:00 A.M. to 5:00 P.M. and Sunday 9:00 A.M. to 4:00 P.M. Extravaganzas are held in May and September.

More than half the market is antiques and collectibles.

Over 400 dealers indoors and 900 dealers outdoors for monthly market in warm weather.

1995 Admission: $1.00. $2.00 for Extravaganza.

Bruce Knight, PO Box 2429, Springfield, OH 45501, (513) 325-0053.

Weekly Flea Markets

Adamstown

Route 272, Adamstown, PA 19501. Sundays.

Antiques, collectibles, secondhand material, and junk.

1995 Admission: Free.

Three major markets.

Black Angus, 8:00 A.M. to 5:00 P.M., year-round, indoor and outdoor; Carl Barto, 2717 Long Farm Lane, Lancaster, PA 17601, (717) 569-3536 or (717) 484-4385.

Renninger's #1, 7:30 A.M. to 5:00 P M , year-round, indoor and outdoor; Renninger's Promotions, 27 Bensinger Drive, Schuylkill Haven, PA 17972. Phone on Sunday: (717) 336-2177.

Shupp's Grove, 7:00 A.M. to 5:00 P.M., April through September, indoor and outdoor; Shupp's Grove, 1686 Dry Tavern Road,

Denver, PA 17517. Information: (717) 484-4115; dealer reservations: (717) 949-3656.

Antique World and Flea Market

10995 Main Street, Clarence, NY 14031. Main Street is part of Route 5.

Every Sunday, 8:00 A.M. to 4:00 P.M.

Three buildings—one devoted to antiques and collectibles, one to flea market material, and one as exhibition building.

350 dealers in winter and 650 dealers in summer. Indoors.

1995 Admission: Free.

Antique World, 10995 Main Street, Clarence, NY 14031. (716) 759-8483.

Atlanta Flea Market

5360 Peachtree Industrial Boulevard, Chamblee, GA 30341.

Friday and Saturday, 11:00 A.M. to 7:00 P.M. and Sunday Noon to 7:00 P.M.

Antiques, collectibles, and gift items.

150 dealers. Indoor.

1995 Admission: Free.

Atlanta Flea Market, 5360 Peachtree Industrial Blvd., Chamblee, GA 30341, (404) 458-0456.

First Monday Trade Days

Canton, TX 75103. Two blocks from downtown square.

Friday through Monday. Friday before the first Monday of each month, 7:00 A.M. to dusk.

Antiques, collectibles, new merchandise, crafts. [*Editor's note:* This belong in the book—not because it is a great source for antiques and collectibles, but because it is the best known swap meet/flea market in the world.]

Over 4,000 booths. Antiques and collectibles located on three-acre plot north of Courthouse.

1995 Admission: Free. Parking: $2.00.

City of Canton, PO Box 245, Canton, TX 75103. (903) 567-6556.

Lambertville Antiques Flea Market

Route 29, 1½ miles south of Lambertville, NJ 08530.

Saturday and Sunday, 6:00 A.M. to 4:00 P.M.

Antiques and collectibles.

150 dealers. Indoor and outdoor.

1995 Admission: Free.

Mr. and Mrs. Errhalt, 324 S. Main St., Pennington, NJ 08534, (609) 397-0456.

Renninger's Antiques Center

Highway 441, Mount Dora, FL 32757.

Saturdays and Sundays, 9:00 A.M. to 5:00 P.M. Indoor opens at 9:00 A.M. Extravaganzas on third weekend of November, January, and February. Friday 10:00 A.M. to 5:00 P.M., Saturday 8:00 A.M. to 6:00 P.M., and Sunday 8:00 A.M. to 5:00 P.M.

Antiques and collectibles.

Over 500 dealers. Indoor and outdoor.

1995 Admission: Free. Extravaganza admission: three-day pass $10.00, Friday $10.00, Saturday $5.00, and Sunday $2.00.

Florida Twin Markets, PO Box 939, Zellwood, FL 32798, (904) 383-8393.

Shipshewana Auction and Flea Market

On State Route 5 near the southern edge of Shipshewana, IN 46565.

Wednesdays, 6:00 A.M. to dusk from May through October, 7:30 A.M. to dusk from November through April.

Antiques, collectibles, new merchandise, and produce. In fact, you name it, they sell it.

Can accommodate up to 800 dealers. Indoor and outdoor.

1995 Admission: Free.

Shipshewana Auction, Inc., PO Box 185, Shipshewana, IN 46565.

Thus far you have learned to identify the various types of flea markets, how to locate them, the keys to evaluating whether or not they are right for you, and my recommendations for getting started. Next you need to develop the skills necessary for flea market survival.

CHAPTER FOUR

Flea Market Survival Guide

Your state of exhaustion at the end of the day is the best gauge that I know to judge the value of a flea market—the greater your exhaustion, the better the flea market. A great flea market keeps you on the go from early morning, in some cases 5:00 A.M., to early evening, often 6:00 P.M.. The key to survival is to do advance homework, have proper equipment, develop and follow a carefully thought-out shopping strategy, and do your follow-up chores as soon as you return home.

If you are a Type-A personality, your survival plan is essentially a battle plan. Your goal is to cover the flea market as thoroughly as possible and secure the objectives (bargains and hard-to-find objects) ahead of your rivals. You do not stop until total victory is achieved. Does not sound like you? No matter. You also need a survival plan if you want to maximize fun and enjoyment.

Advance Homework

Consult the flea market's advertisement or brochure. Make certain that you understand the dates and time. You never know when special circumstances may cause a change in dates and even location. Check the admission policy. It may be possible to buy a ticket in advance to avoid the wait in line at the ticket booth.

Determine if there is an early admission fee and what times are in-

volved. It is a growing practice at flea markets to admit collectors and others to the flea market through the use of an early admission fee. In most cases the fee is the cost of renting a space. The management simply does not insist that you set up. Actually, this practice had been going on for some time before management formalized it. Friends of individuals renting space often tag along as helpers or assistants. Once inside, the urge to shop supersedes their desire to help their friend.

Review the directions. Are they detailed enough to allow you to find the flea market easily? Remember, it still may be dark when you arrive. If you are not certain, call the manager and ask for specific directions. Also, make certain of parking provisions, especially when a flea market takes place within a city or town. Local residents who are not enamored with a flea market in their neighborhood take great pleasure in informing police of illegally parked cars and watching the cars get towed away. In some cases, I have found locating parking to be more of a problem than locating the flea market. Avoid frustration and plan ahead.

Decide if you are going to stay overnight either the evening before the flea market opens or during the days of operation. In many cases local motel accommodations are minimal. It is not uncommon for dealers as well as collectors to commute fifty miles each way to attend Brimfield. The general attitude of most flea market managers is that accommo-

dations are your problem, not their problem. If you are lucky, you can get a list of accommodations from a local chamber of commerce. The American Automobile Association regional guidebooks provide some help. However, if you attend a flea market expecting to find nearby overnight accommodations without a reservation, you are the world's biggest optimist.

If possible, obtain a map of the flea market grounds. Become familiar with the layout of the spaces. If you know some of your favorite dealers are going to set up, call and ask them for their space number. Mark the location of all toilet facilities and refreshment stands. You may not have time for the latter, but sooner or later you are going to need the former.

Finally, try to convince one or more friends, ideally someone whose area of collecting is totally different from yours, to attend the flea market with you. Each becomes another set of eyes for the other. Meeting at predesignated spots makes exchanging information easy. It never hurts to share the driving and expenses. Best of all, war stories can be told and savored immediately.

Flea Market Checklist

In order to have an enjoyable and productive day at the flea market, you need the right equipment, ranging from clothing to packing material for your purchases. What you do not wear can be stored in your car trunk. Make certain that everything is in order the day before your flea market adventure.

Clothing Checklist

____ Hat

____ Sunglasses

____ Light jacket or sweatshirt

____ Poncho or raincoat

____ Waterproof work boots or galoshes

Field Gear Checklist

____ Canvas bag(s)

____ Cash, checkbook, and credit cards

____ Wants lists

____ Address cards

____ Magnifying glass

____ Swiss Army pocket knife

____ Toilet paper

____ Sales receipts

____ Mechanical pencil or ballpoint pen

____ *Warman's Antiques and Their Prices, Warman's Americana and Collectibles,* and this price guide

Car Trunk Checklist

____ Three to six cardboard boxes

____ Newspaper, bubble wrap, diapers, and other appropriate packing material

____ Sun block

____ First-aid kit

____ Cooler with cold beverages

The vast majority of flea markets that you attend will either be outdoors or have an outdoor section. If you are lucky, the sun will be shining. Beware of sunburn. Select a hat with a broad rim. I prefer a hat with an outside hat band as well. First, it provides a place to stick notes, business cards, and other small pieces of paper I would most

likely lose otherwise. Second, it provides a place to stick a feather or some other distinguishing item that allows my friends to spot me in the crowd. Some flea marketeers use the band as a holder for a card expounding their collecting wants. Make certain that your hat fits snugly. Some flea market sites are quite windy. An experienced flea market attendee's hat will look as though it has been through the wars. It has.

I carry sunglasses, but I confess that I rarely use them. I find that taking them on and off is more trouble than they are worth. Further, they distort colors. However, I have found them valuable at windswept and outdoor markets located in large fields. Since I usually misplace a pair a year, I generally buy inexpensive glasses.

The key to dressing for flea markets is a layered, comfortable approach. The early morning and late evening hours are often cool. A light jacket or sweatshirt is suggested. I found a great light jacket that is loaded with pockets. Properly outfitted, it holds all the material I would normally put in my carrying bag.

You must assume that it is going to rain. I have never been to Brimfield when it was not raining. Rain, especially at an outdoor flea market, is a disaster. What is astonishing is how much activity continues in spite of the rain. I prefer a poncho over a raincoat because it covers my purchases as well as my clothing.

Most flea markets offer ponchos for sale when rain starts. They are lightweight and come with a storage bag. Of course, you have to be a genius to fold them small enough to get them back into their original storage bag. The one I purchased at Kane County has lasted four years. Mrs. Robinson, being a shrewd promoter, just happened to have them imprinted with information about her flea market. I had a great time there so I have never objected to being a

walking bulletin board on her behalf.

The ideal footwear for a flea market is a well-broken-in pair of running or walking shoes. However, in the early morning when the ground is wet with dew, a pair of waterproof work boots is a much better choice. I keep my running shoes in the car trunk and usually change into them by 9:00 A.M. at most flea markets.

Rain at outdoor flea markets equals mud. The only defense is a good pair of galoshes. I have been at Brimfield when the rain was coming down so fiercely that dealers set up in tents were using tools to dig water diversion ditches. Cars, which were packed in the nearby fields, sank into the ground. In several cases, local farmers with tractors handsomely supplemented their income.

I always go to a flea market planning to buy something. Since most flea market sellers provide the minimum packaging possible, I carry my own. My preference is a double-handled canvas bag with a flat bottom. It is not as easy an item to find as it sounds. I use one to carry my field gear along with two extra bags that start out folded. I find that I can carry three filled bags comfortably. This avoids the necessity of running back to the car each time a bag is filled.

If you are going to buy something, you have to pay for it. Cash is always preferred by the sellers. I carry my cash in a small white envelope with the amount with which I started marked at the top. I note and deduct each purchase as I go along. If you carry cash, be careful how you display it. Pickpockets and sticky-fingered individuals who cannot resist temptation do attend flea markets.

Since I want a record of my purchases, I pay by check whenever I can. I have tried to control my spending by only taking a few checks. Forget it. I can always borrow money on Monday to cover my weekend purchases. I make certain that I have a minimum of ten checks.

Most flea market sellers will accept checks with proper identification. For this reason, I put my driver's license and a major credit card in the front of my checkbook before entering the flea market. This saves me the trouble of taking out my wallet each time I make a purchase.

A surprising number of flea market sellers are willing to take credit cards. I am amazed at this practice since the only means they have of checking a card's validity is the canceled card booklet they receive each week. They wait until later to get telephone authorization, a potentially dangerous practice.

I buy as much material through the mail as I do at flea markets. One of the principal reasons I attend flea markets is to make contact with dealers. Since flea markets attract many dealers from other parts of the country, I expand my supplier sources at each flea market I attend. The key is to have a wants list ready to give to any flea market seller that admits to doing business by mail. My wants list fills an 8½" × 11" sheet of writing paper. In addition to my wants, it includes my name, post office box address, UPS (i.e., street) address, and office and home telephone number. I also make it a point to get the full name and address of any dealer to whom I give my list. I believe in follow-up.

Not every dealer is willing to take a full-page wants list. For this reason, I have an address (business) card available with my name, street address, phone numbers, and a brief list of my wants. Most take it as a courtesy. However, I have received quotes on a few great items as a result of my efforts.

I carry a simple variety-store ten-power magnifying glass. It is helpful to see marks clearly and to spot cracks in china and glass. Ninety-nine percent of the time I use it merely to confirm something that I saw with the naked eye. Jewelers loupes are overkill unless you are buying jewelry.

Years ago I purchased a good Swiss Army pocket knife, one which contains scissors as part of the blade package. It was one of the smartest investments that I made. No flea market goes by that I do not use the knife for one reason or another. If you do not want to carry a pocket knife, invest in a pair of operating room surgical scissors. They will cut through most anything.

I am a buyer. Why do I carry a book of sales receipts? Alas, many flea market sellers operate in a nontraditional business manner. They are not interested in paper trails, especially when you pay cash. You need a receipt to protect yourself. More on this subject later.

I keep a roll of toilet paper in the car and enough for two sittings in my carrying bag. Do not laugh; I am serious. Most outdoor flea markets have portable toilets. After a few days, the toilet paper supply is exhausted. Even some indoor facilities give out. If I had five dollars from all the people to whom I supplied toilet paper at flea markets, I would be writing this book in Hawaii instead of Pennsylvania.

I carry a mechanical pencil. When I pick up someone's business card, I note why on the back of the card. Use the pencil to mark dealer locations on the flea market map. I do not always buy something when I first spot it. The map helps me relocate items when I wish to go back for a second look. I have wasted hours at flea markets backtracking to find an item that was not located where I thought it was. A ballpoint pen works just as well. The mechanical pencil is a personal preference.

Anyone who tells you they know everything about antiques and collectibles and their prices is a liar. I know the areas in which I collect quite well. But there are many categories where a quick source check never hurts. *Warman's Antiques and Collectibles Price Guide* and *Warman's Americana and Collectibles* are part of my field gear. I could tell you that I carry them out of loyalty to my dad, who edits them. The truth is that I carry them because I have found them more helpful and accurate than other general price guides. I have also scored some major points with dealers and others when I offered to share some of the information found in the category introductions with them.

My car trunk contains a number of cardboard boxes, several of which are archival file boxes with hand inserts on the side. I have them because I want to see that my purchases make it home safe and sound. One of the boxes is filled with newspaper, diapers, and some bubble wrap. It supplements the field wrapping so that I can stack objects on top of one another. I check the trunk seals on a regular basis. A leaking car trunk once ruined several key purchases I made on an antiquing adventure.

A wide-brim hat may protect the face and neck from the sun, but it leaves the arms exposed. I admire those individuals who can wear a long-sleeved shirt year-round. I am not one of them. In the summer, I wear short-sleeved shirts. For this reason, I keep a bottle of sun block in the trunk.

I also have a first-aid kit that includes aspirin. The most used object is a Band-Aid for unexpected cuts and scratches. The aspirin comes in handy when I have spent eight or more hours in the sun. My first-aid kit also contains packaged cleaning towelettes. I always use one before heading home.

It does not take much for me to get a flea market high. When I do, I can go the entire day without eating. The same does not hold true for liquid intake. Just as toilet paper is a precious commodity at flea markets, so is ice. I carry a small cooler in my trunk with six to a dozen cans of my favorite beverage of the moment. The fastest way to seal a friendship with a flea market dealer is to offer him or her a cold drink at the end of a hot day.

How to Shop a Flea Market

After attending flea markets for a number of years, I would like to share some of the things that I do to bag the treasures found in the flea market jungle. Much of what I am about to tell you is no more than common sense, but we all know that this is probably one of the most ignored of all the senses.

Most likely you will drive to the flea market. Parking is often a problem. It does not have to be. The general rule is to park as close to the main gate as possible. However, since most flea markets have a number of gates, I usually try to park near a secondary gate. First, this allows me to get closer than I could by trying for the main gate. Second, I have long recognized whatever gate I use as "my" main gate, and it serves well as home base for my buying operations.

As soon as I arrive at the flea market, I check three things before allowing my buying adrenaline to kick into high gear—the location of the toilets, the location of the refreshment stands, and the relationship between outdoor and indoor facilities. The latter is very important. Dealers who regularly do the flea market are most likely to be indoors. If I miss them this time around, I can catch them the next. Dealers who are just passing through are most likely setup outdoors. If I miss them, I may never see them again.

I spend the first half hour at any flea market doing a quick tour in order to (1) understand how the flea market is organized, (2) spot those dealers that I would like to visit later, and (3) develop a general sense of what is happening. I prefer to start at the point farthest from my car and

work my way to the front, just the opposite of most flea market shoppers. It makes trips back to the car shorter each time and reduces the amount of purchases that I am carrying over an extended period of time.

Whenever I go to a flea market to buy, I try to have one to four specific categories in mind. If one tries to look at everything, one develops "antiques and collectibles" shock. Collectors' minds short-circuit if they try to absorb too much. They never get past the first aisle. With specific goals, a quick look at a booth will tell me whether or not it is likely to feature merchandise of interest. If not, I pass it by.

Since time is always at a premium, I make it a practice to ask every dealer, "Do you have any ——?" If they say "no," I usually go to the next booth. However, I have learned that dealers do not always remember what they have. When I am in a booth that should have the type of merchandise that I am seeking, I take a minute or two to do a quick scan to see if the dealer is right. In about 25% of the cases, I have found at least one example of the type of material for which I am looking.

I eat on the run, if I eat at all. A good breakfast before the market opens carries me until the evening hours when dusk shuts down the market. I am at the flea market to stuff my bag and car trunk, not my face.

When I find a flea market that I like, I try to visit it at least once in the spring and once in the late summer or early fall. In many flea markets the same dealers are located in the same spot each time. This is extremely helpful to a buyer. I note their location on my map of the market. When I return the next time, I ask these dealers if they have brought anything that fills my needs. If they say "yes," I ask them to hold it until I return. In most cases, a dealer will agree to hold a piece for one to two hours. Do not abuse the privilege, but do

not hesitate to take advantage of it either.

There is an adage among antiques and collectibles collectors that "if you bought something at a flea market, you own it." I do my best to prove this adage wrong if I am not happy with a purchase. I am successful most of the time.

I try to get a receipt for every purchase that I make. Since many individuals who sell at outdoor flea markets are part-time dealers, they often are unprepared to give a receipt. No problem. I carry a pad of blank receipts and ask them to fill one out.

In every case, I ask the dealers to include their name, shop name (if any), mailing address, and phone number on the receipt. If I do not think a dealer is telling me the truth, I ask for identification. If they give me any flack, I go to their vehicle (usually located in their booth) or just outside their indoor stand and make note of the license plate number. Flea market dealers, especially the outdoor group, are highly mobile. If a problem develops with the merchandise I bought, I want to reach the dealer in order to solve the problem.

Whenever possible, the receipt should contain a full description of the merchandise along with a completeness and condition statement. I also ask the dealer to write "money back guaranteed, no questions asked" on the receipt. This is the only valid guarantee that I know. Phrases such as "guaranteed as represented" and "money back" are open to interpretation and become relatively meaningless if a dispute develops.

I always shop around. At a good flea market, I expect to see the same merchandise in several booths. Prices will vary, often by several hundred if not several thousand percent. I make a purchase immediately only when a piece is a "real" bargain, priced way below current market value. If a piece is near current market value, I often inspect it, note its location on my map, and walk away. If I do not find another in as good condition, at a cheaper price, or both, I go back and negotiate with the dealer.

I take the time to inspect carefully in natural sunlight any piece that I buy. First, I check for defects such as cracks, nicks, scratches, and signs of normal wear. Second, if the object involves parts, I make certain that it is complete. I have been known to take the time to carefully count parts. The last two times that I did not do this, the objects that I bought turned out to be incomplete when I got them home.

I frequently find myself asking a dealer to clean an object for my inspection. Outdoor flea markets are often quite dusty, especially in July and August. The insides of most indoor markets are generally not much better. Dirt can easily hide flaws. It also can discolor objects. Make certain you know exactly what you are buying.

I force myself to slow down and get to know those dealers from whom I hope to make future purchases. Even though it may mean that I do not visit the entire flea market, I have found that the long-term benefits from this type of contact far outweigh the short-term gain of seeing every booth.

Flea Market Food

Flea market food is best described as overcooked, greasy, and heartburn-inducing. I think I forgot to mention that my first-aid kit contains a roll of antacid pills. Gourmet eating facilities are usually nonexistent. Is it any wonder that I often go without eating?

Several flea markets take place on sites that also house a farmer's market. When this is the case, I take time to shop the market and eat at one of its food counters or buy something that I can eat while sitting in my car. I make a point to spot any fast-food restaurants in the vicinity of the flea market. If I get desperate, I get in the car and drive to one of them.

I do make it a point to inquire among the dealers where they go to have their evening meals. They generally opt for good food, plenty of it, and at inexpensive prices. At the end of the day I am hungry. I do not feel like driving home, cleaning up, and then eating. I want to eat where the clientele can stand the appearance and smell of a flea marketeer. I have rarely been disappointed when I followed a flea market dealer's recommendation.

The best survival tactic is probably to bring your own food. I simply find this too much trouble. I get heartburn just thinking about a lunch sitting for several hours inside a car on a hot summer day. No thanks; I will buy what I need.

Follow-Up

Immediately upon returning home, at worst the next day, unpack and record all your purchases. If you wait, you are going to forget important details. This is not the fun part of collecting. It is easy to ignore. Discipline yourself to do it. Get in the habit. You know it is the right thing to do, so do it.

Review the business cards that you picked up and notes that you made. If letters are required, write them. If telephone calls are necessary, make them. Never lose sight of the fact that one of your principal reasons for going to the flea market is to establish long-term dealer contacts.

Finally, if your experiences at the flea market were positive or if you saw ways to improve the market, write a letter to the manager. He or she will be delighted in both instances. Competition among flea markets for dealers and customers is increasing. Good managers want to make their markets better than their competitors'. Your comments and suggestions will be welcomed.

CHAPTER FIVE

Honing Your Shopping Skills

Earlier I mentioned that most buyers view flea markets as places where bargains and ''steals'' can be found. I have found plenty. However, the truth is that you have to hunt long and hard to find them, and in some cases, they evolve only after intense bargaining. Shopping a flea market properly requires skills. This chapter will help shape and hone your shopping skills and alert you to some of the pitfalls involved with buying at a flea market.

With What Type of Dealer Are You Dealing?

There are essentially three types of dealers found at flea markets: (1) the professional dealer, (2) the weekend dealer, and (3) the once-and-done dealer. Each brings a different level of expertise and merchandise to the flea market. Each offers pluses and minuses. Knowing with which type you are dealing is advantageous.

So many flea markets developed in the 1980s and 1990s that there are now professional flea market dealers who practice their craft on a full-time basis. Within any given week, you may find them at three or four different flea markets. They are the modern American gypsies; their living accommodations and merchandise are usually found within the truck, van, or station

wagon in which they are traveling. These individuals survive on shrewdness and hustle. They want to turn over their merchandise as quickly as possible for the best gain possible and are willing to do whatever is necessary to achieve this end.

Deal with professional flea market dealers with a questioning mind; i.e., question everything they tell you about an object from what it is to what they want for it.

Their knowledge of the market comes from hands-on experience. It is not as great as they think in most cases. They are so busy setting up, buying, selling, and breaking down that they have little time to do research or follow trade literature. More than any other group of dealers in the trade, they are weavers of tales and sellers of dreams.

The professional flea market dealer's circuit can stretch from New England to California, from Michigan to Florida. These ''professionals'' are constantly on the move. If you have a problem with something one of these dealers sold you, finding him or her can prove difficult. Do not buy anything from a professional dealer unless you are absolutely certain about it.

Judge the credibility and integrity of the professional flea market dealer by the quality of the merchandise he or she displays. You should see middle- and high-quality material in better condition than you normally expect to find. If the offerings are heavily damaged and appear poorly maintained, walk away.

Do not interpret what I have said to imply that all professional flea market dealers are dishonest. The vast majority are fine individuals. However, as a whole, this group has the largest share of rotten apples in its barrel—more than any other group of dealers in the flea market field. Since there is no professional organization to police the trade and promoters do not care as long as their space rent is paid, it is up to you to protect yourself.

The antiques and collectibles field works on the principle of *caveat emptor,* ''let the buyer beware.'' Just remember that the key is to beware of the seller as well as the merchandise. It pays to know with whom you are doing business.

Weekend flea market dealers are individuals who have a full-time job elsewhere and are dealing on the weekends to supplement their income. In most cases, their weekday job is outside the antiques and collectibles field. However, with the growth of the antiques mall, some of these weekend dealers are really full-time antiques and collectibles dealers. They spend their weekdays shopping and maintaining their mall locations, while selling on the weekend at their traditional flea market location.

In many cases, these dealers specialize, especially if they are in a large flea market environment. As a result, they are usually familiar with the literature relating to their areas of expertise. They also tend to live within a few hours' drive of the flea market in which they set up. This means that they can be found if the need arises.

Once-and-done dealers range from an individual who is using the flea market to dispose of some inherited family heirlooms or portions of an estate to collectors who have culled their collection and are offering their duplicates and discards for sale. Bargains can often be found in both cases. In the first instance, bargains result from lack of pricing knowledge. However, unless you are an early arrival, chances are that the table will be picked clean by the regular dealers and pickers long before you show up. Bargains originate from the collectors because they know the price levels in their field. They realize that in order to sell their discards and duplicates, they will have to create prices that are tempting to dealer and collector alike.

The once-and-done dealers are the least prepared to conduct sales on a business basis. Most likely they will not have a receipt book or a business card featuring their address and phone number. They almost never attempt to collect applicable sales tax.

There is little long-term gain in spending time getting to know the individual who is selling off a few family treasures. However, do not leave without asking, "Is there anything else you have at home that you are planning to sell?" Do spend time talking with the collector. If you have mutual collecting interests, invite him or her to visit, and view your collection. What you are really fishing for is an invitation to view his or her holdings. You will be surprised how often you will receive one when you show genuine interest.

What Is It?

You need to be concerned with two questions when looking at an object: What is it? and How much is it worth? In order to answer the second question, you need a correct answer to the first. Information provided about objects for sale at flea markets is minimal and often nonexistent. In a great many cases, it is false. The only state of mind that protects you is a defensive one.

There are several reasons for the amount of misidentification of objects at flea markets. The foremost is dealer ignorance. Many dealers simply do not take the time to do proper research. I also suspect that they are quite comfortable with the adage that "ignorance is bliss." As long as an object bears a resemblance to something authentic, it will be touted with the most prestigious label available.

When questioning dealers about an object, beware of phrases such as "I think it is an . . . ," "As best as I can tell," "It looks exactly like," and "I trust your judgment." Push the dealers until you pin them down. The more they vacillate, the more suspicious you should become. Insist that the sales receipt carry a full claim about the object.

In many cases misidentification is passed along from person to person because the dealer who bought the object trusted what was said by the dealer who sold the object. I am always amazed how convinced dealers are that they are right. I have found there is little point in arguing with them in most cases. The only way to preserve both individuals' sanity is to walk away.

If you do not know what something is, do not buy it. The Warman guides that you have in your carrying bag can point you in the right direction, but they are not the final word. If you simply must find out right that minute, consult the listing of references in the Warman guides and then check with the antiques and collectibles book dealer at the market to see if the specific book you need is in stock.

Stories, Stories, and More Stories

A flea market is a place where one's creative imagination and ability to believe what is heard are constantly tested. The number of cleverly crafted stories to explain the origin of pieces and why the condition is not exactly what one expects is endless. The problem is that they all sound plausible. Once again, I come back to the concept upon which flea market survival is founded: a questioning mind.

I often ask dealers to explain the circumstances through which they acquired a piece and what they know about the piece. Note what I said, I am not asking the seller to reveal his or her source. No one should be expected to do that. I am testing the openness and believability of the dealer. If the dealer claims there is something special about an object (e.g., it belonged to a famous person or was illustrated in a book), I ask to see proof. Word-of-mouth stories have no validity in the long run.

Again, there are certain phrases that serve as tip-offs that something may be amiss. "It is the first one I have ever seen," "You will never find another one like it," "I saw one a few aisles over for more money," "One sold at auction a few weeks ago for double what I am asking," and "I am selling it to you for exactly what I paid for it" are just a few examples. If what you are hearing sounds too good to be true, it probably is.

Your best defense is to spend time studying and researching the area in which you want to collect before going to flea markets. Emphasis should be placed equally on object identification and an understanding of the pricing structure within that collecting category. You will not be a happy person if you find that although an object you bought is what the seller claimed it was, you paid far more for it than it is worth.

Period Reproduction, Copycat, Fantasy, or Fake

The number of reproductions, copycats, and fantasy and fake items at flea markets is larger than in any other segment of the field. Antiques and collectibles malls run a close second. In fact, it is not uncommon to find several stands at a flea market selling reproductions, copycats, and fantasy items openly. When you recognize them, take time to study their merchandise. Commit the material to memory. In ten years when the material has begun to age, you will be glad that you did.

Although the above terms are familiar to those who are active in the antiques and collectibles field, they may not be understood by some. A period piece is an example made during the initial period of production. The commonly used term is *real*. However, if you think about it, all objects are real, whether period or not. *Real* is one of those terms that should set your mind to questioning.

A reproduction is an exact copy of a period piece. There may be subtle changes in areas not visible to the naked eye, but essentially it is identical to its period counterpart. A copycat is an object that is similar, but not exactly like the period piece it is emulating. It may vary in size, form, or design elements. In some cases, it is very close to the original. In auction terms, copycats are known as *in the style of*. A fantasy item is a form that was not issued during the initial period of production. An object licensed after Elvis's death would be an Elvis fantasy item. A Chippendale-style coffee table, a

form which did not exist during the first Chippendale period, is another example.

The thing to remember is that reproductions, copycats, and fantasy items are generally mass-produced and start out life honestly. The wholesalers who sell them to dealers in the trade make it clear exactly what they are. Alas, some of the dealers do not do so when they resell them.

Because reproductions, copycats, and fantasy items are mass-produced, they appear in the market in quantity. When you spot a piece in your collecting area that you have never seen before, quickly check through the rest of the market. If the piece is mint, double-check. Handle the piece. Is it the right weight? Does it have the right color? Is it the quality that you expect? If you answer "no" to any of these questions, put it back.

The vast majority of items sold at any flea market are mass-produced, twentieth-century items. Encountering a new influx of never-seen-before items does not necessarily mean they are reproductions, copycats, or fantasy items. Someone may have uncovered a hoard. The trade term is *warehouse find*. A hoard can seriously affect the value of any antique or collectible. All of a sudden the number of available examples rises dramatically. So usually does the condition level. Unless the owner of a hoard is careful, this sudden release of material can drive prices downward.

A fake is an item deliberately meant to deceive. They are usually one-of-a-kind items, with many of them originating in shops of revivalist craftspersons. The folk art and furniture market is flooded with them. Do not assume that because an object is inexpensive, it is all right. You would be surprised how cheaply goods can be made in Third World countries.

It is a common assumption that reproductions, copycats, fantasy

items, and fakes are of poor quality and can be easily spotted. If you subscribe to this theory, you are a fool. There are some excellent reproductions, copycats, fantasy items, and fakes. You probably have read on more than one occasion how a museum was fooled by an object in its collection. If museum curators can be fooled, so can you.

This is not the place for a lengthy dissertation on how to identify and differentiate period objects, reproductions, copycats, fantasies, or fakes. There are books on the subject. Get them and read them. What follows are a few quick tips to put you on the alert:

1. If it looks new, assume it is new.
2. Examine each object carefully, looking for signs of age and repair that should be there.
3. Use all appropriate senses—sight, touch, smell, and hearing—to check an object.
4. Be doubly alert when something appears to be a "steal."
5. Make a copy of any articles from trade papers or other sources that you find about period, reproduction, copycat, fantasy, and fake items and keep them on file.
6. Finally, handle as many authentic objects as possible. The more genuine items you handle, the easier it will be to identify imposters.

What's a Fair Price?

The best selling scenario at a flea market is a buyer and seller who are both extremely happy with the price paid and a seller who has made sufficient profit to allow him or her to stay in business and return to sell another day. Reality is not quite like this. Abundance of merchandise, competition among dealers, and negotiated prices often result in the seller being less than happy with the final price received. Yet the dealers sell because some money is better than no money.

Price haggling is part of the flea market game. In fact, the next section discusses this very subject in detail. The only real value an object has is what someone is willing to pay for it, not what someone asks for it. There is no fixed price for any antique, collectible, or secondhand object. All value is relative.

These considerations aside, there are a few points relating to price and value that the flea marketeer should be aware of. Try to understand these points. Remember, in the antiques and collectibles field there are frequently two or more sides to every issue and rarely any clear-cut right or wrong answer.

First, dealers have a right to an honest profit. If dealers are attempting to make a full-time living in the trade, they must triple their money in order to cover their inventory costs; pay their overhead expenses, which are not inconsequential; and pay themselves. Buy at thirty cents and sell at one dollar. The key problem is that many flea market dealers set up at flea markets not to make money but simply to have a good time. As a result, they willingly sell at much lower profit margins than those who are trying to make a living. It is not really that hard to tell which group is which. Keep the seller's circumstances in mind when haggling.

Second, selling is labor- and capital-intensive. Check a dealer's booth when a flea market opens and again when it closes. Can you spot the missing objects? When a dealer has a "good" flea market, he or she usually sells between fifteen and thirty objects. In most cases, the inventory from which these objects sold consists of hundreds of pieces. Do not think about what the dealer sold, think about what was not sold. What did it cost? How much work is involved in packing, hauling, setting up, and repacking these items until the objects finally sell. Flea market

sellers need a high profit margin to stay in business.

Third, learn to use price guide information correctly. Remember the prices are guides, not price absolutes. For their part, sellers must resist the temptation to become greedy and trap themselves in the assumption that they deserve book price or better for every item they sell. Sellers would do better to focus on what they paid for an object (which, in effect, does determine the final price) rather than on what they think they can get for it (it never sells as quickly as they think). They will make more on volume sales than they will trying to get top dollar for all their items.

Price guide prices represent what a *serious* collector in that category will pay provided he or she does not already own the object. An Elvis Presley guitar in its original box may book for over $500, but it has that value only to an Elvis Presley collector who does not already own one. What this means is that price guide prices tend to be on the high side.

Fourth, the IRS defines fair-market value as a situation where there is a willing buyer and seller and both parties are equally knowledgeable. While the first part of this equation usually applies, the second usually does not. There is no question that knowledge is power in the flea market game and sharing it can cost money. If money were the only issue, I could accept the idea of keeping your mouth shut. However, I like to think that any sale involves transfer of information about the object as well as the object itself. If there were a fuller understanding of the selling situation by both sides, there would be a lot less grousing about prices after the deal is done.

Finally, forget about book value and seller's value. The only value an object has is what it is worth to you. This is the price that you should pay. The only person that can make this judgment is you. It is a decision of

the moment. Never forget that. Do not buy if you do not think the price is fair. Do not look back if you find later that you overpaid. At the moment of purchase, you thought the price was fair. In buying at a flea market, the buck stops in your heart and wallet.

Flea Market Haggling

Few prices at a flea market are firm prices. No matter what anyone tells you, it is standard practice to haggle. You may not be comfortable doing it, but you might as well learn how. The money you save will be your own.

In my mind there are only three prices: a bargain price, a negotiable price, and a ridiculous price. If the price on an object is already a bargain, I pay it. I do this because I like to see the shocked look on a seller's face when I do not haggle. I also do it because I want that dealer to find similar material for me. Nothing encourages this more than paying the price asked.

If the price is ridiculous, marked several times above what it is worth, I simply walk away. No amount of haggling will ever get the price to where I think it belongs. All that will happen is that the dealer and I will become frustrated. Who needs it? Let the dealers sit with their pieces. Sooner or later, the message will become clear.

I firmly believe it is the responsibility of the seller to set the asking price. When an object is not marked with a price, I become suspicious that the dealer is going to set the asking price based on what he or she thinks I can pay. I have tested this theory on more than one occasion by sending several individuals to inquire about the value of an unmarked item. In every case, a variety of prices were reported back to me. Since most of the material that I collect is mass-produced, I walk away from all unpriced merchandise. I will find another example somewhere else. This type of dealer does not deserve my business.

I have too much to do at a flea market to waste time haggling. If I find a piece that is close to what I am willing to pay, I make a counter-offer. I am very clear in what I tell the seller. "I am willing to pay 'x' amount. This is my best offer. Will you take it?" Most dealers are accustomed to responding with "Let's halve the difference." Hard though it is at times, I never agree. I tell the dealer that I made my best offer to save time haggling, and I intend to stick by it.

If the flea market that I am attending is a monthly or weekly, I may follow the object for several months. At the end of four to five months, I speak with the dealer and call attention to the fact that he or she has been unsuccessful in selling the object for the amount that had been asked. I make my counter-offer, which sometimes can be as low as half the value marked on the piece. While the dealer may not be totally happy selling the object at that price, the prospect of any sale is often far better than keeping the object in inventory for several more months.

In Summary

If you are gullible, flea markets may not be for you. While not a Darwinian jungle, the flea market has pitfalls and traps which must be avoided in order for you to be successful. The key is to know that these pitfalls and traps exist.

Furthermore, successful flea marketeering comes from practice. There is no school or seminar where you can learn the skills you need. You fly by the seat of your pants, learn as you go, wing it. The tuition that you pay will be the mistakes that you make along the way. Never get discouraged. Everyone else you see at the flea market has experienced or is experiencing exactly what is happening to you. When you become a seasoned veteran, you will look back upon the learning period and laugh. In the interim, at least try to smile.

CHAPTER SIX

The Flea Market Scene Today

The current status of today's flea markets can be summarized in one sentence: *Little has changed in the past two years*. The points that I discussed in my lengthy analysis of the flea market scene for the second edition of *Price Guide to Flea Market Treasures* remain valid. Repeating them serves little purpose. For those who own a copy of the second edition, I strongly suggest re-reading "Chapter 6: The Flea Market Scene Today." If you do not own a copy, try your local library or a friend. If this fails, send a SASE (self addressed, stamped—$0.32—envelope) to Harry L. Rinker Jr., Rinker Enterprises, Inc. (5093 Vera Cruz Road, Emmaus, PA 18049) for a photocopy.

Perhaps the biggest news from the flea market scene is the growing emphasis on post–World War II material. This comes as no surprise. This is the material that now fills most attics, basements, garages, and sheds. It is also the material that (1) is affordable and (2) is attracting the attention of young collectors.

In fact, the number of items from the late 1940s through the 1950s is decreasing, not increasing. Does this mean that '40s and '50s material is becoming scarce and pricey? I believe it does. As a result, one is more likely to find it in malls, shops, and shows than at flea markets.

The positive side is watching collectors discover the 1960s and 1970s as valid collecting periods. In the early 1990s toys, games, and puzzles from these eras were domi-

nant. In the mid-1990s collectors are expanding their horizons. Dinnerware, novelty glassware, metals (e.g., hammered aluminum), and furniture are selling well. Transistor radios from the 1950s and 1960s have replaced bakelite models from the 1930s and 1940s as the hot radio commodity of the moment.

While not every new collecting category has its origin in the flea market scene, many do. During the past two years, I have spotted several areas that I suspect Dad will eventually have to add to a future edition of *Warman's Americana & Collectibles* (hint, hint).

The first is record album covers from the 1960s and 1970s. Forget the records. Use them as frisbees. The key is the cover art. Record album covers from the 1960s and 1970s are home to some of the best psychedelic art of the period. Prices start at $6.00 and go up. If you do decide to get caught up in this craze, stress condition. Many covers are heavily damaged. Remember— these records were issued in the hundreds of thousands and millions. Covers in fine to excellent condition are plentiful. You just have to hunt for them. Some record album sellers are touting covers featuring artists from Perry Como to Whitney Houston as potential long-term collectibles. I do not buy this argument. Como already has shown he is relatively one-generational and, paraphrasing Secretary of the Treasury Benson: "He is no Elvis."

Second, time to take a look at auto racing collectibles. Admittedly,

auto racing collectibles are stronger in the South and Southwest than other sections of the country, but the collecting trend is spreading nationwide. It is going to take some doing to convince Dad that when he hears Petty he should think *race car driver* and not *pinup illustrator*. He is a quick study. There is hope.

Third, over the past ten years, Dad has quietly collected pocket calculators and early home computers. A collectors' club has been organized within the past year. Pocket calculators and computers are only the tip of the iceberg with respect to microchip collectibles. The first edition of Pong in its original box now sells for over $20.00. Microchip collectibles, as Walt Disney would say, is a whole new world.

Fourth, Dad swears (a lot sometimes) that he will never add PVC (polyvinylchloride) collectibles to a Warman's. There is something about Smurfs and Trolls that drive him mad. Too bad. PVC collectibles are hot. Boggles the mind, doesn't it?

Finally, there are Melmac and Pyrex. The former is still speculative, but the latter is firmly established. There are three price guides devoted exclusively to Pyrex. Early Corning material is highly collectible. Still using it in your kitchen? Stop immediately.

The eclectic nature of interior decorating continues to confuse the flea marketeer—buyer and seller alike. No one decorating look dominates the flea market scene as Country did in the 1970s and early 1980s. At today's flea market Country is found side by side with formal, Western, psychedelic, and junk.

Price Guide to Flea Market Treasures focuses on flea markets with a strong antiques and collectibles orientation. Tragically, their number is diminishing rather than increasing. The reason is simple. As the number of flea markets continues to grow, the competition for renters of booths or space increases. There are not enough antiques and collectibles dealers to fill the available spaces. Faced with the prospect of empty spaces, many flea market owners and managers will rent to anyone willing to pay the setup fee, caring little whether those who rent space are selling crafts or new merchandise. The result is that several antiques and collectibles flea markets now more closely resemble swap meets than flea markets.

The positive side is that many owners and managers separate the antiques and collectibles portion of their market from those where other types of merchandise is sold. In addition, more and more owners are constructing pavilions or buildings to house antiques and collectibles dealers. With increased emphasis among collectors on condition, few dealers can afford to expose their merchandise to the elements any longer.

This is especially true of the paper community, where dealers and collectors alike now recognize the negative effects of exposing paper to sun and dirt for any extended period of time. The amount of paper items found at flea markets in the mid-1990s has decreased significantly from the early 1990s. Flea market field conditions are not the sole reason for the shift. Equally important is the tremendous growth in specialized paper shows across the country.

Most major flea markets now run extravaganza weekends two to three times a year. The goal is to double or triple the usual number of dealers and attendees. While the

concept still has some validity, increased numbers are deluding the quality-dealer base at any one show.

Almost every extravaganza has an *early-buyer's premium,* an amount that allows collectors to shop while dealers are setting up. This concept now has been expanded to monthly and even weekly flea markets. While it makes dealers unhappy, it adds significantly to the pockets of the promoters. Look for more and more promoters to institute an early-buyer's premium in the years ahead.

In this chapter in the second edition of *Price Guide to Flea Market Treasures,* I stated: "Worth noting is the decline in the amount of reproduction and fake folk art items at the flea markets of the early 1990s." I take it back. I must have had my head buried in the sand. Rather than decreasing, the number of reproductions, copycats, fantasy items, fakes, and contemporary folk art has increased significantly. Further, few of the sellers are labeling the items for what they are. The low prices asked clearly reflect the recent origin of the objects. However, the novice collector or casual buyer does not know this. Rather, they believe they are acquiring older items at bargain prices. They are not happy campers when they discover that they have been had; and, they do eventually discover this.

While some individuals fill their entire booth or space with modern items, many dealers mix them with their period pieces. If confronted, they plead ignorance. I am sorry. I do not buy this argument. They know full well what they have. There is only one solution, albeit painful. Do not buy from anyone who has an unmarked reproduction, copycat, fantasy item, or fake in their booth or space. Walk away. Vote with your wallet. Finally, on the way out of the flea market, tell the owner or manager about the dealer and how angry you are that he is allowed to set up.

What happened to the recession of the late 1980s and early 1990s? Has it gone away? Are we on the road to recovery? President Clinton and the Democrats would like the public to believe this is the case. If recovery is in the wind, you could not prove it by most flea market dealers.

The recession is very much alive within the flea market community. Selling remains tough. Finding replacement merchandise at affordable prices is even tougher. Customers demand more for their money—high quality goods at low prices. Even a bargain price cannot tempt a customer whose funds have been tapped out. The amount of discretionary income—the dollars that fuel a strong flea market economy—remains small.

The good news is that dealers and buyers alike have not lost hope. Their numbers remain strong. Gate attendance has stabilized in most markets and started to increase in a few. Dealer count also remains consistent. Everyone is hanging in there.

It probably will take another decade to put behind us the buying conservatism of dealers and collectors brought about by the recession of the late 1980s and early 1990s. In the interim, prices remain stable—not a bad thing if you stop and think about it. Again, to give the picture a positive slant, price decline has stopped. What is needed is an initial push to overcome the inertia that is preventing the market from moving forward. How soon will this happen? At the moment, it is anyone's guess. My own suspicion is sooner, rather than later.

Dad's big on tradition—so am I. When I ended my market analysis in the second edition, I used the final three paragraphs from the market analysis in the first edition of *Price Guide to Flea Market Treasures.* The advice they contain is timeless and written as I want to state it. As a result, they appear here as they will in any future edition of this book that I author.

"Permit me one final thought. The key to having an enjoyable experience at a flea market does not rest with the manager, the dealers, the physical setting, or the merchandise. The key is you. Attend with reasonable expectations in mind. Go to have fun, to make a pleasant day of it. Even if you come home with nothing, savor the contacts that you made and the fact that you spent a few hours or longer among the goodies.

"As a smart flea marketeer, you know the value of customers to keep flea markets alive and functioning. When you find a good flea market, do not keep the information to yourself. Write or call the regional trade papers and ask them to do more stories about the market. Share your news with friends and others. Encourage them to attend. There is plenty for everyone.

"Happy Hunting from my Dad, the Rinkettes, and me."

PART TWO

Flea Market Treasures

Price Notes

Flea market prices for antiques and collectibles are not as firmly established as those at malls, shops, and shows. As a result, it is imperative that you treat the prices found in this book as *guides,* not *absolutes.*

Prices given are based on the national retail price for an object that is complete and in fine condition. *Please Note: These are retail prices.* They are what you would expect to pay to purchase the objects. They do not reflect what you might realize if you were selling objects. A "fair" selling price to a dealer or private collector ranges from 20% to 40% of the book price, depending on how commonly found the object is.

Prices quoted are for objects that show a minimum of wear and no major blemishes to the display surface. The vast majority of flea market objects are mass-produced. As such, they survive in quantity. Do not buy damaged or incomplete objects. It also pays to avoid objects that show signs of heavy use.

Regional pricing is a factor within the flea market area, especially when objects are being sold close to their place of manufacture. When faced with higher prices due to strong regional pricing, I offer the price an object would bring in a neighboring state or geographic area. In truth, regional pricing has all but disappeared due to the large number of nationally oriented antiques and collectibles price guides, magazines, newspapers, and collectors' clubs.

Finally, *you* determine price; it is what *you* are willing to pay. Flea market treasures have no fixed prices. What has value to one person may be totally worthless to another.

Is it possible to make sense out of this chaos? Yes, but in order to do so, you have to jump in feet first: attend flea markets and buy.

Happy Hunting! May all your purchases turn out to be treasures.

Abbreviations

These are standard abbreviations used in the listings in *Price Guide to Flea Market Treasures,* third edition.

3D	three-dimensional	h	height, high	orig	original
adv	advertising	hp	hand painted	oz	ounce or ounces
C	century	illus	illustrated, illustration, or	pc	piece
c	circa		illustrations	pcs	pieces
circ	circular	imp	impressed	pgs	pages
cov	cover or covered	int.	interior	pkg	package
d	diameter or depth	j	jewels	pr	pair
dec	decorated or decoration	K	karat	pt	pint
dj	dust jacket	l	length, long	qt	quart
ed	edition	lb	pound	rect	rectangular
emb	embossed	litho	lithograph or lithographed	sgd	signed
expo	exposition	MBP	mint in bubble pack	SP	silver plated
ext.	exterior	mfg	manufactured	SS	sterling silver
ftd	footed	MIB	mint in box	sq	square
gal	gallon	MIP	mint in package	vol	volume
		MISB	mint in sealed box	w	width, wide
		mkd	marked	yg	yellow gold
		MOC	mint on card	yr	year
		MOP	mother of pearl		
		No	number		

ABINGDON POTTERY

Over the years, Roseville and Weller pottery, favorites of old–time traditionalist collectors of mass–produced pottery wares, have become more and more expensive. In the 1970s and 1980s collectors with limited budgets began concentrating on firms such as Gonder, Hall, Hull, McCoy, Stangl, and Vernon Kiln. Now this material is going up in value. Stretch your dollar by concentrating on some of the firms that also have collector appeal. Abingdon Potteries, Inc., J. A. Bauer Pottery Company, Haeger Potteries, Metlox Potteries, and Pfaltzgraff Pottery Company are a few suggestions. I'll bet you can think of many more.

The Abingdon Sanitary Manufacturing Company began manufacturing bathroom fixtures in 1908 in Abingdon, IL. In 1938, they began production of art pottery made with a vitreous body. This line continued until 1970 and included over 1,000 shapes and pieces. Almost 150 colors were used to decorate these wares. Given these numbers, forget about collecting an example of every form in every color ever made. Find a few forms that you like and concentrate on them. There are some great ones.

Club: Abingdon Pottery Club, 212 South Fourth, Monmouth, IL 61462.

Ashtray, green, Sol Ellis adv **20.00**
Bookends, pr
    Horse Head, black, #441 . . . . **50.00**
    Sea Gull, 6" h **40.00**
Bowl, low, 12" d, blue, flower decals, #518
     . . . . **25.00**
Candlesticks, pr, pink, double, #575   **20.00**
Console Bowl
    9" d, round, blue **8.00**
    18" l, oval, white **18.00**
Cookie Jar
    Daisy, 8" h **30.00**
    Granny, green **135.00**
    Humpty Dumpty, 10½" h **185.00**
    Jack-In-The-Box, 10½" h **295.00**
    Little Miss Muffet, 10½" h **295.00**
    Pineapple, 10½" h, 3664 . . . . **75.00**
Cornucopia, blue, #474 . . . . **15.00**
Dish, oblong, pink, two geese dec . . . **35.00**
Pitcher, ice lip, 2 qt, #200 . . . . **35.00**
Planter
    Cactus, 7" l, bookend type, pr . . . **55.00**
    Scroll and Leaf pattern, 9 × 3½", yellow
     . . . . **6.50**
String Holder, mouse, 8½" d **80.00**
Vase
    Cactus, #669 . . . . **15.00**

Classic, 9⅞" h, blue, emb leaf band, orig
    label **25.00**
Grecian, 8" h, #603 . . . . **25.00**
High Oval, matte pink, #685 . . . . **35.00**
Sang, 10" h, white matte glaze, #304
     . . . . **40.00**
Scroll, 9" h, soft green, flared **10.00**
Sea Horse **18.00**
Tulip, 8" h, yellow **40.00**
Wall Pocket
    Butterfly, #601 . . . . **65.00**
    Leaf, #724 . . . . **40.00**

ACTION FIGURES

Action, action, action is the key to action figures. Action figures show action. You can recognize them because they can be manipulated into an action pose or are modeled into an action pose.

There are a wealth of supporting accessories for most action figures, ranging from clothing to vehicles, that are as collectible as the figures themselves. A good rule is the more pizzazz, the better the piece.

This is a relatively new collecting field. Emphasis is placed on pieces in mint or near–mint condition. The best way to find them is with their original packaging. Better yet, buy some new and stick them away.

Periodicals: *Action Figure News & Toy Review*, 556 Monroe Turnpike, Monroe, CT 06468; *Tomart's Action Figure Digest*, Tomart Publications, 3300 Encrete Lane, Dayton, OH 45439; *Triton: Comic Cards & Collectibles*, Attic Books Ltd, 15 Danbury Rd, Ridgefield, CT 06877.

Action Jackson, Mego, 1974, blonde hair
     . . . . **20.00**
All–Star Wrestlers, Remco, Legion of Doom
    Road Warriors **15.00**
Aquaman, Super Powers Collection, Kenner,
    1984–86 . . . . **20.00**
A–Team, Galoob, 3¾" h, set of four, 1984
     . . . . **30.00**
Bart Simpson, Mattel, 1990 . . . . **5.00**
Black Hole, Mego, 3¾" h, Humanoid, 1980
     . . . . **50.00**
Bruce Wayne, Kenner, #63180, quick
    change Batman costume, 1990 . . . **15.00**
Captain Power, Mattel, 1987
    Captain Power **8.00**
    Corporal Pilot Chase **15.00**
    Sgt Scout Baker **12.00**
    Tritor **35.00**
Carey Mahoney, Police Academy, Kenner,
    1990 . . . . **6.00**
Charon, Clash of the Titans, Mattel, 3¾" h,
    1980 . . . . **15.00**

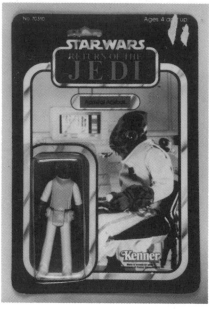

Star Wars, Return of the Jedi, Admiral Ackbar, Kenner, No. 70310, 9 × 6", $20.00.

Chuck Norris, Karate Kommandos, Kenner,
    battle gear, 1986 . . . . **12.00**
Conan the Warrior, Remco, 1984 . . . **15.00**
Dick Tracy, Playmates, #5701, 1990   **5.00**
Dukes of Hazzard, Bo, Mego, 3¾" h, 1981
     . . . . **10.00**
Evel Knievel, Ideal, white outfit, 1973–74
     . . . . **30.00**
Flash Gordon, Mego, 1976 . . . . **50.00**
Grizzly Adams, Mattel, 1978 . . . . . . **25.00**
Hawkeye, M.A.S.H., Tri–Star, large size,
    1970 . . . . **35.00**
Hoss Cartwright, Bonanza, American Character, 1966 . . . . **100.00**
Illya Kuryakin, Man From U.N.C.L.E., Gilbert **200.00**
Indiana Jones, Kenner, #46010, field outfit
    with whip, 1982 . . . . **80.00**
James Bond, Gilbert, 1965–66 . . . . . **150.00**
Johnny West, Best of the West, Marx, quick
    draw, 1965 . . . . **75.00**
Juggernaut, X–Men, Toy Biz, #4909, 5" h,
    power punch action **10.00**
Moon McDare, Gilbert **150.00**
Napoleon Solo, Man From UNCLE, Gilbert,
    1965 . . . . **140.00**
Officer Bowzer and Blitz, C.O.P.S., Hasbro,
    #7687, 1988 . . . . **15.00**
Planet of the Apes, Mego, 1973–75
    Cornelius **35.00**
    Soldier Ape **40.00**
Robin Hood, Mego, 1974 . . . . **85.00**
Robocop, Kenner, 1988 . . . . **8.00**
Sheriff of Nottingham, Robin Hood Prince
    of Thieves, Kenner, #05850, with
    sword, 1991 . . . . **6.00**
Starbuck, Battlestar Galactica, Mattel, 1978
     . . . . **20.00**

Superman, Super Power Collection, Kenner,
1984–86 . . . . **15.00**
Thundercats, LJN, 1985–87 . . . . **10.00**
Tom Selleck, Magnum P.I., LJN, 1983 **12.00**
Wonder Woman, Mego, 12¼" h, 1978
. . . . **75.00**
Zorro, Gabriel, 1982 . . . . **10.00**

ADVENTURE GAMES

Adventure games have been played for hundreds of years. In an adventure game, each player assumes the role of a character. The character's fate is determined by choices that he and other players make. The rules are often very complex; games can last for days, even months.

There are many different game scenarios ranging from sports and entertainment, war and conflict, to finance and fortune. The principal marketing source for current games is the comic book shop. Some comic book shops are also starting to handle discontinued games.

Collectors fall into two groups: those who buy discontinued games to play them and those who buy them solely for the purpose of collecting them. Both groups place strong emphasis on completeness. Many of the games contain more than one hundred different playing pieces. Few take the time to count all the parts. This is why adventure games tend to be relatively inexpensive when found at garage sales and flea markets.

A small group of individuals have begun to collect playing pieces, many of which are hand painted. However, rarely does the price paid exceed the initial cost of the figure.

Chess Set, 19" l hinged wood box opens to
game board, ivory playing pieces **175.00**
Dungeons & Dragons, Gygax & Arneson,
Tactical Studies Rules, orig set, three
volumes: *Men & Magic*, Book 1,
Monsters & Treasure, Book 2, and *The
Underworld & Wilderness Adventures*,
Book 3; 1974, MIB **150.00**
Gettysburg, Avalon Hill, 1958 . . . . . . **30.00**
High-Bid: The Auction Game, 3M (Minnesota Mining and Manufacturing Company), 1965 . . . . **7.50**
Magic: The Gathering, Wizards of the
Coast, 363 cards **125.00**
Management, Avalon Hill, 1960 . . . . **15.00**
Starship Troopers, Robert Heinlein, Avalon
Hill, 1976, MIB **20.00**
Star Wars Star Warriors, West End Games,
1987, MIB **25.00**

Fast Attack Boats, A Game of the Arab-Israeli Naval War, 1973, copyright 1980 Yaquinto Publications Inc., #2205, 12½" sq, opens to 25" l, $5.00.

Strategic Command, Transogram, 1950
. . . . **45.00**
Woman & Man: The Classic Confrontation,
Psychology Today Games, 1971   **12.50**

ADVERTISING ITEMS

Break advertising items into two groups: items used to merchandise a product and items used to promote a product. Merchandising advertising is a favorite with interior decorators and others who want it for its mood-setting ability. It is often big, splashy, and showy. Promotional advertising (giveaways) are primarily collector-driven.

The thing to remember is that almost every piece of advertising is going to appeal to more than one collector. As a result, prices for the same piece will often differ significantly depending on who the seller views as the final purchaser.

Almost all advertising is bought for the purpose of display. As a result, emphasize theme and condition. The vast majority of advertising collectibles are two-dimensional. Place a premium on large three-dimensional objects.

Clubs: Antique Advertising Association of America, PO Box 1121, Morton Grove, IL 60053; The Ephemera Society of America, PO Box 37, Schoharie, NY 12157; The Trade Card Collector's Association, PO Box 284, Marlton, NJ 08053; Tin Container Collectors Association, PO Box 440101, Aurora, CO 80044.

Periodicals: *National Association of Paper and Advertising Collectors (P.A.C.),*

PO Box 500, Mount Joy, PA 17552; *Paper Collectors' Marketplace* (PCM), PO Box 128, Scandinavia, WI 54977.

Bag Rack, Honey Bread **165.00**
Banana Hook, Jacko, boy with banana hair
illus **18.00**
Bank
Blue Bonnet Sue **25.00**
Charlie The Tuna **125.00**
Green Giant, Little Sprout, musical **35.00**
Kool-Aid, 7" h, plastic, mechanical, red,
yellow base, slogan decal, orig box,
1970s **50.00**
Norge Refrigerator, 4" h, metal, painted,
white, black base, 1930s **40.00**
Oscar Mayer, 9" l, figural, Wienermobile, orig box **15.00**
Pillsbury Doughboy, MIB **40.00**
Rival Dog Food, can shape, tin . . . **15.00**
Scrubbin Bubbles **12.00**
Banner, Valen'Ju Orange Drink, 58 × 35",
colorful **65.00**
Beater Jar, Wesson Oil **72.00**
Bill Hook
Ceresota Flour **45.00**
Peacock Roasted Coffee, diecut, full
color cardboard, wire hook . . . **22.00**
Blotter
Beech-Nut Gum, color graphics, 1937
. . . . **22.00**
Blue Coal, The Shadow illus **18.00**
Blue Valley Butter **6.00**
Holstein Milk **9.00**
Kellogg's Rice Krispies, 1940s **22.00**
Morton's Salt **10.00**
Royal Corona Stoves, range illus   **10.00**
Book
Eveready Flash Light Batteries, *Book of
Radio Stars,* illus, includes Groucho
Marx, Jack Benny, and George Burns,
1930 . . . . **38.00**
Kellogg's, *Storybook of Games,* 1931
. . . . **35.00**
Booklet, Colgate, *Jungle Pow-Wow,* 1911
. . . . **18.00**
Bookmark
Acorn Stoves **6.00**
Buckwalter Stoves, celluloid, diecut, figural, teddy bear and stove illus on
back, Whitehead and Hoag, 1907
. . . . **45.00**
Royal Insurance Co, celluloid **15.00**
Bowl
Sample From The Strong Mfg Co, Sebring, Ohio, 3½" d, porcelain
enamelware, green and white, inscription int. **40.00**
Use Jaxon Soap, 6" d, cast iron, bail
handle **75.00**
Box
Baker's Chocolate, wood, dovetailed,
1900 . . . . **45.00**
Dr Baker's Condition Powders, cov,
wood, dovetailed **45.00**
Fairy Soap, five bars, unopened   **65.00**

Imperial Peanut Butter, wood, dovetailed **35.00**

Uncle Tom's Chewing Gum **135.00**

Broadside, Pure Milk, "New System" illus, c1885 ....**32.00**

Broom Rack, Blu–J Brooms, two multi-colored signs **495.00**

Butter Tub, Willow Farm, LaGrange, IL, stoneware **88.00**

Cabinet

Putnam Dye **95.00**

Rit Dye, woman on front, drawers in back **155.00**

Can, Dutch Cleanser, unopened, 1940s **15.00**

Change Tray

Choclat Suchard, glass, colorful St Bernard image **30.00**

C Worz Saloon, 1907 ....**55.00**

Frank Jones Alea **60.00**

Franklin Life **30.00**

Globe Wernicke, couple illus, 1930s **65.00**

Old Reliable Coffee, beautiful woman, 1907 ....**148.00**

Sollwerch Chocalots **50.00**

Charm, Ideal Dog Food, metal **12.00**

Christmas Card, Breyer Ice Cream Company, c1920 ....**20.00**

Cigarette Lighter

Mayflower Moving Service, van illus, Made in Germany **45.00**

TraveLodge Motels, enameled sleepy bear on billboard illus **35.00**

Clipboard, 4 × 5¾", Ludlow–Saylor Wire Co, St Louis, 75th Anniversary, brass, 1931 ....**26.00**

Clock Radio

Pillsbury, Poppin Fresh **50.00**

Raid Bug **285.00**

Condiment Set, creamer, sugar, salt and pepper shakers, Ken–L–Ration Dog **225.00**

Cookie Jar

Alpo dog **85.00**

Keebler Elf Treehouse **38.00**

Nabisco, McCoy **50.00**

Counter Card, National Oats, diecut, girl carrying basket, c1900 ....**35.00**

Creamer, Howard Johnsons **35.00**

Crock, Germ Proof Water Filter, Pasteur Chamberland, Dayton, OH **175.00**

Dispenser, Smith Brothers Cough Drops **225.00**

Display

Chocks Vitamins, counter top, metal **25.00**

Eveready Flashlight Batteries, counter top, litho tin, 1930s **75.00**

Monarch Range Golden Jubilee, counter top, 1896–1946, 14 × 14", double gold coin, orig mailing envelope **40.00**

Nestle's Hot Chocolate, stand–up, cardboard, diecut, girl **550.00**

St Joseph's Aspirin, counter top, tin **75.00**

Sunbeam Bread, counter top, loaf of bread shape, 1940s **15.00**

West Hairnets, 6" sq, counter top, litho tin, 1918 ....**150.00**

White Horse Whiskey, 15" h, counter top, horse shape **85.00**

Display Rack

Eagle Leather Laces **25.00**

Esquire Shoe Polish, metal, revolving **50.00**

Lord Calvert Coffee, tin, holds six containers **200.00**

Uncle Josh Pork Rind **30.00**

Door Push

Colonial Is Good Bread, 3 × 22", adjustable, double sided, blue and black paint **75.00**

Fleischmann's Yeast, porcelain **250.00**

Red Rose Tea **350.00**

Salada Tea, porcelain enamel ...**110.00**

Fan, Symphonies, colorful, 1930s **165.00**

Figure

Charlie Tuna **25.00**

Icee Bear **25.00**

Insulite, 4" h, Bill Drite, leprechaun, cast bronze **125.00**

Michelin Man **30.00**

Mr Bubble **20.00**

RCA Victor Nipper, chalk, logo **45.00**

Regan's Holsum Bread, 9½" h, cardboard, pudgy little girl **25.00**

Speedy Alka-Seltzer **150.00**

Flyswatter, Wittman's hardware, wood handle, 1930s **4.00**

Game, checkers, Standard Oil **60.00**

Glass, Welch's, cartoon scenes, boxed set, 1974 ....**45.00**

Hatchet, Art Stove Co, 4" l **50.00**

Jar, Lik–Em Nuts, counter top, clear glass, hexagonal, raised lettering, ribbed dec, metal screw lid **75.00**

Ledger, pocket type, Chicago Stove Works, heaters and ranges illus, c1900 ... **10.00**

Match Holder

J C Stevens **225.00**

Juicy Fruit **145.00**

Matchsafe, pocket type, Buffum Tools, Louisiana, MO **75.00**

Menu, Wagon Wheel Cafe, 1942 .....**6.00**

Milk Box, metal, Borden's, Elsie illus **80.00**

Mirror

Buckwalter Stoves, pocket, oval, celluloid, detailed stove illus **75.00**

Consolidated Ice Co, polar bear and Eskimo scene **150.00**

Dr. Walker's Bitters, pocket, brass **48.00**

Mug, Speedy Alka-Seltzer **15.00**

Neckerchief, Lee Jeans **65.00**

Needle Threader, Prudential Insurance, tin **6.50**

Pamphlet

Nestles Baby Food, 1922 ....**10.00**

Shredded Wheat, 1918 ....**6.00**

Paper Clip, Venus Pencils, brass **23.00**

Paperweight

Diamond Tool & Horseshoe Co, horseshoe shape **30.00**

King Sales–Memphis, TN, To Forge Our Relationship, brass, anvil shape, emb **25.00**

Star Biscuits, metal, figural mouse and biscuit **85.00**

Pen, Winchester, rifle shaped **10.00**

Pie Plate, Coon Chicken Inn **140.00**

Pinback Button

ABC Soda Crackers, parrot illus, 1896 ....**35.00**

Dandee Bread, tan, black, and white, early 1900s **20.00**

Sunbeam Bread, litho, Sunbeam girl, red, white, and blue, 1930–40 ....**15.00**

Pot Scraper

C D Kenny Teas, Coffees, Sugars, cast iron, S–shape handle, raised lettering **50.00**

Sharples **145.00**

Puzzle, Folgers Coffee can, sealed ... **12.00**

Reamer

C D Kenny Co, Teas, Coffees, Sugars, 3" d, side handle, emb bottom **50.00**

Sunkist, 6" d, milk glass, block letters **30.00**

Record Cleaner, RCA Victor, round, celluloid **20.00**

Ring, Chief Wahoo, Goudey Gum, Indian head **65.00**

Ruler, Old Hood Ice Cream, 12" l, wood **28.00**

Salt and Pepper Shakers, pr, Green Giant **12.00**

Shot Glass, Adlerika Bowel Cleanser **15.00**

Pencil, Renner Bros, Perkasie, PA, pledge of allegiance on celluloid band, used, 4" l, $2.00.

Africana   37_

Sign

Adam's Express Co, reverse painted glass **375.00**

Bell System Public Telephone, round, porcelain **80.00**

Breidbach & Sons, Mfgs of Dyes, brass, c1900 .... **65.00**

Butter–Nut Bread, tin, loaf and bakery kid illus **75.00**

Cranford Dairy, 4 × 9", cardboard, Charles Twelvetrees illus **12.00**

Dauntless Coffee, young Roman soldier illus **55.00**

Drink Krim's For Health, 33 × 14", porcelain **75.00**

Dr Lyna's Hair Grower, cardboard **40.00**

DuPont, 33 × 23", tin, "Generations Have Used DuPont Powders," tin, old man and boy hunting with dogs, sgd "Osthaus" **225.00**

Dutchess Trousers, 20 × 25", tin **65.00**

Fairbanks Scales, porcelain **135.00**

Forthoffers Soda, counter top, color litho, c1905 .... **35.00**

Francisco Auto Heater, tin, framed **1,150.00**

Honeggers Big H Feeds, tin **25.00**

IcyPic, 12 × 19", cardboard, orange IcyPic cake illus, blue and white lettering, framed **45.00**

Independent Lock Co. Lock & Key Products, 14 × 32", tin, double sided, key shape **200.00**

Keen Kutter, tin, hardware adv **48.00**

Korbel Champagne, woman and bottle illus, c1920 .... **195.00**

Kraft Kraylets, tin, diecut pig **195.00**

Sugar Bowl, Purple Cow, Pick–Ohio Hotel, Youngstown, OH, Shenango China, New Castle, PA, $5.00.

Trade Card, Benny Schwartz, 1930s, $12.00.

Lee's Overalls, 36 × 60", Union Made, metal **450.00**

Okay Drug, wood **50.00**

Omega Watch, tin, 1920s **85.00**

Pellegrino Water, porcelain, two bottles illus **385.00**

Penn Special Beverage, 14½ × 20" **150.00**

Polarine, wood, painted, 1910 .... **290.00**

Red Man Chew, tin **35.00**

Sky Chief Supreme, tin, 1962 .... **50.00**

Southern Bread, tin, loaf and child illus **65.00**

Southwestern Bell Telephone, 19 × 5½", porcelain **290.00**

Standard Red Crown, wood, painted, 1910 .... **290.00**

Tom Sawyer Apparel, boy painting sign and hand cutting Elder Products, emb, multicolored **165.00**

United States Fur Co, St Louis, MO, 15 × 21", paper litho **110.00**

Vigorator Hair Tonic, tin **45.00**

Western Union Telegraph & Cable, porcelain **135.00**

White Eagle Beverages, 19 × 3½", tin **10.00**

Spoon

Banner Buggies, tablespoon, buggy in bowl **35.00**

French's Mustard, Hot Dan figure **30.00**

Heinz, child's, silver plated, raised design, early 1900s **15.00**

Towle's Log Cabin, child's, silver plated, early 1900s **12.00**

Stickpin

Doe Wah Jack **20.00**

Dr Bell's Pine Tar Honey **12.00**

Tape Measure, Hoover canister shape **12.00**

Thermos, Carnation Milk, logo **20.00**

Toy Truck, Campbell's Soup, product logos on trailer **45.00**

Trade Card

Allen's Root Beer Extract, 2½ × 2½", girl in bonnet **8.00**

A & P, little girl at market **6.00**

Atmore's Mince Meat, product illus **10.00**

Bunker Hill Harness Oil Spirit of '76 .... **16.00**

Elite Chocolate Creams, woman holding product **8.00**

Emerson Pianos **12.00**

Empire Wringer, anthropomorphic animal wedding **8.00**

Gabler Pianos, Hussar **10.00**

Lutted Cough Drops, Mary and lamb **18.00**

Sea Foam, 2½ × 3½", angel using product **6.00**

Tray, Jersey Creme Soda **100.00**

Whistle, Butter–Nut Bread, c1920 .... **18.00**

Wristwatch, Charlie The Tuna, silvered metal, full color dial, blue vinyl straps, 1973 copyright, Star–Kist Foods **75.00**

Yardstick, Keen Kutter **22.00**

AFRICANA

The bulk of what you see out there is junk—either souvenirs brought home by tourists or decorative pieces sold by discount or department stores. The problem is twofold. First, modern–day African craftsman continue to work in centuries-old traditions, making pieces with the same tools and in the same form as did their ancestors. Second, telling the difference between a piece made a century ago and a piece made a few months ago requires years of study. The only safe assumption is that most flea market dealers do not have the slightest idea which is which.

When buying African art at flea markets, be cheap about it. Never pay more than you can afford to lose. Buy primarily for decoration. When you think that you have found the real thing, have it checked by a museum curator.

Many pieces of African art involve the use of animal hides and tusks. Be extremely cautious about buying any object made from animals that are on the endangered species list.

Quality African art does show up at flea markets. The listings show some possibilities if you spot the real thing.

Bowl, cov, 13¼" d, divided, rim border, incised geometric design with two lizards, relief crouched rabbit finial, c1910 ....**300.00**
Bust, 10" h, king, bronze, Benin style, 1920–30 ....**350.00**
Door Lock, 19 × 19", carved man, crossbar handle, dark brown stain, Mali, 20th C **270.00**
Figure
    Ashanti Fish, 20½" l, bronze, dark patina, 1940s **325.00**
    Bayaka Fetish, 8½" h, wood, carved, wrapped in gauze, 1920–30 **125.00**
    Female, 12" h, bronze, nude, kneeling, Yoruba, 1920–30 ....**210.00**
    Male Effigy, 12" h, punch hole eyes, Nigeria, late 19th C **125.00**
    Grain Scoop, 16¼" l, dark wood, handle tip carved with Dan style face, Liberia, 1930s **175.00**
    Helmet, 15" l, wood, engraved geometric triangular, Bobo, 1920s **170.00**
    Knife, 22½" l, iron blade, wood handle, engraved snakeskin pattern, late 19th/early 20th C **145.00**
Mask, wood, carved
    Dan, oval shaped face, dark brown paint, Liberia Border **300.00**
    Guro Bird, 15½" h, dark brown wood, two birds on top head, gentle facial features head, Ivory Coast ...**100.00**
    Marka, 14½" h, wood, carved, dark brown stain, brass and tin dec, red trade cloth tassels, Mali, Sudan **95.00**
    N'gere, 15" l, wood, carved facial features, cloth border, c1930 ...**175.00**
Staff, 15" l, wood, head–shaped finial, varnished, Yaka Tribe, Zaire, 1940s **125.00**
Stool, 12" h, 17" l, wood, U–shaped seat, brown, openwork dec, 1930–1940 ....**425.00**

AKRO AGATE GLASS

When the Akro Agate Company was founded in 1911, its principal product was marbles. The company was forced to diversify during the 1930s, developing floral ware lines and children's dishes. Some collectors specialize in containers made by Akro Agate Company for the cosmetic industry.

Akro Agate merchandised a great many of its products as sets. Full sets that retain their original packaging command a premium price. Learn what pieces and colors constitute a set. Some dealers will mix and match pieces into a false set, hoping to get a better price.

Most Akro Agate pieces are marked "Made in USA" and have a mold number. Some, but not all, have a small crow flying through an "A" as a mark.

Clubs: Akro Agate Art Association, PO Box 758, Salem, NH 03079; Akro Agate Collector's Club, 10 Bailey St., Clarksburg, WV 26301.

Ashtray, Westite, gray and brown marble, rect playing card, recessed spade **10.00**
Basket, marbleized orange and white, two handles **28.50**
Bell, light blue **65.00**
Bowl
    5" d, marbleized orange and white, emb leaves **35.00**
    6" d, Westite, marbleized brown and white **18.00**
    7½" d, cream and red, tab handle **28.00**
Children's Dishes
    Cereal Bowl, Interior Panel, transparent amber **15.00**
    Creamer, octagonal, green **6.00**
    Cup and Saucer
        Concentric Rib, transparent cobalt blue **50.00**
        Interior Panel, transparent green **19.50**
    Pitcher, Stacked Disc, blue **15.00**
    Plate
        Concentric Ring, opaque lime green **6.00**
        Octagonal, green **8.00**
    Set
        5 pcs, Stacked Disc, bright blue and white, pitcher and four tumblers **25.00**
        8 pcs, Interior Panel, pink, orig box **100.00**
        16 pcs, Concentric Rib, green and white, orig box **85.00**

Plate, children's play size, celery green, opaque, 3⅜" d, $8.00.

Sugar, octagonal, green, white lid, closed handles **12.00**
Teapot, cov, Raised Daisy, blue **65.00**
Tumbler, Raised Daisy, yellow ...**25.00**
Cornucopia, orange and white **5.50**
Flowerpot
    2¾" h, Ribbed Top, yellow **12.00**
    3" h, Stacked Disk, blue and white **10.00**
    4" d, Single Dart, blue and white **15.00**
    5¼" d, Westite, brown and white **15.00**
Jardiniere, 4½" h, Westite, marbleized green and white **17.50**
Match Holder, 3" h, red and white ...**7.00**
Planter
    4½" d, Hexagon, opaque, green **15.00**
    8" l, rect, blue and white, No. 653 **35.00**
Powder Box
    Colonial Lady, pink and white ...**60.00**
    Ribbed, yellow **25.00**
Powder Jar, Scottie, pink **75.00**
Shaving Mug, cov, black **15.00**
Vase
    4½" h, marbleized orange **6.50**
    6¼" h, Graduated Dart, dark green, scalloped top, No. 316 ....**55.00**

ALADDIN

The Mantle Lamp Company of America, founded in 1908 in Chicago, is best known for its lamps. However, in the late 1950s through the 1970s, it also was one of the leading producers of character lunch boxes.

Aladdin deserves a separate category because of the large number of lamp collectors who concentrate almost exclusively on this one company. There is almost as big a market for parts and accessories as for the lamps themselves. Collectors are constantly looking for parts to restore lamps in their possession.

Club: The Mystic Light of the Aladdin Knights, Route 1, Simpson, IL 62985.

LAMPS
Bracket
    Model 11 ....**100.00**
    Model C, aluminum font **45.00**
Caboose, Model 23, aluminum **45.00**
Candle, Aladdinette, stationary shade holder with paper shade **50.00**
Floor
    Model B
        B–271, bronze lacquer and gold, 1936 ....**75.00**
        B–289, oxidized bronze, 1937–38 ....**90.00**
        B–297, satin gold, 1939–40 ....**150.00**

Model 12, #1253, Verde Antique
.... **125.00**
Hanging
Model 4, 203 shade **275.00**
Model 9, 516 shade **225.00**
Model 12, tilt frame, parchment shade
.... **175.00**
Model C–224, Brazil, white paper shade
.... **100.00**
Parlor
Model 3 .... **750.00**
Model 4 .... **450.00**
Shelf, model 23, drape font
Clear, 1975–1982 .... **65.00**
Ruby, no oil fill, 1979 .... **90.00**
Student
Model 4 .... **3,500.00**
Model 23, replica, 1983 .... **350.00**
Table
Model 1, emb foot **500.00**
Model 9 .... **95.00**
Model 12
Brass, slanted sides **65.00**
Crystal, vase, 1243, green Venetian
Art–Craft, 10¼" h, 1930–1935
.... **85.00**
Model 23, aluminum font **35.00**
Model A, Venetian, 1932–33
100, white **75.00**
103, rose **90.00**
Model B
99, Venetian, clear, 1932–33 **175.00**
104, Colonial, clear crystal, 1933
.... **90.00**
109, Cathedral, amber crystal, 1934–
1935 .... **100.00**
B–27, Simplicity, alacite, gold lustre,
1948–53 .... **175.00**
B–53, Washington Drape, clear crystal, 1940–41 .... **65.00**
B–80, Beehive, clear crystal, 1937–
38 .... **75.00**
B–90, Quilt, white moonstone font,
black moonstone foot, 1937
.... **200.00**
B–100, Corinthian, clear crystal,
1935–1936 .... **55.00**
B–121, Majestic, rose moonstone
font, 1935–1936 .... **225.00**
B–130, Orientale, ivory, 1935–36
.... **125.00**
B–137, Treasure, bronze, 1937–53
.... **75.00**
Vase Lamp, Model 12, Crystal, 1930–35
1231U, pale yellow, 10¼" h **125.00**
1241, variegated tan, 12" h **100.00**

PARTS AND ACCESSORIES

Bug Screen, old style **55.00**
Burner
Lumineer **50.00**
Model 6 .... **40.00**
Ceiling Extension Hanger, No. 1, satin brass
.... **100.00**
Chimney Brush **15.00**
Electric Converter, old style **12.00**

Flame Spreader
Model 8 .... **75.00**
Model 11 .... **10.00**
Gallery
Model 3, international patent **50.00**
Model C **10.00**
Match Holder, copper plated, Kone Kap,
Model 3 .... **10.00**
Shade
Glass
21C, English cased, red, 10" d **65.00**
201, opal, white **125.00**
401, fancy, satin white, table lamp
.... **110.00**
516, painted white **100.00**
616F, decorated, poppies, hanging
lamp **500.00**
Paper
Aladdinite Parchment, 20½" d, floor
lamp, 1929–33 .... **175.00**
Whip–o–lite Parchment, Caboose,
12" d, plain white **12.00**
Tripod
Model 6, scallop **15.00**
Model B, 14" w **5.00**
Wall Bracket, Model B, 0179 ...... **25.00**
Wick, orig box
Model 7 .... **20.00**
Model 12A **8.00**
Wick Cleaner, three prong **15.00**
Wick Raiser, model 8 .... **15.00**
Wick Trimmer, brass **4.00**

ALBUMS

The Victorian craze has drawn attention to the Victorian photograph album that enjoyed an honored place in
the parlor. The more common examples
had velvet or leather covers. However,
the ones most eagerly sought by collectors are those featuring a celluloid cover
with motifs ranging from floral to Span-
ish-American War battleships.

Most albums housed "family" photographs, the vast majority of which are
unidentified. If the photographs are head
and shoulders or baby shots, chances are
they have little value unless the individuals are famous. Photographs of military
figures, actors and actresses, and freaks
are worth checking out further.

Cardboard albums still have not
found favor with collectors. However,
check the interior contents. In many
cases, they contain post cards, clippings,
match covers, or photographs that are
worth far more than the album.

Advertising, 5½ × 9", trade cards, album
cards, and pictures, 66 pgs **35.00**
Daguerreotype, gutta percha, baroque motif
cover **45.00**

Cabinet Cards, Victorian
Embossed "Album" and floral design on
celluloid front cov, green and orange
floral pattern on velvet back cov
.... **65.00**
Floral motif on celluloid front cov, red
velvet back cov **65.00**
Leather cover **30.00**
Plain red velvet covers **25.00**
Raised floral design and gold highlights
on red velvet covers **45.00**
Spanish–American War battleship motif
front, celluloid front and back **200.00**
Young maiden dec on celluloid front
cov, red velvet back cover ... **85.00**
Greeting Cards, celluloid cov, multicolored
medallion of Gibson girl portrait center,
1910–20 .... **25.00**
Souvenir, European photos, menus, bill-
heads, booklets, and steamships, 50 pgs,
1930–31 .... **20.00**
Valentines, includes mechanical cards, early
1940s **40.00**

ALIENS

IEEEEKK!! As the cry for extraterres-
trials rises, so does their collectibility.
From *War of the Worlds* to *My Favorite
Martian*, aliens have been landing in our
collections. Aliens have gained in popularity with the influence of television and
advances made in movie special effects.
The *Mork and Mindy* show starring comedian Robin Williams as a fun–loving
extraterrestrial, and the *Star Wars* trilogy,
with its strange alien creatures, are just
two prime examples of alien familiarity.

So what is an alien? The alien is any
creature, character, or being that is not of
this planet. Aliens appear in many
shapes and sizes so be careful—you
never know where an alien will turn up.

Alien
Book, 8 × 11", *Alien The Illustrated
Story*, Heavy Metal Communications
Inc, 1979, 64 pgs **25.00**
Comic Book, *Aliens*, #4, Dark Horse,
Second Series, 1989 .... **1.00**
Costume, Alien, Ben Cooper, 1979
.... **60.00**
Game
Alien Blaster Target Game, H G
Toys, 1979 .... **140.00**
Alien Game, board, Kenner, copy-
right 20th Century Fox Film Corp,
1979 .... **35.00**
This Time It's War, board, Leading
Edge, 1990 .... **35.00**
Jigsaw Puzzle, Alien illus, H G Toys,
1979 .... **20.00**

Model Kit
    Alien Face Hugger, Halcyon, 1991
    . . . . **70.00**
    Alien with teeth, MPC, unassembled,
    orig box **80.00**
    Mug, plastic, logo **5.00**
    Note Pad, "Trust Me I'm the Boss" **4.50**
    Poster, 72" h, Alien Warrior, multi-
    colored, GS, 1988 . . . . **18.00**
    Shirt, Alien Chestburster, 3D, Distortions
    Unlimited **250.00**
Battlestar Galactica
    Chair, inflatable, Cylon **15.00**
    Costume, Cylon **20.00**
    Game, Battlestar Galactica, Parker Broth-
    ers, copyright 1978 Universal City
    Studios Inc., 18" sq playing board,
    playing pieces, and cards, orig box
    . . . . **20.00**
    Helmet Radio, Cylon **25.00**
    Stuffed Toy, Daggit, plush **15.00**
    Wallet, black vinyl, ID card and silver
    plastic badge, orig blister card, Lar-
    ami Corp, copyright 1978 Universal
    City Studios **15.00**
Close Encounters Of The Third Kind
    Figure, alien, Imperial, 1977 . . . . . **12.00**
    Lunch Box, 7 × 9 × 4", metal, color
    illus, King Seeley, 1977–78 . . . **25.00**
    Magazine, 8½ × 11", *Official Poster
    Monthly*, #1, Paradise Press Inc,
    1977 . . . . **12.50**
    Pinback Button, alien illus, "CONTACT"
    . . . . **1.50**
Dune
    Model Kit, Sandworm, Revell, unassem-
    bled, orig box **20.00**
    Pinback Button, Sandworm illus . . . **1.50**
    Poster, Sandworm illus **3.00**
    Vehicle, Sandworm, LJN, battery oper-
    ated, 1984 . . . . **18.00**
E. T.
    Action Figure, wearing robe **3.00**
    Address Book, E. T. and "Addresses" on
    cov **1.00**
    Figure, 3½" h, hard plastic, LJN, copy-
    right 1982 Universal City Studios Inc,
    orig blister card **25.00**
    Finger Light, plastic, battery operated
    . . . . **5.00**
    Glass, Pizza Hut promotional, "Phone
    Home" **2.50**
    Keychain, plastic disc, E. T. face illus
    . . . . **1.50**
    Lunch Box, Aladdin **10.00**
    Stickers, puffy, E. T. engaged in various
    activities, set of 9, orig pkg . . . . . **.75**
    Tea Set, "E. T. Party Set," four tea cups,
    saucers, plates, and spoons, pitcher
    and tray, creamer and sugar, plastic,
    white, color illus, orig box, Chilton–
    Globe Inc, copyright 1982 Universal
    City Studios Inc **25.00**
    Tee Shirt, E. T. illus **9.00**
    Wristwatch, Melody Glow Alarm Watch,
    Nelsonic **12.00**

Gremlins, sleeping bag, 30 × 56", padded,
    red, multicolored image, Ero Leisure,
    copyright 1984 Warner Bros Inc
    . . . . **18.00**
Outer Space, comic book, 7 × 10¼", #6,
    Dell Publishing Co, 1965 . . . . . . **12.00**
Planet Of the Apes
    Activity Album, 10½ × 12½", 24 pgs,
    Saalfield, 1974 . . . . **25.00**
    Dart Game, 11" sq target, two soft plas-
    tic suction darts, orig box,
    Transogram, 1967 Apjac Productions
    Inc **75.00**
    Magazine, 8¼ × 11", Vol 1, #4, Janu-
    ary 1965, 1974 Magazine Manage-
    ment **15.00**

ALUMINUM, HANDWROUGHT

With increasing emphasis on post–World War II collectibles, especially those from the 1950s, handwrought aluminum is enjoying a collecting revival. The bulk of the pieces were sold on the giftware market as decorative accessories.

Do not be confused by the term *handwrought*. The vast majority of the pieces were mass–produced. The two collecting keys appear to be manufacturer and unusualness of form.

There is an enormous difference between flea market prices and prices at a major show within driving distance of New York City. Handwrought aluminum is quite trendy at the moment among the "arty" community.

Newsletter: *The Aluminist*, PO Box 1346, Weatherford, TX 76086.

Basket, Farber & Shlein, china insert with
    Indian Tree pattern and gold border, alu-
    minum frame and handle **20.00**
Beverage Set, 5 pcs, World Hand Forged,

hammered, pitcher with square knot
    handle, four tumblers with flared
    lip **60.00**
Bowl, 11½" d, Arthur Armour, sundial and
    zodiac signs, inscribed "Grow old along
    with me, the best is yet to be" . . . **55.00**
Buffet Server, 10 × 14½", Keystone Ware,
    rect caddy with wrapped handle, six
    square ribbed glass inserts with fruit de-
    sign on lids, No. 606 . . . . **25.00**
Butter Dish, cov, Buenilum, glass insert,
    beaded, double looped finial, castle
    mark **20.00**
Cake Basket, 12" d, Canterbury Arts, floral
    spray design, twisted handle, helmet
    mark faces left **28.00**
Candy Dish, Wrought Farberware, round di-
    vided glass dish with sunburst pattern,
    aluminum lid with camellia and leaf de-
    sign, wood knob finial **12.00**
Casserole, cov, Cromwell, hammered, glass
    liner, ftd **12.00**
Chafing Dish, Rodney Kent **25.00**
Cigarette Box, Arthur Armour, pine bough
    dec **32.00**
Cocktail Shaker, 12" h, Continental, cork
    lined top, No. 530 . . . . **40.00**
Creamer and Sugar, Everlast, hammered,
    open mark, No. 5018 . . . . **12.00**
Ice Bucket, 8" h, Canterbury Arts, ham-
    mered, double walled, rubber seal
    . . . . **45.00**
Lazy Susan, 14½" d, Everlast, Rose and For-
    get–Me–Not pattern, open mark, No.
    5063 . . . . **15.00**
Napkin Holder, Rodney Kent, hammered,
    decorative floral bands and feet **10.00**
Nut Bowl, 11" d, Continental, Wild Rose
    pattern, No. 1011 . . . . **12.00**
Pitcher, 2 qt, Cromwell, hammered, looped
    ice guard **25.00**
Platter, Everlast, rect, oval center well with
    tree, grape leaf dec in corners, two han-
    dles **42.00**
Relish Dish, 7¾" d, Everlast, glass bowl,
    aluminum underliner, Bali Bamboo pat-
    tern, open mark **10.00**
Silent Butler, 6½" d, Buenilum, hammered,
    mkd "Handwrought" **15.00**

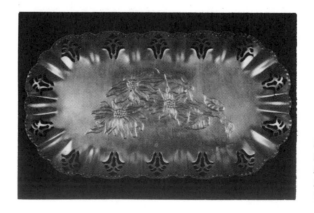

Bread Tray, poinsettia type flower dec, reticulated ruffled sides, marked "Farber & Schlein Inc. Hand Wrought, 1718," 7" w, 12½" l, $20.00.

Tray, incised floral dec, marked "Hand Forged Everlast Metal," with anchor and arm holding hammer in oval, 11⅝" sq, $15.00.

Tray
Sandwich, 11" w, Wendell August Forge, eight–sided, dogwood design   **20.00**
Tidbit, 7½" d, Hammercraft Hand Hammered, grape cluster design, looped finger hold **5.00**
Tiered, Wrought Farberware, two circular tiers with beaded edges, flower, stem, and cascading stamen design handle and stand **14.00**

AMUSEMENT PARKS

From the park at the end of the trolley line to today's gigantic theme parks such as Six Flags Great Adventure, amusement parks have served many generations. No trip to an amusement park was complete without a souvenir, many of which are now collectible.

Prices are still modest in this new collecting field. When an item is returned to the area where the park was located, it often brings a twenty to fifty percent premium.

Baggage Tag, silvered brass, emb "Coney Island," numbered "1904," c1920 .... **25.00**
Book, *Walt Disney's Guide to Disneyland*, 8 × 11½", 28 pgs, 1960, full color **30.00**
Box, 8⅞" l, Goff's Atlantic City Salt Water Taffy, blue, woman wearing orange swimsuit **6.00**
Butter Dish, cov, Lancaster Fair, ruby stained glass, Button Arches pattern, 1916 .... **150.00**
Card Game, Excursion to Coney Island, Milton Bradley, c1885 .... **20.00**
Folder, Coney Island, yellow and green, facts and timetables int., 1879 ... **40.00**
Game
County Fair Game, Parker Bros, orig box, 1891 .... **20.00**

Disneyland Riverboat Game, Parker Bros, 8 × 16 × 1½" box, minor use wear, c1955 .... **50.00**
Hat, Disneyland, Mouseketeers, stiff black felt, large black plastic ears, white, blue, and orange "Disneyland/Mickey Mouse" patch, c1960 .... **25.00**
Magazine, *Disneyland Vacationland Summer 1970*, 8½ × 11", 20 pgs, light general wear **18.50**
Medal, Coney Island, steeplechase face, orig ribbon, 1924 .... **90.00**
Pennant
Coney Island, 24" l, maroon felt, white title, yellow, green, orange, and white scene of Steeplechase Pool, amusement rides, Luna Mill Sky Chaser building, c1930 ...... **20.00**
Hershey Park, felt, brown ground, white letters, c1950 .... **25.00**
Photograph, 8 × 10", Coney Island, glossy, park scene **50.00**
Pinback Button
Asbury Park, 1¼" d, black and white, bathing beach scene, c1900   **10.00**
Coney Island, 1¼" d, multicolored, bathing beauty center, rim reads "Citizens Committee of Coney Island," c1915 .... **35.00**
Dreamland Park, NY, white lettering, red ground, 1900s **5.00**
Hershey Park, multicolored, child emerging from cocoa bean, c1905 .... **35.00**
New Virginia Reel, Luna Park, 1¼" d, two men and four ladies on ride, Bastian Brothers back label   **125.00**
Playing Cards, Dorney Park, Allentown, PA, Alfundo the Clown **5.00**
Post Card
Beach Club, photo **6.00**
Coney Island, 3½ × 5½", black and white, Aerial Swing, Luna Park, July 10, 1906 postmark **25.00**
Life Saving Beach Club, photo ... **10.00**
The Great Allentown Fair, Allentown, PA, Dan Patch race horse illus, 1906 .... **75.00**
Poster, 28 × 41", panoramic view of various rides, Riverside Print Co, c1910 .... **175.00**
Sheet Music, *Just Take Me Down To Wonderland*, ride illus on cov, 1907   **20.00**
Sign, 36" l, Coney Island, porcelain, arrow shape **350.00**
Souvenir Book, 10½ × 10½", Disneyland, 32 pgs, copyright 1965 .... **25.00**
Stamp Book, Disneyland, 8½ × 11", 32 pgs, Simon & Schuster, copyright 1956 .... **50.00**
Stereograph
Asbury Park, NJ, 1870s **10.00**
Coney Island, hot air balloon, 1870s **70.00**
Sweater Guard, Disneyland, cardboard case, clear plastic slipcover, bright brass

chain, two brass star–shaped charms with pink glass stones, "Disneyland" spelled out in brass, c1960 ..... **40.00**
Ticket
Coney Island, Steeplechase **30.00**
Disneyland, paper, black and purple illus, $4.75 adult admission ticket, checklist of attractions on back, c1960 .... **15.00**
Token, 1⅜" d, carousel ride, aluminum, "Good For One Ride," T O Newman, 1920s **50.00**
Toy, windup
Double Loop–the–Loop Roller Coaster, McDowell, figural man driving car, 1920s, MIB **425.00**
Ferris Wheel, Chein, 1930s **350.00**
Mickey Mouse Ferris Wheel, Chein **450.00**

ANIMAL DISHES, COVERED

Covered animal dishes were a favorite of housewives during the first half of the twentieth century. Grandmother Rinker and her sisters had numerous hens on nests scattered throughout their homes. They liked the form. It did not make any difference how old or new they were. Reproductions and copycats abound. You have to be alert for these late examples.

Look for unusual animals and forms. Many early examples were enhanced through hand-painted decorations. Pieces with painting in excellent condition command a premium.

Cat, crystal, glass eyes, lacy base ... **120.00**
Chick and Eggs, emerging chick, white milk glass, Atterbury, 11" h **185.00**
Doe, irid glass **23.00**
Dog, white milk glass, patterned quilt top, sgd Vallerystahl **175.00**
Duck, Mama Quack, crystal, hp eyes and bill, Jeannette Glass Co, 1950s, 6" l **15.00**
Eagle on Nest, white milk glass, "The American Hen" inscribed on banner **85.00**
Elephant, amber glass **150.00**
Fish, walking, white milk glass, red glass eyes, detailed scales, 8¾" l **175.00**
Frog, sitting, green glass, Co–Operative Flint Glass Co, 1920s–30s **85.00**
Hen on Nest
Blue Frosted Glass, quilted base, 6½" l **75.00**
China, Metlox, California Provincial pattern **65.00**
Marbleized Glass, white and deep blue, lacy base, Atterbury, 7½" l   **165.00**
White Milk Glass, 6⅞" l **50.00**

Hen on nest, blue frosted glass, Kemple, marked "K" on base, 8½" l, 6" w, 6" h, $30.00.

Jumbo the Elephant
    Crystal, Indiana Glass Co, reissue, 1981,
        4 × 7" **20.00**
    Ruby Glass, Co–Operative Flint Glass
        Co, 1920s–30s, 6 × 13" **200.00**
Lonesome Elephant, black glass **195.00**
Lovebirds, blue milk glass **55.00**
Owl, caramel slag glass, Imperial **40.00**
Rabbit
    Pink Frosted Glass, emb features, footed,
      rect, marked "Dermay–Fifth Avenue–
      New York–970," 4½" l **225.00**
    White Frosted Glass, 6" l **70.00**
Rin–Tin–Tin, green glass **225.00**
Scottie Dog, Akro Agate
    Turquoise **65.00**
    White **85.00**

ANIMAL FIGURINES

Animal collectors are a breed apart. Collecting is a love affair. As long as their favorite animal is pictured or modeled, they willingly buy the item. In many cases, they own a real-life counterpart to go with their objects. My personal zoo includes a tarantula, lovebird, two rabbits, a Golden Ball python, and three tanks of tropical fish.

Clubs: Canine Collectibles Club of America, Suite 314, 736 N Western Ave, Lake Forest, IL 60045; Cat Collectors,

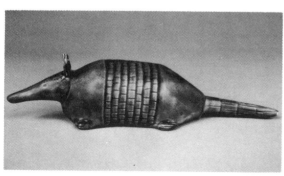

Armadillo, ceramic, gray, 7" l, $4.00.

33161 Wendy Drive, Sterling Heights, MI 48310; The Frog Pond, PO Box 193, Beech Grove, IN 46107; The National Elephant Collectors Society, 380 Medford St, Somerville, MA 02145.

Bird, chalk, old worn polychrome paint,
    6" h **215.00**
Boxer Dog
    Ceramic, sitting, Morten **75.00**
    Crystal, reclining, Haley **55.00**
Brittany Spaniel, porcelain, Goebel   **18.00**
Cat, china
    Beswick **55.00**
    Stylized, black matte, Royal Dux Bohe-
      mia triangle mark, 7½" h **21.00**
Chanticleer, crystal, Fostoria **195.00**
Dachshund, china, Beswick, early, 9" l
    .... **53.00**
Deer, crystal, Fostoria **42.00**
Eagle, bisque, marked "Bald Eagle by An-
    drea, Japan," 15" h **85.00**
Egret, crystal, Imperial **225.00**
Elephant
    China, white, numbered, 3" h, price for
      pair **17.00**
    Pink Quartz, wood base, 2⅝" l .. **45.00**
Elephant, glass
    Amber, Co–Operative Flint Glass Co
    .... **85.00**
    Black, Co–Operative Flint Glass Co
    .... **125.00**
    Caramel Slag, Imperial, 4" h **45.00**
    Crystal, New Martinsville **95.00**
Fish, tall and narrow, amber glass, New
    Martinsville Epic Line **40.00**
Giraffe, amber, Heisey **400.00**
Goose
    Caramel Slag, wings up, Imperial   **30.00**
    Crystal, fat, Duncan **225.00**
Horse, jumping, crystal, Haley **45.00**
Lamb, china, pink roses and bows,
    Cordelia, 4½" h **18.00**
Mamma Bear, crystal, New Martinsville
    .... **95.00**
Monkey, bronze, stylized, Hagenauer, Aus-
    tria, c1925, 3¾" h **470.00**
Owl, wood, carved, old brown finish, round
    base, 3¾" h **45.00**
Parrot, porcelain, polychrome, marked
    "Germany," 13" h **125.00**

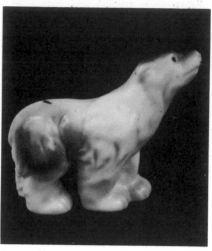

Bear, white, gray spots, black nose and eyes, marked "Japan," 3½" w, 2½" h, $10.00.

Percheron Horse, china, 10½" h, unmarked
    .... **14.00**
Poodle, ceramic, black, Goebel, 1977, 7" h
    .... **85.00**
Rooster, frosted blue glass, Paden City
    .... **195.00**
Siamese Cat, sitting, bisque, rust and black,
    4" h **18.00**
Tiger, jade, Heisey **80.00**

APPLIANCES, ELECTRICAL

Nothing shows our ability to take a relatively simple task (e.g., toast a piece of bread) and create a wealth of different forms to achieve it. Electrical appliances are viewed as one of the best documents of stylistic design in utilitarian form.

Collectors tend to concentrate on one form. Toasters are the most commonly collected, largely because several books have been written about them. Electric fans have a strong following. Waffle irons are pressing toasters for popularity. Modernistic collectors seek bar drink blenders from the 1930s through the 1950s.

Clubs: American Fan Collectors Association, PO Box 804, South Bend, IN 46624; Electric Breakfast Club, PO Box 306, White Mills, PA 18473.

Blender, 13" h, Home Malt Mixer, chrome, domed motor housing, crinkle green painted base, A C Gilbert, 1930s   **65.00**
Broiler, Royal Master Appliance Co, Miriam, OH, 1930s **25.00**
Bun Warmer, cov, 10" d bowl, Art Deco,

chrome, red, yellow, and green wood ball feet and finial, wire basket, 1930s **25.00**

Butter Churn, Mixmaster, stainless steel, wood paddles, clear glass jar, 4 qt **35.00**

Chafing Dish, American Beauty, 3 pcs, nickel, black wood knob and handles, American Electrical Heater Co, Detroit, MI, 1910 .... **50.00**

Coffee Grinder, Kitchen Aid **65.00**

Coffee Maker
    Dripolator
        Silex, 13" h, 2 pcs, glass, Bakelite holder, 1930s **18.00**
        Westinghouse, 14" h, 2 pcs, black Bakelite handles, 1940s ... **20.00**
    Farberware, Coffee Robot, chrome body, glass bowl, thermostat, S W Farber, Brooklyn, NY, 1937 .... **35.00**
    Percolator
        Royal Rochester, 10" h, nickel plated copper, black wooden handles, #366 B-29, 1920s **15.00**
        United Metal Goods Mfg Inc, 17" w, urn shape, pierced tilting frame, emb spout base, ornate handle, indicator light, 1940s **65.00**
    Sunbeam Coffee Master, 12½" h, 2 pcs, chrome, Bakelite handles and base, 1939–44 .... **25.00**

Coffee Mill, 13¾" h, Kitchen Aid, Hobart model A9, Art Deco style, white motor base, clear glass top threads onto base, threaded black metal lid, 1936 ... **60.00**

Deep Fryer, Betty Crocker, 11 × 7", model 9–A, chrome, black Bakelite base, aluminum basket, General Mills, late 1940s **25.00**

Drink Mixer, Made Rite, Weining Co, Cleveland, OH, 1930s **20.00**

Egg Cooker, Hankscraft Co, Madison, WI, 5¼" d, cream china base, aluminum top, late 1930s **15.00**

Fan
    General Electric
        Brass blade, steel guard **80.00**
        Steel blade, steel guard, 12" h **45.00**
        Whiz, brass blade, steel guard **90.00**
    Polar Cub, A C Gilbert, brass plated blades, steel guard **60.00**
    Starrite, brass plated blades, steel guard **50.00**
    Western Electric, Graybar, counter type, three speeds **85.00**
    Westinghouse
        Brass blades, steel guard **80.00**
        Whirlwind **50.00**

Flour Sifter, Miracle Electric Co, ivory metal body, push button above blue wooden handle, decal label, unused, 1930s **35.00**

Hot Plate, Edison/Hotpoint, New York, Chicago and Ontario, copper heat control, 1910s **25.00**

Iron
    Dover Co–Ed, child's, nickel body, green wood handle, Dover Mfg Co **20.00**
    Never Lift, #966–B, Art Deco, attached cord, heat indicator, Proctor Silex, 1935–37 .... **25.00**
    Sunbeam, "Iron Master," 2¾ lb chrome body, steam attachment, orig box, unused, #52, 1940s **40.00**

Malt Mixer, 18¾" h, model B, Machine Craft, Los Angeles, CA **60.00**

Mixer
    Hamilton Beach, model C, cream color body, black cast iron base, black Bakelite handle, single unit beaters, complete juicer attachments, yellow juicer bowl and two Fenton mixing bowls, 1934 .... **65.00**
    Handymix, 11½" h, #D–121125, stand, two beaters, push button, Mary Dunbar, Chicago Elect Mfg Co, 1930s **16.00**
    Mixmaster, model K, cream metal body, stand with folding handle, green glass bowl/juicer, Sunbeam, Chicago Flexible Shaft Co, 1930 ...... **40.00**

Popcorn Popper, Knapp–Monarch, oil type, aluminum body, wire base, domed glass lid with vented sides, walnut handles, measuring cup, Cat #12A–500B, 1930–1940 .... **20.00**

Teakettle, Mirro, aluminum, 4 qt, nickel chrome domed body, Bakelite handle, 1930s **20.00**

Toaster
    Electrahot Mfg Co, Minneapolis, c1934 .... **20.00**
    Estate Stove Co, model 177, nickel, pierced door rack, 1922 ..... **75.00**
    General Electric, model D–12, white china base, lift–off warming rack, 1908 .... **125.00**

Toaster, Protos, chrome plated, 7¼" l, 3" d, 6⅞" h, $35.00.

Hotpoint Model 115T1, marked "Royal Rochester," 1919–23 .... **65.00**

Sears Kenmore, model #307–6323–1, chrome, rounded body, two slice pop–up, Bakelite handles and knob, early 1940s **15.00**

Star–Rite Extra Fast Toaster, Fitzgerald Mfg Co, Torrington, CT, 1925–30 .... **20.00**

Toastmaster, model 1–A–3, Art Deco, sq, chrome, vertical fluted sides, Waters Genter Co, 1929 .... **35.00**

Waffle Iron, Armstrong, model W, metal, black wood handled, early 1920s **25.00**

Whipper, Sears Kenmore, cream metal dome top, clear glass bottom, dark blue Bakelite knob, 1940s **15.00**

AQUARIUM COLLECTIBLES

You don't have to be all wet to collect aquarium–related items. Old filtering systems, heaters, and decorative accessories as well as the containers themselves provide an overwhelming array of collecting possibilities.

Aquariums aren't just for fish. They also provide a home to air–breathers such as lizards and snakes. Terrariums, with their animal habitats, rock heaters, and strange plants, are reminiscent of a prehistoric tropical forest—a wonderful environment for any collector.

Accessory
    Dragon, ceramic, three parts, Japan **2.00**
    Sunken Ship, plastic, bubble stone **3.00**

Air Pump, Second Nature Whisper 600, 10–15 gal **3.00**

Aquarium Heater, Aquarium Systems, 20–30 gal **15.00**

Goldfish Bowl Stand
    Ceramic, television lamp, black cat, sitting with front paw raised, green tree stump base, 1920s **45.00**
    Chalkware, 9½" h, cat sitting on haunches, peering into bowl, 1930s **65.00**
    Pottery, white cat, sitting, looking in bowl, "Wistful Kitten," Camark Pottery **25.00**

Reptile Heater, Hot Rock, stone **5.00**

Tank
    10 gal **5.00**
    20 gal, high **20.00**

Tank Hood, Perfecto, iridescent light, 10 gal **7.00**

Water Filter System, Whisper Second Nature Power Filter, 15–20 gal **10.00**

ASHTRAYS

Most price guides include ashtrays under advertising. The problem is that there are a number of terrific ashtrays in shapes that have absolutely nothing to do with advertising. Ashtrays get a separate category from me.

With the nonsmoking movement gaining strength, the ashtray is an endangered species. The time to collect them is now.

Club: Ashtray Collectors Club, Box 11652, Houston, TX 77293.

Advertising
Barbasol, 3½" d, 3" h, metal tray with figural eight sided clear glass jar
.... 15.00
Cliff House, San Francisco, shell, litho
.... 15.00
Crane Plumbing, cast iron 20.00
Firestone Tires, 6" d, soft rubber, black, tire shape, 1940–50 .... 20.00
General Electric Motor 15.00
Kelly Springfield, tire form, green insert, heavy duty 30.00
Mountain States Telephone & Telegraph, granite 85.00
Moxie, ceramic, white, Moxie man dec
.... 25.00
Old Judge Coffee, tin 90.00
Old Shay–Fort Pitt Beer, aluminum
.... 14.00
Penn Rubber Co, tire shape 12.00
Resistol Hats, cowboy hat shape 25.00
Royal 58 Beer 12.00
Salem Cigarettes, tin, emb 8.00
Seiberling Tire, tire shape, black glass insert 20.00
Sombrero Tequila 8.00
Winston Cigarettes, tin, emb 8.00

Firestone, black tire rim, center glass ashtray emb Firestone, New York World's Fair, $20.00.

Pickard China, emb gold trim, marked "Pickard," lion mark, #134, 3¼" d, $3.00.

Airplane, chrome 35.00
Bambi, Beswick/Goebel, 1950s 150.00
Bird, chrome, Art Deco, figural 18.00
Black Cat, open mouth, Shafford label
.... 20.00
Cloisonne, 5" d, blue, covered match holder
.... 70.00
Commemorative, 6½" d, china, white, 1961 Civil War Centennial, color center illus and symbols 30.00
Devil Head, bronze, open mouth 75.00
Fiesta Ware, green 25.00
Fire Hydrant, 4 × 7¼", green, water main connection, Hueckel China, El Monte, CA, marked "Berkeley & USA" 80.00
Fish, Frankoma Pottery 15.00
Flintstones, Barney, 8" h, figural, ceramic, raised white image holding bowling ball, 1961 copyright, Arrow Houseware Products Inc 75.00
Frog, 4½" h, porcelain, sitting, Japan 20.00
Hand, leaf dec, yellow, McCoy Pottery, 1941 .... 6.50
Hat, figural, blue 7.50
Lindbergh, photo 50.00
Mack, Bulldog, chrome 25.00
Mae West, 2½ × 4 × 3¼", china, figural, West reclining on chaise lounge, "Come Up And See Me Sometime," Japan, 1930s 125.00
Mermaid, Hull 125.00
Mickey Mouse, 3½ × 5 × 3", china, painted, marked "Made in Japan"
.... 350.00
Pinup girl, tin, Vargas, 1950s 10.00
Saddle on Fence, copper 15.00
Scottish Terrier, 4½" h, 5¾" w, figural, glass insert 25.00
Skillet, Griswold #00 .... 22.00
Spade, 4½" d, dark blue, white cupids dec, marked "Wedgwood" 30.00
Tire, amber insert, cigarette rests 35.00
Triangle Shape, 3½" d, apple blossom dec, marked "Town/Hand Made Aluminum"
.... 4.00

AUTO RACING COLLECTIBLES

Man's quest for speed is as old as time. Automobile racing dates to before the turn of the century. Many of the earliest races took place in Europe. By the first decade of the twentieth century, automobile racing was part of the American scene.

The Indianapolis 500 began in 1911 and was interrupted only by World War II. In addition to Formula 1 racing, the NASCAR circuit has achieved tremendous popularity with American racing fans. Cult heroes such as Richard Petty have become household names.

This is a field of heroes and also fans. Collectors love the winners. A household name counts. Losers are important only when major races are involved. Pre-1945 material is especially desirable because few individuals were into collecting prior to that time.

The field does have problems with reproductions and copycats. Check every item carefully. Beware of paying premium prices for items made within the last twenty years.

Although interest in Indianapolis 500 collectibles remains strong, the market is dominated by NASCAR collectibles. In fact, the market is so strong that racing collectibles have their own separate show circuit and supporting literature. Because racing collecting is in its infancy, price speculation is rampant. Market manipulators abound. In addition, copycat, fantasy, and contemporary limited edition items are being introduced into the market as fast as they can

Bumper Sticker, Miller High Life, white ground, red lettering, black checkerboard flag, green and gold highlights, marked "Miller Brewing Company, Milwaukee, WI," 4" h, 6" l, unused, $1.00.

Game, Turbo, Based On The Arcade Game By SEGA, Milton Bradley, #4318, copyright 1981 Sega Enterprises, Inc., three fold game board, plastic cars and ambulance, $12.00.

be absorbed. A shakeout appears years in the future. In the interim, check your engine and gear up for fast action.

Banner, 19 × 31½", Indianapolis 500, silky fabric, silver, blue printing, early 1973 . . . . **50.00**

Book, *Salute to the 75th Anniversary of the Indianapolis 500,* Marlboro, 1986 **15.00**

Bumper Sticker, Freemont Raceway, CA, red and white **5.00**

Decal, 4 × 5½", Valvoline Racing Oil, 1973 NHRA Spring Nationals **5.00**

Game, Auto Race Game, Milton Bradley, orig box, c1925 . . . . **95.00**

Glass, 5" h, Indianapolis Motor Speedway, frosted glass, black design, red racing car image, 1940s **45.00**

Magazine, *TACH,* American Hot Rod Assoc **6.00**

Matchbook Cover, Lee Petty, Champion adv **5.00**

Mug, Indianapolis 500, frosted glass, wood handle with attached Agajanian racer, 1950s **50.00**

Necktie, Indianapolis 500, 1940s **40.00**

Pass, Indianapolis Motor Speedway, 1939 . . . . **75.00**

Patch, jacket, Indianapolis 500, May 25, 1986 . . . . **10.00**

Pennant, 16" l, William Grove Park and Speedway, felt, green, 1950s **25.00**

Playing Cards, Indy 500, Gulf adv, complete deck **25.00**

Poster, Soapbox Derby Workshop/Clinic, 14 × 22", cardboard, 1967 . . . . **22.00**

Program

Daytona Firecracker 400, NASCAR, July 4, 1963, cov with Tiny Lund **25.00**

East Coast Inaugural Championship Racing Program, Reading, PA, March 28, 1954 . . . . **20.00**

Indianapolis 500, 1976 . . . . **12.00**

Monterey Historic Auto Races, CA, 1979 . . . . **15.00**

Pocono 500, PA, 1971 . . . . **10.00**

Ruler, 12" l, American Racing Wheels, plastic **20.00**

Ticket, Indianapolis 500, 1937 . . . . . **20.00**

AUTOGRAPHS

Collecting autographs is a centuries–old hobby. A good rule to follow is the more recognizable the person, the more likely the autograph is to have value. Content is a big factor in valuing autograph material. A clipped signature is worth far less than a lengthy handwritten document by the same person.

Before spending big money for an autograph, have it authenticated. Many movie and sports stars have secretaries and other individuals sign their material, especially photographs. An autopen is a machine that can sign up to a dozen documents at one time. The best proof that a signature is authentic is to get it from the person who stood there and watched the celebrity sign it.

Clubs: Manuscript Society, 350 N Niagara St, Burbank, CA 95105; Universal Autograph Collectors Club, PO Box 6181, Washington, DC, 20044.

Periodicals: *Autograph Collector,* 510–A S Corona Mall, Corona, CA 91720; *Autographs & Memorabilia,* PO Box 224, Coffeyville, KS 67337; *Autograph Times,* 2303 N 44th St, #255, Phoenix, AZ 85008; *The Autograph Review,* 305 Carlton Rd, Syracuse, NY 13207; *The Collector,* PO Box 255, Hunter, NY 12442.

Aikman, Troy, 24 × 34" poster, full action pose, blue felt tip signature **75.00**

Ali, Muhammed, magazine photo, sgd ''To Larry-Love Muhammed Ali, After Me There Will Never Be Another, 9/28/88'' **25.00**

Anka, Paul, 8 × 10" photo, black and white glossy **10.00**

Bankhead, Tallulah, typed letter, blue ink signature **75.00**

Brothers, Joyce, first day cover **10.00**

Bush, George, 8 × 10" photo, black and white glossy, inscription, sentiment and signature on lower white border **450.00**

Carter, Jimmy, sgd speech, 5 pgs, July 12, 1972, blue ink signature **185.00**

Chamberlain, Wilt, 8 × 10" photo, black and white glossy **30.00**

Close, Glen, magazine, *American Film,* May 1984, sgd cov **15.00**

Connors, Chuck, 8 × 10" photo, black and white, wearing Dodger uniform **75.00**

Crawford, Joan, typed letter **45.00**

Crosby, Cathy Lee, 8 × 10" photo, black and white glossy **10.00**

Cummings, Constance, 3½ × 5½" photo, black and white **10.00**

Davies, Marion, 8 × 10" photo, black and white **60.00**

Devine, Andy, 8 × 10" photo, black and white, bust pose **75.00**

Diller, Phyllis, 5 × 7" photo, black and white glossy **5.00**

Dorr, Julia C, 4 × 3" plain card, four line poem **60.00**

Farrar, Geraldine, 1 pg, typed letter, to Mr James Cook **35.00**

Farrow, Mia, 5 × 7" photo, black and white glossy **10.00**

Forbes, Malcolm, 8 × 10" photo, black and white **75.00**

Ford, Gerald, 11 × 13" photo, color, bust pose **75.00**

Garland, Beverly, 8 × 10" photo, black and white **15.00**

Gaye, Marvin, 8 × 10" photo, black and white glossy, bust pose **350.00**

Glenn, John, Alan Shepard, and Deke Slayton, plain 5 × 3" card, light green **65.00**

Haley, Alex, 5 × 3" card **15.00**

Hoffman, Dustin, 7½ × 9" photo, *Little Big Man* scene **40.00**

Hoover, Herbert, 7 × 10½", typed letter, thank you to Mr. Wilson Mills **145.00**

Jabbar, Kareem Abdul and Julius Irving, first day cover **45.00**

Janney, Russell, book, *The Miracle of the Bells,* sgd on first paper **35.00**

Jones, Carolyn, 8 × 10" photo, black and white, purple ink signature **195.00**

Tie, Andy Williams, Best Wishes, dark blue, light blue, gray, and white stripes on black ground, $20.00.

Larry Seiple, blue plastic toy car with NFL decal, white helmet with Dolphins decal and striping, marked "Sportstoy by Orange Prod, Chatham, NJ," 3½" l, 3" h, $25.00.

Lawford, Peter, photo, snapshot, black and white **65.00**

Liston, Sonny, 4 × 3" paper, inked signature **400.00**

Loy, Myrna, 8 × 10" photo, black and white **75.00**

Madonna, photo, *A League of Their Own* pose, purple ink signature **300.00**

McDowell, Roddy, 5 × 7" photo, color **5.00**

Melba, Nellie, opera singer, 3½ × 6" photo, black and white, framed with letter **175.00**

O'Brien, Hugh, 8 × 10" photo, black and white glossy **10.00**

O'Toole, Peter, 8 × 10" lobby card, *Lawrence of Arabia* scene, 1971 . . **75.00**

Pavarotti, Luciano, 8 × 10" photo, black and white glossy **25.00**

Perot, Ross, 5 × 3" plain white card **75.00**

Price, Vincent, 5 × 7" photo, black and white glossy **5.00**

Quayle, Marilyn, 8 × 10" photo, color **45.00**

Quinn, Anthony, 8 × 10" photo, black and white, *Lawrence of Arabia* scene **25.00**

Rockefeller, John D, 8 × 10", typed letter, business stationery **95.00**

Russell, Jane, 8 × 10" photo, black and white glossy **10.00**

Sandburg, Carl, 5 × 3" card, bold signature **35.00**

Schmelling, Max, 3½ × 5½" photo, black and white **30.00**

Scott, Jerry, cartoonist, 5 × 3" card, black signature **55.00**

Sinatra, Frank, magazine, *Review,* Feb 1984, sgd on cov **95.00**

Snead, Sam, first day cover **50.00**

Stanwick, Barbara, 8 × 10" photo, black and white, early pose **15.00**

Stevens, Thaddeus, 1 pg, letter to Col Frazier, 1850 . . . . **125.00**

Townsend, Pete, 7 × 9" photo, color, silver ink signature, dated "'90" **60.00**

Vinton, Bobby, 8 × 10" photo, black and white glossy **10.00**

Williams, Robin, 8 × 10" photo, black and white glossy, sgd "Happy Thoughts/ Robin Williams" **20.00**

AUTOMOBILE COLLECTIBLES

An automobile swap meet is twenty–five percent cars and seventy–five percent car parts. Restoration and rebuilding of virtually all car models is never–ending. The key is to find the exact part needed.

All too often, auto parts at flea markets are not priced. The seller is going to judge how badly he thinks you want the part before setting the price. You have to keep your cool.

Two areas that are attracting outside collector interest are promotional toy models and hood ornaments. The former have been caught up in the craze for 1950s and 1960s Japanese tin. The latter have been discovered by the art community, which views them as wonderful examples of modern streamlined design.

Clubs: Hubcap Collectors Club, PO Box 54, Buckley, MI 49620; Spark Plug Collectors of America, 14018 N.E. 85th St., Elk River, MN 55330.

Periodicals: *Automobilia News,* PO Box 3528, Glendale, AZ 85311; *Hemmings Motor News,* Box 100, Bennington, VT 05201; *Mobilia,* PO Box 575, Middlebury, VT 05753.

AUTO PARTS AND ACCESSORIES

Ashtray, glass, dark blue and cream swirl, hangs under dash **45.00**

Carburetor, Buick, 1924–1925 . . . . . . **25.00**

Clock, Motor, "Luna," 8–day, luminous dial, brass and bronze, 1914 . . . **120.00**

Curb Feelers, electric buzzer, orig box and instructions **50.00**

Door Guards, plastic, cream, clamp on, MOC **15.00**

Engine
  Maxwell, 1914 . . . . **200.00**
  Packard, 1935 . . . . **800.00**

Fog Lights, chrome, amber lenses, pr **50.00**

Gearshift Knob
  Glass swirl, blue and white **15.00**
  Plastic, red, tapered sides, red jewel center **25.00**

Grill, Packard, 1941 . . . . **125.00**

Headlamp, 12" d, bull's–eye, Marchal **700.00**

Hood Ornament
  Lincoln Continental, paperweight, marble base, orig box **65.00**
  Lion, dated 1924 . . . . **30.00**

Steer Horns **50.00**

Horn, Pierce Arrow, 1915–1920, cowl– mounted, correct bracket **175.00**

Hubcaps, set of four
  Baby Moons, chrome **40.00**
  Plymouth, 1939–1940 . . . . **250.00**

Instruction Manual, Rickenbacker, 1920s **35.00**

License Plate
  Colorado, Bicentennial, Ski Colorado **6.00**
  Massachusetts, four digits, 1911 **70.00**
  North Dakota, orig wrapper, 1933, pr **25.00**

License Plate Emblem, Mobil flying horse, unused **15.00**

Owner's Manual
  Chandler Big Six, 1927 . . . . **55.00**
  Ford, Model T, 1914 . . . . **15.00**
  Rambler, 1927 . . . . **35.00**

Radiator Ornament
  Hubmobile Nash **25.00**
  Pontiac, feather headdress, 1958 **15.00**
  Willys Knight **25.00**

Radio, Cadillac, 1937 . . . . **250.00**

Shop and Parts Manual
  Avanti, Studebaker, 1964 . . . . **50.00**
  Cadillac, 1941 . . . . **110.00**
  DeSoto, master, 1936 . . . . **45.00**

Spark Plug
  Champion Y–4–A, unused, orig box **5.00**
  Spitfire, lightning bolt logo **10.00**

Steering Wheel Knob, plastic, white, clear insert with "Rod and Custom" logo **25.00**

Visor, 1932 Ford, full length **125.00**

Warranty, Owner's Service Policy, Chevrolet, Bel Air, 1955 . . . . **8.00**

SALES AND PROMOTIONAL ITEMS

Ashtray
  Cadillac Motor Car Division, copper, center shield emblem, 1948 **35.00**
  Pontiac–Chief of the Sixes, 3 × 5½", brass, raised image, 1930s **25.00**

Badge, employee plant
  Cadillac Motor Car Division, nickel plated, hexagon shape **85.00**
  Ford Northville Plant **65.00**

Blotter
  Atlantic City Auto Repair, early auto illus **15.00**
  Dodge panel truck, MA dealer, unused, 1925 . . . . **25.00**
  Drive A Ford & Feel The Difference, 1949 . . . . **6.00**
  Kelly Tires, 1910s **28.00**

Book
  The Automobile User's Guide, General Motors **15.00**
  Those Wonderful Old Automobiles, Floyd Clymer, 1953 . . . . **25.00**

Booklet, Chevy, Soap Box Derby Rules, illus, 1939 . . . . **20.00**

Brochure, dealer, fold out
    Buick, 1933, Series 90, orig photos, 8 ×
        10", black and white 7.00
    Chevrolet, 1949 ....25.00
    DeSoto, 1957 ....20.00
    Dodge Brothers Motor Vehicles, 1919
        ....80.00
    Franklin Car, 1921 ....45.00
    Plymouth Valiant, 1970 ....10.00
Calendar
    1954, US Royal Tires, pinup girl 20.00
    1986, *Century of the Automobile*, 14 ×
        22", chronological photos of classic
        automobiles with historical news
        photos, 12 pgs 16.00
Candy Container, car, glass, paper closure,
    includes candy 35.00
Catalog
    Airflow, 1935, 28 pgs 75.00
    Auburn, 9 × 16", part color, 16 pgs,
        1935 ....35.00
    Buick Air Conditioning, 1956, 6 pgs, 10
        × 7" 8.00
    Cadillac, 1927, 8 pgs 175.00
    Plymouth Barracuda 15.00
Checkbook Cover, vinyl, white, Chevrolet
    logo, gold letters 5.00
Coaster, 4" sq, Cadillac dealer, plastic, blue,
    set of four, 1960s 5.00
Flyswatter, Chevrolet, wire, wood handle,
    1940s 15.00
Letter Opener, Oldsmobile, 1950s ...25.00
Match Holder, Exide Battery & Goodyear
    Tire, orig box 35.00

Magazine Tear Sheet, **Ladies' Home Journal, May 1915, Overland Automobile, double page, Coles Phillips color illus, 13½ × 18½", $45.00.**

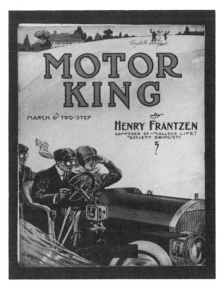

Sheet Music, **Motor King, March & Two–Step, Henry Frantzen, $20.00.**

Mirror, pocket
    Plymouth, PA dealer 20.00
    Studebaker Vehicle Works, South Bend,
        IN, 2¾" oval, 1910 ....125.00
Mug, ceramic, white, stake–bed truck illus,
    gold emblem with "1961 Sales Award"
    ....15.00
Pamphlet, 4 × 8", Mercedes–Benz Delivery
    Program, 10 pgs, 1971 ....7.50
Paperweight, metal, figural, Nash, 50th An-
    niversary of the Nash, 1902–52 95.00
Pen and Pencil Set, Buick, gold script
    ....40.00
Pinback Button
    Buick, "Looking Fine For 39" 45.00
    Chevrolet, 1¼" d, black and white,
        1930s 22.00
Post Card, DeSoto, full color, one with
    four–door sedan, other with two–door
    sedan, 1939, pr 8.00
Poster, Buick, "Kansas City," 25 × 38",
    black and white, 1921–1922, ...85.00
Program, Indy 500, 1953 ....40.00
Routing Chart, 10", movable, orig envelope,
    1936 ....25.00
Shoulder Patch, Oldsmobile Service, em-
    blem, c1940 ....23.00
Sign
    Corvair by Chevrolet, 4 × 11", neon,
        gold and white, early 1960s 350.00
    Ford, dealer's, neon 750.00
    General Motors, 4 × 30", tin, brown,
        yellow letters 90.00
    United Motor, dealer's, neon outline of
        early auto 1,250.00
Tie Tack, 1953 Chevrolet, gold colored
    metal, Chevrolet form, orig card 15.00
Tray, Pontiac, tin, 1957 ....50.00
Watch Fob, Chevrolet, 1939 ....60.00
Yo–Yo, Chevrolet, wood, 1955 .....15.00

AUTUMN LEAF

The Hall China Company devel-oped Autumn Leaf china as a dinnerware premium for the Jewel Tea Company in 1933. The giveaway was extremely suc-cessful. The "Autumn Leaf" name did not originate until 1960. Previously, the pattern was simply known as "Jewel" or "Autumn." Autumn Leaf remained in production until 1978.

Pieces were added and dropped from the line over the years. Limited-production pieces are most desirable. Look for matching accessories in glass, metal, and plastic made by other compa-nies. Jewel Tea toy trucks were also made.

Clubs: Autumn Leaf Reissues Associa-tion, 19238 Dorchester Circle, Strongsville, OH 44136; National Au-tumn Leaf Collector's Club, 7346 Shamrock Dr, Indianapolis, IN 46217.

Berry Bowl, 5½" d 5.00
Bud Vase 150.00
Cake Plate 20.00
Canister Set, sq, 4 pcs 125.00
Casserole Dish 25.00
Cereal Bowl, 6½" d 8.50
Coaster, set of 8 ....45.00
Coffeepot, electrical 240.00
Cookie Jar 165.00
Creamer 8.00
Cup 7.00
Custard Cup 6.50
Drip Jar 20.00
French Baker 8.00
Fruitcake Tin 5.00
Gravy Boat 20.00
Hot Pad, 7¼" d, tin back 30.00
Jug, ball 30.00
Mixing Bowl, nested set of 3 ....40.00
Mug, ftd 75.00
Pie Baker 19.00

Berry Bowl, **5½" d, $5.00.**

Teapot, Aladdin, flame finial, round infuser, gold trim, gold stamped "Hall's Superior Quality Kitchenware, Tested And Approved By Mary Dunbar, Jewel Homemakers Institute," 10½" d, 6½" h, $45.00.

Plate

    6" d, bread and butter **4.00**
    8" d, salad **8.50**
    10" d, dinner **9.00**
Platter, 13½" l **14.00**
Salad Bowl **17.00**
Salt and Pepper Shakers, pr, handled **32.00**
Saucer **4.00**
Soup Bowl, 8½" d **10.00**
Stack Set **75.00**
Sugar, vertical lines **20.00**
Tablecloth, 54" sq, sailcloth, slight damage
    .... **40.00**
Teapot, Aladdin style, round infuser **45.00**
Tea Towel **20.00**
Tidbit Tray, three tiers **40.00**
Toaster Cover, plastic **20.00**
Tray, oval, metal **50.00**

AVIATION COLLECTIBLES

Now is the time to get into aviation collectibles. The airline mergers and bankruptcies have produced a wealth of obsolete material. There were enormous crowds at Eastern's liquidation sale in spring 1991. I have a bunch of stuff from Piedmont and Peoples, two airlines that flew off into the sunset in the 1980s.

The wonderful thing about airline collectibles is that most of them initially were free. I try to make it a point to pick up several items, from bathroom soap to playing cards, each time I fly. Save the things most likely to be thrown out.

Clubs: Aeronautica & Air Label Collectors Club, PO Box 1239, Elgin, IL, 60121; The World Airline Historical Society, 3381 Apple Tree Lane, Erlanger, KY 41018.

Periodical: *Airliners,* PO Box 52–1238, Miami, FL 33152.

Advertising Trade Card, Airship Bonbon
    Candy, 1920s **45.00**
Book
    Airplanes of the USA, John B Walker,
        1944, 60 pgs, color photos ... **18.00**
    Charles Lindbergh, His Life, Dale Van
        Every, 1927, first edition **40.00**
    The Bird Boys, Langworthy, 1912, first
        edition, 3 volumes **50.00**
    The Search For Amelia Earhart, Fred
        Goerner, Doubleday, 1966, dj, 326
        pgs **10.00**
    The Story of Lindbergh, The Lone Eagle,
        Richard J Beamish, 1927, first edition
        .... **40.00**
Bookends, pr, 5½" h, Lindbergh, "The Avia-
    tor," cast iron, 1929 copyright
    .... **100.00**
Booklet, *Man Has Learned To Fly,* 4 × 6",
    Monarch Food Products, copyright 1929,
    24 pgs **25.00**
Bookmark, brass, Wright Bros, early 1900s
    .... **45.00**
Brochure, 8 × 11", Alaska Airlines Inc, 11
    pgs **20.00**
Calendar, 16 × 24", "Fly TWA," spiral
    bound, full color photo for each month
    .... **25.00**
Calendar Plate, 6½" d, biplane, 1912 **35.00**
Card Game, Lindy, Parker Bros, 1927 **55.00**
Chewing Gum Tin, Orville Wright, Peerless
    Chips Violet, illus, early 1900s ... **65.00**
Figure, 4" h, tin **25.00**
Flatware
    Flagship, fork and spoon, SS, streamlined
        propeller plane handles, 1930s **25.00**
    United Airlines, fork, knife, and spoon,
        1950–60 .... **25.00**
Folder, 4 × 6", Beech–Nut Autogyro **45.00**
Game, A Voyage Through The Clouds, J W
    Spear & Sons, London, c1910, orig box
    .... **350.00**
Glass
    Eastern Airlines, 4¾" h, clear, titled "Fly
        Eastern's New Silver Falcon," late
        1930s **25.00**

Cigar Label, Spirit of St Louis, Charles Lindbergh, green and blue, 6½ × 8½", $30.00.

TWA, 3¾" h, clear, weighted bottom,
    red and buff logo on one side, other
    with black lettering, 1960s ... **15.00**
Greeting Card, pop–out air balloon, airship
    Germany, 1909 .... **175.00**
Hostess Wings, TWA **6.00**
Hot Plate, Century of Progress zeppelin,
    Spirit of St Louis **35.00**
Jacket, stewardess, American Airlines, navy,
    seven insignia buttons, designer's label,
    1950s **15.00**
Manual
    Boeing 727 Flight Engineer's, 11 × 8",
        287 pgs, 1978 .... **30.00**
    Northeast Airlines, three ring binder,
        1947 .... **25.00**
Menu, Christmas, Gardner Air Field, CA,
    39th School Squadron Air Corps **12.00**
Necklace, emb aluminum charm, airship
    Akron, enameled beige and black back-
    ground, 1930s **75.00**
Paperweight, United Airlines, sgd "WA Pat-
    terson," bronze **40.00**
Pen, Allegheny Airlines **5.00**
Pilot Wings, US Air Force, senior, wing with
    star, SS **35.00**
Pin
    British Overseas Airways Corps Junior Jet
        Club, brass, wings, blue enameled
        symbol, 1960s **15.00**
    Eastern Airlines, stewardess **25.00**
    Flight Commemorative, *Spirit of St Louis,*
        New York to Paris, May 21, 1927,
        emb, brass **25.00**
    National Air Races, Yuma, AZ, 1928,
        2 × 3", diecut copper, airplane
        shape **75.00**
    Northwest Airlines, US Airmail Official
        Carrier, half wing, 1950s **75.00**
    TWA Junior Pilot, brass, red accented
        initials, 1960s **12.50**
    Western Airlines
        Jr Stewardess, silvered metal, totem
            style wing feathers and Indian
            symbol, 1960s **12.50**
        Wings **5.00**
Pinback Button
    American Air Races, Mechanic, 2½" d,
        red on cream, 1933 .... **50.00**
    USA Bomber, City of Binghamton, oval,
        celluloid, black and gray **50.00**
Plate, 7½" d, hot air balloon dec, Limoges,
    set of 4 .... **75.00**
Playing Cards, Cessna, double deck, full
    color photo of Cessna 120 on one deck,
    other with Cessna 140, orig box, 1940s
    .... **25.00**
Post Card
    Aircraft above pier, sepia photo, mes-
        sage on back, May 8, 1912,
        postmark **25.00**
    Dirigible & Lakehurst, Lakehurst Naval
        Air Station in NJ and USS *Los Ange-
        les Shenandoah* dirigibles scenes,
        numbered, unused, 1930s, set of 12
        .... **200.00**

Propeller, 32" l, wood, marked "Kroehler"
. . . . **50.00**
Puzzle
   American Airlines, 707 jet in flight,
      frame tray, Milton Bradley, 1960
      copyright **15.00**
   Belgian World Airlines, 11½ × 7½",
      1970s **28.00**
Sheet Music, *Amelia Earhart's Last Flight,*
   c1939 . . . . **24.00**
Shot Glass, Eastern Airlines **2.00**
Statue, Air India
   4¼" h, plaster **35.00**
   10" h **60.00**
Tapestry, Charles Lindbergh, New York to
   Paris **325.00**
Toy, Loop The Loop Glider, Ideal, MIB
. . . . **155.00**
Tray, Pan American Airlines, tin litho **30.00**
Umbrella, Capital Airlines **100.00**
Watch Fob
   Eddie Rickenbacker, hat in ring
   . . . . **35.00**
   Spirit of St Louis and airship **65.00**

AVON BOTTLES

Back in the late 1960s, my mother worked briefly as an Avon lady. If only she had saved one example of every product she sold! I am not certain that she would be rich, but she would have one heck of a collection.

Avon products, with the exception of California Perfume Company material, are not found that much at flea markets any longer. The 1970s were the golden age of Avon collectibles. There are still a large number of dedicated collectors, but the legion that fueled the pricing fires of the 1970s has been hard hit by desertions. Avon material today is more likely to be found at garage sales than flea markets.

Clubs: National Association of Avon Collectors, Inc, PO Box 7006, Kansas City, MO 64113; Shawnee Avon Bottle Collectors Club, 1418/32nd NE, Canton, OH 44714; Western World Avon Collectors Club, Box 23785, Pleasant Hills, CA 93535.

Periodical: *Avon Times,* PO Box 9868, Kansas City, MO 64134.

American Belle, Sonnet cologne, 1976–78
. . . . **5.00**
Baby Grand Piano, Perfume Glace, 1971–
   72 . . . . **8.00**
Betsy Ross, white, 1976 . . . . **12.00**
Boot, Miss Lollypop, 1967–69 . . . . **8.00**
Cable Car, green, 1975 . . . . **7.50**
Calculator, black, 1979 . . . . **5.00**

Cardinal, red glass, Bird of Paradise Cologne, 2 fl oz, 32859, orig contents and paper label, 4½" l, 4" h, $7.50.

Cannonball Express 4–6–0, black, Deep
   Woods, 1976–77 . . . . **10.00**
Capitol, milk glass, Spicy, 1976–77 . . . **7.00**
Caseys Lantern, Island Lime After Shave,
   1966–67 . . . . **30.00**
Country Kitchen, Moisture Hand Lotion,
   1973–75 . . . . **4.50**
Dovecote, clear, gold roof, two white
   doves, Bird of Paradise, 1974–76 **4.00**
Dutch Girl Figurine, Somewhere, 1973–74
. . . . **8.00**
Eiffel Tower, clear, gold cap, Rapture, 1970
. . . . **9.00**
Eight Ball, black and white **2.50**
First Class Male, Wild Country After Shave,
   1970–71 . . . . **3.00**
Flower Maiden, yellow paint, 1974 . . . **7.50**
Four Wheel Drive Decanter, black, After
   Shave, 1987 . . . . **8.00**
Golf Cart, green, 1973 . . . . **4.50**
Leisure Hour, Charisma Bath Oil, 1970–72
. . . . **4.50**
Library Lamp, gold plated base, 1976 **5.00**
Little Girl Blue, Cotillion, 1972–73 . . . **7.00**
Longhorn Steer, dark amber, Wild Country,
   1975–76 . . . . **9.00**
Looking Glass, hand mirror shape, 1970
. . . . **3.00**
Partridge, Occur, 1973–75 . . . . **4.50**
Pass Play, blue, white plastic top, Wild
   Country, 1973–75 . . . . **8.00**
Pheasant, brown, green plastic head, 1972
. . . . **7.50**
Pierce Arrow '33, Wild Country, dark blue,
   1975–77 . . . . **8.00**
Pony Post, bronze paint over clear, Tai
   Winds **8.00**
President Lincoln, Tai Winds After Shave,
   1973 . . . . **6.50**
Rainbow Trout, 1973 . . . . **5.00**
Rollin Great Roller Skate, clear, red top,
   Zany, 1980–81 . . . . **4.00**
Royal Coach, Bird of Paradise, 1972–73
. . . . **4.75**
Santa **35.00**

Sea Trophy, Windjammer After Shave, 1972
. . . . **4.50**
Snail Perfume, Brocade, 1968–69 . . . . **8.00**
Spirit of St Louis, silver paint, 1970   **12.00**
Stage Coach, brown **7.50**
Strawberry Bath Foam, 1971–72 . . . . . **3.50**
Sure Winner Racing Car, blue, Wild Coun-
   try, 1972–75 . . . . **7.00**
Swan Lake, Charisma, 8" h, 1972–1976
. . . . **5.00**
Treasure Turtle, Field Flowers Cologne,
   1971–73 . . . . **4.50**
Twenty–Dollar Gold Piece, Windjammer
   After Shave, 1971–72 . . . . **4.25**
Victorian Fashion Figurine, Field Flowers
   Cologne, 1973–74 . . . . **22.00**
Western Boot, Wild Country After Shave,
   1973–75 . . . . **2.50**
Winnebago Motor Home, orig box . . . **8.00**
Yule Tree, green, Sonnet, 1974–79 . . . **3.00**

BADGES

Have you ever tried to save a name tag or badge that attaches directly to your clothing or fits into a plastic holder? We are victims of a throwaway society. This is one case where progress has not been a boon for collectors.

Fortunately, our grandparents and great–grandparents loved to save the membership, convention, parade, and other badges that they acquired. The badge's colorful silk and cotton fabric often contained elaborate calligraphic lettering and lithographed scenes in combination with celluloid and/or metal pinbacks and pins. They were badges of honor, often having an almost military quality about them.

Look for badges with attached three–dimensional miniatures. Regional value is a factor. I found a great Emmaus, Pennsylvania, badge priced at $2.00 at a flea market in Florida; back home, its value is $20.00 plus.

Bicycling, Thistle Cycling Club, link badge,
   1¼ × 2¾", engraved hanger with thistle
   bloom surrounded by wreath of leaves,
   gold plated connecting bar inscribed
   "Sept 15–95," enameled brass disk in-
   scribed "2nd Annual Century/Elgin–
   Aurora–Chicago," second bar inscribed
   "Aug 2–96," 1895 . . . . **85.00**
Chauffeur
   California, 1934–35 . . . . **30.00**
   New York, 1928 . . . . **10.00**
Convention
   Grain Dealers, brass, 3½" h, Minneapo-
     lis name and skyline on hanger bar,
     red, white, and blue ribbon, pendant
     inscribed "24th Annual Convention,
     1920" **10.00**

Convention, IAM, Chicago, 27th Convention, bronze, purple ribbon, Sept 1968, cityscape, red, white, and blue insignia, 4" l, $20.00.

Republican National Convention, celluloid insert on brass bar inscribed "Ass't Sergeant At Arms," red, white, and blue ribbon, celluloid insert on fob inscribed "Republican National Convention, Phila, PA, June 18, 1900" **15.00**
Deputy Constable, silvered brass, 2½" h, embossed design, spring clip metal fastener, 1930s **20.00**
Employee
    New York Port Authority Compressed Air Employee Co, plant **65.00**
    Packard, plant, 1951 .... **10.00**
    899 Union Stockyards & Transit **150.00**
Fireman's, silvered brass, 2¼" h, fire symbols surrounded by inscription "Allison H. & L. Co. 12, Harrisburg, Pa," 1920s **25.00**
Fire Police, Chestertown, NY **35.00**
Guard
    Burns Detective Agency **40.00**
    Sun Oil Co **40.00**
Junior Rifle Corps, Winchester **35.00**
Military
    GAR Commander Staff Aide, bronzed metal, raised portrait of I N Walker, Commander In Chief GAR, inscribed "Walker National Staff, St Paul 1896," unmarked gold fabric ribbon **15.00**
    GAR Veteran, 1¾" d brass pendant, red, white, and blue flag ribbon, brass hanger bar of eagle, crossed cannons, cannonballs, and saber, GAR symbol on pendant and serial number, c1890 .... **20.00**

Newsboy, Bridgeport, CT, 1914 ..... **40.00**
Police
    City
        Boynton Beach **65.00**
        Miami **75.00**
        New Orleans **70.00**
        New York, detective **70.00**
        New York, lieutenant **75.00**
    Special Police, silvered brass, 2½" h, star shaped, black lettering, 1930s **22.00**
    State Police
        Alabama, sergeant **65.00**
        Arizona **85.00**
        New York **90.00**
        Pennsylvania State Police Force, brass, emb, 4½" h, state symbols over starburst shape, early 1900s **45.00**
        Virginia **85.00**
Political, 1924 Progressive Campaign, Robert A LaFollette, Burton K Wheeler, bronze **20.00**
Prohibition Pledge, darkened brass, eagle dec on hanger, red, white, and blue ribbon, aluminum token inscribed "Beautiful Water My Beverage Shall Be," reverse inscribed "Tis Here We Pledge Perpetual Hate, To All That Can Intoxicate," early 1900s **40.00**
Railroad
    Pennsylvania Railroad, coat **35.00**
    Railroad Express, porcelain **95.00**
    Rochester Railway & E **55.00**
Sheriff
    Arkansas **65.00**
    Florida **80.00**
    Las Vegas **80.00**
    Maine **75.00**
    North Carolina **80.00**
    Spec Dept Sheriff, Rennselaer, NY **35.00**

Toy, Junior Fire Marshal Badge, red plastic, Hartford Insurance, 2" l, $.25.

Souvenir
    Columbian Expo, brass, 2" h, "New York" on hanger bar, pendant inscribed "Souvenir World's Columbian Exposition 1893" with central world globe design **30.00**
    Fire Parade, brass, 4" h, two bars, upper bar with "Hackettstown Fire Dept," lower bar with "Elizabeth Oct 11, 1906," hanging celluloid pendant with fireman portrait illus **20.00**
    Parade, 8" l, WW I, brass hanger bar with celluloid insert inscribed "First Regiment," red, white, and blue ribbon with gold lettering "Silk Industry of America and Allied Interests, Citizens Preparedness Parade, May 13th, 1916" **8.00**
Union, Chairman of Committee, 5" l, brass hanger with celluloid insert, red, white, and blue ribbon with gold lettering "Annual Ball Jan 27th, 1940," white metal medallion with celluloid insert inscribed "Bakery Workers Union, Local 50 AF of L" **25.00**

BAKELITE

This is a great example of a collecting category gone price–mad. Bakelite is a trademark used for a variety of synthetic resins and plastics used to manufacture colorful, inexpensive, utilitarian objects. The key word is inexpensive, which can also be interpreted as cheap.

There is nothing cheap about Bakelite collectibles in today's market. Collectors, especially those from large metropolitan areas who consider themselves design–conscious, want Bakelite in whatever form they can find it—from jewelry to radio cases.

Buy a Bakelite piece because you love it. The market has already started to collapse for commonly found material. Can the high–end pieces be far behind?

Bookends, pr, geometric Art Deco style, green and yellow **65.00**
Cake Server, green handle **5.00**
Cigarette Case, hand–shaped closure, France **175.00**
Cigarette Holder, 12" l, Art Deco **35.00**
Cocktail Set, Bakelite and chrome shaker, six cocktails, chrome tray **45.00**
Compact, flower shape, hp dec **10.00**
Dish, chrome accents, sgd "Manning Bowman" **265.00**
Flatware, service for six, red handles, price for 26 pcs **85.00**
Food Chopper, red handle **10.00**
Inkwell, black, streamlined **24.00**
Jewelry
    Bar Pin, red bar, red cherries, green leaves suspended from chain **100.00**

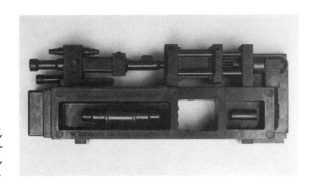

Model, Wuthrich, Switzerland, 150 ton clamp horizontal thermoset injection molding press, 6½" l, 1¼" w, 2½" h, $40.00.

Silk, flag inside wreath of 36 stars, 22 × 25", $80.00.

Bracelet, bangle, bright yellow, red,
   black, and green enamel dec   **25.00**
Necklace, red and black geometric
   shapes, chrome links and spacers
   . . . . **95.00**
Pendant
   Cameo, sterling chain **28.00**
   Rose, yellow flower, green leaves
   . . . . **25.00**
Pin, figural, cherries, cluster of three
   . . . . **20.00**
Mortar and Pestle, yellow and orange swirl
   . . . . **25.00**
Napkin Ring, figural
   Dog **25.00**
   Rabbit, orange **40.00**
Pencil Sharpener
   Charlie McCarthy **45.00**
   Ferdinand the Bull **45.00**
   G–Man Gun, red **45.00**
   Scottie **35.00**
Radio, General Electric **45.00**
Razor, Packare Lifetime, leather case, orig
   box **22.00**
Salt and Pepper Shakers, pr
   Cubes, maroon, handled tray **15.00**
   Half Moon, green and yellow, matching
   tray **18.00**
   Round domed top, red **12.50**
   Shotgun Bullets, green **15.00**
Shaving Brush, green handle **125.00**
Telephone, Kelloggs Series 1000, brown, Art
   Deco style, chrome dial **90.00**

BANDANNAS

Women associate bandannas with keeping their hair in place. Men visualize stagecoach holdups or rags to wipe the sweat from their brow. Neither approach recognizes the colorful and decorative role played by the bandanna.

Some of the earliest bandannas are political. By the turn of the century, bandannas joined pillow cases as the leading souvenir textile found at sites ranging from the beach to museums. Hillary Weiss's *The American Bandanna: Culture on Cloth from George Washington*

to Elvis (Chronicle Books: 1990) provides a visual feast for this highly neglected collecting area.

The bandanna played an important role in the Scouting movement, serving as a neckerchief for Boy and Girl Scouts. Many special neckerchiefs were issued. There is also a close correlation between scarves and the bandanna. Bandanna collectors tend to collect both.

Alice In Wonderland, 22 × 23", silk, multicolored, orig tag "Glentex/All Silk,"
   1950s **25.00**
Davy Crockett, 13½ × 14", cotton, bright
   blue, yellow, red, and white Indian blankets, ranch symbols, spurs, boots, and
   cowboy hat design, center with Davy as
   bronc rider **40.00**
Chessie, Chesapeake & Ohio Railway,
   glossy fabric, full color image, red background, black border, 1940s **75.00**
Eisenhower, 27" sq, "Win with Ike for President" and portrait surrounded by bunting, blue and white **75.00**
Gene Autry, 18 × 21", silk, purple, green,
   dark blue, and white images and design,
   1940s **75.00**
John F. Kennedy, 31" sq, rayon, full color
   portrait on white ground, red, white, and
   blue flag border, 1965 copyright tag
   . . . . **18.00**
Kit Carson, 20 × 22", green and white im-
   ages and Coke symbols, red background,
   c1953 . . . . **50.00**
Lone Ranger, 21 × 23", printed white and
   blue design, bright red ground, portrait,
   rail fence, crossed guns, coiled lasso,
   and horseshoe design, Cheerios premium, 1949–1950 . . . . **65.00**
Mickey Mouse, 22" sq, cotton, black, white,
   and red Mickey, Goofy, Minnie, and
   Donald figures, green border, c1960
   . . . . **35.00**
Orphan Annie, 17 × 19", "Flying W" sym-
   bol surrounded by code letters, four corner portraits, black, white, and red,
   Ovaltine radio premium, c1934   **75.00**
Republican National Convention, 21" sq,
   "Reagan–Bush '84," dark blue, white
   printing and images **20.00**

Roy Rogers, 17" sq, white Roy, Trigger,
   ranch brands, and rope designs on red
   ground, mid 1950s **35.00**
Smokey the Bear, 1950s **45.00**
Straight Arrow, 16½ × 18", red, white, and
   blue image, red background, inscribed
   "Kaneewah Fury," 1949 National Biscuit
   Co copyright **60.00**
Spanish–American War, 17" sq, "Remember
   the Maine," red, white, and blue slogan,
   ship, and flags dec, white ground, c1898
   . . . . **25.00**
Tom Mix, 16½ × 17", Mix on Tony and
   facsimile signature, purple shirt, brown
   horse, red border **60.00**

BANKS, STILL

Banks are classified into two types—mechanical (action) and still (nonaction). Chances are that any mechanical bank that you find at a flea market today is most likely a reproduction. If you find one that you think is real, check it out in one of the mechanical bank books before buying it.

The still or nonaction bank dominates the flea market scene. There is no limit to the way that you can collect still banks. Some favor type (e.g., advertising), others composition (cast iron, tin, plastic, etc.), figural (shaped like something), or theme (Western). Dad collects banks that were used to solicit money. Says something about him, doesn't it?

Beware of still bank reproductions, just as you are with mechanical banks, especially in the cast iron sector. Most banks were used, so look for wear where you expect to find it. Save your money and do not buy if you are not certain that what you are buying is a period original.

Club: Still Bank Collectors Club of America, 1456 Carson Court, Homewood, IL 60430.

Advertising

Bob's Big Boy, 9½" h, soft vinyl, 1970s **75.00**

Borman's Inc, 6¼" h, "Farmer Jack Savings Bank," farmer image, vinyl, Crunch Bird Studios, 1986 copyright **15.00**

Calumet Baking Powder, 4" h, tin **75.00**

Charlie the Tuna, ceramic **25.00**

Cities Service, 2¾" h, oil can shape, tin litho, gold, red, and white **25.00**

Donald Duck Orange Juice, can shape **20.00**

Eveready Battery, figural, cat **5.00**

Exxon Tiger **30.00**

Frito Lay, 1950 panel truck **30.00**

Fulton County Trust, Gloversville, NY, clock **75.00**

Gulf Gas, cardboard, gas pump **15.00**

Gulfpride, 2¾" h, oil can shape, tin litho, blue, white, and orange **25.00**

Humble Oil and Refining Co, figural, tiger **35.00**

Marathon, 2¾" h, oil can shape, litho tin, gold, red, white, and blue **25.00**

McDonald's, 9½ × 14", cardboard, punch-out, restaurant with golden arches shape, c1962, unassembled **100.00**

Mellow Cup Coffee **22.00**

Mr Softee, 4½" h, plastic, pale blue, pig wearing cap image, 1950-60 .... **20.00**

Oreo Cookie, 4¾" h, composition, painted, green base, marked "Korea," 1960s **25.00**

Rival Dog Food **10.00**

Sunoco, 4" h, gas pump, tin, blue, yellow, and red, 1940-60 ...... **35.00**

Thompson Auto Products, Indian, tepee **50.00**

Tootsie Roll, 12" l, cylinder, cardboard and tin, 1960s **12.00**

Underwood Typewriter, 1½" h, white metal, dark gold paint **35.00**

Wolf's Head Oil, can shape **16.00**

Cast Iron

Bank Vault, 5" h, "Fidelity," green and gold **55.00**

Globe, 4⅝" h, worn polychrome paint **135.00**

Lion **85.00**

Mail Box, blue and red, made in US, marked "Iron Art" **46.00**

Mammy **95.00**

Pay Phone, 7¼" h, nickel finish, wood receiver, replaced trap and cord **350.00**

Pig, sgd "Decker's" **85.00**

Reindeer **125.00**

Safe, 6½" h, bronze finish, applied medallions of ladies' heads **50.00**

Celluloid, 3 × 3 × 2½", building, white, red accents, blue roof, green base, black "National Bank," 1930s **50.00**

Ceramic

Camera, 3½ × 3½ × 6", Rolleicord, painted and glazed, opalescent luster, gold name and knobs, marked "PAC/Japan," 1950s **55.00**

Devil, head **16.50**

Character

Baba Louie, Knickerbocker **30.00**

Bullwinkle, 10" h, hard vinyl, glossy painted body, plastic trap, 1977 Ward copyright **75.00**

Buster Brown, 4¼" h, cast iron, early 1900s **210.00**

Casper the Friendly Ghost, Renzi Co **20.00**

Chewbacca, 9½" h, ceramic, painted and glazed, orig trap and "Sigma" sticker, Lucasfilm Ltd copyright 1983 .... **25.00**

Davy Crockett, metal **35.00**

Huckleberry Hound, 15½" h, vinyl, painted, Knickerbocker Toys, 1960 .... **25.00**

Mickey Mouse, 18½" h, plastic, figural **25.00**

Miss Piggy, china, Sigma **45.00**

Penny, 2 × 6 × 7¾", "My Penny Bank," cardboard, brown, schoolbook image, emb image of Penny, mid 1940s **50.00**

Pinocchio, ceramic **75.00**

Porky Pig, 11" h, chalkware, painted, 1940s **30.00**

Road Runner, 8½" h, composition, painted, Japan for Holiday Fair distribution, 1971 Warner Bros copyright **75.00**

Snoopy, ceramic, 40th Anniversary **25.00**

Chalkware, buffalo **15.00**

China

Cat, red sneakers, Kliban **40.00**

Rabbit Head, Napier **75.00**

Glass, figural, pig **10.00**

Metal

Jackpot Dime, 6 × 3½" **20.00**

Mail Box, 9" h, olive green, schedule on front **35.00**

Papier Mache, Beatles, 8" h, rubber plug, Pride Creations **100.00**

Tin, 4" d, 3" h, Uncle Sam's hat, red, white, and blue, trap and key, Chein, 1940s **55.00**

BARBED WIRE

Barbed wire is a farm, Western, and military collectible. It is usually collected in eighteen-inch lengths and displayed mounted on boards. While there are a few rare examples that sell in the hundreds of dollars for a piece, the vast majority of what is found are common types that sell between $2.00 and $5.00 for an example.

Club: American Barbed Wire Collectors Society, 1023 Baldmin Rd, Bakersfield, CA 93304.

Periodical: *Barbed Wire Collector*, 1322 Lark, Lewisville, TX 75067.

Dollars Clock, Kingsbury Mfg Co, cream painted metal case, 7¼" h, $30.00.

Christmas Trees, left: 32" h, $17.50; 16½" h, $12.50.

BARBERSHOP AND BEAUTY PARLOR COLLECTIBLES

Let's not discriminate. This is the age of the unisex hair salon. This category has been male–oriented for far too long. Haven't you wondered where a woman had her hair done in the nineteenth century?

Don't forget drugstore products. Not everyone had the funds or luxury to spend time each day at the barbershop or beauty salon.

Barber Bottle
    Barbicide **20.00**
    Clear glass, enameled dec, stopper
      ....**110.00**
    KDX For Dandruff, 7¾" h, label under
      glass **110.00**
    Kings Barber Barbicide **20.00**
    T Noonan Barber Supply, cobalt blue
      ....**50.00**
    Witch Hazel, 7" h, globular body,
      straight neck, milk glass, floral dec
      ....**60.00**
Barber Pole, top half of floor model, Padar,
    orig hand crank and glass tube, refinished, 1920 ....**300.00**
Blade Bank
    J B Williams, tin litho **23.00**
    Yankee, tin, c1900 ....**55.00**
Bobby Pins, orig card
    Gayla Hold, woman illus on front **2.75**
    Sta–Rite **1.50**
Box, Fairies Bath Perfume, unopened, 1920s
    ....**6.00**
Brochure, Burma Shave, Vol X, 1942 **6.00**
Business Card, 6 × 3¼", man cutting hair,
    "The Newest and Most Sanitary Shop in
    Providence" **10.00**
Catalog
    Emil J Paidar Co, 1928, 32 pgs, barber
      shop and beauty parlor equipment
      ....**25.00**
    Human Hair Goods, 1896, 24 pgs, color
      lithos **65.00**
Chair, pedestal base, Theo Kochs Manufacturer **350.00**
Clippers, Andis, c1940 ....**20.00**
Cologne, stick
    Morning Glory **4.25**
    Zia **4.00**
Hair Groom, Brylcreem **6.00**
Hair Net
    Cameo, c1930 ....**3.00**
    Doloris **4.75**
    Gainsborough **4.25**
    Jal–Net **5.50**
Hair Tonic
    Lan–Tox **12.00**
    Nowland's Lanford Oil **7.50**

Hair Treatment
    Marchand's Hair Rinse **4.25**
    Nestle
      Baby's **7.00**
      Curling Lotion ....**.75**
      Egyptian, hair tent **11.00**
Hair Wax
    Butch Hair Wax, illus of boy with crew
      cut on box, orig case of twelve and
      display sign **70.00**
    Lucky Tiger, large jar **10.00**
Mirror, pocket, "Beautyskin," multicolored
    ....**95.00**
Perm Machine, Duart **50.00**
Post Card, Unsafe Safety Razor, c1910
    ....**12.00**
Poster
    Bickmore Shave Cream, 30 × 21", man
      putting cream on brush, 1930 **22.00**
    Satin Skin Powder, 42 × 26", 1903
      ....**35.00**
Powder
    Lander, Gardenia, 3 pc set **45.00**
    Mavis **30.00**
    Rogers & Gallet Anthea **45.00**
    Stearns Superma Daydream **30.00**
Razor Blade
    Broadway Double Edge **5.00**
    Gold Tone **1.50**
    Pal Double Edge **1.50**
    Treet **1.50**
Razor Sterilizer, chrome and glass ...**55.00**
Shaving Brush, aluminum handle, emb design, c1910 ....**8.50**
Shaving Cream
    Brisk, tin and display box **8.00**
    Krank's Brush Lather Shave **8.00**
    Palmolive **5.00**
    Prep Brushless Shave **8.00**
Shaving Mug, occupational
    Horse–drawn grocer's wagon, 3¾" h,
      gold leaf trim, inscribed "G D
      Pottle" **300.00**
    Telegraph, 3¾" h, laurel surround, gold
      leaf trim, inscribed "C G Albright"
      ....**250.00**
Sign
    Beauty Shop, neon, pink, orig transformer **200.00**
    Dr Linus Hair Grower, 9 × 13", cardboard **30.00**
    Hump Hairpins, 16 × 14", tin, diecut
      ....**150.00**
    Parker's Cold Cream, 7½ × 11½",
      stand-up type, Victorian woman,
      1905 ....**90.00**
    Stephans, 16 × 18", tin **75.00**
Sterilizer, "Antiseptic," clambroth glass,
    metal base, red star mark **45.00**
Strop, Ingersoll, razor blade stropping kit,
    MIB **12.00**
Thermometer, Schick adv, 1950s **75.00**
Tin
    Bermarine Hair Dressing, 1⅝" d, sample,
      round, litho **20.00**

    Colgate's Rapid–Shave Powder, 4" h,
      round, litho **15.00**
    Ex–Cel–Siss Talcum **15.00**
    Gardenia Talcum **5.00**
    Griffen Safety Razor, 2¼" h, rect, litho
      ....**60.00**
    Lander's Lilacs and Roses, talc ...**18.00**
    Peau–Doux Styptic Powder, 2¼" h, oval,
      litho **30.00**
    Stein's Face Powder, 4⅝" d, round, litho
      ....**10.00**
    Tangee Rouge Compact, 1¼" d, sample,
      round, litho **12.00**
    White Witch Talc **12.50**

BARBIE DOLLS

As a doll, Barbie is unique. She burst upon the scene in the late 1950s and remains a major factor in the doll market over forty years later. No other doll has enjoyed this longevity.

Every aspect of Barbie is collectible, from the doll to her clothing to her play accessories. Although collectors place the greatest emphasis on Barbie material from the 1950s and 1960s, there is some great stuff from the 1970s and 1980s that should not be overlooked. Whenever possible, try to get original packaging. This is especially important for Barbie material from the 1980s onward.

Periodicals: *Barbie,* 4578 N Kavanagh, Fresno, CA 93705; *Barbie Bazaar,* 5617 6th Ave, Kenosha, WI 53140; *Barbie Fashions,* 387 Park Avenue South, New York, NY 10016; *Collector's Corner,* 519 Fitzooth Dr, Miamisburg, OH 45342; *Miller's Price Guide & Collectors' Almanac,* West One Summer, #1, Spokane, WA 99204.

Bath Mitt, MIB, 1965 ....**25.00**
Beauty Kit, 1961, MIB **25.00**
Book
    Barbie Solves A Mystery, Random House
      ....**8.00**
    The World of Barbie, Random House
      ....**15.00**
Clothing Accessories
    Barbie
      After Five, #934, 1962 ......**40.00**
      American Airlines Stewardess, #984,
        1961 ....**27.50**
      Barbie–Q Outfit, #962, 1959
        ....**45.00**
      Golden Girl, #911, 1959 ....**45.00**
      Let's Dance, #978 ....**50.00**
      Orange Blossom, #987, 1962
        ....**25.00**
      Peachy Fleecy Coat, #915 ...**50.00**
      Purse Pak, 1962 ....**25.00**

Paper Dolls, "Pos'n' Barbie," Whitman Publishing Co, #1975, 6 pgs, unused, 1972, 7¼ × 15½", $45.00.

Registered Nurse, #991, 1961 **65.00**
Satin Slacks, pink with glitter dots, pink shoes with silver glitter **25.00**
Silken Flame, #977, 1960 .... **40.00**
Ken
  Baseball Cap, ball, mitt, plastic **3.00**
  Corduroy Jacket, 1962 .... **15.00**
  Dreamboat, #785, 1961 ..... **50.00**
  Graduation gown and mortarboard, black **12.50**
  Hunting Cap, red plastic **2.00**
  In Training #780, 1961 ...... **45.00**
  Ken In Mexico, #0778, 1964 **85.00**
  Original Swimsuit, #750 ..... **10.00**
  Rally Day, all–weather coat and hat, #795 .... **8.00**
  Roller Skates **2.50**
  Snorkel Gear, striped suit, green plastic swim fins, face mask, and snorkel, 1963 .... **30.00**
  Sweater, red cotton knit **15.00**
  Time For Tennis, #790 ...... **50.00**
Colorforms Set **7.50**
Cookbook, Random House **45.00**
Display, McDonald's, 1993, Barbie and Hot Wheels **135.00**
Doll
  Barbie
    1962, Bubble Cut Fashion, MIB **90.00**
    1969, light auburn hair, MIB **250.00**
    1986, Fashion Play Barbie **15.00**
    1987, Barbie and The Sensations, bright pink and white outfit, cassette **30.00**

    1988, Mexican Barbie, red and white outfit, white lace mantilla **75.00**
    1990, Happy Holidays, MIB **75.00**
    1992, Holiday, Mattel **27.00**
    1993, Holiday, Mattel **45.00**
  Julia, Twist 'n' Turn, 2 pc uniform, 1969 .... **40.00**
  Ken, 12" h, molded hard plastic, movable head, arms, and legs, flocked blonde hair, orig "Sport Shorts" outfit #783, orig wire pedestal and box, 1961 .... **150.00**
  Midge, poseable legs, 1965 .... **200.00**
Doll Carrying Case, vinyl cov cardboard
  Barbie and Midge, 14 × 18 × 4", light blue, metal snap closure, pink, tan, black and white illus, 1963 Mattel copyright, heavy playwear **25.00**
  Ken, 11 × 13 × 4", olive–yellow, blue, yellow, white, and black illus of Ken, Barbie, and sports car, black plastic handle, 1962 copyright, heavy playwear **30.00**
Doll House
  Barbie's Country Living House, #8662 .... **45.00**
  Dream House, furnished, 1961 ... **55.00**
  The World of Barbie House, #1048 .... **40.00**
Fast Food Giveaways, McDonald's, set of eight
  1992 .... **35.00**
  1993 .... **39.00**
Game, Queen of the Prom **30.00**
Lunch Box, vinyl, 1960 .... **30.00**
Magazine, *Mattel Barbie Magazine,* Jan–Feb 1969, 22 pgs **15.00**
Manicure Set, Barbie Good Grooming Manicure Set, orig box **35.00**
Paper Doll Book, *Barbie and Her Friends,* Whitman #1981, unused, 1975 **14.00**
Record Case, 1961, MIB **20.00**
Sew–Free Fashion Fun, Stardust, #1722, 1965, Mattel **40.00**
Sunglasses, child's, orig pkg, 1978 ... **15.00**
Telephone, Barbie Mattel–a–Phone, pink **50.00**
Thermos, 8½" h, litho metal, red plastic cap, full color illus, black ground, 1962 Mattel copyright **35.00**

BASEBALL CARDS

Collecting baseball cards is not for kids any longer. It is an adult game. Recent trends include buying and stashing away complete boxed sets of cards, placing special emphasis on rookie and other types of cards, and speculation on a few "rare" cards that have a funny habit of turning up in the market far more frequently than one would expect if they were so rare.

Baseball cards date from the late 19th century. The earliest series are tobacco company issues dating between 1909 and 1915. During the 1920s American Caramel, National Caramel, and York Caramel issued cards.

Goudey Gum Company (1933 to 1941) and Gum, Inc. (1939) carried on the tradition in the 1930s. When World War II ended, Bowman Gum of Philadelphia, the successor to Gum, Inc., became the baseball giant. Topps, Inc., of Brooklyn, New York, followed. Topps purchased Bowman in 1956 and enjoyed almost a monopoly in card production until 1981 when Fleer of Philadelphia and Donruss of Memphis challenged its leadership.

In addition to sets produced by these major companies, there were hundreds of other sets issued by a variety of sources ranging from product manufacturers, such as Sunbeam Bread, to minor league teams. There are so many secondary sets now issued annually that it is virtually impossible for a collector to keep up with them.

The field is plagued with reissued sets and cards as well as outright forgeries. The color photocopier has been used to great advantage by unscrupulous dealers. Never buy cards from someone who you can't find six months later.

The listing below is simply designed to give you an idea of prices for baseball cards in good condition and to show you how they change depending on the age of the cards that you wish to collect. For detailed information about card prices consult the following price guides: James Beckett, *Sports Americana Baseball Card Price Guide, No. 16,* Edgewater Book Co., 1994; Gene Florence, *Gene Florence's Standard Baseball Card Price Guide, Revised Sixth Edition,* Collector Books, 1994; Bob Lemke (ed)., *Standard Catalog of Baseball Cards, Fourth Edition,* Krause Publications, 1994; and Sports Collectors Digest, *Baseball Card Price Guide, Eighth Edition,* Krause Publications, 1994. Although Beckett is the name' most often mentioned in connection with price guides, I have found the Krause guides to be much more helpful.

Periodicals: *Beckett Baseball Card Monthly,* Suite 200, 4887 Alpha Rd, Dallas, TX 75244; *Sports Cards,* 700 East State Street, Iola, WI 54990; *Sports Col-*

lectors Digest, 700 East State Street, Iola, WI 54990.

Bowman
  1949
    Complete set **2,000.00**
    1 Vern Bickford **5.50**
    27 Bob Feller **22.00**
    46 Robin Roberts **33.00**
  1952
    Complete set **1,050.00**
    8 Pee Wee Reese **14.50**
    44 Roy Campanella **28.00**
    116 Duke Snider **25.00**
  1954
    Complete set **525.00**
    15 Richie Ashburn **4.70**
    138 Gil Hodges **8.75**
    161 Yogi Berra **22.00**
Donruss, 1981
  Complete set **7.00**
  Common player **01**
Fleer
  1982
    Complete set **11.50**
    Common player **01**
  1984
    Complete set **20.00**
    Common player **02**
Hostess Twinkie, 1976
  Complete set **16.50**
  Common player **10**
Leaf
  1960
    Complete set **150.00**
    27 Brooks Robinson **4.70**
    37 Duke Snider **6.25**
  1990
    Complete set **31.00**
    13 Tom Glavine **1.00**
    245 Ken Griffey Jr **3.10**

Topps, 1971, American League Playoffs, Orioles, $12.00.

Score
  1988
    Complete set **25.00**
    Common player **01**
  1991
    Complete set **2.50**
    Common player **01**
Topps
  1953
    Complete set **1,600.00**
    10 Smokey Burgess **8.25**
    114 Phil Rizzuto **17.50**
    162 Ted Kluszewski **6.00**
    207 Whitey Ford **16.50**
  1958
    Complete set **650.00**
    1 Ted Williams **40.00**
    25 Don Drysdale **10.50**
    70A Al Kaline **10.50**
    187 Sandy Koufax **26.00**
  1966
    Complete set **525.00**
    1 Willie Mays **14.00**
    50 Mickey Mantle **28.00**
    120 Harmon Killebrew **2.30**
    126 Jim Palmer **20.00**
    300 Bob Clemente **12.50**
    365 Roger Maris **7.00**
  1977
    Complete set **50.00**
    10 Reggie Jackson **1.90**
    390 Dave Winfield **3.80**
    450 Pete Rose **1.25**
    580 George Brett **5.00**
  1981
    Complete set **10.50**
    Common player **01**
    240 Nolan Ryan **1.50**
    261 Rickey Henderson **1.50**
    700 George Brett **70**
Upper Deck
  1989
    Complete set **14.00**
    Common player **01**
    1 Ken Griffey Jr **2.80**
    357A Dale Murphy **3.80**
    774 Nolan Ryan **50**
  1991
    Complete set **3.10**
    Common Player **01**

BASEBALL MEMORABILIA

What a feast for the collector! Flea markets often contain caps, bats, gloves, autographed balls, and photos of your favorite all-stars, baseball statues, regular and World Series game programs, and team manuals or rosters. Do not overlook secondary material such as magazine covers with a baseball theme. Condition and personal preference should always guide the eye.

Be careful of autograph forgeries. The general feeling among collectors is that over fifty percent of the autographed baseballs being offered for sale have faked signatures. But do not let this spoil your fun. There is plenty of great, real stuff out there.

Bank
  Braves, 8" h, ceramic, figural, Indian wearing baseball uniform, missing one front tooth, marked "Stanford Pottery/Sebring, OH" **100.00**
  Cleveland Indians, ceramic, 1950s **185.00**
Baseball, autographed
  Bo Jackson **30.00**
  Carl Hubbel, bold black marker signature **30.00**
  Cubs Team, 1986 . . . .**45.00**
  Jimmy Foxx **1,200.00**
  Lou Boudreau, bold blue ink signature **35.00**
  Red Sox Team, 1981 . . . .**45.00**
  Ted Williams, blue ink signature "Best Wishes Ted Williams 1952" **125.00**
Bedspread, chenille, baseball player, twin size **50.00**
Beer Tray, Gil Hodges, round, four coasters, color picture **45.00**
Book
  Bob Feller, How To Pitch, A S Barnes Sports Library, 1948 copyright **18.00**
  Inside Baseball for Little Leaguers, Ted Kluszewski **42.50**
  The Willie Mays Story, 94 pgs, 1954 . . . .**20.00**
Calendar, St Louis Cardinals, 1980 **15.00**
Coin, 1 3/8" d, plastic, Mickey Mantle, black rim, Salada Tea premium, 1962 . . . .**15.00**
Dixie Lid, Joe Medwick/St Louis Cardinals, 2 1/4" d, brown photo, c1937 . . . . . **50.00**
Doll
  Los Angeles Dodgers, 1960 . . . . . . **65.00**
  New York Mets, 7" h, vinyl, movable head, arms, and legs, 1987 copyright **50.00**

Baseball, Joe DiMiaggio autograph, $75.00.

Fan, Pete Rose vs Ty Cobb, cardboard, full color design **15.00**

Game

All–Star Baseball Game, Cadaco–Ellis, 1962 . . . . **15.00**

Big League Baseball Game, 3M Co, copyright 1966 . . . . **20.00**

Los Angeles Dodgers Baseball Card Game, Educards Corp, 1964 **40.00**

The Champion Game of Baseball, Proctor Amusement Co, Cambridge, MA, early 1890s **200.00**

Glass, Rawlings Official League, 5¼" h, clear, weighted bottom, white and red design, 1960s **15.00**

Guide, *1924 Spalding Baseball Guide* **65.00**

Hartland Figure, Hank Aaron, 7" h, bat missing, late 1950s **80.00**

Lapel Pin, Bert & Harry Fan Club **25.00**

Magazine, *Weekly News*

Jackie Robinson, October 6, 1952 **15.00**

Yogi Berra, August 4, 1952 . . . . . . **18.00**

Menu, DiMaggio Restaurant, 6 × 8", glossy stiff paper, early 1950s **15.00**

Mitt, Catfish Hunter **12.00**

Mug, 1968 World Series, 6½" h, plastic, white **12.50**

Napkin, World Series, Los Angeles, 1959, 7 × 5", "Dodgers Win It," Snider and Sherry pictured **10.00**

Nodder

Boston Red Sox, 6" h, composition, green round base, 1962 copyright **55.00**

California Angels, 6½" h, composition, gold round base, orig box, 1967–72 . . . . **75.00**

Kansas City Royals, 6½" h, composition, painted, gold round base, orig box **75.00**

Pennant

Cleveland Indians, felt, red, white lettering, c1950 . . . . **15.00**

Pee Wee Reese, felt, white, red portrait illus and signature, 1950s **45.00**

Philadelphia Athletics, 28" l, navy blue felt, white inscription **50.00**

Photo Button, Indianapolis Champions 1897, 1½" d, sepia, 15 uniformed players **200.00**

Photograph, 13 × 18", Cincinnati team, 1888 . . . . **80.00**

Pinback Button

⅞" d, Miller/Pittsburgh Pirates, Sweet Caporal Cigarettes **20.00**

1¾" d, Brooklyn Dodgers, blue and white, c1945 . . . . **15.00**

Pocketknife, Kansas City Royals 1985 World Champions, presentation box, case **750.00**

Post card, Wrigley Field and Gabby Hartnett photo, linen, 1930s **15.00**

Press Pin, World Series

1943, NY Yankees, ⅞" d, SS, crossed bats beneath baseball, Dieges & Clust, threaded post fastener **300.00**

1967, Chicago White Sox Phantom, 1⅛" d, enameled, gold batter, white stocking, deep red center, deep blue border, Balfour, needle post fastener **80.00**

Program

New York Yankees–Chicago White Sox, 20 pgs, 1956 . . . . **45.00**

Philadelphia Athletics, 1941, 12 pgs **25.00**

St Louis–Yankees, 1926 World Series **600.00**

Yankees vs. Pirates, 1960 World Series, 52 pgs **100.00**

Score Card, St. Louis Cardinals, 1926 World Champions picture, 1951 . . . . **65.00**

Uniform, Athletics, 2 pcs, flannel, #36, gray, royal blue trim and logo **250.00**

Wiffle Ball, plastic, Pete Rose endorsement, orig box, mid 1960s **25.00**

Yearbook, Cubs, 1949 . . . . **75.00**

BASKETBALL

As the price of baseball cards and baseball memorabilia continues to rise, collectors are turning to other sports categories based on the affordability of their material. Basketball and football are new "hot" sport collecting fields.

Collecting generally centers around one team, as it does in most other sport

collecting categories. Items have greater value in their "hometown" than they do "on the road." You know a category is becoming strong when its secondary material is starting to bring strong prices. Check the prices for the games listed in this section.

Periodical: *Beckett Basketball Card Magazine,* Suite 200, 4887 Alpha Rd, Dallas, TX 75244.

Bubble Gum Card

Fleer, 1988–89

Charles Barkley, #85 . . . . **15.00**

Michael Jordan, #120 AS **15.00**

Patrick Ewing, #80 . . . . **7.00**

NBA Hoops, 1989–90, complete set **5.00**

Upper Deck

Larry Johnson, #2, 1991–92 **10.00**

Shaquille O'Neal, #1, 1992–93 . . . . **15.00**

Cereal Box, Wheaties, Michael Jordon, 1½ oz **3.00**

Doll, 15" h, stuffed, New York Nets, 1970s **15.00**

Game

Bas–Ket, Cadaco, 1973 . . . . **25.00**

NBA All–Star Basketball Game, Tudor Metal Products, metal playing board, plastic basketball figures, basketball net, and styrofoam ball, 1968 **45.00**

Mug, 3" h, Milwaukee Bucks, china, cartoon illus, black inscription, 1969–1970 . . . . **15.00**

Nodder

Detroit Pistons, 6½" h, composition, sq gold base, 1969 NBA copyright, orig shrink wrap and box **50.00**

Pinback Button, Baltimore Orioles, World Series, Memorial Stadium, orange and black button and ribbon, 1¾" d button, 4½" l ribbon, $15.00.

Card, Larry Johnson, Forward, statistics on back, 2½" w, 3½" h, $.50.

Fast Food Giveway, NBA Fantasy Packs, McDonald's, foil package, 2¹/₂" w, 4¹/₂" h, $3.00.

Los Angeles Lakers, 7" h, composition, painted, orig cardboard carton, 1960–70 . . . . **50.00**
Millersville, 7" h, composition, holding brown basketball, gold base, 1960s **30.00**
Palm Puzzle, 3" d, styrene plastic case, cardboard center with basketball design, metal ball, 1950s **12.00**
Pen, 6" l, New York Knicks, plastic, orange, clear cylinder with spectator image **15.00**
Pennant, 30" l, Philadelphia Sixers, 1982–83 championship, red, white, and blue felt **20.00**
Program, Harlem Globetrotters
1948–49, 8¹/₂ × 11", 16 pgs **25.00**
1965, 8 × 10¹/₂", Magicians of Basketball Tour, 30 pgs **15.00**
Punchboard, 7¹/₄ × 10", Play Basket Ball, Havana Blend Cigar adv, red, blue, and white, 5¢, 1930s **17.50**
Starting Lineup Figure, orig package, Kenner
Larry Bird, 1988 . . . . **24.00**
Magic Johnson, 1992 . . . . **25.00**
Michael Jordan, Slam Dunk Superstars, 1989 . . . . **100.00**

BASKETS

A tisket, a tasket, who's got the basket? Baskets are always found at flea markets, ranging from the really neat old ones to modern contemporary craft types.

Fireside type, willow, braided rim, ball feet, 23" w, 25" d, 19¹/₂" h, $65.00.

Apple, wide latticework, small painted red apples with green leaves dec, sturdy handle **15.00**
Bicycle, woven plastic cane, white, red and blue stripes, orig leather straps, c1960 . . . . **5.00**
Bushel, stave construction, wrapped with wire bands, wooden rim, bentwood rim handles, old varnish finish, partial paper label **165.00**
Cheese, woven splint, dark brown stained ext **55.00**
Easter, round, colorful, high handle, c1955, marked "Mexico" **5.00**
Egg, woven splint, 16" d **70.00**
Fireside, painted white, wooden base   **10.00**
Laundry, oval, woven splint, bentwood rim handles **50.00**
Market, rect, handle woven as part of basket, worn floral dec **45.00**
Pet, small round wooden feet, worn cushion **25.00**
Picnic, woven splint, swivel handles, wooden lid, worn finish **65.00**
Potato, ash splint, worn base **35.00**
Sewing, cov, round, tightly woven, stained brown, marked "China" **10.00**
Tea, shallow, rect, glass over fabric cov wood bottom, small side handles   **10.00**

BATMAN

"Galloping globs of bat guano, Caped Crusader!" and similar cries may be heard as the Dark Knight and his sidekick are summoned to restore peace to Gotham City.

The saga of the search for Batman & Robin–related items began with Batman's appearance in 1939 in issue #27 of Detective Comics. Today, Boy Wonder and Caped Crusader collectibles are found in almost every medium imaginable. Local flea markets offer a large variety of batgoodies capable of making any batcollector go batty!

Action Figure, plastic
Batman
3" h, Justice League, Ideal, 1966–67 . . . . **50.00**
4³/₄" h, Wall Scaler, Dark Knight, Kenner, #63130, 1990 . . . . . **8.00**
5" h, Super Powers, Kenner, 1984, mini comic **40.00**
Penguin, 4¹/₄" h, missile firing umbrella, long missile, Toy Biz #4409, 1989 . . . . **25.00**
Riddler, Super Amigo, Pacipa, 1989 . . . . **50.00**
Robin, 12¹/₂" h, flyaway action, Mego, 1976 . . . . **140.00**
Activity Book, Paint–By–Numbers, Whitman, 1966 . . . . **45.00**
Alarm Clock, talking, Janex, 1975 . . . **85.00**
Bank
Batman, glazed china, 7" h, 2 × 3" base, 1966 . . . . **60.00**
Robin, ceramic, M U, 1966 . . . . . **65.00**
Batchute, Poynter, 1966 . . . . **65.00**
Batmobile
AHI, battery operated, radio controlled, 1977 . . . . **30.00**
Corgi #267, black diecast car, blue tinted cockpit dome, seated Batman and Robin figures, 1973 . . . . . **80.00**
Ertl #2575, diecast, 1/43 scale **7.50**

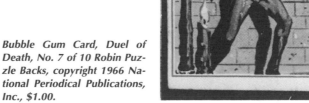

Bubble Gum Card, Duel of Death, No. 7 of 10 Robin Puzzle Backs, copyright 1966 National Periodical Publications, Inc., $1.00.

Matsushiro, radio controlled, 8″ l, 1989
.........................**80.00**
Batphone, 8″ w, hotline, talking, red plastic,
Marx, 1966 ....**225.00**
Bat Ring, Samsons, 1966 ....**25.00**
Bike Reflector, Penguin, Charhill, 1978
............................**15.00**
Book
Batman vs Three Villains of Doom,
Winston Lyon, Signet, first edition,
1966 ....**20.00**
The Batman Murders, Craig Shaw
Gardner, Warner, 1990, first edition
........................**6.00**
Box, Batman Slam Bang Ice Cream, 1966
...........................**20.00**
Carrying Case, Batcave, holds 3″ h figures,
Ideal/Sears, 1966 ....**300.00**
Christmas Ornament, 3¾″ d, Batman, PVC
...........................**9.00**
Colorforms, 1966 ....**25.00**
Desk Set, executive set, Batsharpener, Joker
stapler, and Batcalendar, Janex, 1977
..........................**45.00**
Doll, Batman, 24″ h, cloth, vinyl face, Com-
monwealth, 1966 ....**120.00**
Figure
Joker, hanging figure on suction cup,
Applause, 1989 ....**8.00**
Penguin, diecast, collector card, Ertl
#718, 1990 ....**5.00**
Superhero, bendable, Mego, 5″ h, 1972–
74
Batman **90.00**
Catwoman **175.00**
Joker **150.00**
Robin **75.00**
Flasher Ring, plastic, silver, VariVue, 1966
...........................**16.00**

Fork, Batman, stainless steel, Imperial, 1966
............................**20.00**
Game, Batman Game, Milton Bradley,
1966, orig 20 × 9″ box **35.00**
Glass, Riddler, Pepsi promotion, 1976 **15.00**
Gloves, black vinyl, Batman emblem, Wells
Lamont, 12″ l, 1966 ....**135.00**
Gun, Batman Escape Gun, orig card, 1966
...........................**50.00**
Handcuffs, Batman, Gordy International,
1989 ....**4.00**
Helmet and Cape, plastic and vinyl, Ideal,
full color box, 1966 ....**125.00**
Kite, Ski–Hi, 1979 ....**15.00**
License Plate, Batman Batmobile, Marx,
4″ l, 1966 ....**35.00**
Magic Slate, wood stylus, Whitman, 8½ ×
14″, 1966 ....**35.00**
Memo Pad, Robin, Alco, 1980 ....**9.00**
Model Kit
Batman, Aurora #467, 1964 ....**350.00**
Penguin, Aurora, 1967 ....**700.00**
Mug, Batman logo, 14 oz, 1990 ......**2.50**
Paint Set, Star Dust, Hasbro, 1966   **125.00**
Pencil Sharpener, Robin Super Friends,
1980 ....**12.50**
Periscope, Kelloggs, 14″ l, 1966 .....**45.00**
Playset
Ideal, Batman Shaker Maker, 11 × 9″
box, 1974 ....**65.00**
Mego, Collapsible Bridge, ¾″ h Batman,
Robin, Joker, and Penguin figures,
1975 ....**350.00**
Toy Biz #4417, Batcave, 1989 ...**40.00**
Poster, 41 × 27″, Batman movie serial, Co-
lumbia Pictures, 1954 ....**140.00**
Puzzle
Jigsaw, Batman illus, Whitman, #4608,
150 pcs, 1966 ....**35.00**
Sliding, Batman, American Publishing
Corp, 1977 ....**10.00**
Raincoat, yellow, logo on front, Batman and
Robin on back, Sears, 1975 .....**60.00**
Record, *The Catwoman's Revenge,* 33⅓
RPM, Peter Pan, 1975 ....**10.00**
Rifle, 18″ l, tin, Japan **150.00**
Roller Skates, Laramie, 1970s **50.00**
Soaky Bottle, Robin, Colgate/Palmolive,
1966 ....**50.00**
Towel, Batman bat, 1990 ....**16.00**
Tricycle
Batcycle, Batman and Robin figures, Tai-
wan, 1970 ....**45.00**
Jokercycle, Toy Biz #4437, 1989   **10.00**
Utility Belt, Bat belt grappler, cuffs, clicker
gun, walkie–talkie, orig box, Remco,
1976 ....**120.00**
Viewmaster Reel Set, GAF, 1966 ....**60.00**
Visor, black, logo, 1990 ....**3.00**
Walkie–Talkies, Batman and Robin, figural,
M U, 1974 ....**80.00**
Watch, Joker, Fossil Co, 1989 .....**125.00**

BAUER POTTERY

J. A. Bauer established the Bauer Pottery in Los Angeles, CA, in 1909. Flowerpots were among the first items manufactured, followed by utilitarian items. Dinnerware was introduced in 1930. Artware came a decade later. The firm closed in 1962.

La Linda, 1939–1959
Chop Plate, 13″ d **25.00**
Cup and Saucer **15.00**
Plate, 9″ d, dinner **8.50**
Soup, 7″ d **15.00**
Sugar **15.00**
Teapot, olive green, glossy pastel, Alad-
din **35.00**
Vegetable, 10″ l, oval **25.00**
Monterey, 1936–45
Butter Dish **65.00**
Casserole, cov, 2 qt, chartreuse, metal
frame, crazed lid **35.00**
Creamer **12.00**
Cup, olive green **12.00**
Gravy **35.00**
Plate, 9½″ d, chartreuse **9.00**
Soup Bowl, 7″ d **18.00**
Sugar **20.00**
Teapot, red **65.00**
Tumbler, 8 oz **15.00**
Ring, c1931
Butter Dish, cov, green, round ...**75.00**
Candlestick, spool **35.00**
Coffee Server, wood handle, 6 cup **28.00**
Mixing Bowl
Olive Green, #12 ....**28.00**
Yellow, #24 ....**15.00**
Pie Baker, 9½″ d, turquoise **16.00**
Pitcher, red **75.00**
Plate
6½″ d, yellow **6.00**
7½″ d, orange **10.00**
9½″ d, yellow **12.00**
10½″ d, light blue **20.00**
Ramekin, 4″ d **7.50**
Refrigerator Set, 4 pcs **80.00**
Salad Bowl, yellow **55.00**

Fast Food, plastic drinking cup, McDonald's, Batman Returns, gray frisbee Batdisc top, Louisana Plastics, Inc, St Louis, MO 21A, 1992, 2½″ d, 7″ h, $1.00.

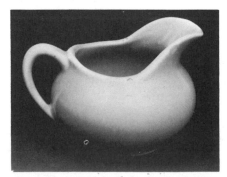

Creamer, La Linda, medium green, imp "Bauer USA" in bottom, 4¾″ w, 3″ h, $10.00.

Shaker, green **12.00**
Souffle Dish **25.00**
Tumbler, 3½" h, cobalt, wood handle
. . . . **25.00**
Vase, 10¼" h, orange **50.00**
Vegetable, oval, divided **50.00**

BEATLES

Ahhh! Look, it's the Fab Four! The collector will never need *Help* to find Beatle memorabilia at a flea market—place mats, dishes, records, posters, and much more. The list is a *Magical Mystery Tour.* John, Paul, George, and Ringo can be found in a variety of shapes and sizes. They are likely to be heavily played with, so their condition will vary from poor to good. Take a good look. You may see *Strawberry Fields Forever.*

Clubs: Beatles Connection, PO Box 1066, Pinellas Park, FL 34665; Beatles Fan Club of Great Britain, Superstore Publications, 123 Marina, St Leonards on Sea, East Sussex, England TN 38 OBN; Working Class Hero Club, 3311 Niagara St, Pittsburgh, PA 15213.

Periodicals: *Beatlefan,* PO Box 33515, Decatur, GA 30033; *Good Day Sunshine,* 397 Edgewood Avenue, New Haven, CT 06511.

Badge, souvenir, 3¾" d, cardboard, black and white image, black and red "I Needed Help! So I Got My Beatles Movie Ticket! Did You?," 1965   **25.00**
Banner, 12" l, rayon, metal staff, photos, "Die Beatles," German **8.00**
Bath Towel, group illus with signatures, Nems 1964 copyright **120.00**
Belt Buckle, 2 × 3", metal, gold, black, and white group picture **25.00**
Comb, 3¼ × 15", plastic, Beatles and signature label, Lido Toys, 1964 . . . . **90.00**
Doll, Paul McCartney, 4½" h, vinyl body, guitar, Remco, 1964 Nems Enterprises, Ltd copyright **90.00**
Figure, set of 4, inflatable, rubber, 1960s
. . . . **120.00**
Headband, orig package **40.00**
Locket Set **35.00**
Lunch Box, Beatles, emb, color illus, Aladdin Industries, copyright 1965 Nems Enterprises Ltd **200.00**
Magazine, *Post,* August 8–15, 1964, 8 page article, color photos **15.00**
Magnet Set, set of four, three dimensional, Beatle's head, marked "Hong Kong"
. . . . **75.00**
Pencil Case, 8" l, vinyl, blue, group picture and autographs, zipper top, Standard Plastic Products **35.00**
Photo Album, Sergeant Pepper **30.00**

Hair Spray, white can, white paper label, facsimile signatures, $35.00.

Photograph
John Lennon, Memory of a Rock Superstar, 1960s **12.00**
Ringo, 1960s **10.00**
Pinback Button, 3½" d, tin litho, black and white photo, 1960s **50.00**
Playing Cards, single deck, orig box   **50.00**
Puzzle, The Beatles Yellow Submarine, Jaymar copyright 1968 King Features Syndicate, orig box **55.00**
Ring Set, flasher type **40.00**
Sheet Music
Day Tripper, 1964 . . . . **40.00**
Help!, 8½ × 11", copyright 1965 Northern Songs Ltd, cover photo . . . **25.00**
She Loves You, red tone and white photo, 1963 copyright **18.00**
Yesterday, 3 pgs, Paul's photo on front cov with inset black and white band photo, copyright 1965 Northern Songs Ltd **10.00**
Stockings, face images on stockings and package, MIP **100.00**
Tapestry, 19 × 29½", linen, black, white, and maroon Beatle illus, purple ground, black and white illus border, marked "Pure Irish Linen/Ulster/Fast Colours," 1960s **125.00**
Thermos, 6½" h, metal, color illus, blue plastic cup **75.00**
Ticket, movie, "The Beatles/Hard Day's Night," cardboard, black and yellow, photo image, Washington Theater, Royal Oak, MI **20.00**

Tie Tack, Ringo, MOC, 1964 . . . . . . **40.00**
Wallpaper, 20½ × 31" section, six photo images, c1964 . . . . **100.00**

BEER CANS

Beer can collecting was very popular in the 1970s. Times have changed. The field is now dominated by the serious collector and most trading and selling goes on at specialized beer "canventions."

The list below contains a number of highly sought-after cans. Do not assume these prices are typical. Most cans fall in the quarter to fifty cent range. Do not pay more unless you are certain of the resale market.

There is no extra value to be gained by having a full beer can. In fact, selling a full can of beer without a license, even if only to a collector, violates the liquor law in a large number of states. Most collectors punch a hole in the bottom of the can and drain out the beer.

Finally, before you ask—Billy Beer, either in individual cans, six packs, or cases, is not worth hundreds or thousands of dollars. The going price for a can among collectors is between fifty cents and $1.00. Billy Beer has lost its fizz.

Club: Beer Can Collectors of America, 747 Merus Court, Fenton, MO 63026.

Altes, National, Detroit, MI, 12 oz, flat top
. . . . **35.00**
Berghoff 1887, Berghoff, Ft Wayne, IN, 16 oz, pull top, red, gold, and white   **18.00**
Blatz Old Heidelberg Castle, Blatz, Milwaukee, WI, 12 oz, cone top **35.00**
Budweiser, Anheuser–Busch, 7 cities, 10 oz, pull top **5.00**
Champagne Velvet, Associated, three cities, 15 oz, pull top **10.00**
Colt 45 malt lager, National, Baltimore, MD, 10 oz, pull top **8.00**
Coors, Golden, CO, 7 oz, flat top **6.00**
Dawson, Lager, Dawson, Hammonton, NJ, 11 oz, pull top **1.50**
Eastside Old Tap, Pabst, Los Angeles, CA, 12 oz, flat top **10.00**
Fehr's Draft, Fehr, Louisville, KY, 11 oz, pull top **15.00**
Fitger's, Fitger, Duluth, MN, 12 oz, pull top
. . . . **10.00**
Grain Belt, Minneapolis, MN, 12 oz, flat top, brown, gold, and white **6.00**
Great Falls Select, Great Falls, MT, 12 oz, flat top **15.00**
Hamm's, St Paul, MN, 12 oz, pull top **2.50**
Heritage House, Pittsburgh, PA, 12 oz, pull top **3.50**

Horlacher, Pilsner, Horlacher, Allentown, PA, 12 oz, flat top **8.00**
Kentucky Malt Lager, Fehr, Louisville, KY, 10 oz, flat top **35.00**
Lucky Lager, San Francisco, CA, 7 oz, flat top **10.00**
Manheim, Reading, PA, 10 oz, flat top **8.00**
Milwaukee's Best, Miller, Milwaukee, WI, 12 oz, pull top **5.00**
Mustang Malt Lager, Pittsburgh, PA, 16 oz, pull top **25.00**
National Bohemian, Detroit, MI, 10 oz, flat top **10.00**
North Star, Associated, 3 cities, 11 oz, pull top **2.00**
Old Export, Cumberland, MD, 12 oz, white and gold **85.00**
Oyster House, Pittsburgh, PA, 12 oz, pull top . . . . **.50**
Pearl Light, San Antonio, TX, 12 oz, brown, red, and white **4.00**
Progress, Oklahoma City, OK, 11 oz, flat top **75.00**
Rahr's, Green Bay, WI, 12 oz, Crowntainer cone top **45.00**
Rheingold, 2 cities, 7 oz, pull top **1.50**
Rolling Rock, Latrobe, PA, 12 oz, pull top **1.00**
Shell's City, Miami, FL, 12 oz, pull top **30.00**
Stag Premium Dry, Griesedieck–Western, 2 cities, 12 oz, cone top **25.00**
Stoney's, Jones, Smithon, PA, 12 oz, pull top **1.00**
Tavern Pale, Atlantic, Chicago, IL, 12 oz, flat top **25.00**
Tudor Ale, Metropolis, NY, 12 oz, green and white **15.00**

Old Ox Head Ale, Standard Brewing Co, Rochester, NY, $325.00.

University Club, Miller, Milwaukee, WI, 8 oz, flat top **15.00**
Valley Forge, Norristown, PA, 10 oz, flat top **15.00**
Weiss Bavarian, Maier, Los Angeles, CA, 15 oz, pull top **20.00**
Ye Tavern, Lafayette, IN, 12 oz, cone top **90.00**

BELLS

Bell collectors are fanatics. They tend to want every bell they can find. Admittedly, most confine themselves to bells that will fit on a shelf, but there are those who derive great pleasure from an old school bell sitting out on their front lawn.

Be alert for wine glasses that have been converted into bells. They are worth much less than bells that began life as bells. Also, collect limited edition bells because you like them, rather than with the hope they will rise in value. Many limited edition bells do not ring true on the resale market.

Club: American Bell Association, PO Box 19443, Indianapolis, IN 46219.

Brass
    Kewpies **60.00**
    Owl, 4" h, emb feathers and features **45.00**
China, figural
    Boy, 6½" h, dressed in white coat, blue trim, blue flowers, orange leaves, holding paper, gold trim **145.00**
    Chef, 3" h, holding wine bottle and glass, Occupied Japan **24.00**
    Cow, 4" h, pale blue, pink roses, gilded handle, Limoges **40.00**
Commemorative, 4½" h, Queen Elizabeth II Silver Jubilee, marked "Aynsley"   **25.00**
Desk, bronze, white marble base, side tap, c1875 . . . . **45.00**
Farm, cast iron, yoke **85.00**
Fire, 12" d, brass **75.00**
Glass
    Bicentennial, canary, Degenhart **15.00**
    Carnival, figural, Southern Belle, white, Imperial **38.00**
    Cranberry, gold edge, acid leaves   **30.00**
    Milk, smocking, marked "Akeo, Made in USA" **22.00**
Hand, brass, figural
    Lady, 3⅝" h, bust, quilted pattern on bell **35.00**
    Turtle, bell bracket and striker on shell **30.00**
Horse, 3" h, brass **15.00**
Hummel
    Hark the Herald, 5¼" h **20.00**
    Heavenly Melody, 4½" h **58.00**

Ship's, emb "W Taylor/Oxford/1847," bronze, 11" d, $695.00.

Ornament, Holiday Heirloom, Hallmark, 1988 . . . . **35.00**
Political, "Ring For Harding and Coolidge," copper finish **20.00**
Railroad, brass, steam locomotive   **700.00**
School, 7½" h, brass, wood handle   **45.00**
Sleigh, four, graduated sizes, shaft type, iron strap **45.00**

BELT BUCKLES

This is a category loaded with reproductions and fakes. Beware of any cast buckle signed Tiffany. Surprisingly, many collectors do not mind the fakes. They like the designs and collect them for what they are.

A great specialized collection can be built around military buckles. These can be quite expensive. Once again, beware of recasts and fakes, especially Nazi buckles.

Colt Revolvers, The World's Right Arm, marked "Tiffany & Co, New York," 2⅜" h, 4" l. This reproduction belt buckle often shows up at flea markets. BEWARE!

Star Wars, C3PO and R2D2, silvered metal, marked "1096," 2³⁄₈ × 3¹⁄₄", $12.00.

Club: Buckle Buddies International, 501 Dauphin St, Riverside, NJ 08075.

Periodical: *Buckle Buddies,* HC 2 Box 5, LaMoure, ND 58458.

Advertising
    Borden, 2 × 3", brass, emb Elsie   **40.00**
    Coors Beer **10.00**
    Hire's Root Beer, "Drink Hires" . . .**5.00**
    Planters Peanuts, metal, gold tone, fig-
        ural Mr Peanut **10.00**
    Stroh's Beer **5.00**
Art Deco, gold wash, double hasp, c1920
    . . . .**85.00**
Brass
    Naval Officer, Indian War, stamped
        "Horstman, Phila" **115.00**
    New York City Police **75.00**
Character
    Buffalo Bill Jr **5.00**
    Davy Crockett, silvered metal, raised
        border, inscription, Old Betsy rifle,
        1¹⁄₂ × 3" **25.00**
    Fonz **4.00**
    Mickey Mouse, Sun Rubber Co, 1937
        . . . .**45.00**
    Red Ryder, silvered brass, cowboy on
        bronc, name spelled twice in rope
        script, 2" sq, 1940s **35.00**
Mother–of–Pearl, chrome hasp, c1930
    . . . .**10.00**
Rhinestone, brass hasp, c1930 . . . . . .**35.00**
Sterling Silver
    Baroque, c1900 . . . .**65.00**
    Filigree with French jet, c1900 . . .**45.00**

BIBLES

The general rule to follow is that any Bible less than two hundred years old has little or no value in the collectibles market. For a number of reasons, individuals are reluctant to buy religious items. Bibles are proof positive that nothing is worth anything without a buyer.

Many have trouble accepting this argument. They see a large late nineteenth-century family Bible filled with engravings of religious scenes and sev-

eral pages containing information about the family. It is old and impressive. It has to be worth money. Alas, it was mass–produced and survived in large quantities. The most valuable thing about it is the family data, and this can be saved simply by copying the few pages involved on a photocopier.

An average price for a large family Bible from the turn of the century is between $25.00 and $50.00. Of course, there are Bibles that sell for a lot more than this. I have listed a few of the heavy hitters from the seventeenth and eighteenth centuries. Bibles such as these tend to remain in private hands. Never speculate when buying a Bible, God would not like it.

1629, Latin, *Biblia Sacra,* Antwerp, six parts, five volumes, early morocco gilt, rubbed
    . . . .**175.00**
1668, English, *Holy Bible,* Cambridge, John Field, engraved title with fine architectural border by John Chantry, Van Hove copperplates, 8 × 10", 18th C mottled calf, neatly rebacked, gilt edges
    . . . .**350.00**
1702, German, *Bible,* Nuremberg, J L Buggel, two engraved titles, over 250 plates, 8 × 10", contemporary calf gilt over wooden boards, loose binding, lacking clasps **350.00**
1798, English, *Bible,* Philadelphia, Thompson & Small, two volumes in one, 12 × 16", contemporary calf binding . . .**65.00**
1805, German, *Biblia, Das 1st: Die Ganze Gottliche Heilige Schrift. . . Erst Auflage,* Reading, PA, Gottlob Jungmann, 1,235 pgs, 8 × 10", contemporary polished calf binding **125.00**
1810, English, *The Christian's New and Complete British Family Bible,* London, A Hogg, 12 × 5", morocco gilt   **195.00**
1846, English, *The Illuminated Bible,* New York, two engraved titles, 1,600 plates, 8 × 10", morocco gilt **250.00**

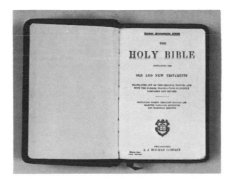

Holman, No. 41X, leather binding, India paper, orig 5³⁄₄ × 8¹⁄₂" green box, 16mo, $10.00.

World Large Print, New Testament and Psalms, #326, orig 6¹⁄₈ × 8¹⁄₄" red box, 1967 confirmation inscription on card, $15.00.

1908, English, *Bible,* London, Groiler Society, 14 vols, orig pigskin, soiled, fitted wooden book box **325.00**

BICENTENNIAL

America's 200th birthday in 1976 was PARTY TIME for the nation. Everyone and everything in the country had something stamped, painted, printed, molded, cast, and pressed with the commemorative dates 1776–1976. The American spirit of "overdo" and "outdo" always puts our nation in a great mood. We certainly overdid it during the Bicentennial.

The average flea market will have a wide variety of Bicentennial goodies. Prices have come down in recent years as the patriotic spirit waned and the only buyers left in the market were the collectors. Remember the Bicentennial was only nineteen years ago. This is one category where you only want to buy in fine or better condition.

Alarm Clock, 8" h, metal, windup, dark copper–bronze finish, inscribed on back "Commemorative Series Registered Edition" **45.00**
Calculator, American Pocket Calculator, Model #1776, 6 digit, red, white, and blue flag box, near mint **15.00**
Drinking Glasses, set of four
    Arby's, Bullwinkle crossing the Delaware, 11 oz **8.00**
    Burger King, 1776–1976 Have It Your Way Collector Series, 5¹⁄₂" h, American Revolution symbols **6.00**
    Coca–Cola, Heritage Collector Series, Revolutionary War heroes **4.00**
Pin, ¹⁄₄ × ¹⁄₂" red, white, and blue enamel on brass flag, orig 1¹⁄₂" sq card inscribed "Official Pin, Quick Chek" **12.00**
Pinback Button, 2³⁄₈" l oval, white Statue of Liberty, brown accents, yellow ground, red and white dates "1776" and "1976," white lettered "Bicentennial"
    . . . .**10.00**

Calendar Plate, 200th Anniversary Year, large eagle over red, white, and blue shields and American flags, calendars around rim, $12.00.

US Federal Reserve Two Dollar Bill, Series 1976 Neff–Simon, fr#1935–b*, New York, signing of the Declaration of Independence scene printed on back   **5.00**

BICYCLES

Bicycles are divided into two groups—antique and classic. Chances of finding an antique bicycle, e.g., a high-wheeler, at a flea market are slim. Chances of spotting a great balloon-tire classic are much greater.

Do not pay much for a bicycle that is incomplete, rusted, or repaired with nonoriginal parts. Replacement of parts that deteriorate, e.g., leather seats, is acceptable. It is not uncommon to heavily restore a bicycle, i.e., to make it look like new. If the amount of original parts is less than fifty percent, question an extremely high price.

There is a great market in secondary material from accessories to paper ephemera in bicycle collectibles. Bicycle fanatics should haunt the automobile flea markets, as well as antiques and collectibles flea markets.

Clubs: Classic Bicycle & Whizzer Club of America, 35769 Simon, Clinton Twp, MI 48035; International Veteran Cycle Association, 248 Highland Dr, Findlay, OH 45840; National Pedal Vehicle Association, 1720 Rupert, NE, Grand Rapids, MI, 49505; The Wheelmen, 55 Bucknell Ave, Trenton, NJ 08619.

Periodicals: *Antique/Classic Bicycle News*, PO Box 1049, Ann Arbor, MI 48106; *Classic Bicycle & Whizzer News*,

PO Box 765, Huntingdon Beach, CA 92648; *National Antique & Classic Bicycle*, PO Box 5600, Pittsburgh, PA 15207.

BICYCLES

Bowden, 300	**6,000.00**
Colson	
Clipper, 1941	**1,500.00**
Packard, 1936	**1,750.00**
Columbia	
3 Star	**600.00**
Model 50, chainless pneumatic, 1898	**850.00**
Victory, 1939	**1,750.00**
Elgin, Sears Roebuck	
Blackhawk	**3,000.00**
Dolly Bike, 1939	**1,250.00**
Skylark	**1,750.00**
Twin 30	**700.00**
Firestone, Deluxe Speed Cruiser, 1959	**450.00**
Gormully & Jeffery, Rambler, man's tandem, c1896	**1,325.00**
Hawthorne, Montgomery Ward, Comet Rollfast, 1936	**1,000.00**
Huffman Dayton, Champion, 1940	**2,000.00**
Huffman (Huffy)	
Coca–Cola Classic, 1987	**300.00**
Dial A Ride, 1952	**1,750.00**
Radiobike, 1950s	**2,500.00**
Sportsman, 26", 1959	**100.00**
Iroquois, Iroquois Cycleworks, 1898	**1,000.00**
Iver Johnson, drop handle racer, 1920s	**1,000.00**
J C Higgins, Sears Roebuck	
1949	**1,250.00**
1953	**500.00**
Kensington, tandem, c1900	**1,000.00**
Marsh & Metz, tandem	**200.00**
Monark	
Coupe De Ville, 1954	**750.00**
Firestone Holiday, 1953	**750.00**
Firestone Super Cruiser, 1953	**1,000.00**
Silver King	
L037	**2,000.00**
M137	**3,000.00**
M237	**1,000.00**
Super Deluxe, 1953	**1,200.00**
Murray, Flatline, c1956	**800.00**
Overman Victor Flyer, c1893	**1,750.00**
Pacemaker, Cleveland Welding Co, 1941	**1,500.00**
Peerless Roadster, c1910	**1,000.00**
Pony–Byk	**1,500.00**
Roadmaster, Cleveland Welding Co	
1941	**2,000.00**
1947	**1,000.00**
1952	**2,000.00**
1965, Flying Falcon	**100.00**
Roamer, No. 36, lady's, 1941	**200.00**
Rollfast, D P Harris Co, Hopalong Cassidy, 20", 1951	**2,500.00**
Rudge, light roadster, 58" high-wheeler, British, 1880s	**4,200.00**

Schwinn	
Corvette, 1955	**300.00**
Flying Star	**225.00**
Hollywood Special	**500.00**
Orange Krate	**400.00**
Pea Picker	**350.00**
Phantom Deluxe, 1950	**1,500.00**
Spitfire	**200.00**
Stingray	**175.00**
Tiger, 1962	**200.00**
Wasp	**200.00**
Shelby	
Flyer	**1,000.00**
Super Airflow, 1937	**800.00**
Star, 52" high–wheeler, 1886	**2,225.00**
Tricycle	
Skyline, 1930s	**100.00**
Tiller, 29" rear wheels, multicolored seat covering	**200.00**
Western Flyer	
Jet Swept, 20", 1960s	**75.00**
Mercury, 1939	**1,500.00**
Sonic Flyer, 1950s	**350.00**
Whizzer, Sportsman, motorized, 1952	**2,500.00**
Winchester, Rollfast, 1936	**1,250.00**

BICYLCE RELATED

Advertising Trade Card	
Columbia Bicycle, mechanical, bike illus, movable dials, 3 × 4"	**60.00**
Pope Mfg Co, Columbia Bicycle, men riding bikes at night illus	**10.00**

Puzzle, Hibiscus Time in Bermuda, Parker Bros for Miss Josephine Flood's Picture Puzzle Mart, New York, NY, 1940s, 266 hand–cut plywood pieces, figural pieces, irregular edge, 9¼ × 5½" cardboard box, 16½ × 10½", $50.00.

Calendar, New Departure Mfg Co, 1902,
  missing two months **80.00**
Catalog
  Mead Cycle Co, 1923, 8½ × 11¼"
  . . . .**14.00**
  Union Cycles, 1896, 8 × 5" **30.00**
Clock, adv, "Columbia Built Bicycles Since
  1877–America's First Bicycle," electric,
  15" d, 1950s **325.00**
Lapel Stud
  Ariston Cycles, white and dark blue
  . . . .**15.00**
  Norwood Bicycles, dark blue, white de-
  sign **12.50**
Magazine Ad, Ideal Bicycles, woman riding
  bike, matted **5.00**
Matchsafe, 6" h, bisque, hp, figural woman
  on bike, 19th C **150.00**
Medal, Pierce Cycle Co, racing, brass
  . . . .**145.00**
Name Plate, 2¾" h, diecut, brass, Oxford
  Bicycle Co, red enamel ground, 1930s
  . . . .**25.00**
Pinback Button
  Lovell Diamond Cycles, white and dark
  purple, black lettering **25.00**
  Mak–Nu/Expressly For Bicycle Use,
  cream, red design **15.00**
  Master Ray Smallest Bicyclest In The
  World, sepia, youngster on bike
  . . . .**25.00**
  Miss Annis Burr Porter On Her Quaker
  Wheel, 1¼" d, black and white **50.00**
Post card, man on high–wheeler leading a
  stagecoach in a parade illus **18.00**
Poster
  E V M Bicycle, 19 × 27", Art Nouveau
  bicycle parts border, c1910
  . . . .**175.00**
  Iver Johnson Bikes, bike illus, 42½ ×
  21½" **275.00**
  "Presto," cyclist and monoplane illus,
  half–sheet **775.00**
Sign
  Monarch Bicycles, 5" h, 43" l, wood,
  gold lettering **250.00**
  Whizzer Bike Motor, 23¾" × 15¾", tin,
  emb, "Ride One–You'll Buy One"
  . . . .**450.00**
Stickpin, Elgin King/Elgin Cycle Co, brass,
  blue enamel crown design on top **35.00**

BINOCULARS

Looking for field glasses or through
them is an eye–opening experience. The
binocular has been in use for more than
two hundred years, continuing to improve our view of things. Though their
greatest use has been by the military,
civilian demand has given binocular production and versatility quite a push.

A flea market stand may not have
that Bausch and Lomb super–deluxe,

see–the–planet–like–it's–next–to–you
model, but they might have an old pair of
WWII spotter's glasses. Take care when
going through a selection of binoculars.
If they are still in the original case, they
are more valuable than if they are just
sitting on a seller's table. Look closely at
the optics to check for cracks and loose
lenses. Happy spotting.

Bausch & Lomb, Zephyr, 7 × 35, orig case
  . . . .**200.00**
Character
  Hopalong Cassidy **50.00**
  Roy Rogers, MIB **45.00**
Opera Glasses, French, mother–of–pearl ex-
  terior, dated 1902, Hmed "Lemaire Fi.,
  Paris" **35.00**
Premium, Kellogg's **60.00**
Voightlander, German, leather neck strap
  and black leatherette carrying case, 8 ×
  36 high power, Hmed Braunschweig address, long range glasses **150.00**
World War I, French officer's, leather carrying case, Hmed, Paris, 8 × 32   **30.00**
World War II, German
  Trench, 15" h, North Africa Corps, tan
  camouflage, orig tripod and dual sun
  shades, lenses swing to different
  widths, base marked "S.F.14z.Gi,H/
  6400," orig lens covers **350.00**
  Tropical Canvas, 6 × 9, neck strap, optics, calibrated range finders on the
  lenses, Hmed "EK, J.E.S." **30.00**

BIRD CAGES

Bird cages, what can be said? There
are as many different kinds of bird cages
as there are birds. With so many to

*Wrought Iron, painted white, reproduction,
34" h, $110.00.*

choose from the buyer must ask himself
"What am I looking for?"

Bird cages are often designed with a
particular species in mind and crafted
with a material that is sufficient to re-
strain that species. Bamboo, wicker, and
wood were used in cages for smaller
birds that did not require a stronger construction. Larger birds such as cockatoos,
parrots, and macaws often were housed
in metal cages. Bird cages are collected
more for their decorative nature, with
less emphasis placed on their construction material.

Bent Wire
  14" h, spherical, heart shape bent wire
  hanger and wood base, decorative
  wire bird on trapeze **15.00**
  31" h, rectangular, turned wood hanging
  finial, tin and wood base, painted
  black and green **250.00**
  34" h, square, peaked roof, painted
  black **175.00**
Brass
  39" h, 18½" d, domed, hanging ring,
  two horizontal braces, circular
  stepped base, c1950 . . . .**500.00**
  41" h, domed, ball finial, three horizontal braces, trapeze, brass food and
  water cups attached to lower perch,
  39" h circular Art Nouveau style copper pedestal base **750.00**
Brass Plated, 28" h, 20½" d, domed, hanging ring, two horizontal braces, trapeze
  and perch, circular dished tray, 62" h
  brass plated arched stand with circular
  stepped base **175.00**
Nickel Plated Brass
  16" h, square, hanging ring attached to
  flattened ball finial, two horizontal
  braces, trapeze, dished tray, hanging
  stand, late 1940s **200.00**
  16½" h, domed, hanging ring attached
  to globular finial, two horizontal
  braces, trapeze and perch, dished
  tray, hanging stand, mid 1940s
  . . . .**225.00**
Wicker
  24" h, 18" d, painted white, conical roof,
  tapering sides, woven gallery wall on
  circular tray, 74" h woven crescent
  moon shape pedestal stand   **300.00**
  63" h, bird cage/fernery combination,
  painted white, bird cage with waisted
  cone shape roof with ornate curlicue
  dec, tapering sides with braided horizontal braces, and woven gallery
  wall on circular tray, fernery with
  openwork arch with stick and ball
  dec, rect planter with braided swags
  dec, and wrapped legs and stretcher,
  late 19th C **700.00**
Wrought Iron, 32" h, 18" d, domed, hanging
  ring **200.00**

BISQUE

Every time I look at a bisque figure, I think of grandmothers. I keep wondering why I never see a flea market table labeled "ONLY THINGS A GRANDMOTHER WOULD LOVE."

Bisque is pottery ware that has only been fired once and not glazed. It is a technique that is centuries old and is still being practiced today. Unfortunately, some of today's figures are exact copies of those made hundreds of years ago. Be especially aware of bisque piano babies.

Collectors differentiate between Continental (mostly German) and Japanese bisque with premiums generally paid for Continental pieces. However, the Japanese made some great bisque. Do not confuse the cheap five-and-dime "Occupied Japan" bisque with the better pieces.

Basket, 8" d, boy seated on rim, barefoot, wearing wide brim hat marked "Germany" **50.00**
Box, egg shape, relief windmill scene, ftd **45.00**
Candy Container, 5½" h, witch, holding vegetables **35.00**
Cigarette Holder, 3½" d, youth on clothesline, marked "Japan" **15.00**
Creamer, figural, cow, Occupied Japan **20.00**
Doll, 6" h, pr, Dutch boy and girl, orig box, Japan **95.00**
Fairy Lamp, 4" h, figural, owl, cat, and dog, glass eyes, clear glass base marked "Clarke" **250.00**
Figure
Bonnie Prince Charlie, 8" h, France **30.00**

Vase, green and violet costume, green bow, molded house scene, bird with envelope, gilt trim, Unger Bros, 9" h, $25.00.

Bride and Groom, 1950s **16.00**
Cat, lying on green pillow with gold tassels, marked "Cappe, Italy" . . . **30.00**
Chicken, 2" h, multicolored, marked "Japan" **5.50**
Dog, 3¼" h, teaching two puppies how to read, tan book base **65.00**
Frog, 3½" h, Occupied Japan **15.00**
Minnie Mouse, 3½" h, carrying first-aid kit, c1930 . . . . **50.00**
Humidor, 8 × 8", baby's head **125.00**
Lamp, 10" h, applied floral dec, Lefton **42.00**
Match Holder, figural
Dog, wearing man's clothing and top hat, Germany **70.00**
Dutch girl, copper and gold trim, includes striker **35.00**
Nodder
Hobo, holding walking stick, green coat, tan pants, bottle in pocket . . . **210.00**
Jester, seated, holding pipe, pastel peach and white, gold trim **75.00**
Piano Baby, 6¾" l, wearing bib, lying on stomach, dog and cat, Germany   **100.00**
Pitcher, miniature, multicolored applied floral spray, pink ground, Occupied Japan **8.00**
Planter
Girl, sitting by well, holding water jug, coral and green **48.00**
Peasant Girl, 6", figural, standing beside leaf covered planter, Occupied Japan **35.00**
Salt, 3" d, figural, wood, cream, branch base, matching spoon **70.00**
Tobacco Jar, figural, boy, hair forms cov, marked "Heubach" **150.00**
Toothbrush Holder, 5" h, Mickey Mouse, one movable arm **200.00**
Toothpick Holder, lady with flower   **35.00**
Vase, 7" h, ftd, emb floral dec, Occupied Japan **18.00**
Wall Pocket, 5" h, cuckoo clock, orange luster, pinecone weights, Occupied Japan **12.00**

BIZARRE ART

Just had to add this category. Dad's books are too stuffy to acknowledge some of the really great stuff you can find at a local bazaar, church rummage sale, etc. Of course, after a few years, this stuff sometimes turns up at flea markets.

Some bazaar craftspeople create really nice stuff and it may even hold some resale value. Other stuff is just "stuff" and can be had for pennies on the dollar. Perhaps some day this tacky stuff will catch a decorator's eye and skyrocket in value!

Ashtray/Candleholder, made from six sq ruby glass ashtrays, center holds votive candle **3.00**

Ashtray, natural shell, wrought iron holder with center black boy which is also a pipe holder, $50.00.

Boo Boo Bear, made from washcloth . . . . **.50**
Bread Basket, rooster, made from plastic jug . . . . **.50**
Christmas Ornaments, handmade
Beadwork **2.00**
Candy Airplane **1.00**
Cinnamon sticks, decorated **1.00**
Pinecone, painted gold, attached ribbon **1.00**
Dish Towels, crocheted top **2.00**
Door Decoration, plastic mesh, Christmas greetings **2.00**
Honey Do List Holder, wood, figural hammer, hp, clip to hold list of things to do **3.00**
Lampshade, plastic bottle with colorful beads and cutout work **2.00**
Pinecone Wreath, large, well made and decorated **5.00**
Plant Hanger, macrame . . . . **.50**
Pot Holder, crocheted **1.00**
Tissue Box Holder, plastic mesh with colorful design **3.00**
Toilet Paper Cover, crocheted
Hat style **2.00**
Poodle style **5.00**
Round **2.00**
Wind Catcher, made with plastic mesh and beads **2.00**
Wishing Well Pencil Holder, made from clothespins . . . . **.25**

BLACK GLASS

This glass gets its name from the fact that when it is sitting on a table, it looks black. When you hold it up to the light, sometimes it actually is a deep purple color. It was extremely popular in the period between World War I and World War II.

Black Glass can be found in several patterns of Depression Era Glass as well as utilitarian and household items such as planters and vases.

Ashtray, 5¾" d, match holder center, Cloverleaf pattern, Hazel Atlas **75.00**

Bowl, 6½" d, Victory pattern, Diamond
Glass Co **26.00**
Candlesticks, pr
Diamond Quilted Pattern, Imperial
. . . . **50.00**
Victory pattern, Diamond Co **90.00**
Candy Dish, cov, Crow's Foot pattern,
Paden City **60.00**
Console Bowl, 11¾" d, Crow's Foot pattern,
Paden City **85.00**
Creamer
Cloverleaf pattern, Hazel Atlas . . . **17.50**
Victory pattern, Diamond Co **45.00**
Cream Soup Bowl, 4¾" d, Diamond Quilted
Pattern, Imperial **18.00**
Cup and Saucer
Cloverleaf pattern, Hazel Atlas . . . **21.00**
Crow's Foot pattern, Paden City
. . . . **16.00**
Victory pattern, Diamond Co **44.00**
Flowerpot, LE Smith, c1930 . . . . **15.00**
Gravy Boat, Crow's Foot pattern, Paden City
. . . . **100.00**
Ice Bucket, Diamond Quilted pattern, Imperial **85.00**
Loving Cup, LE Smith **20.00**
Place Card Holder, 2½" h, Fostoria   **30.00**
Plate
8" d, luncheon, Cloverleaf pattern, Hazel
Atlas **15.00**
10½" d, dinner, Crow's Foot pattern,
Paden City **100.00**
Sandwich Server, center handle, Crow's
Foot pattern, Paden City **75.00**
Sherbet
Cloverleaf pattern, Hazel Atlas . . . **20.00**
Victory pattern, Diamond Glassware
. . . . **25.00**
Sugar, Victory pattern, Diamond Glassware
. . . . **45.00**
Tumbler, Town & Country pattern, Heisey
. . . . **30.00**
Vase
10" h, Orchid pattern, Paden City
. . . . **110.00**
10¼" h, flared, Crow's Foot pattern,
Paden City **75.00**
Whipped Cream Bowl, Crow's Foot pattern,
Paden City **65.00**

BLACK MEMORABILIA

Black memorabilia is enjoying its second renaissance. It is one of the "hot" areas in the present market. The category is viewed quite broadly, ranging from slavery era items to objects showing ethnic stereotypes. Prices range all over the place. It pays to shop around.

Because black memorabilia ranges over a wide variety of forms, the black memorabilia collector is constantly competing with collectors from other areas, e.g., cookie jar, kitchen, and salt and pepper shaker collectors. Surprisingly enough, it is the collectors of black memorabilia who realize the vast amount of material available and tend to resist high prices.

Reproductions, from advertising signs (Bull Durham Tobacco) to mechanical banks (Jolly Nigger), are an increasing problem. Remember—if it looks new, chances are that it is new.

Club: Black Memorabilia Collector's Association, 2482 Devoe Terrace, Bronx, NY 10468.

Periodicals: *Black Ethnic Collectibles*, 1401 Asbury Court, Hyattsville, MD 20782; *Blackin'*, 559 22nd Ave, Rock Island, IL 61201.

Advertising Trade Card, Crescent Tobacco,
black men and mules illus, poem, 4 ×
4" **5.00**
Ashtray, cast iron
Coon Chicken Inn **30.00**
Mammy and Chef, skillet shaped, pr
. . . . **65.00**
Man playing banjo **160.00**
Bank
Book of Knowledge, dentist with black
boy in chair, cast iron, mechanical
. . . . **145.00**
Girl, figural, nodding head **45.00**
Blotter, golf scene with men and alligator,
1920s **10.00**
Book, hard cov
Black Alice, 1968 . . . . **45.00**
Black Boy, Richard Wright **20.00**
Color, 1925 . . . . **130.00**
Epaminonda and His Auntie, 1938
. . . . **115.00**
George Washington Carver, 1943 **80.00**
Heroes of the Dark Continent, 1890
. . . . **150.00**
How Come Christmas, 1948 . . . . **115.00**
Little Black Quibba, 1964 . . . . . . **45.00**
Little Black Sambo and the Monkey People, 1935 . . . . **90.00**
Little Brown Koko, 1940 . . . . **85.00**
Little Jeemes Henry, 1947 . . . . . . **95.00**
Little Nemo in Slumberland, 1941 **75.00**
Little White Cotton, 1928 . . . . . . **125.00**
Lyrics from Cottonland, 1922 . . . **145.00**
*My Undercover Years With The Ku Klux
Klan*, Gary Rowe's **6.00**
Nigger Heaven, Carl Van Vechten, Grossett, 1928 . . . . **25.00**
Old Folks at Home, 1890 . . . . . . **135.00**
Old Mitt Laughs Last, 1944 . . . . . **65.00**
Petunia Be Keerful, 1934 . . . . . . **120.00**
Pinky Marie and Seven Bluebirds, 1939
. . . . **110.00**
Ten Little Colored Boys, 1942 . . . **80.00**
The Negro Question, 1903 . . . . . . **80.00**
Topsy Turvy and the Tin Clown, 1934
. . . . **75.00**
Uncle Tom's Cabin, 1910 . . . . . . **45.00**
Uncle Tom's Children, 1943 . . . . . **50.00**

Bottle, Aunt Dinah, paper label, 1950
. . . . **45.00**
Bottle Opener, man's face **78.00**
Candy Dish, butler's head **400.00**
Candy Jar, Mammy **450.00**
Clock
Black Boy, alarm, metal case, 1940
. . . . **350.00**
Mammy, marked "Red Wing"
. . . . **260.00**
Coffee Bag, Black Plantation Coffee . . . **3.00**
Cookie Jar
Abingdon, Mammy, flowered apron
. . . . **650.00**
Brayton, Mammy
Light blue, hairline crack **950.00**
Yellow **1,350.00**
F & F, Aunt Jemima **395.00**
McCoy, Mammy **125.00**
Mettlach
Mammy, blue **295.00**
Topsy Girl, yellow **350.00**
Pearl China
Chef **450.00**
Mammy **675.00**
Rockingham, Mammy **240.00**
Sears, little girl **475.00**
Unknown Maker, Mammy, gold tooth,
gold trim, polka dot dress, hand dec,
matching salt and pepper shakers,
sgd **185.00**
Creamer
Mammy, full figure **135.00**
Man, figural **35.00**
Creamer and Sugar, plastic, yellow, F & F
. . . . **110.00**
Decanter
Butler **150.00**
Clown **39.00**
Dish Towel **35.00**
Doll, baby, bisque, jointed, 3½" h . . . **35.00**
Drawing, black woman, color pencil on paper, artist Inza Walker **475.00**
Dresser Jar, butler **195.00**
Figure
Dancing Dan, 9" h, jointed, man in front
of lamppost, Mystery Mike causes
figure to dance, orig box **225.00**
Two boys kneeling on base, ceramic, Japan, Pioneer Mfg Co **30.00**
Woman, 8" h, sitting on chair knitting,
German **175.00**
Glass, Coon Chicken Inn **25.00**
Jigsaw Puzzle, Woozie **60.00**
Lamp, Swami with turban sitting on pillow,
holding shade **300.00**
Letter Opener, man in alligator's mouth
. . . . **48.00**
Magazine, *Life*, 1900, cartoon black mother
and child cov **34.00**
Magazine Cover, Mammy, Lyendecker
. . . . **10.00**
Mask, rubber, black man, large features
. . . . **45.00**
Match Holder, adv, Coon Chicken Inn,
metal **250.00**
Memo Pad Holder, Mammy **40.00**

Mug
  Large Mammy face **240.00**
  Muscles Moe **65.00**
Mustard Pot, Chef **165.00**
Nodder
  Bahama Policeman, white uniform, minor paint flakes **85.00**
  Children, pr **65.00**
  Mammy, ceramic **175.00**
  Man **45.00**
Paper Towel Holder, Mammy **125.00**
Pencil Sharpener, man's face **125.00**
Photograph
  Black Boy, Cuban tobacco field **15.00**
  Zulu woman **25.00**
Pinback Button, 2¼" d, Dr Martin Luther King, Jr, January 15th National Holiday, yellow, black and white photo, 1980s **12.00**
Pin, Aunt Jemima, Breakfast Club **15.00**
Pitcher, Mandy **150.00**
Planter
  Banana boat and black man, McCoy **95.00**
  Plaid Mammy **95.00**
Plaque, man **55.00**
Post Card
  Martin Luther King, "Training School For Communists" **22.00**
  Thanksgiving, Mammy serving children **10.00**
Pot Holder Hanger, boy **29.00**
Puppet, Little Black Sambo, dated 1952, MIB **110.00**
Recipe Box, plastic, red **150.00**
Salt and Pepper Shakers, pair
  Boy and Girl
    Sitting in basket, china **95.00**
    Sitting on peanut shell, china **110.00**
  Boy sitting on alligator, china **72.00**
  Boys, sitting on carrots, ceramic **68.00**
  Chef, holding two barrels, wood **65.00**
  Chef and Mammy, holding spoons, 8" h **85.00**
  Children in peanut, Poinsettia Studios **185.00**
  Jonah on whale **95.00**
  Lady with child on back, native **68.00**
  Mammies, chalkware, seated **45.00**
  Mammy and Chef, 8" h **150.00**
  Pickaninny, reclining with melon **55.00**
  Porter, holding suitcases **195.00**
  Suzanne Mammy, plastic, red, F & F **150.00**
Saucer, 6" d, Coon Chicken Inn **135.00**
Scoop, Mammy sitting on end, green, McCoy **110.00**
Shaker
  Mammy, range size, Pearl China **100.00**
  Native on cucumber **35.00**
Sheet Music, *Little Sunshine*, Al Jolson, 1930 .... **25.00**
Sign, porcelain, Pickaninny, black child eating ice cream **385.00**
Soup Bowl, adv, Coon Chicken Inn **195.00**

Spice Set, 5 pcs, jars with raised ceramic figures, wooden rack with wall hanger **350.00**
Spoon rest
  Chef, nodder **150.00**
  Mammy, winking eye **75.00**
Statue, Louis Armstrong **95.00**
String Holder
  Fredericksburg porter **275.00**
  Mammy, Japan **145.00**
Syrup, Aunt Jemima, F & F **48.00**
Target Game, Black Sambo, tin, framed, Wyandotte Toys, 11 × 23½" ... **325.00**
Tea Bell, Aunt Jemima, MIB **90.00**
Teapot
  Mammy, google eye, wire handle **300.00**
  Mammy, polka dot dec, missing lid **275.00**
  Mandy **150.00**
  Young chef **125.00**
Thermometer, boy **26.00**
Thermos, Sambo's Restaurant, includes literature **60.00**
Tin
  Bowery's Hot Chocolate Powder **125.00**
  Luzianne Coffee, white **80.00**
Toaster Cover, Mammy **16.00**
Toy, windup, Mammy, 8" h, tin litho, Lindstrom **200.00**

BLUE RIDGE POTTERY

Southern Potteries of Erwin, TN, produced Blue Ridge dinnerware from the late 1930s until 1956. Four hundred patterns graced eight basic shapes.

Club: Blue Ridge Collectors Club, Rte 3, Box 161, Erwin, TN 37650.

Newsletter: *National Blue Ridge Newsletter*, 144 Highland Dr, Blountville, IN 37617.

Periodical: *The Daze*, PO Box 57, Otisville, MI 48463.

Ashtray, Apple, cigarette rests **25.00**
Batter Jug, cov, Antique Leaf **98.00**
Bowl
  Chanticleer, 6½" d **18.00**
  Crab Apple, oval, 9¼" l **22.00**
  French Peasant, 9¼" d **80.00**
  Norma, berry **6.00**
  Sungold, oval **13.50**
Chocolate Pot, French Peasant **225.00**
Chocolate Set, chocolate pot, creamer, and sugar, Chintz **325.00**
Cigarette Box, Rooster **50.00**
Cigarette Set, box and 4 coasters, Sailboat **115.00**
Creamer and Sugar
  Crab Apple, Colonial **25.00**
  Nocturne, open **38.00**

Berry Bowl, 5½" d, blue flower, $8.00.

Rose Marie **58.00**
Snippet, cov **27.00**
Sunflower **18.00**
Cup and Saucer, French Peasant **48.00**
Demitasse Saucer, Brittany **10.00**
Dish
  Easter Parade, maple leaf **72.00**
  Nove Rose, shell
    Deep **50.00**
    Flat **65.00**
  Palace, shell, flat **70.00**
  Tussie Mussie
    Maple Leaf **70.00**
    Shell, deep **72.00**
  Verna, maple leaf **67.00**
Jug
  Big Blossom **85.00**
  Summertime Virginia **100.00**
  Tralee Rose, swirl **75.00**
Leaf Celery
  French Peasant **75.00**
  Rose O Sharon **40.00**
  Summertime **50.00**
Pitcher
  Antique **65.00**
  Chanticleer **85.00**
  Grace, blue **45.00**
  Scatter Jane **120.00**
  Sculptured Fruit **60.00**
  Spiral, 7" h **65.00**

Cup and Saucer, red flower on 3¾" d, cup, blue flower on 6" d saucer, $10.00.

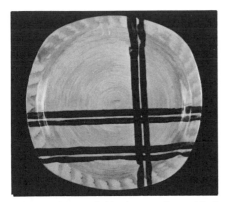

Plate, Piedmont Plaid, piecrust shape, black stamp mark, green ground, brown stripes, 8" w, $4.00.

Plate
   Briar, 9" d **4.50**
   Forest Fruit, dinner **7.00**
   Freedom Ring, 11½" d **42.00**
   French Peasant
     9¼" d, lunch **42.00**
     10" d, dinner **50.00**
   Fruit Punch, divided **32.00**
   Sunflower, dinner **8.50**
   Weathervane Cock, 6" sq **65.00**
Platter, oval
   Crab Apple, 11¾" l **28.00**
   Forest Fruit **12.00**
   Quilted Fruit, 13½" l **42.00**
Relish
   Normandie, Skyline, oval **35.00**
   Nove Rose, 4 pint **82.00**
Salt and Pepper Shakers, pr, Blossom Top
   . . . . **45.00**
Teapot
   Poinsettia Colonial **145.00**
   Rose Bouquet, snub nose **135.00**
Vase
   Dogtooth Violet, 7¾" h **75.00**
   Flo, 9¼" h **80.00**
   Mum, spray handle **82.00**

BOOKENDS

Prices listed below are for pairs. Woe to the dealer who splits pairs apart!

Art Deco, 7" h, cast iron, circle with nude
   in center, gold paint **185.00**
Arts and Crafts, metal, verse **135.00**
Boy with Sailboat, playing with dog,
   Frankart **245.00**
Cat, full figure, pottery, Rookwood, c1923
   . . . . **200.00**
Charles Lindbergh, 1929 . . . . **175.00**
Cheshire Cat, brass, c1930 . . . . **135.00**
Children, kissing, cast iron, Hubley **155.00**
Cornucopia, 5¾" h, glass, New Martinsville
   . . . . **45.00**

Bronze, cat, sgd "DAL" with triangle in a circle, 1925, $70.00.

Daddy Bear, 4½" h, glass, New Martinsville
   . . . . **100.00**
Dolphin, Abingdon Pottery, #444 . . . **65.00**
Donald Duck, 7" h, carrying schoolbooks,
   chalkware **20.00**
Eagle
   Bronze finish, Frankart **35.00**
   Glass, Fostoria **175.00**
Elephants, ivory, teakwood base . . . **165.00**
Fish, glass, Heisey **150.00**
Fleur-de-lis, 10 × 5", copper, Roycroft,
   orb mark **100.00**
Flower Basket, cast iron, painted **50.00**
Flower Urn, soapstone **85.00**
Lincoln Memorial, plaster, bronze finish, de-
   tailed **25.00**
Lion, glass, Cambridge **400.00**
Mongol Head, Goldscheider, 1941 **95.00**
Nudes, 5 × 7", cast iron, bronze finish, full
   figured, kneeling, Art Deco **70.00**
Owl, hp **25.00**
Race Horse and Jockey, white metal, bronze
   finish, Art Deco **75.00**
Roseville
   Peony, yellow **130.00**
   Pine Cone, brown **185.00**
Scottie Dog, Frankart **135.00**
Sentry, 7½" h, brass, Bakelite trim, orb
   mounted base, Chase Chrome and Brass
   Co, impressed mark **165.00**
Setter, pointing, 4½ × 7½", cast iron,
   black, c1920 . . . . **95.00**
Swordfish, pressed wood **15.00**
Terriers, 4¼" h, chrome plated, round back
   and base, c1920 . . . . **100.00**
Tom and Jerry, 8" h, Gorham, 1980 **40.00**
Tooled Design, 6 × 6", leather, wood base,
   Roycroft, orb mark **150.00**

BOOKMARKS

Don't you just hate it when you lose your place in that book you've been reading? Bookmarks will help keep your sanity and can make a neat collectible.

They're easy to find, easy to display, and fun to own.

Bookmark collecting dates back to the early nineteenth century. A bookmark is any object used to mark a reader's place in a book. Bookmarks have been made in a wide variety of material, including celluloid, cloth, cross-stitched needlepoint in punched paper, paper, sterling silver, wood, and woven silk. Heavily embossed leather markers were popular between 1800 and 1860. Advertising markers appeared after 1860.

Woven silk markers are a favorite among collectors. T. Stevens of Coventry, England, manufacturer of Stevengraphs, is among the most famous makers. Paterson, New Jersey, was the silk weaving center in the United States. John Best & Co., Phoenix Silk Manufacturing Company, and Warner Manufacturing Co. produced bookmarks. Other important United States companies that made woven silk bookmarks were J. J. Mannion of Chicago and Tilt & Son of Providence, Rhode Island.

The best place to search for bookmarks is specialized paper shows. Be sure to check all related categories. Most dealers do not have a separate category for bookmarks. Instead they file them under subject headings, e.g., Insurance, Ocean Liners, World's Fairs, etc.

Periodical: *Bookmark Collector*, 1002 West 25th St, Erie, PA 16502.

Advertising
   Austin Young & Co Biscuits, 2 × 7",
     colorful **3.00**
   Climax Catarrah Cure, woman with fur
     coat, colorful **10.00**
   Cracker Jack, 2¾" l, litho tin, brown
     terrier, c1930 . . . . **18.00**
   Hood's Sarsaparilla, 1900, children
     holding books, colorful **10.00**
   Hoyt's German Cologne, diecut, colorful
     . . . . **6.00**
   LePages' Liquid Glue, diecut, codfish
     . . . . **7.50**
   Pear's Soap, 1 × 7", diecut, colorful
     . . . . **2.50**
Bazaar Art, plastic mesh, rect, initial and
   embroidered design . . . . **.50**
Cloisonne, butterfly, metal bookmark hook
   . . . . **2.00**
Cross-stitched, punched paper, sometimes
   found attached to silk ribbon
     Incomplete embroidery . . . . **.50**
     Large, 3⅝ × 7¾" **4.50**
     Small, 3¼ × ⅞" and smaller **3.00**

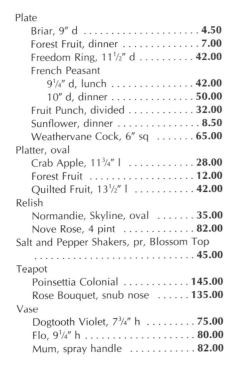

Advertising, Hoyt's German Cologne, adv on back, 2³/₁₆ × 4⁹/₁₆", $4.00.

Silk, woven
  Birthday Greetings
    Contemporary, white, blue flowers,
      blue tassel **1.00**
    Stevengraph, c1860 .... **50.00**
  Home Sweet Home, 2½ × 11", John
    Best & Co **40.00**
Souvenir
  Ocean Grove, NJ, ¾ × 7", SS ... **70.00**
  Pilgrim Hall, Plymouth, MA, 1 × 4¾",
    wood, Mauchline Ware **8.50**
  World's Fair, Pan–American Expo, silk,
    woven, Allen Chesters, Paterson, NJ,
    1901 .... **30.00**

BOOKS

There are millions of books out there. Some are worth a fortune. Most are hardly worth the paper they are printed on. Listing specific titles serves little purpose in a price guide such as this. By following ten guidelines below, you can quickly determine if the books that you have uncovered have value potential.

1. Check your book titles in *American Book Prices Current*, which is published annually by Bancroft–Parkman, Inc., and is available at most libraries, and *Huxford's Old Book Value Guide, Sixth Edition* (Collector Books: 1994). When listing your books in preparation for doing research, include the full name of the author, expanded title, name of publisher, copyright date, and edition and/or printing number.

2. Examine the bindings. Decorators buy handsomely bound books by the foot at prices ranging from $40.00 to $75.00 per foot.

3. Carefully research any children's book. Illustration quality is an important value key. Little Golden Books are one of the hottest book areas in the market today. In the late 1970s and early 1980s Big Little Books were hot.

4. Buy all hardcover books about antiques and collectibles that you find that are cheaply priced, i.e., less than $5.00. There is a growing demand for out–of–print antiques and collectibles books.

5. Check the edition number. Value, in most cases, rests with the first edition. However, not every first edition is valuable. Consult Blank's *Bibliography of American First Editions* or Tannen's *How to Identify and Collect American First Editions*.

6. Look at the multifaceted aspects of the book and the subject that it covers. Books tend to be collected by type, e.g., mysteries, Westerns, etc. Many collectors buy books as supplements to their main collection. A Hopalong Cassidy collector, although focusing primarily on the objects licensed by Bill Boyd, will want to own the Mulford novels in which Hopalong Cassidy originated.

7. Local histories and atlases always have a good market, particularly those printed between 1880 and 1930. Add to

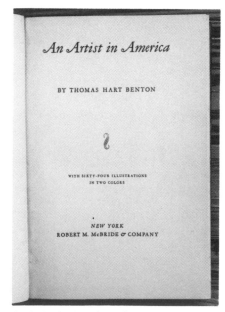

An Artist In America, Thomas Hart Benton, first edition, illus, $250.00.

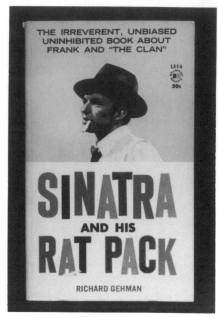

Sinatra And His Rat Pack, Richard Gehman, Elmont Books, multicolored cover, $2.00.

this centennial and other celebration volumes.

8. Check to see if the book was signed by the author. Generally, an author's signature increases the value of the book. However, it was a common practice to put engraved signatures of authors in front of books during the last part of the nineteenth century. The Grant signature in the first volume of his two–volume memoir set is not original, but printed.

9. Book club editions have little or no value with the exception of books done by George and Helen Macy's Limited Editions Club.

10. Accept the fact that the value of most books falls in the 50¢ to $2.00 range and that after all the searching that you have done, this is probably what you have found.

BOOTJACKS

Unless you are into horseback riding, a bootjack is one of the most useless devices that you can have around the house. Why do so many individuals own one? The answer in our area is "just for nice." Actually, they are seen as a major accessory in trying to capture the country look.

Cast iron reproductions are a major problem, especially for "Naughty Nellie" and "Beetle" designs.

Brass, beetle, 10" l **90.00**
Cast Iron
    Beetle, 9¼" l, black **35.00**
    Closed Loop, painted **70.00**
    Cricket, 11¾" l, scroll design, dated
        1873 . . . . **175.00**
    Heart and Circle, open, 13" l, scalloped
        sides **225.00**
    Lyre shape, 10¼" l **48.00**
    Mule's head **40.00**
    Musselmans Plug Tobacco adv, ornate
        . . . . **150.00**
    Pheasants, pr, 19" l **225.00**
    Scissor Action, marked "Pat 1877"
        . . . . **85.00**
    Vine design, 12" l **35.00**
    V–shaped, ornate **45.00**
Wood
    Fish, 19" l, relief carving, red stain **30.00**
    Monkey, 15" l, wearing painted suit,
        c1900 . . . . **30.00**

BOTTLE OPENERS, FIGURAL

Although this listing focuses on cast iron figural bottle openers, the most sought–after type of bottle openers, do not forget the tin advertising openers, also known to some as church keys. The bulk still sell between $2.00 and $10.00, a very affordable price range.

Clubs: Figural Bottle Opener Collectors Club, 117 Basin Hill Rd, Duncannon, PA 17020; Just For Openers, 605 Windsong Lane, Durham, NC 27713.

All are cast iron unless otherwise specified.

Advertising
    Centrum Vitamins, brass, figural, sundial
        . . . . **75.00**
    Dr Brown's Celery Tonic **20.00**
    Effinger Beer, Baraboo, WI, hand shape,
        pointing finger **15.00**
    Medford Lager Beer, dachshund shape,
        nickel plated over cast iron . . . **45.00**
Alligator **30.00**
Bear Head, 3¾" h, 1950 . . . . **110.00**
Billy Goat, 2¾" h, 1950 . . . . **250.00**
Black Boy, hand in air, riding on green alli-
    gator, green base, John Wright Co
    . . . . **165.00**
Bulldog, 4" h, 1947 . . . . **125.00**
Clown
    Brass, 4" h, wall mounted, white bowtie,
        red polka dots, bald head, sgd "495"
        on back, John Wright Co **70.00**
    Cast Iron, mustache, four eyes . . . **35.00**
    Cowboy, 4⅞" h, marked "San Antonio,
        Texas" **225.00**
    Dachshund, brass **50.00**
    Donkey **35.00**

Drunk
    Cactus, figural, 1950 . . . . **195.00**
    Palm Tree, 4" h, polychrome paint **65.00**
    Signpost, polychrome paint, marked
        "Baltimore, MD" **10.00**
English Setter, 2½" h, 1950 . . . . **65.00**
Flamingo, figural **95.00**
Four-Eyed Man, figural **45.00**
Girl, 3⅞" h, buck teeth, polychrome paint,
    marked "Wilton Prod" **50.00**
Horseshoe **25.00**
Madamoiselle and Lamppost, 4½" h, 1960s
    . . . . **35.00**
Mallard Duck, 3¼" h, cast iron, 1947 **95.00**
Nude, reclining, chromed metal **35.00**
Palm Tree **115.00**
Parrot **20.00**
Pelican, 3¾" h, cream colored, orange beak
    and feet, green base, John Wright Co
    . . . . **140.00**
Pretzel, brass **25.00**
Rooster, 3¼" h, polychrome paint . . . **50.00**
Seagull, 3¼" h, on stump, polychrome paint
    . . . . **175.00**
Squirrel, 3" l, 1947 . . . . **110.00**
Steel worker, 3¼" h, polychrome paint
    . . . . **175.00**
Swordfish **65.00**
Teeth, 3⅜" l, polychrome paint **95.00**

BOTTLES

Bottle collecting is such a broad topic that the only way one can hope to survive is by specialization. It is for this reason that several bottle topics are found elsewhere in this book.

Bottles have a bad habit of multiplying. Do not start collecting them until you have plenty of room. I know one person whose entire basement is filled with Coca–Cola bottles bearing the imprint of different cities.

There are many bottle categories that are still relatively inexpensive to collect. In many cases, you can find a free source of supply in old dumps. Before getting too deeply involved, it pays to talk with other bottle collectors and to visit one or more specialized bottle collector shows.

Club: Federation of Historical Bottle Clubs, 14521 Atlantic Ave, Riverdale, IL 60627.

Periodicals: *Antique Bottle And Glass Collector*, PO Box 187, East Greenville, PA 18041; *Bottles & Extras*, PO Box 154, Happy Camp, CA 96039.

BEVERAGES
Alburgh A Springs, qt, yellow amber   **40.00**

Asparagus Gin, Rothenberg Co, clear   **10.00**
Booths High & Dry Gin, 10¼" h, light blue
    . . . . **5.00**
Buster Brown Rye, swirled, enameled **55.00**
Cliquot Soda, paper label **5.00**
Cloverleaf Dairy, Quincy, Mass, qt, emb
    . . . . **35.00**
Congress & Empire Spring Co, Saratoga, em-
    erald green, qt **15.00**
Double Line Soda, Kokomo, IN **6.00**
Fruitbowl Grapefruit Wine **12.00**
Geyser Soda, aqua **20.00**
Gordon Dry Gin, London, England, 9" h,
    light green **5.00**
Grapette Pop **8.00**
Klassy Tops In Taste Pop **8.00**
Knapp Root Beer, labeled **15.00**
Korker The OK Refresher Pop **5.50**
Mission Dry Sparkling, black, crown top
    . . . . **5.00**
Mountain Valley Mineral Water **13.00**
Quality Beverages, Perryton, Texas, green,
    crown top **10.00**
Royal Ruby Beer, 32 oz **35.00**
Stroymers Grape Punch, 12" h, clear, metal
    cap **140.00**
W A Gilbey Silver Stream Schnapps, 8" h,
    clear **6.00**

FOOD
A & S, lemon extract, c1905 . . . . **24.00**
Baker Flavoring Extract, 5" h, clear   **10.00**
Bridal Brand Olives, stoneware **45.00**
Burnetts Standard Flavoring Extract, 5½" h,
    aqua **4.00**
Colgate, vanilla extract, c1910 . . . . . **20.00**
Cross & Blackwell Mint Sauce **3.00**
East India Pickles, qt, aqua **15.00**
Golden Tree Maple Syrup, 20 oz, clear,
    screw top **2.00**
Hanfords Flavoring Extracts, 5¼" h, clear
    . . . . **2.00**
Herberlings, banana flavoring, 8" h, paper
    label **8.00**
HICO Imitation Lemon Flavoring, 8 oz,
    clear **6.00**
Highland Maple Sap Syrup **9.00**
James Chaskel & Co Extract **35.00**
Jumbo Peanut Butter, pt, clear **4.00**
Louis & Co, lemon extract **10.00**
Marceau Spanish Olives, 7¾" h, barrel
    shape, clear **14.00**
Marvel Sweet Pickles **12.00**
McCormick Imitation Pineapple **5.50**
Mrs Chapins Mayonnaise, clear, pt . . . **5.00**
Newmans' Pure Cold Extracts, 5½" h, clear
    . . . . **2.00**
Purity Oats, qt, clear, flower dec, screw cap
    . . . . **12.00**
Sauers Extracts, 6" h, clear **4.00**
Spears Vinegar **8.00**
Thompson & Taylor Root Beer Flavoring,
    4" h, clear **3.00**
Valentines Meat Juice, 3" h, amber . . . **4.00**
Warsaw Salt Co Choice Table Salt, 5¾" h,
    amber **60.00**

HEALTH AND BEAUTY

Altenheim Medical Dispensary For Hair, Scalp, 8" h, clear 8.00
Arnolds Vegetable Hair Balsam, 6⅛" h, clear 18.00
Bono Opto For The Eyes, 3¼" h, clear   4.00
Chattanooga Medicine Co, 8⅜" h, light green, screw top 5.00
Damschinksy Liquid Hair Dye, NY, 4¼" h, aqua 5.00
Drake's Plantation Bitters, 9¾" h, log cabin shape, strawberry puce 135.00
Dr C Grattans Diptheria Remedy, 7" h, aqua 25.00
Ebenezer A Pearls Tincture Of Life, 7¾" h, aqua 8.00
Fish Bitters, 11¾" h, reddish amber   165.00
Fletchers Castoria, 6" h, aqua 5.00
Golden Eye Lotion, Leonardis, Tampa, FL, 4½" h, aqua 8.00
Great English Sweeny Specific, 6" h, aqua 5.00
Hicks Capudine Liquid For Headaches, 8½" h, amber 400.00
Hoods Tooth Powder, C I Hood & Co, 3½" h, clear 5.00
John Wyeth & Brother Liquid Malt Extract, 9" h, amber 10.00
Log Cabin Cough & Consumption Remedy, amber 125.00
Lufkin Eczema Remedy, 7" h, clear, label 8.00
Mrs. Winslows Syrup, paper litho with ladies and angel, unopened 40.00
Oldridge Balm of Columbia For Restoring Hair, 6¼" h, aqua 45.00
Peter Mollers Pure Cod Liver Oil, 5¾" h, clear, label 4.00
Ponds Extract, 5½" h, amethyst 15.00
Rubifoam For The Teeth, 4" h, clear   5.00
Sanitol For The Teeth, 4½" h, clear . . .8.00
Short Stop For Coughs, H M O'Neil, NY, 4" h, sq form, aqua 5.00
Sparks Perfect Health For Kidney & Liver Diseases, 4" h, aqua 8.00
Thompsons Herbal Compound, 6¾" h, aqua, label 8.00
US Marine Hospital Service 20.00
Warners Safe Diabetes Cure, Melbourne, 9½" h, amber 100.00
Woodward Chemist–Nottingham, 6" h, light blue 5.00
Zemo Antiseptic Lotion For Skin & Scalp, 6" h, clear .8.00

HOUSEHOLD

American Bluing Co, NY, 5¼" h, clear   4.00
Bengal Bluing, 5¾" h, aqua 3.00
Black Cat Stove Enamel, 6" h, clear . . .3.00
Cocoa Nut Oil, 5⅞" h, aqua, violin shape, open pontil 100.00
Dutchers Dead Shot For Bed Bugs, 4⅞" h, aqua, label 60.00
Eclipse French Stain Gloss, 4½" h, apple green 5.00
Hercules Disinfectant, 6" h, amber 4.00

Mexican Imperial Bluing, 10 oz, clear, gold cap 7.50
Poison, cobalt blue 28.00
Prices Patent Candle Company Limited, 7⅛" h, cobalt 75.00
Shulife–For Shoes, 3¾" h, olive green   5.00
Snow Bird Liquid Wax, 6 oz, brown bottle, red cap, blue and white label 7.50
Spauldings Glue, aqua, open pontil   12.00
Standardised Disinfectant Co, 4¼" h, light amber 2.00
Triumph Superior Clock Oil, 3½" h, clear 4.00
Uptons Liquid Glue, 2⅞" h, aqua, twelve sided 40.00

BOXES

We have reached the point with some twentieth-century collectibles where the original box may be more valuable than the object that came in it. If the box is colorful and contains a picture of the product, it has value.

Boxes have always been a favorite among advertising collectors. They are three–dimensional and often fairly large in size. The artwork reflects changing period tastes. Decorators like the pizzazz that boxes offer. The wood box with a lithographed label is a fixture in the country household.

Advertising

Aunt Jemima Pancake Flour, 13 × 9 × 14", cardboard 55.00
Baker's Chocolate, 12 lbs, wood, shipping 15.00
Beech–Nut .18.00
Blanar Banana 55.00
Blue Flag Brand Popcorn Midgets, wood 40.00
Bossie's Best Brand Butter, pound   2.00
Cupples Topseal Jar Rings, unused   4.00
Diamond Spring & Cold Spring Brewery, wood 20.00
Dr Johnson's Educator Crackers   35.00
Fairy Soap, individual 22.00
Forbes Co, St Louis, allspice, Buster Brown illus 40.00
Gay Times Soft Drink, children illus 20.00
Hires Extract, wood, 1889 . . . . . . .85.00
Jackson Fly Killer, display, wood   25.00
Loft Candy, wood 20.00
Nabisco, Mickey Mouse Cookies, cardboard, unopened 195.00
Pickney Spice, wood, store size   80.00
Reese Cigars, wood 20.00
Regal Underwear, cardboard 15.00
Royal Baking Powder, wood, shipping, c1800 .125.00
Squirrel Brand Peanut Taffy, wood   30.00

Collar Box, cash register shape, forest motif, oval with musician playing to lady in garden, compartments for collars, cuffs, buttons, etc, orig lavender litho paper covered with celluloid has faded to pink–yellow, c1900, $115.00.

Union Biscuit 20.00
Victory Hair Pins, cardboard, "Help Uncle Sam Save Steel," unopened   4.00
Wrigley's Spearmint Gum, 1929   35.00
Collar, gutta percha, 1876 Centennial 125.00
Pencil
Faber Castell 12.00
Lone Ranger 125.00
Sample, National Lead Co, paint chip samples 15.00
Toy
Marx, Police Siren Motorcycle, empty 170.00
Structo, machinery truck and steam shovel, #402 . . . . .65.00
Tootsietoy, furniture, empty 85.00
Wristwatch, Walt Disney, Mickey Mouse 110.00

BOYD CRYSTAL ART GLASS

The Boyds, Bernard and his son, purchased the Degenhart Glass Factory in 1978. Since that time they have reissued a number of the Degenhart forms. Their productions can be distinguished by the color of the glass and the "D" in a diamond mark. The Boyd family continues to make contemporary collectible glass at its factory in Cambridge, Ohio.

Toothpick Holder, gypsy pot, dark brown slag, $6.00.

Club: Boyd Art Glass Collectors Guild, PO Box 52, Hatboro, PA 19040.

Newsletters: *Boyd's Crystal Art Glass,* PO Box 127, 1203 Morton Ave, Cambridge, OH 43725; *Jody & Darrell's Glass Collectibles,* PO Box 180833, Arlington, TX 76094.

Animal
    Brian Bunny, Cardinal Red Carnival
      . . . . **5.00**
    Bunny on Nest, White Opal **9.00**
    Debbie Duck, English Yew **5.00**
    Fuzzy the Bear, Cashmere Pink . . . **5.00**
    Joey Pony
      Cashmere Pink **18.00**
      Chocolate **30.00**
      Nile Green **15.00**
    Patrick, Balloon Bear, Golden Delight
      . . . . **7.50**
    Rooster, Orange Calico **10.00**
    Skippy, dog, sitting, Light Rose **8.50**
    Suee Pig, Autumn Beige **7.50**
    Willie, mouse, 2" h, Lime Carnival **10.00**
Ashtray, Zodiac, Nile Green **4.00**
Basket, 4¹⁄₂" d, Milk White, hp dec   **20.00**
Bell
    Owl, Violet Slate **15.00**
    Santa, White **25.00**
Candleholder, sleigh, White **22.00**
Colonial Doll, Ruby Red Carnival . . . **18.00**
Hobo Clown, Freddie, Cobalt Blue **10.00**
Louise, doll
    Cashmere Pink, hp dec **25.00**
    Golden Delight **10.00**
Salt
    Duck
      Classic Black Slag **6.00**
      Crown Tuscan **6.00**
      Dove Blue **5.00**
      Lamb, Ruby Red Carnival **10.00**
      Tub, Nile Green **5.00**
    Tractor, 2" h, Spinnaker Blue **10.00**

BOY SCOUTS

This is another collecting area in which adults dominate where you would normally expect to find kids. When my dad was a Boy Scout, emphasis was on swapping material with little concern for value. One for one was the common rule.

Today old Scouting material is viewed in monetary terms. Eagle badge books go for $75.00 or more. The key is to find material that was officially licensed. Unlicensed material is generally snubbed by collectors.

Boy Scout collecting is so sophisticated that it has its own shows and swap meets. Strong retail value for Boy Scout material occurs at these shows. Flea market prices tend to be much lower.

Clubs: American Scouting Traders Association, Inc, PO Box 92, Kentfield, CA 94914; International Badgers Club, 7760 NW 50th St, Lauder Hill, FL 33351; National Scouting Collectors Society, 806 E Scott St, Tuscola, IL 61953.

Bank, orig paint **95.00**
Book
    Boy Scouts in Camp, George Burston
      . . . . **12.00**
    Songs Scouts Sing, 4¹⁄₄ × 6³⁄₄", 104 pgs,
      1931 third printing **25.00**
    Troop Committee, 5¹⁄₂ × 8", 42 pgs,
      1931 Boy Scouts of America copyright **25.00**
Canteen, aluminum, hip type, red canvas
    cov **8.00**
Certificate, Assistant Scout Master, Warren, PA, 1914, sgd by Theodore Roosevelt, framed **100.00**
Container, oval, tin, 1920s **95.00**

Belt, buckle reads "National Scout Jamboree, Virginia, 1981," profile of George Washington and scout, brown leather belt with emb scrolls and scouting emblem, marked "TOOLOCRAFT, Top Grain Cowhide," 32" l, $24.00.

Handbook
    Handbook for Scoutmasters, 1922, blue cov **15.00**
    Lone Scouts of America, 1915–20, 50 pgs, illus **25.00**
    Scouting For Boys, 1935 . . . . **17.50**
Hat, leader's, pin **55.00**
Magazine, *Boy's Life,* Norman Rockwell cov
    . . . . **25.00**
Membership Card, 2¹⁄₂ × 3³⁄₄", typed name and October 31, 1941, orig 2³⁄₄ × 4" brown manila envelope **12.00**
Neckerchief
    Cub Scout Standard, 3rd issue, tenderfoot emblem, band border
      . . . . **4.00**
    National Jamboree, 1973, blue cotton, emblem **5.00**
    National Order of the Arrow Conference, 1967, tan cotton, emblem
      . . . . **18.00**
    World Scouting, purple, white design, white piping **8.50**
Notepad, 2¹⁄₂ × 4", Boy Scout signaling illus on front, 1914 copyright **25.00**
Paperweight, silver, Explorer symbol **5.00**
Patch, 3 × 5", Historic Trails Award, leather, tan and black, emb, unused, 1960s
    . . . . **15.00**
Pennant, 30" l, felt, blue, white inscription, c1940 . . . . **20.00**
Pinback Button
    Do A Good Turn Daily, multicolored portrait, dark blue ground, 1920s
      . . . . **15.00**

Flashlight, olive green, official Boy Scout emblem, belt hanger, 7¹⁄₄" l, $20.00.

National Jamboree, multicolored, 1937
........................**25.00**
1948 Roundup, Boy Scouts of America,
white, red illus and lettering   **25.00**
Plaque
Award, 6 × 9", laminated masonite, full
color Norman Rockwell illus, titled
"Ever Onward," 1961 ....**50.00**
1953 National Jamboree **18.00**
Pocket Watch, dollar type, Ingersol, patented July 2, 1916 ....**350.00**
Scarf Slide, plastic, white, raised red Indian
head, 1951 ....**8.00**
Sheet Music, 11 × 13", *Boy Scout March*,
full color illus on cov, 1912 .....**95.00**

BRASS

Brass is a durable, malleable, and
ductile metal alloy consisting mainly of
copper and zinc. It appears in this guide
because of the wide variety of objects
made from it. I have never met a brass
collector whose interest spans all forms,
but I have met padlock and key collectors.

Ashtray, 4½ × 5", figural, bull's head
...........................**50.00**
Bed Warmer, 44½" l, oversized lid with
tooled designs and heart, turned wood
handle **75.00**
Bell, Kewpie **65.00**
Blotter, rocker shape, knob handle ...**10.00**
Bowl, handles, Dutch **50.00**
Call Bell, 6¼" h, red granite base **25.00**
Candlesticks, pr, 10¾" h, Queen of Dia-
mond pattern, pushups, English   **100.00**
Clothes Tree, four top hooks, four legs, sq
tubular trim on base **45.00**
Door Knocker, basket with flowers   **78.00**
Fireplace Fan, 38" w, 25" h, folding, griffin
detail **65.00**
Knife, Golden Wedding Whiskey adv   **20.00**

*Medical bleeding device, marked "W H
Huthchinson, Sheffield," English, $185.00.*

Letter Opener, Pittsburg Coal Co adv, Indian
head on handle **15.00**
Matchsafe, International Tailoring adv,
nickel plated, emb Indians and lion
...........................**55.00**
Mortar and Pestle, 2½" h **40.00**
Padlock, Keen Kutter, Simmon, plain back
...........................**75.00**
Pail, 9½" d, spun, iron bale handle, marked
"Haydens Patent" **65.00**
Picture Frame, easel type, Art Nouveau
style, gilded, four topaz colored jewels
...........................**175.00**
Plant Stand, gilded, white onyx shelf and
top **50.00**
Teapot, 8¼" h, Oriental dragons and trees
dec **40.00**
Trivet, 7½" d, reticulated top, worn tooling
...........................**100.00**
Wick Trimmer, 9½" l, matching tray   **85.00**

BREAD BOXES

Bread boxes are too much fun to be
hidden in a Kitchen Collectibles category. There are plenty of great examples
both in form and decoration. They have
disappeared from the modern kitchen. I
miss them.

Art Deco, chrome, rect, black wood handle
...........................**10.00**
Graniteware, 19" l, green and white, hinged
lid, 1920s **95.00**
Metal
Betsy Ross Moderne pattern, white, red
trim, Roll-A-Way, E M Meder Co,
1930s **15.00**
Fruit Decal, painted yellow **15.00**
Red Poppy pattern **17.00**
Stenciled "Bread," white enamel paint,
c1900 ....**32.00**
Tin, 12" l, white, red enameled top   **12.00**
Wood, 12½" h, carved "Give Us This Day"
...........................**80.00**

BREAD PLATES

Bread, the staff of life, has been
served on ornate plates of all types, ranging from colored glass of the Victorian
era to the handwrought aluminum of the
1950s. Some bread plates included mot-
tos or commemorated historical events.

Avoid plain examples. A great bread
plate should add class to the table.

Cut Glass, 13½" l, brilliant cut, sgd "Lib-
bey" **175.00**
Majolica, 12¼" l, Oak Leaf with Acorns pat-
tern **120.00**
Pattern Glass
Actress, 7 × 12", HMS Pinafore, frosted
...........................**90.00**
Ashman, clear, motto dec **55.00**

Barley, clear **30.00**
Beaded Grape, emerald green ...**45.00**
Beaded Loop, clear **35.00**
Cape Cod, clear **45.00**
Chain With Star, 11" l, clear, handled
...........................**30.00**
Cupid and Venus, clear **40.00**
Dahlia, amber **55.00**
Daisy and Button, 13" l, blue **35.00**
Finecut and Panel, blue **45.00**
Garden of Eden **75.00**
Kansas, emb "Our Daily Bread"   **45.00**
Lion, 12" l, frosted **90.00**
Maine, 10 × 7¾", oval, clear **30.00**
Maryland, clear, gold dec **25.00**
Moon And Star, rect, clear **45.00**
Palmette **30.00**
Paneled Thistle, clear **40.00**
Question Mark, clear **30.00**
Royal Lady, vaseline **135.00**
Sprig, clear **40.00**
Tennessee, colored jewels **75.00**
US Coin, clear **175.00**
Westward Ho!, clear **175.00**
Silver Plated, grape clusters on self handles
...........................**65.00**
Tin, 14" l, bronze powder stenciled fruit,
flowers, and foliage dec, yellow striping,
orig green paint **55.00**
Wooden, round, "Bread" emb on rim, hand
rubbed oil refinish **15.00**

BREWERIANA

Beer is liquid bread, or so I was told
growing up in Pennsylvania German
country. It is hard to deny German link-
age with the brewing industry when your
home community contained the
Horlacher, Neuweiler, and Uhl breweries.

Brewery signs and trays, especially
from the late nineteenth and early twentieth century, contain some of the finest
advertising lithography of the period.
The three-dimensional advertising figures from the 1930s through the 1970s
are no slouches either.

Brewery advertising has become expensive. Never fear. You can build a
great breweriana collection concentrating on barroom accessories such as foam
scrapers, coasters, and tap knobs.

Clubs: American Breweriana Association, PO Box 11157, Pueblo, CO 81001;
National Association of Breweriana Advertising, 2343 Met-Tu-Wee Lane,
Wauwatosa, WI 53226.

Ashtray, Great Falls Select Beer, white milk
glass **12.00**
Beer Can, Strohs, miniature **4.00**

Blotter, 7½ × 3″, Bergdoll Brewing Co, black and white portrait of Louis Bergdoll, holly dec, 60th anniversary, 1909, unused **50.00**

Bottle
Beckers Beer, Evanston, WY **10.00**
Blatz, figural, fishing lure, MIB ... **35.00**
Calgary Ale **10.00**
Enterprise Brewing Co, qt **8.00**
Fredericksburg Brewery, 11¼″ h, red amber **15.00**
Schwarzenbach Brewing Co, 7¼″ h, clear **3.00**

Bottle Opener, Pabst, metal, figural bottle **7.50**

Butter Pat, Magnolia Brewing, Houston, ornate **32.00**

Change Tray
Angeles Brewing & Malting Co, Port Angeles, WA **100.00**
Billings Brewing Co, Billings, MT **100.00**
Budweiser **8.00**
Miller Beer, duck illus **20.00**
Ryan's Beer, pretty girl **45.00**

Clock
Lowenbrau **18.00**
Old Milwaukee, bar display, ship's bell time **60.00**

Coaster, metal
Knickerbocker Beer **5.00**
Simon Pure Beer **5.00**
Smith Brothers Beer **5.00**

Corkscrew
Anheuser–Busch, encased **75.00**
Pabst, wood handle **22.00**

Dart Board, wood box with Anheuser–Busch Inc logo on front **125.00**

Employee Pin, Miller Brewing Co ... **12.00**

Fishing Lure, Schlitz, bottle shape ... **10.00**

Sign, Columbia Brewing Co, Shenandoah, PA, curved corner type, vitrolite, $7,150.00. Photo courtesy of James D. Julia, Inc.

Foam Scraper
Birk's Beer **18.00**
Hampden Ale **20.00**
Meister Brau, celluloid **20.00**

Foam Scraper Holder, Piel's Beer, metal **65.00**

Ice Pick, Empire Lager, Black Horse Ale **25.00**

Lamp, Budweiser, wall, pr **22.00**

Lapel Pin, Pabst Breweries, enameled 14K gold **25.00**

Matchbook, Stoeckle Beer, oversized, figural matches **20.00**

Matchsafe
Genessee **65.00**
Pabst Beer, pocket **48.00**
Schlitz **55.00**

Mirror, Haaberle Beer, 20 × 12″, Art Deco style **45.00**

Mug
Leisey Brewery, desert scene **58.00**
Stroh's At The Fair, May 1–Oct 31, 1982, Knoxville, TN, marked on bottom "King Wood 44413" **45.00**

Pinback Button
Emil Sick's Select Beer, 1½″ d, red number "6" logo, yellow ground, black letters, gold rim and accents, c1930 .... **20.00**
Poth's Beer, 1″ d, white letters, khaki ground, c1900 .... **12.00**
Schlitz Beer, 1¼″ d, white ground, red letters, crossed key center, early 1900s **20.00**

Poster, Budweiser, Spuds MacKenzie illus **6.00**

Sign
Bavarian Premium Beer, 5 × 9″, tin **25.00**
Old Milwaukee, 13″, glass and metal **25.00**
Piels Beer, Sammy Davis Jr, bus **100.00**
Regal Beer, enamel and tin, chalkboard **150.00**
Schmidt's Malta, bottle illus, unused **125.00**

Statue
Blatz, banjo player, metal, lights up **100.00**
Hamm's, bear, changeable calendar **75.00**
Pabst Blue Ribbon, girl's face, 1957 .... **175.00**

Stein
Blatz, barrel shape, glaze flakes **30.00**
Budweiser, holiday dec, 1980 ... **75.00**
Hamm's Beer, Octoberfest, 1973, McCoy **25.00**
Miller Great Achievements 32, Model T **35.00**
Old Milwaukee **18.00**
Schlitz **18.00**

Tap Knob, Hamm's Beer, metal **15.00**

Tray
Dawson's, couple seated at table **45.00**

Diamond Spring, coat of arms illus, green **75.00**
Ehret Beer, oval **55.00**
Hamm's Beer, bear illus **20.00**
Hampden, man on keg, green, yellow, and brown **40.00**
Holihan's, red and yellow **55.00**
Leinenkugels Brewery
Indian Maiden illus **90.00**
110th Anniversary **50.00**
Meister Brau, Peter Hand Mfg **18.00**
Miller Beer, girl sitting on moon **40.00**
New England Brewing, oval **60.00**
Old Tap, cream, red, and black **60.00**
Pabst, rect, man pouring beer, 1930s **45.00**
Port Townsend Brewing Co, Port Townsend, WA **395.00**
Tadcaster, stagecoach illus **80.00**

BRITISH ROYALTY COMMEMORATIVES

This is one of those categories where you can get in on the ground floor. Every king and queen, potential king and queen, and their spouses is collectible. Buy commemorative items when they are new. I have a few Prince Harry items. We may not have royal blood in common, but. . . .

Most individuals collect by monarch, prince, or princess. Take a different approach—collect by form, e.g., mugs, playing cards, etc. British royalty commemoratives were made at all quality levels. Stick to high–quality examples.

It is fun to find recent issues at flea markets for much less than their original selling price. Picking is competitive. There are a lot of British royalty commemorative collectors.

Ashtray, Edward VIII Coronation, May 12, 1937, round, scalloped edge **25.00**
Bank, Edward VII, Oxo Cubes, tin ... **60.00**
Beaker, Edward VII Coronation, June 28, 1902, transfer printed, portrait, date, and "The King's Coronation Dinner presented by His Majesty," Doulton **100.00**
Bell, 5½″ h, Queen Elizabeth II Silver Jubilee, 1977, applied roses, silver trim, Crown Staffordshire **30.00**
Biscuit Tin
3 × 7″, Queen Elizabeth Coronation, 1953 .... **20.00**
5½ × 4½″, George V Silver Jubilee, 1935, McVitie & Price Biscuit Manufacturers, marked "Free Sample" on bottom **30.00**

Cup, Edward VIII Coronation, multicolored, design by Dame Laura Knight, lion handle, "Myott Son, Made in England" mark, 3¼" h, $60.00.

6 × 10", Queen Elizabeth Coronation, 1953 . . . . **30.00**

Bowl, 6" d, Prince William of Wales Birth, June 21, 1982, color portraits and nursery scenes **35.00**

Candy Tin, 2¼ × 5", Edward VII Coronation, June 28, 1902, rect, Rowntree & Co **35.00**

Cigarette Case, George VI Coronation, May 12, 1937, book type, emb medallion design on front cov, clasp, 1930s . . . **38.00**

Coca–Cola Bottle, Prince Charles Wedding to Lady Diana Spencer, July 29, 1981 . . . . **40.00**

Dish, 5½" d, Prince Charles Investiture as Prince of Wales, July 1, 1969, multicolored coat of arms, ftd, Aynsley **50.00**

Egg Cup, George VI Coronation, May 12, 1937, portrait illus **35.00**

Glass, Edward VIII Coronation, May 12, 1937, clear, etched portrait and inscriptions **35.00**

Lace Panel, Prince Charles Wedding to Lady Diana Spencer, July 29, 1981, Nottingham lace, twenty–point . . . **25.00**

Magazine, Queen Elizabeth II Coronation, *The Illustrated London News* **20.00**

Mug

George VI Coronation, May 12, 1937, tin, portrait illus **35.00**

Prince Charles Wedding to Lady Diana Spencer, July 29, 1981, 3½" h, sepia portraits, color dec, Pall Mall Ware **35.00**

Queen Elizabeth, eightieth birthday, Aug 4, 1980, portrait in floral wreath, inscribed "To Celebrate the 80th Birthday of Her Majesty Queen Elizabeth the Queen Mother, August 4, 1980," Spode **75.00**

Pincushion, Queen Elizabeth II Silver Jubilee, 1977, crown, silvered metal **30.00**

Plate

George V and Queen Mary, Silver Jubilee, 1910–1935, 6" d, Almaware **27.00**

Prince Charles Wedding to Lady Diana Spencer, July 29, 1981, 10 ½" d, black and white portraits, color and gold dec **40.00**

Queen Victoria Diamond Jubilee, 1897, white, color portrait center, raised design border, gold trim, Doulton **225.00**

Queen Victoria Golden Jubilee, 1887, pressed glass, clear, "1887, Year of Jubilee" **100.00**

Playing Cards

Prince Charles Wedding to Lady Diana Spencer, July 29, 1981, double deck, British Monarchs, color portraits, Grimaud **30.00**

Queen Elizabeth II Silver Jubilee, 1977, portrait illus **10.00**

Pocket Watch, 2" d, Queen Elizabeth II Coronation, silvered metal, back engraved with royal family crest **250.00**

Post Card, Prince William of Wales, birth, June 21, 1982 . . . . **2.00**

Program, George V Coronation, June 22, 1911, issued by City of Lincoln **25.00**

Spoon, Prince William of Wales, birth, June 21, 1982, silver plated, picture of Prince and Princess of Wales holding William on handle **12.00**

Stamp Packet, Queen Elizabeth II Coronation, 4 × 6" envelope, two blocks of sixty different stamps, 1953 . . . **20.00**

Teapot, cov, Edward VIII Coronation, May 12, 1937, portrait and shield, gold trim **95.00**

Tea Towel, Prince Charles Wedding to Lady Diana Spencer, July 29, 1981, Irish linen, color portraits **15.00**

Thimble, set of 4, Prince William of Wales, birth, June 21, 1982, Queen Mother, Queen Elizabeth, Princess Diana, and crown illus, Caverswall **60.00**

Trinket Box, cov, 4" w, Prince Charles Wedding to Lady Diana Spencer, July 29, 1981, heart shaped, portrait illus on cov, wedding information inside, Hammersley **35.00**

BROWNIES, PALMER COX

Palmer Cox created *The Brownies,* comical elf–like creatures, for *St. Nicholas* magazine. Each Brownie had a distinct personality and name. Thirteen books were published about them.

Beware of imitation Brownies. The Brownies' success led other illustrators to utilize elf figures in their cartoons. The only way to tell the copies from the originals is to carefully study and memorize the Cox illustrations.

Puzzle, The Brownie Blocks, McLoughlin Brothers, copyright 1891, 20 hollow wood cubes, makes six different pictures, wood frame, 11 × 15" cardboard box, booklet and diagrams, 10 × 12½", $450.00.

Advertising Trade Card, American Machine Co, ice cream freezers **18.00**

Basket, 2 × 4", desk type, brass, Brownie at base **75.00**

Book

Palmer Cox Brownie Yearbook, McLoughlin Bros, 1895 . . . . **190.00**

The Brownies Abroad, 18th printing, dj, 1941 . . . . **35.00**

Booklet, set of 6, *Palmer Cox Primers,* 12 pgs, Jersey Coffee premium **150.00**

Box, Little Buster Popcorn **12.00**

Charm, 1" d, white metal, black finish, vest and cap, c1900 . . . . **35.00**

Creamer, 2½" h, china, Brownies smoking pipe, verse on back **60.00**

Magazine Ad, *Youth's Companion,* April 9, 1885, full page, Ivory Soap adv, four black and white Brownies illus, Palmer Cox **30.00**

Napkin Ring, figural, silver plated . . . **80.00**

Needle Book, Columbian Expo, Brownie Policeman illus, 1893 . . . . **50.00**

Paper Doll, Lion Coffee adv **20.00**

Plate, 6" d, china, three Brownies seated on mushrooms playing musical instruments, 1890s **55.00**

Ruler, Mrs Winslow's Soothing Syrup adv **25.00**

Stickpin, Brownie Policeman **20.00**

Toy, Brownie Trapeze, 7¾" h, wood, mechanical, early 1900s **50.00**

BUBBLE GUM CARDS

Based on the publicity received by baseball cards, you would think that they were the only bubble gum cards sold. Wrong, wrong, wrong! There are a wealth of non–sport bubble gum cards.

Prices for many of these card sets are rather modest. Individual cards often sell for less than $1.00. The classic cards were issued in the 1950s, but I bought a pack of the recent Desert Storm cards just to be on the safe side.

Club: United States Cartophilic Society, PO Box 4020, St Augustine, FL 32085.

Periodicals: *Non–Sport Update,* 4019 Green St, PO Box 5858, Harrisburg, PA 17110; *Non Sports Illustrated,* PO Box 126, Lincoln, MA 01773; *The Non–Sport Report,* PO Box 128, Plover, WI 54467; *The Wrapper,* PO Box 227, Geneva, IL 60134; *Triton: Comic Cards & Collectibles,* Attic Books Ltd, 15 Danbury Rd, Ridgefield, CT 06877.

Andy Griffith, Third series, Pacific Trading Cards, 110 cards, 1991 . . . . **6.00**
Antique Autos, Bowman, 2½ × 3¾″, 48 card set, 1953 . . . . **50.00**
Astronauts, Topps, 55 cards, 1963 **200.00**
Bay City Rollers, Topps, 66 cards, 1975 . . . . **25.00**
Brady Bunch, Topps, 88 cards, 1970 . . . . **150.00**
Buck Rogers, Topps, 88 cards, 22 stickers, 1979 . . . . **12.00**
Civil War News, Topps, 88 cards, 1962 . . . . **175.00**
Combat, Donruss, Series I, 66 cards, 1964 . . . . **55.00**
Daniel Boone, Topps, 55 cards, 1965 **25.00**
Dark Shadows, Series II, Philadelphia Chewing Gum Co, 66 cards, green, 1969 . . . . **80.00**
Desert Storm, Homecoming, Topps, 88 cards, 11 stickers **9.00**
Empire Strikes Back, Series I, Topps, 1980 . . . . **5.00**
Dukes of Hazzard, Donruss, 66 cards, 1980 . . . . **3.50**
Gomer Pyle, Fleer, 66 cards, 1965 . . . **10.00**
Gong Show, Fleer, 66 cards, 10 stickers, 1979 . . . . **5.00**
Hogan's Heroes, Fleer, 66 cards . . . **500.00**
James Bond, Philadelphia Chewing Gum Co, 66 cards, 1965 . . . . **55.00**
Julia, Topps, 33 cards **550.00**
King Kong, Topps, 55 cards, 1965 . . . **20.00**
Labyrinth, Topps, 5 cards, 1986 . . . . . . **6.00**
Mad, Fleer, 128 stickers, 1983 . . . . . . **15.00**
Man From UNCLE, Topps, 55 cards, 1966 . . . . **100.00**
Monkees, Donruss, 44 cards, 1966 **30.00**
Monster Cards, Nu-Card, 84 cards **155.00**
Movie Stars, Bowman, 2¹⁄₁₆ × 1½″, 36 card set, 1948 . . . . **75.00**
My Kookie Klassmates, Fleer, 20 cards, 9 autograph stamp sheets, 1968 . . . . **15.00**
Nintendo, 60 cards, 33 stickers, 1989 **13.00**
Osmonds, Donruss, 66 cards, 1973 **30.00**
Rock Stars, Donruss, 66 cards, 1979 **2.50**
Saturday Night Fever, Donruss, 66 cards, 1978 . . . . **6.50**

Bowman, US Presidents, No 11, Martin Van Buren, 2½ × 3¾″, 1952, $2.00.

Star Trek, Leaf, 72 cards, 1967 . . . . . **550.00**
Tarzan, Philadelphia Chewing Gum Co, 66 cards, 1966 . . . . **40.00**
Terror Tales, Topps, 88 cards, 1967 **440.00**
Transformers, 225 cards, 1987 . . . . . . **17.50**
US Navy Victories, Bowman, 2½ × 3¾″, 48 card set, 1954 . . . . **50.00**
Video City, Topps, 26 cards, 4 stickers, 1983 . . . . **7.00**
Wacky Packages, Topps, 44 stickers, 1985 . . . . **9.00**
World War II, Pacific Trading Cards, 110 cards, 1992, mint **10.00**

BUSTER BROWN

R. F. Outcault could have rested on his Yellow Kid laurels. Fortunately, he did not and created a second great cartoon character—Buster Brown. The strip first appeared in the Sunday, May 4, 1902, *New York Herald.* Buster's fame was closely linked to Tige, his toothily grinning evil–looking bulldog.

Most of us remember Buster Brown and Tige because of Buster Brown Shoes. The shoe advertisements were popular on radio and television shows of the 1950s. "Look for me in there too."

Advertising Trade Card, Buster Brown, Independence Day, 1910 calendar . . . **35.00**
Bandanna, Buster, Tige, Smilen Ed, and Froggy, 1940s, unused **95.00**
Bank, 5″ h, Buster and Tige, cast iron, early 1900s **130.00**
Bike, merry–go–round horse, Buster and Tige advertisement, Hollywood Jr **295.00**
Bill Hook, Buster Brown Shoes adv **65.00**
Book, *Book of Travels,* 1912 . . . . **45.00**
Booklet, Ringen Stove adv, Buster Brown illus, c1905 . . . . **30.00**
Box, socks **20.00**
Calendar Plate, 7″ d, Buster and Tige, 1909 . . . . **48.00**
Cigar **10.00**
Clicker, Buster Brown Hosiery, red, white, and blue, 1930–1940 . . . . **22.00**
Coat Hook **28.00**
Compact, 2″ d, brass, emb logo "Buster Brown Shoes, First Because Of The Last," Buster holding shoe beside Tige, reverse with hinged door and small mirror, c1930 . . . . **65.00**
Cup and Saucer, child's, Buster pouring tea for Tige **120.00**
Dictionary, *Buster Brown Webster Selected Dictionary,* Buster Brown shoe premium **32.00**
Duffle Bag, vinyl **35.00**
Fan, framed **85.00**
Frame, 5 × 7″, good graphic decal, 1950s **30.00**
Game, Pin the Tie on Buster Brown, 24 × 48″ paper sheet, early 1900s **125.00**
Kite **35.00**
Lapel Stud, 1¼″ w, white metal, silver finish, Buster with hand on Tige's head, c1900 . . . . **40.00**
Miniature Pitcher, 3¼″ h **30.00**
Mirror, pocket, 1946 . . . . **22.00**
Periscope, Secret Agent, unused **26.00**
Pin, brass, Buster and Tige head **5.00**
Pinback Button
  ⅞″ d, Buster Brown Gang, multicolored, litho, c1920 . . . . **20.00**
  1″ d, Buster Brown Blue Ribbon Shoes, sepia, photo–like portrait of Buster and Tige, paper text on back, 1902–1910 . . . . **18.00**

Sign, Buster Brown Health Shoes, reverse painted on glass, framed, 9½ × 9¾″, $175.00.

Post Card
Buster and Tige, colorful, Tuck, 1906
...................................25.00
Buster Brown and Yellow Kid, sgd "R F
Outcault" 38.00
Rug, runner, adv, 108" l, 26½" w, Buster
and Tige illus, "For Boys, For Girls,
Buster Brown, Brown built Shoes," de-
sign repeated three times 110.00
Shoe Box, Buster Brown Shoes 15.00
Shoehorn 40.00
Sign, Buster Brown Shoes 45.00
Spice Box, Forbes Co, St Louis, allspice
..................................40.00
Stickpin, diecut, emb, name on hat, c1900
..................................50.00
Valentine, 8" h, diecut, mechanical, Buster
standing behind large walnut shell, "All
in a Nutshell, Valentine Greeting," eyes
roll when nutshell is raised, c1900
..................................20.00
Watch Fob, Buster Brown 200.00

BUTTONS, PINBACK

Around 1893 the Whitehead & Hoag Company filed the first patents for celluloid pinback buttons. By the turn of the century, the celluloid pinback button was used as a promotional tool covering a wide spectrum, ranging from presidential candidates to amusement parks, not that there is much difference between the two.

This category covers advertising pinback buttons. Presidential pinbacks can be found in the Political category. To discover the full range of non-political pinbacks consult Ted Hake and Russ King's *Price Guide To Collectible Pinback Buttons 1896–1986* (Hake's Americana & Collectibles Press: 1986).

American Boy Shoe, red, white, and blue,
1906–07 ....12.00
Aristos Flour, orange, yellow, and black,
1900–12 ....15.00
Bear Brand Hosiery, white, brown bear, red
lettering 18.00
Boston Swift Club, red, white, and blue,
dated July 17, 1926 ....15.00
Bunker Hill Salt, black, white, and red
..................................50.00
Ceresota Flour, multicolored, boy slicing
loaf of bread 50.00
Comfort Soap, 1¾" d, multicolored, portrait
of red headed child, toothy grin, blue
ground, yellow letters, 1901–10 300.00
Diamond C Hams, 1½" d, multicolored,
packaged ham from Cudahy Packing Co,
dark green ground, white rim inscription,
1900–12 ....35.00
Dottie Dimple Shoes, white, green illus
..................................18.00

Advertising Character, The People's Choice, David C. Ruler neatly inked name, Reddy Killowatt, cream, red letters, 4" d, $2.00.

Dutch Boy Paints 25.00
Eat Top–N–Och Bread, orange, blue, and
cream design, 1910 copyright 22.50
Frank Baker Bread Co, red and white, 1930s
..................................15.00
Frigidaire, 1¼" d, blue and white, Frigidaire
delivery man, refrigeration unit on shoulder, c1930 ....15.00
Gold Dust Washing Powder, multicolored,
two black children in sudsy tub, c1896
..................................55.00
Golden Glow Butter, 1¾" d, multicolored,
butter package on blue center, blue lettering on soft yellow border, early 1900s
..................................40.00
Golden Guernsey Products, gold and yellow, black inscriptions, 1930s ...12.50
Golden Sheaf Bread, multicolored .75.00
Hats Off To The New Frigidaire, red, white,
and blue, patriotic Uncle Sam design,
1930–40 ....10.00
Holsum Bakers, white and red design 18.00
Homeopathic Hospital, ⅞" d, black and
white, homeopathic nurse, c1920 15.00
IGA Booster Club, 1" d, red, white, and
blue, pink eagle logo, 1933 .....15.00
I'm For Meadow Gold, white, red and blue
print, 1930s 12.00
Interwoven Stocking Co, black, white, and
red 12.00
Iten's Quality Product, red rim, gold
"Crackers–Biscuits–Wafers–Cake and
Cookies," c1912 ....12.00
It's Cream of Rye That Makes Me Happy,
multicolored 45.00
Jockey Sweaters, oval, lime green, red illus,
1920s 20.00
John Alden Flour, green rim, white lettering,
early 1900s 25.00
Kenton Baking Powder, canister on black
ground, 1898–99 ....30.00
Lion Coffee, 1¼" d, multicolored, white rim
with black lettering, 1903 Indianapolis
celebration 20.00

Mandan Brand Top Hat Turkey, brown turkey, red wattles, black top hat, white
ground, black lettering, 1930s ...18.00
Metropolitan Life Insurance, ⅞" d, light blue
with building center, "Health & Happiness League" on yellow rim, Whitehead
& Hoag 8.00
Mr Pikle Keeps Your Weight Right, red,
white, and green, 1946 ....20.00
National Hotel Cafe, Minneapolis, cream,
red lobster image, black "I Had One Today At The National Hotel Cafe, Minneapolis" 25.00
Parrot Brand Biscuit, parrot eating cracker,
white background, black lettering, c1896
..................................18.00
Ritz Crackers 15.00
Royal Typewriter Co, silvered metal, dark
green enameled symbol, inscribed
"Royal/Accuracy First," 1930s ...10.00
Stephenson Underwear, multicolored, black
lettering 50.00
Sweet Clover Brand Condensed Milk,
1¾" d, multicolored, canned milk container with round clover design label,
pale yellow and green sun rays, early
1900s 65.00
The Best Oatmeal Is Roasted Oats, cream,
black and red logo 15.00
Topsy Doll Club 12.50
Turkey From Henry Ballard's Flock, 1½" d,
multicolored, Puritan hunter displaying
large turkey to wife and daughter, yellow rim lettering, c1925 ....50.00
Twentieth Century Sanitary System, "The
Guarantee of Pure Soda Water," red
cross in center, 1900s 25.00
We All Eat At Baines/Next To Captive Balloon, cream, full color carnation 15.00
Westinghouse Electric & Manufacturing
Company, service award, brass, blue
enameled, logo and inscription, 1930s
..................................12.50

Humor, white, black dog and saying "So What If I Ain't Good Lookin', I'm Faithful," rim marked "Made in USA," 1¾" d, $5.00.

Casio fx-451, orig box, 10" w × 7½" h, $5.00.

CALCULATORS

The Texas Instruments TI–2500 Datamath entered the market in the early 1970s. This electronic calculator, the marvel of its era, performed four functions—addition, subtraction, multiplication, and division. This is all it did. It retailed for over $100.00. Within less than a decade, calculators selling for less than $20.00 were capable of doing five times as many functions.

Early electronic calculators are dinosaurs. They deserve to be preserved. When collecting them, make certain to buy examples that retain their power transformer, instruction booklet, and original box. Make certain any calculator that you buy works. There are few around who know how to repair one.

It is a little too early for a category on home computers. But a few smart collectors are starting to stash away the early Texas Instrument and Commodore models.

Calculator, four functions **10.00**
Calculator, five or more functions **5.00**
Calculator, thirty or more functions **20.00**
Calculator, not working **0.00**
Calculator, solar-powered **3.00**

CALENDAR PLATES

Calendar plates are one of the traditional, affordable collecting categories. A few years ago, they sold in the $10.00

1911, Compliments H B Schanely, Jeweler, Quakertown, PA, calendar on horseshoe, 7" d, $40.00.

to $20.00 range; now that figure has jumped to $35.00 to $50.00.

Value rests with the decorative motif and the place for which it was issued. A fun collection would be to collect the same plate and see how many different merchants and other advertisers utilized it.

1908, harvesting scene, Lowel Fertilizer adv **28.00**
1909, Compliments T J Augustine, Gen Merchandise, Addison, PA, green transfer, gold trim, 9½" d **45.00**
1909, outdoor scenes, General Merchandise, OR, 8½" d **36.00**
1909, souvenir, Abrams, WI, flower girl, 8½" d **40.00**
1910, bust of woman, calendar months, fruit, and floral border **50.00**
1910, high school, bell border **32.00**
1910, purple and green grapes, gold trim, marked "Carnation McNicol" **35.00**
1911, Compliments of Hilding Nelson, New Britain, CT, 7½" d **30.00**
1911, Moose Lake, MN **30.00**
1912, fruits, months around rim, Woodburn, OR, 8¼" d **25.00**
1913, Quebec country scene **30.00**
1913, sweet peas, pink and lavender ground, 8¼" d **45.00**
1915, black boy eating watermelon, 9" d **35.00**
1916, eagle with shield and American flag, 8¼" d **32.00**
1919, Walnut Grove, MN, 9" d **45.00**
1920, The Great War, MO **25.00**
1922, dog watching rabbit **30.00**
1924, flowers, holly, and berries, San Francisco, 9" d **35.00**
1928, deer standing in field, 8¾" d **30.00**
1931, automobile, 8½" d **30.00**

CALENDARS

The primary reason calendars are collected is for the calendar art. Prices

hinge on quality of printing and the pizzazz of the subject. A strong advertising aspect adds to the value.

A highly overlooked calendar collecting area is the modern art and photographic calendar. For whatever reason, there is little interest in calendars dating after 1940. Collectors are making a major mistake. There are some great calendars from this later time period selling for less than $2.00.

"Gentlemen's" calendars did not grace the kitchen wall, but they are very collectible. Illustrations range from the pinup beauties of Elvgren and Moran and the *Esquire* Vargas ladies in the 1930s to the *Playboy* Playmates of the 1960s. Early *Playboy* calendars sell in the $50.00 plus range.

1892, Sing Sing Prison **75.00**
1894, Hoyt's, lady's, perfumed **10.00**
1896
    Metropolitan Life Insurance **125.00**
    Singer Sewing Machine **37.50**
1900, Hood's, full pad, two girls **45.00**
1901, miniature, Colgate, flower illus **15.00**
1903, Grecian maidens, Raphael Tuck **18.00**
1905, Grand Union Tea Co, diecut, litho **90.00**
1906, Youths Companion Minutemen **65.00**
1908
    De Laval Cream Separators, girl hugging cow **175.00**
    Fleischmann's Yeast **125.00**

Pin–Up, 1955, Esquire, January with verse about New Year's resolutions, spiral bound at top, $60.00.

1909, Bank of Waupun, emb lady ... **30.00**
1910, Chinese Student Alliance, rope
    hanger **6.00**
1913, Aunt Jemima Recipe Calendar **85.00**
1915
    Cosgroves Detective Agency, moose
        hunting scene **10.00**
    Magic Yeast, paper litho, barefoot boy
        carrying yeast and stick **225.00**
1916, Putnam Dyes **37.50**
1919, Woodrow Wilson **10.00**
1923
    State Bank of Hilbert, Indian maiden,
        diecut oval mat **20.00**
    Wrigley's Gum, desk style **40.00**
1928
    Artic Ice Machine **15.00**
    Fur Buyers, leopards **65.00**
1929, Compliments of H Buch, Butcher and
    Dealer in Fresh and Smoked Meats,
    color litho illus, full pad **30.00**
1931, Adelaide Hiebel **20.00**
1940, Columbian Rope **40.00**
1943, full color Varga art, spiral bound, orig
    envelope **100.00**
1944, Sinclair Gasoline, twelve color wild-
    life pictures **20.00**
1948, Squirt, pinup girls illus **38.00**
1961, TWA, 16 × 24", six sheet **15.00**
1965, Jayne Mansfield, 9 × 14", full color
    glossy photo **85.00**

CAMBRIDGE GLASS

The Cambridge Glass Company of Cambridge, Ohio, began operation in 1901. Its first products were clear tablewares. Later, color, etched, and engraved pieces were added to the line. Production continued until 1954. The Imperial Glass Company of Bellaire, Ohio, bought some of the Cambridge molds and continued production of these pieces.

Club: National Cambridge Collectors, Inc, PO Box 416, Cambridge, OH 43725.

Ashtray, Caprice, blue, shell **8.00**
Basket, Apple Blossom, pink **18.00**
Bonbon Plate, Diane, 8" d **12.00**
Bowl
    Diane, 11" d **35.00**
    Everglades, 12" d **50.00**
    Rosepoint, 5" d **25.00**
Butter Dish, cov, Rosepoint **200.00**
Cake Plate
    Caprice **65.00**
    Wildflower, 13½" d, handled, 3900/35
    .... **38.00**
Candlesticks, pr, Diane, Keyhole, one light
    .... **35.00**

Candy Dish, blue, gold colored metal handle, 5" w, 7⅞" l, $8.00.

Candy Dish, cov, Crown Tuscan, gold trim,
    three parts **48.00**
Champagne, Wild Flower **30.00**
Cocktail
    Diane, tall **18.00**
    Nude Stem, amber **95.00**
Cocktail Shaker, Chantilly, metal top **95.00**
Compote
    Diane **35.00**
    Elaine, Gadroon etching **58.00**
Console Bowl, Apple Blossom **19.00**
Creamer, Caprice **7.00**
Creamer and Sugar, Chantilly, sterling base
    .... **58.00**
Cruet, Deco, green **75.00**
Cup and Saucer
    Diane, scroll handle **30.00**
    Mt Vernon, set of six cups and saucers
    .... **35.00**
    Rosepoint **45.00**
    Wild Flower **20.00**
Decanter, Mosaic gold and ebony, orig han-
    dle and stopper **165.00**
Figure, 6" h, nude with shell, clear **90.00**
Flower Holder, Bashful Charlotte, 6½" h,
    figural, crystal **85.00**
Goblet, water
    Chantilly **20.00**
    Mt Vernon **9.00**
    Rosepoint **25.00**
Ice Bucket
    Diane, orig tongs **85.00**
    Gloria, pink, chrome handle **65.00**
Iced Tea, Portia **24.00**
Mayonnaise
    Caprice, blue, 2 pc set **60.00**
    Diane **30.00**
Mustard, cov, Caprice, blue **40.00**
Oil Bottle, Diane, 6 oz, orig stopper **10.00**
Pitcher, Wild Flower **95.00**
Plate
    Diane, 8½" d **11.00**
    Caprice, blue, 8½" d **38.00**
    Tally Ho, Carmen, 9½" d **28.00**
    Wild Flower, 10½" d **40.00**
Platter, Decagon, light blue **40.00**
Relish
    Diane, 6½" d, three parts **20.00**
    Elaine, 9" l, three parts, 3900/125 **34.00**
    Everglades, three parts **45.00**

Salt and Pepper Shakers, pr
    Apple Blossom **30.00**
    Diane **30.00**
Sherbet
    Caprice, blue, 3¼" d **30.00**
    Diane, amber, tall **20.00**
    Elaine **17.50**
Sugar
    Caprice, blue **17.50**
    Wild Flower **14.00**
Swan, Crown Tuscan, 3½" h **35.00**
Torte Plate, Diane, 14⅝" d **45.00**
Tumbler, Cascade, 3⅞" h **8.50**
Water, Diane, 11 oz **20.00**

CAMEOS

Cameos are one form of jewelry that has never lost its popularity. They have been made basically the same way for centuries. Most cameos are dated by their settings, although this is risky since historic settings can be duplicated very easily.

Normally one thinks of a cameo as carved from a piece of conch shell. However, the term cameo means a gem carved in relief. You can find cameos carved from gemstones and lava. Lava cameos are especially desirable.

Beware of plastic and other forms of copycat and fake cameos. Look carefully at the side. If you spot layers, shy away. A real cameo is carved from a single piece.

Your best defense when buying a cameo is to buy from a dealer who you can find later and then have the authenticity of the cameo checked by a local retail jeweler. Do not use another antiques jewelry dealer.

Bracelet
    Carved lava, various color panels, Victo-
        rian 14K yg mounting **1,300.00**
    Shell, cuff style, gold wash over silver,
        c1900 .... **275.00**
Brooch, woman, head and shoulders
    Flowers in hair, Victorian carved agate,
        gold knife edge and beadwork frame,
        18K yg setting **800.00**
    Grapevine and leaves entwined in hair,
        14K yg setting **300.00**
    Shell, 14K gold, gypsy setting, c1920
    .... **150.00**
Button, pearl, carved cameo and lily of the
    valley dec **10.00**
Compact, onyx cameo, marcasite ring, yel-
    low guilloche enamel **400.00**
Earrings, hobe shell, rhinestones, smoked
    crystals **45.00**
Hair Ribbon Holder, dated 1913 .... **12.50**
Necklace, hard stone, silver filigree chain
    with jet beads, marked "Czech" **65.00**

Brooch, Victorian, Persephone motif, oval gold frame, artist sgd, $1,800.00.

Pendant
    Bakelite, sterling chain **28.00**
    Plastic, molded, plastic link chain,
      c1920 .... **85.00**
Ring, lady's, 14K yg **30.00**
Stickpin, carved opal, gold frame, rubies
    and diamonds highlights, 14K yg setting,
    marked "Tiffany & Co" **650.00**

CAMERAS

Just because a camera is old does not mean that it is valuable. Rather, assume that the more examples of a camera that were made the less likely it is to be valuable. Collectors are after unusual cameras or examples from companies that failed quickly.

A portion of a camera's value rests on how it works. Check all bellow cameras by shining a strong light over the outside surface while looking at the inside. Check the seating on removable lenses.

It is only recently that collectors have begun to focus in on the 35mm camera. You can still build a collection of early models at a modest cost per camera.

There is a growing market in camera accessories and ephemera. A camera has minimal value if you do not know how it works. Whenever possible, insist on the original instruction booklet as part of the purchase.

Clubs: National Stereoscopic Association, PO Box 14801, Columbus, OH 43214; The Photographic Historical Society, Inc, PO Box 39563, Rochester, NY 14604.

Argus, Argoflex EM, metal body, 1948
    .... **25.00**
Blair Camera Company, Hawk–Eye Junior,
    box, 1895–1900 .... **75.00**
Brownie Jr, 6–20 .... **38.00**

Canon, Dial 35, 35mm, 1963–1967 **50.00**
Character
    Charlie Tuna, figural, 126 ...... **75.00**
    Dick Tracy, 3 × 5", plastic, black,
      Seymore Products, Chicago ... **45.00**
    Hopalong Cassidy **125.00**
    Mickey Mouse, 3 × 3 × 5", plastic,
      black, red plastic straps, uses 127
      film, early 1960s **50.00**
    Roy Rogers and Trigger, 3 × 3¼ ×
      3¼", plastic, black, metal flash at-
      tachment, vinyl carrying strap, Her-
      bert George Company, Chicago,
      1940–1950 .... **100.00**
Cinex Candid Camera, 50mm, bakelite
    .... **23.00**
Conley Camera Company, Kewpie No. 2A,
    box **15.00**
Eastman Kodak Company
    Brownie, Flash IV, box, tan cov, match-
      ing canvas case, 1957–1959
      .... **28.00**
    Buckeye Camera, folding, wood, leather
      cov, c1899 .... **125.00**
    Camp Fire Girls Kodak, folding, Camp
      Fire Girls emblem on front door,
      matching case, 1931–1934
      .... **375.00**
    Duex Camera, helical telescoping front,
      doublet lens, 620 film, 1940–1942
      .... **15.00**
Goerz, Coat Pocket Tenax, 6½ × 9cm,
    1912–25 .... **60.00**
Minolta, 24 Rapid 24 × 24mm, 35mm
    range finder, built–in meter **80.00**
Minox, EC, Point & Shoot, plastic, black
    .... **90.00**
Multiple Toymakers, plastic frame, 127 film,
    orig box, c1973, unassembled ... **15.00**
Olympus, Flex A3.5, 1954–1956 .... **85.00**
Polaroid, Pathfinder 110A, 1957–1960
    .... **50.00**

Sears Roebuck and Co, Tower One Twenty, box, leather strap, 1950s, 2⅞" w, 4⅛" d, 3⅞" h, $8.00.

Book, Kodak Graphic Arts Handbook, $15.00.

Ricoh, 35 Deluxe Rangefinder, c1956
    .... **65.00**
Sanrio Co Ltd, Hello Kitty, 110 film, plastic,
    Japan, c1981 .... **55.00**
Sears, Marvel–flex, c1941 .... **25.00**
Stewart Warner, Hollywood model, movie
    .... **23.00**
Universal
    Roamer I, folding, eight exposures,
      c1948 .... **12.00**
    Uniflash, plastic, Vitar f16/60mm lens,
      orig flash and box, c1940 .... **20.00**
Voigtlander Compur, light meter **23.00**
Yashica
    Atoron Electro, 8 × 11mm, black finish,
      case, flash, filters, and presentation
      box, c1970 .... **50.00**
    Yashimaflex, 6 × 6cm, TLR, c1953
      .... **175.00**

CANDLEWICK

Imperial Glass Corporation issued its No. 400 pattern, Candlewick, in 1936 and continued to produce it until 1982. In 1985 the Candlewick molds were dispersed to a number of sources, e.g., Boyd Crystal Art Glass, through sale.

Over 650 items and sets are known. Shapes include round, oval, oblong, heart, and square. The largest assortment of pieces and sets were made during the late 1940s and early 1950s.

For a list of reproduction Candlewick pieces check the Candlewick category in *Warman's Americana and Collectibles.*

Creamer and sugar, $15.00.

Newsletter: *The National Candlewick Collector Newsletter,* 275 Milledge Terrace, Athens, GA 30606.

Ashtray, 4" l, rect **5.00**
Basket, beaded handle **275.00**
Bowl
    4½" d, two handles **12.00**
    5" d **12.00**
    6" sq **75.00**
    7" d, handle **12.00**
    8½" d, handle **24.50**
    11" d, float **35.00**
Brandy Snifter **135.00**
Butter Dish, cov, quarter pound **25.00**
Cake Stand **58.00**
Canape Set **18.00**
Candleholder
    Flower, 5" h, pr **60.00**
    Mushroom **25.00**
Candy, cov, 7" d **95.00**
Celery Tray, 11" l, oval **55.00**
Champagne **15.00**
Cheese and Cracker Set **45.00**
Cigarette Set, 6 pc **40.00**
Coaster, round **4.00**
Coffee Cup **6.50**
Compote, 5½" d, four beaded stem **18.00**
Condiment Set, 4 pcs **65.00**
Creamer and Sugar, 8 oz, beaded foot
    .... **30.00**
Cream Soup **40.00**
Cup and Saucer, beaded handle cup, 5½" d
    saucer **8.50**
Demitasse Cup and Saucer **22.00**
Deviled Egg Plate **110.00**
Dish
    5" w, heart, handle **18.50**
    10" d **25.00**
Fruit Bowl, 5" d **9.00**
Goblet, 10 oz **18.00**
Iced Tea Tumbler, 12 oz **48.00**
Juice Tumbler **10.00**
Lemon Dish **35.00**
Marmalade, 4 pc set, orig label **30.00**
Mayonnaise, 2 pc set **25.00**
Nappy, 4¾" d, two handles, orig label **8.50**
Parfait, 6 oz **45.00**
Pitcher, 80 oz **100.00**

Plate
    6" d **6.00**
    7" d, indent **15.00**
    8" d **12.50**
    9" d **15.00**
    10" d **40.00**
Platter, 13" l, oval **70.00**
Relish
    6½" d, 2 part **10.00**
    13" d, 5 part, handled **60.00**
Salad Fork and Spoon **30.00**
Salt and Pepper Shakers, pr, bulbous,
    beaded foot, plastic tops **22.00**
Sandwich Plate, 12½" d, center handle
    .... **18.00**
Saucer **6.00**
Seafood Cocktails, 3½ oz, set of 6 ... **30.00**
Sherbet, low **14.00**
Sugar, cov, 3¼" d **8.00**
Tea Cup **6.50**
Tidbit, two tiers **60.00**
Tray, 10" d **40.00**
Tumbler
    10 oz **11.00**
    12 oz **14.00**
Vase
    4" h, bud **35.00**
    7" h **45.00**
    8" h, fan, beaded handles ... **28.00**
Wafer Tray **22.00**

CANDY COLLECTIBLES

Who doesn't love some form of candy? Forget the chocoholics. I'm a Juicy Fruit man.

Once you start looking for candy-related material, you are quickly overwhelmed by how much is available. Do not forget the boxes. They are usually discarded. Ask your local drugstore or candy shop to save the more decorative ones for you. What is free today may be worth money tomorrow.

Advertising Trade Card
    Monarch Teenie Weenie Toffies
    .... **15.00**

Wilbur's Chocolate & Cocoa, diecut,
    boy and girl, multicolored front and
    back, c1890 .... **20.00**
Bank, 12" h, Tootsie Roll, cylinder, card-
    board and tin, 1960s **12.00**
Bonbon Tongs, candy store, tin **4.00**
Box
    Milky Way, 24 5¢ bars **6.00**
    Old Nick Candy Bars **7.00**
Candy Bar Mold, Clark Bar, multiple open-
    ings **15.00**
Candy Bucket, green glass, hammered alu-
    minum handle **12.00**
Candy Container
    Chicken, round base **150.00**
    George Washington, composition **95.00**
    Hat, milk glass, tin brim **60.00**
    Pelican, papier mache **58.00**
    Rabbit, seated, white, carrot in mouth,
        Germany **40.00**
    Santa Claus, 8½" h, paper and composi-
        tion, red velvet accents, cone hat
        .... **150.00**
    Suitcase, glass, tin closure, wire handle
        .... **55.00**
Candy Scale, large scoop, 1877 .... **225.00**
Candy Wrapper, Home Run Candy, base-
    ball game illus, 1936 .... **45.00**
Catalog, Savage Bros Candy Machinery &
    Copper Work, early 1900s, 144 pgs
    .... **60.00**
Change Receiver, Teaberry Gum **75.00**
Display, Whitman's Chocolates, wood,
    painted, movable hand, blue dress,
    c1930 .... **120.00**
Display Rack, Beech-Nut Beechies, metal,
    two shelves **20.00**

Candy Container, glass, man, plaid jacket, black plastic hat, 3⅜" h, $20.00.

Puzzle, Baby Ruth, Curtiss Candy Co, Chicago, IL, 1930s, 45 diecut cardboard pieces, reverse with array of Curtiss products, J F Kernan, artist, 5½ × 7½", $35.00.

Display Stand, Clark's Teaberry Gum, vaseline glass **75.00**
Eraser, Hershey's miniature candy wrapper, mint **10.00**
Game, Tootsie Roll Train Game, Hasbro, orig box, 1962–63 . . . . **18.00**
Giveaway, Zatek Chocolate, Indian girl, cutout, multicolored, 1918, uncut . . . **20.00**
Gum Wrapper, Wrigley's, yellow, purple, and gold **10.00**
Hammer, 3½" l, Seeds Candies adv **20.00**
Jar, Kiss Me Gum **85.00**
Mirror, Stacey Chocolates, sunset over water scene **35.00**
Pennant, Jacob's Chocolates, "Made Last Night," felt, 14 × 33" **35.00**
Pinback Button
    Baker's Chocolate, oval, pretty lady **30.00**
    McDonald's Merry Widow Chocolates, 1¼" d, lady wearing exaggerated feather hat, pr of well-dressed suitors, black and white, light blue accents, 1900–1912 . . . . **30.00**
    Sommer-Richardson's Candies, 1" d, red "Red Cross" logo, white ground, blue letters, early 1900s **15.00**
    Zig Zag Modern Confection, 1¼" d, multicolored, 1903–1905 . . . . **50.00**
Ruler, Clark Bars, wood **6.00**
Sign
    Kibber's Candies, 9 × 8", brass **50.00**
    Ox Heart Chocolate, tin **75.00**
    Sweet Maris Gum, diecut **45.00**
Tape Dispenser, Baby Ruth **25.00**
Teddy Bear, Hershey's Chocolate, holding silver Kiss, dark brown **28.00**
Tin
    Fireside Gems Candy, 8" d, round, girl sitting on bench **10.00**
    Mellow-mint, 3¾" d **10.00**
    Orange Mellow-mints **15.00**
    Up To Date Pure Candy, 5 lb, 5" d, tropic scene, orange lettering, 1920–50 . . . . **15.00**
Tray, Teaberry & Beech-Nut Gum, glass, green, decals **38.00**

CAP PISTOLS

Classic collectors collect the one-shot, cast iron pistols manufactured during the first third of the twentieth century. Kids of the 1950s collect roll cap pistols. Children of the 1990s do not know what they are missing.

Prices for roll cap pistols are skyrocketing. Buy them only if they are in working order. Ideally, acquire them with their appropriate accessories, e.g., holsters, fake bullets, etc.

Club: Toy Gun Purveyors, Box 243, Burke, VA 22015.

Newsletter: *Toy Gun Collectors of America Newsletter,* 312 Starling Way, Anaheim, CA 92807.

Buck 'N Bronc, 10" l, pr, silvered metal, dark bronze plastic grips, tan leather holster with silvered metal rivets and disks, George Schmidt Co **100.00**
Cowboy King, 9" l, pr, silvered cast iron, ivory plastic grips with red inset glass stone, one with raised Indian image, other with cowboy, "Cowboy King" inscription **100.00**
Dent, Villa, cast iron, 4¾" l, 1934 . . . **60.00**
Gene Autry, 9" l, metal, gold finish, ivory plastic grips, raised images dec **150.00**
Halco, The Texan, 9½" l, pr, silver, ivory grained grips, holster, orig box, 1950s **125.00**
Hubley
    Cap Firing Colt Detective Special, 4" l, 1958 . . . . **60.00**
    Cap Firing Flintlock, 9" l, 1950s **45.00**
    Dagger Derringer, 7" l, double barrel, silvered metal, black plastic grips, 1960s **50.00**
    Golden Agent, 6" l, metal, gold finish, holster, 1950s **50.00**
    Pirate, die cast zinc, 9⅜" l, 1941 **50.00**
    Ric-O-Shay, 12" l, silvered metal, black plastic grips, late 1950s **55.00**
    Trooper, 5⅛" l, 1938 . . . . **50.00**
    Western, 9" l, silvered metal, white plastic grips, raised steer head image, unused **45.00**
    Zip, cast iron, 5" l, 1930 **45.00**
James Bond, 100 Shot Repeater, Lone Star, 1965 . . . . **200.00**
Kenton, Dixie, 6¼" l, 1935 . . . . **60.00**
Kilgore
    American, cast iron, 9⅝" l, 1940 **120.00**
    Border Patrol, 4¼" l, 1935 . . . . . **40.00**
    Hi-Ho, cast iron, 6½" l, 1940 . . . **50.00**
    Kit Carson, 9½" l, silvered metal, black plastic grips, raised portrait image, orig box **75.00**
    Rotor Fifty, 6⅛" l, 1930 . . . . **70.00**

Lone Ranger, 10" l, silvered metal, grained white plastic grips, black leather holsters with silvered metal dec with inset red plastic stones, orig box, Esquire Novelty Co, 1947 . . . . **375.00**
Marshal, 10½" l, silvered metal, ivory plastic grips, white plastic belt with six bullets, 1960s **75.00**
Mattel
    Fanner 50, 11" l, metal, chrome finish, white plastic grips, raised image, late 1950s **55.00**
    Tommy Burb, 24" l, 1950s **45.00**
National, Bunker Hill, 5¼" l, 1925 **55.00**
Nicholas Stallion, 38 six-shooter, orig box **195.00**
Pony Boy, two guns in double holster **30.00**
Roy Rogers
    2½" l, gold finish metal, "RR" symbol on each grip, black leather holster, 1950s **50.00**
    8½" l, silvered metal, metal inset grips with raised Roy on Trigger image, "RR" symbol with red accent, unused **100.00**
Stevens
    Bang-O Cast Iron Cap Pistol, 7" l, 1938 . . . . **40.00**
    Buffalo Bill, cast iron, orig box **165.00**
Texan
    Cast Iron, orig box **135.00**
    Junior **30.00**
Texas Ranger gun and holster set **125.00**
Westerner, 9½" l, gray luster finish, ivory plastic grips **25.00**

CAPTAIN ACTION

This 12" tall fully poseable action figure was made by the Ideal Toy Company from 1966 to 1968. Captain Action had thirteen costume sets, numerous accessories, a youthful counterpart, Action Boy, and an evil villain, Dr. Evil.

A number of the Captain Action costume sets were used to transform Captain Action into a different super hero such as DC Comics' Superman, Batman, or Aquaman and Marvel Comics' Spiderman, Captain America, or Sergeant Fury.

Club: Captain Action Collectors Club, PO Box 2095, Halesite, NY 11743.

Action Figure, 12" h
    Action Boy, first issue, 3420, 1967 . . . . **800.00**
    Captain Action
        First Issue **500.00**
        Second Issue, 3400, 1967 . . . **600.00**
        Dr Evil, photo box **800.00**

Action Figure Accessories
   Action Cave Carrying Case **500.00**
   Anti–Gravitational Power Pack, 3455
      .... **300.00**
   Dr Evil Sanctuary **700.00**
   Inter–Galactic Jet Mortar, 3452 **300.00**
   Inter–Spacial Directional Communicator,
      3454 .... **300.00**
   Parachute Set, 4", 3453 .... **300.00**
   Quick Change Chamber, Sears
      .... **750.00**
   Silver Streak Car **1,200.00**
   Silver Streak Garage, hide-out, Sears ex-
      clusive **1,500.00**
   Survival Kit, 20 pcs, 3450 ...... **350.00**
   Weapons Arsenal, 10 pcs, 3451 **300.00**
Action Figure Outfit
   Aqualad, Action Boy outfit, Octo the
      Octopus, 3423, 1967 .... **600.00**
   Aquaman, 1966 .... **400.00**
   Batman, 1966 .... **500.00**
   Buck Rogers, videomatic ring, 3416,
      1967 .... **1,600.00**
   Captain America, 1966 .... **400.00**
   Flash Gordon, 1966 .... **475.00**
   Lone Ranger, blue shirt with ring, 3406,
      1967 .... **900.00**
   Phantom, 1966 .... **450.00**
   Robin, Action Boy outfit, 3421, 1967
      .... **750.00**
   Steve Canyon, videomatic ring, 3405,
      1967 ....~......... **350.00**
   Superboy, Action Boy outfit, 3422, 1967
      .... **700.00**
   Superman, videomatic ring, 3401, 1967
      .... **700.00**
Costume **150.00**
Model Kit, Aurora **150.00**

CAPTAIN AMERICA

Stars and Stripes Forever, as America's Super Hero helps preserve the American way from the onslaught of super villains.

Captain America was created in March 1941, by Marvel Comics' artists Jack Kirby and Joe Simon. He became one of the leading manifestations of American patriotism during World War II. With his sidekick, Bucky, Captain America fought Nazis and "Japs" on all fronts.

Action Figure
   Just Toys, Marvel Super Heroes Bend–
      em, 12062, 1991 .... **6.00**
   Lakeside, bendie **120.00**
   Marx, 6" h, plastic, 1966 .... **15.00**
   Mego
      8" h, orig box, 1974 .... **175.00**
      12½" h, flyaway action, 1979 **125.00**
   Remco, 9" h, energized **60.00**
   Transogram, flying figure **70.00**
Badge, Sentinels of Liberty **325.00**

Coloring Book, Whitman, 1966 ..... **35.00**
Comic Book
   100, Avengers appearance, Jack Kirby,
      1968 .... **275.00**
   117, introduction of Falcon, Gene Colan
      and Joe Sinnott **12.00**
   138, Spider–Man appearance, John
      Romita **10.00**
   241, Punisher appearance **65.00**
   264, X–Men, pencils by Mike Zeck
      .... **3.00**
   332, Rogers resignation, Bop McLeod
      .... **12.00**
   383, 50th anniversary, Jim Lee and Ron
      Lim, 64 pgs **4.00**
   384, Jack Frost appearance, Ron Lim
      .... **1.00**
Costume Accessory Playset, Toy Biz, 1991
   .... **15.00**
Iron–On Transfer, Kirby Art, unused, 1960s
   .... **10.00**
Jigsaw Puzzle, Whitman, attacking Zombies
   illus, 14 × 18" orig box, 1976 ... **20.00**
Pennant, 6½" l, vinyl sleeve over cardboard,
   Marvel Comics, 1966 .... **15.00**
Pez Dispenser, 4" h, plastic, blue body and
   helmet, white wings, marked "Made in
   Austria," 1978 .... **50.00**
Vehicle
   Captain Americar, fits 8" figure, Mego
      .... **225.00**
   Jetmobile, Corgi **30.00**
   Rocket Racer, Buddy–L, Secret Wars, re-
      mote controlled, battery operated,
      1984 .... **40.00**
   Turbo Coupe, Toy Biz, 1990 ..... **15.00**

CARNIVAL CHALKWARE

Carnival chalkware is my candidate for the kitsch collectible of the 1990s. No one uses *quality* to describe these inexpensive prizes given out by games of chance at carnivals, amusement parks, and ocean boardwalks.

The best pieces are those depicting a specific individual or character. Since most were bootlegged (made without permission), they often appear with a fictitious name, e.g., "Smile Doll" is really supposed to be Shirley Temple. The other strong collecting subcategory is animal figures. As long as the object comes close to capturing the appearance of a pet, collectors buy.

Figure
   Betty Boop, 15" h, painted, 1930s
      .... **150.00**
   Drum Majorette, 16" h **30.00**
   Gorilla, 14" h **40.00**
   Indian Brave, 19" h **40.00**

Kewpie, 7" h, sitting with elbows on
   knees and hands under chin, painted,
   1930s **30.00**
King Kong, 6¼" h, 1940s **18.00**
Kitten, 7" h, with ball of yarn, 1930–
   1945 .... **8.00**
Lion, 8 × 9", 1940–1950 .... **20.00**
Mae West, 13" h, 1934 .... **65.00**
Majorette, 12" h, marked "El Segundo
   Novelty Co," 1949 .... **25.00**
Mickey Mouse, 8½" h, 1930–35 **75.00**
Parrot, 13½" h, 1935–1945 ..... **35.00**
Paul Revere, 14½" h, 1935–1945 **25.00**
Pinocchio, 16" h, 1950 .... **75.00**
Popeye, 9¾" h, 1929–1950 ..... **35.00**
Sailor Girl, 14" h, 1925–1935 ... **70.00**
Scottie Dog, 5½" h, 1935–1945
   .... **10.00**
Snuffy Smith, 9¼" h, 1934–1945 **65.00**
Superman, 15" h, painted, 1940s
   .... **150.00**
Windmill, 10¾" h, 1935–1940 ... **20.00**
String Holder, 9" h, figural, Indian head,
   1935–1945 .... **60.00**

CARTOON COLLECTIBLES

This is a category with something for each generation. The characters represented here enjoyed a life in comic books and newspaper pages. Many also had a second career on movie screens and television.

Every collector has a favorite. Buy examples that bring back pleasant memories. "That's All Folks."

Badge, Dick Tracy Secret Service, silver fin-
   ish, 1930s **60.00**
Ball, juggler, Popeye, litho tin, 1929 **55.00**
Bank
   Betty Boop **30.00**
   Casper, glow in the dark, 1967 ... **75.00**
   Krazy Kat, graduation outfit **55.00**
   Popeye, plaster, King Features Syndicate
      .... **200.00**
   Speedy Gonzales **25.00**
Barrette, Li'l Abner, 2⅛" l, oval, brass, die-
   cut, 1940s **18.00**
Beach Ball, Popeye, MIP **18.00**
Book
   Mighty Mouse, Santa's Helper, Treasure
      Book, 1955 .... **25.00**
   Woody Woodpecker's Peck of Trouble,
      Whitman, 1951 .... **5.00**
Breakfast Set, Woody Woodpecker, mug
   and log shape cereal bowl, F & F Mold
   Co **50.00**
Bubble Making Set, Popeye, 1936, MIB
   .... **38.00**
Candy Bar Wrapper, Dick Tracy, color pic-
   ture, premium offer, 1950s **10.00**
Card Game, Popeye, 1934, MIB **28.00**

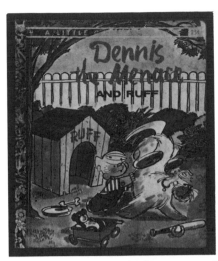

Little Golden Book, Dennis The Menace and Ruff, *$6.50.*

Chalk, Popeye, white and colored pieces, unused, 1953, MIB **24.00**

Charm, Popeye, 1¼" w, celluloid, brass loop, orange, pink, black, and green, Japan, 1930s **20.00**

Christmas Light Set, Betty Boop **55.00**

Christmas Ornament, Garfield, round, 1981, orig box **9.00**

Clicker, Felix the Cat, litho tin, Germany, 1929 . . . . **25.00**

Clock
    Betty Boop, alarm, animated, boxed **45.00**
    Popeye, animated, revolving Sweetpea, Smith, England, 1960s **225.00**
    Woody Woodpecker, animated, 1960s **145.00**

Coloring Book
    Blondie, 8½ × 11", 1954, Dell Publishing, unused **20.00**
    Bugs Bunny and Porky Pig, 1946 **65.00**

Cookie Jar
    Casper the Ghost **850.00**
    Popeye, Vandor **450.00**
    Yogi Bear, felt tongue **195.00**

Dish, Pink Panther, plastic, three sections **30.00**

Doll
    Barney Google, Snuffy Smith, 17" h, stuffed, felt, movable head, amber and black eyes, 1930s **150.00**
    George Jetson, 12" h, cloth **19.00**
    Little Lulu, 15" h, stuffed cloth, black felt and yarn hair, Western outfit, 1940s **80.00**
    Mr Magoo, no shoes, 1962 . . . . . . **65.00**

Dollmaker Kit, Little Lulu, Whitman **14.00**

Egg Carton, Felix **60.00**

Figure
    Barney Google, Syroco, sailor suit **75.00**
    Elmer Fudd, hiding behind tree, Shaw **95.00**
    Huckleberry Hound, ceramic **55.00**

Scooby Doo, 7" h, hard plastic, orange, black accents, movable tail and head, 1970s copyright **50.00**
Speedy Gonzales, 1970 . . . . **22.00**
Tweety Bird **15.00**

Game
    Dino The Dinosaur Game, Transogram, 1961 copyright **50.00**
    Harold Teen, spinner and orig tokens, boxed, 1930s **15.00**
    Huckleberry Hound Bumps **38.00**
    Popeye Ring Toss, MIB **65.00**
    Popeye Tiddly Winks, MIB **275.00**
    Quick Draw McGraw Private Eye, Milton Bradley, 1960 . . . . **40.00**

Greeting Card, Popeye, Christmas, 1951, unused **12.00**

Handkerchief, Foxy Grandpa, 1920 **40.00**

Ice Cream Mold, Yellow Kid, 4¾" h, full figure, hinged **185.00**

Key Chain, Winnie Winkle, characters on each side, 1940s **15.00**

Lunch Box
    Bullwinkle and Rocky, steel, Jay Ward Productions copyright, Universal, c1962 . . . . **200.00**
    Joe Palooka, litho tin, 1948 . . . . . . **45.00**
    Underdog **300.00**

Magic Tracer Set, Yogi & Friends, orig box, Milton Bradley, 1962 copyright **75.00**

Mug
    Betty Boop **22.00**
    Popeye **25.00**

Music Box
    Bambi and Thumper **45.00**
    Betty Boop **45.00**
    Wimpy, on hamburger **55.00**

Napkins, paper, Popeye, 1978, MIP . . . **7.00**

Necktie, 10½" l, Bugs Bunny, clip-on, c1940 . . . . **50.00**

Nodder
    Moon Mullins, 3⅞" h, bisque, Germany **60.00**
    Smitty, bisque **85.00**

Paint Book, Blondie and Dagwood, 1940 . . . . **12.00**

Pegboard, Popeye, orig box, 1934 . . . **35.00**

Pencil, mechanical, Popeye, Eagle brand, oversized, 1929, MIB **35.00**

Pencil Sharpener, Popeye, tin, dated 1929 . . . . **95.00**

Plaque, 7" h, Andy Panda, ceramic, figural, marked "Napco Ceramics," 1958 **55.00**

Poster, 27 × 41", Hey There, It's Yogi Bear, full color, Hanna-Barbera, Columbia Pictures, 1964 . . . . **75.00**

Record, Deputy Dawg, 78 rpm, full color glossy envelope, Peter Pan Records, 1962 Terrytoons copyright **20.00**

Salt and Pepper Shakers, pr
    Maggie and Jiggs, 2½" h, figural, marked "Made In Japan," 1930s **65.00**
    Popeye and Olive Oyl, Vandor . . . **35.00**

Sandwich Bag, Dagwood, waxed paper, large Bumstead image, 1952 . . . . . **25.00**

Thermos, Casper the Friendly Ghost, metal **60.00**

Toothbrush Holder, Skippy, bisque, jointed arm, painted **75.00**

Toy
    Jetsons, Turnover Tank, windup, litho tin, marked "Made in China," c1970 . . . . **300.00**
    Magilla Gorilla, inflatable, vinyl, orig TV Cartoon Blow-Ups card **25.00**

Popeye
    Barrel Walker, windup, litho tin, Chein, 1930s **375.00**
    Sand See-Saw, litho tin, Chein, 1940s **145.00**
    Sparkler, Chein, 1956, MIB **400.00**
    Spinach Can, tin, pop-up head **95.00**
    Porky Pig, 5½" h, rubber, marked "Sun Rubber Co" **45.00**

Tray, Popeye, tin, 1980 . . . . **14.00**

CASH REGISTERS

If you want to buy a cash register, you had better be prepared to put plenty of money in the till. Most are bought for decorative purposes. Serious collectors would go broke in a big hurry if they had to pay the prices listed below for every machine they buy.

Beware of modern reproductions. Cash registers were meant to be used. Signs of use should be present. There is also a tendency to restore machines to their original appearance through re-plating and rebuilding. Well and good. But when all is said and done, how do you tell the refurbished machine from a modern reproduction? When you cannot, it is hard to sustain long-term value.

Improved Sun, No 10, oak, transparent celluloid keys, change drawer with six coin and three bill compartments **300.00**

McCaskey, oak, orig decal, metal account files, two drawers, refinished, 23 × 23 × 27" **150.00**

Michigan #1, twenty-two keys **200.00**

National
    Model 4, brass, candy store type **900.00**
    Model 7, brass, detailed design **325.00**
    Model 311, brass **650.00**
    Model 317, marble change shelf, printer, 5¢ to $1.00, 16" h **1,200.00**
    Model 321, brass, extended base, 17¼ × 17 × 16", 1916 . . . . **650.00**
    Model 342, brass, crank operated, drawer, 24" h **600.00**
    Model 349, two drawers, 1910 **800.00**
    Model 421, crank-operated, oak cash drawer, receipt machine on side, 23" h **650.00**
    Model 552-5, brass, oak base **450.00**

NCR, Model 3, wood, light color, carved
  wildflower dec, drawer **725.00**
Peninsula, Muren, nickel plated, c1912
  . . . .**250.00**

CASSETTE TAPES

Flea markets thrive on two types of
goods—those that are collectible and
those that serve a secondhand function.
Cassette tapes fall into the latter group.
Buy them for the purpose of playing
them.

The one exception is when the promotional pamphlet covering the tape
shows a famous singer or group. In this
case, you are really buying the piece of
paper ephemera more than the tape, but
you might as well have the whole shooting match.

Several times within recent years
there have been a number of articles in
the trade papers about collecting eight–
tracks. When was the last time you saw
an eight–track machine? They are going
to be as popular in thirty years as the wire
tape recorder is today. Interesting idea—
too bad it bombed.

Average price . . . . **50¢ to $2.00**

CAST IRON

This is a category where you should
be suspicious that virtually everything
you see is a reproduction or copycat.
More often than not, the object will not
be original. They are even reproducing
cast iron frying pans.

One of the keys to spotting the
newer material is the rust. If it is orange
in color and consists of small pinpoint
flakes, forget it. Also check paint patina.
It should have a mellow tone from years
of exposure to air. Bright paint should be
suspect.

Cast iron is a favorite of the country
collector. It evokes memories of the great
open kitchen fireplaces and wood/coal
burning stoves of our ancestors. Unfortunately, few discover what a great cooking utensil cast iron can really be.

Periodicals: *Cast Iron Cookware News,*
28 Angela Ave, San Anselmo, CA 94960;
*Griswold Cast Iron Collectors News &
Marketplace,* PO Box 521, North East,
PA 16428; *Kettles 'n Cookware,* PO Box
B, Perrysburg, NY 14129.

Airplane, 4" wingspan, orig paint **65.00**

*Boot Scraper, harp, fluted base, painted
black, 7¹⁄₂" h, $28.00.*

Bottle Opener
  3⁵⁄₈" l, donkey, polychrome traces **65.00**
  5¹⁄₂" l, cockatoo on perch, polychrome
    dec **75.00**
Cake Mold, 8¹⁄₂ × 14 × 5", lamb, two part
  . . . .**140.00**
Cigarette Dispenser, 8¹⁄₂" l, elephant, bronze
  repaint **30.00**
Dipper, 12" l, swivel lid, wrought handle
  . . . . **85.00**
Door Knocker
  Basket of flowers
    2¹⁄₂" l, painted **70.00**
    3³⁄₄" l, orig polychrome paint **30.00**
  Parrot **65.00**
Fence, 43" h, 70" l, four sections, old green
  paint **240.00**
Figure, 3¹⁄₂" l, whale, painted **20.00**
Fire Alarm Box, "Chicago" on back, miss-
  ing int. and front door **75.00**
Garden Urn, 28¹⁄₂" h, removable ears, white
  repaint **290.00**
Hitching Post, 62¹⁄₂" h, tree form, branch
  stubs, marked "Patent" **100.00**
Kettle, 5" d, caldron style, three short legs
  . . . . **75.00**
Lawn Ornament, jockey, polychrome re-
  paint **100.00**
Lock, 4¹⁄₄ × 7", box type **40.00**
Match Holder, boot shape **65.00**
Shooting Gallery Target, 4¹⁄₄" l, bird   **40.00**
Skillet, 9³⁄₄" d, three short feet, 9¹⁄₄" l handle
  . . . . **35.00**
Spittoon, 5¹⁄₂" h, 8¹⁄₂" d, white porcelain int,
  c1850 . . . . **45.00**
String Holder, beehive shape **70.00**

CAT COLLECTIBLES

It is hard to think of a collecting
category that does not have one or more
cat–related items in it. Chessie the Cat is
railroad oriented; Felix is a cartoon,
comic, and toy collectible. There rests

the problem. The poor cat collector is
always competing with an outside collector for a favorite cat item.

Cat collectors are apparently as
stubborn as their pets because I have
never seen a small cat collectibles collection. One additional thing that I have
noticed is that, unlike most dog collectibles collectors, cat collectors are more
willing to collect objects portraying other
breeds of cats than the one that they
own.

Club: Cat Collectors, 33161 Wendy
Drive, Sterling Heights, MI 48310.

Advertising Trade Card
  Carter's Little Liver Pills, four striped cats
    playing with yarn, Mayer, Merkell &
    Ottmann Litho **5.00**
  Choose Black Cat Reinforced Hosiery,
    multicolored diecut **15.00**
  Clarks Mile End Spool Cotton, cat walk-
    ing over spool, calendar on back,
    1881 . . . .**10.00**
Ashtray
  4" d, black cat face, bow, #16 Shafford,
    1953 . . . .**20.00**
  5" l, ceramic, brown crouching cat, front
    paws extended, marked "Made in
    China" **20.00**
Bank, Lucifer The Cat, musical, Schmid
  . . . . **35.00**
Bottle, glass, clear, blue bow, painted facial
  features, marked "Smiley" **48.00**
Calendar, wall, three parts, several peeking
  cat faces, titled "Little Mischief," Tuck,
  1903 . . . . **25.00**
Children's Book
  Adventure's of Mrs. Tabitha's Kittens,
    1928 . . . .**60.00**
  Felix The Cat, Big Little Book, Whitman,
    #1129, 1936 . . . .**50.00**

*Tile, A Mother's Lullaby, handpainted by
"AS," 1881, sepia on white, marked "Min-
ton/Hollins/Co/Patent/Tile/Works; Stoke on/
Trent," modern frame, 6" sq, $35.00.*

Trouble Of The Careless Kitten, 1945
.........................**60.00**
Cookie Jar, Kliban **150.00**
Door Knocker, brass, Cheshire Cat, engraved, c1920, England **55.00**
Egg Cup, 3" h, black cat, Japan, paper label
.........................**20.00**
Game
    Funny Fortunes, 10½ × 19¾" checkerboard type, playing pcs, orig box with cat illus **28.00**
    Kitty Kat Cup Ball, Rosebud Art Co, 1930s **35.00**
    Match Holder, cat scene, ftd, marked "Wavecrest" **225.00**
Mirror, pocket, White Cat Union Suits adv, 2¾" l, black and white, celluloid, cartoon illus, early 1900s **65.00**
Pencil Box, ¾ × 6 × 8½", Felix The Cat, cardboard, deep blue, inscriptions, American Pencil Co **45.00**
Pinback Button
    Black Cat Stove and Shoe Polish, yellow, black and white dec, c1915
        ....**25.00**
    Cat's Paw Heels, ⅞" d, yellow and black, early 1900s **15.00**
    Groovy Cat, 1⅜" d, red, white, and blue, c1940 ....**10.00**
    Morris For President, 2¼" d, multicolored photo portrait, bright red, white, and blue border, Nine Lives Cat Food, 1988 ....**10.00**
Planter, 6¾" h, kitten with basket, Hull
    ....**15.00**
Plaque, kitchen, 12" h, figural, Kliban cat, Sigma **60.00**
Print, 14 × 11", two cats in hat, titled "A Love Song," J Ottmann Litho, 1894
    ....**25.00**
Salt and Pepper Shakers, pr
    3¾" h, teapot shape, black cat illus, Japan label **15.00**
    4" h, comical Siamese, paper label marked "Norcrest Japan" **10.00**
Toothpick Holder, kitten and boot ...**10.00**
Toy, windup, tin, cat with ball, rolls over, made in US Zone Germany **200.00**
Yarn Holder, 6½ × 6½", Felix the Cat, wood paddle, black images and inscription, 1930s **50.00**

CAUSE COLLECTIBLES

Social cause collectibles are just now coming into their own as a collecting category. Perhaps this is because the social activists of the 1960s have mortgages, children, and money in their pocket to buy back the representations of their youth. In doing so, they are looking back past their own protest movements to all forms of social protest that took place in the twentieth century.

Great collections can be built around a single cause, e.g., women's suffrage or the right to vote. Much of the surviving material tends to be two-dimensional. Stress three-dimensional items the moment you begin to collect. As years pass, these are the objects most likely to rise in value.

Autograph
    Pamphlet, 5 × 7", "The National First Aid Association of America," sgd Clara Barton photo **250.00**
    Quotation, 4 × 3", Anna E Dickinson, suffrage leader **25.00**
Medal, 1¾" d, Peace, emb brass, Angel of Peace waving palm branch, text on back with dates of beginning and ending of World War I **15.00**
Pinback Button
    Equality, 1" d, black and white, 1965
        ....**15.00**
    ERA/Equal Rights Amendment–Vote Yes, red, white, and blue **12.00**
    Give Us Liberty–Down With The Corrupt Political Machine, 1¼" d, red, white, and blue **50.00**
    Stop The War, 1¼" d, green, black lettering **10.00**
    Support Victims Of The Seaside Massacre–I Have!, 1" d, gold, black lettering **25.00**
    Uppity Women Unite, white, black lettering, 1970s **10.00**

Convention, IAM, 28th Convention, Los Angeles, bronze, purple ribbon with "Delegate" printed on front, figural building lapel pin with 1972, cityscape, red, white, and blue insignia, 4" l, $20.00.

Volunteer Hospital Service, pin, gold plated, blue trim, ¾" d, $5.00.

Votes For Women, gold, black lettering
    ....**25.00**
Win With Women, white, red and black lettering, 1974 ....**12.50**
Post Card, 3½ × 5½", prohibition, "I'm On The Water Wagon Now," black, white, red, and yellow illus, 1906 ......**25.00**
Poster
    Bridge of Peace, 16 × 22", Anti–War, children of all nations illus, c1936
        ....**125.00**
    Give–Welfare Federation, 14 × 22", Jessie Wilcox Smith illus, little girl and two babies, green and yellow ground, c1920 ....**165.00**
    Lend Your Strength To The Red Triangle, 20 × 30", Gil Spear, man lifting YMCA stone **50.00**
    Vietnam, Anti–War, 23 × 27", anonymous, black and white montage, c1967 ....**85.00**
Sheet Music, 7 × 10", *I Am Not Crazy Enough To Want A War*, Anti–Nazi, 1942 ....**75.00**
Sign, 4½ × 8", Bring Back Prosperity, tin, diecut and emb, beer glass shape, letter "B" shaped like twisted pretzel, made by De Vo Novelty Co, Asbury Park, NJ, c1932 ....**80.00**
Watch Fob, Transport Workers Union **10.00**

CELLULOID

Celluloid is the trade name for a thin, tough, flammable material made of cellulose nitrate and camphor. Originally used for toilet articles, it quickly found a use as inexpensive jewelry, figurines, vases, and other household items. In the 1920s and 1930s, it was used heavily by the toy industry.

Be on the lookout for dealers who break apart sets and sell the pieces individually as a way of getting more money. Also check any ivory or tortoise shell piece that is offered to you. Both were well imitated by quality celluloid.

Animal
  Camel, 1½″ h **8.00**
  Deer, Christmas
    4″ l **15.00**
    4½″ l, Occupied Japan **30.00**
  Pig, 2″ l **6.00**
  Reindeer, Occupied Japan **22.00**
  Swan, white **5.00**
Bangle Bracelet, mottled brown, tortoise
  shell imitation, rhinestones **25.00**
Candlestick, 8½″ h, pr **35.00**
Cigar Bowl, football player, Tampa, FL, Oc-
  cupied Japan **25.00**
Clothespin Set, miniature **15.00**
Compact, Rex Fifth Avenue, round, floral
  transfer on lid, 1939–40 .... **65.00**
Doll
  Bridal, MIB, 1940s **100.00**
  Cowboy, 7½″ h, Japan, 1940–50 **24.00**
  German, orig dress **45.00**
Dresser Set, Art Deco, green, 7 pcs **25.00**
Dresser Tray, jeweled dec **20.00**
Figure
  Baby, crawling **40.00**
  Baseball Player, jointed, holds ball and
    glove, "#1" on back, Occupied Ja-
    pan **125.00**
  Policeman, movable head and arms, Ja-
    pan **22.00**
Glove Box, light blue **25.00**
Lamp, shade **45.00**
Manicure Set, leather roll-up case, eight
  pcs **9.00**
Matchbook Cover, Evansville Hat Works
  adv, celluloid on metal **15.00**
Matchsafe, Merry Christmas & Happy New
  Year, Compliments of Roth & Scanlan,
  Fine Wines, Liquors & Cigars, 115 E 1st
  St, Rushville, Ind **135.00**
Mirror, Buckwalter Stove Co, Royersford, PA
  .... **65.00**
Nodder, goose, stamped "Germany" **30.00**

Playing Card Box, enameled club, spade, heart, and diamond card on cov, molded, ivory grained, c1910, 2¾ × 3⅝ × ¾″, $20.00.

Novelty, flip-it, Golden Orangeade adv,
  mechanical, diecut, pin-on, orange,
  1910s **25.00**
Pencil Clip, Diamond Edge, ⅞″ d, black,
  white, and red, silvered tin clip, early
  1900s **10.00**
Pencil Sharpener, clock, amber, German
  .... **20.00**
Pin, Uncle Sam, diecut, movable arms and
  legs **35.00**
Place Card Holder, snowman, angels, and
  elves, set of eight, MIB **17.50**
Rattle
  Cupid in wreath, 4½″ l **15.00**
  Five Faces **12.00**
  Teething Ring, silhouette pictures, dated
    1916 .... **85.00**
Sewing Kit, red stripes **8.00**
Sharpening Stone, Circle Service Station,
  Hanover, PA **40.00**
Sign, Coon Range Kentucky Whiskey adv
  .... **95.00**
Stamp Case, Tom Moore Cigar adv **35.00**
Tape Measure, fish **25.00**
Toothbrush Holder, young girl, 1920s
  .... **40.00**
Toy
  Boy, riding tricycle, Occupied Japan,
    MIB **95.00**
  Hawaiian Dancer, MIB **150.00**

CEREAL BOXES

There is no better example of a collectible category gone mad than cereal boxes. Cereal boxes from the first half of the twentieth century sell in the $15.00 to $50.00 range. Cereal boxes from the 1950s through the 1970s sell in the $50.00 range and up. Where's the sense?

The answer rests in the fact that the post–World War II cereal box market is being manipulated by a shrewd speculator who is drawing upon his past experience with the lunch box market. Eventually, the bubble will burst. Don't get involved unless you have money to burn.

Periodicals: *Flake,* PO Box 481, Cambridge, MA 02140; *Free Inside,* PO Box 178844, San Diego, CA 92117.

All Bran, Kellogg's, Art Linkletter on back,
  1959 .... **30.00**
Alpha Bits, Post, premium offer, 1960s
  .... **20.00**
Apple Jacks, Kellogg's, Banana Splits
  flashlight offer, 1970 .... **100.00**
Batman, Ralston, shrink wrapped plastic
  bank on front, 1989 .... **10.00**
Cap'n Crunch, Quaker, breakfast games,
  1988 .... **10.00**
Cheerios, General Mills
  American Airlines Game Kit, 1956 **20.00**

Kellogg's Special K, Kristi Yamaguchi, 1992 Olympic Gold Medalist Women's Figure Skating, 8″ w, 12″ h, $12.00.

  Lone Ranger front and back, 1940s
  .... **300.00**
Cocoa Krispies, Kellogg's, Ogg the
  Caveman, 1973 .... **50.00**
Cocoa Pebbles, Post, Bedrock Bike Race
  poster, 1987 .... **3.00**
Cocoa Puffs, General Mills, Harlem Globe-
  trotters trading cards **20.00**
Cookie Crisp, Ralston, Great Mouse Detec-
  tive stickers in pack, 1985 .... **10.00**
Corn Flakes, Kellogg's, Norman Rockwell
  illus, Atomic Sub offer, 1955 .... **50.00**
Cracker Jack, Ralston, Disney World offer,
  surprise in pack, 1983 .... **10.00**
Ghostbusters, Ralston, frisbee offer, 1985
  .... **10.00**
Grape Nuts, Post, baseball cards on back,
  1960s **75.00**
Honey Comb, Superman Action poster,
  1978 .... **20.00**
Honey Smacks, Kellogg's, Hot Wheels offer,
  1989 .... **10.00**
Kix, General Mills, Railroad model cutouts
  on back, 1947 .... **30.00**
Life, Quaker, premium offer, 1960s **25.00**
Lucky Charms, General Mills, Magic Secrets
  Video offer **3.00**
Post Toasties, Post, giant economy size,
  1937 .... **50.00**
Puffed Rice, Quaker, Bugs Bunny comic
  book offer, 1940s **125.00**
Quisp, Quaker, space trivia game on back,
  1985 .... **25.00**
Raisin Bran
  Kellogg's, 1950s **30.00**
  Post, Monkees Mobile Car offer, 1970
  .... **100.00**
Rainbow Brite, Ralston, Crazy Chain offer,
  1985 .... **30.00**

Rice Krispies, Kellogg's
    Cloth doll offer, 1948 .... **30.00**
    Dennis the Menace comic on back,
       1960 .... **50.00**
Smurfberry Crunch, Post, game cutout on
    back, 1986 .... **10.00**
Sugar Crisp, Post, Dick Tracy Decoder offer,
    1958 .... **100.00**
Sugar Frosted Flakes, Kellogg's, Tony The
    Tiger Sky Ride offer, 1973 ...... **20.00**
Sugar Pops, Kellogg's, Fun Niks offer, 1970
    .... **50.00**
Sugar Smacks, Kellogg's, Magic Moon Gar-
    den offer, 1964 .... **20.00**
Trix, General Mills, Trix Plush rabbit offer,
    1985 .... **10.00**
Wheaties, General Mills
    Fun at the Breakfast Table Games &
       Trivia, 1933 .... **50.00**
    Johnny Bench Commemorative, 1989
       .... **10.00**
    Mickey Mouse Club record offer, 1956
       .... **75.00**
    Skeeter the Monkey cutout mask, 1946
       .... **30.00**

CEREAL PREMIUMS

Forget cereal boxes. The fun rests with the goodies inside the box that you got for buying the cereal in the first place. Cereal premiums have changed a great deal over the past decade. No self-respecting manufacturer in the 1950s would have included a tube of toothpaste as their premium. Yuck!

Collectors make a distinction between premiums that came with the box and those for which you had to send away. The latter group is valued more highly because the items are often more elaborate and better made. My dad keeps telling me about all the neat things he received through the mail as a kid. I think my generation has missed something.

Periodicals: *Flake,* PO Box 481, Cambridge, MA 02140; *Free Inside,* PO Box 178844, San Diego, CA 92117.

Adventure Kit, Fury, Post Cereals, 1950s
    .... **400.00**
Astronaut Moon Buggy, 2¼ × 3¼", hard
    plastic, blue, gray wheels, two figures,
    rubber band windup mechanism, Post
    Cereal **25.00**
Booklet, *The Frolie Grasshopper Circus,*
    multicolored, grasshoppers and clowns,
    whimsical scenes, American Cereal Co,
    Quaker Oats, 1895 .... **65.00**
Car, Magno-Power, '50 Ford, 3" l, plastic,
    blue, Mystery Control ring and 4 × 5"
    instruction sheet **100.00**

Wheaties, Western Pacific, black, red, and white, 1953, 3" sq, $2.00.

Card, pop out, Dale Evans, Post Cereals,
    unused, mint **15.00**
Comic Book
    Sergeant Preston of the Yukon, 2½ × 7",
       full color, 12 pgs, copyright 1956
       .... **25.00**
    Sugar Bear In The Race For Outer Space,
       2½ × 4¹/₁₂", 12 pgs, Post Cereal,
       1960s **15.00**
Creamer, Kellogg's Correct Cereal ... **18.00**
Disappearing Coin Trick, Kellogg's Rice
    Krispies, MIP **1.00**
Doll, cloth, Snap, Krackle, and Pop, uncut,
    1946, Rice Krispies, Kellogg's, set of 3
    .... **180.00**
Figure, 7" h, rubber, Snap, Crackle, and
    Pop, Rice Krispies, Kellogg's, set of 3
    .... **50.00**
Flasher Card, Danny Thomas winks eye,
    Post Corn Flakes, 1950s **24.00**
Glass, cartoon, Toucan Sam, Fruit Loops,
    Kellogg's, 1977 .... **6.50**
Handbook, *Kellogg's Cadet Aviation Corps,*
    6 × 9", 28 pgs, copyright 1938   **25.00**
Hike-o-meter, orig mailer, Wheaties **40.00**
Jet Ring, Kellogg's, 1950s **15.00**
License Plate, Kellogg's, 1973 .... **8.00**
Mask, 4½ × 9" unpunched cardboard
    sheet, #4, Post Sugar Crisp, 1960s **25.00**
Model, punch-out, C–54 Skymaster war
    plane, Kellogg's Pep, WWII **24.00**
Plate, Kellogg's, 1985 .... **25.00**
Quisp's Quazy Moon Mobile, vinyl glow-
    in the dark sheet of complete parts, in
    struction sheet, 1970s **75.00**
Ring, Flash Gordon, Post Cereal **20.00**
Yo-Yo, Teddy Grahams Breakfast Bears,
    MIP **1.00**

CHASE CHROME AND BRASS COMPANY

The Chase Chrome and Brass Company was founded in the late 1870s by Augustus S. Chase and some partners. Through numerous mergers and acquisitions, the company grew and grew. The mergers helped to expand the product line into chrome, copper, brass, and other metals. Several name changes occurred until the company was sold as a subsidiary of Kennecott Corp in its merger with Standard Oil in 1981.

One of the most popular products this company made was the chrome Art Deco line which really appealed to housewives in the 1930–1942 period.

Chase items can be found with some really neat styling and are usually marked. Just like the aluminum wares, they do not need polishing and are becoming just as hot with today's collectors.

Ashtray, sombrero shape, 3 piece set **45.00**
Ashtray Set, ashtray, cigarette holder, and
    tray, red paint, red Bakelite handles
    .... **45.00**
Bank, barrel shape, brass, chromium finish,
    double bolt lock, key **9.00**
Bookends, pr, Art Deco, arch **185.00**
Buffet Warming Oven, electric, 10¼" l, pol-
    ished chromium cylinder, door slides
    back, walnut fluted handles and legs,
    heating element in base, designed by
    Charles Arcularius **40.00**
Candy Dish, two part
    Rect, handles, glass inserts, pr ... **65.00**
    Round, upside down whale in middle,
       circular handle **45.00**
Champagne Bucket, 9¼" h, Bacchus, Rock-
    well Kent **500.00**
Cigarette Holder, black paint dec **22.00**
Cocktail Set, 5 pc **35.00**
Crumber, polished copper, scraper, tray,
    white plastic handles with two metal
    stars **20.00**
Flashlight, Airalite, vest pocket size, pol-
    ished nickel, colored inlays **25.00**
Lamp, 8" h, copper, #01001 .... **65.00**
Mustard and Catsup Set, chrome, white
    frosted glass inserts, glass spoons **65.00**

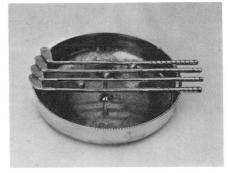

Ashtray, four figural golf clubs, 5" d, 4¹/₈" h, $30.00.

Salt and Pepper Shakers, pr, spherical, polished chromium **8.00**

Snack Set, plate with matching cup, rainbow colors, set of 8 . . . . **185.00**

Tray, heart shape, polished chromium, white plastic ring handle **12.00**

Tumbler, rainbow colors, set of 7 . . . **20.00**

Vase, bud, chromium, central tube with three applied tubes, stepped circular base **45.00**

CHILDREN'S COLLECTIBLES

Mothers of the world unite. This category is for you. The children who used it hardly remember it. It's the kind of stuff that keeps your children forever young in your mind.

There is virtually nothing written about this collecting category so what to collect is wide open. One collector I know has hundreds of baby planters. To each their own.

Club: Children's Things Collectors Society, PO Box 983, Durant, IA 52747.

Baby Bathtub, green and ivory, nursery rhymes and illus **65.00**

Baby Bonnet, Victorian, white **38.00**

Baby Bottle, Barney Rubble **10.00**

Baby Bottle Warmer, Art Deco design **18.00**

Baby Brush, SS, ornate design, unused **25.00**

Baby Plate, Humpty Dumpty, colorful, Beswick, 1950s **250.00**

Baby Record Book, Maud Humphrey illus, some staining **195.00**

Baby Scale, pink, 1940s **38.00**

Baby Spoon, curved handle, kitten dec, Rogers **35.00**

Baptism Set, 3 pcs, gown, slip, and matching cap, cotton, white, c1920 . . . . **85.00**

Bedspread, twin size, chenille, chicks coming out of eggs scene **35.00**

Blackboard, Cress Education Boards, patented October 15, 1912 . . . . **95.00**

Book

A Kiss For Little Bear, E H Minarik, Harper & Row, 1968 . . . . **15.00**

In Wink–A–Way Land, Eugene Field, 1930 . . . . **15.00**

Little Tots ABC Book, c1900, linen **18.00**

Mickey Mouse Alphabet Book, 1936 . . . . **75.00**

The Tale Of Cuffy Bear, Arthur Scott Bailey, Grossett & Dunlap, 1915, 112 pgs **10.00**

Carriage, wicker, serpentine edges, natural finish, orig velvet upholstery, c1890 . . . . **450.00**

Catalog, Best & Co Lilliputian Bazaar, 1935, 48 pgs, children and infants speciality shop **20.00**

Clock Radio, three mice, Fisher–Price **20.00**

Creamer and Sugar, milk glass, Thumbelina **25.00**

Crib Blanket, woven, nursery rhymes, Marseilles **200.00**

Cup, SS **22.50**

Desk, lift top **115.00**

Feeding Dish

Bunnykins **100.00**

Campbell Kid illus, Buffalo Pottery **85.00**

Clown, pink **22.00**

Divided, 8" d, three sections, Patriot China **50.00**

Iron, The Pearl, matching trivet . . . **125.00**

Mug, Victorian, resilvered, engraved **75.00**

Music Box, Victorian, pretty children lithos, 3 × 4 × 2" **110.00**

Nursing Bottle, Talwar, opening on both ends, 4 oz **32.00**

Pail, wood, metal bail handle, 4" h, 1890s **68.00**

Phonograph, metal, ruby red enamel, nursery rhymes, one speed switch, General Electric Electronic Toys, 1930s **185.00**

Plate, Juvenile, chicks dec, Roseville **110.00**

Quilt, infant, handmade **45.00**

Rattle, SS, includes birth record **20.00**

Rocking Horse, straw stuffed, red wheels **275.00**

Sheet Music, *Whistle While You Work*, Walt Disney, 1937 . . . . **20.00**

Shoes, infant's, pr

Leather, ankle strap, white **35.00**

Victorian, high top, black and white **75.00**

Toy

Busy Box, 14 × 20", twelve movable gadgets, Gabriel **15.00**

Dippee Bug, pull, rubber, multicolored, MIB **40.00**

Jack–In–The–Box, red, white, and blue box, painted plaster head . . . **110.00**

Player Piano, eight muppets, Fisher–Price **45.00**

Singer Sew Handy #20, MIB . . . **175.00**

Toot Toot Train, pull, Fisher–Price **15.00**

Wawky Tawky String Phone, 1940s **10.00**

Toy Chest, pirate chest shape, Little Tykes **50.00**

Toy Dishes

Coffeepot, aluminum, red metal handle **7.50**

Cookware Set, aluminum, 8 pcs, boxed **110.00**

Cup and Saucer, Akro Agate, Interior Panel, oxblood and white **35.00**

Flour Sifter, aluminum, red metal handle, Bromwell **10.50**

Plate, Akro Agate, Interior Panel, oxblood and white **35.00**

Punch Bowl Set, glass, bowl and six cups, Diamond pattern, 1920s **85.00**

Tea Kettle, aluminum, red metal handle, whistle spout **6.00**

Tea Set

Akro Agate, transparent green, 21 pcs **155.00**

FAO Schwartz **60.00**

German, porcelain, maroon luster, 13 pcs **210.00**

Graniteware, blue, 15 pcs . . . **350.00**

Hazel Atlas Little Hostess, glass, 16 pcs **140.00**

Mirro, aluminum, 30 pcs, orig box, 1930s **175.00**

Staffordshire, blue and white, nursery rhymes and characters . . . **700.00**

CHRISTMAS AND EASTER SEALS

Collecting Christmas and Easter Seals is one of the most inexpensive "stamp" hobbies. Sheets usually sell for between 50¢ and $1.00. Most collectors do not buy single stamps, except for the very earliest Christmas seals.

Club: Christmas Seal and Charity Stamp Society, 5825 Dorchester Avenue, Chicago, IL 60637.

Children's Dishes, tea set, little girl pouring milk for kitty, teapot, creamer, cov sugar, two cups and saucers and plates, luster finish, marked "Made in Japan," orig fitted box, $45.00.

Sign, "Buy Christmas Seals Fight Tuberculosis," 1931, 11 × 14", $40.00.

CHRISTMAS COLLECTIBLES

Of all the holiday collectibles, Christmas items are the most popular. It has grown so large as a category that many collectors specialize in only one area, e.g., Santa Claus figures or tree ornaments.

Anything Victorian is "hot." The Victorians popularized Christmas. Many collectors love to recapture that spirit. However, prices for Victorian items, from feather trees to ornaments, are quickly moving out of sight.

This is a field where knowledgeable individuals can find bargains. Learn to tell a late nineteenth/early twentieth-century ornament from a modern example. A surprising number of dealers cannot. If a dealer thinks a historic ornament is modern and prices it accordingly, he is actually playing Santa Claus by giving you a present. Ho, Ho, Ho!

Club: Christmas Year 'Round, Box 5708, Coralville, IA 52241

Periodicals: *Golden Glow of Christmas Past*, 6401 Winsdale St, Golden Valley, MN 55427; *Ornament Collector*, RR #1, Canton, IL 61520.

Book
  A Northern Christmas, Kent Rockwell, American Artists Group Inc, 1941 . . . . **7.00**
  Christmas In Action, pop–up, orig box, 1949 . . . . **24.00**

Visions of St Nick, E A Bradford, 1950, Phillip Publishing, pop–up . . . **20.00**
Candy Container
  Elf, 8" h, cylinder type, wire neck   **25.00**
  Santa, 13" h, cardboard, spring head, West Germany **60.00**
  Snowman, 7¹/₂" h, papier mache, West Germany, 1950s **22.00**
Card Book, flocked, 1950s **20.00**
Christmas Card, set of 5, Disney characters, Walt Disney Productions **25.00**
Cookie Jar, 10" h, Santa head, plastic, sealed with orig plastic **48.00**
Display
  Hanging, Santa, cardboard, 1940s **30.00**
  Pop-Up, Twelve Days of Christmas, 1920s **150.00**
  Stand–Up, Pepsi, Norman Rockwell Santa illus, 1950s **65.00**
Doll, 8¹/₂" h, felt, press–me voice **95.00**
Earrings, pr, Christmas bells, screw type **10.00**
Figure
  Boot, 5¹/₂" h **24.00**
  Santa on skis, metal, Barclay **40.00**
  Snowman, papier mache, set of 6, MIB **225.00**
Greeting Card
  "A Merry Christmas," three children under umbrella, Wolf & Co, NY   **2.50**
  "Wishing You A Happy Christmas," sepia tones, Raphael Tuck & Sons, London **3.00**
Hatbox, Stetson, continuous small–town Christmas scene **115.00**
Light Set
  Milk Glass, figural, Santa, painted, 10 bulbs **95.00**
  Noma Bubble Lite, boxed set **27.00**
Nativity Set
  Ideal Toy Corp, The Most Wonderful Story, 9" h rubber doll, Jesus in manger, orig 16 × 12 × 4¹/₂" box, 1951 . . . . **135.00**
  Marx, orig box **45.00**
Ornament
  Balls, miniature, boxed set of 12   **12.00**
  Barton Cross, Reed, 1974 . . . . **38.00**
  Cat in Shoe, glass **38.00**
  Clown, glass, painted face, Germany **38.00**
  Flamingo, blue mercury glass **40.00**
  French Hens, Towle, 1973 . . . . . . **34.00**
  Kugel, cobalt blue **55.00**

Ornament, angel, wax over composition, wavy blond hair, painted facial features, spun glass wings, red net skirt, 4" l, $80.00.

  Santa, figural, honeycomb **8.00**
  Snake **32.00**
Pinback Button, adv, Santa illus
  Emery's, mulitcolored, dark blue lettering **50.00**
  Foster, Ross & Company, multicolored, early 1900s **75.00**
  Home Again/Wanamaker's, multicolored, early 1900s **150.00**
  Rudge & Guenzel, multicolored, black lettering, 1930s **45.00**
  Webbs City Inc, black, white, and red, 1930–40 . . . . **25.00**
Post Card, Santa with red suit **8.00**
Putz Items
  Animal
    Cow, 3" h, celluloid, brown, USA **7.00**
    Dog, 1" h, celluloid, brown, marked "Japan" **5.00**
    Horse, 3¹/₂" h, brown and tan, rubber, USA **7.00**
    Sheep, 1³/₄" h, composition, wool coat, wood legs, Germany   **20.00**
  Bank, 3" h, chalk, white, marked "Made in Japan" **10.00**
  Church, 6" h, cardboard, litho, frosted roof **8.00**
  Fence, 2¹/₂" h, eight 6" sections, wood, red and green **30.00**
  House
    2¹/₂" h, cardboard, frosted roof, marked "Japan" **4.50**
    3" h, log type, frosted roof, marked "Germany" **10.00**

Putz Animals, German, composition, painted facial features, 3" h lion, 2¹/₄" h bear, $10.00 each.

Wagon, wood, driver and horses, Germany **38.00**
Puzzle, pr, children hanging stockings, other with Santa waving, McLoughlin **175.00**
Reflectors, copper foil, Germany, set of 10 .... **20.00**
Snowdome, chimney, red brick, water–filled fireplace, Santa, gifts, tree **20.00**
Tin, color litho, 1930s **85.00**
Toy, Santa
    Battery Operated, remote control, celluloid face, rings bell, beats drum **150.00**
    Squeaker, 7" h, papier mache, red coat, fur beard **55.00**
Tree
    9" h, brush, green, glass bead dec, red base **15.00**
    15" h, cellophane **15.00**
    18" h, feather, green, white base, Germany, 1920s **150.00**
    54" h, berry tipped branches, white square wood stand, poinsettia decals, orig Sears shipping carton ... **250.00**
    60" h, feather, Germany **350.00**
Tree Stand
    Cast Iron, poinsettia dec **45.00**
    Revolving **20.00**
Tree Topper, Angel, lighted, orig box **18.00**
Utensil Set, spoon and fork, A Michelsen, large tablespoon size, SS, heavy gold plate, cloisonne handles
    1946, holly leaves and berries ... **85.00**
    1949, Christmas wreath and candles **85.00**
    1955, green and red spots **75.00**
    1966, Madonna riding on donkey **75.00**

CIGARETTE AND CIGAR COLLECTIBLES

Cigarette products contain a warning that they might be hazardous to your health. Cigarette and cigar memorabilia should contain a warning that they may be hazardous to your pocketbook. With each passing year, the price for cigarette and cigar–related material goes higher and higher. If it ever stabilizes and then drops, a number of collectors are going to see their collections go up in smoke.

The vast majority of cigarette and cigar material is two–dimensional, from advertising trade cards to posters. Seek out three–dimensional pieces. There are some great cigarette and cigar tins.

Clubs: Cigarette Pack Collectors' Assoc, 61 Searle St, Georgetown, MA 01833; International Seal, Label & Cigar Band Society, 8915 East Bellevue St, Tuscon, AZ 85715.

Advertisement, Cabana Cigarettes, standing harem girl illus, framed **200.00**
Advertising Card, store type, Rumin Red Devil Flints **20.00**
Ashtray
    Fatima Cigarettes, matchbox holder, marked "Nippon" **100.00**
    LaMinerva Cigars, goddess dec ... **12.00**
    Winston Cigarettes, tin **5.00**
Bookmark, Old Gold Cigarettes, plastic **20.00**
Chair, Piedmont Cigarettes, folding **225.00**
Change Tray, Tom Moore Cigars **20.00**
Cigar Box
    Charles V **8.00**
    Delavana Cigars, orig contents, 1938 .... **24.00**
    General Pershing Commander ... **20.00**
    The Overland, unopened **32.00**
Cigar Case, Superior, leather **10.00**
Cigar Cutter
    Figural, anchor, UPC **28.00**
    Mother–of–pearl, pocket **125.00**
    United **15.00**
Cigarette Case, etched, "Gilbralter" **20.00**
Cigarette Dispenser, music box shape, lift lid **185.00**
Cigarette Jar
    Cut Glass, 6½" h, marked "#10" **150.00**
    Heisey, 6" h, clear, sgd **85.00**
Cigarette Maker, E–Z Maker, 1933 **35.00**
Cigarette Pack
    Condax, Turkish, full pack **25.00**
    Lucky Strike, green, unopened ... **25.00**
    Prosperity Island, round, unopened **65.00**
    Ramsese Cigarettes, unopened ... **15.00**
Cigar Holder, velvet lined case, Meerschaum **45.00**
Cigar Lighter, counter top, electric ... **35.00**
Cooler, vinyl, Joe Camel **20.00**
Counter Display, Corina Cigars, glass and copper **75.00**
Flip Book
    Fatima Cigarettes **15.00**
    Liggett Myers Sultan Cigarettes ... **42.00**
Jar, R G Dun Cigars, glass **15.00**
Match Holder
    Kool Cigarettes, tin **25.00**
    Philip Morris, tin **75.00**
Mirror, pocket, Philip Morris **20.00**
Pinback Button
    Philip Morris, 1" d, celluloid, Johnny, c1930 .... **18.00**
    Union Made Cigars, 1¼" d, red, white, blue, and black, light green cigar label, c1890 .... **20.00**
Pocket Notebook, Black Maria **10.00**
Poster
    Booster Cigars, 27 × 30", black man and lady adjusting garter, framed **175.00**
    Chesterfield Cigarettes, cardboard **18.00**
    Kool Cigarettes, 12 × 18", smoking penguin points to pack, c1933 **35.00**

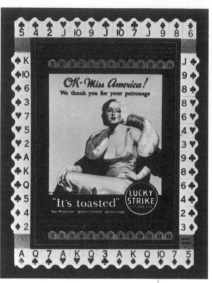

Contract Bridge Score Card, Lucky Strike Cigarettes, 1930s, $20.00.

    Raleigh Cigarettes, 12 × 18", paper, full color glossy portrait **20.00**
Punchboard, Big Smokes, 10½" d ... **25.00**
Sign
    Blue Ribbon Cigars, stand–up **45.00**
    Chesterfield Cigarettes, Lucille Norman illus, 20 × 43" **55.00**
    Dark Horse Cigar, 12 × 23", paper, two trotting racehorses **65.00**
    Denby Cigar, tin, man with cigar illus **375.00**
    El Wadora Cigars, 24 × 36", tin, c1930 .... **45.00**
    Hambone Cigar, 7" d, round, cardboard, two sided, hanging, caricature of black man wearing aviator goggles in tiny airplane **48.50**
    Kool Cigarettes, tin, penguin illus **55.00**
    Marvel Cigarettes **15.00**
    Nickel King Cigars, 16 × 18", cardboard **35.00**
    Old Gold Cigarettes, 12 × 4", tin, emb dancing box **25.00**
    Philip Morris Cigarettes, tin **35.00**
    Piedmont Cigarettes, 30 × 46", porcelain **165.00**
    Pollocks Cigar, riverboats unloading and commercial buildings **175.00**
    Raleigh Cigarettes, tin **95.00**
    Red Dot Cigar, figural **52.00**
    Viceroy Cigarettes, neon, red and yellow **180.00**
Smoking Jacket, cigar ribbons **250.00**
Tee Shirt, adv, Camel Cigarettes, Joe Camel **9.00**
Thermometer
    Kool Cigarettes **35.00**
    Winston Cigarettes **35.00**
Tin
    Cuban Daisy Cigar **45.00**

Good Cheer Cigar, handled **60.00**
In–B–Tween Cigars **20.00**
Little Tom Cigar **22.50**
Omar Cigarettes **35.00**
Reichard's Cadet Cigar **65.00**
Sweet Afton Virginia Cigarettes . . . **20.00**
Tobacco Players, "Tawney" **28.00**
Wills Gold Flake **30.00**
Tray, Will's Wild Woodbines Cigarettes
. . . . **35.00**

CIRCUS COLLECTIBLES

The only circus that I ever saw was at a theme park in Florida. Dad keeps telling me about traveling tent circuses and how exciting they really were. Based on the memorabilia that they left behind, I think he might be right.

Dad keeps threatening to take me to see the great annual circus parade in Milwaukee featuring the equipment from the Circus World Museum in Baraboo, Wisconsin. The reason that I get to be his traveling companion is that Connie, his wife, wants nothing to do with his circus fantasies. She says living with him is all the circus that she needs.

Clubs: Circus Fans Association of America, PO Box 59710, Potomac, MD 20859; The Circus Historical Society, 743 Beverly Park Place, Jackson, MI 49203; The Circus Model Builders International, 347 Lonsdale Avenue, Dayton, OH 45419.

Book, *Randy Starr Leading Air Circus,* Eugene Martin, Saalfield Publishing, 1932 . . . . **15.00**
Calendar, Circus World Museum, 1974
. . . . **5.00**
Circus Wagon, horse–drawn, cast iron
. . . . **55.00**
Game, Emmett Kelly's Circus, orig box, All–Fair, 1953 . . . . **45.00**
Lunch Box, Ringling Bros and Barnum & Bailey Circus, 7 × 9 × 4", vinyl, color illus, thermos, King Seeley, 1970 **375.00**

Poster, Ringling Bros and Barnum & Bailey, 16 × 28", $85.00.

Puzzle, Toy Carnival, Miller Rubber Products Co, Akron, OH, 1933, 50 diecut cardboard pieces, 8 × 10" paper envelope, 7½ × 9¾", $25.00.

Menu, Greatest Show on Earth, Nov 12, 1898, full color **100.00**
Pinback Button
　Clyde Beatty Circus, man holding chair and lion illus **30.00**
　Super Circus Club, 1½" d, Canada Dry adv, pictures Mary Hartline, c1950
　. . . . . **20.00**
Post Card, Ringling Brothers, Freak Fisher Family **35.00**
Poster
　Cole Bros, All The Marvels, animals in cages, Erie Litho **210.00**
　Hunt Bros Circus and Wild West Show, 21 × 28", wild West scene
　. . . . . **200.00**
　Ringling Bros and Barnum & Bailey, The Greatest Wild Animal Display, presents Terrell Jacobs, World's Foremost Trainer, Strobridge Litho, 1938
　. . . . . **625.00**
Program
　Barnum & Bailey, 1953 . . . . **10.00**
　Ringling Bros and Barnum & Bailey, 1953 . . . . **12.00**
Stereograph, Windsor & Whipple, Olean, NY, people with elephant **35.00**
Ticket
　Ringling Brothers, Railroad Dept complimentary ticket, 1956 . . . . **2.00**
　Von Brothers Circus **4.00**

CLICKERS

If you need a clicker, you would probably spend hours trying to locate a modern one. I am certain they exist. You can find a clicker at a flea market in a matter of minutes. As an experiment, I tried looking up the word in a dictionary. It was not there. Times change.

Clickers make noise, a slight sharp sound. I believe their principal purpose was to drive parents crazy. I understand they played a major role at parochial

school, but cannot attest to the fact since I attended public school.

Advertising
　Allen's Parlor Furnace, reddish–brown heating stove illus, yellow ground
　. . . . . **20.00**
　Benzo–Gas, red, blue, white, and lime green, "Does What Gasoline Can't" slogan **18.00**
　Calvert Whiskey, red and white, 1950s
　. . . . . **8.00**
　Chain Tread Tire, US Rubber Co, round, black, white, and blue **30.00**
　Chevrolet/Steel Turret–Top, 2" l, tin, black image, 1930s **25.00**
　Endicott Johnson Shoes, yellow and black **12.00**
　Gridley Milk, baby face in milk bottle, red ground **25.00**
　Humpty Dumpty Shoes, 2" l, litho tin, c1930 . . . . **25.00**
　Mule–Hide Roofing and Shingles, yellow and black, logo symbol **22.00**
　New and True Coffee, c1930 . . . . . **15.00**
　Peter's Weatherbird Shoes, ¾ × 1¾", litho tin, multicolored, 1930s **25.00**
　Poll Parrot Shoes, red, yellow, and green, 1950s **25.00**
　Real–Kill Bug Killer **18.00**
　Red Goose Shoes, ¾ × 1¾", litho tin, red goose, yellow lettering and ground, 1930s **22.50**
　Secret Guard, 2½" l, red, white, and blue, 1941 . . . . **50.00**
　Studebaker/The Car With A Snap, blue and white, round, Whitehead & Hoag, 1904 copyright **45.00**
　Twinkies Shoes For Boys and Girls, Twinkie character, blue ground **18.00**
　Weatherbird Shoes, red, yellow, and black **15.00**
Banjo, figural, 1930s **15.00**
Birds feeding babies, tin litho **30.00**
Boy, gold wash, holding rectangle for ad label, 1930s **20.00**
Cartoon Character
　Felix, 1¾" l, black and white, dark brown ground, caption "Fancy You Fancying Me Felix!", 1930s **50.00**
　Mickey Mouse, playing drum **35.00**
Clown, 1½ × 2¼", multicolored, Japan
. . . . **3.00**
Cricket, yellow and black, insect design
. . . . **10.00**
Halloween, witch and pumpkin, orange, black, and white **15.00**
Political, Click with Dick, 1¾" l, white and dark blue **12.00**

CLOCKS

Look for clocks that are fun (have motion actions) or that are terrific in a decorating scheme (a schoolhouse clock in a country setting). Clocks are bought to be seen and used.

Avoid buying any clock that does not work. You do not know whether it is going to cost $5.00, $50.00, or $500.00 to repair. Are you prepared to risk the higher numbers? Likewise, avoid clocks that need extensive repair work to the case. There are plenty of clocks in fine condition awaiting purchase.

Club: National Association of Watch and Clock Collectors, Inc, 514 Poplar, Columbia, PA 17512.

Advertising
  Calumet Baking Powder, oak case
    .... **995.00**
  Coca–Cola, round, metal, silver and red, c1950 .... **150.00**
  Frostie Root Beer, cuckoo, Frostie on pendulum **125.00**
  Golden Secret, Jefferson **50.00**
  Jacob Lucks Clothier, Watkins, NY, figural, dog, black man holding sign above **160.00**
  Orange Crush, Spartus, MIB, 1960s
    .... **125.00**
  Purina Poultry Chows, electric, three dials, red, white, and blue checkerboard bag **40.00**
  Valvoline Motor Oil, lights up **125.00**
  Vernors, lights up, little man with cap and beard **125.00**
Alarm
  Art Deco, 3″ h, white metal case, silvered dial, 30–hour time and alarm movement, Westclox **30.00**

Alarm, My Little Pony, white plastic body, pink and purple mane and tail, dial marked "My Little Pony, Nelsonic Quartz copyright 1985 Hasbro Bradley, Inc.", back marked "Made in Hong Kong," 10″ w, 10″ h, $15.00.

  Brass, double bells, Bradley, Germany
    .... **35.00**
  Metal, 10¼″ h, Seth Thomas, 1910–1920 .... **50.00**
Banjo, 17⅝″ h, inlaid mahogany case, eagle finial, New Haven Clock Co, c1920
  .... **150.00**
Beehive, 5¼″ h, brass, porcelain dial, Chelsea, c1900 .... **50.00**
Carriage, bronze, Ansonia **250.00**
Character
  Big Bird, animated arms, Bradley **40.00**
  Cinderella, 2½ × 4½ × 4″, alarm, windup, white metal case, orig box, Westclox **50.00**
  Donald Duck, 2 × 4½ × 4½″, alarm, metal case, light blue, orig box, Bayard **250.00**
  Mickey Mouse
    Bayard, Mickey's head wags, 1964
      .... **150.00**
    Ingersoll, cathedral plastic case, orig graphic color box, 1949
      .... **475.00**
  Pluto, 4 × 5 × 9½″ h, hard plastic, eyes and tongue move, orig box, Allied Mfg Co, c1955 ...... **400.00**
  Popeye and Swee' Pea, alarm, ivory enameled steel case, color illus on dial, Smiths, c1968 .... **100.00**
  Raggedy Ann & Andy, talking, Janex
    .... **40.00**
  Roy Rogers, alarm, windup, metal case, animated, Ingraham, c1951 **300.00**
  Strawberry Shortcake, alarm, orig box
    .... **25.00**
Cuckoo, 19″ h, carved case, bird with glass eyes on top, two doors, dancing figures, Germany, 1940 .... **110.00**
Electric, chrome, 5 × 5″, General Electric, 1920s **80.00**
Figural
  Birdhouse, two celluloid birds popping out of windows, United **135.00**
  Refrigerator, 8½″ h, white metal, GE label, Warren Telechron Co, Ashland, MA **185.00**
  Ship, walnut hull, chrome plated sails and rigs, lighted portholes, United Clock Co, 1955 .... **90.00**
  Tape Measure, black, Lux **30.00**
Kitchen
  Oak, Ansonia, Belmont **265.00**
  Walnut, New Haven Clock Co, Clarita
    .... **250.00**
Mantel
  Black Marble, 19¼″ h, incised gold dec, mounted figure on top, black and gold dial, Sozet, 1890 .... **30.00**
  Fruitwood, Chelsea, c1910 ...... **80.00**
  Rosewood, 10½″ h, veneered case, Seth Thomas, c1880 .... **75.00**
Schoolhouse
  Sessions, 19½″ h, oak, orig label, Sessions Clock Co, 1915–1920 **300.00**
  Seth Thomas, oak case, 8 day ... **150.00**

Wall, Ansonia General, walnut case, 71″ l, $1,900.00.

  Waterbury Clock Co, 24″ h, mahogany, veneered case, Waterbury Clock Co, c1890 .... **200.00**
Stove, 9¾″ h, cast iron, 30–hour time and alarm hairspring movement, c1900
  .... **100.00**

CLOTHING AND ACCESSORIES

Decide from the beginning whether you are buying clothing and accessories for use or display. If you are buying for use, apply very strict standards with respect to condition and long-term survival prospects. If you only want the items for display, you can be a little less fussy about condition.

Vintage clothing was a hot collectible craze in the 1980s. Things seem to have cooled off a bit. Emphasis in the 1990s seems to be on accessories, with plastic purses from the 1950s leading the parade.

I love the wide ties from the late 1950s and early 1960s, but they have become so trendy and pricy that I find myself more often than not passing them by. Besides, Dad has a closet full at home that belonged to him as a young adult. He's come a long way in his tastes since then.

Club: The Costume Society of America, 55 Edgewater Dr, PO Box 73, Earleville, MD 21919.

Newsletters: *Lilli's Vintage Clothing Newsletter,* 19 Jamestown Dr, Cincinnati, OH 45241; *Vintage Clothing Newsletter,* PO Box 1422, Corvallis, OR 97339.

Periodicals: *Lady's Gallery,* PO Box 1761, Independence, MO 64055; *The Glass Slipper,* 653 S Orange Ave, Sarasota, Fl 34236; *The Vintage Gazette,* 194 Amity St, Amherst, MA 01002.

Baby Gown, string tie at neck **6.00**
Baby Pants, Playtex Waterproof Dress–eez, snap, orig box **6.00**
Bed Jacket, blue, satin, lace trim **20.00**
Bloomers, crepe satin, peach, silk embroidery, lace **20.00**
Blouse, white, cotton, Victorian cutwork **20.00**
Change Purse
  Mesh
    Art Nouveau head **45.00**
    Coins surrounding head **40.00**
    Mother–of–Pearl **15.00**
    Tin, small face, mouth opens for change **35.00**
Coat
  Cashmere, silver fox collar, c1940 **45.00**
  Muskrat, bell shaped sleeves **95.00**
Collar
  Beaded, white **15.00**
  Linen, sq cutwork corners **25.00**
Dress
  Chiffon, blue, braid edge trim, 1925 . . . . **40.00**
  Crepe, brown, evening, matching velvet capelet, feather trim, c1930 . . . **45.00**
  Psychedelic, Mollie Parnis, 1960s **85.00**
  Silk, black, chiffon sleeves, embroidered, 1923 . . . . **50.00**
  Victorian, teenager's, white, French lace insertions, tucks of embroidery **135.00**
Dressing Gown, ruby red, satin, ruffled edges, 1930 . . . . **30.00**
Gloves, pr
  Lady's, leather, France **15.00**
  Opera length, kid leather **20.00**
Handbag
  Alligator
    9½" w, 7" h, wedge shape, strap handle, black, "American Designer Award Lesco Lona" label **85.00**
    17" w, 9½" h, large tortoise shell type handles, "JR of Florida" label **85.00**
  Beaded, celluloid compact top and chain **225.00**
  Enameled, Mandalian **95.00**
  Gold mesh, German silver frame, pink coral stones, silk lining **68.00**

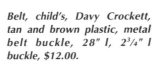
Belt, child's, Davy Crockett, tan and brown plastic, metal belt buckle, 28" l, 2¾" l buckle, $12.00.

Plastic, Lucite, pearlized, round lid, twisted handle, seashell dec **18.00**
Shaggy, beaded, wristband, silk lining **58.00**
Silk, clutch, black, cut steel beads, marked "France," c1930 . . . . . **40.00**
Hat, top, Victorian, beaver **65.00**
Jacket, Sir Jac, The Crest of Outerware, small **5.00**
Measuring Book, *English Town Clothes,* custom tailoring book, A Sagner & Sons, Inc **12.00**
Necktie
  Bolo, Zorro, 15" l, black strings, silvered tin disk with black portrait and red name, late 1950s **25.00**
  Marilyn Monroe, *The Seven Year Itch,* black, colorful stitched image, Made in England, mid 1950s **75.00**
  Oleg Cassini, 1960s **6.00**
  President Nixon Now More Than Ever, white, dark blue, and red print, unused **15.00**
  Reddy Kilowatt, bluish–charcoal slate, printed red and white images, stitched label "Made Expressly For Reddy Kilowatt Your Electric Servant" **150.00**
Pajamas
  Child's, Nitey–Nite, size 4, ftd **5.50**
  Men's, flannel, medium, Harwick **16.00**
Panties, satin, Biltrite, size medium . . . **6.50**
Petticoat, Victorian, white **10.00**

Collar, celluloid, marked "Boniface Rubber," for size 16, $25.00.

Prom Gown, pink, net and taffeta, layered skirt, bow trim, c1950 . . . . **35.00**
Roller Skates, child's, strap–on **12.00**
Shoes
  Child's, Birth–Right, white, strap, hard sole, size 6, orig box **12.00**
  Men's, canvas, 1880s **75.00**
  Women's
    Alligator, pumps, 2" heel, size 7, Emilio of Milan label **85.00**
    Leather, high button **85.00**
Skirt
  Poodle dec, pink, felt **25.00**
  Victorian, embroidered panels with French lace insert **60.00**
Skirt Hoop, Victorian, wire and tape **85.00**
Sleep Cap, lady's, silk, unused **60.00**
Snow Shoes, military style, 54" l, 10" toe curl, complete with boot harness **110.00**
Spats, gray, wool, c1900 . . . . **25.00**
Stockings, BV May, May Hosiery Mills, unused **6.50**
Sweater, cashmere, white pearl trim **35.00**

COCA–COLA COLLECTIBLES

John Pemberton, a pharmacist from Atlanta, Georgia, is credited with creating the formula for Coca–Cola in 1886. Less than two years later, he sold out to Asa G. Chandler. Chandler improved the formula and began advertising. By the 1890s America was Coca–Cola conscious.

Coke, a term first used in 1941, is now recognized worldwide. American collectors still focus primarily on Coca–Cola material designed for the American market. Although it would take a little effort to obtain, a collection of foreign Coke advertising would make a terrific display. What a perfect excuse to fly to the Orient.

Club: The Coca–Cola Collectors Club International, PO Box 49166, Atlanta, GA 30359.

Annual Report, 1935 . . . . **5.00**
Banner, 1 × 3′, plastic, 100th Anniversary
. . . . **26.00**
Belt Buckle/Cigar Cutter, heavy brass, nun
on outside, naked lady inside, c1915
. . . . **50.00**
Blotter
1903 . . . . **30.00**
1942, girl sitting on blanket and beach
scene **8.00**
1947 . . . . **35.00**
1952 . . . . **15.00**
Booklet, *The Truth About Coca–Cola,* 1912
. . . . **30.00**
Bottle, brown, Huntington, WV, 1918
. . . . **35.00**
Bottle Opener, hand **10.00**
Bridge Score Pad **5.00**
Bubble Bath, bottle shape **10.00**
Can, diamond with bottle center dec, c1960
. . . . **15.00**
Carrier, cardboard **12.00**
Cassette Player **25.00**
Charm Bracelet, 6½″ l, brass, NFL, four
miniature charms, punter, football, NFL
logo, Coke logo, enamel accents, c1970
. . . . **20.00**
Check, Coca–Cola Bottling Co, 1948   **6.00**
Clock, round, metal, silver and red, c1950
. . . . **150.00**
Clothing, bell–bottom pants, 1970s   **40.00**
Cribbage Game, MIB **55.00**
Dish, souvenir 1964 New York World's Fair
. . . . **65.00**
Fan, cardboard, 1940s **22.00**
Festoon, sports car, 1958 . . . . **400.00**
Flyswatter **9.00**
Hat, beanie type, c1960 . . . . **7.00**
Ice Scraper **8.00**
Key Chain
Fish shape **4.00**
Miniature bottle, c1950 . . . . **6.00**
Marbles, bag, 1950s **25.00**
Matchbook, c1930 . . . . **5.00**

Menu, girl holding serving tray, unused
. . . . **30.00**
Pencil, bullet shape **4.00**
Pinback Button
1⅛″ d, red and white, "Drink Coca–
Cola," c1950 . . . . **10.00**
1¼″ d, red and white, "Coca–Cola Big
Wheels Club," *Cleveland Press*
newspaper, ship's wheel center,
c1930s **50.00**
Plate, lunch, china, 1931 . . . . **220.00**
Playing Cards
Autumn girl, MIB, 1943 . . . . . . **200.00**
Party girl, complete deck, 1951   **135.00**
Santa Claus, complete deck **12.00**
World War II girl, MIB, 1943 . . . **225.00**
Pocket Watch, E Ingraham, pat 1907
. . . . **250.00**
Post Card, showing c1940 Coke truck **18.00**
Punchboard, small **8.00**
Radiator Plate, 1920s **175.00**
Radio, bottle shape, MIB **35.00**
Sign
19 × 54″, tin, Ice Cold Coca–Cola, bot-
tle shape **400.00**
30″ h, figural, bottle shape **250.00**
45″ d, round, porcelain, bottle illus
. . . . **200.00**
Syrup Jug, gal, paper label, 1950s . . . **18.00**
Telephone **35.00**
Thermometer
12″ d, round **100.00**
17″ l, bottle shape **90.00**
Timer, sand type **10.00**
Toy
Frisbee **20.00**
Pop Gun **4.00**
Truck, Buddy L, 1960s, MIB **200.00**
Tray
Barefoot boy with dog, 1931 . . . **425.00**
Betty, 1914 . . . . **235.00**
Cheese and snacks, 1956 . . . . **20.00**
Girl in afternoon, 1938 . . . . **125.00**
Girl in menu, 1955 . . . . **40.00**
Ice Skater, 1940 . . . . **200.00**
Pansy Garden, 1961 . . . . **20.00**
Picnic Basket, 1958 . . . . **25.00**
Santa, 1973 . . . . **15.00**
Thanksgiving, TV, 1961 . . . . **20.00**
Umbrella **25.00**
Whistle, 1960s **7.00**

COIN–OPERATED MACHINES

This category covers any machine operated by inserting a coin, from arcade games to player pianos to vending machines. Since all these machines are mechanical, it is important to buy only machines in operating order. The techniques to repair them rest in the hands of a few enthusiasts. Many repair parts need to be made by hand.

Many museums, recognizing the long–term collectibility of coin–operated games, have already begun to acquire some of the early video games. Imagine Pacman in a museum. It doesn't seem so long ago that I was playing it in an arcade.

Newsletters: *Coin–Op Newsletter,* 909 26th St, NW, Washington, DC 20037; *Jukebox Collector,* 2545 SE 60th St, Des Moines, IA 50317.

Periodicals: *Around The Vending Wheel,* 5417 Castana Ave, Lakewood, CA 90712; *Coin–Op Classics,* 17844 Toiyabe St, Fountain Valley, CA 92708.

Dispenser, Dixie–Vortex Cup, one cent, long glass domed cylinder, orig cardboard box, 36″ h **400.00**
Jukebox
Rockola, Model 1422, coin operated, twenty selections, rebuilt amplifier, orig records, light–up plastic columns, flashing lights, early 1940s, 29 × 60 × 30″ **2,150.00**
Wurlitzer, Model 1650, 48 selections, light–up side columns, 55″ h, 1954
. . . . **500.00**
Mutoscope, one cent, optical card viewer, original marquee insert promoting "nature's beauties," 14 × 74 × 18″
. . . . **1,250.00**
Pinball Machine, The Empire Billiard Machine, vertical, ornate wood case with galleried top, orig play card, 48″ h
. . . . **200.00**
Skill Game
Challenger, shoot balls for points, 10½ × 16 × 24″ **85.00**

Serving Tray, 1922, 10½ × 13¼″, $550.00.

Slot Machine, Mill's Jackpot, c1930, $1,500.00.

Champion's Basketball, one cent, five shots per play, wood case, glass panel with basketball motif, 21 × 26½ × 11" **120.00**

Master Target Practice, one cent, ball gum vendor, cast metal and wood, place penny in gun and shoot at target, 10 × 14¾ × 22" ... **325.00**

Skill Jump, one cent, skiers juggle ball down steps, Groetchen Mnfct Co, 1940s, 21 × 73 × 12" **225.00**

Stamping Machine, Roovers Stamping Machine, five cent, cast iron wheel with alphabet and numbers prints metal tags, Brooklyn, NY, 12 × 57 x 20" ... **700.00**

Trade Stimulator

Ball Flip, one cent, wood case, pedestal base, 9 × 15 × 15" **175.00**

Cent–A–Pack, cigarettes and gum balls, three wheels, 10 × 12 × 9½" **135.00**

5 Jacks Skill Flip, one cent, Pace Mfg Co, Chicago, 19 × 19 × 10" **750.00**

Hercules Midget Baseball, one cent, battery operated lights, cast iron front and marquee, Hercules Novelty Co, Chicago, 16¼ × 21½ × 9" **1,800.00**

Kicker and Catcher, one cent, maple case, 14 × 17½" × 12" **600.00**

Star Advertiser, cigar, one cent, oak case, Drobisch Bros, IL, 1890s, 13½ × 19 × 6½" **775.00**

Tally, ball gum, five cent, Art Deco design, three wheels, 10 × 14 x 9" **225.00**

Try It Dice, ball gum, five cent, 11¼ × 7¾ × 7¾" **200.00**

Wizard Fortune Teller, one cent, cast metal front with raised wizard, orig card, 14 × 18½ × 6" **900.00**

Vending Machine

Basketball, one cent, gum vendor, flip gum ball into basket, 11 × 15½ × 7" **75.00**

Breath Ball Vendor, one cent, bulb shaped globe, push slide mechanism, octagonal plated metal body, cast iron base with three legs, 6 × 11 × 10" **2,850.00**

Pulver's Chocolate, Cocoa and Gum, one cent, emb tin, 10½ × 24 × 5½" **3,500.00**

Zeno Chewing Gum, one cent, porcelain, wall mounted, 7 × 16½ × 6" **400.00**

COINS, AMERICAN

Just because a coin is old does not mean that it is valuable. Value often depends more on condition than on age. This being the case, the first step in deciding if any of your coins are valuable is to grade them. Coins are graded on a scale of 70, with 70 being the best and 1 being the worst.

Start your research by acquiring Marc Hudgeons's *The Official 1995 Blackbook Price Guide To United States Coins, Thirty–Third Edition* (House of Collectibles: 1994). Resist the temptation to look up your coins immediately. Read the hundred–page introduction, over half of which deals with the question of grading.

Do not overlook the melt (weight) value of silver content coins. In many cases, weight value will be far greater than collectible value. If only we'd sold when the industry was paying twenty times face value in the midst of the 1980s silver craze!

Club: American Numismatic Association, 818 North Cascade Avenue, Colorado Springs, CO 80903.

COINS, FOREIGN

The foreign coins that you are most likely to find at a flea market are the leftover change that someone brought back with them from their travels. Since the coins were in circulation, they are common and of a low grade. In some countries, they have been withdrawn from circulation and cannot even be redeemed for face value.

If you are a dreamer and think you have uncovered hidden wealth, use Chester L. Krause and Clifford Mishler's *1993 Edition Standard Catalog of World Coins* (Krause Publications: 1992). This book covers world coinage from 1801 through 1991.

Avoid any ancient coinage. There are excellent fakes on the market. You need to be an expert to tell the good from the bad. Coins are one of those categories where it pays to walk away when the deal is too good. Honest coin dealers work on very small margins. They cannot afford to give away anything of value.

COLLEGE COLLECTIBLES

Rah, rah, sis–boom–bah! The Yuppies made a college education respectable again. They tout their old alma mater. They usually have a souvenir of their college days in their office at home or work.

You will not find a Harvard graduate with a room full of Yale memorabilia and vice versa. These items have value only to someone who attended the school. The exception is sport–related college memorabilia. This has a much broader appeal, either to a conference collector or a general sports collector.

Periodical: *Sports Collectors Digest*, 700 East State St, Iola, WI 54990.

Book, *Stanford, The Story of A University*, Edith Mirriles, 1959, 255 pgs, sgd by author **17.50**

Calendar, University of Wisconsin, Madison, Bascom Hall photo, 1916 **100.00**

Compact, Lehigh University, camera shape, sealed **45.00**

Folder, Yale Athletic Association Fall Meeting, three panels, violet, black lettering, 1874 .... **40.00**

Magazine, Phi Gamma Delta, 1955 **10.00**

Nodder, 7" h, basketball player, composition, rounded gold base, sticker inscribed "Millersville," 1960s **22.00**

Padlock, University of Colorado, Yale **75.00**

Pinback Button

Oregon vs WSC, yellow, dark green illus **15.00**

Penn State, 2¼" d, Orange Bowl, bowl of oranges **18.00**

Rockne of Notre Dame, black and white photo, 1930s **15.00**

Sugar Bowl, Fordham, New Orleans, LA, purple, 1942 .... **5.00**

Plate, 10" d, William and Mary College, Wren building, Jonroth **10.00**

Program

Illinois–Notre Dame Football Game, 8 × 11", 20 pgs, Oct 9, 1937 **25.00**

University of Iowa, 5 × 5¼", commencement, steel engraving, 3 pgs, 1891 .... **10.00**

Sheet Music, *Everybody Loves A College Girl*, Kerry Mills, 1911 .... **3.00**

Souvenir Spoon

Cornell University, Art Nouveau woman **50.00**

Pinback Button, Basketball, State Champions, Kutztown Univ, 1916–17, $15.00.

Iowa State College, Indian Chief, SS
.... **28.00**
Notre Dame **100.00**
State Normal School, Superior, Wisconsin **25.00**
Wellesley College, woman in cap and gown handle **50.00**
Tie Clip, Yale, 2" l, key shape, bright gold colored plating, inscribed "The Yale & Towne Mfg Co" and "First For Ike," issued by Yale Ike Club, 1952 ..... **75.00**
Yearbook
Iowa State Teachers College, 1940 **10.00**
Princeton University, 1942 ...... **28.00**
University of Texas, 1918, 480 pgs **12.00**

COLORING BOOKS

The key is to find these gems uncolored. Some collectors will accept a few pages colored, but the coloring had better be neat. If it is scribbled, forget it.

Most of the value rests on the outside cover. The closer the image is to the actual character or personality featured, the higher the value. The inside pages of most coloring books consist of cheap newsprint. It yellows and becomes brittle over time. However, resist buying only the cover. Collectors prefer to have the entire book.

Annie Oakley, 11 × 14", Whitman, unused, 1955 .... **18.00**
Barnie Google, 1968 .... **10.00**
Blondie, 8½ × 11", Dell Publishing, 1954, unused **20.00**
Boo Boo Bear, 8 × 11", Watkins–Strathmore, copyright 1963, 96 pgs **25.00**
Bugs Bunny and Porky Pig, 1946 .... **65.00**

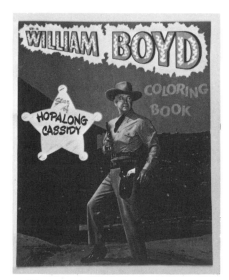

William Boyd, Star of Hopalong Cassidy, #1231–15, 10½" w, 13½" h, $20.00.

Buster Crabbe Foreign Legionnaire ... **45.00**
Charlie Chaplin, 10 × 17", Donohue & Co, copyright 1917 .... **80.00**
Daniel Boone, 8½ × 10¾", Whitman, copyright 1961 .... **75.00**
Dennis The Menace, 1960, unused **12.50**
Dick Tracy, 8¼ × 11", Saalfield, #2536, copyright 1946 .... **25.00**
Disneyland, 11 × 13½", Whitman, copyright 1956 .... **50.00**
Donald Duck, 7½ × 8½", Whitman, 1946, unused **20.00**
Esso Oil Drop **25.00**
Fonzie, 8¼ × 10¾", Treasure Books, copyright 1976 Paramount Pictures Corp
.... **15.00**
Garrison's Gorillas, 8 × 10¼", Whitman, copyright 1968 Selmur Productions Inc
.... **25.00**
Hee Haw, 8½ × 11", Saalfield Publishing Co, copyright 1970 Columbia Broadcasting System Inc **25.00**
Hong Kong Phooey, 8½ × 11", Saalfield, copyright 1975, 32 pgs, unused **15.00**
Hopalong Cassidy, 5¼ × 5¼", "William Boyd/Star of Hopalong Cassidy/On The Range," 48 pgs, Samuel Lowe Co, copyright 1951 .... **25.00**
Howdy Doody, some colored pages **15.00**
Indian Scout Kit Carson, 8 × 11", Abbott Publishing Co, copyright 1957 ... **25.00**
Jughead, 8 × 11", Whitman, Archie Comic Publications Inc copyright 1972, 10 pgs
.... **25.00**
Leave It To Beaver, 8 × 10¾", Saalfield Publishing Co, copyright 1958 ... **75.00**
Li'l Abner, 8 × 11", Saalfield, #209, 80 pgs, copyright 1941 .... **30.00**
Lone Ranger, 8½ × 11", Whitman, 64 pgs, Cheerios premium, 1956 .... **75.00**
Partridge Family, 8½ × 11", Saalfield, copyright 1971 Columbia Pictures Industries Inc. **25.00**
Planet of the Apes, 8½ × 11", Saalfield, Apjac Productions copyright 1974, unused **15.00**
Rocky and Bullwinkle, "Bullwinkle's How To Have Fun Outdoors Without Getting Clobbered," unused **20.00**
Roy Rogers, 15 × 11", Roy Rogers and Dale Evans, 1952 .... **20.00**
Shazam, 11 × 14", Whitman, pinup poster on back cov, National Periodical Publications, copyright 1975 .... **12.00**
Shirley Temple, Great Big Coloring Book, 1936 .... **75.00**

Spiderman, large size **18.00**
Straight Arrow, 10¾ × 14¼", Stephens Publishing Co, National Biscuit Co copyright 1949, 20 pgs **25.00**
Superman, 8 × 11", Whitman, National Periodical Publications copyright 1966, unused **25.00**
Tom & Jerry, 8 × 11", Watkins–Strathmore, copyright 1957, 192 pgs, unused **45.00**
Tom Mix, 11 × 14", Whitman, 96 pgs, 1935 .... **50.00**
Walt Disney
Christmas, 8¼ × 10¾", Dell Publishing Co, copyright 1954, 80 pgs ... **45.00**
Mickey Mouse Club, 11 × 13", Whitman, copyright 1955, 164 pages, unused **50.00**
Welcome Back Kotter, 8 × 11", Whitman, copyright 1977 Wolper Organization Inc
.... **15.00**

COMBS

The form is pretty basic. Value rests in how and in what material the comb is presented. Some hair combs are fairly elaborate and actually should be considered as jewelry accessories.

Beware of combs being sold separately that were originally part of larger dresser sets. Their value is less than combs that were meant to stand alone.

You can build an interesting collection inexpensively by collecting giveaway combs. You will be amazed to see how many individuals and businesses used this advertising media, from politicians to funeral parlors.

Club: Antique Fancy Comb Collectors Club, 4901 Grandview, Ypsilanti, MI 48197.

Advertising, Denver House, pocket size, aluminum, diecut, handsaw shape **28.00**
Political, Muskie, "Vote Muskie, Comb Nixon Out of Your Hair," blue plastic, inscriptions both sides, 7" l **15.00**
Purse Comb, folding
Brass
Embossed cracker barrel design **35.00**
Rhinestone covered case **50.00**
Enameled, rhinestone champagne glass motif **50.00**

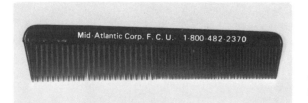

Mid–Atlantic Corp, FCU, telephone number, green, white lettering, 5" l, $.50.

Lucite, gold speckled case, Curry Arts
.... 25.00
Mother–of–Pearl, Wiesner of Miami
.... 50.00
Plastic, faux mother–of–pearl, Marhill,
1960s 25.00
Side Comb
  Celluloid, butterscotch colored, rhine-
    stone band, c1900 .... 10.00
  Faux Tortoise Shell, pierced floral design
  .... 45.00
  Gutta Percha, black, chain link design
  .... 150.00
  Horn, black, white glass beaded band,
    early 20th C 45.00
  Jet, faceted bead design, England, c1890
  .... 45.00
  Plastic
    Crown design, brilliant rhinestones,
      faux tortoise shell, 1940s   35.00
    Eagle design, brilliant rhinestones set
      in brass frame, faux tortoise shell,
      5½" w, 4" l 45.00
    Floral spray design, ornate, green and
      blue rhinestones, 1960s ... 20.00
    Rhinestone band with pearl end
    .... 25.00
    Tiara design, silver colored metal,
      brilliant rhinestones, hinged, clear
    .... 30.00
Tuck Comb
  Celluloid, faux tortoise shell
    Amethyst–colored rhinestones 75.00
    Double Arches, cobalt blue rhine-
      stones around edges 80.00
    Peacock motif, rhinestone accents,
      early 1900s 40.00
    Spade shape, rhinestones around
      edge, 1900–1915 .... 40.00
  Horn, yellow, cut steel flower and rope
    dec 175.00
  Tortoise Shell, domed top, etched leaf
    design, nine rhinestones, 1920s
    .... 28.00

COMEDIAN COLLECTIBLES

    Laughter is said to be the best medi-
cine. If this is true, why does it hurt so
much when Abbott & Costello meet the
Mummy?
    Comedians of all eras have gifted
the public with the pleasures of laughter.
In return the public has made them stars.
    Comedian collectibles range
throughout the known mediums of radio,
vaudeville, television, standup, and cin-
ema. The plight of Charlie Chaplin
echoes in the antics of Whoopie Goldberg. Comedian collectibles also reflect
the diversity of those mediums. So feel
free to laugh out loud the next time you

find a Groucho Marx eyeglass and mus-
tache mask—I do.

Abbott & Costello, pinback button, 1939
  New York World's Fair, 1¼" d, "Lou
  I'm a Bad Boy' Costello for Mayor of
  World's Fair Midway/Abbott for Com-
  missioner of Laffs," portrait illus, blue
  and white 65.00
Bob Newhart, script, TV series, signed
  "Bob" 25.00
Charlie Weaver, book, *Charlie Weaver's
  Letters From Mama,* Cliff Arquette, 1959,
  64 pgs 15.00
Dobie Gillis, nodder, 7" h, composition,
  1960s 100.00
Jackie Gleason
  Bus, Wolverine, steel, wood wheels,
    14" l, 1955 .... 500.00
  Climbing Toy, Poor Soul, c1955 120.00
  Cocktail Napkins, Honeymooners, set of
    50, orig box, 1955 .... 40.00
  Game, Jackie Gleason's Awa-A-A-A-Y
    We Go, orig box, Transogram, 1956
    .... 125.00
Johnny Carson, tablet, 8 × 10", full color
  photo cov, 1960s 10.00
Laurel & Hardy
  Bank, figural Hardy, hard vinyl, multi-
    colored, Play Pal Plastics, 7½" h,
    1974 .... 30.00
  Doll, pr, 23" h Laurel and 20" h Hardy,
    bisque head and shoulders, forearms,
    and lower legs, stuffed cloth body,
    1970s 100.00
  Figure, pr, 8" h Laurel, 7½" h Hardy,
    hard plastic, vinyl head, R Dakin &
    Co, c1974 .... 100.00
  Mask, pr, 6½ × 10", Laurel & Hardy
    faces, molded plastic, 1960s   35.00
  Pencil Sharpener, 1½" h, plastic, Laurel
    head, orig blister card, Larry Harmon
    copyright, 1970s 50.00
  Puzzle, 11½ × 14½", frame tray, Whit-
    man, Laurel, Hardy, and gorilla car-
    toon illus, 1967 .... 14.00
  Sign, 18 × 31½", Anco Wiper Blades
    adv, diecut and emb hard plastic,
    portrait illus 65.00
Lucille Ball
  Book, *Lucy and The Madcap Mystery,*
    Whitman, 212 pgs, copyright 1963
    Desilu Productions Inc 15.00
  Doll, 27" h, stuffed cloth, molded plastic
    face, yellow yarn hair, red and white
    fabric outfit, 1950s 150.00
  Notebook, 6 × 9", 40 pgs, black and
    white and color photos of Lucy and
    Desi, recipes, 1950s 25.00
  Paper Doll, Lucy, Desi, and Little Ricky,
    Whitman, copyright 1953 .... 75.00
  TV Guide, December 10, 1955, color
    photo on cov and three–page article
    .... 25.00
Marx Brothers
  Game, Groucho TV Quiz, Pressman
    .... 75.00

Groucho Goggles and Cigar, plastic,
    carded, 1955 .... 40.00
  Sheet Music, 9 × 12", *Ev'ryone Says I
    Love You,* "Horse Feathers," 1932
    .... 25.00
  TV Guide, July 18, 1952, cover photo
    .... 20.00
Milton Berle
  Book, *Milton Berle's Jumbo Fun Book,*
    48 pgs, illus, jokes, games, and reci-
    pes, copyright 1940 The Quaker
    Oats Co 15.00
  Sign, 13 × 19½", cardboard, "The
    Texaco Star Theater Presents The
    Milton Berle Show," white, black
    and white photo, red design, green
    stars 75.00
  TV Guide, Volume 4, Number 21, May
    23–29, 1952, cover photo and article
    .... 25.00
Robin Williams
  Action Figure, 4" h, Mork From Ork
    Eggship, poseable, Mattel, copyright
    1979 Paramount Pictues Corp
    .... 25.00
  Doll, 9" h, Mork, plastic, poseable, red
    plastic backpack talking unit, Mattel
    copyright 1979 Paramount Pictures
    Corp 25.00
  Game, Mork & Mindy, Parker Brothers,
    1979 .... 15.00
  Lunch Box, King–Seeley Thermos, steel
    box, plastic thermos, 1979 ... 30.00
  Tee shirt, white, "Na Nu, Na Nu," size
    M 12.00
Pinky Lee
  Game, Pinky Lee Game Time, orig box,
    Pressman Toys, early 1950s ... 30.00
  Tray, 10½ × 14½", tin, full color litho
    .... 20.00
Rowan & Martin, Laugh–In
  Game, Squeeze Your Bippy, orig box,
    Hasbro, 1968 .... 35.00
  Magazine, *Laugh–In,* Volume 1, Number
    2, November, 1968 .... 15.00
  Paper Doll Book, Saalfield #1325, 8¼
    × 11½", 1969 .... 20.00
  Waste Can, 13" h, litho steel, photos,
    illus, and phrases 25.00
Smothers Brothers, pinback button, 1¼" d,
  "The Smothers Brothers Comedy Hour/
  Mom Always Liked You Best," white,
  red print, late 1960s 15.00
Soupy Sales
  Autograph, "Sincerely Soupy Sales,"
    black and white glossy photo post
    card 20.00
  Game, Soupy Sales Mini Board Card
    Game, Ideal, 1965 .... 25.00
  Magazine, *Soupy Sales,* Volume 1,
    Number 1, Fall 1965, 68 pgs
    .... 30.00
  Pinback Button, 3½" d, Charter Member/
    Soupy Sales Society, 1960 .... 15.00
  Wallet, 3½ × 4", vinyl, snap closure,
    blue with black, white, and red de-
    sign 50.00

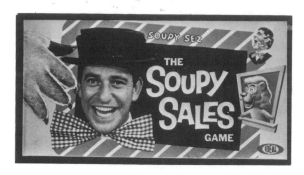

Game, The Soupy Sales Game, Ideal, copyright 1965 Soupy Sales WMC, $20.00.

Steve Allen, balloon, ''Goo–Goo Steve Allen–Star of NBC–TV Tonight,'' yellow, mid 1950s **10.00**
Three Stooges
　Badge, 3'' d, celluloid, white, black and white illus, red and blue inscription, ''Collector Cups'' promotion
　. . . . . **15.00**
　Bubble Gum Card, 2¹/₂ × 3¹/₂'', #54, Fleer, 1966 . . . . **50.00**
　Game, Fun House, Lowell Toy Corp, 1959 . . . . **200.00**
　Poster, 27 × 41'', *Three Stooges Meet Hercules,* Columbia Pictures, 1961
　. . . . . **60.00**
　Record, 45 rpm, *Yuletide Songs,* cardboard sleeve, 1959 copyright, Norman Maurer Productions **25.00**

COMIC BOOKS

　Comic books come in all shapes and sizes. The number that have survived is almost endless. Although there were reprint books of cartoon strips in the 1910s, 1920s, and 1930s, the modern comic book had its origin in June 1938 when DC issued Action Comics No. 1, marking the first appearance of Superman.

　Comics are divided into Golden Age, Silver Age, and Contemporary titles. Before you begin buying, read John Hegenberger's *Collector's Guide To Comic Books* (Wallace–Homestead: 1990) and D. W. Howard's *Investing In Comics* (The World of Yesterday: 1988).

　The dominant price guide for comics is Robert Overstreet's *The Official Overstreet Comic Book Price Guide* (Avon Books). However, more and more you see obsolete comics being offered in shops and at conventions for ten to twenty–five percent less than Overstreet's prices. The comic book market may be facing a revaluation crisis similar to what happened in the stamp market several years ago when the editors of the Scott catalog significantly lowered the values for many stamps.

Periodicals: *Comic Book Market Place,* PO 180900, Coronado, CA 92178; *Comic Buyers Guide,* 700 E State St, Iola, WI 54990; *Comics Values Monthly,* Attic Books, 15 Danbury Rd, Ridgefield, CT 06877; *Overstreet's Comic Book Marketplace,* 801 20th St NW, Suite 3, Cleveland, TN 37311.

Note: Most comics, due to condition, are not worth more than 50¢ to a couple of dollars. Very strict grading standards are applied to comics less than ten years old. The following list shows the potential in the market. You need to check each comic book separately.

Aquaman, Battle of the Rival Aquaman, DC, #27 . . . . **25.00**
Archie, Adventures of the Fly, #6 . . . **45.00**
Avengers, Marvel, #62 . . . . **10.00**
Batman, #110 . . . . **40.00**
Beetle Bailey, Harvey, #2 . . . . **1.25**
Bewitched, Dell, #7, Dec 1966, 7 × 10''
　. . . . . **10.00**
Buster Brown, #37, mint **12.50**
Captain America, Marvel Comic, Vol 1, #100, April 1968 . . . . **10.00**
Captain Incredible, DC Action, #354 **7.00**
Captain Marvel, ''Captain Marvel Adventure,'' Wheaties adv and Bob Feller photo on back, 1964 copyright, 6¹/₂ × 8¹/₄'' **30.00**
Casper & Friends, Harvey, #4 . . . . . . **1.00**
Cheyenne, Dell, #9, Nov–Jan 1959 **12.00**
Conan The Barbarian, Shadow in the Tomb, Marvel, #31 . . . . **4.00**
Defenders, Tunnel World, Marvel, #79
　. . . . . **2.50**
Dr Jekyll and Mr Hyde, Classics Illustrated, #8 . . . . **3.75**
Fantastic Four, Mole Man, Marvel, #329
　. . . . . **1.50**
Gene Autry Comics, Dell, Vol 1, #20, Oct 1948 . . . . **18.00**
GI Joe, Vol 2, #18, winter 1952, 7 × 10''
　. . . . . **20.00**
Gunsmoke, 1958 . . . . **14.00**
Hawkman, Zatanna, #5 . . . . **6.00**
Hopalong Cassidy, Fawcett, Vol 5, #29, March 1949 . . . . **55.00**

Fawcett Pub, Sweethearts, *Oct 1949, Vol 14, No 80, $3.00.*

Hulk, Trapped in Space, Marvel, #281 **2.00**
Johnny Quest, Comico, #6 . . . . **2.00**
Little Lulu, premium, 16 pgs, Marjorie Henderson Buell 1964 copyright, 5 × 7¹/₄''
　. . . . . **20.00**
Outer Limits, #1 . . . . **30.00**
Rin–Tin–Tin and Rusty, Dell, #31, Aug–Oct **15.00**
Roy Rogers Comics, Dell, Vol 1, #17, May 1949 . . . . **80.00**
Spiderwoman, Killer Clown, Marvel, #22
　. . . . . **1.50**
The Danny Thomas Show, #1249, Nov–Jan 1962, 7¹/₂ × 10'' **12.00**
Thor, Hercules, Marvel, #229 . . . . **3.50**
Twilight Zone, #1 . . . . **42.00**
Walt Disney, Chip 'N Dale, #7 . . . . . . **2.50**
X–Men, Morlocks, Marvel, #292 . . . . . **1.50**

COMMEMORATIVE GLASSES

　Before there were modern promotional drinking glasses (the kind you get from a fast food restaurant, gas station, or by eating the contents of a glass food container) people bought glasses as souvenirs. The earliest examples have acid–etched decorations. Although these are tough to find, they are not all that expensive. One collector I know specializes in advertising spirit glasses. Her collection numbers in the hundreds.

Advertising Spirit Glasses
　Compliments of Jos Spand, 589 Atlantic Avenue, Boston, MA, 2³/₈'' h, c1910
　. . . . . **18.00**

Green Mill Whiskey, S M Denison, Wholesale Liquor Dealer, Chillicothe, OH, 2¼" h, c1910 . . . 15.00

Rose Valley Whiskey, 4" h, etched product name 15.00

Seattle Liquor Co, 1123 First Avenue, Seattle, WA, 2⁵⁄₁₆" h, gold rim, c1908 . . . . 20.00

Juice, Moon Landing, 3¼" h, clear, red, white, and blue illus and inscriptions 15.00

Tumbler

Apollo 12 Moon Mission, 4" h, red, white, and blue illus, pr 12.50

Bicentennial Presidents and Patriots Collector's Series, 5¼" h, image and biographical sketch on front, 1975 Burger Chef Systems, Inc 8.00

Bryan/Sewell, "Sixteen To One," 3¾" h, clear, frosted white portraits, 1896 . . . . 80.00

End of Prohibition, 3⅝" h, clear, GOP elephant and DEM donkey on beer keg illus, "At Last! 1933" 30.00

Heritage Collector Series, 1976, 6" h, sixteen different American history issues, Coca–Cola Company 5.00

Historical Mission Series, 5⅝" h, mission illus, Coca–Cola Company 7.00

Knoxville, Tennessee World's Fair, 1982, 5⅝" h, red and black design . . . 5.00

McKinley and Teddy Roosevelt, 3¾" h, clear, frosted portraits and slogan "Integrity, Inspiration, Industry," gold rim 80.00

Michigan 150th Anniversary, 5⁹⁄₁₆" h, red numerals encircled by white lettering, red and blue Pepsi logo on back 4.00

Minstrel Show, 5¼" h, clear, weighted bottom, black caricature performers, music and words from "Dixie's Land," 1930–1945 . . . . 15.00

National Sports Festival, Indianapolis, July 23–31, 1982, 5½" h, flared, red, white, and blue 6.00

New York World's Fair, 1939, 4½" h, clear, Theme Building and Court of Communications illus 25.00

Remember Pearl Harbor, 4¾" h, clear, red slogan, white date, red, white, and blue airplanes, warships, Hawaiian island, and Pearl Harbor Bay 75.00

Space Spectaculars of the United States, 5½" h, clear, Atlas D launch vehicle and Mercury 6 space capsule illus, red, white, and blue 12.00

Texas Centennial Exposition, 1936, 3½" h, clear, dark blue seal and cowboy on rearing horse illus 22.00

William McKinley, 3¾" h, clear, frosted image, c1896 . . . . 30.00

World Series, 5¾" h, clear, weighted bottom, white lettering, list of World Series winners from 1924 through 1951, gold batter illus 20.00

1933, 4% Beer, etched political mascots, red rim, 3⁹⁄₁₆" h, $20.00.

World War II, 4¾" h, clear, blue "Victory" over large "V" symbol 25.00

Wright–Patterson Air Force Base, 5½" h, clear, weighted bottom, Wright Brothers plane, jets, and Air Force Museum insignia, late 1950s . . . 8.00

COMMEMORATIVE MEDALS

From the late nineteenth century through the 1930s, commemorative medals were highly prized possessions. The U.S. Mint and other mints still carry on the tradition today, but to a far lesser degree.

Distinguish between medals issued in mass and those struck for a limited purpose, in some cases in issues of one for presentation. An old medal should have a surface patina that has developed over the years causing it to have a very mellow appearance. Never, never clean a medal. Collectors like the patina.

In most medals, the metal content has little value. However, medals were struck in both silver and gold. If you are not certain, have the metal tested.

Club: Token and Medal Society, Inc, PO Box 951988, Lake Mary, FL 32795–1988.

Anti–Slavery, brass, kneeling black woman, slogan "Am I Not A Woman & Sister/1838," wreath design on back with motto 70.00

Apollo XII, November 19–20, 1969, "Return To The Moon," gold colored metal, raised portraits 12.50

Centennial, US, 1⅜" d, brass shell, New Mexico trading post, inscribed "J E Barrow & Co/Post Traders/Fort Union/New Mexico," reverse with Miss Liberty and 1776 date 50.00

Civil War, 1¼" d, copper, Major General George McClellan, USA, eagle, shield, and flag design, slogan on back "I Am Born To Defend My Country" . . . 35.00

Exposition

Alaska Yukon Pacific, 1909, 1½" d, emb "Virgin Utah Copper," Utah exhibit on front, inscribed rim, reverse with state seal 20.00

Cincinnati Industrial, 1883, Brewery Award, 1¼" d, brass, six sided, "Complimentary Grand Medal" and George Washington profile on front, reverse with date, expo title, and "The Christian Moerlein Brewing Co, Cincinnati O" 60.00

Columbian, 1893

⅜" d, aluminum, raised detailed image of Manufacturers and Liberal Arts Building, Berry Brothers Varnishes adv 10.00

1½" d, bronze, raised scene of Columbus, reverse with trumpeting angels, ship, and commemorative text 40.00

2" d, white metal, raised bust portrait of Columbus, rim inscribed "Souvenir World's Columbian Exposition, Chicago, USA, 1892–1893," worn silver flashing 25.00

Cotton States, 1895, 2" d, white metal, dark finish, Phoenix bird, center inscribed "Resurgens/Atlanta, Ga," rim inscribed "Cotton States and International Exposition/Sept 18th to Dec 31st" 30.00

Civilian Conservation Corps, 50th Anniversary, 1933, 1983, gold colored medallion, gold colored bolo tie mounting, 1½" d medal, $15.00.

George Washington Bicentennial, 3″ d, brass, bust portrait, female Liberty figure on reverse with "Proclaim Liberty Throughout All The Land" inscription, orig box with blue velveteen holder
. . . . **50.00**

Hall of Fame Induction, Carl Yastrzemski, Boston Red Sox, July 23, 1989, 1½″ d, bronze colored, baseball and portrait on front, reverse with Kahn's Meats and Hillshire Farm sponsor logos **8.00**

Hudson–Fulton Celebration, 2″ d, aluminum, emb, Robert Fulton portrait above three seated goddesses on front, reverse with Hudson River discovery scene and text **20.00**

Lindberg Flight, brass, portrait and rim inscription **12.00**

Political

Andrew Johnson Inauguration, white metal, silver luster, portrait on front, reverse with "Andrew Johnson, 17 President U S" **45.00**

Harrison Campaign, brass, name, birth date, and portrait on front, reverse with log cabin and "The People's Choice In The Year 1840" . . . **10.00**

Hoover Inauguration, 3″ d, metal, dark brass finish, name, portrait, and 1929 date on front, reverse with female figure and "Inaugurated March 4, 1929, Engineer, Scholar, Statesman, Humanist" **15.00**

John Fitzgerald Kennedy Memorial, 1½″ d, brass, orig box and four page insert **15.00**

Lincoln Campaign, eagle and "Success To Republican Principles" on front, reverse with "Millions For Freedom Not One Cent For Slavery," 1860
. . . . **65.00**

Sesquicentennial, Hamden, CT, 1¼″ d, brass, emb "Eli Whitney Arms Plant" and details, 1936 . . . . **15.00**

World's Fair

Chicago, 1934, 1¼″ d, brass, emb, Travel and Transport building on front, reverse with Century of Progress symbol **10.00**

New York, 1964, white metal, Unisphere, theme slogan and dates on front, back with 300th anniversary of New York City and seal inscription
. . . . **12.50**

COMMEMORATIVE (SOUVENIR) SPOONS

Collecting commemorative spoons was extremely popular from the last decade of the nineteenth century through 1940. Actually, it has never gone completely out of fashion. You can still buy commemorative spoons at many historical and city tourist sites.

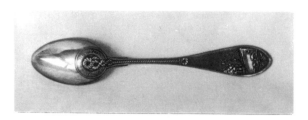

Red Star Lines, German silver, 5½″ l, $75.00.

The first thing that you want to check is for metal content. Sterling silver was a popular medium for commemorative spoons. Fine enamel work adds to value.

Clubs: American Spoon Collectors, 4922 State Line, Westwood Hills, KS 66205; The Scoop Club, 84 Oak Ave, Shelton, CT 06484.

Albuquerque, NM, kneeling Indian on handle **40.00**
Armour **12.00**
Battle Monument, Trenton, NJ **25.00**
Ben Franklin, Philadelphia **40.00**
Buffalo, NY, demitasse **15.00**
Callaway County Courthouse, Fulton, MO, SS, enameled dec, dated 1938 . . . **65.00**
Canada, SS **25.00**
Cheyenne, WY, state capital cutout **30.00**
Chief Seattle, totem pole **22.00**
Cleveland, OH **17.00**
Columbian Exposition, 1893, inverted anchor handle, standing warrior goddess and "World's Fair 1893" in bowl, 4½″ l, SP **15.00**
Columbus, bust, SP **15.00**
Denver, Colorado **18.00**
Denver, Columbine handle **16.50**
Dionne Quintuplets, set of 5, standing figure and first name on handle, 6″ h, SP
. . . . **75.00**
Duba, Morro castle **40.00**
Flint, MI, Public Library **20.00**
Fort Dearborn, SS **12.00**
Fredericton, New Brunswick, spiral handle, gold wash bowl **30.00**
GAR Encampment, 31st National Encampment of Grand Army of the Republic in Buffalo, NY, 1897, GAR symbol, war monument statue and buffalo head on handle, 4½″ l, SP **18.00**
Golden Gate, San Francisco **30.00**
Grand Canyon, AZ, full–figure nude in canoe **35.00**
Indianapolis, Soldier's & Sailor's Monument
. . . . **18.00**
Jamestown Exposition **35.00**
Lake Worth, Palm Beach, Florida **58.00**
Mackinack Island, MI, Arch Rock, demitasse
. . . . **18.00**
Madison, WI **10.00**
Mt Vernon **10.00**
New York Peace Monument, Lookout Mountain, TN, picture bowl **25.00**

Notre Dame **110.00**
Old Hickory, Jackson Monument **55.00**
Palm Springs Aerial Tramway, SP, John Brown, marked "Antico" **100.00**
Pan–American Expo, 1901, "Pan–American Candy Co" on handle, standing buffalo in bowl, 4″ l, silvered brass **15.00**
Pittsburgh, Ft Pitt **38.00**
Put–In–Bay, EGH, demitasse, 1902 **20.00**
Quebec, openwork handle **15.00**
Queen Elizabeth, 1953 Coronation **15.00**
Rochester, NY **35.00**
Salt Lake City, UT **38.00**
San Francisco, Mission Dolores 1776, bear on dec handle, gold bowl **35.00**
Settle Memorial Church, Owensboro, KY
. . . . **25.00**
Statue of Liberty, Tiffany **60.00**
Tacoma, WA, demitasse, rhododendrons
. . . . **20.00**
Teddy Roosevelt, riding horse, full–figure handle **85.00**
Three Sisters, OR **15.00**
Ticonderoga, NY, SS **48.00**
Washington, DC, capitol **28.00**

COMPACTS

The jewelry market is now so sophisticated that you have to look to its components to find out what is hot and what is not. Compacts are hot. They increased significantly in price in the 1980s. They are still rising in value.

Look for compacts that are major design statements or have gadget mechanisms. Many compacts came with elaborate boxes and pouches. These must be present if the compact is going to be viewed as complete.

Club: Compact Collectors Club, PO Box Letter S, Lynbrook, NY 11563.

Art Deco, ebony enamel, goldtone design
. . . . **30.00**
Avon, oval, lid dec with blue and green checkerboard pattern **25.00**
Bojouis, Evening in Paris, chrome, navy enamel, pie shaped wedges **30.00**
Coty, sq, chromium plated, scenic Rio center design made from butterfly wing
. . . . **55.00**
Eisenberg Original, damaged mirror **125.00**

Elgin, American
Goldtone, shell shape **55.00**
Musical, "Oh How We Danced," 1940s
. . . . **90.00**
Rectangular, engraved script "Mother"
. . . . **80.00**
Estee Lauder, round, mother–of–pearl,
goldtone medallion center **50.00**
Evans Case Company, rect, goldtone,
watchcase, plaid design, 1940s **160.00**
Finberg Manufacturing Company, round, SS,
enameled, pink flowers on yellow
ground **100.00**
Gold, three pearl dec **5.00**
Harriet Hubbard Ayers, pink enamel,
shamrocks dec **10.00**
John Wanamaker, round, plastic, pink,
flower basket design on foil paper insert,
1930s **50.00**
Kotler and Kopit, rect, goldtone, rhinestone
encrusted lid **85.00**
Lin–Bren, oval, goldtone, multicolored
rhinestones on grid design **65.00**
Majestic, gold, calla lily dec **12.00**
Marhill, round, Bakelite, green, gold plated
band with engraved floral design **80.00**
Revlon, round, goldtone, paisley design,
case designed by Van Cleef & Arpels
. . . . **90.00**
Rex Fifth Avenue, goldtone, round, geometric design **40.00**
Richard Hudnut
Petite double, silver, floral design, MIB
. . . . **55.00**
Rectangular, gold plated, DuBarry, emb
leaf design **75.00**
Rowenta, oval, brown enamel, petit point
. . . . **40.00**
Schildkraut, sq, tortoise shell **95.00**
Souvenir
New York World's Fair 1939, wood, tapestry design **80.00**
Sesquicentennial International Exposition, Philadelphia, PA, 1926, silvered
metal, George Washington portrait
. . . . **25.00**

Pilcher, brass, enameled cov, black, gray,
white, and red geometric design, 2⁷⁄₈" sq,
$35.00.

Volupte, silver, woman tennis player, double sifter **55.00**
Wadsworth, round, gold plated, enameled
playing card motif on lid **60.00**
Woodworth, Karess, polished goldtone,
corset shape **25.00**

CONSTRUCTION SETS

Children love to build things. Building block sets originated in the nineteenth century. They exist in modern form as Legos and Lego imitators.

Construction toys also are popular, especially with young boys who aspire to be engineers. The best known is the Erector Set, but it also had plenty of imitators. Alfred Carlton Gilbert, Jr. began his business by producing magic sets as the Mysto Manufacturing Company. With the help of his father, he bought out his partner and created the A. C. Gilbert Company located on Erector Square in New Haven, Connecticut.

Clubs: A C Gilbert Heritage Society, 594 Front St, Marion, MA 02738; Anchor Block Foundation, 980 Plymouth St, Pelham, NY 10803; Southern California Meccano & Erector Club, 9661 Sabre Ave, Garden Grove, CA 92644.

A C Gilbert, Erector Set
No. 1, complete with box **150.00**
No. 4, 1930 . . . . **250.00**
No. 6½, Electric engine **55.00**
No. 7½, Engineers Set, early 1950s
. . . . **55.00**
No. 8½ **70.00**
No. 10½, Merry–Go–Round **100.00**
No. 77, Trumodel Set, Sears, 1929
. . . . **125.00**
No. 10021 . . . . **30.00**
No. 10032 . . . . **30.00**
No. 10042, Radar Scope Set **35.00**
No. 10053, Rocket Launcher Set **90.00**
No. 10062, Steam Engine Set **35.00**
No. 10093, Master Builder Set
. . . . **300.00**
No. 10181, Action Helicopter
. . . . **100.00**
No. 10621, 5 in 1 . . . . **50.00**
Mysto Erector Set, No. 1 . . . . **150.00**
Remote Control Senior Power Line, 1971
. . . . **80.00**
Auburn
Flexi–Blocks, No. 949 . . . . **45.00**
Plexi Bricks **60.00**
Bilt–E–Z, Skyscraper Building Blocks, Scott
Manufacturing, Chicago, c1925 **125.00**
Chautauqua Architectural Building Blocks,
No. 510, 1920s **150.00**
Cozzone, No 500 Construction Set, metal
parts, electric motor, orig box . . . **250.00**

Crandall's Building Blocks, No. 3, patented
1867 . . . . **75.00**
Elgo, American Plastic Bricks, No. 715,
1950s **30.00**
Embossing Co, Stabuilt Blocks, 1916 **50.00**
Gilbert
No. 3, Junior Engineer's Outfit **110.00**
No. 6, In The Big Red Chest With The
Steam Boiler **110.00**
No. 7½, The Set That Builds The Chassis
. . . . **175.00**
Hai–San, Hewn American Logs, No. 815
. . . . **30.00**
Halsam
American Plastic Bricks
No. 60, 1939 . . . . **75.00**
No. 705 . . . . **40.00**
Logs, Senior Size, No. 815 . . . . . . **30.00**
New American Bricks, No. 725 **50.00**
Hasbro, Astrolite **70.00**
Ideal, Super City, No. 3361–3 . . . . . **30.00**
Ives Struktiron, motorized, 1915 . . . **125.00**
Kenner
Girder and Panel
No. 2, 1950s **55.00**
No. 72000 . . . . **30.00**
Girder and Panel Airport Set **40.00**
Girder and Panel Bridge and Turnpike
Motorized Set, 1960 . . . . **120.00**
Girder and Power, Build A Home and
Subdivision **200.00**
Girder Bridge and Highway Set, No. 6
. . . . **90.00**
Lincoln Logs
No. 1A, 1920 . . . . **20.00**
No. 1C **70.00**
No. 29 . . . . **125.00**
Marx, Riverside Construction Set, 1960s
. . . . **120.00**

American Plastic Bricks, tin screw–on lid,
paper box, Halsam, Set No. 715, 208 pieces,
4" d, 15½" h, $40.00.

Meccano
    No. 1, 1914 . . . . **50.00**
    Engineering Erector Set **20.00**
M–I Toys, Building Bricks, No. 955   **40.00**
Pressman, Crystal Climbers **30.00**
Remco, Jumbo Construction Set, 1968
    . . . . **125.00**
Richter & Co, Richter's Anchor Blocks,
    No. 7 . . . . **125.00**
Scott Manufacturing, Bilt–E–Z Skyscraper
    Building Blocks, c1925 . . . . **175.00**
Structo, No. 3 . . . . **150.00**
Tinkertoy
    No. 104 . . . . **30.00**
    Wonder Builder **40.00**
Union Building Blocks, No. 7 . . . . . **150.00**

COOKBOOKS

There are eighteenth- and nine-teenth-century cookbooks. But, they are expensive, very expensive. It pays to look through old piles of books in hopes that a dealer has overlooked one of these gems. But, in truth, you are going to go unrewarded ninety–nine percent or more of the time.

The cookbooks that you are most likely to find date from the twentieth century. Most were promotional giveaways. A fair number came with appliances. Some were associated with famous authors.

A few years ago, you could buy them in the 50¢ to $1.00 range and had a large selection from which to choose. No longer. These later cookbooks have been discovered. Now you are going to pay between $2.00 and $10.00 for most of them.

Cover art does effect price. Most are bought for display purposes. Seek out the ones that feature a recognizable personality on the cover.

Club: Cookbook Collectors Club of America, Inc, PO Box 56, St James, MO 65559.

Periodical: *Cookbook Collectors' Exchange*, PO Box 32369, San Jose, CA 95152.

A Few Choice Recipes, Rumford, 10 pgs,
    3½ × 5" **18.00**
ABC Casserole, Peter Pauper Press, 1954,
    61 pgs **3.50**
American Home Cookbook by Ladies of
    Detroit, 1878 . . . . **45.00**
Anyone Can Bake, Royal Baking Powder,
    1929, 100 pgs **6.50**
Ball Blue Book, Russel, 1930, 56 pgs   **15.00**
Better Homes and Gardens, 1953 . . . **16.00**
Book of Valuable Recipes, Arm & Hammer
    Baking Soda, 32 pgs, 3½ × 6", 1900
    . . . . **12.00**
Campbell's Main Dishes **8.00**
Ceresota Cookbook, Northwestern Consoli-
    dated Milling Co, 29 pgs, 5½ × 9",
    1900s **35.00**
Cleveland's Superior Recipes, Cleveland
    Baking Powder Co, 72 pgs, 1900s   **12.00**
Cross Creek Cookey, Marjorie Kinnan Rawl-
    ings, 1942 . . . . **35.00**
Desserts of the World, Jell–O **5.00**

Dishes For All Year Round, S Rorer, 1903,
    62 pgs **6.00**
Duncan Hines Food Odyssey, 1955, 274
    pgs **5.00**
Economy Administration Cookbook, 1913,
    696 pgs **45.00**
Electric Cooking with Your Kenmore, 1941
    . . . . **2.00**
Food Favorites, Kraft, 1951, 32 pgs . . . **1.50**
Gold Label Recipes, Gold Label Baking
    Powder, 16 pgs, 5 × 7" **7.50**
Guardian Service Tested Recipes, 72 pgs,
    5½ × 8½", 1940 . . . . **12.00**
Handy Cook Book, Kerosine Soap, 1897
    . . . . **15.00**
Housekeeping in Old Virginia, slave recipes
    by Mozis Addams, 1965 reprint
    . . . . **35.00**
How To Eat Canned Salmon, Argo Red
    Salmon, 36 pgs, 4 × 5½", 1904   **12.00**
Joys of Jell–O **5.00**
Knox Gelatin, black child cov illus, 1915
    . . . . **5.00**
Maxwell House Coffee, 22 pgs, 1927   **7.00**
Maytag Dutch Oven Cookbook, 49 pgs
    . . . . **5.50**
New Royal Cookbook, 49 pgs, 5 × 8",
    1922 . . . . **12.00**
Norge Recipe Book, 1930 . . . . **2.00**
Old Shaker Recipes, Bear Wallow, 1982, 30
    pgs **3.00**
Pillsbury Family Cookbook, 1963 . . . **10.00**
Proven Recipes, Corn Products Refining Co,
    1930 . . . . **5.00**
Prudential, little girl giving tea party with
    two teddy bears on cov, 1910 . . . **39.00**
Quaker Cereal Products and How To Use
    Them, 56 pgs, 5 × 7" **35.00**
Royal Baking Powder, Making Biscuits, 14
    pgs, 1923 . . . . **12.00**

Betty Crocker's Frankly Fancy Foods Recipe Book, copyright 1959 General Mills, 26 pgs, 6½ × 9¾", $5.00.

Enjoy Good Eating Every Day The Easy Spry Way, Aunt Jenny, copyright 1949, Lever Bros, Cambridge, MA, 48 pgs, 6 × 8¼", $6.50.

Recipes for Good Eating, Crisco, copyright 1945 Procter & Gamble, 64 pages, 5½ × 8", $5.00.

Royal Cream of Tartar Baking Powder, A Guide To Royal Success in Baking, 22 pgs, 1944 . . . . **10.00**
Rumford Southern Recipes, M Wilson, 1894, 65 pgs **7.00**
Searchlight Recipe Book **20.00**
Simply Elegant Desserts, American Dairy Association, 23 pgs **1.00**
Sourdough Jack's **8.00**
Sunset Cookbook for Entertaining, 1968, 210 pgs **4.50**
The Recipe Book For Club Aluminum Ware, 35 pgs, 5½ × 8½", 1928 . . . . . **6.00**
The Southern Cookbook of Fine Old Recipes, 49 pgs, 6 × 9, 1960 . . . . . . **30.00**
Treasure of Great Recipes, Price **30.00**
Universal Cookbooks, Jeanie L Taylor, 1888, 185 pgs **15.00**
Vermont Maple Recipes, 1952, 87 pgs **5.00**

COOKIE CUTTERS

When most individuals think of cookie cutters, they envision the metal cutters, often mass-produced, that were popular during the nineteenth century and first third of the twentieth century. This is too narrow a view. Do not overlook the plastic cutter of recent years. Not only are they colorful, but they come in a variety of shapes quite different from their metal counterparts.

If you want to build a great specialized collection, look for cutters that were giveaway premiums by flour and baking related businesses. Most of these cutters are in the $10.00 to $40.00 range.

Club: Cookie Cutter Collectors Club, 1167 Teal Rd SW, Dellroy, OH 44620.

Periodical: *Cookies,* 5426 27th St NW, Washington, DC 20015.

Advertising
 Betty Crocker, plastic, gingerbread boy, blue **1.50**
 Garland Stoves and Ranges, flame shape **22.00**
 Pioneer Seed Company, plastic, white **1.00**
 Quaker Oats, plastic, standing bear, yellow **3.00**
 Swans Down Cake Flour, aluminum, premium **22.00**
Angel, plastic, Nord Cutters **2.50**
Arrow, plastic, hot pink, Wilton **1.00**
Bear, 2½ × 3", handcrafted, tin, irregular back, missing handle **10.00**
Bird, 4½" l, spread wings, tin **15.00**
Camel, marbleized, multicolored, sgd "Kleeware, England" **3.50**
Clock, plastic, Nord Cutters **2.50**
Cowboy, plastic, red, McB's **3.50**

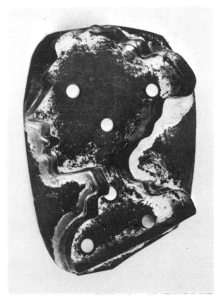

Tin, profile of woman's face, galvanized, 3 × 4⅛" h, $10.00.

Dog, 4½" l, tin **20.00**
Duck, metal, Depression glass eye, hand made in Nazareth, PA **125.00**
Dutchman, 5¼" h, tin **115.00**
Goblet, 4" h, tin **100.00**
Leprechaun, plastic, green and tan, Hallmark, 1979 . . . . **2.00**
Man, 3 × 5½", handcrafted, tin, hat and coat, handle removed **85.00**
Penn State University mascot, lion, plastic, white and blue, Monogram Plastics **3.00**
Pitcher, 4¼" h, tin **110.00**
Pretzel, metal, handle **3.00**
Question Mark, plastic, white, Wilton **.50**
Reindeer, 5 × 6", handcrafted, tin, irregular back, four legs, grouped antlers **115.00**
Scissors, 5¼" l, tin **100.00**
Sprinkling Can, metal, Wilton **2.50**
Star, plastic, red, Southwest Indian Foundation, orig card **5.00**
Strawberry Shortcake, Hallmark **10.00**
Tom & Jerry, dated 1956 . . . . **10.00**
Tree, plastic, green, Southwest Indian Foundation, orig card **5.00**
Twelve Days of Christmas, set, dated 1978 . . . . **45.00**
Whale, 3¾" l, tin **20.00**

COOKIE JARS

Talk about categories that have gone nuts over the past years. Thanks to the Andy Warhol sale, cookie jars became the talk of the town. Unfortunately, the prices reported for the Warhol cookie jars were so far removed from reality that many individuals were deceived into believing their cookie jars are far more valuable than they really are.

The market seems to be having trouble finding the right pricing structure. A recent cookie jar price guide lowballed a large number of jar prices. Big-city dealers are trying to sell cookie jars as art objects at high prices instead of the kitsch they really are. You have to be the judge. Remember, all you are buying is a place to store your cookies.

Club: The Cookie Jar Collector's Club, 595 Cross River Rd, Katonah, NY 10536.

Periodicals: *Cookie Jarrin',* RR 2, Box 504, Walterboro, SC 29488; *Crazed Over Cookie Jars,* PO Box 254, Savanna, IL 61074.

Arc, Metlox **100.00**
Aunt Jemima, F & F **295.00**
Baking Angel **650.00**
Bandit Raccoon, Metlox **75.00**
Barn, Twin Winton **45.00**
Bartender, tan, Napco **80.00**
Baseball Boy, Treasure Craft **45.00**
Bear and Beehive, McCoy **55.00**
Beer Mug, Doranne **60.00**
Blue Bonnet Sue **30.00**
Brown Bear, Brush **65.00**
Brown Cow, Treasure Craft **65.00**
Bulldog Cafe, Treasure Craft **60.00**
C-3PO, int rim chip, Roman Ceramics **145.00**
Caboose, McCoy **75.00**
Cat, green, Doranne **75.00**
Cat Head, wearing hat, Metlox **85.00**
Chef's head **40.00**
Churn, American Bisque **25.00**
Cinderella, Napco **300.00**
Cinderella's Pumpkin, Brush **275.00**
Clown on Alphabet Block, American Bisque **80.00**
Coffee Grinder **9.00**
Collegiate Owl, American Bisque . . . **80.00**
Cookie Cabin, McCoy **60.00**
Cookie Kettle, American Bisque **45.00**
Cookie Truck, American Bisque **80.00**
Corn, Metlox **145.00**
Cow, tan, Brush–McCoy **110.00**
Dalmatian **50.00**
Dog, sitting, tan, Metlox **95.00**
Donald Duck, American Bisque **250.00**
Donkey, Twin Winton **40.00**
Dutch Boy, Shawnee **200.00**
Dutch Girl, Pottery Guild **65.00**
Elf, wearing green hat **40.00**
Elephant
 McCoy **125.00**
 Twin Winton **40.00**
Emmett Kelly, Japan **135.00**
Farmyard Follie Chicken, Doranne . . . **45.00**
Fat Boy, Abingdon **550.00**
Fiver's Doghouse **225.00**

Flasher Clown, American Bisque, painted
   face, missing flasher **120.00**
Fox, Treasure Craft **50.00**
Frontier Family, McCoy **50.00**
Frosty Penguin, Metlox **145.00**
Grandma, Treasure Craft **55.00**
Granny, red skirt, McCoy **90.00**
Granny Ann, lavender, Shawnee **85.00**
Grease Monkey **75.00**
Gumball Machine, yellow **60.00**
Have A Happy Day, McCoy **35.00**
Hippopotamus, white, Abingdon . . . **165.00**
Honey Bear, McCoy **70.00**
Humpty Dumpty, wearing cowboy hat,
   Brush **245.00**
Ice Cream Soda, Doranne **75.00**
Indian Tepee **45.00**
Jack Frost, Red Wing **250.00**
Keebler Elf, sitting **75.00**
Kissing Penguins, McCoy **45.00**
Kitchen Witch, bisque face **100.00**
Kitten Head, Lefton **60.00**
Koala Bear
   McCoy **35.00**
   Metlox **95.00**
Kraft Bear, Regal **175.00**
Lantern, Brush–McCoy **185.00**
Little Red Riding Hood, Hull, closed basket
   . . . . **180.00**
Lucky Elephant, gold, Shawnee **400.00**
Magic Bunny **40.00**
Mallard, Treasure Craft **50.00**
Maurice Shoe House **50.00**
Milk Bone Doghouse **225.00**
Monk, Twin Winton **40.00**
Mouse Mobile, Metlox **245.00**
Mr Rabbit, standing, American Bisque
   . . . . **60.00**
Mrs Fields **35.00**
Noah's Ark, Treasure Craft **60.00**
Owl, Shawnee **95.00**
Pennsylvania Dutch, Shawnee **175.00**
Pepperidge Farm, cookie bag, MIB   **60.00**
Peter Max **475.00**
Peter Rabbit, Sigma **150.00**
Pinky Lee **700.00**

*Shawnee, basket of fruit, yellow basketweave
base, 7³⁄₈" d, $35.00.*

Pinocchio, Metlox **450.00**
Poodle Head, white **75.00**
Popeye, McCoy **85.00**
Porky Pig, sitting in chair **75.00**
Potbelly Stove, McCoy **25.00**
Puss 'N Boots, Shawnee **135.00**
Quaker Oats, Regal **130.00**
Queen of Hearts, Fitz & Floyd **125.00**
R2–D2 . . . . **100.00**
Raggedy Ann
   California Originals **195.00**
   McCoy **85.00**
   Metlox **145.00**
Ranger Bear, Twin Winton **40.00**
Red Baron, California Originals **625.00**
Rocking Chair Dalmatian **300.00**
Rooster, American Bisque **80.00**
Sailor, gold, Shawnee **650.00**
Santa, Japan **50.00**
School Bus, yellow **40.00**
Shoe, Doranne **75.00**
Sir Frances Drake, Metlox **70.00**
Smiley Pig, Shawnee
   Pink flowers **250.00**
   Shamrocks **200.00**
Snail, worm in hat **75.00**
Spice, Treasure Craft **55.00**
Squirrel
   Metlox, with pinecone **70.00**
   Twin Winton **35.00**
Stanforware Corn, RRP **75.00**
Sugar and Spice, Treasure Craft **55.00**
Taxi, California Originals **100.00**
Three Little Kittens, McCoy **65.00**
Tiger Head, California Originals **185.00**
Timmy Tortoise, McCoy **35.00**
Toy Soldier, standing in guard house
   . . . . **100.00**
Train
   Pfaltzgraff **145.00**
   Twin Winton **100.00**
Wagon Train, McCoy **95.00**
Walrus, Maurice **40.00**
Winking Owl, gold **235.00**
Winnie the Pooh, California Originals
   . . . . **90.00**
Yogi Bear, American Bisque **450.00**

COPPER PAINTINGS

Copper paintings, actually pictures
stamped out of copper or copper foil,
deserve a prize as one of the finest
"ticky–tacky" collectibles ever created.
My dad remembers getting a four–
picture set from a bank as a premium in
the late 1950s or early 1960s. He takes
great pride in noting that this is one of the
few things that he has no regrets about
throwing out.

However, to each his own—
somewhere out there are individuals
who like this unique form of mass–
produced art. Their treasures generally

cost them in the $15.00 to $50.00 range
depending on subject.

COSTUMES

Remember how much fun it was to
play dress–up as a kid? Seems silly to
only do it once a year around Halloween. Down South and in Europe, Mardi
Gras provides an excuse; but, in my area,
we eat doughnuts instead.

Collectors are beginning to discover
children's Halloween costumes. I'll bet
you are staggered by some of the prices
listed in this section. Yet, I see costumes
traded at these prices all the time.

There doesn't seem to be much market in adult costumes, those used in the
theater and for theme parties. Costume
rental shops are used to picking them up
for a few dollars each.

Addams Family, Uncle Fester, Ben Cooper,
   1965 . . . . **150.00**
Astronaut, Collegeville, 1962 . . . . . . **40.00**
Bambi, Ben Cooper, 1950s **40.00**
Beetle Bailey, Spook Town Halloween cos-
   tume, orig box, 1960s **50.00**
Betsy Ross, Ben Cooper **30.00**
Blondie, Collegeville, 1960s **75.00**
Brady Bunch, Collegeville, 1969 . . . **125.00**
Bugs Bunny, Collegeville, 1965 . . . . **60.00**
Casper the Friendly Ghost, Ben Cooper,
   1961 . . . . **50.00**
Cecil, orig box, Ben Cooper, 1962–65
   . . . . **100.00**
Centurion Ace McCloud, Ben Cooper, 1982
   . . . . **15.00**
Daniel Boone, Ben Cooper, 1960s . . . **80.00**
Deputy Dawg, Ben Cooper, 1961 . . . **65.00**
Devil, Masquerade, 1960 . . . . **40.00**
Donald Duck, Ben Cooper, 1962 . . . . **75.00**
Donny Osmond, Collegeville, 1977   **35.00**
Dracula, plastic mask, one–piece synthetic
   fabric suit, orig box, Ben Cooper copy-
   right U P Co 1960s **75.00**
Farmer Alfalfa, 1950s **45.00**
Flipper, Ben Cooper, 1964 . . . . **50.00**
Fonzie, Ben Cooper **30.00**
Frankenstein, Universal, 1980 . . . . . . **30.00**
Ghastly Gertie, Ben Cooper, 1962 . . . **50.00**
Girl From UNCLE, MGM, 1967 . . . . **275.00**
Grandpa Munster, Ben Cooper, 1964
   . . . . **225.00**
Green Hornet, Ben Cooper, 1966   **425.00**
Green Lantern, 1960s **60.00**
Harlem Globetrotters, Meadowlark Lemon,
   Ben Cooper, 1971 . . . . **25.00**
Hee Haw, 1976 . . . . **20.00**
Hong Kong Fooey, 1974 . . . . **35.00**
H R Puf–n–stuf, Collegeville, 1971   **75.00**
Huckleberry Hound, Ben Cooper, 1960
   . . . . **50.00**
Illya Kuryakin, Halco, 1965 . . . . **150.00**

Indiana Jones, Ben Cooper, 1982 . . . . **35.00**
Inspector, Pink Panther, 1970 . . . . **35.00**
Jackie Gleason, bus driver, Empire Plastic, gray hat, money changer, 15 plastic coins, bus transfer sheet booklet, ticket punch, mid 1950s **350.00**
Jeannie, I Dream of Jeannie, 1974 . . . **30.00**
Jet Man, Ben Cooper, 1950s **45.00**
Jetsons
    Jane Jetson, Austin Art, 1972 . . . **150.00**
    Rosie the Robot, Ben Cooper, 1963 . . . . **225.00**
Jughead, Halco **60.00**
King Kong, Ben Cooper, 1976 . . . . . . **30.00**
Koko the Clown, 1960s **65.00**
Land of the Giants/Giant Professor, plastic mask, one–piece synthetic suit, orig box, Ben Cooper copyright 1968 Kent Productions **125.00**
Little Audrey, Collegeville, 1959 . . . . **75.00**
Lost in Space, Ben Cooper, 1966 . . . **250.00**
Luke Duke, Ben Cooper **6.00**
Man On the Moon, 1970 . . . . **25.00**
MASH, Klinger, Ben Cooper, 1981   **75.00**
Monkees, Mickey Dolenz, 1960s . . . **150.00**
Mork, Mork & Mindy, Ben Cooper, 1978 . . . . **20.00**
Mouseketeer Sheriff, Ben Cooper, 1950s **90.00**
Mummy, Ben Cooper, 1973 . . . . **30.00**
Munsters, Herman, Ben Cooper, 1964 . . . . **225.00**
Mutant, Universal Studios, 1980 . . . . **25.00**
Peter Potamus, Ben Cooper, 1965 . . . **50.00**
Phantom, Collegeville, 1956 . . . . **250.00**
Pink Panther, Kusan, 1969 . . . . **75.00**
Popeye, Collegeville, 1958 . . . . **60.00**
Roger Rabbit, Ben Cooper, 1980s . . . **40.00**
Santa, 1950s **55.00**
Scooby Doo, Ben Cooper, 1973 . . . . . **25.00**

Secret Squirrel, 1965 . . . . **125.00**
Shari Lewis, one piece vinyl suit with puppet illus, autographed, Ben Cooper Inc **50.00**
Six Million Dollar Man, Ben Cooper, 1978 . . . . **35.00**
Steve Canyon, Halco, 1959 . . . . **50.00**
Strawberry Shortcake **15.00**
Superman, cotton outfit, shirt, pants, and cape, orig box, Ben Cooper, copyright Superman Inc, 1950s **75.00**
Tarzan, Collegeville, 1967 . . . . **50.00**
The Shadow, plastic mask, synthetic fabric suit, Collegeville copyright 1973 Conde Nast Publications Inc **100.00**
Tom, Tom & Jerry, Halco, 1952 . . . . . **40.00**
Uncle Sam, Ben Cooper **30.00**
Underdog, Collegeville, 1975 . . . . **70.00**
Vampira, Collegeville, 1972 . . . . **30.00**
Wile E Coyote, 1974 . . . . **25.00**
Witchie Poo, Collegeville, 1971 . . . . . **65.00**
Woody Woodpecker, Collegeville, 1950 . . . . **50.00**
Zorro, orig box, Ben Cooper, copyright 1965 . . . . **125.00**

COUNTRY STORE

There is something special about country stores. My favorite is Bergstresser's in Wassergass, Pennsylvania. There is probably one near you that you feel as strongly about. Perhaps the appeal is that they continue to deny the present. I am always amazed at what a country store owner can dig out of the back room, basement, or barn.

Country store collectibles focus heavily on front-counter and back-counter material from the last quarter of the nineteenth century and first quarter of the twentieth century. The look is tied in closely with Country. It also has a strong small-town, rural emphasis.

Drop in and prop your feet up on the potbelly stove. Don't visit a country store if you are in a hurry.

Cabinet
  Adams Pepsin Tutti–Frutti, oak case with pressed oak marquee, glass front, mirrored back, 12½ × 17½ × 6" **700.00**
  Corticelli Spool, oak, gallery top, glass door, shelved int, two drawers below, refinished, 23" w, 39" h, 19" d **300.00**
  J & P Coats' Spool Cotton, figural spool with composition thread, four drawers, 22" l, 19 1/2" h **600.00**
Cash Register, National, brass
  317, candy store, side tape dispenser, 12½ × 16 × 16" **475.00**

442, oak base, single drawer, ornate open grillwork tape dispenser on side, 20 × 24 × 17" **325.00**
Ceiling Fan, electric, Tuerk type C, orig wooden paddles, 56" d **250.00**
Coffee Mill, Enterprise, small size, orig paint and decals, c1879, refitted as lamp, 11 × 12 × 9" **475.00**
Coin Changer, oak and iron, one cent to one dollar, 12½ × 10¼ × 10½"   **25.00**
Display
  Chase and Sanborn, metal, adjustable–height horizontal shelf on vertical stand, green and gold lettering, 15½" w shelf, 33" h stand **95.00**
  Dutch Boy Paints, figural Dutch Boy carrying bucket, papier mache and composition, 29" h **300.00**
  Hood Rubber and Canvas Footwear, standup, diecut red–jacketed Hood man holding flag, pointing to oval trademark, 19 × 13½ × 4½" **300.00**
  Wrigley's Chewing Gum, diecut tin, standing moon faced figure with arms stretched to support display racks, 14 × 13¼ × 7" **300.00**
Display Case, Boston Garter, etched glass, int glass shelves, 14¼" w, 14" h, 7¼" d **250.00**
Peanut Warmer, The Defiance Peanut Warmer, tin, stenciled letters, 18½ × 21½ × 18" **200.00**
Seedbox, Shakers Choice Vegetable Seeds, divided wood box, litho paper labels, 22 × 4½ × 9¼" **275.00**

Sesame Street, Oscar the Grouch, Ben Cooper, CTW trademark, orig box and price sticker, $15.00.

Package, Quick Mothers Oats, Quaker Oats Co, cardboard box, nutritional information on back, $12.00.

Showcase
  18″ w, 33½″ h, 4½″ d, wall mount, three
    shelves, made from ornate clock case
    . . . . **175.00**
  48½″ w, 14″ h, 25″ d, countertop, nar-
    row oak frame, glass paneled top,
    front, and sides, mirrored sliding
    back door **120.00**
  58″ w, 34″ h, 27½″ d, wood countertop,
    glass panels in front and sides, mir-
    rored back **300.00**
Sign
  Boston Garter, paper, early baseball
    players Fred Clarke and F L Chase
    using garters, 20¾ x 11″ . . . **4,000.00**
  Campbell's Soup, soup can, hangs in
    corner, curved bracket, 14 × 22″
    . . . . **2,300.00**
  Coleman's Mustard, paper, two small
    children climbing up to peer into top
    of giant mustard tin, 16½ × 22″
    . . . . **105.00**
  Knox Desserts, cardboard, "Dainty Des-
    serts for Dainty People," little girl
    serving gelatin dessert at table, 20 ×
    36″ **200.00**
  The People's Store, brass, etched letters,
    77½″ l, 8″ h **350.00**
  W Baker Cocoa, paper, color litho, ea-
    gle, shield, factory and shipping vi-
    gnettes, 24 × 20″, framed . . . **200.00**
  Wrigley's Chewing Gum, paper, trade-
    mark moon faced man with pointed
    head holding stick of gum, 21 × 11″
    . . . . **205.00**
String Holder
  Heinz Pickle adv, tin, hanging figural
    pickle holds spool below two sided
    sign "Pure Foods, '57' Varieties,"
    17″ w, 14″ h **7,500.00**
  Red Goose Shoes adv, tin, diecut goose
    hangs above suspended string spool,
    16″ w, 28″ h **2,600.00**

COUNTRY WESTERN COLLECTIBLES

You don't have to be a *rhinestone cowboy* to enjoy Country Western music and you don't have to travel to Nashville to find its memorabilia. With a large assortment of items available such as sheet music, signed photographs, and record albums, Country Western collectibles won't bring ya' back home empty-handed. So go ahead and enjoy yourselves, and "Ya'll come back now, ya' hear?"

Periodicals: *Country Music Reporter,* 112 Widmar Place, Clayton, CA 94517; *Disc Collector,* PO Box 315, Cheswold, DE 19936.

Autograph
  Atkins, Chet, record album cover, sgd
    . . . . **35.00**
  Britt, Elton, 78 rpm record album cover,
    sgd and dated 1951 . . . . **15.00**
  Davis, Jimmie, sgd calling card **5.00**
  Ritter, Tex, letter, 1 pg, c1936 . . . **35.00**
  Snow, Hank, letter, future plans, 1931
    . . . . **28.00**
  Tubb, Ernest, sgd 45 rpm record sleeve
    . . . . **3.00**
  Williams, Hank, letter, orig envelope,
    1945 . . . . **100.00**
Catalog, Ernest Tubb Record Shop issue,
  Nashville, TN, 1972 . . . . **2.50**
Lobby Card, Tex Ritter, 27 × 41″   **100.00**
Lunch Box, Hee Haw, metal, colorful illus
  front and back, very minor wear, 1970
  . . . . **120.00**
Magazine, *TV Guide,* sgd by Grandpa
  Jones, *Hee Haw* feature **6.50**
Membership Card
  Hank Snow Fan Club **8.00**
  Tex Ritter Fan Club **15.00**
Paper Dolls
  Hee Haw, punch–out, Saalfield, #5139,
    Gunilla, Lulu, Kathy, and Jeannie
    dolls, uncut, 1971 . . . . **12.00**
  Hootenanny, punch–out, Saalfield,
    #4440, four dolls, uncut, 1964 **18.00**
Photograph
  Allen, Rex, 8 × 10″, sgd **12.00**
  Carlisle, Cliff, 8 × 10″, sgd **15.00**
  Carter, Wilf, 8 × 10″, sgd "Montana
    Slim" **18.00**
  Gayle, Crystal, 8 × 10″, sgd, framed
    . . . . **8.00**
  Kincaid, Bradley, standing on stage, sgd,
    1930s **15.00**
  Nelson, Willie, 8 × 10″, sgd **20.00**
  Parton, Dolly, 8 × 10″, sgd **24.00**

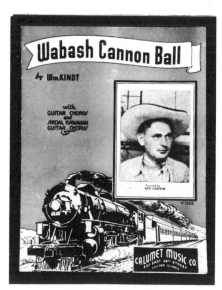

Sheet Music, Wabash Cannon Ball, **Rex Griffin, Calumet Music Co, 1939, 9 × 12″, $8.00.**

Pride, Charley, 6 × 7″, sgd and in-
  scribed **15.00**
Ritter, Tex, 8 × 10″, sgd and inscribed
  . . . . **25.00**
Tanner, Gid, playing fiddle, sgd
  . . . . **60.00**
Pinback Button, Rex Allen, photo and name
  . . . . **5.00**
Poster, Grand Old Opry, Chet Atkins   **20.00**
Record
  Ain't We Crazy/The Little Shirt That
    Mother Made For Me, 78 rpm, Brad-
    ley Kincaid, Decca **8.00**
  Are You Thinking of Me Darling/I Called
    and Nobody Answered, 78 rpm, Roy
    Acuff, Columbia **5.00**
  I Believe It for My Mother Told Me So/
    Hey! Hey! I'm Memphis Bound, 78
    rpm, Delmore Brothers, Bluebird
    . . . . **40.00**
  I'm a Convict with Old Glory in My
    Heart/The Best of Travel, 78 rpm,
    Elton Britt, Bluebird **10.00**
  I'm Only a Dude in Cowboy Clothes/My
    Honeymoon Bridge Broke Down, 78
    rpm, Wilf Carter, Bluebird **35.00**
  I Will Always Love You, 45 rpm, Dolly
    Parton, photo sleeve **8.00**
  Merry Hee Haw Christmas, 33 rpm
    . . . . **10.00**
  Mommy, Please Stay Home With Me/
    Many Tears Ago, 78 rpm, Eddy Ar-
    nold, Bluebird **30.00**
  My Son Calls Another Man Daddy/Long
    Ago Lonesome Blues, 78 rpm, Hank
    Williams, Sterling **15.00**
  Never Trust a Man/Take it Back and
    Change it for a Boy, 78 rpm, Rosalie
    Allen, Bluebird **10.00**
  The Honest Farmer/Taxes on the Farmer
    Feeds Them All, 78 rpm, Fiddlin'
    John Carson, Bluebird **85.00**
  You Laughed and I Cried/It's Too Late to
    Change Your Mind, 78 rpm, Jack
    Guthrie, Capitol **12.00**
Sheet Music
  Copas, Cowboy, *Filipino Baby,* sgd
    . . . . **30.00**
  Dexter, Al, *Pistol Packin' Mama,* sgd
    . . . . **18.00**
  Ritter, Tex, *Old Chisum Trail,* sgd   **30.00**
  Tubb, Ernest, *Walking the Floor Over
    You,* sgd **25.00**
Ticket Stub, Willie Nelson, concert, c1977
  . . . . **15.00**
Wallet, inscribed "Ernest Tubb" and "Music
  City USA" **25.00**

COW COLLECTIBLES

Holy cow! This is a moovelous category, as entrenched collectors already know.

Newsletter: *The MOOsletter,* 240 Wahl Ave, Evans City, PA 16033.

Bank, figural, marked "Metlox Calif USA" **40.00**

Book, *Walt Disney's Story of Clarabell Cow*, Whitman, 1938, 5 × 5½", hardcover **50.00**

Bowl, 10¼" d, china, full color Elsie and family portraits, Universal–Cambridge Pottery, Borden copyright 1940s **100.00**

Box, Dwight Soda, wood, cow illus, adv on sides **25.00**

Butter Stamp, 4¼" d, cow, turned handle **150.00**

Can Opener, figural, head, nickel plated **45.00**

Cookie Cutter, 4½" l, tin, missing handle **5.00**

Cookie Jar
Cow jumping over moon, gold, RRP Co **80.00**
Elsie **350.00**

Creamer, figural, Occupied Japan ...**25.00**

Display, standup, 6" l, Holstein adv, tin, cow shape, black and white **75.00**

Doll, 12" h, Elsie the Cow, plush and vinyl, orig stitched tag, My–Toy Co, 1950–1960 ....**75.00**

Figure, 3" h, metal **15.00**

Footstool, cow–horn legs, needlepoint top **60.00**

Milk Bottle, ½ pint, Hillcrest Farm, cow illus **15.00**

Mug, 3" h, white china, Elsie dancing through meadow of daisies, Continental Kilns signature, Borden Co copyright, late 1930s **50.00**

Pin
Dominion Washing Sodas adv, enameled cow symbol, dark cherry red background, early 1900s **15.00**
Horlicks, cow and milkmaid **20.00**

Pinback Button
Aberdeen Angus, 1¾" d, cow's head with ring in nose, c1900 .....**25.00**
St Charles Evaporated Milk, multicolored, cow illus **30.00**

Pitcher, ceramic, white, cow shape **15.00**

Plaque, 6 × 7", Elsie, figural, head, plaster, painted, c1940s **75.00**

Print, 20 × 16", cattle scene, ornate gold frame, ES Porter, 1908 ....**195.00**

Doorstop, black and white, pink accents, green base, reproduction, 13" l, 9" h, $25.00.

Toy, litho tin windup, black and white, Japan, 5½" l, 4" h, $35.00.

Puppet, 10" h, Ferdinand the Bull, composition head, black and white fabric body, marked "Crown Toy Co," Walt Disney Enterprises copyright **50.00**

Sharpening Stone, Bull Brand's Feeds adv, cow illus **16.00**

Sign, Dwight's Soda Swiss Cow, 15 × 19", paperboard, oak frame **175.00**

Stereograph, cows and sheep, Kilburn #739, 1870s **4.00**

Tee Shirt, blue, black and white cow on front, rear view on back, vertical lettering front and back, "Vermont" **4.00**

Toy,
Fisher–Price, cow, #132 ....**20.00**
Push, 5½" h, felt, brown and white, glass eyes, wood wheels **65.00**

Tray, 3½ × 5½", Carnation Milk adv, oval, cows in pasture **20.00**

Watch Fob, Happy Cow Feed, celluloid **49.00**

COWAN POTTERY

R. Guy Cowan founded the Cowan Pottery in 1913 in Cleveland, Ohio. It remained in almost continuous operation until financial difficulties forced it to close in 1931. Initially utilitarian redware was produced. Cowan began experimenting with glazes, resulting in a unique lusterware glaze.

Bowl, 6 × 7½", mottled tan glaze ...**60.00**

Console Bowl, 16" l, canoe shaped, molded sea horse dec, mottled blue glaze **110.00**

Flower Frog, deer **175.00**

Lamp, table, 14" h, relief–molded flowers on blue lustre glazed base, dragon handles **750.00**

Match Holder, ivory, sea horses **45.00**

Paperweight, elephant, blue–green glaze **325.00**

Soap Dish, 4" d, sea horse, blue **35.00**

Teapot, 7¼", white glaze **75.00**

Vase, 5" h, turquoise glaze **150.00**

Vase, green, sea horse standard, imp mark, 7⅛" h, $50.00.

COWBOY HERO COLLECTIBLES

The cowboy heroes in this category rode the range in movies and on television. In a way, they were larger than their real-life counterparts, shaping the image of how the West was won in the minds of several generations. Contemporary Westerns may be historically correct, but they do not measure up in sense of rightness.

The movie and television cowboy heroes were pioneers in merchandise licensing. If you were a child in the 1949 to 1951 period and did not own a Hopalong Cassidy item, you were deprived.

Collectors tend to favor one cowboy hero. My dad owns a few Roy Rogers and Gene Autry items, but he would never admit it publicly. As far as the world knows, he's a Hoppy man.

Club: Westerns & Serials Fan Club, Rt 1, Box 103, Vernon Center, MN 56090.

Annie Oakley
Clothing, shirt and vest **45.00**
Game **25.00**
Buffalo Bill, cabinet photo, William F Cody **180.00**
Daniel Boone
Decanter, 10" h, ceramic, figural, inscribed "Liquer Bottle/Japan," mid 1960s **50.00**

Lunch Box, King–Seeley Co, copyright
   1965, American Tradition Co **100.00**
Thermos, 6½" h, steel, red plastic cup
   . . . . **50.00**

Davy Crockett
   Badge, frontier, orig card **25.00**
   Bowl **15.00**
   Game, Walt Disney Fess Parker Indian
      Scouting Game, board, orig box
      . . . . **75.00**
   Iron–on Transfer, set of 3, titled images,
      "Great Hunter," "Indian Fighter,"
      and "Wild Frontier" **50.00**
   Lamp, composition, Davy sitting, hold-
      ing long rifle **125.00**
   Mug, 3" h, plastic, red, tan lid, relief
      portrait image, mid 1950s **75.00**
   Rifle, metal and plastic, brown . . . **25.00**
   Shirt, child's **28.00**
   Toolbox, tin, Fess Parker **75.00**
   Wristwatch **110.00**

Gene Autry
   Better Little Book, *Gene Autry In Special
      Ranger Rule,* Whitman, #1456, 1945
      . . . . **25.00**
   Boots, rubber, orig box, pr **125.00**
   Box, 1½ × 5 × 11", Gene Autry Pistol,
      cardboard **100.00**
   Comic Book, 1955 . . . . **16.00**
   Guitar, Emenee, MIB **175.00**
   Holster and Texan Jr Cap Gun . . . **75.00**
   Magazine, 8½ × 11", *Movie Thrills,*
      Sept 1950, full color cover photo, 96
      pgs **50.00**
   Movie Poster
      Silver Canyon **60.00**
      Wagon Team, 27 × 41", full color,
         Columbia Pictures, 1952
         . . . . **75.00**
   Pinback Button, photo, 1930s–early
      1940s **25.00**
   Post Card, Mile City, MT, roundup
      . . . . **18.00**
   Puzzle, 9½ × 11½", full color close–up
      photo, Whitman, 1950 copyright
      . . . . **25.00**
   Song Folio **20.00**
   Wristwatch, chrome metal case, en-
      graved "Always Your Pal" and
      "Gene Autry" on back of case,
      brown leather straps, c1948   **110.00**

**Comic Art, Tex Taylor In An Exciting Adven-
ture at the Gold Mine, *Vital Publications,
Inc.,* NY, 1950, 24 pgs, 7 × 3½", $12.00.**

Hopalong Cassidy
   Badge, teller's, Hopalong Cassidy Saving
      Club **30.00**
   Barrette **6.00**
   Bedspread, chenille, Hoppy scenes
      . . . . **225.00**
   Binoculars, decals **65.00**
   Birthday Card, 5¼ × 6¼", mechanical,
      full color, diecut disk wheel, Buzza
      Cardozo, c1950 . . . . **25.00**
   Bread Loaf Wrapper, Butter–Nut Bread
      . . . . **65.00**
   Calendar, 1952 . . . . **225.00**
   Camera, 2 × 2½ × 5", metal, black,
      black and silver circular title plate,
      Glater Products Co, late 1940s **75.00**
   Coloring Book, 10½ × 14¾", Abbott,
      20 unused pgs, c1950 . . . . **50.00**
   Crayon and Stencil Set, orig box
      . . . . **95.00**
   Cuff Links, pr **10.00**
   Figure, lead **45.00**
   Folder, Hoppy and Topper on cov, in-
      cludes writing paper and envelopes,
      Hoppy bust on stationery **95.00**
   Hunting Knife, 4" l, scabbard . . . **120.00**
   Ice Cream Carton, 6½" h, Quality Bulk
      Style Ice Cream, waxed cardboard,
      c1950 . . . . **45.00**
   Lobby Card, 11 × 14", *Hopalong
      Cassidy Enters,* 1935 . . . . **25.00**
   Marble, black, Hoppy illus **15.00**
   Pennant, 20" l, black, white, inscription
      and trim band, c1950 . . . . **25.00**
   Pin, gun and holster **50.00**
   Pinback Button, Hopalong Cassidy Daily
      News **9.00**
   Plate, bread, milk glass **60.00**
   Post Card, Chrysler adv, 1942 . . . . **8.00**
   Press Book, 9½ × 14½", *Renegade
      Trail,* Paramount Film **75.00**
   Radio, red **390.00**
   Ring, club, metal **45.00**
   Scrapbook, 12 × 15", leather, cov with
      engraved color Hoppy on Topper
      . . . . **150.00**
   Sign, tin, radio adv **55.00**
   Stationery Set, 8½ × 11½", cardboard
      folder, envelopes and four unused
      stationery sheets, Whitman, copyright
      1950 . . . . **75.00**
   Sweater, Hoppy on front, Topper on
      back **100.00**
   Wristwatch, US Time, 1950 . . . . **350.00**

John Wayne
   Belt Buckle, brass, portrait from *True
      Grit* **45.00**
   Knife, pearl finish **16.00**
   Playing Cards, 1956 . . . . **20.00**

Lone Ranger
   Belt, glow-in-the-dark, orig box and in-
      structions **185.00**
   Book, *The Lone Ranger On Powderhorn
      Trail,* No. 11, 207 pgs, copyright
      1949 . . . . **25.00**

Clicker Pistol, 8" l, tin and steel, glossy
   black enamel finish, silvered cham-
   ber, decal, 1938 copyright . . . **75.00**
Coloring Book, 8½ × 11", Whitman,
   128 pgs, 1953 . . . . **50.00**
Cut–Outs, Merita Bread premium **225.00**
Game, target, tin, Marx, 1938 . . . . **75.00**
Guitar, Tonto and Silver, MIB . . . **145.00**
Manual, 5¼ × 8¼", Lone Ranger Safety
   Club, 28 pgs, Weber's Bread, copy-
   right 1939 . . . . **200.00**
Map, 13 × 17", Lone Ranger Hunt Map,
   full color illus, orig mailing envelope,
   Silvercup Bread, c1938 . . . . . **200.00**
Pedometer, 2¾" d, aluminum, Cheerios
   premium, c1948 . . . . **30.00**
Ring, filmstrip, saddle shape, includes
   filmstrip **175.00**
Sheet Music, *Hi-Yo Silver,* 9 × 12",
   copyright 1938 . . . . **25.00**
Snowdome, Lone Ranger lassoing calf,
   orig decal **95.00**
Toothbrush Holder, 4" h, plaster, figural,
   painted, 1928 Lone Ranger Inc copy-
   right **75.00**
Water Gun Set, 9" l plastic pistol, water
   reservoir, thin vinyl black mask,
   cardboard star badge, and vinyl belt,
   H–G Industries, copyright 1981
   . . . . **40.00**

Red Ryder
   Game, target, orig box, complete   **39.00**
   Mittens, unopened, orig pkg, pr   **75.00**

Rifleman
   Comic Book, 1962 . . . . **14.00**
   Game, complete **40.00**
   Puzzle, photo **15.00**

Roy Rogers
   Bank, 5½" h, white metal, coppery
      bronze finish, raised image Roy on
      rearing Trigger, Alma Metal Arts,
      1950s **75.00**
   Belt, leather, buckle **35.00**
   Binoculars, Roy and Trigger, three
      power, MIB **150.00**
   Camera **50.00**
   Cigarette Lighter, Dale Evans, horse head
      . . . . **15.00**
   Guitar, red, orig box **145.00**
   Jewelry Set, pr cuff links and tie bar,
      gold finished metal, cowboy boot
      shape cuff links, relief western saddle
      design tie bar, orig card, mid 1950s
      . . . . **45.00**
   Lantern, ranch, orig box **200.00**
   Little Golden Book, *Dale Evans And The
      Lost Gold Mine,* 28 pgs, copyright
      1954 . . . . **15.00**
   Lunch Box, Roy Rogers and Dale Evans,
      thermos **120.00**
   Microscope Ring **125.00**
   Paint Set **150.00**
   Plate, 6" d, china, full color illus of Roy
      on Trigger, marked "Rodeo By Uni-
      versal," 1950s **25.00**

Pocket Knife, 3¼" l, steel, plastic insert
panels, Colonial, 1950s **55.00**
Record Album, *Songs of the Old West*,
colorful cov **28.00**
Ring, branding iron **45.00**
Tablet, 8 × 10", full color cov, unused,
early 1950s **45.00**
Telephone, wall, crank type **95.00**
Toy, Trigger and Trigger Jr, tin horse
trailer truck, back and side doors,
Marx **195.00**

Tom Mix
Arrow, Lucite **85.00**
Belt Buckle, decoder, secret compart-
ment **95.00**
Big Little Book, *Tom Mix And The
Stranger From The South*, Whitman,
1936 .... **25.00**
Booklet, *Secret Writing Manual*, 4 pgs,
Ralston premium, 1938 ...... **75.00**
Decoder, 2¾" d, cardboard disk, red,
white, and blue, Secret Ink Writing
Set premium, Ralston, c1938
.... **55.00**
Letter, typewritten on letterhead, to Dent
Hardware Co, Fullerton, PA, Febru-
ary 15, 1935 .... **125.00**
Periscope, mailer **75.00**
Poster, safety, 17 × 22", 1947 ... **15.00**
Ring, branded "TM" **125.00**
Spinner, Good Luck **30.00**
Telegraph, mailer **75.00**

Wild Bill Hickock
Lunch Box, 7 × 8 × 4", Wild Bill
Hickock and Jingles, steel, front and
back illus, Aladdin Industries, copyright 1955 .... **100.00**
View–Master Reel, 4 × 5½" envelope,
three color view cards, #T–2, #T–
18, and #T–19, 1956 copyright
.... **50.00**

Magazine, Look, Aug 29, 1950, $45.00.

Wyatt Earp
Coloring Book, Hugh O'Brien cov,
unused **35.00**
Mug, milk glass **22.00**
Puzzle, photo **15.00**

CRACKER JACK COLLECTIBLES

You can still buy Cracker Jack with a prize in every box. The only problem is that when you compare today's prizes with those from decades ago, you feel cheated. Modern prizes simply do not measure up. For this reason, collectors tend to focus on prizes put in the box prior to 1960.

Most Cracker Jack prizes were not marked. As a result, many dealers have Cracker Jack prizes without even knowing it. This allows an experienced collector to get some terrific bargains at flea markets. Alex Jaramillo's *Cracker Jack Prizes* (Abbeville Press: 1989) provides a wonderful survey of what prizes were available.

Army Tank **35.00**
Booklet, 1½ × 2½", 1933 World's Fair, 8
pgs, Cracker Jack adv **75.00**
Bookmark, 2¾" l, diecut litho tin, c1930
.... **15.00**
Bubble Gum Card, Cracker Jack in baseball
uniform, 1915 .... **17.50**
Bus **70.00**
Cereal Bowl and Cup Set **25.00**
Charm, die cast lead, ring
Boat **5.00**
Candlestick **5.00**
Cannon **5.00**
Fish **5.00**
Plane **5.00**
Shoe **5.00**
Stork and Baby **5.00**
Teddy Bear **5.00**
Thimble **5.00**
Wrench **5.00**
Clicker, aluminum **15.00**
Cookbook, 4 × 6", "Angelus Recipes,"
black and white, 14 pgs **15.00**
Doll, stuffed cloth body, vinyl head, Vogue
Dolls, 1980 copyright, unopened display
card **25.00**
Fire Truck **52.00**
Freight Car **42.00**
Hat, paper, "Me For Cracker Jack," red,
white, and blue design, early 1900s
.... **65.00**
Horse–Drawn Wagon, "More You Eat"
.... **88.00**
Lunch Box **35.00**
Mask, 8½ × 10", "Cracker Jack" on front,
c1960 .... **15.00**

Boxcar, plastic, red, $5.00.

Midget Auto Race, 2 × 3¼", cardboard, full
color, grommeted disk, instructions on
bottom margin, 1940s **50.00**
Panel Van, Quick Delivery **38.00**
Pencil, wood **15.00**
Plate, 1¾" d, tin, silver, "Cracker Jack" in
center **30.00**
Pocket Watch **50.00**
Puzzle Book, 2½ × 4", 4 pgs, Series One,
1917 copyright **75.00**
Radio, orig box **38.00**
Roadster, open, #348 .... **70.00**
Top, 1½" d, tin, silver, wood peg **25.00**
Truck, "More You Eat" **80.00**
Whistle
Plastic **18.00**
Tin **30.00**
Yellow Cab, litho tin **90.00**

CUFF LINKS

Many people consider cuff links to be the ideal collectible. Besides being available, affordable, and easy to display and store, cuff links are educational and offer windows to history. They have been around for centuries and have always reflected the styles, economics, and technologies of their era. Cuff link collecting can be profitable, rare or unusual finds can be worth substantial dollars. Most serious collectors have had the thrill of buying a pair for "pennies" that turned out to be worth a great deal.

Many cuff link collectors specialize in their collections. Some areas of specialization are size, shape, and closure type. Other collectors specialize by subject. Examples of this are cuff links that show animals, sports, advertising logos, cars, boats, etc.

Cuff link collecting can be a family project; many parents and their children spend weekends at flea markets and garage sales. Indeed, there are many reasons to collect cuff links. That's why cuff link collecting is the fastest growing hobby in the country.

Club: National Cuff Link Society, PO Box 346, Prospect Heights, IL 60070.

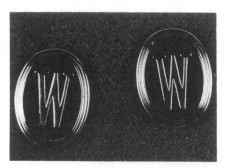

Swank, monogram "W," silver, black ground, matching tie bar, 1" l, $12.00.

Chance Cuff Button, bracelet style cuff holder, spring band, c1924, orig box **35.00**
Coin, set
Indian Head Penny, pr cuff links and collar stud, copper circular setting, clear celluloid disk **100.00**
Mercury Dime, pr cuff links and tie tack, 1930s **40.00**
Hickock, ¾" d, gold filled findings, powder blue glass dec, early 1930s **10.00**
Jem Snap Link, Art Deco, sq metal base, green celluloid with center mother–of–pearl circle dec, orig card, 1920s **25.00**
Krementz, ¾" d, acrylic, paperweight type, fish hook tied with red feather, 1950s **10.00**
Oriental, Japan
½ × ¾", rectangular, Obsidian, carved letters **38.00**
⅝" d, round, black glass disk with center pearl dec, silver base, chased intaglio rim **45.00**
1 × 1½", figural, demon head, hand carved ivory, sterling toggle, 1950s **35.00**
Spiedel, pr cuff links and tie clip, gold tone findings, rect, round corners, black glass, molded Centurian motif, 1960s ... **7.50**
Swank, gold tone findings, late 1930s
⅜" d, paperweight type, fishing hook tied with white feather, mother–of–pearl ground **20.00**
¾" l, rect, paperweight type, reverse painted hunter with raised gun and hunting dog, mother–of–pearl ground **25.00**
⅝" d, rosette, simulated carbuncle dec **8.00**
Unmarked
Round, ½" d, silver tone, white celluloid center, alternate celluloid ring and carved metal ring border **6.00**
Set, pr cuff links and tie pin, octagonal shape, silver tone, center ivory celluloid disk set with rhinestones, 1920s **30.00**
Square
⅜" d, gold tone findings, simulated acrylic moonstone dec **5.00**

½" d, Art Deco, silver tone, celluloid with mother–of–pearl center circle dec, 1920s **15.00**
Triangular shape, black matte ground, simulated pearl and rows of gold beads dec, patent number 2,472,958, c1949 .... **7.50**
Zentall, 1" d, lady's, brass, gold wash, mound of irregular beaded dec, 1940s **12.00**

CUPIDS

Be suspicious of naked infants bearing bows and arrows. It is not clear if their arrows are tipped with passion or poison.

Advertising Trade Card, Hoods Sarsaparilla, cupid with trumpet **6.00**
Booklet, Diamond Dyes, two rabbits watching cupid blowing bubbles, 6 × 8", 1901 .... **18.00**
Candy Box, cardboard, cupid with wheelbarrow **15.00**
Centerpiece, composition, cupid holding quiver of arrows, foil cardboard arrows, early 20th C **50.00**
Christmas Ornament, white cupid, gold trim, gold hanger, plastic, 4" h **5.00**
Creamer, cupid dec **20.00**
Diecut, emb, cupids with flowers, K & B No. 1830, 6 × 3", set of four **12.00**
Dresser Scarf, linen, embroidered dec **45.00**
Fan, cardboard, cupids in center, "Diamond Candy Store, manufacturers of Ice Cream, Springfield, Mass," gilded edge **30.00**
Garden Statuette, sitting, legs crossed, wings folded around body, stone, antique finish, 12" h **28.00**
Napkin Ring, figural, sitting, legs crossed, combination candleholder and napkin ring, SP **175.00**
Nut Cup, red crepe paper, cupid dec **4.00**
Post Card
Happy New Year, sgd "Rosie O'Neill" **26.00**
Valentine, hearts with arrows, cupid, and flowers dec, early 20th C **10.00**
Print
6 × 8", Cupid Awake, Cupid Asleep, Taber Prang, 1897 copyright, unframed, pr **22.00**
8 × 10", woman in gauze dress with cupid on rock **30.00**
13 × 17", Cupid Awake, Taber Prang, 1897 copyright, unframed **48.00**
Toothpick Holder, cupid holding flower basket, bisque **35.00**
Valentine
4½ × 7", two cupids and heart faces in snow, diecut int, Ellen Clapsaddle **20.00**

Valentine, three dimensional, cupid playing violin atop topiary tree, 3½" w, 5¾" h, $12.00.

7" l, fold down, three layers, cupid behind couple holding hands ... **12.00**
7 × 7½", heart shape, cupid shooting arrow, rose silk fringe dec **35.00**
Wall Hanging, 7 × 8", diecut, heart, cupids listening to phonograph, Ellen Clapsaddle **40.00**

Post Card, Affectionate Greetings, two cupids mailing love letter, white mail box, blue flowers, divided back, $2.00.

CUSPIDORS

After examining the interiors of some of the cuspidors for sale at flea markets, I am glad I have never been in a bar where people "spit." Most collectors are enamored by the brass cuspidor. The form came in many other varieties as well. You could build a marvelous collection focusing on pottery cuspidors.

Within the past year a large number of fake cuspidors have entered the market. I have seen them at flea markets across the United States. Double–check any cuspidor with a railroad marking and totally discount any with a Wells Fargo marking.

Advertising, Redskin Cut Plug Chewing Tobacco, brass **110.00**
Bennington Pottery, 10" d, 4" h, Shell pattern, mottled brown Rockingham glaze **200.00**
Cast Iron, porcelainized, light gray, white int, marked "Valley RR" **95.00**
Graniteware, blue **55.00**
Nickel Plated Brass, 7½" d, Arcade, Model No 401 . . . . **250.00**
Nippon, lady's hand, violets, turquoise beading, green M in wreath mark **150.00**
Pewter, 8" d, Gleason, Roswell, Dorchester, MA, c1850 . . . . **200.00**
Pottery, 4½" h, pansies, marked "Loy–Nel Art" **100.00**
Redware, 8 × 4¼", tooled bands, brown and green running glaze with brown dashes **250.00**
Roseville
   Donatello **110.00**
   Ivory, 5" h, ink stamp **150.00**
Salt Glazed, 8½" d, brown highlights **55.00**
Spatterware, 5 × 7½", blue stripes **65.00**
Spongeware
   Blue sponging, white ground, molded basketweave dec **150.00**
   Yellow and brown dec **65.00**
Stoneware
   Cobalt blue leaf and floral motif, 8" d **175.00**
   Emb sponged blue earthworm pattern **120.00**
Tin, 8¼" d, smoked white, red stripes and gold stenciled dec **70.00**

CUT GLASS

Collectors have placed so much emphasis on American Brilliant Cut Glass (1880 to 1917) that they completely overlook some of the finer cut glass of the post–World War I period. Admittedly, much cut glass in this later period was mass-produced and rather ordinary. But, if you look hard enough, you will find some great pieces.

The big news in the cut glass market at the end of the 1980s was the revelation that many of the rare pieces that had been uncovered in the 1980s were of recent origin. Reproductions, copycats, and fakes abound. This is one category where you had better read a great deal and look at hundreds of pieces before you start buying.

Condition is also critical. Do not pay high prices for damaged pieces. Look for chips, dings, fractures, and knife marks. Sometimes these defects can be removed, but consider the cost of the repair when purchasing a damaged piece. Of course, signed pieces command a higher dollar value.

Remember, the antiques and collectibles market is governed by *caveat emptor* (let the buyer beware).

Club: American Cut Glass Assoc, 1603 SE 19th, Suite 112, Edmond Professional Bldg, Edmond, OK, 73013.

Atomizer, 8" h, Harvard pattern, gold washed atomizer **100.00**
Bell, hobstars, fan, and strawberry diamond **275.00**
Bonbon, 8" d, Broadway pattern, minor flakes **125.00**
Bowl
   5" d, cross cut diamond and fan **40.00**
   8¼" d, swirled primrose, sgd "Tuthill" **500.00**
Candlestick, 9½" h, teardrop stem, hobstar base **200.00**
Cheese and Cracker Dish, SS rim . . . **150.00**
Compote, Ribbon Star, rayed foot **275.00**
Door Knob, facet cut **25.00**
Goblet, Russian, facet cut teardrop stem, rayed base **125.00**
Mustard, cov, Renaissance pattern, matching underplate **150.00**

Dish, sawtooth edges, pinwheel and hobstar cutting, 6" l, several chips, $2.50.

Pitcher, 11½" h, cane and hobstar cut, 24 point hobstar base **275.00**
Plate, Hindoo pattern, Hoare **115.00**
Punch Bowl Ladle, 11½" l, cut and notched prism handle, SS emb shell dec **150.00**
Punch Cup, hobstars, pedestal, handle **75.00**
Salt, feather **15.00**
Sherbet, Chicago pattern, Fry **75.00**
Toothpick Holder, 2½" h, prism cut **35.00**
Tray, 12" d, pinwheels, hobstars, and florals **115.00**
Vase, 5" h, Brazilian pattern, trumpet shape, Hawkes **155.00**
Wine, hobstars, fans, and strawberry diamond **35.00**

CZECHOSLOVAKIAN OBJECTS

Czechoslovakia was created at the end of World War I out of the area of Bohemia, Moravia, and Austrian Silesia. Although best known for glass products, Czechoslovakia also produced a large number of pottery and porcelain wares for export.

Czechoslovakian objects do not enjoy a great reputation for quality, but I think they deserve a second look. They certainly reflect what was found in the average American's home from the 1920s through the 1950s.

Box, cov, 4" d, 3" h, cut glass, engraved **45.00**
Card Holder, 2¾" h, ornate gold metal frame and base, green ground, glass cameo **40.00**
Christmas Ornament, clip–on, Santa **48.00**
Cologne Bottle, 4" h, blue, glossy, bow front **12.00**
Container, head, fisherman, hat lid **75.00**
Creamer and Sugar
   Orange lustre, pink roses **55.00**
   Swans, white and green, sgd **95.00**
Cup and Saucer, pheasant **32.50**
Decanter, 11" h, Art Nouveau, 4 part **40.00**
Dish, frosted, cameo inset, filigree, ftd **45.00**
Perfume Bottle, 5" h, engraved design, amber frosted flowers, stopper **25.00**
Pitcher
   4" h, red, black handle **15.00**
   10" h, sheep and shepherdess dec **55.00**
Plate
   9" d, pr, Bartered Bride, hp **50.00**
   13" d, 18th C romantic scene, green border, gilt ornate carved frame **95.00**
Rolling Pin, wood, carved **35.00**
Salt and Pepper Shakers, pr, 2" h, figural, duck, clear glass bodies, orange porcelain tops **42.00**

Tablecloth, 50 × 70", eight matching napkins, ecru, pull work, brown tones, cross–stitch deer pattern, paper label "Moravian Art Linen," unused
.............................**125.00**

DAIRY ITEMS

For decades the dairy industry has been doing a good job of encouraging us to drink our milk and eat only real butter. The objects used to get this message across as well as the packaging for dairy products has long been a favorite with collectors.

Concentrate on the material associated with a single dairy, region, or national firm. If you tried to collect one example of every milk bottle used, you simply would not succeed. The amount of dairy collectibles is enormous.

Clubs: Creamer Separator Assoc, Rt 3, Box 189, Arcadia, WI 54612; National Assoc of Milk Bottle Collectors Inc, 4 Ox Bow Rd, Westport, CT 06800.

Periodicals: *Creamers,* PO Box 11, Lake Villa, IL 60046; *The Udder Collectibles,* HC 73 Box 1, Smithville Flats, NY 13841.

Advertising Trade Card, Borden's Milk, girl and pug dog illus **8.00**
Box
     Bing Crosby Ice Cream **5.00**
     Borden's Process Cheese Food, 4 × 12 × 4", wood, red and green logo, 1950s **18.00**
Brochure, Eskimo Pie, premium, c1952
     ....**15.00**
Broom Holder, 4 × 4", De Laval Cream Separators, tin, orig envelope ...**115.00**
Bucket, Sunny Field Lard, 4 lbs **28.00**
Calendar
     De Laval, 1932 ....**45.00**
     Melotte Cream Separators, 1903, 18 × 23" frame **65.00**
     Sharples Tubular Cream Separators, 1922 ....**110.00**
Change Tray
     De Laval **85.00**
     Merit Separator Co, emb, cream separator illus, fluted edges **175.00**
Clicker, "Gridley Milk Did It!," color milk bottle with baby face, red ground **25.00**
Clock
     Dinsmore Dairy **150.00**
     Foremost Ice Cream, light up ...**170.00**
     Garst Bros Dairy, double globe **125.00**
     Sealtest Milk **75.00**
Cookbook
     Borden's Eagle Brand Book of Recipes, 32 pgs **15.00**
     Carnation Milk, 32 pgs, 1915 ....**10.00**

Dairy Cap, Produced in Florida, Grade A Raw Milk, red and green letters, 1⅝" d, $.25.

Creamer
     Anthony's Cream **13.00**
     Elsie, figural **35.00**
     Rosebud Dairy **9.00**
Cream Separator, McCormick–Deering, stainless steel, maroon paint, manual crank, 1940s **175.00**
Doilies, Carver Ice Cream, linen–like, emb, Christmas, 1920s, pkg of 12 .....**10.00**
Doll, Elsie, 12" h, plush **40.00**
Figure, cow, De Laval, glued–on legs
     ....**125.00**
Flashlight, miniature, Eagle Brand Ice Cream carton shape **4.00**
Game, Elsie, Selchow Righter, 1941   **68.00**
Letter Opener, De Laval, brass, 1878–1928
     ....**38.00**
Match Holder
     De Laval **50.00**
     Sharples Tubular Cream Separators, 7 × 2", tin litho, diecut, mother and cow illus **350.00**
Milk Bottle
     Borden's, Elsie illus **8.00**
     Borden Weiland, emb, round, qt   **20.00**
     Dairylea **6.00**
     Forresters, round, red print and illus, ½ gal **15.00**
     Gail Borden, amber, 1½ gal **22.00**
     Hood, qt **4.00**
     Peterson's Dairy, qt **20.00**
     VM&I Co, emb, amber, qt **50.00**
Milk Bottle Cap, Deerfoot Farms, Southborough, MA **5.00**
Milk Box, metal, Borden's, Elsie illus
     ....**80.00**
Milk Can, plain **10.00**
Mirror, pocket, Ice Cream Dairy Co, Springfield, IL **45.00**
Mug, Elsie in daisy on outside, Elsie head on inside bottom **35.00**
Pinback Button
     Drink Aristocrat Milk, red and white, 1930s **10.00**
     Land O' Lakes, oval, Indian princess serving turkey on platter dec, 1930s
     ....**50.00**

Post Card, Elsie **8.00**
Poster, 29 × 42", Sharples tubular Cream Separators, paper, comical farmer and wife scene **300.00**
Push Puppet, Elsie, 5" h **285.00**
Ruler, Breyer Ice Cream, colorful **15.00**
Sign
     Borden's Condensed Milk, 15 × 11", cardboard, little girl wearing witch's hat, kittens, 1893 ....**450.00**
     De Laval, blue and yellow **40.00**
     Meiers Ice Cream, porcelain **65.00**
Thermometer, Sharples Tubular Cream Separators, 14 × 10", tin, emb, "The World's Best" **55.00**
Tin, Mohican Pure Cream Cheese, Indian logo, 30 lb **80.00**

DAKIN FIGURES

The term "Dakin" refers to a type of hollow vinyl figure produced by the R. Dakin Company. These figures are found with a number of variations—molded or cloth costumed, jointed or nonjointed— and range in size from 5 to 10" high.

As with any popular and profitable product, Dakin figures were copied. There are a number of Dakin–like figures found on the market. Produced by Sutton & Son Inc, Knickerbocker Toy Company, and a production company for Hanna–Barbera, these figures are also collectible and are often mistaken for the original Dakin products. Be careful when purchasing.

Baby Puss, 5" h, figure, vinyl, copyright 1971 ....**110.00**
Bozo, figure, 7½" h, plastic and vinyl, movable head and arms, orange hair, blue body, white gloves, 1974 ......**12.00**
Bugs Bunny, gray and white body, yellow gloves
     Bank, 10" h, standing on yellow basket filled with carrots, holding carrot, hard plastic and vinyl, movable head and arms, 1971 ....**35.00**
     Figure
          7" h, vinyl **15.00**
          10" h, holding carrot, hard plastic and vinyl, movable head, arms, and legs, 1971 ....**18.00**
Bullwinkle, figure, 7½" h, TV Cartoon Theater series, holding megaphone, hard plastic and vinyl, movable head, arms, and legs, tan and brown body, ivory gloves, red "B" on green sweater, "What's–A–Matta U" on green megaphone, 1976, orig box **35.00**
Cool Cat, figure, 9" h, hard plastic and vinyl, movable head, arms, and legs, green beret and tie, orange and white body, black markings, 1968 .....**25.00**

Deputy Dawg, figure, 6" h, Fun Farm series, hard plastic and vinyl, movable head, arms, and upper torso, white body, glossy black plastic hat and vest, blue trousers, yellow badge, orange belt and holster, 1977, orig pkg **30.00**

Dudley Do-Right, figure, Cartoon Theater **20.00**

Dumbo, figure **12.00**

Elmer Fudd, figure, 7" h, vinyl, plastic double-barreled shotgun over one arm, orig tag, 1968 copyright **125.00**

Foghorn Leghorn, figure **50.00**

Hokey Wolf, figure, 8" h, vinyl, movable head, arms, feet, and tail, brown body, tan and black markings, 1971 .... **20.00**

Little Liberty Bell, figure, 7" h, vinyl, orig tag, copyright 1975 .... **55.00**

Mickey Mouse, figure, 5½" h, hard plastic and vinyl, movable head, arms, and legs, black body, yellow shirt, red pants, white gloves, orange shoes **20.00**

Mouse, figure, 8" h, standing on pedestal, holding champagne glass, Goofy Grams series, vinyl, movable head, arms, and upper torso, W C Fields likeness, gray body, red nose, black and gray top hat, maroon and white fabric jacket, "I'll drink to that!" on marbleized base, 1971 .... **35.00**

Oliver Hardy, figure, 7½" h, hard plastic and vinyl, movable head and arms, brown hat, black hair, lavender fabric jacket, white fabric shirt, blue fabric tie, blue trousers, black shoes, 1960s   **35.00**

Olive Oyl, figure, 9" h, vinyl, orig tag, 1960s **75.00**

Pebbles Flintstone, figure, 8" h, vinyl, movable head, arms, and legs, orange hair, purple and black fabric outfit, 1970 .... **28.00**

Porky Pig, figure
    5" h, vinyl, pink cap and shirt, black jacket, white gloves, blue and white polka dot bow tie **15.00**
    6½" h, vinyl, orig box, 1976 copyright **50.00**

Road Runner, figure, 10" h, hard plastic and vinyl, movable head, light and dark blue body, yellow beak, orange legs, 1968 .... **20.00**

Rocky Squirrel, figure, 6½" h, TV Cartoon Theater series, hard plastic and vinyl, movable head, arms, legs, and tail, gray body, blue aviator's cap, 1976, orig box **35.00**

Smokey Bear, figure, 8" h, hard plastic and vinyl, movable head and arms, yellow hat, brown body and belt, blue denim fabric jeans, 1960s **28.00**

Speedy Gonzales, brown body, yellow sombrero, green shirt, white trousers, red neckerchief
    Bank, 9¾" h, standing on cheese wedge, hard plastic and vinyl, movable head, arms, and tail, fabric outfit, 1970 .... **20.00**

Figure
    5" h, vinyl **15.00**
    7" h, standing on pedestal, hard plastic and vinyl, Goofy Gram series, "Have A Speedy Recovery" on white pedestal, 1971 ..... **28.00**

Sylvester, black and white body
    Bank, 11" h, standing on blue sea chest, hard plastic and vinyl, movable head, arms, tail, and upper torso, 1969, orig pkg **25.00**
    Figure, vinyl, red nose
        5½" h **15.00**
        8" h, movable head, arms, legs, and tail, 1969, orig pkg **20.00**

Tweety Bird, 6" h, movable head, yellow body, orange beak and feet, blue eyes
    Bank, hard plastic, 1976 .... **10.00**
    Figure, vinyl, 1969, orig pkg **25.00**

Underdog, figure, 6" h, vinyl, mid 1960s **75.00**

Wile E Coyote
    Bank, standing on explosives crate, holding bomb, hard plastic and vinyl, movable head, arms, and upper torso, dark brown and tan, "Acme Explosives" and "Handle With Care" on base, 10" h, 1971 .... **35.00**
    Figure, 8" h, vinyl, orig box, 1976 copyright **50.00**

Woodsy Owl **30.00**

Woody Woodpecker, Warner Brothers **40.00**

Yogi Bear, figure, Hanna Barbera **30.00**

Yosemite Sam, blue hat and trousers, yellow shirt, orange hair, black gun belt and boots
    Bank, 7" h, standing on brown trunk, hard plastic and vinyl, movable arms, yellow painted hair, orange "cotton" beard, fabric outfit, 1970 ..... **30.00**
    Figure, 6½" h, Fun Farm series, vinyl, red neckerchief, movable arms and upper torso, silver gun, 1977–1978, orig pkg **28.00**

DEARLY DEPARTED

I know this category is a little morbid, but the stuff is collected. Several museums have staged special exhibitions devoted to mourning art and jewelry. Funeral parlors need to advertise for business.

I did not put one in the listing, but do you know what makes a great coffee table? A coffin carrier or coffin stand. Just put a piece of glass over the top. Its the right size, has legroom underneath, and makes one heck of a conversation piece.

Advertising Trade Card, Geo A Cunley Monumental & Granite Works, black and green, cemetery scene **50.00**

Booklet, *Incineration*, John B Beugless, United States Cremation Company, Ltd, 9¾" × 6", Portland vase pictured on front, 14 pgs, wraps **18.00**

Bottle
    Dr George Lenninger's Formaldehyde Generator, 5½" h, sq **125.00**
    Coffin Poison, 4½" h, cobalt blue, diamond design, emb "Poison" **40.00**
    Warner Co Poison, 3" h, triangle, skull, and crossbones, blue, paper label **35.00**

Casket Plate, brass, "Rest in Peace," mounted **27.00**

Catalog
    Crane & Breed Funeral Supplies, Cincinnati, OH, 1906, 36 pgs, 10½ × 14" **35.00**
    F H Hill Co, Chicago, IL, "Illus Catalogue of Wood Finished, Cloth Covered and Metallic Caskets," 1886, 108 pgs, illus, cloth cover, 8 × 10" **50.00**
    H S Eckels and Co, Philadelphia, PA, "Derma Surgery with Complete Catalog of Embalmer's Supplies," c1927, 324 pgs, 9 × 12" **35.00**
    Keystone Coffin Works, Allegheny, PA, 1875, coffins and caskets, color illus **45.00**
    Monumental Bronze Co, Bridgeport, CT, 1884, 134 pgs **30.00**
    National Metal Products, Connersville, IN, 1929, 72 pgs, casket hardware **35.00**

Fan, cardboard, advertising on reverse
    Sisler Bros, Inc, Fine Monuments, 8½ × 7½", multicolored, garden and mountain scene, 11" l wooden handle **25.00**
    Swallow Funeral Home, four panel, folding, floral bouquet illustration **30.00**

Skull, tobacco jar, X handle on lid, ceramic, late 19th C, $190.00.

Grave Marker, 1898 Cuba War **15.00**

Memorial, 3⅜ × 4¼", abalone shell, watercolor, applied straw, paper willow, tomb, German inscription, black lacquered frame **55.00**

Mortician's Basket, woven, adult size **125.00**

Mourning Jewelry

Ring, 18K gold, seed pearls, one diamond, locket on inside of shank, enamel "In Memory Of" on shank, English **300.00**

Stickpin, gold, round, black enamel "In Memory Of," lock of hair under glass, 19th C **165.00**

Mourning Picture, 8⅜ × 10⅜", watercolor, paper memorial, tomb, inscription, matted, gilt frame, dated 1810 . . . . . . **65.00**

Pinback Button, adv

Pan–American, Pass Bearer One Way, Rock Falls Mfg Co, Sterling, IL, 1¼" d, funeral wagon, 1901–1910 . . . . **12.50**

This Man Died From Overwork, Trying To Beat The Parsons Feeder, 1¾" d, multicolored, man lying in coffin, two tall candlesticks, wheat, 1896–1900 . . . . **85.00**

Post–Mortem Set, saws, scalpels, and hooks, mahogany case **485.00**

Remembrance Card, 4⅛ × 6⅜", cardboard, diecut, gold lettering and illus on black ground, 1888 . . . . **6.00**

Sheet Music, *Funeral March*, Eclipse Publishing Co, c1914 . . . . **12.00**

Sign, emb steel, oval, "Funeral Space" on one side, back reads "Funeral, No Parking" **35.00**

tures. Benjamin Franklin signed a number of Pennsylvania deeds. These are worth a great deal more than $10.00. Third, check the location of the deed, the current property owner may like to acquire it.

Finally, a number of early deeds have an elaborate wax seal at the bottom. Framed, these make wonderful display pieces in attorneys' offices. When a deed is to be used for this purpose, the price charged has little to do with the intrinsic worth of the deed. Sock it to the attorney—charge decorator prices.

Baptismal Certificate, 6" sq, handcolored, Germany, 1830 . . . . **10.00**

Bill of Lading

Pittsburgh, Cincinnati & St Louis RR Co, 1886, green **10.00**

Union Line RR, 1886, red print **12.00**

Confirmation Certificate, 11½ × 16", Abingdon Press, NY and Cincinnati, No. 80, 1926 . . . . **8.00**

Dog License, City of Fitchburg, MA, 1887, dog's name and information **15.00**

Land Grant, 14 × 20", sgd by President Grant, framed, 1862 . . . . **225.00**

Marriage Certificate, 13 × 17", Ernst Kaufmann, NY, No. 105, 1898 . . . . . . **15.00**

Receipt

American Bank Note Co, War, Liberty & Museum, Building Fund of the War, 1892, $25 . . . . **12.00**

Tierney Bros Bicycle Store, Saginaw, MI, 1899 . . . . **15.00**

Reward of Merit

Card of Honor, Model Scholar, Jackson Daily Citizen, 1874 . . . . **20.00**

Reward Card, Joyful be thy Days, black, gold, and white, floral dec center, coated stock **12.00**

Stock Certificate

Altex Petroleum Co, Delaware, 1921, orange and black, oil well vignettes **10.00**

Baltimore & Ohio Railroad Co, 1922, canceled **10.00**

Bank of Binghamton, 1859, 10 shares, $100 each **20.00**

Dubuque & Sioux City Railroad Co, 1873, used **12.00**

Missouri, Kansas & Texas Railway Co, 1907, orange and black **15.00**

DEGENHART GLASS

Degenhart pressed glass novelties are collected by mold, by individual color, or by group of colors. Hundreds of colors, some almost identical, were produced between 1947 and 1978. Prior to 1972 most pieces were unmarked. After that date a "D" or "D" in a heart was used.

Club: The Friends of Degenhart, Degenhart Paperweight and Glass Museum, Inc, 65323 Highland Hills Rd, PO Box 186, Cambridge, OH 43725.

Animal Dishes, covered

Hen, 3" h, dark green **25.00**

Lamb, cobalt blue **40.00**

Turkey, custard **60.00**

Basket, cobalt blue **18.00**

Bicentennial Bell, canary **15.00**

Boot, Daisy and Button **25.00**

DEEDS AND DOCUMENTS

A document is any printed paper that shows evidence or proof of something. Subject matter ranges from baptismal certificates to scholastic awards to stocks and bonds. Flea markets are loaded with old documents. Though they generally have minimal value and are usually copies of the original forms, it makes good sense to check before discarding. It may be of value to descendents of the original owner or to a paper ephemera collector.

Many eighteenth- and early nineteenth-century deeds are on parchment. In most cases, value is minimal, ranging from a few dollars to a high of $10.00.

First, most of the deeds are copies. The actual document is often on file in the courthouse. Second, check the signa-

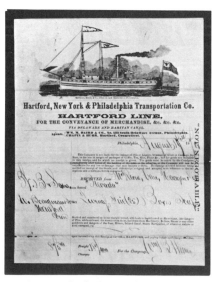

Receipt, Hartford, New York & Philadelphia Transportation Co, pink ground, 1870, 7¾ × 10", $45.00.

Goblet, Old Chocolate, $40.00.

Candy Dish, cov, wildflower, crystal **15.00**
Creamer and Sugar, Texas, pink **45.00**
Cup Plate, Heart and Lyre, gold **9.00**
Gypsy Pot, Blue Jay **20.00**
Hand
    Amethyst **8.50**
    Frosty Jade **15.00**
Hat, Daisy and Button
    Amethyst **8.00**
    Opalescent **12.00**
Jewelry Box, heart
    Blue Jay **25.00**
    Fawn **18.00**
    Old Lavender **25.00**
Owl
    Bluebell **30.00**
    Charcoal **40.00**
    Frosty Jade **45.00**
    Midnight Sun **30.00**
    Sunset **25.00**
    Willow Blue **48.00**
Paperweight, name **50.00**
Pooch
    Canary **15.00**
    Ivory Slag **20.00**
Salt
    Daisy and Button, lime ice **15.00**
    Star and Dew Drop
        Aqua **15.00**
        Forest Green **12.00**
Salt and Pepper Shakers, pr, birds, gun
  metal **18.00**
Shoe, figural, high button, light blue **25.00**
Slipper
    Bow, caramel **30.00**
    Kat, sapphire **15.00**
Toothpick Holder
    Basket, sparrow slag **15.00**
    Beaded Oval, old lavender **20.00**
    Colonial Drape and Heart, ruby
        .... **20.00**
    Daisy and Button, light blue slag **25.00**
    Forget–Me–Not, caramel **8.50**
    Gypsy Pot, blue fire **15.00**
    Heart, crystal **7.50**

DEPRESSION ERA GLASS

Depression Era Glass refers to glassware made between the 1920s and 1940s. It was mass-produced by a number of different companies. It was sold cheaply and often given away as a purchasing premium.

Specialize in one pattern or color. Once again, there is no way that you can own every piece made. Also, because Depression Era Glass was produced in vast quantities, buy only pieces in excellent or better condition.

A number of patterns have been reproduced. See Gene Florence's *The Col-*

lector's *Encyclopedia of Depression Glass* (Collector Books, revised annually) for a complete list of reproductions.

Clubs: The National Depression Glass Assoc, PO Box 69843, Odessa, TX 69843; 20-30-40 Society, Inc, PO Box 856, La Grange, IL 60525.

Newspaper: *The Daze,* PO Box 57, Otisville, MI 48463.

AMERICAN PIONEER

Made by Liberty Works, 1931–1934. Made in amber, crystal, green, and pink.

Bowl, 5" d, handle
    Crystal **14.00**
    Green **17.00**
    Pink **14.50**
Candlesticks, pr, 6½" h
    Crystal **60.00**
    Green **80.00**
    Pink **65.00**
Candy Dish, cov, 1 lb
    Crystal **75.00**
    Green **95.00**
    Pink **78.00**
Creamer, 3½" h
    Amber **40.00**
    Crystal **18.50**
    Green **21.00**
    Pink **20.00**
Cup and Saucer
    Amber **30.00**
    Crystal **15.00**
    Green **18.50**
    Pink **15.00**
Plate, 8" d, luncheon
    Amber **20.00**
    Crystal **10.00**
    Green **11.00**
    Pink **10.00**
Sherbet, 4¾" h
    Crystal **30.00**
    Green **35.00**
    Pink **32.00**
Sugar, 3½" h
    Amber **36.00**
    Crystal **18.00**
    Green **21.00**
    Pink **20.00**
Tumbler, 4" h, 8 oz
    Crystal **25.00**
    Green **45.00**
    Pink **25.00**

AUNT POLLY

Made by US Glass Co, late 1920s. Made in blue, green, and iridescent.

Bowl, 4¾" d, berry
    Blue **17.50**
    Green **8.00**
    Iridescent **7.50**

Butter Dish, cov
    Blue **185.00**
    Green **210.00**
    Iridescent **200.00**
Candy Dish, cov, two handles
    Green **60.00**
    Iridescent **60.00**
Creamer
    Blue **42.00**
    Green **26.00**
    Iridescent **25.00**
Plate
    Blue, 8" d, luncheon **18.00**
    Green, 6" d, sherbet **6.50**
    Iridescent, 6" d, sherbet **6.00**
Sherbet
    Blue **12.00**
    Green **10.00**
    Iridescent **9.00**
Sugar
    Blue **30.00**
    Green **23.00**
    Iridescent **23.00**
Tumbler, 3⅝" h, 8 oz, blue **26.00**
Vase, 6½" h, ftd
    Blue **37.50**
    Green **27.50**
    Iridescent **27.50**

BOWKNOT

Made by an unknown manufacturer in the late 1920s. Made only in green.

Bowl
    4½" d, berry **14.00**
    5½" d, cereal **18.00**
Cup **7.50**
Plate, 7" d **12.00**
Sherbet, low **14.00**
Tumbler, 5" h, 10 oz, ftd **16.00**

CAMEO (BALLERINA, DANCING GIRL)

Made by Hocking Glass Co, 1930–1934. Made in crystal (with a platinum rim), green, pink, and yellow. Heavily reproduced.

Bowl, 5½" d, cereal
    Crystal **6.50**
    Green **28.00**
    Pink **150.00**
    Yellow **28.00**
Butter Dish, cov
    Green **185.00**
    Yellow **1,500.00**
Cake Plate, 10½" d
    Green **90.00**
    Pink **130.00**
Creamer, 3¼" h
    Green **25.00**
    Yellow **17.50**
Cup and Saucer
    Green **17.50**
    Pink **150.00**
    Yellow **12.00**
Plate, 9½" d, dinner
    Green **16.00**
    Pink **60.00**
    Yellow **10.00**

Sherbet, 3⅛" h
   Green 12.50
   Pink 65.00
   Yellow 38.00
Sugar, 3¼" h
   Green 17.00
   Yellow 14.00
Tumbler, 4" h, 9 oz
   Crystal 9.00
   Green 24.00
   Pink 75.00

CLOVERLEAF

Made by Hazel Atlas Glass Co, 1930–1936. Made in black, crystal, green, pink, and yellow.

Ashtray, 5¾" d, match holder center, black
. . . . 75.00
Bowl, 4" d, dessert
   Green 18.00
   Pink 12.00
   Yellow 24.00
Candy Dish, cov
   Green 48.00
   Yellow 98.00
Creamer, 3⅝" h, ftd
   Black 17.50
   Green 10.00
   Yellow 16.00
Cup and Saucer
   Black 21.00
   Green 12.00
   Pink 15.00
   Yellow 18.00
Plate, 8" d, luncheon
   Black 15.00
   Green 8.00
   Pink 7.00
   Yellow 14.00
Sherbet, 3" h
   Black 20.00
   Green 7.00
   Pink 6.50
   Yellow 11.00
Sugar, 3⅝" h, ftd, green 45.00
Tumbler, 3¾" h, 10 oz, flared
   Green 35.00
   Pink 20.00

DOGWOOD (APPLE BLOSSOM, WILD ROSE)

Made by MacBeth–Evans, 1929–1932. Made in cremax, crystal, green, monax, pink, and yellow.

Bowl, 8½" d, berry
   Cremax 36.00
   Green 95.00
   Monax 50.00
   Pink 36.00
Cake Plate, 13" d
   Cremax 165.00
   Green 85.00
   Monax 160.00
   Pink 90.00

Dogwood, grill plate, pink, $15.00.

Creamer, 2½" h, thin
   Green 45.00
   Pink 16.00
Cup and Saucer
   Green 45.00
   Pink 25.00
Plate, 8" d, luncheon
   Green 8.00
   Pink 7.50
   Yellow 55.00
Sherbet
   Green 90.00
   Pink 35.00
Sugar, 2½" h, thin
   Green 45.00
   Pink 18.00
Tumbler, 4" h, 10 oz, dec
   Green 75.00
   Pink 35.00

DORIC AND PANSY

Made by Jeannette Glass Co, 1937–1938. Made in crystal, green, pink, and ultramarine (teal).

Bowl, 4½" d, berry
   Crystal 8.00
   Green 15.00
   Pink 8.00
   Ultramarine 15.50
Butter Dish, cov, ultramarine 475.00
Creamer
   Crystal 70.00
   Green 115.00
   Pink 75.00
   Ultramarine 118.00
Cup and Saucer
   Crystal 15.00
   Green 24.00
   Pink 15.00
   Ultramarine 25.00
Plate, 9" d, dinner
   Crystal 7.50
   Green 27.50
   Pink 7.50
   Ultramarine 28.50

Doric and Pansy, tumbler, ultramarine, $72.00.

Sugar, open
   Crystal 65.00
   Green 110.00
   Pink 65.00
   Ultramarine 115.00
Tumbler
   Green 70.00
   Ultramarine 72.00

FLORENTINE #1 (OLD FLORENTINE, POPPY NO. 1)

Made by Hazel Atlas Glass Co, 1932–1935. Made in cobalt blue, crystal, green, pink, and yellow. Salt and pepper shakers have been reproduced.

Ashtray, 5½" d
   Crystal 22.00
   Green 22.00
   Pink 26.00
   Yellow 26.00
Bowl, 8½" d, berry
   Crystal 20.00
   Green 21.00
   Pink 26.00
   Yellow 26.00
Butter Dish, cov
   Crystal 120.00
   Green 120.00
   Pink 150.00
   Yellow 155.00
Coaster, 3¾" d
   Crystal 16.00
   Green 16.50
   Pink 23.00
   Yellow 18.00
Compote, 3½" d, ruffled
   Cobalt Blue 55.00
   Crystal 20.00
   Green 21.00
   Pink 18.00

Creamer
    Crystal **9.50**
    Green **10.00**
    Pink **17.00**
    Yellow **18.00**
Cup and Saucer
    Cobalt Blue **90.00**
    Crystal **12.00**
    Green **12.50**
    Pink **15.00**
    Yellow **14.00**
Plate, 10" d, dinner
    Crystal **15.00**
    Green **15.00**
    Pink **21.00**
    Yellow **20.00**
Sherbet
    Crystal **10.00**
    Green **10.00**
    Pink **10.00**
    Yellow **11.00**
Sugar, cov
    Crystal **22.00**
    Green **24.00**
    Pink **34.00**
    Yellow **36.00**
Tumbler, 4¾" h, 10 oz, ftd
    Crystal **21.00**
    Green **21.00**
    Pink **22.00**
    Yellow **20.00**

GEORGIAN (LOVEBIRDS)

Made by Federal Glass Co, 1931–1935. Made in green.

Bowl
    4½" d, berry **8.00**
    5¾" d, cereal **22.50**
    9" l, vegetable, oval **60.00**
Butter Dish, cov **70.00**
Creamer, 4" h, ftd **14.00**
Cup and Saucer **14.00**
Hot Plate, 5" d, center design **45.00**
Plate
    6" d, sherbet **6.00**
    8" d, luncheon **9.00**
    9¼" d, dinner **25.00**

Georgian, creamer, green, $14.00.

Sherbet **12.00**
Sugar, cov, 4" h, ftd **110.00**
Tumbler, 4", 9 oz **50.00**

JUBILEE

Made by Lancaster Glass Co, early 1930s. Made in pink and yellow.

Bowl, 11½" d, fruit
    Pink **195.00**
    Yellow **165.00**
Candlesticks, pr
    Pink **185.00**
    Yellow **175.00**
Cheese and Cracker Set
    Pink **255.00**
    Yellow **250.00**
Creamer
    Pink **35.00**
    Yellow **25.00**
Cup and Saucer
    Pink **42.00**
    Yellow **24.00**
Plate, 8¾" d, luncheon
    Pink **27.50**
    Yellow **17.50**
Sandwich Tray, 11" d, center handle
    Pink **195.00**
    Yellow **200.00**
Sugar
    Pink **35.00**
    Yellow **22.00**
Tumbler, 6" h, 10 oz
    Pink **75.00**
    Yellow **42.00**

MADRID

Made by Federal Glass Co, 1932–1939. Made in amber, blue, crystal, green, and pink. Heavily reproduced.

Bowl, 5" d, sauce
    Amber **6.00**
    Green **6.50**
    Pink **6.50**
Butter Dish, cov
    Amber **68.00**
    Green **80.00**
Cookie Jar, cov
    Amber **45.00**
    Pink **30.00**
Creamer, ftd
    Amber **8.50**
    Blue **20.00**
    Green **12.00**
Cup and Saucer
    Amber **11.00**
    Blue **27.00**
    Green **14.00**
    Pink **12.50**
Pitcher, 8" h, 60 oz, sq
    Amber **45.00**
    Blue **150.00**
    Crystal **150.00**
    Green **135.00**
    Pink **35.00**

Madrid, pitcher, amber, 5¾" h, $45.00.

Plate, 8⅛" d, luncheon
    Amber **8.00**
    Blue **18.00**
    Green **9.00**
    Pink **7.50**
Sherbet
    Amber **7.50**
    Blue **15.00**
    Green **12.00**
Soup Bowl, 7" d
    Amber **15.00**
    Blue **30.00**
    Green **16.00**
Sugar, cov
    Amber **45.50**
    Blue **170.00**
    Green **50.00**
Tumbler, 4¼" h, 9 oz
    Amber **15.00**
    Blue **25.00**
    Green **20.00**
    Pink **15.00**

MANHATTAN (HORIZONTAL RIBBED)

Made by Anchor Hocking Glass Co, 1938–1943. Made in crystal, green, and pink.

Ashtray, 4" d, round, crystal **10.00**
Bowl, 5⅜" d
    Crystal **17.50**
    Pink **17.50**
Candy Dish, cov, crystal **36.00**
Compote, 5¾" d
    Crystal **30.00**
    Pink **30.00**
Creamer
    Crystal **10.00**
    Pink **10.00**
Cup and Saucer
    Crystal **25.00**
    Pink **190.00**
Plate, 10¼" d, dinner
    Crystal **20.00**
    Pink **110.00**
Sherbet
    Crystal **9.00**
    Pink **15.00**

Manhattan, plate, clear, 6" d, $3.50.

Sugar
  Crystal **10.00**
  Pink **12.00**
Tumbler, 10 oz, ftd
  Crystal **16.00**
  Green **15.00**
  Pink **17.50**

NEWPORT (HAIRPIN)

Made by Hazel Atlas Glass Co, 1936–1940. Made in amethyst, cobalt blue, fired–on colors, pink, and platonite white.

Bowl, 4¾" d
  Amethyst **13.00**
  Cobalt Blue **16.50**
  Fired–On Colors **5.50**
  Platonite White **4.00**
Creamer
  Amethyst **13.50**
  Cobalt Blue **15.00**
  Fired–On Colors **7.50**
  Platonite White **4.50**
Cup and Saucer
  Amethyst **16.00**
  Cobalt Blue **15.00**
  Fired–On Colors **7.50**
  Platonite White **6.50**
Plate, 8½" d, luncheon
  Amethyst **11.50**
  Cobalt Blue **12.50**
  Fired–On Colors **5.00**
  Platonite White **3.50**
Sherbet
  Amethyst **14.00**
  Cobalt Blue **16.00**
  Fired–On Colors **5.50**
  Platonite White **3.50**
Sugar
  Amethyst **14.00**
  Cobalt Blue **16.00**
  Fired–On Colors **8.00**
  Platonite White **7.00**
Tumbler, 4½" h, 9 oz
  Amethyst **30.00**
  Cobalt Blue **32.00**
  Fired–On Colors **12.00**

OLD COLONY (LACE EDGE, OPEN LACE)

Made by Hocking Glass Co, 1935–1938. Made in pink.

Bowl, 7¾" d, salad, ribbed **45.00**
Butter Dish, cov **60.00**
Candy Jar, cov **45.00**
Compote, cov, 7" d **45.00**
Cookie Jar, cov **55.00**
Creamer **21.00**
Cup and Saucer **35.00**
Fish Bowl, crystal **26.00**
Plate
  8¾" d, luncheon **17.50**
  10½" grill **18.00**
Relish Dish, 7½" d, 3 parts **55.00**
Sherbet **75.00**
Sugar **21.00**
Tumbler, 4½" h, 9 oz **17.50**

PATRICK

Made by Lancaster Glass Co, early 1930s. Made in pink and yellow.

Bowl, 9" d
  Pink **125.00**
  Yellow **50.00**
Candy Dish
  Pink **115.00**
  Yellow **75.00**
Cheese and Cracker Set
  Pink **140.00**
  Yellow **95.00**
Creamer
  Pink **75.00**
  Yellow **40.00**
Cup and Saucer
  Pink **95.00**
  Yellow **52.00**
Plate, 8" d, luncheon
  Pink **45.00**
  Yellow **30.00**
Sherbet
  Pink **60.00**
  Yellow **45.00**
Sugar
  Pink **75.00**
  Yellow **40.00**
Tray, 11" d, two handles
  Pink **75.00**
  Yellow **60.00**

PRINCESS

Made by Hocking Glass Co, 1931–1935. Made in apricot yellow, green, pink, topaz yellow.

Bowl, 5" d
  Apricot Yellow **28.00**
  Green **22.00**
  Pink **24.00**
  Topaz Yellow **28.00**
Butter Dish, cov
  Apricot Yellow **600.00**
  Green **85.00**
  Pink **85.00**
  Topaz Yellow **600.00**

Cake Plate, 10" d
  Green **24.00**
  Pink **28.00**
Coaster
  Apricot Yellow **85.00**
  Green **32.00**
  Pink **64.00**
  Topaz Yellow **85.00**
Cookie Jar, cov
  Green **50.00**
  Pink **55.00**
Creamer
  Apricot Yellow **14.00**
  Green **14.00**
  Pink **15.00**
  Topaz Yellow **14.00**
Cup and Saucer
  Apricot Yellow **12.50**
  Green **22.00**
  Pink **24.00**
  Topaz Yellow **14.00**
Plate, 9½" d, dinner
  Apricot Yellow **14.50**
  Green **24.00**
  Pink **22.00**
  Topaz Yellow **15.00**
Sherbet
  Apricot Yellow **35.00**
  Green **20.00**
  Pink **20.00**
  Topaz Yellow **35.00**
Sugar
  Apricot Yellow **8.50**
  Green **10.00**
  Pink **12.00**
  Topaz Yellow **9.00**
Tumbler, 4" h, 9 oz
  Apricot Yellow **22.00**
  Green **25.00**
  Pink **26.00**
  Topaz Yellow **24.00**

RADIANCE

Made by New Martinsville Glass Co, 1936–1939. Made in amber, cobalt blue, crystal, emerald green, ice blue, pink, and red.

Bonbon, 6" d
  Amber **10.00**
  Crystal **5.00**
  Ice Blue **17.50**
  Red **18.00**
Bowl, 10" d, crimped
  Amber **18.00**
  Crystal **10.00**
  Ice Blue **24.00**
  Red **25.00**
Butter Dish, cov
  Amber **185.00**
  Crystal **100.00**
  Ice Blue **400.00**
  Red **400.00**
Cheese and Cracker Set
  Amber **25.00**
  Crystal **16.00**
  Ice Blue **48.00**
  Red **48.00**

Creamer
 Amber **14.00**
 Crystal **6.00**
 Ice Blue **24.00**
 Red **22.00**

Cup and Saucer
 Amber **17.50**
 Crystal **10.00**
 Ice Blue **25.00**
 Red **25.00**

Plate, 8" d, luncheon
 Amber **10.00**
 Crystal **5.00**
 Ice Blue **16.00**
 Red **16.00**

Punch Bowl
 Amber **100.00**
 Crystal **50.00**
 Emerald Green **125.00**
 Ice Blue **175.00**
 Red **175.00**

Punch Cup
 Amber **8.00**
 Crystal **5.00**
 Ice Blue **17.50**
 Red **15.00**

Salt and Pepper Shakers, pr
 Amber **50.00**
 Crystal **25.00**
 Ice Blue **80.00**
 Red **80.00**

Sugar
 Amber **12.00**
 Crystal **7.50**
 Ice Blue **20.00**
 Red **21.00**

Tumbler, 9 oz
 Amber **17.50**
 Cobalt Blue **28.00**
 Crystal **8.50**
 Ice Blue **28.00**
 Red **26.00**

RING (BANDED RINGS)

Made by Hocking Glass Co, 1927-1933. Made in crystal with colored rings of black, blue, orange, pink, red, and silver, and plain crystal and plain green.

Bowl, 5" d
 Colored Rings **5.00**
 Crystal **3.50**
 Green **5.00**

Butter Tub
 Colored Rings **30.00**
 Crystal **18.00**
 Green **30.00**

Cocktail Shaker
 Colored Rings **24.00**
 Crystal **18.00**
 Green **20.00**

Creamer
 Colored Rings **6.00**
 Crystal **4.00**
 Green **5.00**

Cup and Saucer
 Colored Rings **7.00**
 Crystal **6.00**
 Green **6.50**

Plate, 8" d, luncheon
 Colored Rings **4.50**
 Crystal **2.50**
 Green **4.00**

Sherbet, 4¾" h
 Colored Rings **9.00**
 Crystal **5.00**
 Green **7.50**

Sugar, ftd
 Colored Rings **5.50**
 Crystal **4.50**
 Green **5.00**

Tumbler, 4¼" h, 9 oz
 Colored Rings **10.00**
 Crystal **5.00**
 Green **10.00**

STAR

Made by Federal Glass Co, 1950s. Made in amber and crystal.

Bowl, 4⅜" d
 Amber **4.00**
 Crystal **3.50**

Iced Tea Tumbler, 5⅛" h, 12 oz
 Amber **7.50**
 Crystal **7.00**

Juice Tumbler, 3⅜" h, 4½ oz
 Amber **4.00**
 Crystal **4.00**

Pitcher, 36 oz
 Amber **8.00**
 Crystal **7.50**

Plate, 9⅜" d, dinner
 Amber **5.00**
 Crystal **5.00**

Tumbler, 3⅞" h, 9 oz
 Amber **5.50**
 Crystal **5.00**

Vegetable Bowl, 8¾" d
 Amber **9.00**
 Crystal **8.00**

Whiskey Tumbler, 2¼" h, 1½ oz
 Amber **3.00**
 Crystal **2.50**

STRAWBERRY

Made by US Glass Co, early 1930s. Made in crystal, green, iridescent, and pink.

Bowl, 6½" d
 Crystal **15.00**
 Green **18.00**
 Iridescent **15.00**
 Pink **18.00**

Butter Dish, cov
 Crystal **135.00**
 Green **150.00**
 Iridescent **135.00**
 Pink **150.00**

Compote
 Crystal **15.00**
 Green **20.00**
 Iridescent **18.00**
 Pink **20.00**

Creamer, 4⅝"
 Crystal **22.50**
 Green **30.00**
 Iridescent **24.00**
 Pink **35.00**

Olive Dish, 5" l
 Crystal **8.50**
 Green **12.00**
 Iridescent **8.00**
 Pink **13.00**

Plate, 7½" d
 Crystal **10.00**
 Green **13.00**
 Iridescent **10.00**
 Pink **13.00**

Sherbet
 Crystal **6.00**
 Green **7.00**
 Iridescent **6.50**
 Pink **8.00**

Sugar
 Crystal **24.00**
 Green **32.00**
 Iridescent **25.00**
 Pink **35.00**

Tumbler, 3⅝" h, 8 oz
 Crystal **18.00**
 Green **28.00**
 Iridescent **20.00**
 Pink **30.00**

SWIRL (PETAL SWIRL)

Made by Jeannette Glass Co, 1937–1938. Made in delphite, pink, and ultramarine, limited production in amber and ice blue.

Bowl, 9" d
 Delphite **27.50**
 Pink **18.00**
 Ultramarine **25.00**

Candy Dish, cov
 Pink **100.00**
 Ultramarine **135.00**

Coaster
 Pink **9.50**
 Ultramarine **12.50**

Creamer, ftd
 Delphite **12.00**
 Pink **8.00**
 Ultramarine **15.00**

Cup and Saucer
 Delphite **15.00**
 Pink **14.00**
 Ultramarine **20.00**

Plate, 9¼" d, dinner
 Delphite **12.00**
 Pink **14.00**
 Ultramarine **18.00**

Sherbet
 Pink **10.00**
 Ultramarine **15.00**

Sugar, ftd
  Delphite .12.00
  Pink 10.00
  Ultramarine 15.00
Tumbler, 4⅝" h, 9 oz, pink 16.00

TEA ROOM

Made by Indiana Glass Co, 1926-1931.
Made in green and pink.

Bowl, 8¾" d
  Green 80.00
  Pink 65.00
Candlesticks, pr
  Green 48.00
  Pink 45.00
Creamer, 3¼" h
  Green 25.00
  Pink 27.00
Cup and Saucer
  Green 75.00
  Pink 75.00
Plate, 8¼" d
  Green 35.00
  Pink 30.00
Sherbet, low, flared
  Green 30.00
  Pink 28.00
Sugar, cov, 3" h
  Green 100.00
  Pink 90.00
Tumbler, 4¼" h, 8 oz
  Green 85.00
  Pink 75.00

VICTORY

Made by Diamond Glassware Co,
1929–1932. Made in amber, black, cobalt
blue, green, and pink.

Bowl, 6½" d
  Amber 11.00
  Black 26.00
  Cobalt Blue 26.00
  Green 12.00
  Pink 12.00
Candlesticks, pr, 3" h
  Amber 30.00
  Black 90.00
  Cobalt Blue 90.00
  Green 30.00
  Pink 30.00
Cheese and Cracker Set
  Amber 40.00
  Green 45.00
  Pink 45.00
Creamer
  Amber 15.00
  Black 45.00
  Cobalt Blue 45.00
  Green 15.00
  Pink 15.00
Cup and Saucer
  Amber 13.00
  Black 44.00
  Cobalt Blue 44.00

Green 14.00
Pink 15.00
Plate, 8" d, luncheon
  Amber 7.00
  Black 25.00
  Cobalt Blue 25.00
  Green 7.50
  Pink 8.00
Sherbet
  Amber 14.00
  Black 25.00
  Cobalt Blue 25.00
  Green 15.00
  Pink 15.00
Sugar
  Amber 15.00
  Black 45.00
  Cobalt Blue 45.00
  Green 15.00
  Pink 15.00

DIONNE QUINTUPLETS COLLECTIBLES

On May 28, 1934, on a small farm
in Callander, Ontario, Canada, five baby
girls weighing a total of 10 pounds 1¼
ounces were delivered into this world
with the help of Dr. DaFoe and two
midwives: The Dionne Quintuplets.

Due to their parents' poor circumstances and the public's curiosity, the
quintuplets were put on display. For a
small fee, the world was invited to come
and see the quints at play in their custom–built home or to buy a souvenir to
mark their birth.

The field of collectibles for Dionne
Quintuplets memorabilia is a very fertile
one!

Club: Dionne Quints Collectors, PO Box
2527, Woburn, MA 01888.

Book
  *Dionne Quintuplets Picture Album, The
    Complete Story of Their First Two
    Years,* Dell, 1936 . . . . .28.00
  Dionne Quintuplets Play Mother Goose,
    Dell, 1938 . . . . .25.00
  Now We're Two Years Old, Whitman,
    1936 . . . . .30.00
  *Soon We'll Be Three Years Old: The
    Five Dionne Quintuplets Book,* Whit-
    man, 1936 . . . . .22.00
  The Dionne Quintuplets Growing Up,
    8½ × 11", brown and white cov,
    1935 . . . . .40.00
Booklet, 4½ × 5½", adv, "Lysol vs.
  Germs," Dionne photos inside, 30 pgs,
  Lehn & Fink Products Corp, 1938 15.00
Box, candy
  Baby Ruth, 2 × 8 × 11", cardboard,
    "Baby Ruth–First and Only Candy
    Served the Dionne Quints" . . .75.00

Dionne Pops, 4 × 10½ × 1", Vitamin
  Candy Co, Providence, RI, 1936
  . . . . .125.00
Calendar
  1937, Robotman & Sons Dairy, quints
    wearing pink dresses 15.00
  1943, Sunny Day, beach illus 25.00
Cake Plate, 11½" d, china, white, gold ma-
  ple leaf at top, red rim, center color por-
  traits titled "Dionne Quintuplets, Born
  May 28, 1934, Callander, Ontario, Can-
  ada" 135.00
Cereal Bowl, 5⅞" d, chrome plated metal,
  Quaker Oats premium, late 1935 25.00
Coloring Book, 10 × 15", *The Dionne
  Quintuplets Pictures to Paint,* Merrill,
  1940 . . . . .40.00
Doll, 7½" h, mohair wig, painted brown
  eyes, Madame Alexander, 1936 250.00
Fan, 8¼ × 8¾", diecut cardboard, tinted
  color photo portraits, light blue ground,
  funeral parlor adv reverse, 1936 18.00
Handkerchief, 8" sq, linen weave cotton,
  three quints playing, two with birthday
  cakes, sgd "Tom Lamb," 1936–37
  . . . . .25.00
Keychain, 3" l, celluloid, dark green, gold
  lettering, "Souvenir of Quint Land,
  Callander, Canada" 30.00
Lobby Card, 11 × 14", "Five Of A Kind,"
  color, girls playing piano, 1938
  . . . . .70.00
Magazine, *Woman's World,* Feb 1937
  . . . . .10.00
Palm Puzzle, steel balls, glass cov, place
  quints in buggy 35.00

*Fan, cardboard, multicolored, copyright
1936 NEA Service, Inc., St Paul, MN,
#17000, adv for the Stonington Furniture Co
on back, $15.00.*

Paper Doll Book, 9½ × 10½", Annette,
    Whitman, 1936 . . . . **100.00**
Photograph, 7¼ × 9", tinted color, first
    year, 10 × 12" glass frame with card-
    board easel **25.00**
Playing Cards, double deck, orig cellophane
    and box, 1936 . . . . **150.00**
Poster, 14 × 32", "Today the Dionne
    Quints Had Quaker Oats," 1935 **65.00**
Program, theater, promotion for *The Coun-
    try Doctor,* 1936 . . . . **20.00**
Sheet Music, *Quintuplets' Lullaby,* tinted
    photo front cov, 6 pgs **10.00**
Spoons, set of five **125.00**
Thermometer, 4 × 6", Cupp's Dairy, card-
    board, multicolored **25.00**

DISNEYANA

"Steamboat Willie" introduced
Mickey Mouse to the world in 1928.
Walt and Roy Disney, brothers, worked
together to create an entertainment
empire filled with a myriad of memora-
ble characters ranging from Donald
Duck to Zorro.

Early Disney is getting very expensive. No problem. Disney continues to
license material. In thirty years the stuff
from the 1960s and 1970s is going to be
scarce and eagerly sought after. Now is
the time to buy it.

Clubs: National Fantasy Fan Club for
Disneyana Collectors & Enthusiasts, PO
Box 19212, Irvine, CA 92713; The
Mouse Club, 2056 Cirone Way, San
Jose, CA 95124.

Periodicals: *Mouse Rap Monthly,* PO
Box 1724, Ojai, CA 93024; *Tomart's
Disneyana Digest,* 3300 Encrete Ln,
West Carrollton, OH 45439.

Advertising Fan, Silly Symphonies, colored
    scenes of Disney characters picnicking,
    1936 . . . . **175.00**
Bank
    Dopey, dime register, tin, dated 1939
    . . . . **145.00**
    Pinocchio **30.00**
Book
    Snow White and the Seven Dwarfs,
        hardback, 1938 . . . . **95.00**
    Winnie the Pooh, scratch and sniff
    . . . . **10.00**
Box, Mickey Mouse Straws, 1960s . . . **15.00**
Butterfly Net, Mickey Mouse **85.00**
Button, Seven Dwarfs, Bakelite, red . . . **9.50**
Camera, figural, Mickey Mouse, train engi-
    neer, Helm Toy Co, MIB **55.00**
Ceiling Fixture, 11" d, round globe, Donald
    Duck and Pluto chasing butterflies
    . . . . **295.00**
Charm Bracelet, enameled metal figures
    . . . . **35.00**

*Disneyland, CA, charm, Magic Castle, gold
toned sterling silver, orig case, c1970, 1" d,
$7.50.*

Children's Tea Set
    Disneyland, tin litho, 7 pcs, orig box
    . . . . **195.00**
    Donald Duck, porcelain, 13 pcs, orig
        box **395.00**
    Mickey Mouse
        Porcelain, 23 pcs, tan lustre, orig box
        . . . . **475.00**
        Tin, litho, 7 pcs, Happynak, orig box
        . . . . **375.00**
Christmas Bulb Covers, Mickey Mouse, set
    of 8 . . . . **75.00**
Christmas Light Set, Mickey Mouse, shades,
    no string, orig box, Noma **165.00**
Clock Radio, Mickey Mouse, General Elec-
    tric, Youth Electronics, 1950s . . . **175.00**
Cookie Jar
    Alice In Wonderland, Japan **195.00**
    Donald Duck and Nephews **95.00**
    Dumbo, mouse finial **95.00**
    Mickey Mouse on Drum **195.00**
    Winnie the Pooh, Walt Disney Produc-
        tions **85.00**
Drawing Set, Walt Disney Electric Drawing
    Set, carrying case, dated 1961
    . . . . **115.00**
Figure
    Donald Duck, bisque, strutting . . . **68.00**
    Dopey, 5½" h, bisque **65.00**
    Mickey and Minnie, china, 1940s **55.00**
    Mickey Mouse, jointed, decal, early
        1920s **275.00**
    Snow White and Seven Dwarfs, bisque,
        1938 . . . . **325.00**
    Three Little Pigs, musicians, bisque
    . . . . **145.00**
Fork and Spoon, Mickey and Minnie, SP,
    pie eyes **60.00**
Lamp, scent, Bambi, porcelain, Goebel
    . . . . **295.00**
Lantern, Pluto, tin, Line Mar, 1950s **325.00**
Map
    Mickey Mouse and Donald Duck, Race
        to Treasure Island, no stamps, 1939
    . . . . **60.00**

*Donald Duck, children's feeding dish, pink,
hot water reservoir, 6¾ × 8", $30.00.*

Mickey Mouse Travel Club Star Bakery,
    1938 . . . . **95.00**
Movie Poster, one sheet
    Fantasia **25.00**
    Jungle Book **300.00**
    Lady & The Tramp **100.00**
Napkin, linen
    Happy, bathing, name on soap dish
    . . . . **25.00**
    Snow White with Dopey, Disney label
    . . . . **25.00**
Nodder
    Donald Duck, 6½" h **45.00**
    Mickey Mouse **65.00**
    Pluto, orig tag **55.00**
Paint Box, Alice In Wonderland, tin, orig
    paints **30.00**
Pattern, Cinderella, apron, paper **8.00**
Pencil Box, Mickey Mouse, Dixon . . . **75.00**
Pencil Sharpener, Ferdinand, Bakelite
    . . . . **70.00**

*Mickey Mouse, figurine, blue jacket, red
pants, oversized yellow shoes, tan base,
Schmid, orig red and white 4¾" h box, imp
"Disney," marked "copyright The Walt Disney Company, Schmid, Taiwan," 4" h,
$18.00.*

Phonograph, Alice In Wonderland, 1951
. . . . **150.00**
Plate, 7" d, Mickey Mouse, tin enamel, red
and blue **110.00**
Press Box, Alice In Wonderland, uncut,
1974 . . . . **15.00**
Puppet, Ferdinand the Bull, composition
head, flower in hand **120.00**
Purse, Snow White, 1938 . . . . **60.00**
Puzzle, jigsaw, orig box, set of 4 . . . **125.00**
Record Album, Mickey Mouse Club, *Who's
The Leader,* 1955 . . . . **55.00**
Record Player, Alice In Wonderland, 45
rpm, RCA **85.00**
Salt and Pepper Shakers, pr Pinocchio,
1940s **45.00**
Sand Pail, Mickey Mouse Happynak, color-
ful character portraits, England, 1940s
. . . . **95.00**
Scrapbook, Mickey Mouse Club, unused,
1952 . . . . **55.00**
Sheet Music, *Snow White,* Walt Disney En-
terprises, 1938 . . . . **40.00**
Song Album, *Alice in Wonderland,* 20 pgs,
1951 . . . . **95.00**
Stuffed Toy
Dopey, Knickerbocker, 1930s . . . **175.00**
Pluto, 14" h, velvet, black leather collar,
orig label **110.00**
Suitcase, overnight, Alice in Wonderland,
colorful illus ext and int **115.00**
Tablecloth, child's, Alice In Wonderland,
color storybook illus, 1950s **65.00**
Tea Set, Alice in Wonderland, china, orig
box **45.00**
Tie Bar, Mickey Mouse **15.00**
Transfer, color, Davy Crockett, unused,
1955 . . . . **30.00**

Toy
Watering Can, Snow White and Seven
Dwarfs, Ohio Art Co, 1938   **145.00**
Windup
Mickey Mouse, climbing fireman,
orig box **95.00**
Nautilus, 20,000 Leagues Under the
Sea, tin, orig box, 1930s
. . . . **295.00**
Pinocchio, tin, walking figure, Line
Mar **395.00**
Wristwatch
Alice in Wonderland, 1958 . . . . . **225.00**
Mickey Mouse
Bradley **350.00**
US Time **75.00**

DOG COLLECTIBLES

The easiest way to curb your collection is to concentrate on the representations for a single breed. Many collectors
focus only on three–dimensional figures.
Whatever approach you take, buy pieces
because you love them. Try to develop
some restraint and taste and not buy every piece you see. Easy to say, hard to
do!

Clubs: Canine Collectibles Club of
America, Suite 314, 736 N Western Ave,
Lake Forest, IL 60045; Wee Scots, Inc,
PO Box 1512, Columbus, IN 47202.

Advertising Trade Card
Bogues Soap, figural, dog **20.00**
Compliments of Imperial Granum, baby
and puppies, 6¹⁄₂ × 9¹⁄₂" **12.00**
Ashtray
Mack Bulldog, full figure with tray, stain-
less steel **40.00**
Scottie, black full figure with tray   **20.00**
Bank, dog on barrel, McCoy **35.00**
Bookend, porcelain, Terrier dogs, black and
white **150.00**
Bookmark, 2³⁄₄" l, Cracker Jack adv, brown
and black dog **15.00**

*Tankard, Golden Retriever decal, white, gold
trim, Swank Tankard Collection, #3419,
1968, 5" h, $15.00.*

Calendar, 1909, Hoods, Family Medicine,
4¹⁄₂ × 10" **15.00**
Calendar Plate, 8⁵⁄₈" d, white, boxer, gold
trim, 1910 . . . . **45.00**
Cookie Jar, Dalmatian, McCoy **425.00**
Doorstop
German Shepherd, standing **40.00**
Wirehaired Terrier, orig paint, c1929
. . . . **115.00**
Figure, porcelain
Boxer, 3¹⁄₂" h **5.00**
Collie, 5¹⁄₂ × 8¹⁄₄", "Made in Japan"
. . . . **10.00**
Poodle, 9¹⁄₂ × 9¹⁄₂", "Made in Austria"
. . . . **75.00**
Napkin Ring, dog pulling sled, SP   **250.00**
Pin, Scottie, Bakelite, black **75.00**
Planter, 5 × 6", Scottie, chalkware   **10.00**
Post Card, wood burned, dog with baby
bottle **8.00**
Record, *Train Your Dog,* Lee Duncan, 12¹⁄₄"
sq cardboard album, 33¹⁄₃ rpm, 1961,
produced by Carlton Record Corp   **15.00**
Sign
10 × 14", Old Vitality Dog Food   **85.00**

*Mickey Mouse, stuffed toy, drum major,
green jacket, yellow hands, red papier–
mache shoes, orig hat and baton, heavily
played with condition, $95.00.*

*Puzzle, His Master's Voice, RCA Victor,
copyright 1933, 165 diecut cardboard
pieces, figural pieces, 5¹⁄₄ × 3¹⁄₄" cardboard
box with radio on cov, 10 × 13", $75.00.*

*Pull Toy, Cocker Spaniel, pressed cardboard,
painted brown and black, heavily played with
condition, 11" l, 7" h, $12.00.*

23 × 23", Old Boston Beer, cardboard,
 dog illus **25.00**
25 × 17", Sensation Cut Plug, card-
 board, man restraining dogs, framed
 . . . . **85.00**
Stuffed Toy, 4½" h, Cocker Spaniel   **30.00**
Tape Measure, Armco Steel, red and white,
 collie and company slogan on one side,
 logo on other, inscribed "Lyle Culvert
 and Road Equipment Co, Minneapolis"
 . . . . **18.00**
Tie Tack, brass, Mack bulldog, 1950s
 . . . . **12.50**
Tobacco Jar, Pug **75.00**
Toy, windup
 Happy Pup, rubber tail, plush ears, orig
  box, Mikuni, Japan, 1960s . . . **125.00**
 Romping Puppy, plush, black, tin litho
  bone in mouth, orig box, T N, Japan,
  1950s **75.00**
Valentine, 7" h, mechanical, dog, eyes and
 tongue move, easel back, Sam Gabriel
 . . . . **15.00**
Watch Fob, Mack Trucks, brass, relief bulldog image, slogan on back, 1960s **15.00**

DOLLS

People buy dolls primarily on the basis of sentiment and condition. Most begin by buying back the dolls with which they remember playing as a child.

Speculating in dolls is risky business. The doll market is subject to crazes. The doll that is in today may be out tomorrow.

Place great emphasis on originality. Make certain that every doll you buy has the complete original costume. Ideally, the box or packing also should be present. Remember, you are not buying these dolls to play with. You are buying them for display.

Clubs: Ideal Doll Collector's Club, PO Box 623, Lexington, MA 02173; Madame Alexander Fan Club, PO Box 330, Mundeline, IL 60060; United Federation of Doll Clubs, 8B East St, PO Box 14146, Parkville, MO 64152.

Periodicals: *Doll Reader,* 6405 Flank Dr, Harrisburg, PA 17112; *Dolls The Collectors Magazine,* 170 Fifth Ave, 12th Floor, New York, NY 10010.

Note: The dolls listed date from the 1930s through the present. For information about antique dolls, see Jan Foulke's *11th Blue Book Dolls and Values* (Hobby House Press: 1993) and R. Lane Herron's *Herron's Price Guide To Dolls* (Wallace-Homestead: 1990).

Acme, 26" h, girl, composition head and
 limbs, cloth body, tin sleep eyes **150.00**
Advertising
 Blue Bonnet Sue, 12" h, cloth **25.00**
 Campbell Soup, 10" h, 1963 . . . . . **95.00**
 Ceresota Flour, 13" h, cloth **135.00**
 Chicken of the Sea, mermaid **12.00**
 Chiquita Banana **20.00**
 Del Monte
  Shoo Shoo Trudy **15.00**
  Sweet Pea, 12" h **10.00**
 Green Giant, 6½" h, Little Sprout, vinyl
  . . . . **20.00**
 Jack Frost, 19" h **12.00**
 Lee Jeans **175.00**
 Little Debbie, 25th Anniversary   **40.00**
 Mr Clean, 8" h, vinyl, Procter & Gamble
  . . . . **110.00**
 Mrs Butterworth's Syrup, 11" h **5.00**
 Northern Bathroom Tissue Girl, 15" h
  . . . . **35.00**
 Pillsbury, Poppin Fresh
  Molded soft vinyl, 6" h **10.00**
  Plush, 25th Anniversary **40.00**
 Rice Krispies, Pop, squeeze, 1975 **30.00**
 Swiss Miss, 17" h, cloth **15.00**
 Vermont Maid Syrup, 15" h, vinyl **30.00**
American Character
 9" h, Toddler, soft vinyl, baby style hair
  and clothes **30.00**
 11½" h, Mary Make-Up, vinyl, ward-
  robe booklet and order sheet, c1966
  . . . . **55.00**
 12" h, Tiny Tears, vinyl **160.00**
 14½" h, Sweet Sue **40.00**
Arranbee
 8" h, Baby Marie, vinyl head, arms, and
  legs, plastic body, 1963 . . . . . . **18.00**
 12" h, My Dream Baby, bisque solid
  head, cloth body **400.00**
 19" h, Rosie, composition swivel head
  on shoulder plate, cloth body
  . . . . **80.00**
Cameo
 12" h, Kewpie, composition, flowered
  sun dress and bonnet, c1940 **125.00**
 19" h, Miss Peeps, vinyl, brown skin,
  1973 . . . . **35.00**
Coleco, Cabbage Patch, 16" h, cowgirl, vi-
 nyl head, cowgirl outfit **85.00**
Deluxe Toys
 6" h, Dawn, blonde hair, vinyl body
  . . . . **15.00**
 18" h, Baby Catch A Ball, vinyl head,
  plastic body, battery operated, throws
  ball, 1969 . . . . **30.00**
Eegee
 11" h, Tina, vinyl head, hard plastic
  body, walker, 1959 . . . . **15.00**
 16" h, Newborn Baby, vinyl head and
  limbs, cloth body, 1963 . . . . . . **20.00**
Effanbee
 14" h, Patsy, composition, painted eyes,
  orig clothing **75.00**
 18" h, Rosemary, composition head and
  limbs, cloth body, tin sleep eyes, orig
  mohair wig and clothing **250.00**

American Character, Hedda Get Better, marked "Whimsie/Amer Doll & Toy Corp, 1960," 20½" h, $85.00.

20" h, girl, composition, tin sleep eyes,
 orig wig, replaced body parts **45.00**
22" h, Ann Shirley, composition, sleep
 eyes, orig wig **60.00**
30" h, Mae Star, composition head and
 limbs, cloth body, tin sleep eyes, orig
 wig and clothing **400.00**
Goebel, 7" h, bisque socket head, composition body, molded hair, intaglio eyes,
 molded shoes **255.00**
Gund
 Mad Hatter, 11½" h, stuffed body,
  molded plastic face, orig "Gund"
  tag, 1950s **200.00**
 Minnie Mouse, 14" h, plush body,
  molded black and white face, orig
  tag, 1940s **225.00**
Hasbro, Charlie's Angels, Kelly, 11½" h,
 orig card, copyright 1977 Spelling-
 Goldberg Productions **25.00**
Horsman
 12" h, Billiken, plush jointed body
  . . . . **350.00**
 16" h, Baby Dimples, composition head
  and limbs, soft cloth body, redressed,
  1930 . . . . **150.00**
Ideal
 10½" h, Pinocchio, composition body,
  wood arms and legs, c1940   **200.00**
 11" h, Shirley Temple, composition,
  sleep eyes, replaced wig **60.00**
 12" h, Betsy Wetsy, composition head,
  rubber body **75.00**
 14" h, Miss Curity, orig nurse's uniform
  and play nurse kit **75.00**
 17" h, Saucy Walker, hard plastic head,
  walker, c1951, MIB **150.00**

19" h, Crissy, vinyl, orig box, 1970
.... **50.00**
22" h, Shirley Temple, composition, orig
mohair wig and clothing **295.00**
Knickerbocker
Holly Hobbie, 24" h **15.00**
W C Fields, talking **22.00**
LaMotte, 9" h
Girl, bisque, google eyes, Bessie Kerney
clothing **85.00**
Kewpie, bisque, 1978 .... **20.00**
Madame Alexander
9" h, McGuffey Ana, composition,
painted features, orig mohair wig and
tagged clothing **175.00**
12" h, Scarlett, composition, sleep eyes,
orig wig and tagged clothing **175.00**
14" h, composition, sleep eyes, orig
mohair wig, tagged clothing, crazing
and paint peeling **15.00**
17" h, Madeline, composition, sleep
eyes, orig wig and tagged clothing,
crazing **40.00**
20" h, Princess Elizabeth, composition,
sleep eyes, orig wig and clothing
.... **100.00**
21" h, Bridesmaid, composition, sleep
eyes, orig mohair wig and under
clothing **200.00**
Mattel, Inc
10" h, Barbie, Sweet 16, vinyl, 1975,
MIB **75.00**
11½" h, Donny Osmond, poseable, orig
box, copyright 1976 Osbro Productions Inc **75.00**
Nancy Ann Storybook, hard plastic **10.00**
Roberts, Xavier, 16" h, Georgia Dee, Cabbage Patch, porcelain head, limited edition, 1985 .... **350.00**
Sonja Bryer, 5" h, bisque head and limbs,
cloth body, pouty expression, 1979
.... **75.00**

*Cookin' with Alf, furry, chef's hat and apron,
$15.00.*

Sun Rubber
10" h, Peter Pan, 1953 .... **35.00**
11" h, Gerber Baby, molded rubber
.... **45.00**
17" h, Sun–Dee, vinyl, dark skin, 1956
.... **48.00**
Terri Lee
15½" h, Terri Lee, vinyl **100.00**
17" h, Cowgirl, plastic, orig cowgirl outfit, 1950 .... **225.00**

DOORSTOPS

Cast iron doorstops have gone
through a number of collecting crazes
over the past twenty years. The last craze
occurred just a few years ago and drove
prices up to a level where you now are
more likely to find doorstops at an antiques show than at a flea market.

Reproductions abound. A few helpful clues are: (1) check size (many reproductions are slightly smaller than the period piece); (2) check detail (the lesser
the detail, the more suspicious you need
to be); and (3) check rust (a bright orange
rust indicates a new piece).

Club: Doorstop Collectors of America,
2413 Madison Ave, Vineland, NJ 08630.

Basket, 11" h, handle with bow, sgd
"Hubley 121" **135.00**
Black Cat, lying on pillow, red ribbon and
bow **125.00**
Bowl, 7 × 7", blue–green, fruit, sgd
"Hubley, 456" **100.00**
Cinderella's Carriage, 9¾ × 19" ... **175.00**
Conestoga Wagon, 8 × 11" **95.00**
Cornucopia and Roses, 10¼" h, orig paint
.... **85.00**
Cottage, Cape Cod style **145.00**
Dog
Boston Terrier, 8¼" h **75.00**
Cocker Spaniel, bronze, relief detail,
worn green patina **150.00**
German Shepherd, sitting **165.00**
St Bernard, wearing keg **145.00**
Whippet, 6¾" h **110.00**
Wirehaired Terrier, bushes, orig paint,
c1929 .... **115.00**
Doll on Base, 4½ × 4⅞" **100.00**
Elephant, 14" h, pulling coconut from tree
.... **145.00**
Fish, 9¾" h, three–fan tail, orig paint, sgd
"Hubley 464" **125.00**
Flower, cast iron, marked "WS–1926"
.... **160.00**
Flower Basket, 5⅞ × 5⅝", National
Foundry **75.00**
Fraternal, Independent Order of Odd Fel-
lows, white bird, gold chain, red base
.... **85.00**
Frog, 3" h, sitting, yellow and green **40.00**
Girl, 9" h, holding skirt out, sgd "Hubley
23" **125.00**

Holy Bible, marble, 5 × 6¼ × 2", $15.00.

High Heel Shoe **75.00**
Horse, black, dated 1949 .... **125.00**
House, 6" h, sgd "Eastern Spec Co" **165.00**
Mammy, 8½" h, red dress, white apron, sgd
"Hubley 327" **150.00**
Pansy Bowl, 7 × 6½", Hubley **125.00**
Parrot, sitting on ring, 8 × 7" ... **100.00**
Peacock, 6¼ × 6¼" **150.00**
Pineapple, 13" h, cast brass **115.00**
Poppies and Cornflowers, 7¼ × 6½",
Hubley **115.00**
Rabbit, 12" h, black repaint, pink and white
trim **125.00**
Rooster, 7" h, black, colorful detail **135.00**
Ship, 5¼" h, clipper, sgd "CJO" **50.00**
Windmill, 6¾" h, ivory, red roof, green base
.... **95.00**
Woman, 8½" h, minuet **175.00**

DRESSER SETS

While growing up, I remember visiting my grandmother and wondering
about all those bottles and little containers on her dresser. They seemed to
contain such exotic things and were always arranged neatly. A small tray held
her comb and brush and sometimes even
a piece of jewelry or two.

Now that I'm older and wiser, I have
learned to recognize these things as
dresser sets and accessories, a fast growing collectible category. Her powder jar
with the Scottie on top always held a big
fluffy powder puff that was just perfect
for bombing my little sister when she
least expected it. Sure beats trying to peel
the child–proof protective tops off of today's powder containers.

Atomizer, black amethyst, goldtone spider web dec, DeVilbiss **90.00**
Bath Set, scented, original package reads: "Starts the Day on a Fresh and Joyful Path" **18.00**
Bottle, Desert Flower Beauty Clean For Deep Skin Cleansing, 5 oz bottle   **8.75**
Brush and Comb
    Celluloid, pink, hand painted flowers, 1920s **40.00**
    Silver Plated, emb florals and scrolls, monogram, worn bristles **35.00**
Cologne Bottle, orig stopper
    Baccarat, 5⅞" h, clear, panel cut   **75.00**
    Fenton, Aqua Crest, melon rib . . . **60.00**
    Heisey, Horizontal Rib, crystal . . . **70.00**
    Pairpoint, 8" h, applied vertical cranberry ribbing, flower form stopper **110.00**
    Porcelain, 4" h, glossy blue, bow on front, Czechoslovakia **12.00**
Dresser Box
    Celluloid **75.00**
    Royal Bayreuth, 3¼" d, rose tapestry, pink and yellow roses **275.00**
Dresser Tray
    Belleek, roses dec **115.00**
    Ceramic, hand painted, forget–me–nots and pink ribbon dec **45.00**
    Custard Glass, Winged Scroll, hp dec **165.00**
    Mirror, round, pierced metal frame, four small feet **15.00**
Hair Receiver
  Ceramic
    Carlsbad, 4" d, cobalt blue flowers, emb basketweave on top, gold trim **30.00**
    Limoges, small blue flowers and butterflies, gold trim **75.00**
    RS Prussia, pink roses, white ground, green border, red mark . . . **65.00**
  Glass
    Custard, Winged Scroll **125.00**
    Fostoria, American pattern **85.00**
Nail File, celluloid, figural, lady's leg, painted high heel and garter, folds in center **35.00**
Perfume, original contents
    Aimant Mist, Coty, 8 oz bottle . . . **11.00**
    Chanel No. 5, 1½ oz bottle **12.00**
    Tussy Midnight Cologne, 2 oz bottle **8.50**
Powder Box
    Bohemian, 4¼" d, ruby flashed top with etched cov with leaping stag, clear base **100.00**
  Cobalt
    Gold leaves, marked "Bavaria KPM, Handarbeit Echt" **95.00**
    Peacock, marked "Japan" **65.00**
Powder Jar, cov, glass, figural
    Bambi, iridescent **25.00**
    Bulldog, pink, frosted **65.00**
    Dancing Girls, transparent blue   **250.00**
    Elephant, crystal **16.00**
    Lady, Akro Agate, pink **75.00**

Hair Receiver, Noritake Tree in the Meadow pattern, blue mark, 3⅛" × 2¼", $30.00.

    Lovebirds, pink, frosted **65.00**
    Melon Base, blue overlay, Fenton   **45.00**
    Sailboat, crystal **30.00**
    Scottie, pink **45.00**
Puff Box, cov, round, glass
    Duncan & Miller, 4" d, pink opalescent **85.00**
    New Martinsville, amethyst, gold dec **50.00**
Sachet, powder, original Avon envelopes, 1908 . . . . **35.00**
Set
    Bakelite, yellow and orange, enameled Art Deco dec, brush, comb, manicure accessories, and mirror   **75.00**
    Belleek, cov powder box, pin tray, buffer and container, nailbrush, and pincushion, hp violets, sgd "MR Willets" **550.00**
  Celluloid
    3 pcs, blue, rosebuds **22.00**
    5 pcs, amberoid, Art Deco design **35.00**
    11 pcs, ivory, orig case **85.00**
  Glass
    New Martinsville, #18, crystal and black, 3 pcs **85.00**
    Pattern, Daisy and Button, amethyst, 3 pcs **125.00**
    Westmoreland, Paneled Grape, milk glass, 7 pcs **282.50**
    Porcelain, tray, pin tray, powder, and hair receiver, blue and white floral dec, B & Co France, 4 pcs   **135.00**
Trinket Box, glass, Sandwich pattern, Duncan & Miller, 3¾" × 5" **85.00**
Vanity Box, cov, glass, blue, Fostoria **100.00**

DRINKING GLASSES, PROMOTIONAL

It is time to start dealing seriously with promotional glasses given away by fast food restaurants, garages, and other merchants. This category also includes drinking glasses that start out life as product containers.

Most glasses are issued in a series. If you collect one, you better plan on keeping at it until you have the complete series. Also, many of the promotions are regional. A collector in Denver is not likely to find a Philadelphia Eagles glass at his favorite restaurant.

Just a few washings in a dishwasher can seriously change the color on promotional drinking glasses. Collectors insist on unused, unwashed glasses whenever possible. Get the glass, drink your drink out of a paper cup.

Newsletter: *Collector Glass News,* PO Box 208, Slippery Rock, PA 16057.

Archie, Welch's **6.00**
Batman, mug, black and white, 1966   **15.00**
Big Boy, 50th anniversary **3.00**
Big Mac on roller skates, McDonaldland Series, 5⅝" h, 1977, McDonald's **3.50**
Billy Beetle **15.00**
Brian Sipe, Cleveland Browns, 1981, Wendy's **5.00**
Burger Chef and Jeff Go Trail Riding, 1976, Burger Chef **8.00**
Camp Snoopy, 1983, McDonald's . . . **3.00**
Chuck E Cheese, Pizza Time Theater   **5.00**
Coke, German **5.00**
Davy Crockett, Indian Fighter, 5⅞" h   **15.00**
Elsie The Cow, dutch costume, Borden's **10.00**
ET Collector Series, Be Good, 1982, Pizza Hut **2.50**

Kentucky Derby, Churchill Downs, 1979, 5¼" h, 2¾" d, $20.00.

Flintstones, Fred & Barney Play Golf, 1962,
  Welch's **6.50**
Howdy Doody **10.00**
Kentucky Derby
  1948 ....**150.00**
  1959 ....**45.00**
  1964 ....**35.00**
  1967 ....**30.00**
  1978 ....**10.00**
Kentucky Fried Chicken, bucket and balloon
  ....**6.50**
King Louie, Jungle Book, Canada **45.00**
Mr Magoo, 1962, Welch's Jelly **7.00**
Noid at the Beach, Domino's Pizza ...**3.00**
Norman Rockwell, Grandpa's Girl, Saturday
  Evening Post scene, Country Time Lem-
  onade **5.00**
Oz, logo **10.00**
See These Burgers, 1978, Burger King **11.00**
Sleeping Beauty, #2, Canada **15.00**
Snow White **22.00**
Star Trek, four different designs, Taco Bell
  ....**5.00**
Star Wars **4.00**
Superman in Action '64, 4¼" h **40.00**
Swee' Pea, 1979, Popeye's Fried Chicken
  ....**10.00**
Warner Sports Series, set of four **8.00**

DRUGSTORE COLLECTIBLES

The corner drugstore, especially one with a soda fountain, was a major hangout center in almost every small town in the United States. Almost all of them dispensed much more than drugs. They were the 7–11's of their era.

This category documents the wide variety of material that you could acquire in a drugstore. It barely scratches the surface. This is a new collecting approach that has real promise.

Advertising Trade Card
  Burdock Blood Bitters, Invalid Ladies!
    This Is For You **10.00**
  Hibbard's Rheumatic Syrup, Greatest
    Blood Purifier Known & Testimonials
    int, litho **25.00**
  Johnson's Anodyne Liniment **10.00**
  Royal Elixir, multicolored **8.00**
Bag, 4¼ × 8¼", Black Draught Family Lax-
  ative, paper, brown, illus **4.00**
Book, *Hand Book of Pharmacy & Therapeu-
  tics,* Eli Lilley & Co **85.00**
Booklet, Royal Tooth Powder, 1890s **23.00**
Bookmark, Climax Catarrh Cure, woman
  wearing fur coat **10.00**
Bottle
  Eli Lilley & Co, Gentian, 1 pt **16.00**
  Wallace Laboratories, Brunswick, NJ,
    Soma Carisoprodol **6.50**
Bottle Opener, Dr Brown's Celery Tonic
  ....**20.00**

Box
  Cutex Deluxe, wood, Art Deco, gift set
    ....**85.00**
  Dr Hobson's Ox Marrow Pomade, 3½
    × 2 × 2", lady illus, includes bottle
    ....**15.00**
  Feen–A–Mint Chewing Gum Laxative
    ....**20.00**
  Lydia Pinkham's Pills for Constipation,
    2½ × 1¼ × 1¼", includes bottle
    and pills **10.00**
  Smith Brothers Cough Drops, 39 × 18
    × 10", wood **75.00**
Calendar, 1901, Colgate, miniature, flower
  ....**15.00**
Catalog, Brewer & Co, 1938, pharmaceuti-
  cal **20.00**
Clock, Rexall, double face, electric **155.00**
Container, 4¼" d, Rexall Cold Cream, red,
  turquoise letters **11.00**
Cookbook, *Dr Ward's Medical Co Cook
  Book,* tonics and patent medicines,
  c1920 ....**3.00**
Counter Card, Dr Carman's Dentalaid, full
  color illus, late 19th C **15.00**
Display, Peter Rabbit Safety Pins, colorful
  cartoon **25.00**
Fan
  666 Laxative **17.50**
  Tums, 1920s **18.50**
Glass, Bromo Seltzer **25.00**
Label, pill box, Dr Blumer's Torpedo Pellets,
  7 × 4½" **1.00**
Liniment, Banalag Mild Non–Greasy, ½ oz
  bottle **6.00**
Mirror
  Nature's Remedy Tablets, 2½" d, white
    lettering, red rim **55.00**
  People's Drug, birthstones, pocket **20.00**
  Star Soap, pocket **20.00**

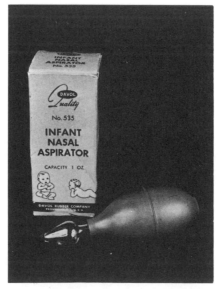

*Davol Infant Nasal Aspirator, Davol Rubber
Co, Providence, RI, light blue, dark blue, and
tan box, orig instruction sheet, $6.50.*

Needle Case, Bromo Seltzer **10.00**
Pinback Button, Lane's Pills Are Best For
  The Liver, ⅞" d, blonde youngster, light
  blue ground, 1907–20 ....**40.00**
Playing Cards, Speedy Alka Seltzer **30.00**
Post Card, Speedy Alka Seltzer **15.00**
Sign
  Dolly Madison Cigar, 6 × 20", tin **20.00**
  Nature's Remedy, porcelain **265.00**
  Professional Pharmacists, brass ...**18.00**
  Sozodont Tooth Powder, 8½ × 13", pa-
    per, smiling woman **100.00**
Thermometer
  Abbott's Bitters, 21" h, wood, yellow,
    blue outline, black letters ...**185.00**
  Doan's Pills, wood **175.00**
  Ex–Lax, 8 × 36", porcelain **135.00**
  Ramon's Kidney & Laxative Pills, 8½ ×
    21", wood, c1930 ....**175.00**
Tin
  Bayer's Aspirin, 7" d **100.00**
  Century Tobacco, factory graphics, flat,
    pocket **110.00**
  Dearso Respicoal Ointment **15.00**
  Golden Pheasant Condom **88.00**
  Hope Denture Powder **35.00**
  Hygenol Violet Talcum, litho image,
    chartreuse, green, and red, 1920s
    ....**25.00**
  Lauxes Tablets **15.00**
  Mentholatum, 1½" d, litho, young nurse
    illus, 1920–30 ....**25.00**
  Ramsey's Condoms, 1929 ....**60.00**
  Rexall Foot Powder, blue **15.00**
  Smith's Rosebud Salve **20.00**
  Three Merry Widows, condoms
    ....**25.00**
  Velvet Night Talc **26.00**
Vitamins
  Beta–Concemin Ferrated Vitamins, Wm
    S Merrill Co, 100 capsules **8.75**
  Gelatric Vitamin–Mineral Supplement,
    Premo Pharm Lab, 100 capsules **8.75**

EASTER COLLECTIBLES

Now that Christmas and Halloween collectibles have been collected to death, holiday collectors are finally turning their attention to Easter Collectibles. The old Easter bonnet still hangs in the Clothing Collectibles closet, but chicken and rabbit collectors now have to contend with Easter enthusiasts for their favorite animal collectible.

Basket
  Metal, round, 1940s **15.00**
  Reeded, 6" h, pink, handle, Germany
    ....**20.00**
  Wicker, oval, colored band, 1940s
    ....**25.00**
Bell, ceramic, rabbit handle, "Happy Easter
  1979" **15.00**

Book, *The Tale of Peter Rabbit*, Edna M
Aldredge and Jessie F McKee, Harter
Publishing Co, 1931 ....**18.00**
Box, Kauffman's Egg Dye, wood, early
1900s **75.00**
Candy Box, cardboard, egg shape, chick
emerging from egg illus, yellow, purple
flowers, 1940s **20.00**
Candy Container
Basket, cardboard, rect, two chicks on
each end, marked "Ertel Bros
Wmspt, PA" **18.00**
Duck, 4" h, yellow composition, ribbon
around neck, standing on 3" d round
cardboard box, opens at base, Germany **35.00**
Egg Shape, papier mache, litho of little
girl and St Bernard, marked "Germany" **40.00**
Rabbit, 8" h, potbelly, white, head and
ears on wire spring, white glass
beaded trim, separates at belt line,
marked "US Zone, Germany" **15.00**
Decoration, honeycomb fold-up type, rabbit with eggs and flowers, 1940s **35.00**
Egg
Glass, 5" l, white, opaque, painted
spring scene, "Happy Easter" painted
in gold trim **25.00**
Porcelain, daisies, gold dec, Dresden
.........................**35.00**
Egg Dye Packet, PAAS, 1930–40 ....**10.00**
Magazine, *Donahoe's*, Easter, 1900 **25.00**
Post Card
"Bright and Happy Easter for You,"
Gibson Girl kissing chick in garden
.........................**1.25**
"Easter Greetings," children watching
two rabbits kissing, 1910 ......**2.00**

*Planters, female, blue egg, bonnet and um-
brella, pink dress and ears, 4¾ × 2½ × 8" h,
male, brown hat and pants, blue nest, yellow
egg, pink ears, yellow-orange carrot, 4¾ ×
2½ × 7½" h, Morton Pottery Co, $12.00.*

Rabbit
1½" h, diecut, multicolored, marked
"Germany" **1.25**
5" h, plastic, hard, mother rabbit dressed
in yellow, brown glasses **7.00**
Record, child's, Easter Parade, colorful illus
sleeve, 1957, mint condition **15.00**
Toy, pip squeak, egg shape, rabbit dec,
Grand Toys, 1960s **8.00**

EGG CUPS

Where modern Americans would
be hard-pressed to recognize, let alone
know how to use, an egg cup, their European counterparts still utilize the form as
an everyday breakfast utensil. Their
greatest period of popularity in America
was between 1875 and 1950—long before cholesterol became a four-letter
word.

A plain white porcelain egg cup
works just as well as a fancifully decorated one. The fact that so many different
and highly decorative egg cups exist
shows our unwillingness to accept the
mundane at the breakfast table.

Collectors place a premium on
character egg cups. You can make a
great collection consisting of egg cups
from breakfast services of hotels, railroads, steamships, or restaurants. As
tourists, many of our ancestors had a bad
case of sticky fingers.

Finally, do not forget the various
scissor-like devices designed to
decapitate the egg. Would you even recognize one if you saw one? I saw one
once at a flea market marked as a cir-
cumcision device. Ouch!

Newsletter: *Eggcup Collectors' Corner,*
67 Stevens Ave, Old Bridge, NJ 08857.

Belleek, Irish, basketweave, pink rim, first
black mark **150.00**
Character, ceramic
Lone Ranger, 2½" h, raised portrait,
Lone Ranger Inc. copyright on base,
c1950 ....**35.00**
Supercar, 2¼" h, white, raised Supercar,
marked "Keele St Pty Co, Ltd, England," 1962 AP Film Ltd copyright
.........................**80.00**
French Porcelain, blue floral dec, white
ground, marked "Made In France," pr
.........................**30.00**
Homer Laughlin, Yellowstone pattern,
Southwestern motif decal **20.00**
John Maddock & Sons, Ltd, Indian Tree pattern, 4" h **25.00**
Limoges, France, multicolored florals, 2½" h
.........................**12.00**

Meissen, Blue Onion pattern **20.00**
Quimper, peasant man, yellow ground,
marked "Henriot Quimper, France"
.........................**35.00**
Southern Potteries, Blue Ridge, green and
red floral design, white ground ...**25.00**
Taylor, Smith & Taylor, Lu Ray pattern,
Sharon Pink **18.00**
Universal Pottery, Ballerina pattern, Jade
Green **12.00**
Watcombe Pottery, Torquay pattern, cottage
dec, motto "Straight From the Nest,"
1¾" h **12.00**
Wedgwood, Caneware, brown scrolling
vine dec, c1820 ....**275.00**
Willow Ware, blue, marked "Wood and
Sons" **15.00**
W S George Co, Petalware, light blue **14.00**

ELEPHANT COLLECTIBLES

Public television's unending series
of documentaries on African wildlife has
destroyed the fascination associated with
wild animals. By the time parents take
their children to the zoo or circus, elephants are old hat, blase. Boo, hiss to
public television—those pompous
pachyderms. We want the mystery and
excitement of wildlife returned to us.

Things were different for the pre-
television generations. The elephant
held a fascination that is difficult for
modern generations to comprehend.
When Barnum brought Jumbo from England to America, English children (and a
fair amount of adults) wept.

There are a few elephant-related
political collectibles listed. It is hard to
escape the G.O.P. standard-bearer.
However, real elephant collectors focus
on the magnificent beasts themselves or
cartoon representations ranging from
Dumbo to Colonel Hathi.

Club: The National Elephant Collector's
Society, 380 Medford St, Somerville, MA
02145.

Periodical: *Jumbo Jargon,* 1002 W 25th
St, Erie, PA 16502.

Advertising Trade Card, Clark's O N T
Spool Cotton, Jumbo Aesthetic, elephant
walking on hind legs **5.00**
Book, *Walt Disney's Dumbo of The Circus,*
Garden City, 1941, 10 × 11", 52 pgs
.........................**50.00**
Cheese Cutting Board, 8 × 13", elephant
shape, cherry hardwood **85.00**
Chocolate Mold, tin, three cavities ...**75.00**
Doorstop, 10" h, cast iron **25.00**

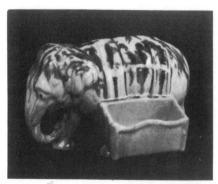

Planter, Cliftwood Art Pottery, 1920–40, $15.00.

Figure
   Circus, celluloid, standing on chair
      ....**15.00**
   Dumbo, 3½ × 4 × 4″, painted, Goebel,
      Disney copyright, 1950s **375.00**
   Elephant trio, celluloid **15.00**
   Fantasia Elephant, 5½″ h, ceramic, wear-
      ing pink dress, American Pottery
      ....**150.00**
Ink Blotter, 6⅛ × 3⅜″, Hummel Ware-
   house Co, elephant and monkey illus
   and 1941 calendar on cov **4.00**
Pencil Sharpener, figural, elephant on globe
      ....**55.00**
Pin, 1″ d, elephant shape, inscribed
   "Carlsberg Beer," diecut, silvered brass
      ....**15.00**
Pinback Button
   Coolidge and Dawes, white and dark
      blue, red, white, and blue elephant
      with names on blanket **15.00**
   Dewey In 1948, 2½″ d, white, dark blue
      elephant illus **25.00**
Pincushion, SS **85.00**
Pitcher, Dumbo, ceramic, white, pink and
   blue dec, Leeds China, marked "Walt
   Disney Dumbo 2 Qt Jug," 1947 **85.00**
Tea Set, child's, 11 pcs, elephant dec **35.00**
Toy
   Pull, 7″ h, wood, diecut, green base with
      wheels, 1930s **55.00**
   Squeaker, 6½″ h, Dumbo, rubber, mova-
      ble head, Walt Disney Productions
      copyright, 1950s **20.00**
Windup
   Expander Elephant, blue plush, tin li-
      tho ears and eyes, built–in key,
      orig box, T N, Japan, 1960s
      ....**75.00**
   Musical Elephant, gray plush, plastic
      tusks, orig box, Alps, Japan,
      c1956 ....**100.00**

ELVIS

Dad grew up with Elvis and ignored him. Always knew Dad was a bit of a prude. Fortunately, millions of others did not. Elvis was hot, is hot, and promises to be hot well into the future. Elvis is a collectible that is bought from the heart, not the head. A great deal of totally tacky material has been forgiven by his devoted fans.

Elvis material breaks down into two groups: (1) items licensed while Elvis was alive and (2) items licensed after his death. The latter are known as "fantasy" items. Fantasy Elvis is collectible, but real value rests with the material licensed during his lifetime.

Beware of any limited edition Elvis. It was manufactured in such large numbers that its long–term prospects are very poor. If you love it, fine. If you expect it to pay for your retirement, forget it.

Club: Graceland News Fan Club, PO Box 452, Rutherford, NJ 07070.

Album, stiff paper cov, Elvis signature front
   cov, glossy paper pages with black and
   white and color photos, signatures, and
   track listings, 21″ l color pinup centerfold, 12 pgs, 1963, 8 1/2 x 11″ ...**30.00**
Bangle Bracelet, brass, photo portrait, 1960s
      ....**85.00**
Book, *Elvis Special 1964,* hard cov, World
   Distributors, Ltd, England, 108 pgs, 7½ x
   10″........................**10.00**
Bubble Gum Cards, set of 66, 1978 **60.00**
Calendar, pocket size, glossy stiff paper,
   color photo, 1964, 2¼ × 4″ **5.00**
Charm Bracelet, gold colored metal, four
   metal charms, picture frame with black
   and white photo, guitar, hound dog, and
   heart, 1956, 6″ l **60.00**

Bubble Gum Card, Elvis seated in MGM chair, copyright Boxcar Enterprises, $5.00.

Flasher Button, close–up color portrait and
   second color portrait, Elvis with guitar at
   microphone, 1956 Elvis Presley Enterprises copyright, Pictorial Productions
   Inc., Tuckahoe, NY, earliest version,
   2½″ d **18.00**
Hat, fabric, black top and brim, wide band
   with multicolored song titles and portrait
   illus, Magnet Hat and Cap Corp, copyright 1956 Elvis Presley Enterprises, orig
   cardboard tag, 8½″ l **60.00**
Keychain Viewer, plastic, purple and clear,
   attached chain, color Elvis photo, wearing red shirt, early 1970s, 2″ l **12.50**
Lipstick Tube, brass, facsimile signature
   stamped on side, red and white paper
   label, Teen–ager Lipstick Corp, Beverly
   Hills, CA, c1956, 2¼″ l, empty **150.00**
Lobby Card, *That's The Way It Is,* copyright
   1971 Metro–Goldwyn–Mayer Inc, set of
   eight different Elvis photos **30.00**
Magazine Article, *Hep Cats,* Vol 2, #2,
   Most Publication Ltd, 10 page Elvis article with black and white movie photos,
   color photos front and back cov, Elvis
   doll, lipstick, and statuette adv, 8 ×
   10¼″ **12.00**
Menu, hotel, 1971 ....**20.00**
Movie Poster, *Girls! Girls! Girls!,* Paramount
   Pictures, 1960 ....**20.00**
Overnight Case, simulated leather over
   cardboard, Elvis portrait photos and sig-
   natures design, 1956 Elvis Presley Enterprises copyright, 9 × 12½ × 7″ **250.00**
Pennant, blue felt, white printed "Elvis The
   King Of Rock And Roll" and picture
   frame, black and white photo of Elvis
   holding crown attached to front, white
   trim, 1970s, 9 × 24″ **18.00**
Pinback Button
   Gold record with black and white Elvis
      photo center, litho, 1956, ⅞″ d **20.00**
   I Like Elvis, red and black ground, pink
      lettering, 1956, ⅞″ d **25.00**
Pocket Knife, memorial, front grip with
   color portrait and birth and death dates
   on pale blue ground, dark red plastic
   grip on back, two blades, unused, late
   1970s, 3½″ l **15.00**

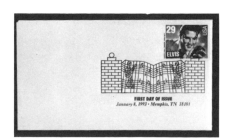

First Day Cover, Elvis stamp, black stamp reads "First Day of Issue, January 8, 1993, Memphis, TN 38101," orig stamp order blank inside, $5.00.

Post Card, glossy black and white Elvis'
Gold Car photo, "On Tour For RCA Victor Records," early 1960s, 3½ × 5½"
......................................**10.00**
Record, *Don't, I Beg of You*, 45 rpm, RCA
Victor, #47–7150, Jan 1958, color paper sleeve **8.00**
Record Case, stiff cardboard, lid with Elvis,
hound dog, and hearts raised design,
Elvis Presley Enterprises, 7¾ × 7¾ ×
2½" **75.00**
Record Player, paper covered wood, Elvis
signature on top, RCA Victor, 1950s, 12
× 12½ × 7" **350.00**
Record Sleeve, Hound Dog, 45 rpm   **48.00**
Sheet Music, *Love Me Tender*, pink–tone
photo front cov, copyright 1956 Elvis
Presley Music Inc, 2 pgs, 9 × 12" **15.00**
Tab, litho tin, "Elvis We Love You," blue
and red lettering, bright yellow ground,
1970s, 2⅛" d, unbent **12.00**

ERTL BANKS

This is another one of those highly
speculative areas that are addressed as
the need arises. The 1980s and 1990s
saw a surge in cast iron banks that were
produced by several companies, Ertl being the most dominate. These banks
were often made to commemorate a special event, used as a promotion, or fundraising effort for local charities.

Most of the Ertl banks are recently
made and are manufactured in Hong
Kong in large numbers. They should only
be purchased in fine or better condition,
with original packaging. All of the banks
are marked and numbered. Avoid any
that are not marked. The serial numbers
and series numbers are important in cataloging and pricing these items.

Antique Power, Chevy Truck, 1923, #9432
..................................**18.00**
Atlantic, Diamond T Tanker, 1930, #9666B
..................................**24.00**
Baltimore Gas & Electric, Utility Bucket
Truck, 1993, #3814 ....**22.00**
Banjo Matthews, Ford Panel, 1932, #2784
..................................**55.00**
British American #3, Wrecker, #3808
..................................**30.00**
Champion Spark Plug, Ford Runabout,
1918, #9067 ....**35.00**
Check the Oil, Chevy Panel, 1938, #4 in
series, #3226 ....**28.50**
Coca–Cola, Hawkeye Box Truck, 1931,
#2919 ....**20.00**
Coors Malt Milk, Model T, 1917, #9543
..................................**13.50**
Dairy Queen, School Bus, #3257 ...**28.50**
Delaware Valley, Ford, 1905, #9522 **20.00**

Delco Radio, Chevy Panel, 1950, #9082
..................................**85.00**
Diamond Walnut, Hawkeye Box Truck,
1931, #9881 ....**34.00**
Dominos Pizza, Chevy Panel, 1950, #9460
..................................**34.00**
Dr Pepper
    Chevy, 1923, #3907 ....**17.50**
    Mack Truck, 1926, #9235 .....**35.00**
Eastwood, #9, Cameo Pickup, 1955, #9747
..................................**75.00**
Esso Imperial #2, Diamond T Tanker, 1930,
#B124 ....**31.75**
Happy Birthday, Hawkeye, 1931, #9450
..................................**16.00**
Heatcraft, Mack Truck, 1926, #7562 **20.00**
Hersheys, Trolly, 100th Anniversary, #310
..................................**21.00**
Humble Oil, Kenworth Tanker, 1925, #3 in
series, #3839 ....**20.00**
Jimmy's Auto Parts, Fram Filter, #2951
..................................**27.50**
John Deere
    Cameo Pickup, 1955, #5614 ....**18.50**
    Seagraves Fire Engine, #1 in series,
    #5710 ....**21.00**
Lea & Perrins, Model T, 1913, #9170B
..................................**32.50**
Missouri Tourism, Ford, 1905, #2143 **24.00**
Phillips 66, Mack Tanker, 1926, #9787
..................................**35.00**
Seven–Eleven, Model T, 1913, #9153B
..................................**32.50**
Slice, Step Van, #9709 ....**24.00**
Steamtown USA, Mack Tanker, 1926,
#9167B **75.00**
Sunoco, Tanker, 1931, #2 in series, #3791
..................................**28.50**
Terminix, Ford, 1905, #9086 ....**20.00**
Texaco
    Diamond T Tanker, 1930, #7 in series,
    #9330V0 ....**50.00**
    Dodge, 1939, #10 in series, #9500
    ....**17.95**
    Ford, 1905, #4 in series, #9321 **125.00**
    Ford Runabout, 1918, #5 in series,
    #9740 ....**90.00**
    Horse and Wagon, #8 in series, #9390
    ....**25.00**

*Allied Van Lines, orange body, black top and
running boards, white rubber tires, marked
"Replica Ford 1917 Model T Van," numbered, 6" l, 2½" h, $20.00.*

Kenworth, 1925, #9 in series, #9385
..................................**25.00**
Mack Truck Box, 1926, #6 in series,
#9040 ....**60.00**
United Airlines, Model T, 1913, #9223
..................................**27.00**
West Wyommissing Fire Engine, Ahrens Fox
Fire Engine, #1 in series, #3221   **45.00**

FAIRY TALE COLLECTIBLES

Thank goodness for fairies. They
keep the line between myth and reality
blurred. Where would children be without the tooth fairy or Cinderella without
her fairy godmother? I have told some
fairy tales in my time that I hoped the
listener would believe were true.

This category is a celebration of the
characters and the tales. It also celebrates the spirit of fairy tales—the hopes
and dreams. There is a pot of gold at the
end of the rainbow, isn't there?

Baby Dish, Little Red Riding Hood, porcelain, 1930s, England **115.00**
Baby Plate, Little Red Riding Hood, England, 1920s **55.00**
Baby Warming Dish, Little Red Riding
Hood, china bowl attached to chrome
heating plate, 1930s **175.00**
Bank, Little Red Riding Hood, ceramic
..................................**600.00**
Biscuit Tin, Beatrix Potter, pastel litho,
child's game, England, 1930s ...**145.00**
Book
    Alice's Adventures in Wonderland,
    Lewis Carroll, Garden City, 216 pgs
    ....**12.00**
    Beautiful Stories for Children, Charles
    Dickens, 1908 ....**5.00**
    Favorite Fairy Tales Told in Italy, Virginia Haviland, Little Brown, 1965,
    90 pgs **15.00**
    Hansel & Gretel, 1908 ....**7.00**
    Little Red Riding Hood, pop–up, Blue
    Ribbon, 1934 ....**125.00**
    Mother Goose Picture Book, linen, 1958
    ....**10.00**
    Once Upon A Monday, Dixie Willson,
    Volland, 1931 ....**16.00**
    Rumpelstiltskin, Edith Tarcov, Four
    Winds, 1974, 46 pgs **45.00**
    *The Happy Prince and Other Fairy
    Tales*, Oscar Wilde, 1913, 204 pgs
    ....**225.00**
    The Land of Oz, Rand McNally, 1939
    copyright, 64 pgs **40.00**
    The Three Bears, Platt & Munk ...**15.00**
Bracelet, "Who's Afraid of the Big Bad
Wolf," silvered brass, black, green, and
yellow accents, early 1930s **125.00**

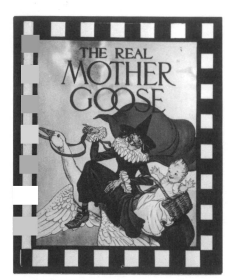

Book, The Real Mother Goose, *multicolored cover, black and white checkered border, illus by Blanche Fisher Wright, Rand McNally & Co Chicago, copyright 1916, renewal copyright 1944, $15.00.*

Butter Dish, Little Red Riding Hood, Hull
. . . . **290.00**
Carrying Case, Alice In Wonderland, 4 ×
    11 × 8¹/₂", heavy cardboard, white plastic handle, Neevel, Disney copyright
    1951 . . . . **40.00**
Child's Dinnerware Set, Alice in Wonderland, 17 pcs, service for four, beige,
    Plasco **40.00**
Chocolate Tin, 13 × 8", Little Red Riding
    Hood and wolf, color forest scene,
    1930s **325.00**
Christmas Card, Peter Pan, 4 × 5", diecut,
    orig envelope, c1953 . . . . **10.00**
Cookie Jar
    Goldilocks **195.00**
    Humpty Dumpty, Clay Art **75.00**
    Little Red Riding Hood, Brush
    . . . . **425.00**

Little Golden Book, King Mitch Had An Itch, *Big Little Golden Book, #10264, copyright 1987 by Jerry Harston, Western Publishing Co, Inc., $4.00.*

Old King Cole **395.00**
Cup and Saucer, Humpty Dumpty, England,
    1930s **65.00**
Doll
    Limited Edition, Edwin M. Knowles, Heroines from the Fairy Tale Forests of
    the Brother's Grimm
    Goldilocks, 1989 . . . . **65.00**
    Little Red Riding Hood **70.00**
    Madam Alexander, Snow White, 14" h,
    plastic, green plastic sleep eyes, real
    lashes, painted features, closed
    mouth, orig tagged ivory satin gown,
    marked "Walt Disney Snow White
    Madam Alexander USA," c1952
    . . . . **500.00**
    Wolf, cloth body, papier mache head,
    wearing Grandma's clothing . . **150.00**
Figure, Snow White, 5" h, china, Japan,
    c1960 . . . . **20.00**
Game, The Wonderful Game of Oz, Parker
    Brothers, 1921 . . . . **300.00**
Hot Water Bottle, baby, This Little Pig, light
    blue **20.00**
Mug
    Little Miss Muffet, colorful transfers and
    verse **45.00**
    Little Red Riding Hood, color image, England, 1930s **45.00**
Picture, Hansel & Gretel, pr, ornate, 11 ×
    13" **45.00**
Plaque, 13 × 16", figural, Cinderella, diecut
    laminated cardboard, 1951 copyright
    . . . . **20.00**
Puppet, hand, Pinocchio, 10" h, velvet
    body, molded cardboard head with
    flocking, c1940 . . . . **125.00**
Radio Books, *Wizard of Oz,* Jell-O premium, 1933 . . . . **65.00**
Salt and Pepper Shakers, pr, Goldilocks
    . . . . **15.00**
Sheet Music
    Over The Rainbow, 9¹/₄ × 12¹/₄", brown
    tone photo **30.00**
    So This Is Love, Cinderella, 9 × 12",
    white and pink cov, 1949 . . . . **20.00**
Snowdome, souvenir, Story Land, plastic,
    fairy tale characters, 1960s **8.00**
Teapot
    Hickory Dickory Dock, England, 1930s
    . . . . **95.00**
    Old MacDonald, Regal China . . . **295.00**
Tea Set
    Aluminum, nursery rhyme dec, 15 pcs
    . . . . **22.00**
    Tin, Snow White, 8 pcs, orig box, Ohio
    Art **125.00**
Toothbrush Holder, Three Little Pigs, figural,
    porcelain, Maw, London **150.00**

FARM COLLECTIBLES

The agrarian myth of the rugged individual pitting his or her mental and physical talents against the elements re-

mains a strong part of the American character in the 1990s. There is something pure about returning to the soil.

The Country look heavily utilizes the objects of rural life, from cast iron seats to wooden rakes. This is one collectible where collectors want an aged, i.e., well-worn, appearance. Although most of the items were factory–made, they have a handcrafted look. The key is to find objects that have character, a look that gives them a sense of individuality.

Club: Cast Iron Seat Collectors Assoc, PO Box 14, Ionia, MO 65335.

Periodical: *Farm Antique News,* 812 N Third St, Tarkio, MO 64491.

Advertisement, D M Ferry & Co Standard
    Seeds, woman with vegetables, dog pulling skirt **35.00**
Advertising Trade Card
    Champion, Harvesting Machine Factories **6.00**
    Empire Binders, Reapers & Mowers,
    Sunrise, 1884 Krebs Litho **6.00**
    Minneapolis Threshing Machine Co
    . . . . **10.00**
Bin, 17¹/₂ × 34", Wilbur's Seed Meal for
    Horse & Cattle Food, yellow, black stencil lettering **795.00**
Calendar
    1899, Listers Fertilizers, woman with
    sheaves of wheat, farm background
    . . . . **125.00**
    1914, McCormick Machinery . . . **175.00**
    1920s, John Deere **35.00**
    1929, Minnesota Binders, DeLavel Separators, Oliver Implements, flapper girl
    illus **28.00**
Catalog
    International Harvester, 1934, 112 pgs,
    6³/₄ × 9¹/₂" **25.00**
    Kraus Farm Cultivators, 1911, 62 pgs
    . . . . **20.00**
    Leroy Plow Co, 1913, 20 pgs, 3¹/₂ × 6"
    . . . . **28.00**
    Oliver Chilled Plow Works, 1924, 18
    pgs, 4 × 8¹/₂" **24.00**
    Walter A Wood, M & R M Co, 1923, 16
    pgs, 6 × 9" **45.00**
    Wiard Plow Co, Batavia, NY, 32 pgs,
    6³/₄ × 9³/₄" **27.00**
Chick Feeder, tin **15.00**
Corn Dryer, wrought iron **15.00**
Corn Sheller
    F F Company **800.00**
    Gray Brothers **350.00**
Egg Candler, 8" h, tin, kerosene burner,
    mica window **20.00**
Feed Bag, cotton, black illus of sheep . **7.50**
Hay Rake, varnished, 48¹/₂" l **50.00**
Hinge, barn, wrought iron, strap, 27" l
    . . . . **60.00**

Medallion
  John Deere Centennial, 1937 .... **10.00**
  Syracuse Chilled Plow, plow and Admiral Dewey illus **12.00**
Milking Stool, wooden, three short legs
  .... **50.00**
Pinback Button
  Deering Harvester Company, multicolored, farmer on horse–drawn mower, black inscriptions **50.00**
  Frick Company, red, white, gold, and lavender, Eclispe farm tractor **15.00**
  Globe Poultry Feed, color image **75.00**
  International Harvester Co, yellow, black, and white, February 1938 issue **12.50**
  Minneapolis–Moline Co, 1944 union member **25.00**
  New Idea Manure Spreader, 1⅛" d, celluloid, multicolored **70.00**
  P & O Canton Plows, 1¼" d, celluloid, multicolored **70.00**
  Rock Island Plow Co, green, red, black, and white, 1920s **15.00**
  Rumley Oil Pull Tractor, multicolored, tractor image **100.00**
  The Huber, yellow, red harvester, black lettering **50.00**
  Twin City Tractors, red, white, and blue, 1920s **50.00**
Shovel, cast iron, wooden handle ... **25.00**
Sign, Goodyear Farm Tires, porcelain, two–sided, diecut **225.00**
Stickpin
  John Deere, brass **35.00**
  Moline Plow, brass **35.00**
  P & O Canton, plow shape **20.00**
Tape Measure
  Blue Seal Grain Products, blue and white, 1950s **20.00**
  Bone Fertilizers, multicolored illus of Griffith & Boyd's fertilizer bag, blue text on other side **25.00**
Thermometer, John Deere, 150th Anniversary Commemorative **45.00**
Watch Fob
  Allis Chalmers, tractor **28.00**
  Gardner Denver Jackhammer **25.00**
  Lima Shovels, Draglines **22.00**

Weather Vane, horse, cast iron, Black Hawk, sgd "Harris & Co," 26" w, $6,500.00.

FARM TOYS

The average age of those who play with farm toys is probably well over thirty. Farm toys are adult toys. Collectors number in the tens of thousands. The annual farm toy show in Dyersville, Ohio, draws a crowd in excess of 15,000.

Beware of recent limited and special edition farm toys. The number of each toy being produced hardly qualifies them as limited. If you buy them other than for enjoyment, you are speculating. No strong resale market has been established. Collectors who are not careful are going to be plowed under.

Clubs: Antique Engine, Tractor & Toy Club, Inc, 5731 Paradise Rd, Slatington, PA 18080; CTM Farm Toy & Collectors Club, PO Box 489, Rocanville, Saskatchewan SOA 3LO Canada; Ertl Collectors' Club, Highways 136 and 20, Dyersville, IA 52040; Farm Toy Collectors Club, PO Box 38, Boxholm, IA 50040.

Newsletters: *Spec–Tacular News,* PO Box 324, Dyersville, IA 52040; *Turtle River Toy News & Oliver Collector's News,* RR1, Box 44, Manvel, ND 58256-9763.

Periodicals: *The Toy Tractor Times,* PO Box 156, Osage, IA 50461; *Toy Farmer,* HC2, Box 5, LaMoure, ND 58458; *Tractor Classics,* PO Box 191, Listowel, Ontario N4H 3HE Canada.

Baler, International Harvester, diecast, 1:16 scale, four bales, Ertl, 1967 ...... **18.00**
Combine Harvester, Corgi, #1111–A, 1959–63 .... **85.00**
Corn Picker, Tru–Scale, pressed steel, 1:16 scale, Carter, 1971 .... **70.00**
Dairy Farm Set, Buddy L, No. 5050, includes blue No. 5210 Milkman Truck, red and gray No. 5260 Milk Tanker, and orange No. 5270 Farm Tractor, boxed set, 1961 .... **65.00**
Disc, International Harvester, diecast, 1:16 scale, sure–lock hitch blades, Ertl, 1965 .... **20.00**
Elevator, John Deere, pressed steel, 1:16 scale, Carter, 1960 .... **85.00**
Farm Machinery Hauler, trailer and truck, Buddy L, No. 5586, 31½" l, 1956–58 .... **95.00**
Farmyard Animals, Dinky, No. 2, pre–1933 .... **35.00**
Furrow Plow, Corgi, #56–A1, four furrows, 1961–63 .... **20.00**
Grain Truck, Great Lakes, 1951 Ford, First Gear, 1:34 scale **30.00**

Hay Rake, Dinky, #27–K, 1953 ..... **20.00**
Horse–Drawn Farm Wagon, pull–n–ride, Buddy L, No. 1809, paper litho horse, steel wagon and seat, black rubber wheels, "Buddy L Farms" decals on wagon sides, 10" h, 23¾" l, 1952 **75.00**
Lawn and Garden Tractor, SCA, Ford **12.00**
Livestock Trailer Truck
  Dodge, Corgi, #484–A, 1967–72 **50.00**
  Indian Head Trademark, Japan, friction, litho tin, black rubber tires, rear door opens, 9½" l, 1960s **90.00**
Manure Spreader, Dinky, #27–C, 1949
  .... **45.00**
Milk Truck and Trailer, Corgi, #21–A, 1962–66 .... **85.00**
Planter, White **15.00**
Tandem Disc Harrow, Corgi, #71–A, 1967–72 .... **18.00**
Tipping Trailer, Corgi, #62–A, 1965–72
  .... **22.00**
Tractor
  Ertl
    Case 800, #2616 .... **6.00**
    Deutz–Allis 6620 All Wheel, #2332
    .... **3.00**
    English Fordson, #2526 .... **6.00**
    Fordson Super Major, 1:16 scale, #0307 .... **19.00**
    IH Farmall Int Cub Tractor, #0653
    .... **19.00**
    John Deere, 1:64 scale, #5606 **6.00**
    Massey Ferguson #3070, #1107 **4.00**
    McCormick Farmall Super–A, #0250
    .... **9.00**
  Hubley, c1950 .... **75.00**
  SCA
    Allis Chalmers, AC D–17, #FB–1592
    .... **65.00**
    Allis Chalmers, D–17, 1:16 scale, #FF–0136 .... **35.00**
    Allis Chalmers, U, Farm Show, #FT–0456 .... **60.00**
    Avery, 1:16 scale, #FT–0158 **45.00**
    Ford 846 4WD, 1:32 scale, #JLE–333 .... **22.00**
    Ford 976, 4WD, 1:64 scale, #FA–0001 .... **8.00**
    Ford TW–25, dual wheels, 1:16 scale, #FF–0117 .... **30.00**
    MF 135, 1:16 scale, #FB–1609 **50.00**
    Oliver 70, 1:16 scale, #FF–0138
    .... **32.00**
    Rumely #6, 1:16 scale, #FC–1020
    .... **50.00**
    White 185, 1:16 scale, #FA–004
    .... **4.00**
Tractor and Cultivator, Ertl, John Deere, Model A, #290 cultivator, #5633
  .... **140.00**
Tractor and Trailer
  Marx, litho tin, multicolored, self–reversing, orig box, 1936 ..... **85.00**
  Matchbox, TP108–2, yellow **5.00**
Triple Gang Mower, Dinky, #27–J, 1952
  .... **60.00**

Tractor, International, metal and plastic, red body, rubber tires, Ertl, 1:32 scale, $60.00.

Wagon, Minneapolis Moline, Slik, pressed
   steel, 1:32 scale, rubber wheels, 1950
   .... **20.00**

FAST FOOD COLLECTIBLES

   If you haunt fast food restaurants for the food, you are a true fast food junkie. Most collectors haunt them for the giveaways. If you stop and think about it, fast food collectibles are the radio and cereal premiums of the second half of the twentieth century. Look at what you have to eat to get them.

   Whenever possible, try to preserve the original packaging of the premiums. Also, save those things which are most likely to be thrown out. I see a great many Happy Meals toys and few Happy Meals boxes. Dad saves fast food company bags. There is no accounting for taste.

Clubs: Fast Food Collectors Express, PO Box 221, Mayview, MO 64071; For Here or To Go, 2773 Curtis Way, Sacramento, CA 95818; McDonald's Collectors Club, 424 White Rd, Fremont, OH 43420.

Newsletter: *Collecting Tips Newsletter,* PO Box 633, Joplin, MO 64802.

Bank, figural
   Bear, Shoney's **20.00**
   Chuck E Cheese **10.00**
   McDonald's restaurant shape, cardboard,
      litho, punch out, 1978 .... **28.00**
Calendar, McDonald's, 1994 See America
   series, set of twelve **10.00**
Clock, prototype, Ronald McDonald below
   dial, hamburgers replace numerals, elec-
   tric, 12" w, 28" h **125.00**
Comic Book, *Adventures of the Big Boy,* Big
   Boy Restaurants, 1973 .... **10.00**
Crown, cardboard, jewel–like design,
   Burger King "Have It Your Way" slogan
   .... **7.00**
Dinner Set, Melmac, plate, cup, and bowl,
   McDonald's, colorful graphics ... **10.00**

Burger King, record, The Many Faces of Alf, 33¹⁄₃ rpm, cardboard, premium offer on back, 5³⁄₄" d, $3.00.

Doll, cloth
   Burger King, red, yellow, flesh, black,
      and white, 16" h **7.50**
   Wendy's, 11¹⁄₂" h **5.00**
Figure
   Big Boy, soft rubber **10.00**
   Chuck E Cheese, bendie **10.00**
   Colonel Sanders, Kentucky Fried
      Chicken, 12" h **20.00**
   Ronald McDonald, 1980, MIP ...**15.00**
Football, rubber, Georgia Tech, poly bag
   marked "McD" **10.00**
Frisbee, plastic, emb Burger King character,
   3³⁄₄" d **6.50**
Glass
   Big Mac, Captain Crook, Grimace, Ham-
      burglar, Mayor McCheese, and Ron-
      ald McDonald, Collector Series, mid
      1970s, 5⁵⁄₈" h, set of six **25.00**
   Domino's Pizza, frosted design and logo,
      4¹⁄₈" h **2.00**
   Little Miss Dairy Queen and red and
      white logo, 5⁵⁄₈" h **2.00**
   Wendy's, white, black, and pink
      "Where's The Beef?" design, 1984,
      5⁷⁄₈" h **6.00**

Little Caesar's Pizza, doll, fabric, stuffed, $3.50.

McDonald's Happy Meal, Crayola stencils, unopened, set 3 and set 4, copyright 1986, yellow and green, 7" w, 7¹⁄₂" h, $3.00.

Meal Box, cardboard
   "Colonel's Kids," features Foghorn
      Leghorn, Kentucky Fried Chicken,
      1987 .... **2.00**
   Star Flyer, flying saucer, Carl's Jr, 1985
      .... **2.50**
Mug, ceramic, white
   McDonald's golden arches and red let-
      tering, 4⁷⁄₈" h **7.00**
   Wendy's, red, white, and black design,
      3⁷⁄₈" h **4.00**
Night Light, Big Boy **95.00**
Nodder, Colonel Sanders, Kentucky Fried
   Chicken **135.00**
Pin, metal, enameled, egg–shaped, yellow
   arches on red center band, "We
   Hatched Egg McMuffin, Santa Barbara
   California," McDonald's, 1980s **20.00**
Pinback Button, metal, "Happy Face," eyes
   made of the Burger King Corporate logo,
   ³⁄₄" d **3.50**
Plate, Howard Johnson **20.00**
Ring
   Plastic, Fun Flyer, Wendy's, 3¹⁄₂" d **1.00**
   Plastic, Happy Star character in center of
      circle, Carl's Jr **2.75**
Toy, Noid, plastic, poseable and bendable,
   Domino's Pizza, 1987, 5" h **5.00**
Waste Basket, plastic, McDonaldland, 1975
   .... **7.50**

FEMININE HYGIENE

   Another subject I know nothing about, honest. Talk about the things the staff makes me do! However, I have noticed an increase in these type of items at flea markets as well as more drugstore type items. Condom collectors have always been on the scene too. How come nobody brags about this type of collection? Bet it can be a real conversation piece when displayed in your powder room!

Beltex Personal Belt, Beltex Corp, St Louis,
   MO, blue, light blue background, lady
   dressed in blue formal on front, 4¹⁄₂ ×
   3³⁄₄" rect cardboard box **5.00**

Nappons, Nappons Laboratories, Chicago, IL, full box of ten, light blue box, 6¹⁄₈ × 3⁵⁄₈ × 1¹⁄₂", $7.00.

Ceeryn Vaginal Suppositories, Wm S Merrell Co, full unopened box **12.00**

Female Prescription, Baltzly Co, full 14 fluid oz bottle **23.00**

Fibs Tampons, Kimberly–Clark Corp, Neenah, WI, gray blue 3³⁄₄ × 2¹⁄₄ × 1³⁄₈" rect cardboard box **8.00**

Foromex Douche Powder, Holland–Rantes Co, orig package with twelve individual pages **8.00**

Freshettes, The Handy Deodorant, empty round can **13.00**

Gynecology, Parsons and Sommers, 1962, hardback cov book, 1,250 pages   **1.50**

Hy–Geen Douche Powder, full 6 oz jar **11.00**

Hygenic P.M.C. Powder, Thomas & Thompson Co, Baltimore, MD, amber glass bottle, light blue ground, dark blue lettering, 2¹⁄₄ × 4" cylinder, 4 fl oz **8.00**

Lygel, Vaginal Antiseptic, 3 oz tube, box **6.75**

Midol, Glenbrook Laboratories, Div of Sterling Drug, Inc, New York, NY, dark blue, white, 3 × ¹⁄₄ × 1" rect tin, 12 tablets **5.00**

Perfection Pessary, womb supporter . . . **8.25**

Picragol Vaginal Suppositories, Wyeth, Philadelphia, orig carton **8.50**

Pursettes, black plastic personal carrying case, silhouette of lady in long gown **10.00**

Sanapak Sanitary Napkins, Doeskin Products, Inc, New York, NY, dark blue, white lettering, 8¹⁄₄ × 2³⁄₄ × 7¹⁄₄" rect cardboard box **12.00**

Tassette, Menstrual Cup, soft rubber, drawstring bag, orig cardboard and plastic case **12.00**

Vaginal Cones, Henry K Wampolie & Co, full unopened box **14.00**

Valgene Douche Powder, Valgene Laboratories, full unopened box **12.00**

Wearever Hotwater Bottle, orig box   **12.00**

FENTON ART GLASS

Frank L. Fenton founded the Fenton Art Glass Company as a glass–cutting operation in Martins Ferry, Ohio, in 1905. In 1906 construction began on a plant in Williamstown, West Virginia. Production began in 1907 and has been continuing ever since.

The list of Fenton glass products is endless. Early production included carnival, chocolate, custard, pressed, and opalescent glass. In the 1920s stretch glass, Fenton dolphins, and art glass were added. Hobnail, opalescent, and two–color overlay pieces were popular in the 1940s. In the 1950s Fenton began reproducing Burmese and other early glass types.

Throughout its production period, Fenton has made reproductions and copycats of famous glass types and patterns. Today these reproductions and copycats are collectible in their own right. Check out Dorothy Hammond's *Confusing Collectibles: A Guide to the Identification of Contemporary Objects* (Wallace–Homestead: 1979, revised edition) for clues to spotting the reproductions and copycats of Fenton and other glass manufacturers of the 1950s and 1960s.

Clubs: Fenton Art Glass Collectors of America, Inc, PO Box 384, Williamstown, WV 26187; National Fenton Glass Society, PO Box 4008, Marietta, OH 45750.

Newsletter: *The Butterfly Net,* PO Box 384, Williamstown, WV 26187.

Ashtray, Lincoln Inn, cobalt blue **17.00**
Basket
    4" h, Hobnail French Opalescent   **45.00**
    6¹⁄₂" h, Silver Crest **37.50**
    7" h, Hobnail Blue Opalescent . . . **60.00**
    8¹⁄₂" h, red carnival, dated 1994, sgd "Tom Fenton" **55.00**
Bonbon
    5" d, Hobnail French Opalescent, handle **17.00**
    8" d, Silver Crest **11.00**
Bowl
    5" d, Lincoln Inn, green **8.00**
    8" d, Thistle, carnival, marigold, ruffled edge **90.00**
    11" d, Silver Crest **48.00**
Cake Plate, 13" h, Silver Crest, ftd . . . **48.00**
Candlesticks, pr
    Hobnail Blue Opalescent, 3¹⁄₂" h, cornucopia **42.00**
    Silver Crest, low, ruffled **20.00**
Candy Dish, Lincoln Inn, ftd, oval, black **25.00**
Champagne, Hobnail French Opalescent **18.00**

Compote, ftd
    6" d, Emerald Crest **38.00**
    7" d, Apple Blossom Crest, dec . . . **45.00**
Condiment Set, Hobnail Blue Opalescent, individual size creamer, sugar, and mustard **37.00**
Creamer
    Hobnail Blue Opalescent **22.00**
    Lincoln Inn, pink **15.00**
    Silver Crest, clear reeded handle   **17.50**
    Turquoise Crest **50.00**
Cruet, Hobnail Blue Opalescent, orig stopper **32.00**
Cup and Saucer, Emerald Crest **48.00**
Epergne Set, Silver Crest, bowl and three horn vases **120.00**
Figure, Happiness Bird, black satin   **25.00**
Flowerpot, Emerald Crest, attached saucer **70.00**
Hat
    3¹⁄₂" h, Hobnail Blue Opalescent   **22.00**
    4" h, Polka Dot French Opalescent **95.00**
    4¹⁄₂" h, Spiral Snow Crest, emerald green **80.00**
Juice Set, 5¹⁄₄" h squatty jug, six 5 oz juice tumblers, Hobnail French Opalescent **110.00**
Juice Tumbler, Hobnail Blue Opalescent **13.00**
Jug, 6" h, Hobnail Blue Opalescent, handle **37.00**
Lamp Base, 9" h, Dancing Lady, Mongolian green **375.00**
Mayonnaise and Liner, Hobnail Blue Opalescent **75.00**
Mustard, orig lid
    Emerald Crest, orig spoon **75.00**
    Hobnail French Opalescent **24.00**
Plate
    Lincoln Inn, 8" d, amethyst   **7.00**
    Silver Crest, 6" d **6.50**

Fairy Lamp, three pieces, clear candle cup, Burmese, satin finish, Persian design, 6¹⁄₂" h, 5" d ruffled base, $50.00.

Puff Jar, cov, Hobnail French Opalescent
. . . . **37.00**
Punch Cup, Silver Crest **12.00**
Relish Dish, Silver Crest, heart shaped, handle **25.00**
Rose Bowl, Waffle, green opalescent **37.00**
Salt and Pepper Shakers, pr, Hobnail Blue
Opalescent **45.00**
Sherbet, Emerald Crest **24.00**
Shoe, Hobnail Blue Opalescent **24.00**
Sugar
Hobnail Blue Opalescent **22.00**
Silver Crest, ruffled top **45.00**
Tid Bit Tray, Silver Crest, 3 tier **48.00**
Tumbler
Hobnail Blue Opalescent **24.00**
Lincoln Inn, red **25.00**
Vase
3³/₄" h, fan, Hobnail French Opalescent
. . . . **30.00**
4" h, Apple Blossom Crest, dec . . . **40.00**
4¹/₄" h, Waffle, green opalescent **40.00**
4¹/₂" h, Silver Crest, fan **12.00**
6¹/₄" h, Jade, ebony vase, hand dec
. . . . **425.00**
8" h, bulbous, Emerald Crest **60.00**
10" h, Apple Tree, white milk glass
. . . . **125.00**
11" h, custard, melon shape, daisy dec
. . . . **45.00**
12" h, Lincoln Inn, amber **85.00**

FIESTA WARE

Fiesta was the Melmac ware of the mid 1930s. The Homer Laughlin China Company introduced Fiesta dinnerware in January 1936, at the Pottery and Glass Show in Pittsburgh, Pennsylvania. It was a huge success.

The original five colors were red, dark blue, light green (with a trace of blue), brilliant yellow, and ivory. Other colors were added later. Fiesta was redesigned in 1960, discontinued in 1972–1973, and reintroduced in 1986. It appears destined to go on forever.

Value rests in form and color. Forget the rumors about the uranium content of early red–colored Fiesta. No one died of radiation poisoning from using Fiesta. However, rumor has it that they glowed in the dark when they went to bed at night.

Newsletter: *Fiesta Collectors Quarterly,* 19238 Dorchester Circle, Strongsville, OH 44136.

Ashtray
Chartreuse **95.00**
Dark Green **90.00**
Medium Green **200.00**

Bowl
4¹/₂" d
Chartreuse **22.00**
Gray **22.00**
Turquoise **18.00**
4³/₄" d
Chartreuse **20.00**
Cobalt Blue **18.00**
Green **15.00**
Turquoise **15.00**
5¹/₂" d
Green **15.00**
Turquoise **18.00**
Bud Vase, red **95.00**
Cake Server, light green, Kitchen Kraft
. . . . **165.00**
Casserole, cov
Chartreuse **195.00**
Dark Green **325.00**
Light Green **165.00**
Medium Green **650.00**
Chop Plate
13" d
Light Green **25.00**
Medium Green **125.00**
Yellow **20.00**
15" d, dark green **125.00**
Coffeepot, cov
Chartreuse **450.00**
Cobalt Blue **210.00**
Gray **475.00**
Ivory **150.00**
Light Green **150.00**
Red **210.00**
Rose **475.00**
Turquoise **150.00**
Compote, large, light green **165.00**
Creamer
Dark Green **25.00**
Light Green, stick handle **40.00**
Turquoise **15.00**
Cream Soup
Gray **75.00**
Red **70.00**
Cup and Saucer, cobalt blue **25.00**
Deep Plate
Chartreuse **40.00**
Cobalt Blue **30.00**
Dark Green **50.00**
Medium Green **75.00**
Turquoise **24.00**
Yellow **24.00**
Demitasse Coffeepot, light green . . . **325.00**
Demitasse Cup and Saucer
Chartreuse **390.00**
Cobalt Blue **80.00**
Dark Green **390.00**
Ivory **55.00**
Light Green **55.00**
Red **80.00**
Rose **390.00**
Turquoise **55.00**
Yellow **55.00**
Egg cup
Chartreuse **165.00**
Light Green **45.00**

Jug, 2 pint, dark green **135.00**
Mixing Bowl Lid
#1
Red **800.00**
Yellow **700.00**
#4, light green **700.00**
Mug
Ivory, Tom & Jerry, gold letters . . . **40.00**
Yellow **35.00**
Nappy
5¹/₂" d, medium green **70.00**
8¹/₂" d
Medium Green **125.00**
Red **65.00**
9¹/₂" d, light green **75.00**
Pitcher, disc
Chartreuse **165.00**
Cobalt Blue, water **105.00**
Dark Green **185.00**
Plate
6" d, bread and butter
Green **2.50**
Ivory **7.00**
9" d, lunch
Ivory **16.00**
Turquoise **15.00**
Yellow **15.00**
10" d, dinner
Ivory **38.00**
Light Green, divided **40.00**
Medium Green **100.00**
Red **40.00**
10¹/₂" d
Chartreuse, divided **75.00**
Light Green **18.00**
12" d, light green, divided **45.00**
15" d, grill
Green **22.00**
Turquoise **22.00**
Platter
Cobalt Blue **25.00**
Medium Green **165.00**
Salad, individual, medium green . . . **110.00**
Sauce Boat
Chartreuse **45.00**
Dark Green **95.00**
Gray **85.00**
Medium Green **160.00**
Turquoise **40.00**

Teapot, light gray, $85.00.

Shaker
   Green, Kitchen Kraft **35.00**
   Red **12.00**
Sugar, cov, chartreuse **50.00**
Syrup
   Cobalt Blue **375.00**
   Ivory **325.00**
   Light Green **325.00**
   Red **375.00**
   Turquoise **325.00**
   Yellow **325.00**
Teacup, light green **15.00**
Teapot, cov, medium size
   Light Green **75.00**
   Medium Green **650.00**
Tumbler, juice
   Turquoise **20.00**
   Yellow **28.00**

FIGURINES

Looking for a "small" with character? Try collecting ceramic figurines. Collecting interest in the colorful figurines produced by firms such as Ceramic Arts Studio, Florence Ceramics, Vernon Kilns, and others has grown considerably during the past ten years. Pieces are starting to become pricy. However, there are still bargains to be found. A surprising number of these figurines are found at garage sales and flea markets at prices below $10.00.

Abingdon Pottery
   Fruit Girl, 10" h **90.00**
   Nude, kneeling, 7" h **160.00**
Brayton Laguna, Arthur, boy with chicken
   . . . . **35.00**
Ceramic Arts Studio
   Archibald the Dragon **70.00**
   Dutch Girl **33.00**
   Lamb **10.00**
Cliftwood Art Potteries, elephant, standing on log, ginger jar on back, chocolate drip glaze, 6½" h **60.00**
Florence Ceramics
   Camille **180.00**
   Choir Boys **35.00**
   Eugenia **225.00**
   Eve & Charles, pr **350.00**
   Grace **195.00**
   Jim and Irene, pr **125.00**
   Linda Lou **95.00**
   Marie Antoinette and Louis XVI, pr
   . . . . **500.00**
   Pat and Mike, pr **125.00**
   Pinky and Blue Boy, pr **450.00**
   Roberta **125.00**
   Sarah Bernhardt, 13¼" h **375.00**
Gonder Pottery
   Collie, gray, 9" l **15.00**
   Cowboy on Bronco, black, gold dec, 7½" h, 1940–1944 . . . . **25.00**

Horse's Head, bluish–green, 13" h **35.00**
Oriental Coolie, pink and green glaze, 8" h **18.00**
Panther, jade green, 18¼" l **90.00**
Hagen Renaker, donkey, 2" h, 1986 **10.00**
Hedi Schoop, girl with poodle **85.00**
Japan, kitten, white, on brown shoe, 3" l
   . . . . **9.00**
McCarley, CA, Oriental boy and girl, 7¼" h boy with large hat and baskets, 6½" h girl with parasol and baskets, pr
   . . . . **15.00**
Midwest Potteries
   Bear, brown spray glaze, 10" h, 1940– 1944 . . . . **30.00**
   Goose, long neck, white, yellow dec, 5¾" h, 1940–1944 . . . . **8.00**
   Parrot, perched on stump, blue, yellow, and white, brown spray glaze on white, 4½" h, 1940–1944 . . . . **12.00**
   Stallion, rearing, gold, 10¾" h, 1940– 1944 . . . . **25.00**
Morton Potteries
   Kangaroo, burgundy, 2½" h **6.50**
   Swordfish, yellow, 5" h **8.00**
   Whippet, c1940 . . . . **80.00**
Niloak Pottery
   Frog **20.00**
   Polar Bear, white matte **35.00**
Pennsbury Pottery, hen, cream body, brown trim, 11" h **225.00**
Royal Doulton, cat, Persian, white, #2539
   . . . . **150.00**
Shaw, Dumbo, Disney elephant, seated, wearing yellow bonnet, 5½" h . . . **60.00**
Unknown
   Caroline Kennedy, 1964 . . . . **145.00**
   John John Kennedy, saluting, 1964
   . . . . **145.00**
Vernon Kilns
   Sprite **135.00**
   Unicorn, black, Disney movie "Fantasia" **200.00**
Wade, England, pony, miniature, Tom Smith artist **15.00**
Weller, boy, fishing **215.00**
Will George, peasant girl, 5½" h **45.00**

Birthday Girl, bisque, orig gold foil sticker, orig paper tag reads "A Josef Original," birthstone in center of flower, $5.00.

FIREARMS

A majority of Americans own firearms. However, many have them and do not use them. Neglecting to properly care for a firearm can seriously damage its value. Avoid any weapons that show excessive use or heavy signs of rust.

Before selling or buying a handgun, check federal, state, and local laws. (A discreet call to your local state police or a local gun dealer will provide you with much needed information). Modern handguns may be sold only by a licensed federal firearms dealer. Do not take a chance by selling outside the law.

Gun collectors are a world unto their own. They buy and sell through specialized gun shows. Check your local paper for the one closest to you.

A surprising number of firearms have low value. Do not be deceived by age. Age alone does not make a gun valuable. The key is collectibility.

The following sampling barly scratches the surface. For antique firearms consult Norman Flayderman's *Flayderman's Guide To Antique American Firearms . . . . And Their Values, 5th Edition* (DBI Books: 1990). For modern weapons, see Russell and Steve Quertermous's *Modern Guns: Identification & Values, Revised 9th Edition* (Collector Books: 1993).

Newspaper: *Gun List*, 700 E State St, Iola, WI 54990.

Handgun
   Beretta Model 1923, .9mm Luger, semi– automatic, exposed hammer, 9–shot magazine, 4" barrel, blued, wood grips **250.00**
   Charter Arms Bulldog, .44 Special, single action, 5–shot swing out cylinder, 4" barrel, blued, checkered walnut bull- dog grips **135.00**
   Cobray Mac–11 .9mm, semi–automatic pistol, 5¼" barrel with machined threads for barrel extension or sup- pressor, 12– and 32–shot staggered magazines, O. D. green cotton web sling with mounting clips . . . **250.00**
   Colt Peacemaker, .22 caliber, single ac- tion, 6–shot cylinder, side load, 7½" barrel, case–hardened frame, black composite rubber grips **175.00**
   C. V. A. Colt Walter, .44 caliber percus- sion black powder pistol, blued steel frame, engraved cylinder, walnut grips, brass trigger guard, 9" barrel, 4 lbs 11 oz, 15½" l overall **165.00**

Japanese, Nambu, Osaka Arsenal, Mod. 14, 8mm cal, 1941, $295.00.

High Standard Sentinel Mark II, swing out cylinder, 4" barrel, blued, checkered walnut grips **150.00**

Ruger Mark I Target, .22 caliber long rifle, semi–automatic, concealed hammer thumb safety, 9–shot magazine, 6" tapered round barrel, blued, checkered hard rubber grips **125.00**

Sterling, Model 283, .22 caliber long rifle, semi–automatic, exposed hammer, adjustable trigger, rear safety lock, 10–shot magazine, 8" heavy bull barrel, blued, checkered plastic grips **120.00**

Rifle

Colt Coltsman, Sako–Medium, .308 Winchester, medium stroke, Sako–type bolt action, repeating, 5–shot box, 24" blued barrel, checkered walnut Monte Carlo one piece pistol grip stock **275.00**

Military, British, Lee–Enfield, No. 1 SMLE MK1, .303 caliber, bolt action, curved bolt handle, 10–shot detachable box magazine, cut–off 25¼" barrel, plain wood military stock **140.00**

Military, United States, U.S. M1 Carbine, .30 caliber, semi–automatic, 30–shot staggered row detachable box magazine, 18" barrel, one piece wood stock and forearm **350.00**

Remington Nylon 11, .22 caliber, bolt action, repeating, 10–shot magazine, 19½" round barrel, polished brown nylon one piece stock **75.00**

Shotgun

Beretta Model A–301, 12 gauge, semi–automatic, hammerless, 3–shot tubular, 30" full barrel, checkered walnut pistol grip stock and forearm **300.00**

High Standard Supermatic Field, 20 gauge, semi–automatic, hammerless, 3–shot tube magazine, 26" barrel, plain walnut semi–pistol grip stock and fluted forearm **150.00**

Remington Model 27, 20 gauge, pump action, hammerless, bottom ejection, repeating, 3–shot tube magazine, 32" steel barrel, checkered walnut pistol grip and forearm **225.00**

Savage, 12 gauge, regular, pump action, hammerless, 4–shot tube magazine, 28" modified barrel, hardwood semi–pistol grip stock and grooved side handle **150.00**

Winchester, Model 23 Pigeon Grade, lightweight, 20 gauge, magnum, box lock, break open top lever, hammerless, selective automatic ejectors, double, 26" modified barrel, Winchoke, checkered walnut semi–pistol grip stock and forearm **900.00**

FIRE-KING

Remember those great coffee mugs you used to find at diners? Those nice big warm cups filled to the brim by a smiling waitress, not the styrofoam of this decade. Chances are they were Fire–King mugs. Made by the Anchor Hocking Glass Corporation, Fire–King dinnerware and ovenware was sold in sets in the 1940s through the 1970s. The manufacturer guaranteed to replace broken pieces, making the colorful wares quite popular with housewives. While Fire–King has been around for many years, collectors are now discovering quantities at flea markets and many are enjoying this new collecting area.

Club: Fire–King Collectors Club, 2156 Carlmont Dr, #6, Belmont, CA 94002.

Alice, blue and white, saucer **3.00**
Charm Square, azurite
    Cup and Saucer **3.00**
    Plate
        6⅝" d **5.00**
        Dinner **20.00**
Coupe Shape, white, silver border
    Cup **3.00**
    Plate
        7¼" d **12.50**
        10" d **9.00**
    Platter, oval, 12" l **12.50**
Black Dots, mixing bowl, 9½" d **18.00**
Fruits, hp, white ground
    Refrigerator Jar, cov
        4⅛" sq **8.50**
        4¼" × 8¼", rect **14.00**
    Mixing Bowl, Colonial, 6" d **7.50**
Golden Shell
    Cup **3.00**
    Plate, dinner **4.00**
    Saucer .... **.50**
Ivory Swirl
    Plate
        Dinner **4.50**
        Salad **3.00**
    Soup Bowl **4.00**
    Sugar, cov **7.00**
Jadite, emb dec
    Coffee Mug **7.00**

Refrigerator Jar, cov
    4½ × 5" **28.00**
    5⅛ × 9⅛" **40.00**
Shaving Mug **27.00**
Jane Ray, jadite
    Bowl
        Cereal **7.00**
        Dessert **3.50**
    Creamer and Sugar, cov **16.00**
    Cup and Saucer **4.00**
    Plate
        7½" d **6.00**
        9⅛" d, dinner **8.00**
    Platter, oval **12.00**
    Saucer **1.50**
    Sugar Lid **7.00**
    Soup **12.00**
    Vegetable, 8½" d **15.00**
Lustre Shell, demitasse cup and saucer
    .... **10.00**
Peach Lustre, plate, 7½" d **2.00**
Pink Dogwood, hp
    Casserole, cov
        1 pint **10.00**
        1½ quart **18.00**
    Coffee Mug **6.50**
Primrose
    Dessert Bowl **2.50**
    Luncheon Set, snack plate and cup **6.00**
    Platter **12.00**
Restaurantware, jadite
    Mug, thin style **6.00**
    Plate, 9" d, lunch **14.00**
Sapphire Blue
    Casserole, individual, 10 oz, tab handle
    .... **13.00**
    Custard, 5 oz **3.00**
    Juice Saver **130.00**
    Lid, 7¼" d, knob handle **10.00**
    Loaf Pan, 9⅛" × 5⅛" **18.00**
    Measuring Cup, 8 oz
        1 spout **20.00**
        3 spout **25.00**
    Mug **25.00**
    Nurser, 4 oz **9.00**
    Pie Baker
        7" d, cov **9.00**
        9" d **8.50**
    Roaster, 10⅜" l **65.00**

Custard Cup, ovenware, light blue, 3½" d, reads "Fire-King Oven Glass," $2.00.

Utility Bowl
    8³/₈″ d **16.00**
    10¹/₈″ d **20.00**
  Utility Pan, 10¹/₂ × 2″ **20.00**
Swirl Azurite
  Creamer **6.00**
  Platter **14.00**
  Sugar **6.00**
Swirl Jadite
  Cup **4.50**
  Plate, dinner **10.00**
  Vegetable Bowl, large **8.50**
Tulips, white, mixing bowl
    7¹/₂″ d **10.00**
    8¹/₂″ d **15.00**
    9¹/₂″ d **18.00**
Turquoise Blue
  Bowl, 8″ d **14.00**
  Luncheon Set, snack plate and cup **9.00**
  Plate, 9″ d **9.00**
  Sugar **5.00**
White Swirl, gold trim
  Mixing Bowl
    7″ d **5.00**
    Set of five **40.00**
  Plate
    7¹/₂″ d **2.50**
    10″ d **4.00**
  Saucer . . . . **.50**

FISHER-PRICE TOYS

In 1930 Herman Guy Fisher, Helen Schelle, and Irving R. Price founded the Fisher-Price Toy Company in Birmingham, New York. From that year forward Fisher-Price Toys were built with a five-point creed: intrinsic play value, ingenuity, strong construction, good value for the money, and action. With these principles and manufacturing contributions, the Fisher-Price Toy Company has successfully produced quality and creativity in the toy market.

The collectibility of Fisher-Price toys is a direct reflection upon their desirability due to their unique characteristics and subject matter.

Club: Fisher-Price Collectors Club, 142 N Ogden, Mesa, AZ 85205.

Allie Gator, #653, 1960 . . . . **125.00**
Big Bill Pelican, fish in bill, #794, 1961
  . . . . **150.00**
Bouncy Racer, #8, 1960 . . . . **45.00**
Bunny Cart, #10, 1940 . . . . **100.00**
Bunny Drummer, bell in cart, red, #505,
  1948 . . . . **250.00**
Chatter Telephone, wood wheels, #747,
  1962 . . . . **25.00**
Circus Train, engine, two cars, caboose, animals, and people **45.00**
Concrete Mixer Truck, #926, 1959 **225.00**

Squeaky The Clown, No. 777, paper litho on wood, 1958–60, 6¹/₂″ l, 9″ h, $150.00.

Dinkey Engine, #642, 1959 . . . . **50.00**
Family Play Barn, 1969 . . . . **15.00**
Farmer In The Dell, #166, 1963 . . . . **35.00**
Husky Dump Truck, #145, 1961 . . . . **75.00**
Katy Kackler, #140, 1954 . . . . **85.00**
Leo The Drummer, #480, 1952 . . . **225.00**
Little Snoopy, #693, 1965 . . . . **10.00**
Looky Chug–Chug, #220, 1953 . . . **125.00**
Merry Mousewife, #662, 1962 . . . . **175.00**
Moo–oo Cow, #155, 1958 . . . . . . **150.00**
Musical Sweeper, #225, 1953 . . . . . **85.00**
Musical Tick Tock Clock, #997, 1962
  . . . . **75.00**
Nosey Pup, #445, 1956 . . . . **175.00**
Playland Express, #192, 1962 . . . . . . **85.00**
Pudgy Pig, #478, 1962 . . . . **50.00**
Push Bunny Cart, #401, 1942 . . . . . **225.00**
Quaky Family, felt beaks, wood dowels,
  #799, 1946 . . . . **125.00**
Rainbow Stack, #446, 1960 . . . . **15.00**
Roller Chime, green, #124, 1961 . . . **55.00**
Scottie Dog, 2 × 6 × 5¹/₂″, wood, red
  wood wheels, 1950s **75.00**
Shaggy Zilo, #738, 1960 . . . . **150.00**
Snap Lock Beads, #760, 1957 . . . . . **12.00**
Suzie Seal, with ball, #460, 1961 . . . **50.00**
Tailspin Tabby, 455, 1939 . . . . **85.00**
Talky Parrot, #698, 1963 . . . . **125.00**
Toot Toot, #643, 1964 . . . . **7.50**
Uncle Timmy Turtle, #125, 1956 **150.00**
Whistling Engine, #617, 1957 . . . . **175.00**

FISHING COLLECTIBLES

There has been a lot written recently about the increasing value of fishing tackle of all types. What has not been said is that high-ticket items are very limited in number. The vast majority of items sell below $5.00.

Fishing collectors place strong emphasis on condition. If a rod, reel, lure, or accessory shows heavy use, chances are that its value is minimal. The original box and packaging are also important, often doubling value.

You will make a good catch if you find early wooden plugs made before 1920 (most that survive were made long after that date), split bamboo fly rods made by master craftsmen (not much value for commercial rods), and reels constructed of German silver with special detail and unique mechanical action. Fishing collectors also like to supplement their collection with advertising and other paper ephemera. Find a pile of this material and you have a lucky strike.

Club: National Fishing Lure Collectors Club, PO Box 0184, Chicago, IL 60690.

Periodical: *Fishing Collectibles Magazine,* 2005 Tree House Lane, Plano, TX 75023.

ADVERTISING AND RELATED ITEMS
Ashtray, Pennsylvania Fishing Tackle, emb
  . . . . **18.00**
Book, *Fishing For Fun and To Wash Your
  Soul,* Random House, copyright 1963,
  86 pgs, hard cov, dj **12.00**
Calendar, Bristol Steel Rod Co, 1935, 14 ×
  18″ **55.00**
Catalog
  Heddon Co, color illus, 1934 . . . . **45.00**
  South Bend Fishing Tackle, 1934 **37.50**
License, pinback button
  1931, Michigan, resident trout fishing license, blue and white ground, black
    serial number **25.00**
  1948, Pennsylvania, resident fishing license, maroon and white ground,
    black serial number **15.00**
Pin, silvered brass, replica speckled fish, inscribed ''Illinois'' **10.00**
Sign, South Bend Co, boy holding stringer
  of fish **65.00**
Store Display, Spiral Wind Fishing Reels,
  ''Get's Double Results,'' two 1¹/₂ lb yellow perch stuffed and suspended on
  painted background of man fishing in
  backwoods stream, hand blown glass
  dome covers fish, painted frame,
  30¹/₄″ w, 22″ h **500.00**

Creel, wicker, leather trim, strap handle, buckle closure, 11″ w, 7¹/₂″ h, $75.00.

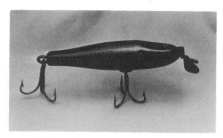

Lure, Baby Pikie Minnow, Series 908, white, yellow, red, and silver–blue body, glass eyes, treble hooks, Creek Chub Bait Co, Garrett, IN, 3¼" l, $15.00.

FISHING GEAR

Bobber, panfish float, hp, black, red, and
  white stripes, 5" l **10.00**
Creel
  Crushed Willow, leather bound, 14 × 9
    × 7" **24.00**
  Wicker **45.00**
Decoy
  Oliver Reigstad, 1960 . . . . **17.00**
  Sletten, cast aluminum, unopened,
    1950s **22.00**
Fly Rod, Horrocks & Ibbotson, 3 pc, split
  bamboo, two tips, maroon wraps, 9' l
  . . . . **40.00**
Lure, wood
  Creek Chub Co, baby beetle, yellow and
    green wings **35.00**
  Heddon, Frog pattern, crazy crawler,
    wood **35.00**
  Paw Paw, underwater minnow, green
    and black, tack eyes, three hooks
    . . . . **15.00**
  Shakespeare Co, Mouse, white and red,
    thin body, glass eyes, 3⅝" l . . . **27.00**
Minnow Trap, Orvis, clear glass, emb name,
  metal hardware, 1 gallon **65.00**
Net, collapsible, leather pouch **25.00**
Reel
  Hendryx, raised pillar type, multiplying,
    nickel plated brass, fancy handle,
    horn knob, two buttons on back
    plate drag/click **25.00**
  Takapart, No. 480, A F Meisselbach
    Mfg, patent 1904–09 . . . . **40.00**
  Winchester, Model #1135, fly, black
    finish **60.00**
Rod, split cane
  Edwards, Quadrate, spinning, 2:1, 7' l,
    orig bag and tube **200.00**
  F E Thomas, Special Fly, 3:2, 9' l, orig
    bag and tube **325.00**

FLAGS AND FLAG COLLECTIBLES

There certainly has been a great deal of flag waving as a result of Operations Desert Shield and Desert Storm. Collectors have already salted away "yellow ribbon" flags. They have forgotten a basic rule of collecting—the more made, the less likely to have value in the future. Ask anyone who owns a forty–eight star flag.

Flags themselves are difficult to display. Old flags are quite fragile. Hanging them often leads to deterioration. If you own flags, you should be aware of flag etiquette as outlined in Public Law 829, 7th Congress, approved December 22, 1942.

Many collectors do not collect flags themselves but items that display the flag as a decorative motif. A flag–related sheet music collection is one example.

Club: North American Vexilological Assoc, Suite 225, 1977 N Olden Ave, Trenton, NJ 08618.

Advertising Trade Card, Major's Cement, 3
  × 4¼", two American flags decorating
  display, full color, adv "Major's Leather
  Cement–For Sale by Druggists and
  Crockery Dealers" **15.00**
Calendar Plate, Betsy Ross sewing flag,
  1919 . . . . **28.00**
Card Game, The Flag Game, McLoughlin
  Bros, 1887 copyright **48.00**
Catalog, Detra Flag Company, #24, New
  York and Los Angeles, 6½ × 9", 1941
  . . . . **100.00**
Certificate, 12 × 16", Betsy Ross Flag Asso-
  ciation, serial #38181, Series N, C H
  Weisgerber painting, 1917 . . . . . . **45.00**
Fan, 9 × 14", Admiral Dewey, flags, admi-
  rals, and ships, lace trim **125.00**
Flag
  36 stars, 21½ × 36", parade flag,
    mounted on stick, five point star de-
    sign, 6,6,6,6,6,6 star pattern **125.00**
  44 stars, 3½ × 2¼", child's parade flag,
    8,7,7,7,7,8 star pattern and five point
    star **40.00**
  46 stars, 4 × 5', 1908–12, stars sewn
    on, Oklahoma **100.00**
  48 stars, 4 × 5', nylon **85.00**
Lapel Pin, crossed flags, "76" in center, orig
  card **3.50**
Magic Lantern Slide, 42 star flag, hand
  tinted, wood frame, c1889 . . . . . . **30.00**
Palm Puzzle, 2¾" d, blue plastic bottom,
  transparent cov, red, white, and blue paper game insert titled "Keep America
  Free/Keep Out The Red," three blue
  balls, one red ball, illus of flag, Capitol,
  White House, and factory, late 1940s
  . . . . **40.00**
Pinback Button, ½" d, red, white, and blue,
  inscribed "Thank God I Am Not A Bol-
  shevist," American flag furls in center,
  orig 3½ × 4½" white card with red and
  blue striping, patriotic verse, c1920
  . . . . **75.00**

Puzzle, Hoods Four–In–One Puzzle, C I Hood Co, Lowell, MA, copyright 1896, 34 diecut cardboard pieces, 5 × 7" cardboard box, 32 page booklet, 11¼ × 18½", $45.00.

Print, 11¼ × 15½", The Star Spangled Banner, Currier and Ives #481 . . . . . **250.00**
Sheet Music, *Stars and Stripes Forever
  March,* John Phillip Sousa portrait in upper left hand corner, Old Glory in center, published by John Church Co **40.00**

FLINTSTONES COLLECTIBLES

"Yabba Dabba Doo," collecting Hanna–Barbera Studios' number one selling cartoon characters can be fun for you.

The Flintstones first aired as a prime-time television show on CBS in the fall of 1960. It was an instant success and started a prehistoric craze for the baubles of Bedrock. The rubble never settled after the 1964 cancellation. The overwhelming popularity grew as the show was syndicated the following year and continued to air.

Toy companies were eager to capitalize on the popular personalities of Fred and Wilma Flintstone along with their wacky neighbors Barney and Betty Rubble. The demand for Flintstone items has led collectors on a fossil hunt for neat goodies.

In 1965 a movie release of The Flintstones, entitled *A Man Called Flintstone,* helped to keep the interest alive. In 1994 Universal Studios released a new *Flintstones* movie starring live actors. The collectibles market responded with new issues of cookie jars, hats, teeshirts, and toys.

Advertising Display, Itty Bitty Figures, complete with 44 figures, 1964 . . . . . **125.00**
Ashtray, 8 × 5½", ceramic, raised relief image of dancing Fred and Wilma, brown
  and white, Arrow Houseware, 1961
  . . . . **60.00**

Bank
  Bamm–Bamm and Dino, Vandor   **90.00**
  Barney and Bamm–Bamm, 12¹/₂" h, hard
    vinyl **30.00**
  Dino, 8¹/₂" h, ceramic, Dino carrying
    golf bag, mid 1960s **200.00**
  Fred, 8¹/₂" h, hard vinyl **15.00**
  Fred and Wilma **435.00**
  Pebbles, 1973 . . . . **25.00**
Bath Soap, Bubble Club Fun, 12 oz box, li-
  tho of Fred giving bath to Pebbles and
  Bamm-Bamm, 1965 . . . . **145.00**
Battery Operated Toy, Fred riding plush
  Dino, 1960s **325.00**
Bubble Gum Machine, figural, Fred Flint-
  stone head **40.00**
Camera, figural, plastic, Fred's face fitted
  over lens, uses Kodak 126 film, 1976
  . . . . **32.00**
Card Game, Rummy, Flintstones illus on
  each card, tray, orig box, 1961 . . . **45.00**
Children's Book, Wonder Book
  Fred Flintstone, Fix It, 1976, fine condi-
    tion **12.00**
  *Pebbles and Bamm–Bamm, Things To
    Do,* 1976, very good condition **10.00**
  The Flintstones, Egg 1976, fine condition
    . . . . **12.00**
Colorforms Set, 1972 . . . . **20.00**
Coloring Book, Fred Flintstone **135.00**
Doll, cloth, Knickerbocker, 1972, individu-
  ally boxed
  Bamm–Bamm **20.00**
  Barney **20.00**
  Fred Flintstone **20.00**
Figure
  Dino, Dakin, dog tag missing, 1970
    . . . . **30.00**
  Fred, three dimensional standup, wood,
    caveman boxer outfit, oversized
    gloves attached to flexible rope arms,
    6" h **100.00**
Game
  Dino The Dinosaur Game, Transogram,
    1961 copyright **50.00**
  Flintstones Stone Age Game,
    Transogram, 1961 . . . . **35.00**
Juice Glass, Welches, 1960 . . . . **10.00**
Lunch Box, Dino, 1962 . . . . **85.00**
Magnet, figural, Fred **7.00**
Mug
  Ceramic, Fred **4.00**
  Plastic, Flintstones Vitamins
    Dino, 1968 . . . . **10.00**
    Fred, 1968 . . . . **9.00**
    Pebbles, 1972 . . . . **8.00**
Pillow Kit, 1970, MIB
  Dino **20.00**
  Fred **25.00**
Plate, Melmac, super glossy, white back-
  ground, Fred, Wilma, Barney, and Betty
  watching kids play **25.00**
Punch–Out Book, 11¹/₄ × 22¹/₄", Whitman,
  copyright 1961, bright, full color illus of
  Fred on front cov, Barney on back,
  unused **45.00**

***Bank, Dino and Pebbles, molded plastic,
Homecraft Products, Vinyl Prod Corp, 1971,
7³/₄" w, 13" h, $45.00.***

Puppet, push, Kohner, early 1960s
  Bamm–Bamm **25.00**
  Fred **30.00**
Sticker Book, 10 × 22", The Flintstones Va-
  cation Sticker Fun Book, Whitman,
  #1692, unused, 1965 . . . . **95.00**
Tambourine, 8" d, clear plastic, center illus
  of Fred and Barney in top hat and tails,
  Australia's Wonderland, 1987 . . . . **25.00**
Toy
  Car, 4" l, Fred riding in colorful tin litho
    car, vinyl head, Marx **525.00**

***Clock, Fred, alarm, colorful ceramic body,
dial marked "Sheffield, The Flintstones
Alarm, Western Germany," 5" w, 8¹/₂" h,
$150.00.***

Circus, 10¹/₂ × 13", plastic snap together
  parts, Kohner, c1965 . . . . . . **200.00**
Dino, Fred riding on back, colorful tin li-
  tho, windup, vinyl head, orig box
  marked "Flintstone Pals on Dino,"
  Marx **585.00**
Give–A–Show Projector **70.00**
Playset, Marx, 1962
  Canadian Edition, 90% complete
    . . . . **395.00**
  US Edition **265.00**
Squeaker, Fred, MIP **25.00**
Tank, 4" l, Turnover, Flintstone images
  on all sides, Linemar, orig box with
  some damage **650.00**
Tricycle, windup, Wilma **450.00**
View–Master Set, 3 reels and story booklet,
  colorful photo cover, 1966 . . . . . **18.00**
Vitamins, bottle, 4" h, 1969, light label wear
  . . . . **32.00**
Wristwatch, vinyl, 1986, MIP **20.00**
Yo–Yo, plastic, molded head, Fred, 1975,
  unused **18.00**

FLUE COVERS

When someone hears "flu" in the
1990s, they immediately think of a cold.
There aren't many individuals left who
remember wood- and coal-burning
kitchen and parlor stoves. When the
stovepipe was removed for the summer
for cleaning or repair, the exhaust flue in
the wall needed to be covered. The answer was a flue cover.

A flue cover is generally round with
a small section of chain attached to the
back so that the cover can be hung from
a nail in the wall. They were made from a
variety of materials. Covers that sport a
pretty woman or advertising have the
most value.

Brass, rural winter landscape **15.00**
Glass
  Girl Holding Flowers **30.00**
  Mountain Landscape **38.00**
  Victorian Parlor Scene, 9" d **40.00**
Tin, stamped
  Cottage and Flowers, emb yellow border
    . . . . **8.00**
  Four Seasons, multicolored **15.00**
  Playful Puppies, multicolored **20.00**

FOOD MOLDS

Commercial ice cream and chocolate molds appear to be the collectors'
favorites. Buying them is now a bit risky
because of the large number of reproductions. Beware of all Santa and rabbit
molds.

Country collectors have long touted the vast array of kitchen food molds, ranging from butter prints to Turk's-head cake molds. Look for molds with signs of use and patina.

Do not forget the Jell–O molds. If you grew up in the 1950s or 1960s, you ate Jell–O and plenty of it. The aluminum Jell–O molds came in a tremendous variety of shapes and sizes. Most sell between 10¢ and $1.00, cheap by any stretch of the imagination.

Butter, rect, cherry, deep carved geometric design **110.00**
Cake, Santa Shape–A–Cake, orig instructions, MIB **8.50**
Cheese, 5 × 13", wood, carved design, branded "Los," carved date 1893 **45.00**
Chocolate
    Chicken, tin, clamp type **20.00**
    Cowboy, tin, clamp type **48.00**
    Rabbit, six 3" h cavities, hinged **125.00**
    Turkey, pewter **35.00**
Cookie
    Cast Iron, 4 × 6", oval, basket with leaves and grape hyacinths, c1830 . . . . **165.00**
    Pewter, wood back, six classical heads **45.00**
Ice Cream
    Basket, pewter, replaced hinge pins **20.00**
    Castle, chess game piece, marked "S & Co" **60.00**
    Shoe, lady's, 5¾" l, pewter **65.00**
    Smoking Pipe, pewter **30.00**
Maple Candy, wood, fruit and foliage design, two parts **28.00**
Pudding, tin and copper, oval, pineapple **65.00**

Ice Cream, strawberry medallion, pewter, $30.00.

FOOTBALL CARDS

Football cards are "hot." It was bound to happen. The price of baseball cards has reached the point where even some of the common cards are outside the price range of the average collector. If you cannot afford baseball, why not try football?

Football card collecting is not as sophisticated as baseball card collecting. However, it will be. Smart collectors who see a similarity between the two collecting areas are beginning to stress Pro–Bowlers and NFL All–Stars. Stay away from World Football material. The league is a loser among collectors, just as it was in real life.

Cards in good condition are listed in this section.

Periodicals: *Beckett Football Card Magazine,* 4887 Alpha Rd, Suite 200, Dallas, TX 75244; *Sports Cards,* 700 E State St, Iola, WI 54990.

Bowman Gum Company
  1948
    Complete Set **800.00**
    Common Card **2.00**
    12 Charley Conerly **31.00**
    60 Elbert Nickel **14.50**
    99 Harry Gilmer **17.00**
  1950
    Complete Set **475.00**
    Common Card **3.00**
    1 Doak Walker **10.00**
    45 Otto Graham **57.50**
  1952
    Complete Set **550.00**
    Common Card **2.25**
    1 Norm VanBrocklin **14.00**
    16 Frank Gifford **57.50**
    127 Ollie Matson **12.50**
  1955
    Complete Set **190.00**
    Common Card . . . . **.55**
    32 Norm VanBrocklin **3.80**
    71 Bobby Lane **5.00**
    152 Tom Landry **23.00**

Bowman, assortment of cards, 1950, 2 × 2½", $3.00.

Fleer Gum Company
  1960
    Complete Set **85.00**
    Common Card . . . . **.30**
    20 Sammy Baugh **4.40**
    58 George Blanda **4.40**
    124 Jack Kemp **45.00**
  1963
    Complete Set **230.00**
    Common Card . . . . **.85**
    6 Charles Long **31.00**
    15 Don Maynard **5.75**
    47 Len Dawson **25.00**
Philadelphia Gum Company
  1964
    Complete Set **115.00**
    Common Card . . . . **.22**
    30 Jim Brown **9.50**
    51 Don Meredith **4.00**
    109 Fran Tarkenton **5.00**
  1966
    Complete Set **115.00**
    Common Card . . . . **.19**
    31 Dick Butkas **22.00**
    41 Jim Brown **8.25**
    114 Fran Tarkenton **3.80**
  1967
    Complete Set **80.00**
    Common Card . . . . **.19**
    23 John Unitas **3.80**
    35 Gale Sayers **10.50**
Pinnacle, 1991
    Complete Set **4.00**
    Common Card . . . . **.01**
Playoff, 1993
    Complete Set **8.25**
    Common Card . . . . **.02**
Score, 1989
    Complete Set **22.00**
    Common Card . . . . **.01**
    211 Thurman Thomas **3.80**
    257 Barry Sanders **5.75**
    270 Troy Aikman **5.75**
Topps Chewing Gum Inc
  1956
    Complete Set **210.00**
    Common Card . . . . **.06**
    9 Lou Groza **3.10**
    11 George Blanda **6.25**
  1958
    Complete Set **160.00**
    Common Card . . . . **.40**
    22 John Unitas **19.00**
    73 Frank Gifford **8.25**
  1960
    Complete Set **85.00**
    Common Card . . . . **.25**
    23 Jim Brown **12.50**
    56 Forrest Gregg **4.00**
  1964
    Complete Set **160.00**
    Common Card . . . . **.40**
    30 Jack Kemp **20.00**
    96 Len Dawson **9.50**
  1966
    Complete Set **160.00**

Common Card . . . .**.40**
48 George Blanda **5.00**
96 Joe Namath **38.00**
1969
Complete Set **70.00**
Common Card . . . .**.15**
26 Brian Piccolo **8.25**
120 Larry Csonka **10.00**
161 Bob Griese **3.40**
1973
Complete Set **52.50**
Common Card . . . .**.05**
60 Fran Tarkenton **1.90**
89 Franco Harris **7.50**
475 Roger Staubach **4.00**
1976
Complete Set **47.50**
Common Card . . . .**.03**
75 Terry Bradshaw **1.00**
148 Walter Payton **25.00**
1984
Complete Set **15.00**
Common Card . . . .**.01**
63 John Elway **3.10**
123 Dan Marino **8.25**

FOOTBALL COLLECTIBLES

At the moment, this category is heavily weighted toward professional football. Do not overlook some great college memorabilia.

Local pride dominates most collecting. Taking an item back to its "hometown" often doubles its value. Because of their limited production and the tendency of most individuals to discard them within a short time, some of the hardest things to find are game promotional giveaways. Also check the breweriana collectors. A surprising number of beer companies sponsor football broadcasts. Go Bud Light!

Periodical: *Sports Collectors Digest,* 700 E State St, Iola, WI 54990.

Bank, 6" h, Pittsburgh Steelers, helmet shape, plastic, 1970s **24.00**
Beer Can, 5" h, 1975 Steelers Commemorative, aluminum, Iron City Beer, 12 oz
. . . .**15.00**
Book, *King Football; The Vulgarization of American Colleges,* R Harris, Vanguard Press, 254 pgs, first edition **6.50**
Bubble Gum Card, Joe Namath, #96, Topps Chewing Gum, 1966 . . . .**12.00**
Catalog, A J Reach Fall & Winter Catalogue, Philadelphia, PA, 1912–13, 32 pgs, football and other sporting equipment
. . . .**25.00**
Cigarette Lighter, Baltimore Colts, musical, MIB **75.00**
Game, Vince Lombardi's Game, Research Games Inc, 1960s **40.00**
Jug, Who Will Win, made for Michigan–Minnesota Football Game, Red Wing
. . . . **195.00**
Magazine, *Illustrated Football Annual,* 1938
. . . .**40.00**
Nodder, 5½" h, composition
Baltimore Colts, 1961–62 NFL series
. . . .**75.00**
Green Bay Packers, inked "1961 Champions" **50.00**
Pennant
Los Angeles Rams, 29½" l, blue and white felt, National Football League logo and 1967 date **20.00**

St Louis Cardinals, red and white felt, c1967 . . . .**15.00**
Program
AFC Division, Baltimore vs Cincinnati, 1970 . . . .**28.00**
Iowa vs Notre Dame, 1951 . . . . . .**50.00**
Lincoln University vs Howard University, 1949 . . . .**15.00**
Notre Dame vs Navy, 1940s–1950s
. . . .**12.00**
Stadium Cushion, 11 × 16", vinyl, stuffed, red, NFL team names and mascot illus, orig tag, unused, 1950s **18.00**
Ticket, AFC Wild Card, Houston vs Miami, 1976 . . . .**10.00**
Wristwatch, Pittsburgh Steelers, chrome metal case, helmet illus on dial, Lafayette Watch Co, 1960s **30.00**

FOSTORIA GLASS

The Fostoria Glass Company began in Fostoria, Ohio, and moved to Moundsville, West Virginia, in 1891. In 1983 Lancaster Colony purchased the company and produced glass under the Fostoria trademark.

Fostoria is collected by pattern, with the American pattern the most common and sought after. Other patterns include Baroque, Georgian, Holly, Midnight Rose, Navarre, Rhapsody, and Wister. Hazel Weatherman's *Fostoria, Its First Fifty Years,* published by the author about 1972, helps identify patterns.

Club: Fostoria Glass Society of America, PO Box 826, Moundsville, WV 26041.

Newsletter: *Facets of Fostoria,* PO Box 826, Moundsville, WV 26041.

Almond dish, American, 3¾" l, oval **18.00**
Ashtray, Coin, Line #1372, 7½" d, coin center, amber **20.00**
Basket
American, reed handle **95.00**
Century, 10" l, oval **100.00**
Bonbon
American, 6" d, ftd **17.00**
Century, 7" d, round **20.00**
Colony, Line #2412, 7" d **14.00**
Bowl
American
11" d, 3 corner **35.00**
13" d, shallow **47.00**
Century, 10½" d, 3 ftd, rolled **55.00**
Coin, Line #1372, 8" d, blue **50.00**
Colony, Line #2412, 12" d, shallow
. . . .**35.00**
Heirloom, yellow opalescent crinkle
. . . .**55.00**
Pinecone, 12" d, flared **45.00**
Butter, cov, American, ¼ lb **30.00**
Cake Plate, American, 3 toes **22.00**

Magazine Cover, **Saturday Evening Post,** *Nov 15, 1913, J C Leyendecker illus, sepia and red, 10¼ × 14", $35.00.*

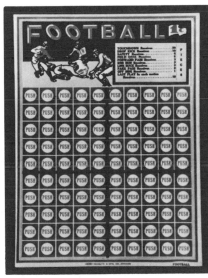

Punchboard, 1¢, red, blue, yellow, and white, 1930s, 7¼ × 10", $20.00.

Cake Salver, American, sq, ftd **125.00**
Candlesticks, pr
  American, 6½" h **32.00**
  Coin, Line #1372, 4½" h **40.00**
  Colony, Line #2412, 2 light **60.00**
  Heirloom, pink opalescent **35.00**
  Meadow Rose, 2 light **32.00**
Candy Dish, cov, Century, ftd **50.00**
Celery, three part
  Century, 9¼" l **34.00**
  Colony, Line #2412 .... **25.00**
Cheese and Cracker Set, American   **50.00**
Cheese Compote
  American **20.00**
  Century, bouquet dec **27.00**
Cigarette Box, cov, Coin, Line #1372, amber **50.00**
Coaster, Pioneer, green **6.00**
Cocktail
  American, 3½ oz, cone **9.00**
  Colony, Line #2412 .... **14.00**
  Vesper, 4⅞" h, amber **25.00**
Compote
  Century **22.00**
  Vesper, 3" h, green **30.00**
Cordial
  Heather, #6037 .... **40.00**
  Versailles, green **60.00**
Creamer and Sugar
  Century **30.00**
  Coin, Line #1372, olive green ... **45.00**
Cruet, orig stopper
  American **35.00**
  Century **50.00**
  Coin, Line #1372, blue **100.00**
Cup and Saucer
  American **12.00**
  Century **18.50**
  Colony, Line #2412 .... **10.00**
  Vesper, green **20.00**
Float Bowl, Century, 9" d **37.00**
Fruit Bowl, Heirloom, 12 × 8½", ruby **55.00**
Goblet, American, 5½" h, luncheon size **10.00**
Hat, American, 3" h **20.00**

Sandwich server, Trojan pattern, yellow, $35.00.

Iced Tea Tumbler
  American, 5" h **20.00**
  Coin, Line #1372 .... **35.00**
Ice Bucket, Century, handle missing   **60.00**
Ice Tub, American, 5½" h **37.00**
Jelly, cov
  American **30.00**
  Coin, Line #1372 .... **15.00**
Juice Tumbler
  American, 3¾" h **13.00**
  Colony, Line #2412 .... **13.00**
Lemon Dish, Colony, Line #2412 ... **15.00**
Mayonnaise, American, ftd **32.00**
Muffin Tray, Colony, Line #2412 ... **38.00**
Nappy
  Coin, Line #1372, 5⅜" d, green, handle **40.00**
  Pinecone, 7" d **19.00**
Perfume Bottle, orig stopper, American **75.00**
Pickle
  Century, 8¼" l **21.00**
  Heather, Line #6037, 6½" l **21.00**
Pitcher
  Colony, Line #2412, blown, 2 qt **95.00**
  Heirloom, 9" h, yellow opalescent **85.00**
Plate
  American, 7¾" d **9.00**
  Coin, Line #1372, 8" d, ruby   **40.00**
  Fairfax, 9" d, topaz **9.00**
  Heirloom, 8½" d, bittersweet **30.00**
  Pioneer, 9½" d, green **7.00**
  Vesper, 10¼" d, amber **32.00**
Platter
  American, 12½" l, oval **50.00**
  Century, 12" l **85.00**
  Colony, Line #2412, dinner **22.00**
  Vesper, 11" l, green **100.00**
Punch Bowl Set, American, 14" d, 11 pcs **300.00**
Relish, three part
  American, 9½" l, oval **37.00**
  Century, 11" d **34.00**
Salt and Pepper Shakers, pr
  Century **20.00**
  Fairfax, topaz **65.00**
  Heather, Line #6037 .... **50.00**
Sandwich Server, Colony, Line #2412, center handle **30.00**
Sherbet
  Century **14.00**
  Coin, Line #1372 .... **20.00**
Shrimp Bowl, American **410.00**
Sundae, American **10.00**
Sweet Pea Vase, American **85.00**
Syrup, American, glass lid **110.00**
Tidbit Tray, Century, bouquet dec .. **18.00**
Tomato Juice Tumbler, American, blown **14.00**
Toothpick Holder, American **25.00**
Torte Plate, American, 14" d **32.00**
Tumbler, Century, 6" h, ftd **30.00**
Urn Vase, Century, bouquet dec ... **85.00**
Vase
  American, 6" h, sq, ftd **34.00**

Coin, Line #1372, 8" h, bud, blue **40.00**
  Colony, Line #2412, 6" h, bud .. **15.00**
Vegetable, American, 10" l, oval, 2 part **32.00**
Water Goblet
  Colony, Line #2412 .... **15.00**
  Heather, Line #6037, 8" h **30.00**
  Vesper, 7" h, amber **30.00**
Whiskey Decanter, orig stopper, American **75.00**
Wine
  American, hex base **14.00**
  Coin, Line #1372, olive green ... **45.00**
  Heather, Line #6037 .... **35.00**

FRANCISCAN WARE

Charles Gladding, Peter McBean, and George Chambers organized the Gladding, McBean and Company pottery in 1875. Located in California, the firm's early products included sewer pipes and architectural items. In 1934 the company began producing dinnerware under the Franciscan trademark. The earliest forms consisted of plain shapes and bright colors. Later, the company developed molded, underglaze patterns such as Desert Rose, Apple, and Ivy.

Franciscan ware can be found with a great variety of marks—over eighty were used. Many of the marks include the pattern name and patent dates and numbers.

Apple
  Bowl
    5¾" d, cereal **15.00**
    8" d, low **55.00**
    10" d, salad **95.00**
  Butter Dish **30.00**
  Candlestick **55.00**
  Child's Plate **110.00**
  Chocolate Mug, 10 oz **125.00**
  Cigarette Box **175.00**
  Coffeepot **90.00**
  Cookie Jar **250.00**
  Creamer and Sugar, jumbo **65.00**
  Cup and Saucer **12.00**
  Gravy Boat **45.00**
  Grill Plate **85.00**
  Jam Jar **85.00**
  Mixing Bowl, large **150.00**
  Mug, 12 oz **40.00**
  Napkin Ring **50.00**
  Platter
    12½" l **30.00**
    14" l **50.00**
    Turkey **250.00**
  Salt and Pepper Shakers, pr, bulbous **225.00**

Sherbet **30.00**
Soup, flat **18.00**
Tumbler, 10 oz **35.00**
Tureen
    Footed **595.00**
    Small **425.00**
Vegetable Bowl
    7¹/₂" d **35.00**
    Divided **55.00**
Wine Glass, hp **15.00**
Coronado
    Bowl, turquoise, satin **15.00**
    Cream Soup, underplate **20.00**
    Demitasse Cup and Saucer, yellow,
      glossy **14.00**
    Soup, flat, 8¹/₂" d
      Blue **10.00**
      Coral, satin **14.00**
Desert Rose
    Baking Dish, sq **195.00**
    Bowl
      5¹/₄" d **14.00**
      5¹/₂" d, cereal **22.00**
      10" d, salad **95.00**
    Bud Vase **125.00**
    Candleholders, pr **125.00**
    Casserole, 1¹/₂ quart **250.00**
    Compote **85.00**
    Cup and Saucer **12.00**
    Demitasse Coffeepot **350.00**
    Dinner Bell **150.00**
    Hurricane Lamp **225.00**
    Plate
      6" d, salad **5.00**
      8" d, lunch **6.00**
      10" d, dinner **12.00**
    Salad, crescent **40.00**
    Salt and Pepper Shakers, pr, bulbous
     . . . . **225.00**
    Sherbet, ftd **30.00**
    Soup, flared rim **30.00**
    Thimble **75.00**
    Tile, 6" sq, orig box **110.00**
    Tureen, flat bottom **650.00**

Westwood pattern, white ground, light green int rim stripe, green and gold floral center, 10¹/₂" d, $9.00.

Vegetable, oval, 2 pint **40.00**
Duet Rose
    Ashtray
      Individual **10.00**
      Large **35.00**
    Berry Bowl **6.00**
    Canister, small **95.00**
    Cup and Saucer **10.00**
    Gravy **15.00**
    Pepper Mill **65.00**
    Pitcher, large **55.00**
    Plate
      Dinner **10.00**
      Salad **8.00**
    Teapot **95.00**
    Vegetable, oval **18.00**
Ivy
    Ashtray, individual **30.00**
    Bowl
      Cereal **25.00**
      Salad, 11" d **150.00**
    Buffet Plate, 11" d **95.00**
    Cup and Saucer **40.00**
    Plate, salad **25.00**
    Sherbet **35.00**
    Tumbler, water **40.00**
    Vegetable, cov **150.00**
Poppy
    Cup and Saucer **40.00**
    Gravy **65.00**
    Plate
      6¹/₂" d, bread and butter **20.00**
      10" d, dinner **40.00**
    Platter, 13¹/₂" l **95.00**
    Vegetable Bowl, 8¹/₂" d **75.00**
Strawberry Fair, cereal bowl **10.00**

FRANKART

Every time there is an Art Deco revival, Frankart gets rediscovered. Frankart was founded by Arthur Von Frankenberg, a sculptor and artist, in the mid-1920s. The key is to remember that his pieces were mass–produced.

Frankart figures are identified through form and style, not specific features. Do I have to tell you that the nudes are the most collectible? Probably not. Nudes are always collectible. Do not overlook other animal and human figures.

Almost every Frankart piece is marked with the company name followed by a patent number of "pat. appl. for." Avoid unmarked pieces that dealers are trying to pass as Frankart. Frankenberg experienced plenty of reproductions during the late 1920s and early 1930s.

Ashtray, 5" h, stylized duck, outstretched
    wings, green glass ashtray **90.00**

Figure, elk, bronze patina finish, 6¹/₄" h, $125.00.

Bookends, pr
    Angel Fish, stylized, exaggerated fins
     . . . . **90.00**
    Horse Heads, flowing manes **45.00**
    Scotties **135.00**
Candlesticks, pr, 12¹/₂" h, nude figures
    standing on tiptoes, holding candle cup
    over heads **365.00**
Figure
    Elk, 6¹/₄" h, bronze patina finish   **120.00**
    Mexican riding on donkey, ceramic hat,
      dated 1928 . . . . **295.00**
Incense Burner, cov, 10" h, draped figure
    holds burner **250.00**
Lamp, nude holding globe, #L210   **500.00**
Night Light, 11" h, sailor leaning against
    lamppost, bronze patina, orig shade
    . . . . **250.00**
Wall Pocket, 12" h, seated nude supported
    by wrought iron metal framework, metal
    flower pan **285.00**

FRANKOMA

This is one of those pottery groups, such as Gonder and Hull, that runs hot and cold. Last edition, I suggested it was freezing. There has been a mild thaw, especially in the Midwest. Frankoma is great fifties. It's just that collectors and dealers have not yet discovered it as such.

In 1933 John N. Frank, a ceramic art instructor at Oklahoma University, founded Frankoma, Oklahoma's first commercial pottery. Originally located in Norman, it eventually moved to Sapulpa, Oklahoma, in 1938. A series of disastrous fires, the last in 1983, struck the plant. Look for pieces bearing a pacing leopard mark. These pieces are earlier than pieces marked "FRANK-OMA."

Ashtray, fish **15.00**
Bean Pot, cov, Plainsman, green and brown
.... **10.00**
Bird Feeder **20.00**
Bookends, pr, boots, #433 .... **24.00**
Bowl, 10" d, cactus, carved **40.00**
Candleholder, three arms, orange, label
.... **25.00**
Chip and Dip Set **20.00**
Christmas Card
    1948 .... **75.00**
    1984, Grace Lee & Milton Smith **35.00**
Compote, Gracetone, pine cone, #85 **20.00**
Dish, leaf shape, Gracetone **15.00**
Figure
    English Setter, 5" h **48.00**
    Gardener Girl, 5¾" h, #701 ..... **95.00**
    Panther, 7½" l, green, sgd, early **40.00**
    Swan, 9" h, open tail, brown glaze
    .... **20.00**
Jewelry, pin **10.00**
Match Holder, 1¾" h, #89–A **15.00**
Mug, Donkey, red and white, 1976 **18.00**
Planter, 9½" l, mallard **8.00**
Plate, Bicentennial Series, 1976 ...... **7.00**
Salt and Pepper Shakers, pr, wagon wheels
.... **10.00**
Toby Mug, 4½" h, cowboy **8.00**
Vase, #43, Ada Clay **40.00**
Wall Pocket, acorn **20.00**

FRATERNAL ORDER COLLECTIBLES

In the 1990s few individuals understand the dominant societal role played by fraternal orders and benevolent societies between 1850 and 1950. Because many had membership qualifications that were prejudicial, these "secret" societies often were targets for the social activists of the 1960s.

As the twentieth century ends, America as a nation of joiners also seems to be ending. Many fraternal and benevolent organizations have disbanded. A surprising amount of their material has worked its way into the market. Lodge hall material is often given a "folk art" label and correspondingly high price. There are lots of common items, don't be lured into paying big prices. Same goes for ornamental swords.

Benevolent & Protective Order of Elks (BPOE)
    Badge, Salt Lake City Elks Reunion, 1902 .... **18.00**
    Bookmark, emb, elk's head, SS ... **18.00**

Cigar Box Label, Elks Temple, multi-colored, emb gold trim **25.00**
Plate, 10" d, elk's head, BPOE & 463, Johnson Bros, England **45.00**
Textile, 10" l, silk, relief elk's head
.... **40.00**
Tie Tack, SS, jeweled dec **28.00**
Fraternal Order of Eagles (FOE)
    Ashtray **12.00**
    Shaving Mug, eagle standing on rock, "Liberty, Truth, Justice, Equality"
    .... **15.00**
    Watch Fob, bronze, FOE, Liberty, Truth, Justice, Equality, 1918 .... **8.00**
Independent Order of Odd Fellows (IOOF)
    Banner, 18 × 30", white silk, metallic gold braid border, wood pole at top, 19th C **75.00**
    Ribbon, Michigan, September 1893, red and black **25.00**
    Teaspoon, IOOF, SS, 1915 ...... **25.00**
Knights of Columbus
    Plate, Vienna Art, 1905 .... **38.00**
    Shaving Mug, gold trim, black and gold lettering, red, white, blue, and gold shield **50.00**
    Sword, brass, ivory handle, fancy scabbard **125.00**
Loyal Order of Moose
    Razor, chrome case, Ever Ready, emb on outside of case **25.00**
    Robe, officer, velvet **120.00**
Masonic
    Belt Buckle, SP **22.00**
    Desk Accessory, cigarette lighter and letter opener combination **25.00**
    Mug, enamel, three handles, Syria, 1905
    .... **60.00**
    Shot Glass, 3" h, cut glass, enclosed bottom holds three dice **150.00**
Order of Eastern Star (OES)
    Cup and Saucer, emblem, marked "Lefton" **15.00**
    Pencil, mechanical **10.00**

Shriners, pinback button, Shrine Circus, white ground, red hat, green letters, 1¾" d, $10.00.

Pendant, gold tone, heart shape, multi-colored enameled symbol in center, ring for hanging **35.00**
Shrine
    Fez Hat, brass scarab **22.00**
    Letter Opener, 32nd emblem, c1920
    .... **20.00**
    Tie Tack, gold, jeweled dec **28.00**
    Vase, Limoges, 1921 .... **48.00**

FROG COLLECTIBLES

A frog collector I know keeps her collection in the guest bathroom. All the fixtures are green also. How long do you think it took me to find the toilet? Thank goodness I have good bladder control.

In fairy tales frogs usually received good press. Not true for their cousin, the toad. Television introduced us to Kermit the Frog, thus putting to rest the villainous frog image of Froggy the Gremlin. I am willing to bet Froggy's "magic twanger" would not get past today's TV censors.

Club: The Frog Pond, PO Box 193, Beech Grove, IN 46107.

Advertising Trade Card
    Lancaster Dental Powders, 4¼ × 3¹/₁₆"
    .... **6.00**
    Semon Ice Cream, 14" l, diecut, printed on both sides **25.00**
Ashtray, 4½" d, porcelain, sitting frog with wide mouth, Japan **20.00**
Bank, 4" h, figural, pottery **40.00**
Cane Handle, 5½" h, figural, silvered white metal, inset glass eyes, early 1900s
.... **50.00**
Clicker, yellow, green, and red **2.00**
Colorforms, Kermit The Frog, 8 × 12½ × 1", 1980 Henson Associates copyright
.... **10.00**
Doorstop, 3" h, full figure, sitting, yellow and green **50.00**
Figure, reclining, wearing jacket **15.00**
Game, Frog Pond, 1895–97 .... **45.00**
Key Chain, 1" d, metal, frog riding bicycle, c1940 .... **8.00**
Mug, ceramic, white, small green frog sitting in bottom, c1972 .... **5.00**
Pez Dispenser, Merry Music Makers, 1980s
.... **10.00**
Planter, seated on lily pad, green and brown, glossy, marked "Shawnee 726"
.... **18.00**
Stuffed Animal
    8" h, smoking pipe **45.00**
    9" h, green, velvet top, white satin bottom, c1960 .... **12.00**
Toothpick Holder, glass, amber, pulling snail shell **40.00**
Toy, rubber, Froggy the Gremlin, Sun Rubber **30.00**

Cookie Cutter, plastic, frog shape, orig card, $2.00.

Ideal Ball, quart, aqua, $5.00.

FRUIT JARS

Most fruit jars that you find are worth less than $1.00. Their value rests in reuse through canning, rather than in the collectors' market. Do not be fooled by patent dates that appear on the jar. Over fifty different types of jars bear a patent date of 1858 and many were made as much as fifty years later.

However, there are some expensive fruit jars. A good price guide is Alice M. Creswick's *Red Book No. 6: The Collector's Guide To Old Fruit Jars* published privately by the author in 1990.

Newsletter: *Fruit Jar Newsletter,* 364 Gregory Ave, West Orange, NJ 07052.

Ball, Masons' Patent 1858, green, qt   5.00
Bulach, green, glass lid, wire clip, qt   3.00
Clark's Peerless, aqua, glass lid, qt . . . **10.00**
Double Safety, pt **5.00**
Globe, amber, pint **88.00**
Lightning, amber, half gallon **55.00**
Mason's
   Improved, light green, qt **15.00**
   Mason's VII, 1858 . . . . **28.00**
   Shield Union, aqua, mismatched zinc lid
      . . . . **240.00**
Pearl, aqua, handmade, emb "The Pearl,"
   qt **25.00**
Reverse Ball, aqua, qt **5.00**
Swayees Improved Mason, amber, quart
   . . . . **38.00**
Texas Mason, clear, qt **15.00**
Trademark Lightning, Putnam 909, on base,
   3¹/₈" d, 7¹/₄" h **55.00**

Victory, clear, glass lid, top emb "Victory
   Reg'd 1925," pt **5.00**
Weir, As You Like It, horseradish trademark,
   minor roughness inside lid **50.00**

FURNITURE

I am not going to compete with my father. If you want to learn about antique or collectible furniture, consult his *Warman's Furniture,* one of the many great volumes in the Warman's Encyclopedia of Antiques and Collectibles. (Psst! Pop, now do I get my raise?)

Much of the furniture found at flea markets is of the secondhand variety. Just remember, all the furniture in my Dad's book was once at this level too.

Bed, cast iron, painted white, double size
   . . . . **65.00**
Bedroom Suite, maple, twin bed, chest of
   drawers, matching wall mirror, night
   stand with one drawer **125.00**
Blanket Chest
   Cherry, maple, and walnut rect blocks,
      dovetailed, hand made from RCA
      cabinet scraps, brass side handles,
      c1920, refinished **165.00**
   Walnut veneer, cedar lined, diamond
      shaped molding on front, Lane,
      1930s **150.00**
Bookcase, oak, stacking, four sections, glass
   sliding doors, drawer in base, orig paper
   labels **425.00**
Chair
   Child's, Sunday School type, rounded
      back, spindles, plank seat, worn dark
      finish **30.00**

Dining, Windsor type, painted floral dec
   and striping, worn stretchers and feet
   . . . . **90.00**
Ladderback, armchair, maple, acorn fin-
   ials, four slats, woven splint seat,
   44" h **75.00**
Chest of Drawers, mahogany, line inlaid
   drawers, two short drawers and two long
   drawers, 42" w, 38" h, 1920s . . . **275.00**
China Cabinet, oak, bow front, convex glass
   side panels, four shelves, mirrored back,
   38" w, 60" h, 1920s **575.00**
Coffee Table, kidney shaped, blue glass top,
   walnut frame **175.00**
Curio Cabinet, oak, hanging, glass door, six
   shelves, 38" h **150.00**
Desk, child's, oak, roll top, three drawers,
   matching chair **125.00**
Dining Table
   Duncan Phyfe style, mahogany, drop
      leaves, brass caps and castors, 42" w,
      1940s **225.00**
   Extension, walnut veneer, molded apron,
      six legs, U–shaped stretchers, 60" w,
      1925 . . . . **175.00**
   Pedestal, oak veneer, circular top, gar-
      goyle feet, two leaves, 1920s . **325.00**
Dry Sink, pine, shallow well, two paneled
   doors, feet missing, 36" w **350.00**
File Cabinet, oak, two drawers **85.00**
Garden Bench, cast iron, grape design,
   painted white, 42" l **300.00**
High Chair, oak, pressed back, cane seat,
   40" h **175.00**
Hoosier Style Cabinet, Sellers, pine panels,
   oak frame, tambour door, flour bin, sliding porcelain work surface, bread
   drawer, sliding cutting board, painted
   white **450.00**
Jelly Cupboard, oak, shaped crest with small
   shelf, two drawers over two paneled
   doors, two int shelves, wood pulls, small
   cast iron latch, refinished **375.00**

Cabinet, oak, refinished with green stain, 20" w, 13¹/₂" d, 32" h, $125.00.

Rocking Chair, poplar base, oak spindles, refinished with brown stain, remnants of stenciling on back splat, 24" w, 26" d, 44" h, $150.00.

Kitchen Table, black and white porcelain top, painted legs **75.00**
Library Table, Empire style, oak, pillar base, scroll feet, 48" w, 28" h, 1920s   **400.00**
Parlor Suite, sofa and two chairs, overstuffed, ball feet, floral upholstery, 1930s **250.00**
Parlor Table, oak, square top, spiral turned legs, base shelf, claw and ball feet **175.00**
Piano Bench, oak, rect top, square legs, 40" w **125.00**
Plant Stand, oak, 12" square top, cutout keyhole design in legs **90.00**
Porch Rocker, woven splint back and seat, wide arms **95.00**
Potty Chair, child's, rocking, pine, cutout carrying handle in back, arms . . . **125.00**
Rocker, oak, pressed back, minor split in seat, worn finish **150.00**
Sewing Stand, Priscilla type, painted red, dark trim, floral decal, rod carrying handle, 25" h, 1930s **28.00**
Smoking Stand, walnut veneer, brass gallery on top, figured veneer on door, base shelf, zinc lined **85.00**
Washstand, oak, floral carved back, single long drawer, three side drawers, paneled carved door, refinished **295.00**

GAMBLING COLLECTIBLES

Casino and other types of gambling are spreading across the country, just as they did over a century ago. Gaming

devices, gaming accessories, and souvenirs from gambling establishments from hotels to riverboats, are all collectible.

Gambling collectors compete with Western collectors for the same material. Sometimes the gunfight gets bloody. With the price of old, i.e., late nineteenth and early twentieth-century, gambling material skyrocketing, many new collectors are focusing on more modern material dating from the speakeasies of the 1920s to the glitz of Las Vegas in the 1950s and 1960s.

You might as well pick up modern examples when you can. Some places last only slightly longer than a throw of the dice. Atlantic City has already seen the Atlantis and Playboy disappear. Is Trump's Taj Mahal next?

Card Counter, plated, imitation ivory face, black lettering **18.00**
Card Press, 9½ × 4½ × 3", dovetailed, holds ten decks, handle **140.00**
Catalog, KC Card Co, Blue Book No. 520, Gambling Equipment, 68 pgs **40.00**
Dice
    Poker, celluloid, set of 5 . . . . **24.00**
    Weighted, always total 12, set of 3 . . . . **35.00**
Faro Cards, sq corners, Samuel Hart & Co, New York, complete **110.00**
Poker Chip
    Inlaid, four crosses **4.00**
    Ivory, scrimshawed, eagle **30.00**
    Molded Rubber, dollar **4.00**
Poker Chip Rack, 11½ × 4", revolving, wood, holds four decks of cards and 400 chips **35.00**
Roulette Ball, set of three, one metal, two composition **15.00**

Punchboard, musical, Queen of All Cats, $20.00.

Puzzle, Gambling's Gang, Thom McAn, 1932, 100 diecut cardboard pieces, double sided, Thom McAn shoes adv on reverse, 10¼ × 13", $35.00.

Roulette Wheel, wood, inlaid dec, F Denzler, Denver, CO, 31½" d . . . **75.00**
Shot Glass, ribbed dec, porcelain dice in bottom **24.00**
Slot Machine, Mills
    1¢, Q T, diamond fronted, 12½ × 18½ × 13" **550.00**
    5¢, Operators Bell, cast iron, gooseneck, orig tin strips and award card, 1915, 16 × 25 × 16½" **1,450.00**
    25¢, hightop, watermelon feature, two/ five payout, 16 × 26 × 16", 1940s **1,425.00**
Trade Stimulator, 1¢, Penny Drop, oak case, sectioned int cash drawer, 14 × 18½ × 8½" **125.00**
Wheel of Fortune
    20½" d, wood, 15 numbers, stenciled dec **30.00**
    48" d, wood, automotive midget racer motif **300.00**
    60½" d, vertical, arcade dice motif, reverse glass center with star dec, orig painted wood and iron stand, orig packing crate, 90" h stand **1,000.00**

GAMES

Many game collectors distinguish between classic games, those made between 1840 and 1940, and modern games, those dating after 1940. This is the type of snobbishness that gives collecting a bad name. In time 1990s games will be one hundred years old. I can just imagine a collector in 2090 asking dealers at a toy show for a copy of the Morton Downey "Loudmouth" game. I am one of the few who have one put aside in mint condition.

Condition is everything. Games that have been taped or have price tags stickered to the face of their covers should be avoided. Beware of games at flea markets where exposure to sunlight

Boy Scout Lotto, Spear Works, Bavaria, $35.00.

and dirt causes fading, warping, and decay.

Avoid common games, e.g., "Go to the Head of the Class," "Monopoly," and "Rook." They were produced in such vast quantities that they hold little attraction for collectors.

Most boxed board games are found in heavily used condition. Box lids have excessive wear, tears, and are warped. Pieces are missing. In this condition, most games are in the $2.00 to $10.00 range. However, the minute a game is available in fine condition or better, value jumps considerably.

Club: American Game Collectors Assoc, 49 Brooks Ave, Lewiston, ME 04240.

Newsletter: *Gamers Alliance Report,* PO Box 197, East Meadow, NY 11554.

Annie, Parker Bros, 1981 . . . . 30.00
Barbie Keys To Fame Career Game, Mattel, 1963 . . . . 40.00
Battle Cry, Milton Bradley, 1962 . . . . 30.00
Batman, Hasbro, 1978 . . . . 28.00
Beachhead Invasion Game, Built–Rite, Korean War invasion scene cov, 1950s
. . . . 65.00
Big Business, Transogram, 1936, separate board and pieces box 30.00
Bionic Woman, Parker Bros, 1976 . . . 38.00
Bugaloos, Milton Bradley, 1971, piece of tape and slight water spotting on box
. . . . 30.00
Camelot, Parker Bros, 1931, small tear in box 20.00
Chutes and Ladders, Milton Bradley, 1943, first edition 30.00
Combat, Ideal, 1963, tape and tears to box, worn pieces 32.00
Concentration, Milton Bradley, 1959, orig edition, one missing piece 55.00
Dark Shadows, Whitman, 1968 . . . . . 50.00
Dogfight, Milton Bradley, 1962 . . . . . 35.00
Dondi Potato Race Game, Hassenfeld Bros, 1950s, water stain, minor tears . . . 35.00
Dr Kildare, Ideal, 1962 . . . . 35.00
Dukes of Hazzard, Ideal, 1981 . . . . . . 10.00

Easy Money, Milton Bradley, 1936   **30.00**
Fish Pond, National Games, W Springfield, MA, 1950s 60.00
Game of Oil, Parker Bros, 1939, missing 1/5 flap 155.00
Goldfinger, Milton Bradley, 1966, corner split 45.00
Gunsmoke, Lowell, 1958 . . . . . . 45.00
Margie, Milton Bradley, 1961 . . . . . . 35.00
McHales Navy, Transogram, 1962 . . . 20.00
Men In Space, Milton Bradley, 1960 **120.00**
Mr Doodles Dog, Selchow & Righter, c1940, Junior Edition, missing pieces, no instructions 35.00
Pro Quarterback, Championship Games, 1965 . . . . 30.00
Smurf Game, Milton Bradley, 1981   **38.00**
Snagglepuss, Transogram, 1961 . . . . . 80.00
Space 1999, Milton Bradley, 1976 . . . 45.00
Stratego, Milton Bradley, 1961, good condition box, wooden pieces 55.00
Supercar To The Rescue, Milton Bradley, box and board only 55.00
Tabit, John Norton Co, 1954 . . . . 40.00
The Fall Guy, Milton Bradley, 1982 . . 22.00
Wicket the Ewok, Parker, 1983 . . . . . 16.00
Wildlife, E S Lowe, 1971 . . . . 60.00
You Don't Say, Milton Bradley, 1963, corner splits, few scattered stains, price sticker upper right corner **28.00**

GAS STATION COLLECTIBLES

Approach this from two perspectives—items associated with gas stations and gasoline company giveaways. Competition for this material is fierce. Advertising collectors want the advertising; automobile collectors want material to supplement their collections.

Beware of reproductions ranging from advertising signs to pump globes. Do not accept too much restoration and repair. There were hundreds of thousands of gasoline stations across America. Not all their back rooms have been exhausted.

Clubs: International Petroliana Collectors Assoc, PO Box 1000, Westerville, OH 43081; World Oil Can Collector's Organization, 20 Worley Rd, Marshall, NC 28753.

Periodical: *Hemmings Motor News,* Box 100, Bennington, VT 05201.

Banner, 36 × 59", Quaker Antifreeze, oilcloth, 1957 . . . . **45.00**
Display, Kanotex Oil, hanging dirigible, flexible electrical fan mounted underneath, 58" w, 12" h **600.00**
License Attachment, Tydol Man and Flying Horse **35.00**
Paperweight, Richfield Gasoline, figural, airplane engine and propellors shape, "The Gasoline of Power," 5 1/4" w, 6 1/2" h
. . . . **300.00**
Pump Globe
Atlantic Premium, red and blue glass inserts, milk glass body, hanging "Atlantic" sign, 15" d **200.00**
Blue Sunoco, blue and yellow glass inserts, metal body, blue lettering on yellow diamond, 16" d **175.00**
Ethyl, glass inserts, milk glass body, olympic runner, "Best in the Long Run," 15" d **300.00**
Lion, black and orange glass inserts, milk glass body, lion poised above lettering, 15" d **425.00**
Mobilgas Special, glass inserts, metal body, Pegasus flying above lettering, 18" d **400.00**
Mutual Gasoline, glass inserts, plastic body, running rabbit image, blue and red, 15" d **100.00**
Radio, Champion Spark Plug, figural spark plug, plastic, Japan, 5" w, 14 1/2" h
. . . . **100.00**
Sign
Conoco Gasoline, round, colonial soldier illus, 25" d **850.00**

Globe, People's Choice Supply Co, 16" d, $150.00.

City Garage, tin, woman driving auto,
"—— Miles to City Garage, Pleasant
Hill, OH, Phone 104," hand color-
ing, 12 × 36" **210.00**
Red Crown Gasoline, porcelain, red,
white, and blue, double sided, 1915
. . . . **950.00**
Valvoline, 24" d, round, green   **120.00**

GEISHA GIRL PORCELAIN

Geisha Girl porcelain is a Japanese
export ware whose production began in
the last quarter of the 19th century and
continues today. Manufacturing came to
a standstill during World War II.

Collectors have identified over 150
different patterns from over 100 manufacturers. When buying a set, check the
pattern of the pieces carefully. Dealers
will mix and match in an effort to
achieve a complete set.

Beware of reproductions that have a
very white porcelain, minimal background washes, sparse detail coloring,
no gold, or very bright gold enameling.
Some of these reproductions come from
Czechoslovakia.

Berry Set, Porch, master bowl, five individual serving bowls, scalloped edge   **40.00**
Bowl
6½" d, Flag, red, gold trim **24.00**
7½" d, Bamboo Trellis, ftd **35.00**
8" d, Ikebana in Rickshaw, yellow, ftd
. . . . **40.00**
Celery Set, Porch, rect master dish, five
matching individual salts, marked "Torii
Nippon" **35.00**
Chocolate Set, Bamboo Trellis, chocolate
pot, six cups and saucers, cobalt blue,
lattice work background **225.00**
Creamer, Long Stemmed Peony, slender,
fluted, blue and gold, marked "Made in
Japan" **10.00**

Plate, Bamboo Tree pattern, 7¼" d, $10.00.

Cup and Saucer
Bamboo Tree, marked "Made in Japan"
. . . . **8.50**
Bird Cage, floral frame int **15.00**
Kite A, brown and gold **15.00**
Egg Cup, Long Stemmed Peony, orange
. . . . **5.00**
Mustard Pot, Bamboo Trellis, blue, scal-
loped **25.00**
Plate, 6" d, Bird Cage, red–orange, gold
trim **9.00**
Salt and Pepper Shakers, pr
Ikebana in Rickshaw, grass green   **15.00**
Visiting with Baby, blue and gold   **20.00**
Teapot, Bamboo Tree **12.00**

G.I. JOE

The first G.I. Joe 12" tall poseable
action figures for boys were produced in
1964 by the Hasbro Manufacturing
Company. The original line was made up
of one male action figure for each branch
of military service. Their outfits were
styled after World War II, Korean Conflict, and Vietnam Conflict military uniforms.

In 1965 the first black figure was
introduced. The year 1967 saw two addi-
tions to the line—a female nurse and
Talking G.I. Joe. To stay abreast of the
changing times, Joe was given flocked
hair and beard in 1970.

The creation of the G.I. Joe Adventure Team made Joe the marveled explorer, hunter, deep-sea diver, and astronaut, rather than just an American
serviceman. Due to the Arab oil embargo
in 1976, the figure was reduced in size to
8" tall and was renamed the Super Joe. In
1977 production stopped.

It wasn't until 1982 that G.I. Joe
made his comeback, with a few changes
made to the character line and to the way
in which the Joe team was viewed. "The
Great American Hero" is now a
poseable 3¾" tall plastic figure with code
names corresponding to his various costumes. The new Joe must deal with both
current and futuristic villains and issues.

G. I. Joe has reached his 30th birthday—way to go Joe! Should be an exciting year for G.I. Joe collectors.

Club: G I Joe Collectors Club, 150 S
Glenoaks Blvd, Burbank, CA 91510.

Periodicals: *The Barracks: The G I Joe
Collectors Magazine,* 14 Bostwick Place,
New Milford, CT 06776; *G I Joe Patrol,*
PO Box 2362, Hot Springs, AR 71914.

Action Figure
Action Pilot, Scramble Pilot, flight suit,
complete, all accessories, painted
hair, mint **495.00**
Action Soldier Sabbotage, uniform,
boots, life raft, TNT, binoculars, wool
knit stocking cap, gas mask, signal
light, flare gun, radio, submachine
gun, oar with yellow tips, mint
. . . . **475.00**
Adventurer, Negro, #7404
Figure in orig box, MIB **275.00**
Figure only **175.00**
Air Adventurer, #7287, MIB **245.00**
Air Cadet, Parade Dress, #7822, jacket,
pants, garrison cap, dress shoes,
chest and belt sash, white M–1 rifle,
saber, scabbard, complete, all accessories, painted hair, mint **375.00**
Air Force, Dress Uniform, #7803, complete, all accessories, painted hair,
mint **295.00**
Annapolis Cadet, Parade Dress, #7624,
complete, all accessories, painted
hair, mint **375.00**
Astronaut, talking, #7915, near MIB
. . . . **675.00**
Australian Jungle Fighter, #8105, com-
plete, all accessories, mint . . . **350.00**
British Commando, #8104, complete,
all accessories, mint **395.00**
Demolition, complete, all accessories,
mint **175.00**
Eight Ropes of Danger, complete, all accessories, mint **275.00**
French Resistance, #8103, complete, all
accessories, mint **350.00**
Frogman, #7602, complete scuba outfit,
all accessories, painted hair, mint
. . . . **395.00**
German Soldier, #8100, complete, all
accessories, mint **395.00**
GI Joe, Hasbro, mark 1, 1964, no
clothes **52.00**
Green Beret, camouflage tunic, green
jacket and pants, beret with emblem,
grenades, pistol, holster, pistol belt,
radio, M–16 rifle, bazooka with
shells, complete, all accessories,
painted hair, mint **375.00**
Heavy Weapons, complete, all acces-
sories, mint **395.00**

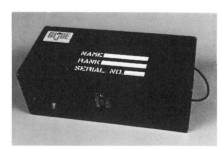

***GI Joe Foot Locker, green wood box, orig
contents, 13¼" l, 5" h, 6½" w. $75.00.***

High Voltage Escape, complete, all accessories, mint **175.00**
Japanese Imperial Soldier, #8101, complete, all accessories, mint . . . **625.00**
Land Adventurer, #7401, MIB   **225.00**
Landing Signal Officer, #7621, complete, all accessories, mint **295.00**
Man of Action, #7284, MIB **225.00**
Marine Dress Parade Set, #7710, complete, all accessories, painted hair, mint **275.00**
Marine Jungle Fighter, #7732, complete uniform, campaign hat, field telephone, knife, sheath, flame thrower, pistol belt, holster, canteen and cov, painted hair, mint **850.00**
Marine Medic, complete, all accessories, mint **375.00**
Military Police Set, #7512, brown uniform, MP arm band and helmet, duffel bag, red tunic, pistol holder and belt, tall brown boots, dog tag, painted hair, mint **375.00**
Race Car Driver, complete, all accessories, mint **195.00**
Russian Infantry Man, #8102, complete, all accessories, mint **395.00**
Sea Adventurer, #7492, MIB . . . **245.00**
Secret Agent, complete, all accessories, mint **195.00**
Shore Patrol, complete, all accessories, mint **375.00**
Ski Patrol and Mountain Troops, complete, all accessories, painted hair, mint **375.00**
Sky Dive to Danger, complete, all accessories, mint **275.00**
Tanker, complete, leather jacket, helmet with visor, emblem, radio, tripod, machine gun, ammo box, painted hair, mint **650.00**
West Point Cadet, Parade Dress, #7537, complete, all accessories, painted hair, mint **350.00**
Activity Book, unused **95.00**
Clothing and Accessories
    Air vest, orange **8.00**
    Ammo Belt, green **12.00**
    Astronaut Accessories, mint in orig bag **35.00**
    Boots
        Brown, short **20.00**
        Silver **10.00**
    Cap, sailor **10.00**
    Carbine with sling **7.00**
    Dress Outfit, complete outfit
        Medic **135.00**
        Navy, orig tie **75.00**
    Helmet, astronaut **25.00**
    Medic Bag **15.00**
    Netting Set, MOC **15.00**
    Pants
        Arctic Explorer **20.00**
        MP, tan **25.00**
    Parka, Snow Troops **20.00**

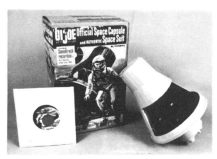

GI Joe Official Space Capsule and Authentic Space Suit, orig gray capsule, record, some accessories missing, #8020, 1966, Hasbro, gold and blue box with multicolored paper label, 10" l, 10" w, 16½" h, $125.00.

    Radio Bag Pack, green **20.00**
    Rifle, M1 . . . . **7.00**
    Shirt and pants, Sailor, work **15.00**
    Tunic
        Green Beret **25.00**
        MP **20.00**
Coloring Book, used **40.00**
Dog Tag, membership **50.00**
Duffel Bag, USN **23.00**
Figure, 3¾" h, unpackaged, near mint, orig file card
    Airborne, 1983 . . . . **15.00**
    Blowtorch, 1984 . . . . **9.00**
    Cobra Commander, 1982, mail premium **50.00**
    Doc, 1983 . . . . **15.00**
    Duke, 1984 . . . . **9.00**
    Firefly, 1984 . . . . **14.00**
    Flash, 1982 . . . . **20.00**
    Grunt, 1982 . . . . **18.00**
    Gung Ho, 1983 . . . . **14.00**
    Recondo, 1984 . . . . **9.00**
    Rock & Roll, 1982 . . . . **20.00**
    Scarlett, 1982 . . . . **35.00**
    Snake Eyes, 1982 . . . . **30.00**
    Snow Job, 1983 . . . . **15.00**
    Stalker, 1982 . . . . **20.00**
    Zap, 1982 . . . . **20.00**
Game
    GI Joe Combat Infantry, MIB **175.00**
    GI Joe Combat Navy Frogman, MIB **175.00**
    Sea Wolf Submarine, MIB **295.00**
Playing Cards, mint **95.00**
Play Set
    GI Joe Training Center, 99% complete **100.00**
    Special Training Center, Sears, MIB **300.00**
    White Tiger Hunt, MIB **195.00**
Puzzle, 221 pcs, Mural
    Scene #2, 1985 . . . . **3.00**
    Scene #2, 1988 . . . . **5.00**
    Scene #3, 1985 . . . . **3.00**
    Scene #4, 1988 . . . . **5.00**
Table Centerpiece, honeycomb, 1986, sealed **4.00**

Jigsaw Puzzle, Whitman No. 4647, 150 pieces, 8½ × 11" box, $15.00.

TV Commercial, #4, The Adventures of GI Joe Eight Ropes of Danger/Mouth of Doom, fair picture quality **30.00**
Vehicle
    APC, complete, MIB **30.00**
    Armadillo, ... **15.00**
    Buggy, 1970s **20.00**
    Cobra Hiss, complete, orig box **60.00**
    Crew Fire truck **35.00**
    Desert Patrol Jeep, MIB **900.00**
    Helicopter, includes orig accessories, 1970s **68.00**
    Mamba, complete, orig box **30.00**
    Mobile Command Vehicle, MIB   **195.00**
    Motorcycle, side car **135.00**
    Night Raven, complete, orig box   **45.00**
    Parasite, complete, MIB **15.00**
    Rattler, complete, orig box **60.00**
    Slugger, complete, orig box **35.00**
    Snow Cat, complete, MIB **20.00**
    Thunderclap, complete, MIB **25.00**
    Tomahawk **50.00**
    Water Moccasin **25.00**
    Weapon Transport **10.00**
    Zortan, complete, MIB **50.00**

GOLD

Twenty–four karat gold is pure gold. Twelve karat gold is fifty percent gold and fifty percent other elements. Many gold items have more weight value than antique or collectible value. The gold weight scale is different from our regular English pounds scale. Learn the proper conversion procedure. Review the value of an ounce of gold once a week and practice keeping that figure in your mind.

Pieces with gold wash, gold gilding, and gold bands have no weight value. Value rests in other areas. In many cases the gold is applied on the surface. Washing and handling leads to its removal.

Take time to research and learn the difference between gold and gold plating before starting your collection. This is not an area in which to speculate. How many times have you heard that an old pocket watch has to be worth a lot of money because it has a gold case? Many people cannot tell the difference between gold and gold plating. In most cases, the gold value is much less than you think.

Gold coinage is a whole other story. Every coin suspected of being gold should first be checked with a jeweler and then in coin price guides.

GOLF COLLECTIBLES

Golf was first played in Scotland in the 15th century. The game achieved popularity in the late 1840s when the "gutty" ball was introduced. Although golf was played in America before the Revolution, it gained a strong foothold in the recreational area only after 1890.

The problem with most golf collectibles is that they are common while their owners think they are rare. This is an area where homework pays, especially when trying to determine the value of clubs.

Do not limit yourself only to items used on the course. Books about golf, decorative accessories with a golf motif, and clubhouse collectibles are eagerly sought by collectors. This is a great sports collectible to tee off on.

Club: Golf Collectors' Society, PO Box 491, Shawnee Mission, KS 66201; The Golf Club Collectors Assoc, 640 E Liberty St, Girard, OH 44420.

Newsletter: *US Golf Classics & Heritage Hickories,* 5407 Pennock Point Rd, Jupiter, FL 33458.

Ashtray, metal, trophy, figural golfer **45.00**
Autograph Book, includes J C Snead, Bob Murphy, Johnny Miller, Gay Brewer, George Archer, and Gib Gilbert, some entertainer autographs included, each page dated, mid 1970s–early 1980s, 5 × 6½ **75.00**
Bag, leather, Tony Lema, 1964 British Open Champion **50.00**

Ball
  Autographed
    Arnold Palmer **45.00**
    Gary Player **40.00**
    Lee Trevino **45.00**
  Bramble Ball, The Crown **15.00**
  Chemico Bob, yellow dot **35.00**
  Gutty, Mitchell, Manchester **35.00**
Book, Barnes, James, *Guide To Good Golf* **25.00**
Bookends, pr, golfer in relief, 4 × 6" **55.00**
Cigarette Box, bronze, Art Deco, Silver Crest **130.00**
Cigarette Lighter, figural, golf bag ...**45.00**
Club
  Iron, Burke juvenile mashie, wood shaft **22.00**
  Putter, Spalding Cash–in, steel shaft **45.00**
  Wood, set of four **50.00**
Doorstop, golfer swinging club **375.00**
Figure, diecut celluloid, flat, lady golfer in backswing position, yellow cap, red sweater, green and white checkered skirt, black shoes, brown club, tube attached to back, 1930s, 3" h **35.00**
Flask, pocket, figural, golfer on green with two ladies, nickel silver, 5½ × 4" **195.00**
Game, Golf–o–matics, Royal London **18.00**
Golf Ball Pail, Billy Casper **15.00**
Locker Tag, brass, Waterbury CC **25.00**
Matchsafe, SS, golfer swinging club motif, 2½ × 1¾ × ¼" **110.00**
Noisemaker, litho tin, male golfer, smoking pipe, addressing ball, ball attached to spring rod on front and back, Germany, 1930s, 2¾" d, 6½" h **20.00**

Hand Towel, Independent Insurance adv, Youth Golf Classic, red and black lettering, white ground, cotton, Dundee, 16 × 24", $12.00.

Paperweight, glass, US Open, 1980 **25.00**
Pinback Button, "B P O E '93' Country Club Caddy, Hamilton, Ohio," sample 000 serial number, black lettering, dark red ground, 1930s, 1¾" d **10.00**
Pipe Stand, bronze golf bag with chrome clubs, wooden rack **125.00**
Plate , cobalt blue, Morgantown Glass Co, 7½" d **18.00**
Press Badge, Chicago Area Golf Tournament, 1950–60 ....**12.00**
Score Pad, celluloid cov, unused, 1900s, 2½ × 4" **15.00**
Souvenir Spoon, SS, golfer, Milford, PA **80.00**
Tablecloth Set, linen, appliqued golfers, greens, bags, and clubhouse, twelve napkins, 68 × 104" **395.00**
Tie Bar and Cuff Links Set, golfers ...**20.00**
Utensils, bar type, silver and chrome, Art Deco **125.00**

GONDER POTTERY

In 1941 Lawton Gonder established Gonder Ceramic Arts, Inc., at Zanesville, Ohio. The company is known for its glazes, such as Chinese crackle, gold crackle, and flambé. Pieces are clearly marked. Gonder manufactured lamp bases at a second plant and marketed them under the trademark "Eglee." Gonder Ceramic Arts, Inc., ceased production in 1957.

Newsletter: *Gonder Pottery Collectors' Newsletter,* PO Box 3174, Shawnee, KS 66203.

Basket, 8" w, leaf pattern, turquoise, pink coral int **25.00**
Bowl, 7" d, blue and brown, swirl ...**15.00**
Candlesticks, pr, 4¾" h, turquoise, pink coral int, marked "E-14 Gonder" **20.00**
Cornucopia, 7½" d, brown and pink, leafy, scrolled **15.00**

Mark, "Gonder E–14"

Ewer
    7½" h, bulbous, mottled maroon   **25.00**
    9" h, matte finish, green, marked
       "Gonder USA H34" **20.00**
Figurine
    Collie, 9" l, gray **15.00**
    Elephant, 10½" h, raised trunk, gray and
       rose **40.00**
    Oriental Coolie, 8" h, pink and green
       glaze **20.00**
Pitcher, 7" h, blue and wine, high pointed
    handle and spout **12.00**
Planter, 7" h, swan, shaded blue, pink int
    . . . . **14.00**
Vase
    6" h, mottled green, twisted **12.00**
    11" h, blue, petal and leaf **24.00**

GOOFUS GLASS

Goofus glass is a patterned glass where the reverse of the principal portion of the pattern is colored in red or green and covered with a metallic gold ground. It was distributed at carnivals between 1820 and 1920. There are no records of it being manufactured after that date. Among the companies who made Goofus Glass are: Crescent Glass Company, Imperial Glass Corporation, La Belle Glass Works, and Northwood Glass Company.

Value rests with pieces that have both the main color and ground color still intact. The reverse painting often wore off. It is not uncommon to find the clear pattern glass blank with no painting on it whatsoever.

Newsletter: *Goofus Glass Gazette,* 9 Lindenwood Ct, Sterling, VA 20165.

Oil Lamp, raised floral design, yellow and red flowers, green highlights, $15.00.

Ashtray, adv, red rose dec **8.50**
Bonbon, 4" d, red and green strawberry dec,
    gold ground **35.00**
Bowl
    8½" d, red floral dec, gold ground
    . . . . **20.00**
    10½" d, water lilies dec, gold ground
    . . . . **50.00**
Candy Dish, 8½" d, figure "8" design, serrated rim, dome foot **55.00**
Coaster, 3" d, red floral dec, gold ground
    . . . . **8.00**
Decanter, single red rose dec, gold basketweave type ground, emb rose stopper
    . . . . **48.00**
Dresser Tray, 6½" l, oval, red and black florals **15.00**
Jewel Box, cov, single red rose dec, gold
    ground **45.00**
Mug, Cabbage Rose, gold ground . . . **30.00**
Plate
    7¾" d, red carnations, gold ground
    . . . . **18.00**
    10¾" d, red flowers, gold ground   **12.00**
Salt Shaker, red poppy blossom, silver
    ground **35.00**
Vase, 7¼" h, purple and green grape dec,
    gold ground **25.00**

GRANITEWARE

Graniteware, also know as agateware, is the name commonly given to iron or steel kitchenware covered with an enamel coating. American production began in the 1860s and is still going on today.

White and gray are the most common colors. However, wares can be found in shades of blue, brown, cream, green, red, and violet. Mottled pieces, those combining swirls of color, are especially desirable.

For the past few years a deliberate attempt to drive prices upward has been taking place. The dealers behind it were quite successful until the 1990 recession. Never lose sight of the fact that graniteware was inexpensive utilitarian kitchen and household ware. Modern prices should reflect this humble origin.

Club: National Graniteware Society, PO Box 10013, Cedar Rapids, IA 52410.

Berry Bucket, black and white speckled, tin
    lid, bail handle **40.00**
Bucket, miniature, bail handle, gray   **30.00**
Bundt Pan, gray **15.00**
Chamber Pot
    Child's, gray, paper label **20.00**
    Covered, gray, labeled **12.00**
Coffeepot, child's, blue, missing lid   **50.00**

Teapot, 1904 St Louis Expo, robin's–egg blue, speckled, gooseneck spout, 4¾" h, $60.00.

Colander
    10½" d **45.00**
    11½" d, gray **55.00**
Cup, child's, green, cat on side **22.00**
Dipper
    Gray and White **20.00**
    Red and White **15.00**
Double Boiler, red, blue trim **45.00**
Dry Measure, light blue and white . . . **35.00**
Funnel, gray mottled **20.00**
Lunch Pail, gray, with cup **90.00**
Measure, gray, 8" h **40.00**
Milk Pan, blue and white swirl **45.00**
Muffin Pan, 8 × 15", gray **35.00**
Pie Pan, gray **20.00**
Pitcher and Bowl Set
    Blue, large **195.00**
    White, black trim **45.00**
Plate
    Blue and white swirl **15.00**
    Gray mottled **9.00**
Potty, child's, light blue **12.50**
Pudding Pan, emerald green, white specks,
    10⅝" × 7¾" **35.00**
Roaster
    Cobalt and white specks, liner, large,
       "Juicy Crisp" **25.00**
    Cream and red, large **30.00**
Skimmer, gray **28.00**
Soap Dish, blue and white swirl **25.00**
Soup Ladle, red and white **22.00**
Spittoon, blue **35.00**
Strainer Insert, 8½" d, wire bail, brown and
    white, large mottle, straight sides   **55.00**
Tube Pan, 12" d, 3¾" h, cobalt marbleized,
    white int **50.00**

GREETING CARDS

Greeting cards still fall largely under the wing of post card collectors and dealers. They deserve to be a collecting group of their own.

At the moment, high-ticket greeting cards are character–related. But someday collectors will discover Hallmark and other greeting cards as social barometers of their era. Meanwhile, enjoy picking them up for 25¢ or less.

Christmas

"A Merry Christmas," three children huddled beneath umbrella, Wolf & Co, NY **2.50**

Elvis, wearing Army uniform, 1959 .... **15.00**

Flash Gordon, 1951, unused **12.00**

Lady And The Tramp, 4 × 5½", stiff paper, beaver carrying basket of Christmas ornaments illus, Lady and Tramp and beaver dec tree int, unused, orig envelope, Gibson, 1950s **15.00**

"Merry Christmas and Happy New Year," flowers and birds, four pgs **12.00**

"My Lips May Give a Message," Kate Greenaway, girl holding letter, c1880 .... **50.00**

"With Best Christmas Wishes," Raphael Tuck and Sons, girl holding flowers, c1890 .... **15.00**

Easter

Angels, Whitney, NY, 19th C **5.00**

Floral Cross, Germany, 19th C **5.50**

Religious, floral, Tuck **12.00**

Get Well

Amos 'n' Andy, 4½ × 5½", black and white photo, Hall Bros, 1951 **30.00**

Mickey Mouse, 4 × 5", pale pink, three black images, unused, Hall Brothers Inc, 1930s **25.00**

Greetings, children's heads in flowerpot, 19th C **3.00**

Happy Birthday

Amos 'n' Andy, brown portraits, message includes song title "Check and Double Check," inked birthday note, Rust Craft **20.00**

Dagwood, 5 × 6", Hallmark, 1939 .... **15.00**

Hopalong Cassidy, 6½ × 7½", diecut, inscribed "Shoot The Works! It's Your Birthday!," slot holds diecut pistol, Buzza Cardozo, early 1950s **40.00**

Snow White and the Seven Dwarfs, c1938 .... **40.00**

Space Patrol Man, 5" sq, full color, diecut, small green transparent helmet, orig envelope **20.00**

Mother's Day, Cracker Jack, diecut, full color, puppy, c1940 .... **40.00**

New Year, girl holding bird, palm tree, 19th C **4.50**

Thanksgiving Day, "Happy Thanksgiving," turkey, illus, mid 20th **5.00**

Valentine's Day

Fold–out, heart with girls head center, flowers with lace dec, 1940 **15.00**

Mechanical, winter scene with boy on skis, verse **25.00**

HALL CHINA

In 1903 Robert Hall founded the Hall China Company in East Liverpool, Ohio. Upon his death in 1904, Robert T. Hall, his son, succeeded him. Hall produced a large selection of kitchenware and dinnerware in a wide variety of patterns, as well as refrigerator sets. The company was a major supplier of institutional (hotel and restaurant) ware.

Hall also manufactured some patterns on an exclusive basis: Autumn Leaf for Jewel Tea, Blue Bouquet for the Standard Coffee Company of New Orleans, and Red Poppy for the Grand Union Tea Company. Hall teapots are a favorite among teapot collectors.

For the past several years, Hall has been reissuing a number of its solid-color pieces as an "Americana" line. Items featuring a decal or gold decoration have not been reproduced. Because of the difficulty in distinguishing old from new solid color pieces, prices on many older pieces have dropped.

Periodical: *The Hall China Encore,* 317 N Pleasant St, Oberlin, OH 44074.

Blue Blossom, teapot, cov
Morning **295.00**
Streamline **395.00**
Monticello
Cup and Saucer **6.00**
Soup, flat, 8" d **10.00**
Vegetable, cov **45.00**
Peach Blossom
Bowl
5¾" d, berry **8.00**
6" d, cereal **12.00**
9" d, soup **17.00**
12" d **28.00**

Casserole, cov, 10" d **65.00**
Creamer **15.00**
Cup and Saucer **15.00**
Gravy, no ladle **40.00**
Plate, 6" d **3.00**
Platter, 15" l **40.00**
Pinecone, E style
Bowl, 5¼" d, berry **6.00**
Cup and Saucer **9.00**
Plate, 9¼" d **9.00**
Poppy and Wheat
Casserole, 5 band **90.00**
Jug
#5, cov **125.00**
#6, open **60.00**
Refrigerator, sq, Radiance **125.00**
Red Poppy
Bowl
5½" d, berry **5.00**
6" d, cereal **15.00**
Casserole, cov **28.00**
Cup **9.00**
Pie Baker **38.00**
Plate
7¼" d, salad **15.00**
9" d, lunch **10.00**
Salt and Pepper Shakers, pr
Range **25.00**
Small, teardrop **28.00**
Soup, flat, 8½" d **15.00**
Sugar, open **33.00**
Teapot, cov, infusor, Aladdin ... **135.00**
Rose Parade
Bowl, salad **22.00**
Creamer, Pert, 5" h **15.00**
Shaker **10.00**
Springtime
Bowl, 5½" d, berry **4.00**
Cup and Saucer **9.00**
Gravy **30.00**
Plate
6" d **3.00**
7¼" d **9.00**
9" d **9.00**
Soup, flat, 8½" d **12.50**
Sugar, open **13.00**
Taverne, pretzel jar **85.00**

Christmas Wishes, US Army Air Corps, printed color cov, satin ribbon dec, 1940s, 5 × 5¾", $15.00.

Silhouette, pitcher, cream ground, silver gilding, two marks, 7" h, $30.00.

Wildfire
  Bowl, 6" d, cereal **15.00**
  Casserole, cov, tab handle **35.00**
  Cup and Saucer **13.00**
  Plate
    7¼" d **11.00**
    9" d **12.00**
  Salt Shaker, range **16.00**
  Soup, flat, 8½" d **17.00**
  Vegetable, oval **33.00**

HARDWARE

The first thing one should realize about computer systems... Wait!...Stop...! Sorry, wrong kind of hardware. Here we're talking about architectural and carpentry hardware. Any self–respecting flea market will have an abundance of assorted items capable of pleasing any collector.

Club: The Antique Doorknob Collectors of America, PO Box 126, Eola, IL 60519.

Barn Hinges, 32" l, pr **50.00**
Carriage Step, cast iron, c1870 . . . . . **22.50**
Carriage Trim, cast iron, 1800s **22.50**
Door Bell, brass, spheres hanging from
  metal netting, mounting bracket **85.00**
Door Knob, faceted crystal, 2½" d, brass
  hardware **2.00**
Door Knocker
  Basket of Flowers, 3¾" l, cast iron, orig
    polychrome paint **30.00**
  Dog's Head, figural, 7" h, brass **65.00**
  Eagle, figural, brass **55.00**
  English Setter, 4 × 5", bronzed metal
    . . . . **20.00**

Doorknocker, cast iron, parrot, painted green and yellow, $55.00.

Fox's Head, figural, 5½" h, cast iron,
  ring hanging from mouth **85.00**
Lion's Head, figural, bronze, ring hang-
  ing from mouth **50.00**
Ram's Head, cast iron, England **65.00**
Door Latch, butterfly shaped, iron . . . **75.00**
Flagpole Finial, 7" w, spread wing eagle,
  brass **25.00**
Garden Stake, 30" h, sunburst and scrolls,
  wrought iron **250.00**
Hook, cast iron, ornate **12.00**
Lock, 4 × 6", iron, turn handle with key,
  c1840 . . . . **100.00**
Padlock, wrought iron, key and fastening
  spikes **75.00**
Shelf Brackets, pr, 5½" h, iron, swivel
  . . . . **18.00**
Shutter Dogs, 8½" l, cast iron, marked "Bre-
  vete SGDG" with anchor, set of four
  . . . . **150.00**
Snowbirds, pr, 5¼" h, eagles, figural, cast
  iron **125.00**
Wall Spike, cast iron, ornate **18.00**
Window Pulley, cast iron, emb "M W &
  Co, New Haven," 1880s **25.00**

HARKER POTTERY

In 1840 Benjamin Harker of East Liverpool, Ohio, built a kiln and produced yellow ware products. During the Civil War, David Boyce managed the firm. Harker and Boyce played important roles in the management of the firm through much of its history. In 1931 the company moved to Chester, West Virginia. Eventually Jeannette Glass Company purchased Harker, closing the plant in March 1972.

Much of Harker's wares were utilitarian. The company introduced Cameoware in 1945 and a Rockingham ware line in 1960. A wide range of backstamps and names were used.

Cameo, plate, blue and white, bear and balloon, 7¾" d, $6.00.

Newspaper: *The Daze,* PO Box 57, Otisville, MI 48463.

Cameoware
  Bowl, berry **3.50**
  Casserole, cov **15.00**
  Cup and Saucer **9.00**
  Plate, 10" d, dinner **10.00**
  Salt and Pepper Shakers, pr, Skyscraper
    . . . . **15.00**
Colonial Lady
  Cereal Bowl **10.00**
  Cup and Saucer **12.00**
  Fork **25.00**
  Plate, 7" d, salad **6.00**
  Spoon **25.00**
  Vegetable Bowl **22.00**
Mallow
  Bowl, 5" d **15.00**
  Lifter **25.00**
  Plate, 8" d, luncheon **10.00**
  Spoon **25.00**
Pastel Tulip, lifter **25.00**
Pinecone
  Cake Set, plate and server **20.00**
  Tidbit Tray, 2 tier **20.00**
Red Apple
  Mixing Bowl, 10" d **30.00**
  Pie Server **20.00**
  Utility Plate **20.00**
  Vegetable Bowl, 9" d **28.00**

HATPINS AND HATPIN HOLDERS

Hatpins were used by women to hold on their hats. Since a woman was likely to own many and they were rather large, special holders were developed for them. Hatpins became a fashion accessory in themselves. The ends were decorated in a wide variety of materials ranging from gemstones to china.

Clubs: American Hatpin Society, 28227 Paseo El Siena, Laguna Niguel, CA 92677; International Club for Collectors of Hatpins and Hatpin Holders, 15237 Chanera Ave, Gardena, CA 90249.

HOLDERS
Bavarian, mother–of–pearl dec, marked "H
  & C Bavaria" **65.00**
Hand Painted China
  1½" h, floral dec, artist sgd, Austria
    . . . . **75.00**
  7" h, Bavaria **95.00**
Nippon, 5" h, relief serpent dec, mottled
  ground **165.00**
Royal Bayreuth, courting couple, cutout
  base with gold dec, blue mark **395.00**
Royal Rudolstadt, lavender and roses dec
  . . . . **25.00**
Schafer & Vater, 5" h, Jasperware medallion,
  woman's profile **125.00**

Schlegelmilch
    RS Germany, 4½" h, poppy pattern
    .... **110.00**
    RS Prussia, floral and scroll dec, gold accents, ftd **170.00**

PINS
Advertising, 10" l, Economy Stoves and
    Ranges **45.00**
Art Deco, 8½" l, brass, knob design   **95.00**
Art Nouveau
    8" l, silver tone head, female profile
    .... **110.00**
    12" l, SS, four sided **85.00**
Bakelite, black fluted disc, rhinestone dec,
    silver accents **35.00**
Black Glass, 8" l, faceted ball, painted top
    .... **25.00**
Carnival Glass, figural, rooster, amber
    .... **35.00**
Ivory, ball shape, carved dec **65.00**
Kewpie **50.00**
Mother-of-Pearl, snake motif, ruby head,
    gold top, USA **175.00**
Peking Glass, ¾" oval head, roses and gold
    dec, turquoise background **135.00**
Porcelain, scenic design, ornate mounting
    .... **35.00**
Rhinestone, figural, butterfly, blue body
    .... **30.00**
Silver Filigree, 12" l, lotus blossom   **23.00**
St Louis World's Fair, 1904, enamel dec
    .... **30.00**
Tortoise Shell, 1¼" l, pear shape, ribboned
    pique work **120.00**

HATS AND CAPS

No clothing accessory, except jewelry, mirrors changing fashion tastes better than a hat. Hats also express our individuality. How else do you explain some of the hats that grace people's heads? Hang twenty on a wall as decoration for a surefire conversation piece.

Formal hats are fine. Want some real fun? Start a collection of advertising baseball-style caps. The source is endless—from truck stops to farm equipment dealers. Why, you can even collect baseball team hats. New, they cost between $5.00 and $20.00. At flea markets you can acquire them for a couple of dollars each.

Baby Bonnet, Victorian, white **38.00**
Baseball Cap, San Francisco Giants,
    ballpark giveaway, 1980 .... **5.00**
Boudoir Cap, crocheted, pink rosettes **12.00**
Campaign, 11 × 13 × 3½", plastic,
    molded, white, red, and blue paper
    band brim, "Kennedy For President"
    .... **50.00**
Cloche, velvet, brown **15.00**

Coonskin Cap, 6 × 9", Davy Crockett,
    brown and black, marked "Davy
    Crockett/Made With New Fur," orig tag,
    1950s **75.00**
Crew Cap, canvas, white, blue, and orange
    panels, front panel with Trylon, ship's
    tiller wheel, and sea gull illus above
    "New York World's Fair 1939" inscription, adult size **40.00**
Derby, black **18.00**
Hat
    Felt, Gabby Hayes, black, upturned brim
        with white lettering, 1950s ... **75.00**
    Heavy Paper, Statue of Liberty, red,
        white, and blue, c1918 ...... **20.00**
    Silk, black, large brim, ribbons, flowers,
        and chartreuse feather trim ... **65.00**
    Velvet, black, MIB, 1939 .... **28.00**
Hopalong Cassidy Cap, fabric, small bill,
    blue, white center panel with red, blue,
    and yellow Hoppy illus, white top button and piping, lined **60.00**
Motorcycle Cap
    Boy's, embroidered blue wheel dec
        .... **15.00**
    Harley Davidson, canvas, white, orange,
        black, and white patch, late 1930s
        .... **100.00**
Pillbox
    Leopard Skin, matching purse ... **100.00**
    Satin, black, netting **18.00**
Railroad
    Agent, Boston & Maine, gold finish,
        curved top **38.00**
    Conductor, LIRR **25.00**
Sombrero, Cisco Kid, 15" d, 5" h, felt,
    green, white piping, wood slide on
    green and white cord, large **45.00**
Straw
    Boater's, 1930s **35.00**
    Lady's, finely woven, worn silk lining
        .... **135.00**
Visor, Toronto Blue Jays, ballpark giveaway,
    1982 .... **5.00**

HEISEY GLASS

A. H. Heisey Company of Newark, Ohio, began operations in 1896. Within a short period of time, it was one of the major suppliers of glass to middle America. Its many blown and molded patterns were produced in crystal, colored, milk (opalescent), and Ivorina Verde (custard). Pieces also featured cutting, etching, and silver deposit decoration. Glass figurines were made between 1933 and 1957.

Not all Heisey glass is marked. Marked pieces have an "H" within a diamond. However, I have seen some non-Heisey pieces with this same marking at several flea markets.

The key to Heisey glass is to identify

the pattern. Neila Brederhoft's *The Collector's Encyclopedia of Heisey Glass, 1925–1938* (Collector Books: 1986) is helpful for early material. The best help for post–World War II patterns are old Heisey catalogs.

Club: Heisey Collectors of America, 169 W Church St, Newark, OH 43055.

Newsletters: *The Heisey News,* 169 W Church St, Newark, OH 43055; *The Newscaster,* PO Box 102, Plymouth, OH 44865.

Ashtray, Orchid, sq **30.00**
Basket, Crystolite **170.00**
Bookends, pr, fish **165.00**
Bowl
    Lariat, 12" d **25.00**
    Provincial, crystal, 12" d, rolled edge
        .... **35.00**
Box, 7" d, Crystolite, brass lid with glass lily
    .... **75.00**
Candlesticks, pr, Crystolite, crystal, sq base
    .... **50.00**
Champagne, Colonial, crystal **10.00**
Cheese Compote, Crystolite, crystal   **24.00**
Coaster, Colonial, crystal **10.00**
Cocktail, Arcadia, crystal **16.00**
Cocktail Shaker, Rooster, 3 pcs **130.00**
Compote, Old Sandwich, green, 6" d **80.00**
Creamer and Sugar, Lariat, crystal ... **18.00**
Creamer, individual, Crystolite, crystal
    .... **10.00**
Cruet, orig stopper
    Pleat and Panel, green **75.00**
    Ridgeleigh, crystal **50.00**
Custard, Colonial, crystal **5.00**
Finger Bowl, Colonial, crystal **12.00**
Goblet
    Arcadia, crystal **18.00**
    Colonial, 7 oz **25.00**
Iced Tea Tumbler, Orchid Etch, crystal
    .... **50.00**
Juice Tumbler, Provincial, crystal **12.00**
Mayonnaise, Waverly, crystal, orchid foot
    .... **85.00**
Mustard, cov, Colonial, crystal **40.00**
Nappy, Provincial, crystal **15.00**
Plate
    Colonial, crystal, 4½" d **8.00**
    Old Colony, Sahara, 8½" sq **25.00**
    Provincial, crystal, 7" d **9.00**
Relish, Crystolite, crystal, round, 5 parts
    .... **40.00**
Sherbet
    Arcadia, crystal **12.00**
    Orchid Etch, crystal **30.00**
Sherry, Colonial, crystal **10.00**
Sugar, cov, individual, Crystolite, crystal
    .... **12.00**
Torte Plate
    Crystolite, crystal, 13½" d **30.00**
    Waverly, crystal **24.00**
Tumbler, New Era, crystal **24.00**

HEISEY GLASS ANIMALS

Heisey produced glass animals between 1937 and 1957. It is difficult to date an animal because many remained in production for decades.

Although the animal line was introduced in 1937, some forms made in the 1920s featured animal motifs, e.g., dolphin–footed and dolphin finial articles and a lion's-head bowl with paw feet, marketed under the pattern name Empress, later Queen Anne. Other examples are the kingfisher and duck flower frogs. Collectors believe the dolphin candlestick was made from molds obtained from the Sandwich Glass Company.

Royal Hickman and Horace King were two of the Heisey employees who were involved in the design of the animal figures. Many of King's designs resulted in animal-head stoppers.

The most commonly found color is crystal. The price listings here are for crystal unless otherwise noted. Many other colors were used. In order of rarity, these colors are Tangerine, Vaseline, Cobalt, Alexandrite, Amber, Limelight, Dawn, Marigold, Moongleam, Sahara, and Flamingo.

One final note: Collecting Heisey animal figures is not for those with a limited pocketbook. As you can see from the prices listed in this section, they are on the expensive side.

Club: Heisey Collectors of America, 169 W Church St, Newark, OH 43055.

Chick, head down **70.00**
Cygnet, black **60.00**
Donkey **250.00**
Duckling, floating **150.00**
Elephant **350.00**
Fish, green, bookend **100.00**
Giraffe, amber **400.00**
Goose, wings up **90.00**
Hen, yellow **125.00**
Horse
    Clydesdale **350.00**
    Colt
        Balking **175.00**
        Standing **80.00**
    Filly, head backward **1,200.00**
Mallard, amber **200.00**
Piglets, pr, ruby **80.00**
Rabbit, head down **175.00**
Rooster **350.00**
Sow, ruby **250.00**
Tiger, jade **80.00**

HOLIDAY COLLECTIBLES

Holidays play an important part in American life. Besides providing a break from work, they allow time for patriotism, religious renewal, and fun. Because of America's size and ethnic diversity, there are many holiday events of a regional nature. Attend some of them and pick up their collectibles. I have started a Fastnacht Day collection.

This listing is confined to national holidays. If I included special days, from Secretary's Day to Public Speaker's Day, I would fill this book with holiday collectibles alone. Besides, in fifty years is anyone going to care about Public Speaker's Day? No one does now.

Newsletter: *Trick or Treat Trader*, PO Box 499, Winchester, NH 03470.

Club: National Valentine Collectors Assoc, PO Box 1404, Santa Ana, CA 92702.

FOURTH OF JULY

Bottle Opener, Uncle Sam, cast iron, painted, early 20th C **35.00**
Candy Box, $2^1/_4 \times 2^1/_2''$, shield shape, red, white, and blue **10.00**
Flag, 10" h, 48 stars, wood stick **2.00**
Menu, $6^1/_2 \times 9^1/_2''$, Hotel Edgemere, Asbury Park, NJ, full color cov, 1909 . . . . **25.00**
Pinback Button
    July 4th, multicolored Miss Liberty, 1906–07 . . . . **30.00**
    Safe and Sane 4th of July, multicolored, red lettering **25.00**
Post Card, "4th of July Greeting," red, white, and blue, gold ground, Germany, 1910 . . . . **2.00**

HALLOWEEN

Bank, tin, skeleton, lying in coffin, Japan, mid 20th C **45.00**
Candy Container, papier–mache, cone shaped, West Germany
    Devil, 7" h **28.00**
    Witch, $7^1/_2''$ h **26.00**

Halloween, jack–o–lantern, pressed paper, orange, black and white eyes, c1950, $4^1/_2''$ h, $40.00.

Centerpiece, cat, 12" h **15.00**
Costume
    Clown, homemade, baggy, yellow and black, trimmed in bells, matching pointed clown hat with bells, 1940s **8.00**
    Wicked Witch, Wizard of Oz, orig box **50.00**
Diecut, 14" h, copyright H E Lehrs, cat on moon **35.00**
Jack–O–Lantern
    Glass Globe, tin base, bail handle, battery operated **45.00**
    Papier–Mache, gruesome features, 1930–40 . . . . **50.00**
Lantern, 7" h, papier–mache, devil head, two–tone red, paper insert behind cutout eyes and mouth, wire bail handle, Germany **100.00**
Mask
    Clown, papier–mache, painted features, early 20th C **35.00**
    Pirate, papier–mache, string ties, marked "Germany" **10.00**
Noisemaker, 3" d, rattle, round, tin, wooden handle, orange, white, and green, pumpkin and cats litho, USA **7.50**
Post Card, "Halloween Greetings," woman bobbing for apples, jack–o'–lantern border, E C Banks, 1909 . . . . **12.00**

Halloween, sign, White Castle Halloween Castle Meal, Pez premiums, $25.00.

Trick or Treat Bag, paper, litho pumpkin head and "Happy Halloween," 1940 .... **18.00**

NEW YEAR'S DAY

Banner, "Happy New Year," paper, silver border, 1930 .... **10.00**
Hat, headband type, silver, plume in center, glitter dec, 1920 .... **10.00**
Noisemaker, litho tin, wood handle, Kirchhof **20.00**

PRESIDENT'S DAY

Bank, Abraham Lincoln, glass, bottle shape, tin closure **25.00**
Candy Container, stump, 3" h, George Washington, papier–mache, surrounded by cherries, marked "Germany"   **45.00**
Diecut, 2½" h, George Washington, three different scenes, set of 3 .... **8.00**
Post Card
 Lincoln Centennial Souvenir, Lincoln's Birthday Series 1, emb, gilt highlights, 1908 copyright **6.00**
 "Three Cheers for George Washington," children waving flag beneath Washington's portrait, 1909 .... **1.75**
 "Washington The Father of His Country," 1912 .... **2.00**

ST PATRICK'S DAY

Candy Container, 4½" h, Irish girl holding harp, standing on box, marked "Germany" **32.00**
Diecut, 3" h, gold harp entwined with shamrocks and green ribbon, marked "Germany" **1.50**
Nut Cup, crepe paper, green and white, double frill, cardboard shamrock   **5.00**
Pin, shamrock shape, emb tin, silver luster, early 1900s **20.00**
Pinback Button, green shamrock with red, white, and blue American flag, 1930s **15.00**
Place Card, name tag and leprechaun with pot of gold dec **5.00**
Post Card
 "Ireland Forever," shamrock with view of Ireland in each leaf, marked "Germany" **1.00**
 "To My Little Colleen," girl dressed in green, large shamrock for hair bow, marked "London" **1.50**
Sheet Music, *When Irish Eyes Are Smiling,* 1930s **10.00**

THANKSGIVING

Apron, "Happy Thanksgiving," fabric, leaf border **5.00**
Candy Container, papier–mache, Germany
 Hen Turkey
  4½" h **12.00**
  6¾" h **35.00**
 Tom Turkey
  2¾" h **12.00**
  7¼" h **40.00**

Chocolate Mold, 8" h, turkey, Germany **30.00**
Figure, 4" h
 Pilgrim Couple, composition, man and woman, marked "Germany" **45.00**
 Turkey, celluloid, white, pink, and blue, weighted bottom, marked "Irwin, USA" **25.00**
Platter, 10½" l, multicolored transfer scene, Johnson Brothers, England **50.00**
Post Card
 "A Thanksgiving Greeting," large harvest pumpkin in background, three turkeys eating from dish outside a home, 1910 .... **1.00**
 "Thanksgiving Greetings," children playing with turkeys, 1909 .... **2.50**
 "With Thanksgiving Greeting," turkey and maiden, John Winsch, copyright 1911 .... **25.00**
Salt and Pepper Shakers, pr, pottery, turkey, brown and red, mid 20th C **10.00**

VALENTINE'S DAY

Candy Box, 3½" l, heart shape, red   **14.00**
Chocolate Mold, aluminum, heart shape, emb "Happy Valentine's Day," 1940 .... **10.00**
Greeting Card
 "Best Wishes," folding, shades of blue, picture of bird in center, poem beneath, no greeting inside, 4½" h **5.00**
 "To My Sweetheart," folding, small girl in green dress and hat, red wild rose border, verse inside, 6½" h ... **10.00**
 "To My Sweetheart," stand–up, white dog, envelope in mouth, 6" h, marked "Germany" **3.50**

Valentine's Day, puzzle, A Valentine For You, Hallmark Cards, 1940s, 29 diecut cardboard pieces, figural pieces, 4 × 3" cloth mailing sack, 6½ × 5¼", $30.00.

Post Card
 Cupid on swing of roses, bordered by red hearts and gold scroll work, small verse, marked "E Nash"   **1.25**
 "February 14th," trimmed in green ivy, cupids shooting hearts and arrows at two lovers, enclosed in heart, marked "Germany, 1910" **1.50**
 Hearts with arrows, cupid, and flowers, early 20th C **10.00**
 "To My Dear Valentine," monk child with wings **8.00**
Sheet Music, *My Funny Valentine* **4.00**

HOMER LAUGHLIN CHINA COMPANY

Homer Laughlin and his brother, Shakespeare, built two pottery kilns in East Liverpool, Ohio, in 1871. Laughlin became one of the first firms to produce American-made whiteware.

In 1896, William Wills and a Pittsburgh group led by Marcus Aaron bought the Laughlin firm. New plants were built in Laughlin Station, Ohio, and Newell, West Virginia. Plant advances included continuous tunnel kilns, spray glazing, and mechanical jiggering.

The original trademark used from 1871 to 1890 merely identified the products as "Laughlin Brothers." The next trademark featured the American eagle astride the prostrate British lion. The third mark featured a monogram of "HLC" which has appeared, with slight variations, on all dinnerware produced since about 1900. The 1900 trademark contained a number which identified month, year, and plant at which the product was made. Letter codes were used in later periods.

Prices for Homer Laughlin china (with the possible exception of Virginia Rose) are still moderate. Some of the patterns from the 1930 to 1940 period have contemporary designs that are highly artistic.

Newspaper: *The Daze,* 10271 State Rd., PO Box 57, Otisville, MI 48463.

REPRODUCTION ALERT. Harlequin and Fiesta lines were reissued in 1978 and marked accordingly.
See: Fiesta

Amberstone
 Berry Bowl **3.50**
 Creamer **4.50**
 Plate
  Bread and Butter **1.50**
  Dinner **5.00**

Conchita
    Cake Plate, Kitchen Kraft **55.00**
    Cake Server, Kitchen Kraft **95.00**
    Casserole, Kitchen Kraft **125.00**
Epicure
    Gravy **20.00**
    Ladle, white **18.00**
    Plate
        6½" d **8.00**
        10" d **14.00**
    Saucer **4.00**
Harlequin
    Ashtray, spruce **50.00**
    Ball Jug
        Forest Green **110.00**
        Maroon **55.00**
        Turquoise **40.00**
    Bowl, 9" d, spruce **25.00**
    Casserole, oval, maroon **30.00**
    Cereal, forest **15.00**
    Creamer
        Mauve **10.00**
        Red, novelty **30.00**
    Cream Soup, turquoise **10.00**
    Egg cup, double
        Forest Green **17.00**
        Maroon **22.00**
    Gravy
        Rose **18.00**
        Yellow **15.00**
    Marmalade, mauve **225.00**
    Oatmeal Bowl
        Forest Green **18.00**
        Gray **20.00**
        Medium Green **25.00**
    Platter, oval
        Large, maroon **40.00**
        Small, yellow **15.00**
    Relish, 5 part, multicolor **210.00**
    Salad, individual, maroon **45.00**
    Salt and Pepper Shakers, pr, gray   **20.00**
    Saucer, after dinner, red **20.00**
    Sugar, cov, mauve **15.00**
    Syrup, cov, red **175.00**
    Tea Cup
        Chartreuse **6.00**
        Dark Green **6.00**
        Red **6.00**
        Spruce **6.00**
        Turquoise **5.00**
        Yellow **5.00**
    Teapot, mauve **60.00**
    Teapot Lid
        Gray **50.00**
        Turquoise **40.00**
    Tumbler
        Maroon **45.00**
        Mauve **35.00**
        Red **38.00**
Mexicana
    Berry Bowl **12.00**
    Casserole
        Individual, Kitchen Kraft **125.00**
        Large **175.00**
    Creamer **22.00**
    Cup and Saucer **18.00**

Virginia Rose, berry dish, marked "33N8," $2.00.

    Gravy Boat **35.00**
    Jar, cov, large, Kitchen Kraft **275.00**
    Nappy **25.00**
    Pie Baker **35.00**
    Plate
        Bread and butter **9.00**
        Deep **22.00**
        7" d **18.00**
        9" d **18.00**
        10" d **45.00**
    Platter
        11½" l **35.00**
        13" l **65.00**
        15" l **95.00**
    Soup, lug handle **75.00**
    Sugar, cov **35.00**
Priscilla Eggshell, Nautilus shape, 67 pc ser-
    vice for eight, 11 serving pcs including
    teapot, Kitchen Kraft water jug, and
    Kitchen Kraft coffeepot, like new   **345.00**
Rhythm, teapot, yellow **45.00**
Riviera
    Batter Jug, open
        Mauve **95.00**
        Yellow **75.00**
    Berry Bowl, 5" d, yellow **8.00**
    Butter Dish, ¼ lb, turquoise **345.00**
    Casserole, cov
        Blue **60.00**
        Ivory **125.00**
    Dinner Service, 20 pc set, red, yellow,
        green, mauve, four each cups and
        saucers, 4½" bowls, 7" plates, and 9"
        plates, orig box **170.00**
    Pitcher, juice, yellow **185.00**
    Plate, 6" d, bread and butter, yellow
        . . . . **6.00**
    Salt and Pepper Shakers, pr, ivory
        . . . . **20.00**
    Saucer, green **2.00**
    Teapot, ivory **180.00**
    Tumbler, juice
        Green **95.00**
        Mauve **85.00**
        Turquoise **95.00**
Serenade, teapot, blue **110.00**

HORSE COLLECTIBLES

This is one of those collectible categories where you can collect the real thing, riding equipment ranging from bridles to wagons, and/or representational items. It is also a category where the predominant number of collectors are women.

The figurine is the most favored collectible. However, horse–related items can be found in almost every collectible category from Western movie posters to souvenir spoons. As long as there is a horse on it, it is collectible.

A neglected area among collectors is the rodeo. I am amazed at how much rodeo material I find at East Coast flea markets. I never realized how big the eastern rodeo circuit was.

Periodical: *Just About Horses,* 34 Owens Dr, Wayne, NJ 07470.

Ashtray, figural, horse head, White Horse
    Whiskey adv, white china, painted
    . . . . **10.00**
Bank, 4" h, cast iron, figural, emb "Beauty"
    on one side, painted black, Arcade,
    early 1900s **80.00**
Belt Buckle, Roy Rogers and Trigger   **35.00**
Bookends, pr, aluminum, square, emb horse
    head, sgd "Bruce Cox" **100.00**
Bridle, braided leather strips, 1930s   **45.00**
Brush, leather back, stamped "US," patent
    date 1860s, Herbert Brush Mfg . . . **60.00**
Christmas Ornament, hobby horse, Dresden
    . . . . **80.00**
Cigarette Lighter, Dale Evans, horse head
    . . . . **15.00**
Comb, mane and tail, marked "Oliver Slant
    Tooth," 1940s **15.00**
Decanter, Appaloosa, Jim Beam, Regal
    China, 1974 . . . . **25.00**

Plate, Royal Doulton, gold glaze, 1907, 9¾" d, $45.00.

Doorstop, 5" l, cast iron, horse figure,
 Hubley **175.00**
Figure, horse jumping fence, Breyer   **45.00**
Game, Derby Day, board folds out to 72",
 six wooden horses and hurdles, Parker
 Brothers, copyright 1959 . . . . **40.00**
Horseshoe, Hopalong Cassidy, "Good
 Luck," orig insert card, 1950 . . . . **20.00**
Lunch Box, Trigger **45.00**
Medal, Ohio horseshoer's, ribbon, 1917
 . . . . **57.50**
Photo, rancher on horse, mountain scene
 . . . . **15.00**
Pinback Button
 Horse portrait, black and white, blue
  ground, white border, c1940 . . . **8.00**
 Rochester, NH Fair, triple horse head
  illus, black and white, 1909
  . . . . **30.00**
 Souvenir of Rodeo, "Let 'er Buck,"
  1¼" d, bucking bronco illus, red and
  black, white ground, 1930s **5.00**
Pincushion, metal, horseshoe shape   **10.00**
Saddle, Rocky Mountain cross–tree type,
 pack saddle, weathered wood supports
 . . . . **75.00**
Saddle Ring, SS **35.00**
Souvenir Spoon, Cheyenne, WY, bucking
 horse, SS **22.00**
Stirrup, wood, rounded bottom, worn lea-
 ther cover **15.00**
Toy
 Pull, 16" h, horsehair mane and tail,
  glass eyes, wood base, red wood
  wheels, late 19th C **600.00**
 Stuffed, mule, collar inscription "One of
  the Twenty Mule Team," Borax pro-
  motion, 1980s **15.00**
 Windup, tin, Lone Ranger on rearing
  horse **95.00**
Tray, horseback riders and roadster scene,
 Coca–Cola adv **35.00**
Wagon Seat, leather cov, springs and steel
 frame **150.00**

HORSE RACING COLLECTIBLES

The history of horse racing dates
back to the domestication of the horse
itself. Prehistoric cave drawings show
horse racing. The Greeks engaged in
chariot racing as early as 600 B.C. As
civilization spread, so did the racing of
horses. Each ethnic group and culture
added its own unique slant.

The British developed the concept
of the thoroughbreds, a group of horses
that are descendants of three great Arabian stallions: Carley Arabian, Byerley
Turk, and Goldolphin Arabian. Receiv-
ing royal sponsorship, horse racing became the Sport of Kings.

Horse racing reached America dur-

ing the colonial period. By the 1800s
four-mile match races between regional
champions were common. In 1863 Saratoga Race Track was built. The first
Belmont Stakes was run at Jerome Park in
1867. As the nineteenth century ended
over 300 race tracks operated a seasonal
card. By 1908, society's strong reaction
against gambling reduced the number of
American race tracks to twenty–five.

Of course, the premier American
horse race is the Kentucky Derby. Programs date from 1924 and glasses, a favorite with collectors, from the late
1930s.

There are so many horse racing collectibles that one needs to specialize
from the beginning. Collector focuses include a particular horse racing type or a
specific horse race, a breed or specific
horse, or racing prints and images. Each
year there are a number of specialized
auctions devoted to horse racing, ranging from sporting prints sales at the major
New York auction houses to benefit auctions for the Thoroughbred Retirement
Foundation.

Periodicals: *Collectors World,* NATEX
Publishing, PO Box 562029, Charlotte,
NC 28256; *Racing Collectibles Price
Guide,* SportsStars Inc, PO Box 608114,
Orlando, FL 32860.

Beer Sign, standup, Lucky Debonair portrait,
 1965 Kentucky Derby winner, glossy paper over laminated cardboard, Rolling
 Rock Beer, 11 × 14" **25.00**
Disk, Prince Alert, celluloid, two sided,
 black and white, engraving style portrait
 on front, back with text for 1901 Allentown Fair, 1¾" d **30.00**
Game, Kentucky Derby Racing Game,
 11 × 7" **35.00**
Glass
 Kentucky Derby
  1959 . . . . **32.50**
  1961 . . . . **45.00**
  1963 . . . . **45.00**
  1972 . . . . **30.00**
  1973 . . . . **25.00**
  1986, 5¼" h, clear, frosted white
   panel, red roses and green leaf
   accents, red and green inscription
   . . . . **10.00**
 Pimlico, 1974 Preakness, frosted white,
  black portraits of famous Triple
  Crown winners, lists winners from
  1873 through 1973, 5¼" h . . . **15.00**
Hartland Statue, horse and jockey, dark
 brown horse with wrapped ankles and
 bobbed tail, jockey wearing red jacket,
 white cap and trousers, black boots
 . . . . **85.00**

*Game, Tudor, Tru–Action Electric Horse
Race Game, white, black, and orange box,
red, blue, yellow, and green jockey and
horses race on brown track, green ground,
27" l, 15¾" w, $35.00.*

Mug, 1983 Kentucky Derby, clear plastic,
 blue lettering and General Electric logo,
 5½" h **18.00**
Pennant, 18" l, Derby Day, felt, red, white
 lettering, red and white design with pink
 accents, 1939 . . . . **15.00**
Pinback Button
 Atlantic King, trotter, sepia photo portrait, back paper with text on owner's
  farm, early 1900s **25.00**
 Bergen, jockey, yellow polka dotted
  shirt, "Celebrated American Jockey,"
  American Pepsin Gum text on back,
  c1900, ⅞" d **15.00**
 Dan Patch, harness racing, portrait, International Stock Food adv, multicolored, c1905, 1½" d **125.00**
 Foolish Pleasure, brown photo portrait,
  green lettering, "The Great Match,"
  New York Racing Assoc, 1965,
  2¼" d **20.00**
 Joe Joker, harness racing, black and
  white portrait, tin rim, early 1900s,
  1¾" d **65.00**
Ribbon, Marion Mills, Record 2:06¼, Republican Day, Michigan State Fair, Sept
 10, 1896, pink fabric, gold inscriptions
 and horse head, 2¼" w, 7" l **35.00**
Tray, 100th Running Kentucky Derby, litho
 tin, full color race scene, lists derby winners and times from 1865 through 1973,
 issued 1974, 21½" l **25.00**

HOT WHEELS

In 1968 Mattel introduced a line of
2" long plastic and diecast metal cars.
Dubbed "Hot Wheels," there were originally sixteen cars, eight playsets, and two
collector sets.

Hot Wheels are identified by the
name of the model and its year cast on
the bottom of each vehicle. The most
desirable Hot Wheels cars have red striping on the tires. These early vehicles are
the toughest to find and were produced
from 1968 to 1978. In 1979 black tires
became standard on all models. The

most valuable Hot Wheels are usually those with production runs limited to a single year or those of a rare color.

Hot Wheels in original packages or bubble packs command a slightly higher price. MBP means mint in the bubble pack. MOC means mint on original card. Promotional Hot Wheels with specific advertisements are quite popular with collectors right now.

So hop in your own set of wheels and race off to your nearest flea market to find your own hot collectibles.

Advertising Display, Barbie and Hot Wheels, 1993, McDonalds **135.00**
Cars and Trucks
   Alive '55, 1974, light blue **40.00**
   AMX, custom, red, MOC **90.00**
   Army Staff Car, green **125.00**
   Backwoods Bomb, light blue **40.00**
   Beatnik Bandit, magenta, MOC
   . . . . **50.00**
   Buick Wildcat, Demolition Man Series, MBP **5.00**
   Continental Mark III, custom, green
   . . . . **20.00**
   Cool One, plum **10.00**
   Corvette Sting Ray III, Demolition Man Series, MBP **6.00**
   Cougar, custom, orange **35.00**
   Dune Daddy, dark green **60.00**
   El Dorado, custom, green **35.00**
   Ferrari 512–S, metallic red **50.00**
   Fleetside, custom, green **35.00**
   Grass Hopper, magenta **30.00**
   Gremlin Grinder, green **30.00**
   Grim Gripper, MBP **10.00**
   Inferno, yellow **35.00**
   Jet Threat, light green **40.00**
   Light My Firebird, blue, 1970, red line tires, MOC **45.00**
   Lola GT70, dark green enamel, 1969, red line tires, MOB **35.00**
   Low Down, light blue **25.00**
   Mercedes Benz, 1976, red **25.00**
   Mighty Maverick, 1975, dark blue
   . . . . **40.00**
   Monte Carlo Stocker, yellow **40.00**
   Mustang, light blue, Vintage II **5.00**
   Oldsmobile Aurora, Demolition Man Series, MBP **20.00**
   Prowler, enamel yellow **100.00**

Playset, Builder Set, dock, ferry, tollgate and bridge, classic auto dealer, and fast food restaurant, MIB, $20.00.

Rolls Royce Silver Shadow, 1969, red line tires, MOC **48.00**
Sir Rodney Roadster, 1974, yellow
   . . . . **40.00**
Special Delivery, light blue **30.00**
Steam Roller, white **30.00**
Sweet Sixteen, dark blue **60.00**
T–Bird, custom, metallic aqua . . . **35.00**
Tri–Baby, metallic pink **30.00**
Warpath, white **35.00**
Promotional Issued Car
   Deep Purple, Nomad, white wall tires, MBP **10.00**
   Getty Oil, custom Corvette, black body
   . . . . **10.00**
   Gulf Gasoline, set of four different cars
   . . . . **40.00**
   Jack Baldwin Camaro, certificate, MBP
   . . . . **15.00**
   Kool Aid, '63 split window Corvette, white body **10.00**
   Roses, Buick Stocker, blue body, Jiffy Lube logo, MBP **10.00**
   Shell Oil, Ferrari, red body **7.00**
   Toys "R" Us, Geoffrey Toys, Bronco, white **45.00**
   Ziploc, Indy Racer, blue and green body
   . . . . **8.00**

HOWDY DOODY COLLECTIBLES

The Howdy Doody show is the most famous of early television's children's programs. Created by "Buffalo" Bob Smith, the show ran for 2,343 performances between December 27, 1947, and September 30, 1960. Among the puppet characters were Howdy Doody, Mr. Bluster, Flub–A–Dub, and Dilly–Dally. Princess Summerfall–Winterspring and Clarabelle, the clown, were played by humans.

There is a whole generation out there who knows there is only one answer to the question: "What time is it?"

Club: Howdy Doody Memorabilia Collectors Club, 8 Hunt Ct, Flemington, NJ 08822.

Alarm Clock, figural, Howdy sitting on Clarabelle, Bob Smith wake up voice, MIB **135.00**
Badge, 3½" d, Howdy Doody's 40th Birthday, red, white, and blue, 1987 **20.00**
Bag, 4 × 5¼", Howdy Doody Fudge Bar, red, white, and blue, waxed paper, premium offer on back, unused **18.00**
Bank, figural, head, Vandor **75.00**
Belt Buckle, 1950s **8.00**
Bubble Pipe Set, Howdy and Clarabelle
   . . . . **95.00**
Cake Decorations, 9 × 9", birthday cake image, diecut, red, white, and blue, six

pink plastic character candle holders, Kagran, 1951–56 . . . . **75.00**
Catalog, 1955, products and illus, 22 pgs, reprint **10.00**
Detective Disguises, cutouts, uncut, Poll Parrot Shoes premium, mint **70.00**
Dinner Set, 3 pcs, plate, mug, and bowl, porcelain, mint **155.00**
Doll, 12½" h, wood, jointed, painted composition head, Bob Smith copyright, 1948–51 . . . . **400.00**
Football, white **75.00**
Game
   Bean Bag **125.00**
   Bowling, flip over, Howdy and four characters **145.00**
   Flub–A–Dub Flip A Ring, orig pkg
   . . . . **95.00**
   Howdy Doody's TV Game, Milton Bradley, playing board, Howdy shape spinner, six cardboard figures, Kagran copyright, 1951–56 . . . . **110.00**
   Howdy Doody's 3–Ring Circus, Harett–Gilmar, orig box, Kargran copyright, 1951–56 . . . . **75.00**
Ice Cream Spoon, 3" l wood paddle type spoon, waxed paper wrapper, Howdy Doody Ice Cream, Kagran copyright, 1951–56 . . . . **15.00**
Iron–On Transfer, unused **30.00**
Little Golden Book, *Howdy Doody And The Princess,* 28 pgs, 1952, 6½ × 8" **15.00**
Magazine, *Jack and Jill,* January 1960, full color cover, six page article **25.00**
Marionette, orig box **275.00**
Model Clay Kit, three red, white, and blue diecut cardboard figures, thin plastic mold sheet **25.00**
Mug, 3¼" h, plastic, red, full color decal, Ovaltine premium **50.00**
Night Lamp, figural **145.00**
Photo Album, 8½ × 11", 8 pgs, Poll Parrot Shoes premium, c1950 . . . . **100.00**
Plaque, 14" d, Howdy with Santa, orig box, 1950 . . . . **95.00**

Shoe Bag, child's, plastic, Howdy Doody characters, yellow and black dec, red ground, 14½" sq, $40.00.

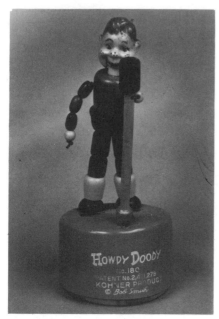

Toy, Kohner Products, No. 180, squeeze type, articulated Howdy standing next to NBC microphone, $25.00.

Puppet, hand **45.00**
Puzzle, 9¼ × 11½", Whitman, Howdy and
  Clarabelle, full color, titled "Skiing With
  Clarabelle," Kagran copyright 1951–56
  . . . . **25.00**
Record Album, 78 rpm, *Howdy Doody and
  The Air-O-Doodle*, glossy paper sleeve
  . . . . **50.00**
Shoe Polish, orig box **45.00**
Spoon, 7" l, SP, raised portrait image on
  handle, Kagran copyright, 1951–56
  . . . . **25.00**
Sticker Book **22.00**
Toy
  Mechanical, standing behind NBC mi-
    crophone, wood, jointed **120.00**
  Squeeze, 13" h, wearing cowboy outfit
    . . . . **125.00**
  Wall Walker **35.00**

HULL POTTERY

Hull Pottery traces its beginnings to the 1905 purchase of the Acme Pottery Company of Crooksville, Ohio, by Addis E. Hull. By 1917 a line of art pottery designed specifically for flower and gift shops was added to Hull's standard fare of novelties, kitchenware, and stoneware. A flood and fire destroyed the plant in 1950. When the plant reopened in 1952, Hull products had a newer glossy finish.

Most Hull pieces are marked. Pre-1950 pieces have a numbering system to identify pattern and height. Post-1950 pieces have "hull" or "Hull" in large script writing.

Newsletters: *Hull Pottery Newsletter*, 11023 Tunnell Hill NE, New Lexington, OH 43764; *The Hull Pottery News*, 466 Foreston Place, St Louis, MO 63119.

Bank, Corky Pig, multicolored **65.00**
Basket
  Bow Knot, B–21, 10½" d **350.00**
  Ebbtide, E–5 . . . . **110.00**
  Iris
    #408, rose and peach, 7" d   **225.00**
    #412, hanging, 4" d **50.00**
  Magnolia, matte, #10 . . . . **150.00**
  Sunglow, pink, #84, 6¼" d **25.00**
  Water Lily, tan and brown, L–14   **235.00**
Bowl
  Iris, oval, #409, 12" d **95.00**
  Poppy, boat shape, #604, 8" d . . . **75.00**
Bud Vase, Woodland, double, W–15, 8½" h
  . . . . **50.00**
Candleholder
  Camelia, doves, #117, 6½" h, pr   **90.00**
  Water Lily, L–22, pr **50.00**
  Wildflower, double, #69, 4" h . . . **75.00**
Clock, Bluebird, electric, Sessions   **250.00**
Console Bowl
  Camelia, bird handles, #116, 12" d
    . . . . **125.00**
  Dogwood, cream and aqua, #511,
    11½" d **165.00**
Console Set, Woodland, pink, 3 pcs   **150.00**
Cookie Jar, apple **35.00**
Cornucopia
  Butterfly, B–2, 6½" l **40.00**
  Parchment & Pine **30.00**
  Wildflower, pink and blue, W–7, 7½" l
    . . . . **55.00**
Ewer
  Bow knot, turquoise to blue, B–1, 5½" h
    . . . . **100.00**
  Magnolia, #5, 7" h **130.00**
  Rosella **40.00**
  Tokay, pink, tall **150.00**
  Wildflower, pink and blue, W–11,
    8½" h **100.00**
Flowerpot, Tulip, #116–33, 6" h **75.00**
Jar, Camelia, ram handles, 8½" h . . . **285.00**
Jardiniere
  Bow Knot, B–18, 5¾" h **65.00**
  Poppy, #603, 4¾" h **50.00**
  Tulip, blue, #117–30–5 . . . . **95.00**
Pitcher
  Camelia, #128, 4¾" h **35.00**
  Rosella, R, 6½" h **45.00**
  Wildflower, W–2, 5½" h **55.00**
Planter
  Bow Knot **110.00**
  Tokay, 6" h **20.00**
  Woodland, W–14, 10" h **55.00**
Teapot, Magnolia, #23, 6½" h, orig paper
  label **55.00**
Vase
  Bow Knot, B–8, 8½" h **195.00**

Iris, pink and blue, #402, 8½" h   **100.00**
Magnolia
  #1, 8½" h **115.00**
  #15, 6¼" h **52.00**
Telephone, gold trim, #50 . . . . . . **32.00**
Tulip, handles, 6½" h **32.00**
Wildflower
  W–4, 6½" h **65.00**
  W–6, 7½" h **78.00**
  W–13, yellow and cream, 9½" h
    . . . . **100.00**

Wall Pocket
  Bow Knot **195.00**
  Sunglow **35.00**
  Woodland, pink, glossy **55.00**

HUMMELS

Hummel items are the original creations of Berta Hummel, a German artist. At the age of 18, she enrolled in the Academy of Fine Arts in Munich. In 1934 Berta Hummel entered the Convent of Siessen and became Sister Maria Innocentia. She continued to draw.

In 1935, W. Goebel Co. of Rodental, Germany, used some of her sketches as the basis for three-dimensional figures. American distribution was handled by the Schmid Brothers of Randolph, Massachusetts. In 1967 a controversy developed between the two companies involving the Hummel family and the convent. The German courts decided The Convent had the rights to Berta Hummel's sketches made between 1934 and her death in 1964. Schmid Bros could deal directly with the family for reproduction rights to any sketches made before 1934.

All authentic Hummels bear both the M. I. Hummel signature and a Goebel trademark. Various trademarks were used to identify the year of production. The Crown Mark (trademark 1) was used from 1935–1949, Full Bee (trademark 2) 1950–1959, Stylized Bee (trademark 3) 1957–1972, Three Line Mark (trademark 4) 1964–1972, Last Bee Mark (trademark 5) 1972–1980, Missing Bee Mark (trademark 6) 1979–1990, and the Current Mark or New Crown Mark (trademark 7) from 1991 to the present.

Hummel lovers are emotional collectors. They do not like to read or hear anything negative about their treasure. At the moment, they are very unhappy campers. The Hummel market for ordinary pieces is flat, with little signs of recovery in the years ahead.

Hummel material was copied

widely. These copycats also are attracting interest among collectors. For more information about them, see Lawrence L. Wonsch's *Hummel Copycats With Values* (Wallace–Homestead: 1987).

Clubs: Hummel Collector's Club, Inc., PO Box 257, Yardley, PA 19067; M I Hummel Club, Goebel Plaza, Rte. 31, PO Box 11, Pennington, NJ 08534.

Bell
    Farewell, Hum–701, 1979 ...... **50.00**
    In Tune, Hum–703, 1981 .... **65.00**
    Thoughtful, Hum–702, 1980 .... **50.00**
Figurine
    Apple Tree Boy, 143, trademark 5, 4" h
    .... **130.00**
    Apple Tree Girl, 141, trademark 5, 4" h
    .... **130.00**
    Birthday Serenade, 218, trademark 3, 4¾" h **500.00**
    Chick Girl, two chicks, 57, trademark 3, 3½" h **155.00**
    Happy Birthday, 176, trademark 5, 5¼" h **195.00**
    Happy Pastime, 69, trademark 5, 3½" h
    .... **145.00**
    Heavenly Angel, 21, trademark 5, 6" h
    .... **190.00**
    Little Hiker, 16, trademark 3 .... **200.00**
    Meditation, 13, trademark 4, 4½" h
    .... **135.00**
    Postman, 119, trademark 3, 5" h **180.00**
    School Boy, 82, trademark 5, 4½" h
    .... **130.00**

    School Girl, 81, trademark 5, 5" h
    .... **175.00**
    Singing Lessons, 63, trademark 5, 2¾" h
    .... **110.00**
    Sister, 98, trademark 3, 5¾" h **180.00**
    Surprise, 94, trademark 3, 4" h **140.00**
    Trumpet Boy, 97, trademark 5, 4¾" h
    .... **120.00**
    Umbrella Boy, 152, trademark 5, 4¾" h
    .... **495.00**
    Umbrella Girl, 152, trademark 5, 4¾" h
    .... **495.00**
Plaque
    Child, looking right, 137B, trademark 5
    .... **60.00**
    Smiling, 690, 1978 .... **250.00**
Plate
    Happy Pastime, 271, 1978 ...... **95.00**
    Merry Wanderer, 11, 1977, white **25.00**

HUNTING COLLECTIBLES

The hunt is on and the only foxes are good flea market shoppers. It is time to take back the fields and exhibit those beautiful trophies and hunting displays. I do not care what the animal activists say; I love it. Old ammunition boxes, clothes, signs, stuffed beasts, photographs of the old hunting cabins or trips, and the great array of animal calling devices. Oh–yea, this is the stuff that adventures and memories are made from.

Care and condition are the prime characteristics for collecting hunting-related items. Weapons should always be securely displayed, insect deterrents and padded hangers are best for clothing or accessories, and humidity-controlled areas are suggested for paper ephemera.

Good luck and happy hunting.

Periodical: *Sporting Collector's Monthly*, PO Box 305, Camden, DE 19934.

Banner, shooting gallery, canvas, Peters Ammunition, "Come On In And Shoot," big–game hunter illus, 27 × 54"
    .... **950.00**
Bearskin Rug
    With head **195.00**
    Without head **475.00**
Book, *National Field Trial Champions, 1896–1955,* 120 pgs **60.00**
Decal Set, hunting dog, orig sheet **9.00**
Disk, brass, "Shot With A Remington Rifle" one side, "Shot With A Kleanbore Remington Cartridge" other side **12.00**
Keychain, "Smith & Wesson," silvered metal, miniature six–shooter handgun, single folding knife blade, keychain loop on grip **30.00**

Pinback Button, left: Peters Shotgun Shell, white ground, "Shoot Peters Shells," celluloid, ⅞" d, $25.00; right: Peters Cartridges "Experts Use," pictures bullet on light green ground, celluloid, ⅞" d, $20.00.

Key Tag, brass, rect, Hercules Powder Co, emb Hercules profile, 1962 50th anniversary inscription **30.00**
Lapel Stud, "UMC," miniature pinback button, celluloid, red ground, white letters, ½" d **20.00**
License, pinback button
    1927, New York State, resident hunting, trapping, and fishing license, peach, black, and white **15.00**
    1932, Wisconsin, resident hunting license, black and white **50.00**
Magazine, *Hunting and Fishing,* complete set Jan–Dec 1933, 12 issues **25.00**
Pinback Button, adv
    Du Pont Smokeless Powder, multi-colored quail illus center, black border, white letters **65.00**
    Infallible Smokeless Shotgun, multi-colored, flag in wreath **50.00**
    Peters No 12 Target, red and yellow version, pink bulls–eye center in large "P" **125.00**
    Winchester Marksman, man's portrait, "C G Spencer, The Man, The Gun And The Shell That Made It," oval
    .... **90.00**
Shot Dispenser, store model, wooden case holds various sizes birdshot, early 20th C, 25" w, 17½" h **300.00**
Sign
    Boston Cartridge Company, paper, 1901 image entitled "Comrades," hunter with bird and dogs, orig metal strips top and bottom, 20 × 26" **550.00**
    Du Pont Powders, tin, self framed, two setters in field, 28¼ × 22¼" **750.00**
    Remington Arms, paper, hunter with dogs, pump shotgun leaning on fence, orig metal strips top and bottom, 17 × 25" **450.00**
Stickpin, brass, rolled thin brass replica shotgun shell, "Shoot Winchester Shells, Winchester No 12 Leader" on red enameled ground **80.00**
Tin, Du Pont Indian Rifle Gunpowder, red, chromolithograph paper label, Indian with rifle, 1908 .... **195.00**

Figurine, Kiss Me, #311, three line mark, 6⅛" h, $295.00.

ICE BOXES

You know the play "The Ice Man Cometh." Well, this listing is the legitimate reason why the ice man came. Never offer to help an ice box collector move!

Acme, ash, extra high, brass locks   **750.00**
Economy, elm, golden finish, galvanized
  steel lining, brass hinges, 45 pound ice
  capacity, 41¼" h **500.00**
Lapland Monitor, Ramey Refrigerator Co,
  Greenville, MI, oak, three paneled
  doors, paneled ends, square feet, metal
  name plate, 35" w, 20" d, 48" h   **575.00**
Northey Duplex, oak, four doors, 74½" h
  . . . . **425.00**
North Pole, oak, applied dec on two pan-
  eled doors, paneled ends, bracket feet,
  zinc lined, orig hardware, metal name
  plate, 25" w, 19" d, 55" h **475.00**
Victor, Challenge Refrigerator Co, Grand
  Haven, MI, oak, single raised panel
  door, paneled ends, zinc lined, orig
  hardware, metal name plate, 22" w,
  15" d, 40" h **500.00**

ICE SKATES AND ICE SKATING COLLECTIBLES

I hope that I am not skating on thin ice by adding this category to the book, but the staff has found many skating-related items and they were hard to ignore. Since ice skating has been around for centuries and is something I have never gotten the knack of, I can only hope that this is better than letting all these goodies go unnoticed.

Book, *Wings On My Feet*, Sonja Henie,
  1940 . . . . **35.00**
Box, Sonja Henie Knitwear, winter cap,
  c1940, 9 × 10 × 2" **15.00**
Coloring Book, features Sonja Henie, Merrill
  Publishing Co, 1941 . . . . **50.00**
Paper Dolls, Sonja Henie, Merrill Publishing
  Co, No 3418, 1941, uncut **50.00**
Pinback Button, Ice Capades, Donna
  Atwood photo portrait, yellow ground,
  black lettering, late 1950s **12.00**
Program, Fifth Transcontinental Tour, Sonja
  Henie, Presented by Hollywood Ice Pro-
  ductions, Chicago, 1941–42 . . . . . **25.00**
Sheet Music, *Let's Bring New Glory to Old
  Glory,* from movie *Iceland,* 1942   **15.00**
Skates, pr
  Clarke's, Syracuse, NY, child's, curved
    prow, bell shaped stanchions, wood
    footplate, 1860s **225.00**
  Douglas Rogers & Co, Norwich, CT,
    Blondin skate, wood footplate, 1860
    . . . . **600.00**

Imperial Glass Console Set, irid blue stretch glass, 10¼" d bowl, 3¼" candlesticks, $85.00.

Dutch
  Child's, plain blade, wood footplate,
    leather straps, 1950s **40.00**
  Touring skate, long heeled, wood
    footplate, early 1800s **185.00**
German, Jackson Haines era, clamp at-
  tachment, c1848 . . . . **250.00**
Raymond Skate Co, Boston, MA, torpedo
  skate, small cast toe and heel plates,
  leather straps, blade stamped "War-
  ranted Tool Steel," 1800s . . . **250.00**
Samuel Winslow, Worcester, MA, plain
  flat blade, wood footplate, 1886
  . . . . **175.00**
Union Hardware, Torrington, CT
  Child's, clamp-on, tighten with key,
    all metal, metal toe and heel
    plates, c1900 . . . . **45.00**
  Donoghue Racing Skate, red paint,
    1860s **195.00**
  Hockey Skate, clamp-on, early
    1900s **95.00**
Unknown Origin
  High stanchions, notched blades,
    wood footplate, early **425.00**
  Thick extended prow, curly maple
    footplate, toe and heel with brass
    trim, mid 1800s **250.00**
  Torpedo racing skate, small toe and
    heel plates, holes punched in
    blade for weight reduction, 1800s
    . . . . **210.00**
Whelpley, Boston, MA, racing skate,
  wood footplate, mid 1800s   **350.00**
Wm Hawkins, Derby, CT, clamp-on,
  metal, ornate, c1860 . . . . . . **275.00**
Wright & Ditson, shoe skate, tuxedo
  model, blade marked "Synthite Steel
  Tempered," early 1900s **60.00**
Tote Bag, white canvas, 1984 Olympic USA
  Figure Skating Team one side, Campbell's Kids skaters illus other side,
  unused, 14 × 14", orig mailing enve-
  lope **25.00**

IMPERIAL GLASS

The history of Imperial Glass dates back to 1901. Initially the company produced pattern and carnival glass. In 1916 an art glass line, "Free-Hand," was introduced. However, Imperial's reputa-

tion rests primarily on a wide variety of household glassware products.

Imperial was responsible for some neat Depression Era Glassware patterns. They were practical, plentiful, and very affordable. Today their bright colors delight collectors.

Imperial made a practice of acquiring molds from companies that went out of business, e.g., Central, Cambridge, and Heisey. The company used a variety of marks over time. Beware of an interlaced "I" and "G" mark on carnival glass. This is an Imperial reproduction.

Animal Dish, cov, hen on nest, amethyst
  slag **115.00**
Ashtray, 6" sq, purple slag **25.00**
Bell, Suzanne, lemon, frosted **35.00**
Bowl
  4½" d, Beaded Block, lily, red
    . . . . **100.00**
  5" d, Laced Edge, opalescent **35.00**
  5½" sq, Beaded Block, amber **7.50**
  6¾" d, Beaded Block, milk white   **16.00**
Butter Dish, cov, Cape Cod, crystal   **30.00**
Cake Plate, Molly, opalescent green   **45.00**
Champagne Goblet, 6" h, 9 oz, Diamond
  Quilted, green **10.00**
Cocktail Shaker, Big Shot, red **75.00**
Cream Soup Bowl, 4¾" d, Diamond
  Quilted, green **8.00**
Goblet, Tradition, crystal **15.00**
Iced Tea Tumbler, Cape Cod, crystal   **12.00**
Jelly Compote, 4½" d, Beaded Block, pink
  . . . . **10.00**
Mayonnaise Set, Laced Edge, opalescent, 3
  pc set **130.00**
Plate, 10" d, Laced Edge, opalescent   **80.00**
Sandwich Server, center handle, Diamond
  Quilted, blue **45.00**
Sherbet, Victorian, yellow **10.00**
Tumbler, Big Shot, red **20.00**
Whiskey, Cape Cod, crystal **10.00**

INK BOTTLES

In the eighteenth and early nineteenth centuries, individuals mixed their own ink. With the development of the untippable bottle in the middle of the

Glass, clear, dug, flat spot on one side for easy pouring, 2½" d, 1½" h, screw type top, $.50.

nineteenth century, the small individual ink bottle was introduced. Ink bottles are found in a variety of shapes ranging from umbrella style to turtles. When the fountain pen arrived on the scene, ink bottles became increasingly plain.

Periodicals: *Antique Bottle and Glass Collector*, PO Box 187, East Greenville, PA 18041.

Automatic Constant Inkwell, 3⅜" h, clear
. . . . **100.00**
Bertinguoit, 2¼ × 2½", black **75.00**
Billings, J T & Son, aqua **7.00**
Carter's Ink, amethyst, mold blown, applied
lip **4.00**

Stoneware, unmarked, sq neck, $15.00.

Drapers Improved Patent, clear, 3 × 4"
. . . . **100.00**
Dunbars Black Ink, 6¾" h, aqua, open pontil **50.00**
Eells Writing Fluid, Mansfield, pottery,
4⅜" h **55.00**
Greenwood's, clear, sheared top **8.00**
Higgins Inks, Brooklyn, NY, amethyst **4.00**
Moses Brickett, olive green **12.00**
Paul's, aqua **12.00**
Sanford, clear, round, crown top **2.00**
Shaws Inks Are The Best, octagonal, aqua
. . . . **20.00**
Signet Ink, cobalt blue **18.00**
Thaddeus Davids & Co Steel Pen Ink, 6" h,
blue green **70.00**
Todd, W B, green **6.00**
Umbrella Ink, blue green, eight sided,
2¼" h **40.00**
Woods Black Ink Portland, 2½" h, aqua,
open pontil **125.00**

INKWELLS

Inkwells enjoyed a "golden age" between 1870 and 1920. They were a sign of wealth and office. The common man dipped his ink directly from the bottle. The arrival of the fountain pen and ballpoint pen led to their demise.

Inkwells were made from a wide variety of materials. Collectors seem to have the most fun collecting figural inkwells—but beware, there are some modern reproductions.

Newsletter: *The Stained Finger,* The Society of Inkwell Collectors, 5136 Thomas Ave So, Minneapolis, MN 55410.

Advertising, Carter's Cubewell **55.00**
Blown Three Mold, 1¾ × 2¼", yellow amber, open pontil **60.00**
Brass
Art Nouveau, glass insert, hinged lid
. . . . **80.00**
Bradley & Hubbard **45.00**
Egyptian Bust, glass insert, hinged lid
. . . . **60.00**
Cast Iron, double well, storks on sides
. . . . **50.00**
Cast Metal, camel, painted **275.00**
Cut Glass, 4¾" h, brass collar, glass stopper
. . . . **95.00**
Glass
1½ × 2½", ringed, deep olive, open
pontil **150.00**
1⅞" h, funnel shape, olive amber, open
pontil **60.00**
1⅞ × 3¾", turtle shape, clear **145.00**
2⅞ × 3", boot shape, turquoise blue
. . . . **100.00**
6 × 7", two screw-in hexagonal inkwells, attached cast metal George Washington statuette standing beside horse, wood stand **125.00**

Porcelain, adv, marked "Purnelle Nivernaise C Dugnas Nevers," marked "Depost," 3¼" sq, 1⅝" h, $42.00.

Metal, cat's head on tray, glass insert **70.00**
Pewter, pen rest with cherub dec, glass insert, floral dec on cov **65.00**
Porcelain
Domed, multicolored floral dec, white
glaze, metal cap **30.00**
Figural, two children playing, Germany
. . . . **85.00**
Red, green, and blue floral design,
3⅛" h **50.00**
Wood, maple, cobalt blue glass liner **15.00**

INSULATORS

This trendy collectible of the 1960s has rested primarily in the collectors' realm since the early 1970s. As a result, prices have been stable.

Insulators are sold by "CD" numbers and color. Check N. R. Woodward's *The Glass Insulator In America* (privately printed, 1973) to determine the correct "CD" number. Beware of "rare" colors. Unfortunately, some collectors and dealers have altered the color by using heat and chemicals to increase the rarity value. The National Insulators Association is leading the movement to identify and stop this practice. They are one of the few clubs in the field that take their "policing" role seriously.

Club: National Insulator Assoc, 5 Brownstone Rd, East Grandby, CT 06026.

Periodical: *Crown Jewels Of The Wire,* PO Box 1003, St Charles, IL 60174.

Threaded
CD 101, Brookfield, aqua, black streak
. . . . **10.00**
CD 102, Diamond, smooth base, root
beer amber **5.00**
CD 102, NEGM, bluish-aqua, milky
swirls **12.00**
CD 104, New England Tel & Tel Co,
smooth base, aqua **12.00**

CD 105, Am Ins Co, plain dome, light aqua **70.00**

CD 106, Ayala, round drip points, light green **35.00**

CD 107, Whitall Tatum No. 9, light olive **15.00**

CD 121, AT & T Co, smooth base, dark aqua **2.00**

CD 131, Tillotson & Co, NY, smooth base, light aqua **225.00**

CD 134, California, smooth base, light rose **185.00**

CD 134, Fall River Police Signal, ding at top **55.00**

CD 143, Canadian Pacific RR, royal purple **125.00**

CD 145, Northern Pacific RR, 3 date base, emb Americans, American blue **7.50**

CD 147, Patented Oct 8th, 1907, emerald green, some amber swirls **15.00**

CD 151, HGC, petticoat, aqua **3.00**

CD 152, hoop skirt, Brookfield, emerald **4.00**

CD 154, Lynchburg, round drip points, green **8.00**

CD 162, Hemingray 19, Made in USA, light golden amber **28.00**

CD 167, Armstrong, corrugated base, root beer amber **4.00**

CD 185, Jeffrey, SDP, aqua, base bruise **105.00**

CD 200, Star, smooth base, yellow–green **275.00**

CD 208, California, smoke purple, base grind mark **50.00**

CD 239, Kimble, corrugated base, clear **4.00**

CD 252, Knowles, smooth base, light green **20.00**

CD 257, Hemingray–60, Made in USA, RDP, clear **6.00**

CD 263, Columbia, smooth base, light aqua **75.00**

Hemingray #60, aqua, Mickey Mouse ears, 5" h, $5.00.

CD 297, Locke No. 16, yellow–green **40.00**

CD 317, Chambers, smooth base, dark aqua **150.00**

CD 320, Pyrex, smooth base, carnival **35.00**

Threadless

CD 701.6, unmarked, smooth base, olive black glass **225.00**

CD 723.3, Wade, minor chips, bruise **200.00**

CD 731, Tillotson, green aqua, skirt fracture and chip **150.00**

CD 735, Chester, NY, smooth base, ice aqua **450.00**

CD 740, No Name, olive black **300.00**

IRONS

Country and kitchen collectors have kept non–electric iron collecting alive. The form changed little for centuries. Some types were produced for decades. Age is not as important as appearance— the more unusual or decorated the iron, the more likely its value will be high.

There are still bargains to be found, but cast iron and brass irons are becoming expensive. The iron collectible of the future is the electric.

Clubs: Club Of The Friends of Ancient Smoothing Irons, Box 215 Carlsbad, CA 92008; Midwest Sad Iron Collectors Club, 2828 West Ave, Burlington IA 52601.

Alcohol, Sun Gas Machine Co, cylinder tank on side **140.00**

Charcoal, Eclipse, single damper, two–tier top with handle, patent 1903 . . . . **35.00**

Electric, Wolverine **10.00**

Flat Iron and Sad Irons

Carver, Racine, WI, combination flat and reversible fluter, pointed ends, patent 1898 . . . . **50.00**

Mexican, wrought, expanded hollow handle, various sizes and shapes, Berney #21 A–B **50.00**

Nelson Streeter, Sensible, various sizes, Glissman Fig 179 . . . . **20.00**

Weida, iron handle disengages at one end, 1870, Berney #32A–B **110.00**

Fluter

English Boxwood Pleater, fluted rolling pin and board, 4½ × 3" base, Berney #37A **250.00**

Geneva **75.00**

Hewitt Revolving Iron, fluter attachment **170.00**

New Geneva, rocker style **50.00**

The Best, rocker style **65.00**

Gasoline

Coleman, round rear tank, pressure pump, plastic handle **25.00**

Slug, cast iron, turned and incised wood handle, cast iron slub, c1850, $95.00.

Montgomery Ward, pump in handle, triangular tank in rear **70.00**

Natural Gas

Clefton Plumbing & Heating Co, spout on front, Berney #166A **120.00**

Imperial, hose coupling at rear, five holes on each side of base . . . **55.00**

Sleeve, Grand Union Tea Co, 8" l, charcoal, detachable bentwood handle **45.00**

Slug

Bless and Drake, combination fluter and flat iron **55.00**

Star, American Machine Co, fluter, cast iron base, crank type **75.00**

IRONSTONE POTTERY

This was the common household china of the last half of the nineteenth century and first two decades of the twentieth century. Its name came because the ceramic ware was supposed to wear like iron. Many different manufacturers used "ironstone" when marking their pieces. However, the vast majority of pieces do not bear the "ironstone" mark.

When a piece is plain white and has a pattern, it is known as "White Pat-

Plate, floral decal, 8½" d, $5.00.

Tureen, white, rope finial and handles, "John Maddock & Sons, Royal Semi Porcelain" mark, 14" l, 9" w, 10½" h, $115.00.

terned Ironstone." A decorative appearance was achieved by using the transfer process.

Cake Plate, white, 9" d, Brocade, Mason
.... **125.00**
Chamber Pot, cov, white, Wheat and Blackberry, Meakin **35.00**
Creamer
   Transfer, 4" h, Oriental style shape,
     marked "Mason's Patent Ironstone"
     .... **75.00**
   White
     Fig, Davenport **60.00**
     Wheat and Clover pattern, Turner &
       Tomkinson **60.00**
Cup and Saucer
   Oriental transfer, polychrome enamel
     .... **25.00**
   White, Ceres, Elsmore & Forster, handleless **48.00**
Gravy Boat, white, 5" h, Wheat and Blackberry, Meakin, 1860s **40.00**
Pitcher
   Transfer, 5" h, red rooster, iris, and
     leaves, marked "Regout & Co,
     Haan" **65.00**
   White, 8½" h, Wheat pattern, ribbed
     .... **30.00**
Plate
   Transfer, 9¼" d, purple transfer, polychrome enamel, Maastricht ... **20.00**
   White, 8½" d, Ceres, Elsmore and Forster **12.00**
Platter, white, 14½" l, Lily of the Valley, Alfred Meakin **40.00**
Sauce Tureen, white, 6⅝" h, oval, Ribbed Bud, 1860s **220.00**
Soup Plate, transfer, 9" d, blue transfer, marked "Adams" **20.00**
Toothbrush Holder, white, Bellflower, Burgess **45.00**

IVORY

Ivory is a yellowish–white organic material that comes from the teeth and tusks of animals. In many cases, it is now protected under the Endangered Species Act of 1973, amended in 1978, which limited the importation and sale of antique ivory and tortoise shell items. Make certain that any ivory that you buy is being sold within the provisions of this law.

Vegetable ivory, bone, stag horn, and plastic are ivory substitutes. Do not be fooled. Most plastic substitutes do not approach the density of ivory nor do they have crosshatched patterns. Learn the grain patterns of ivory, tusk, teeth, and bone. Once you have, a good magnifying glass will quickly tell you if you have the real thing.

Newsletter: *Netsuke & Ivory Carving Newsletter,* 3203 Adams Way, Ambler, PA 19002.

Box, 4¼" h, bust form, floral headdress, carved, Chinese **110.00**
Button, ¾" sq, stylized bird **8.00**
Cane, 36½" l, bamboo form, horse foreleg shape handle, 19th C **250.00**
Cigarette Holder, 2" l, ivory, 14K gold ferrule, black hinged case **30.00**
Crochet Hook, carved **12.50**
Darning Egg, 1¼" l, miniature, mushroom shape **12.00**
Figure
   Apple, 3" h, carved scene inside **120.00**
   Buddha, 3" h, sitting **95.00**
   Elephant, 1¾" h **40.00**
   Monkeys, 2½" h, three evils **200.00**
Hatpin, carved, bird motif, steel pin, England, c1830 .... **300.00**
Knitting Needles, pr, 14" l, black heads
     .... **25.00**
Memo Pad, 1½ × 2¾", silver fittings **25.00**
Napkin Ring, 2" d, relief carved bird **12.00**
Needle Case, cylinder, carved basketweave pattern **85.00**
Netsuke, 1¼" h, musician with stringed instrument, sgd, Japan, early 20th C
     .... **175.00**
Pendant, 1 × 1½ × 2¼", double dragon design, orig silk chord **150.00**
Pen Holder, 4" h, three carved monkeys and tree **180.00**
Pincushion, 2" h, red velvet cushion, pedestal base **40.00**
Ruler, carved demarcations **150.00**

Pie Crimper, ivory wheel, wood handle, 1850, $75.00.

Sewing Box, cov, small **65.00**
Stickpin, carved dog, gold pin, 19th C
     .... **275.00**
Stiletto, 3" l, turned top **32.00**
Tape Measure, spinning top shape ... **50.00**
Tatting Shuttle, carved geometric lines
     .... **40.00**
Thimble Case, 1½" h, barrel shape, carved lines **55.00**
Thread Winder, snowflake shape **45.00**

JAMES BOND COLLECTIBLES

The name is "Bond—James Bond." Women swoon, men grin, and children clap as Agent 007 works his way through another dangerous assignment for Her Majesty's Secret Service. The collector only wishes that Mr. Bond wasn't so elusive at flea markets.

The character of James Bond was invented by Ian Fleming and made famous by MGM/US movie studios. Over the years a number of different actors have portrayed the suave "undercover" agent—Sean Connery and Roger Moore being the most popular. The Bond adventures are also noted for the unique and descriptive names given to the sinister villains and voluptuous females in distress.

Collectors need only know that Her Majesty wishes them luck in the event of their being captured by Bond collectible fever.

Accessories, Gilbert
   For 3" h action figure, 1964
     Dr No's Dragon Tank/Largo's Yacht
      .... **30.00**
     Secret Map Pool Table/Lazer Table
      .... **40.00**
   For 12" h action figure, 1965
     Disguise Kit #1, boxed **125.00**
     Scuba Outfit #2, scuba jacket, headpiece, decoy duck, spring–action spear, three spears, dagger, boxed
      .... **120.00**
     Tuxedo Set, boxed **150.00**
Action Figure
   3" h
     Dr No, Gilbert, 1964 .... **15.00**
     James Bond, wearing tuxedo, Gilbert, 1964 .... **18.00**
   12" h
     Holly Goodhead, Mego, 1979 **160.00**
     James Bond, Ideal, 1966 .... **150.00**
     Jaws, Mego, 1979 .... **550.00**
     Odd Job, Gilbert, 1965 ..... **425.00**
Attache Case, 11 × 17", black plastic, gold plastic combination lock, includes play items, Multiple Toys, 1965 ..... **400.00**
Badge, 1⅛" h, silvered tin, "Special Police 007," 1960s **12.00**

Book, Ian Fleming
  Diamonds Are Forever, Pocket Perma
    M3084, 1957 . . . . **24.00**
  Live and Let Die, Pocket Perma M3048,
    1955 . . . . **38.00**
  Moonraker, Signet S1850, 1960 . . . **8.00**
Bookmark, LLS Ltd, 1987 . . . . **6.00**
Bubble Gum Cards
  Moonraker,, Topps, 2½ × 3½", set of
    99 cards, 22 stickers, 1979 . . . **30.00**
  Thunderball, Philadelphia Gum, set of
    66, 1965 . . . . **250.00**
Camera, Bond–X Automatic Shooting, Mul-
  tiple Toymakers, 1966 . . . . **200.00**
Cap Gun, Lone Star, 100 shot repeater,
  1965 . . . . **200.00**
Card Game, Somportex
  Exciting World of James Bond, 50 cards,
    1965 . . . . **275.00**
  Thunderball, 72 cards, 1965 . . . . **160.00**
  You Only Live Twice, 78 cards, 1967
    . . . . **300.00**
Code–O–Matic, Multiple Toymakers, 1965
  . . . . **60.00**
Cologne Bottle, 007 Aftershave, Colgate–
  Palmolive, 4½" h, black glass, orig silver
  box, 1960s **25.00**
Display, Warner Home Video, *Never Say
  Never Again,* 8½ × 10", cardboard, ea-
  sel back, Sean Connery flanked by two
  women illus, multicolored **20.00**
Dog Tags, Imperial, 1980s **5.00**
Doll, 12" h, Jaws, hard plastic, soft vinyl
  head, fabric clothing, marked "Copyright
  1979 Eon Productions Ltd" **115.00**
Drawing Set, electric, Lakeside, 1965
  . . . . **100.00**
Game
  Agent 007 Game, Milton Bradley, 1966
    . . . . **50.00**
  Bond Message From M Game, orig game
    pieces and box, Ideal, copyright
    1966 Gildrose Productions
    . . . . **200.00**
  Goldfinger, Milton Bradley, 1966 **40.00**
  Secret Agent Game, Milton Bradley,
    1964 . . . . **25.00**
  Thunderball, Milton Bradley, 1965 **45.00**
Gift Set, *License to Kill,* Matchbox, 1989
  . . . . **50.00**
Glass, *A View to a Kill* **10.00**
Gun
  Automatic 100, *For Your Eyes Only,*
    diecast, Crescent, 1982 . . . . . **200.00**
  Submachine Gun, 9mm, Imperial, 1984
    . . . . **15.00**
Lunch Box, 7 × 8 × 4", metal, emb, multi-
  colored illus, Aladdin, 1966 . . . . . **85.00**
Magazine, 8 × 11", *James Bond,* 32 pgs,
  glossy, Dell **45.00**
Model Kit
  Aston Martin, Airfix, 1965 . . . . . . **120.00**
  Autogyro, Airfix, 1967 . . . . **375.00**
  Dr No, with Bond and Honey, Imai,
    1984 . . . . **250.00**

James Bond and Odd Job, Airfix–12, Se-
  ries 4, 1966 . . . . **225.00**
Moonraker Shuttle, Revell, 1979 **30.00**
Movie Poster, 14 × 36", *Goldfinger,* stiff
  paper, color photos, copyright 1964
  United Artists Corp **75.00**
Pistol
  Hideaway Pistol, Coibel, 1985 . . . **25.00**
  Mayday Pistol, *A View to a Kill,* 1980s
    . . . . **30.00**
  SA Automatic Pistol, Multiple Toymak-
    ers, 1965 . . . . **225.00**
  Thunderball Pistol, Coibel, 1985 **25.00**
  Water Pistol, Multiple Toys, 1965 **75.00**
Press Kit, *From Russia with Love,* 1963
  . . . . **50.00**
Puppet, Odd Job, Gilbert, 1965 . . . . **200.00**
Puzzle, jigsaw
  H G Toys, Bond kicking Jaws in mouth
    illus, orig box **25.00**
  Milton Bradley, Goldfinger, 1965 **35.00**
Rifle/Pistol Set, Secret Seven, Multiple
  Toymakers, 1965 . . . . **225.00**
Sheet Music
  Goldfinger, 9 × 12", 2 pgs, copyright
    1964 United Artists Music Ltd **25.00**
  Thunderball, 9 × 12", 3 pgs, Bond un-
    derwater in scuba outfit cov illus,
    1965 . . . . **25.00**
Shoes, pr, Hush puppies, 1965 . . . . . **175.00**
Sticker Book, *A View to a Kill,* Dajaq, 100
  stickers, 1985 . . . . **45.00**
Vehicle
  Aston Martin, slot car, Gilbert, 1965
    . . . . **35.00**
  Helicopter, Corgi, *The Spy Who Loved
    Me,* diecast metal replica, 3" l, black
    and yellow, 1976 . . . . **30.00**
  Lotus Esprit, 3" l, *Spy Who Loved Me,*
    die cast metal and plastic, copyright
    Corgi, 1977 United Artists, orig blis-
    ter card **25.00**
  Moonraker Jet Ranger, Corgi, 1970
    . . . . **75.00**
  Mustang Mach 1, Corgi, 1972 **350.00**
  Toyota 2000, *You Only Live Twice,*
    Corgi, 4" l, 1967 . . . . **100.00**
View–master Pack, *Live and Let Die,* 1973
  . . . . **25.00**

**Bubble Gum Card, James Bond, Secret Agent
007, Enemies At The Gambling Table, copyright 1966, Glidrose Productions and Eon
Productions, $1.25.**

Walkie–Talkie, Secret Service, Imperial,
  1984 . . . . **20.00**
Wristwatch
  Secret Wristwatch Radio, Vanity Fair,
    1970s **75.00**
  Spy Watch, plastic case, "007" logo,
    black and silver, nylon straps, copy-
    right 1965 Gildrose Productions Ltd
    . . . . **150.00**

JEWELRY

All jewelry is collectible. Check the prices on costume jewelry from as late as the 1980s. You will be amazed. In the current market, "antique" jewelry refers to pieces that are one hundred years old or older, although an awful lot of jewelry from the 1920s and 1930s is passed as "antique." "Heirloom/estate" jewelry normally refers to pieces between twenty–five and one hundred years old. "Costume" refers to quality and type, not age. Costume jewelry exists for every historical period.

The first step to determining value is to identify the classification of jewelry. Have stones and settings checked by a jeweler or gemologist. If a piece is unmarked, do not create hope where none deserves to be.

Finally, never buy from an individual who you will not be able to find six months later. The market is flooded with reproductions, copycats, fakes, and newly made pieces. Get a receipt that clearly spells out what you believe you bought. Do not hesitate to have it checked. If it is not what it is supposed to be, insist that the seller refund your money.

Bar Pin
  Gold, 15K, set with three cabochon
    garnets **200.00**
  Sterling Silver, "MIZPAH" and ribbon
    motif, English hallmarks **45.00**

**Bracelet, solid silver, Islamic Tribal, 16th C,
4⅛" d, $2,500.00.**

Bracelet
> Art Nouveau, 18K yg, enameled blue and green dec, Tiffany **285.00**
> Bangle, gold filled, etched band dec **75.00**
> Flexible, 22K, engraved sections, fancy clasp **475.00**

Brooch
> Porcelain
>> Handpainted portrait, gold filled frame **250.00**
>> Victorian, hp **58.00**
> Sash type, Victorian **90.00**

Brooch/Pendant, tri–color 14K yg, filigree mounting, Wedgwood **185.00**

Cuff Links, pr
> Ball motif, 14K yg **90.00**
> Shamrock motif, SS **80.00**

Earrings, small hoop, 14K yg **130.00**

Locket
> Gold, yellow, oval painted miniature, half pearl floral frame **225.00**
> Silver, black onyx shield centered by turquoise and half pearl floral basket **200.00**

Necklace, Art Deco, enamel dec, SS links, set with lapis color glass **165.00**

Pendant, figural, carved lava, gold fittings **250.00**

Pin
> Art Deco, antelope motif, SS **55.00**
> Arts and Crafts, SS, round orange petaled flowers, star points, hallmarked and stamped "JF," 1½" d, pr **140.00**
> Victorian, ivory, carved floral design **35.00**

Pocket Watch, lady's, 14K tricolor gold, hunting case, emb background, applied birds, Elgin **650.00**

Ring
> Platinum, .45 pt dark blue sapphire, filigree spokes radiating to eight sided mounting with sixteen 2 pt cut diamonds **450.00**
> Yellow Gold, 10K, rose cut garnet stones **140.00**

Scarf Pin, gold, Etruscan bead work, pietra dura center **175.00**

Stick Pin, 14K yg, gargoyle motif, set with ruby **125.00**

JEWELRY, COSTUME

Diamonds might be a girl's best friend, but costume jewelry is what most women own. Costume jewelry is design and form gone mad. There is a piece for everyone's taste—good, bad, or indifferent.

Collect it by period or design—highbrow or lowbrow. Remember that it is mass–produced. If you do not like the price the first time you see a piece, shop around. Most sellers put a high price on the pieces that appeal to them and a lower price on those that do not. Since people's tastes differ, so do the prices on identical pieces.

Club: Vintage Fashion/Costume Jewelry Club, PO Box 265, Glen Oaks, NY 11004.

Ankle Bracelet, double heart plaque, 10½" l chain **32.00**

Bangle Bracelet
> Bakelite
>> Brown, carved, rope design, ⅜" w **35.00**
>> Butterscotch, plain **20.00**
>> Green, carved, ¼" w **25.00**
>> Jade green, carved, 1" w **75.00**
> Plastic
>> Clear, hinged, spangles and stones **75.00**
>> Ivory Color, carved, flower, ⅝" w **30.00**
>> Neon Color, multi hinged, 1½" w **45.00**

Bracelet
> Coro, chrome **15.00**
> Mosaic, souvenir, framed photos of Pope, Italy **30.00**
> Rhinestone, stretch type **50.00**
> Trifari
>> Enamel pastel and cabochon **25.00**
>> Gold toned, 22 open aqua stones **45.00**

Brooch
> Carnegie, seed pearls **20.00**
> Coro, SS, winged Gryphon, tassels **200.00**
> Trifari, deep red stones **75.00**

Buckle, bakelite, pinkish–ivory rays, center carved floral design **50.00**

Charm, church with steeple, Stanhope view of Lourdes **55.00**

Clip
> Bakelite
>> Brown, carved daisies **40.00**
>> Butterscotch, carved feather, double **65.00**
>> Ivory, arrow, rhinestone edges **85.00**

Celluloid, carved flower, multicolored, pr **45.00**
> Sterling, Trifari **100.00**

Duette, gold, blue stones, Coro **60.00**

Earrings, pr
> Bakelite
>> Amber tone, carved **30.00**
>> Green, disc, concave **18.00**
>> Green marbleized and rhinestone, hoop, screw back **30.00**
>> Ivory and rhinestone, dice, screw back **35.00**
>> Red, double hoop dangles, screw back **25.00**
> Plastic
>> Aqua, floral disc, aqua, rhinestones, large **35.00**
>> Clear, disc, spangles, large ... **25.00**
>> Red, floral drops, carved, rhinestones **25.00**
> Porcelain, Delft, round drops **28.00**
> Rhinestone
>> Castlecliff, loop, bead trim, large **20.00**
>> Weiss, amber **35.00**

Identification Bracelet, child's, 14K yellow gold, 5" l, single link chain **22.00**

Lapel Button, bakelite
> Hand, black, red nails **75.00**
> Horse Head, brown **65.00**

Lapel Watch, Avalon, 1940s, ice cube motif hanging from gold filled bow pin **100.00**

Locket, ¾" oval **60.00**

Necklace
> Bakelite, 20" l, varicolored loops separated by brass filigree rounds **65.00**
> Beads, Czechoslovakian, crystal, long strand **65.00**
> Niello, Siam, fan shaped segments, white **85.00**
> Pearl, Haskell **135.00**
> Plastic, black cameo on lucite plaque, celluloid chain **85.00**

Pendant, Trifari, "Cartier" style **45.00**

Charm bracelet, silver, zodiac disc, turtle, high school pennant, key, heart, guitar, piano, typewriter, and desk, 1960s, $35.00.

Pendant, Siam, sterling silver design, ½" l, $40.00.

Tie Tac, Champion Spark Plugs, ¾" h, $2.00.

Pin
  Bakelite
    Bar, twisted colors **65.00**
    Bow, geometric, red and white,
      rhinestone set bar **65.00**
    Bow tie, marbleized cream and green
      . . . . **50.00**
    Butterfly **45.00**
    Cherries on log **75.00**
    Flower, large carved custard colored
      flower, leaves **85.00**
  Celluloid
    Carved, flower, coral **25.00**
    Scottie Dog **15.00**
  Enamel, Dutch Girl, Czechoslovakian
    . . . . **25.00**
  Niello, Siam, figural dancer **40.00**
  Plastic
    Accordion, marked "Made in Italy,
      Noble" **35.00**
    Bird, pearly finish **25.00**
    Black Woman, profile, purple turban
      and ruff **45.00**
    Bow, red, lucite **40.00**
    Circle, aqua, applied daisies **25.00**
    Indian, lucite and colored plastic,
      4" h **125.00**
    Spanish Dancer **20.00**
  Porcelain, French poodle, Doliet **40.00**
  Rhinestones, flower, Weiss **35.00**
  Sterling
    Butterfly, Hobe **50.00**
    Flower, tulip, bow motif, Hobe
      . . . . **295.00**
    Lizard, 2⅜" l, Beau **35.00**
    Ship, masts, hand hammered, 1⅜ ×
      1½", Porter **125.00**
    Sterling and gold filled, bow, cameo
      center, Hobe **175.00**
    Sterling and moonstone, flower, Coro
      . . . . **50.00**
Ring
  Amber Tone, dome, embedded ant, size
    7½ **35.00**
  Celluloid, carved coral, size 6 . . **25.00**
  Man's, class **75.00**

Trifari, changeable jewels, orig box
  . . . . **65.00**
Vendome, rhinestone **65.00**
Tie Bar, Kalo **120.00**

JUGTOWN POTTERY

Jugtown is the pottery that refused to die. Founded in 1920 in Moore County, North Carolina, by Jacques and Julianna Busbee, the pottery continued under Julianna and Ben Owens when Jacque died in 1947. It closed in 1958 only to reopen in 1960. It is now run by Country Roads, Inc., a nonprofit organization.

The principal difficulty is that the pottery continues to produce the same type of wares using the same glazes as it did decades ago. Even the mark is the same. Since it takes an expert to tell the newer pieces from the older pieces, this is a category that novices should avoid until they have done a fair amount of study.

Carolina pottery is developing a dedicated core group of collectors. For more information read Charles G. Zug III's *Turners and Burners: The Folk Potters of North Carolina* (University of North Carolina Press: 1986).

Bean Pot, cov, orange, late **45.00**
Bowl, 10⅝" d, Chinese blue glaze, honey
  brown stain, marked **175.00**
Cookie Jar, cov, 12" h, ovoid, strap handles
  . . . . **95.00**
Creamer, cov, 4¾" h, yellow, marked
  . . . . **45.00**
Jar, cov, 6" h, green glaze **95.00**
Mug, brown glaze **25.00**
Pie Plate, 9½" d, orange ground, black concentric circles dec **70.00**

Pitcher, tan, incised dec, 7" w, 6¼" h, $85.00.

Pitcher, 6½" h, incised dec **90.00**
Rose Jar, cov, 4½" h, blended olive green
  glaze **50.00**
Sugar, cov, 3¾" h, Tobacco Spit glaze,
  marked **35.00**
Vase
  3¾" h, brown glaze, two handles **35.00**
  6" h, brown, drippy yellow dec, three
    handles, circular mark **95.00**

JUICERS

Dad lists them as "Reamers" in *Warman's Americana and Collectibles.* Here I call them "Juicers." Finding them in mint condition is next to impossible. The variety of material in which they are found is staggering, ranging from wood to sterling silver. As in many other categories, the fun examples are figural.

Reamers are identified by a number system developed by Ken and Linda Ricketts in 1974. This cataloging system was continued by Mary Walker in her two books on reamers.

Edna Barnes has reproduced a number of reamers in limited editions. These are marked with a "B" in a circle.

Club: National Reamer Collectors Assoc, 405 Benson Rd N, Frederic, WI 54837.

China
  Baby's Orange, 4½" h, blue and white,
    Japan **25.00**
  Duck, 2¾" h, white and yellow, Japan
    . . . . **28.00**
  Happy Face, 2 pcs, lemon rind textured
    surface, yellow spots, green leaves
    and handle, painted face, white
    ground, Japan, c1950 . . . . **50.00**
  Orange Shape, 3¼" h, 2 pcs, figural, orange body, green leaves, England
    . . . . **24.00**
Glass
  Amber, ribbed, loop handle, Federal
    . . . . **20.00**
  Black, fired on, ribbed, tab handle, Anchor Hocking **12.00**
  Clambroth, Hocking, tab handle **90.00**
  Clear
    Easley Mfg Co, baby, 1 pc, four
      blades, basket pattern, rope border, c1902 . . . . **35.00**
    Fenton, baby, 2 pcs, red and white
      elephant and "Orange" inscription on base **75.00**
    Ideal, baby, patent 1888 . . . . . **25.00**
    Westmoreland, baby, 2 pcs, painted
      flowers and "Baby's Orange" inscription on base, c1900 **30.00**
  Cobalt Blue, Hazel Atlas, tab handle
    . . . . **225.00**

Delphite, Jeannette, loop handle, small
.... **60.00**
Green
   Federal, pointed cone, tab handle
.... **30.00**
   Fry, 1 pc, tab handle **25.00**
   Light Jadite, Jeannette, loop handle, large
.... **20.00**
Milk Glass
   Hazel Atlas, 2 pcs, blue dots dec
.... **35.00**
   McKee, "Sunkist" in block letters
.... **20.00**
Pink
   Hazel Atlas, tab handle, large size
.... **30.00**
   US Glass, two-cup pitcher set **35.00**
Metal
  Aluminum
    Handy Andy, 10½" h, 6⅞" d, table
type, crank, red base **20.00**
    Knapp's, crank at top, hand held,
patent 1930 .... **10.00**
    Mason's Sealed Sweet Juicer, wall
mounted, 1930s **10.00**
    Rival Mfg Co, Kansas City, MO, lever
action, c1935 .... **40.00**
    Wearever E-12-1, Ebaloy Inc,
Rockford, IL, 6" h, 20th C   **6.00**
    Stainless Steel, 2½" h, 2 pcs, flat, Hong
Kong **8.50**
    Steel and Aluminum, Kwikway Products,
Inc, St Louis, MO, hand held, wire
reamer, domed lid with crank,
hinged handles, patent 1929 **18.00**
Plastic, figural chef, combination reamer/
lemon slicer, red, c1950 .... **5.00**

Juice-O-Mat, Rival Mfg Co, cast aluminum, chromed and painted iron, patent 1937, 7⅞" h, $17.50.

KEWPIES

Kewpies are the creation of Rose Cecil O'Neill (1876–1944), artist, novelist, illustrator, poet, and sculptor. The Kewpie first appeared in the December 1909 issue of *Ladies Home Journal.* The first Kewpie doll followed in 1913.

Many early Kewpie items were made in Germany. An attached label enhances value. Kewpie items also were made in the United States and Japan. The generations that grew up with Kewpie dolls are dying off. O'Neill's memory and products are being kept alive by a small but dedicated group of collectors.

Club: International Rose O'Neill Club, PO Box 668, Branson, MO 65616.

Newsletter: *Traveler,* PO Box 4032, Portland, OR 97208.

Baby Spoon and Fork, SS, hallmarked "Paye & Baker," marked "P" and "B" in equal size hearts **250.00**
Bank, 5½ × 5", "Koin Keeper," bisque, pink, six white Kewpies illus **175.00**
Cake Top Decorations, 2½" h, pr, bride and groom, celluloid **45.00**
Candy Container **40.00**
Display
   12" h, counter, Santa, sgd "Rose O'Neill," 1913 .... **45.00**
   13" h, Royal Society, Christmas, easel back, 1913 .... **150.00**
Doll
   5" h, bisque, O'Neill **60.00**
   6" h, bisque, Rose O'Neill **200.00**
   8" h, Ragsy, MIB **45.00**
   11" h, composition, red heart, orig clothes and shoes **130.00**
Flour Sifter, child's, tin **45.00**

Plate, sgd "Rose O'Neill," marked "Royal Rudolstadt," 8⅝" d, $165.00.

Paper Dolls, Kewpies in Kewpieland, uncut book **20.00**
Pin, 2" d, cameo **50.00**
Post Card, 3½ × 5½", Valentine, Kewpie pair snuggled on chair, Gibson Art Co, c1920 .... **30.00**
Recipe Book, Jell-O **30.00**
Sugar and Creamer, china, hp **95.00**

KEY CHAINS

Talk about an inexpensive collecting category. Most examples sell under $10.00. If you are really cheap, you can pick up plenty of modern examples for free. Why not? They are going to be collectible in thirty years and antiques in a hundred. Who knows, maybe you will live that long!

One of the favorite charity fundraising gimmicks in the 1940s and 1950s was the license plate key chain tag. There is a collectors' club devoted to this single topic.

Clubs: Key Collectors International, PO Box 9397, Phoenix, AZ 85068; License Plate Key Chain & Mini License Plate Collectors, 888 8th Ave, New York, NY 10019.

Advertising
   Camel Cigarettes, 1¼" d silvered brass pendant with trademark camel and Spanish inscription, silvered brass chain, 1930s **24.00**
   Coca-Cola, gold finished, bottle shape, c1950 .... **15.00**
   Esso Gasoline, 1⅜" d, gold finished metal, raised tiger head symbol, Esso logo under slogan "Put A Tiger In Your Tank," 1960s, serial number on back for Happy Motoring Club
.... **8.00**
   Hercules Powder Co, 1¼" l, rect, brass, logo and company name, reverse with "Fiftieth Anniversary 1912–1962" **12.00**
   Seagrams Gin **5.00**
   Swift Premium Hams, enamel **12.00**
Automobile
   Chrysler, ⅞ × 1¾", emb copper, Airflow model, inscription on back to return to owner, 1934 .... **20.00**
   Packard, metal key holder, attached metal ring, shades of gold and silver, blue, white, and black enamel of convertible titled "Packard Panther," brass Packard logo, late 1950s
.... **20.00**
Good Luck, 1½" h, aluminum, 1946 penny insert, inscribed "Keep Me And Never Go Broke," back "Parts Boys, Auto Specialty Co" **10.00**

IAM, Tool & Die Makers Lodge 688, St Louis, MO, back inscribed "1933 Half Century of Craftsmanship 1983," 3½" l, $7.50.

Motorcycle, American Motorcycle Assoc, 1940 Gypsy Tour, 1½ × 1½", brass, raised image of cycle rider, worn enamel, mail drop guarantee on back **45.00**

Political
John F Kennedy, metal, brass finish, diecut initials, brass chain **15.00**
Richard Nixon, brass case, two pull knife blades, white plastic sides, red and blue lettering reads "President Nixon. Now more than ever." **15.00**

Premium, P F Sneakers, 3" l, ivory plastic, large animal–tooth shape, logo and antelope head dec, built–in siren whistle, sun dial, and alphabet code, 1960s **25.00**

World's Fair, New York
1939, Micro–Lite pen flashlight, orange barrel, circular blue symbol, silver and blue design bands, orig bulb **50.00**
1964, domed acrylic over silver and black unisphere, title, dates, flat silvered metal back, worn **15.00**

KEYS

There are millions of keys. Focus on a special type of key, e.g., automobile, railroad switch, etc. Few keys are rare, prices above $10.00 are unusual.

Collect keys with a strong decorative motif. These range from keys with advertising logos to cast keys with animal or interlocking scroll decorations. Be suspicious if someone offers you a key to King Tut's Tomb, Newgate Prison, or the Tower of London.

Club: Key Collectors International, PO Box 9397, Phoenix, AZ 85068.

Cabinet, barrel type
Brass
Decorative bow, 1½" l **3.00**
Standard bow and bit, 3" l **3.50**
Bronze, dolphin design, 2½" l . . . **12.00**

Iron, painted, Art Deco plastic bow, 3" l **9.50**
Nickel Plated, Art Deco bow, 2½" l **5.00**
Steel
Art Deco, 2" l **6.00**
Standard bow and bit, 3" l . . . . . .**.75**
Car
Basco, steel, flat, early **1.50**
Edsel, any maker **2.50**
Ford, Model "T," brass, crown mark **8.00**
Studebaker, Eagle Lock Co, logo key **1.50**
Car, special
Auto Dealer Presentation Keys, gold plated **1.50**
Crest Key, common cars **1.50**
Casting Plate, bronze, 4" l **22.00**
Door
Brass, standard bow and bit, 6" l   **12.00**
Bronze, special logo bow, 6" l . . . **15.00**
Steel, Keen Kutter bow **3.50**
Folding, jackknife
Bronze and Steel, bit cuts, maker's name, 5" l **18.00**
Steel, bit cuts, Graham, 5½" l **6.50**
Gate, iron, bit type, 6" l **4.00**
Hotel
White Metal, bit type, silhouette of hotel, 4" l **10.00**
Steel, bit type, bronze tag, 4" l **3.50**
Jail
Nickel–Silver, pin tumbler, Yale Mogul, uncut blank **12.00**
Spike Key, steel plated bow, serial number, Yale, 5½" l **40.00**
Steel, flat, lever tumbler, Folger–Adams, cut **18.00**
Keys to the City, presentation, antique bronze, 6" l **15.00**
Pocket Door, bow folds sideways, nickel plated, Art Nouveau, oval bow . . . **15.00**

Door, left: bronze, 3½" l, $3.00; center: Corbin, nickel plated, 3½" l, $3.25; R & E Iron, 3½" l, $3.75.

Railroad
B&M RR, Boston & Maine **20.00**
IC RR, Illinois Central **10.00**
Ship
Bit Type, bronze, foreign ship tag   **6.00**
Pin Tumbler Type, US Coast Guard tag **3.00**
Watch, brass, plain, swivel **2.00**

KITCHEN COLLECTIBLES

Kitchen collectibles are closely linked to Country, where the concentration is on the 1860–1900 period. This approach is far too narrow. There are a lot of great kitchen utensils and gadgets from the 1900 to 1940 period. Do not overlook them.

Kitchen collectibles were used. While collectors appreciate the used look, they also want an item in very good or better condition. It is a difficult balancing act in many cases. The field is broad, so it pays to specialize. Tomato slicers are not for me; I am more of a chopping knife person.

Club: Jelly Jammers, 110 White Oak Dr, Butler, PA 16001.

Newsletters: *Kettles 'n Cookware,* PO Box B, Perrysville, NY 14129; *Kitchen Antiques & Collectibles News,* 4645 Laurel Ridge Dr, Harrisburg, PA 17110.

Basting Spoon, granite, cobalt handle **12.00**
Bread Mixer, Landers Frary, tin **40.00**
Breakfast Skillet, sq **40.00**
Butter Churn, table top type, stave construction, handle **110.00**
Butter Dish, Criss Cross, ½ lb **15.00**
Cake Mold, Griswold, lamb **125.00**

Batter Pitcher, ceramic, blue, $12.00.

Can Opener, cast iron, Universal Dazey, pat
pend **87.00**
Cleanser Shaker, Kleanser Kate, figural girl
.... **18.00**
Coffee Canister, glass, clear, emb zipper
pattern **22.00**
Coffee Grinder
  Counter top, 11" h, cast iron, crank han-
  dle, orig paint, Landers **120.00**
  Lap type, wood **20.00**
  Wall, windmill design, blue and white
  .... **75.00**
Corn Stick Pan, Griswold #273, red and
white, 13" l **50.00**
Cream Can, cov, aluminum, wood bail han-
dle **10.00**
Cutlery Tray, tin, center handle **25.00**
Dish Towels, embroidered days of week, set
of 6 .... **15.00**
Dutch Oven, Wagnerware, No. 9 ... **40.00**
Eggbeater, red Bakelite trim, Androck **25.00**
Flour Sifter, wood, mechanical, Blood's Pat,
Sept 17, 1861, partial label **325.00**
Food Chopper, Universal **6.00**
Frying Pan, Griswold #12, emblem **50.00**
Griddle, Griswold, handled **35.00**
Kettle, light blue swirl, marked "Wrought
Iron Range" **235.00**
Meat Fork, marked "Vintage" **18.00**
Muffin Pan, Griswold #10 .... **35.00**
Onion Chopper, glass jar, paper label
.... **10.00**
Pea Sheller, iron, crank handle **27.50**
Popover Pan, Griswold #10 .... **75.00**
Pudding Mold, cov, tin, tapered pail shape
horn center, 7 cup **55.00**
Recipe Box, metal, blue, includes recipes
.... **10.00**
Refrigerator Dish, cov, rect, glass, green
.... **12.00**
Tea Canister, glass, white, Anchor Hocking
.... **20.00**

KNOWLES CHINA

In 1900 Edwin M. Knowles established the Edwin M. Knowles China
Company in Chester, West Virginia.
Company offices were located in East
Liverpool, Ohio. The company made
semi–porcelain dinnerware, kitchenware, specialties, and toilet wares and
was known for its commitment to having
the most modern and best equipped
plants in the industry.

In 1913 a second plant in Newell,
West Virginia, was opened. The company operated its Chester, West Virginia,
pottery until 1931, at which time the
plant was sold to the Harker Pottery
Company. Production continued at the
Newell pottery. Edwin M. Knowles
China Company ceased operations in
1963.

Knowles dinnerware lines enjoyed
modest sales success. No one line dominated. Some of the more popular lines
with collectors are Deanna (a solid color
line occasionally found with decals—
introduced in 1938), Esquire (designed
by Russel Wright and manufactured between 1956 and 1962), and Yorktown (a
modernistic line introduced in 1936).
Yorktown can be found in a variety of
decal patterns such as Bar Harbor,
Golden Wheat, Penthouse, and Water
Lily.

When collecting decal pieces, buy
only pieces whose decals are complete
and still retain their vivid colors. Edwin
M. Knowles China Company also made
a Utility Ware line that has found some
favor with collectors. Prices for Utility
Ware range between half and two–thirds
of the prices for similar pieces in the dinnerware patterns.

Do not confuse Edwin M. Knowles
China Company with Knowles, Taylor,
and Knowles, also a manufacturer of fine
dinnerware. They are two separate companies. The only Edwin M. Knowles
China Company mark that might be confusing is "Knowles" spelled with a large
"K"

Deanna
  Coffee Server
    Green **35.00**
    Stripes **37.00**
  Creamer and Sugar, light blue ... **25.00**
  Cup and Saucer, yellow **10.00**
  Lug Soup, yellow **5.00**
  Plate, 10" d, dinner, dark blue ... **10.00**
  Platter, Daisies **8.00**
  Shaker, Plaid **8.00**
Fruits
  Pitcher, cov, Utility Ware **25.00**
  Shaker **12.00**
Pink Pastel, creamer **3.00**
Tia Juana
  Bowl, 9" d **12.00**
  Mixing Bowl **30.00**
  Plate
    6" d **3.00**
    9½" d **6.00**
  Platter **12.00**
  Serving Tray, Utility Ware **20.00**
  Shaker **8.00**
  Soup, flat, 8" d **15.00**
  Stack Set, Utility Ware, set of 3
  .... **15.00**
Tulip
  Cookie Jar, Utility Ware **35.00**
  Pie Plate, Utility Ware **15.00**
Tuliptime
  Platter, octagonal **10.00**
  Vegetable Bowl, octagonal **12.00**

Yorktown
  Cereal Bowl, 6" d, green **6.00**
  Chop Plate, 10¾" d, burgundy ... **18.00**
  Coaster, white **8.00**
  Cup and Saucer, orange–red **8.00**
  Gravy Boat, Penthouse **10.00**
  Plate, 10" d, dinner, Picket Fence **10.00**
  Teapot, cov, Mango red **45.00**

LABELS

The first fruit crate art was created
by California fruit growers about 1880.
The labels became very colorful and
covered many subjects. Most depict the
type of fruit held in the box. With the
advent of cardboard boxes in the 1940s,
fruit crate art ended and their labels became collectible.

When collecting fruit crate labels, or
any other paper label, condition is extremely important. Damaged, trimmed,
or torn labels are significantly less valuable than labels in mint condition.

Club: The Citrus Label Society, 131
Miramonte Dr, Fullerton, CA 92365.

Beverage
  Old Craft Brew, four brewery workers
  making beer, gilt dec ....**.50**
  Palm Springs Soda, silver Art Deco de-
  sign, black and gold ground, dated
  1935 ....**.50**
Broom, Indian Queen Broom, Indian lady in
forest, tepees ....**.50**
Carpet, Bibb Manufacturing Co, 5 × 15",
"carpet warp, 20 cuts, long reel," Beatty
& Co Litho, NY **20.00**
Cigar
  Buzzier, ornate butterfly with cigar body
  .... **3.00**
  La Boda, wedding ceremony **2.00**
  Uncle Jake's Nickel Seegar, comical
  man with beard and cat, c1925 **3.00**

*Soda Bottle, Ritz Orange Soda, Ritz Beverage
Co, St Louis, MO, orange and black, 5 × 5",
$.50.*

Food

Butterfly Golden Sweet Corn, bowl of
corn **1.00**

Elkay Cocoa, emb, cup of cocoa, dark
blue, gold, and white **10.00**

Preston Lima Beans, pods, leaves, black
and red ground **1.00**

Fruit Crate

American Beauty, big red rose, dark
green ground **2.00**

Better 'N Ever, half sliced grapefruit,
blue ground .... **.50**

Blue Parrot, green and blue parrot on
flowering pear branch .... **.75**

Coed, smiling girl graduate with oranges,
purple ground, Claremont, CA **2.50**

Don't Worry, little boy holding apple,
black ground **1.00**

Eat One, arrow pointing to juicy orange,
aqua ground, Lindsay **2.00**

Forever First, red holly berries, greens,
and plump juicy pears, blue ground
.... **2.00**

Great Valley, scenic, orange orchard,
Orange Cove **1.00**

L–Z, smiling boy holding green grapes
.... **.50**

Old Mission, Spanish Mission scene,
mission bells, green grapes, 1920s
.... **.50**

Red Diamond, red and yellow apples,
red diamond, blue ground **1.00**

Sea Coast, two lemons, blue triangle,
brown ground, Ventura **2.00**

Sunkist California Lemons, lemon, yellow letters, black ground **1.00**

Wilko, red apple, red border, yellow
ground **1.00**

Medicine, Dr B D Eldridge's Forest Leaf
Compound, Indian maiden illus, gold
trim, black and white **10.00**

Tobacco

Cora, child seated by giant flowers, 7 ×
14" **37.50**

Welcome Nugget, gold miner holding
up giant nugget, 11 × 11" ... **65.00**

LACE

While there are collectors of lace,
most old lace is still bought for use.
Those buying lace for reuse are not willing to pay high prices. A general rule is
the larger the amount or piece in a single
pattern, the higher the price is likely to
be. In this instance, price is directly related to supply and demand.

On the other hand, items decorated
with lace that can be used in their exist-
ing form, e.g., costumes and tablecloths,
have value that transcends the lace itself.
Learn to differentiate between handmade and machine–made lace. Value
for these pieces rests on the item as a
whole, not the lace.

Ask yourself one basic question.
When was the last time you used any
lace or anything with lace on it? Enough
said.

Club: International Old Lacers, Inc, PO
Box 481223, Denver, CO 80248.

Periodical: *The Lace Collector,* PO Box
222, Plainwell, MI 49080.

LADY HEAD VASES

Heart-shaped lips and dark
eyelashes mark the charm of the typical
lady head vase. Manufactured in the
early 1950s, these semi–porcelain,
glazed, or matte-finished vases, were
produced in Japan and the United States.
The sizes of lady head vases range from
4¹/₂" to 7" high. The decoration is
thoughtfully done with a flare for the
modeled feminine form. Many of the
vases have the character shown from the
shoulders up with elaborate jewelry, delicate gloves, and a stylized hair–do or
decorated hat. A majority of the head
vases are marked on the base with the
company and place of manufacture.

Newsletter: *Head Hunters Newsletter,*
Head Vase Society, PO Box 83H,
Scarsdale, NY 10583.

Baby, 5³/₄" h, blond hair, open eyes, pink
cheeks, open mouth, pink ruffled bonnet
tied under chin, pink dress, unmarked
.... **15.00**

Black Lady, 5" h, young, downcast eyes,
yellow turban, red sarong, large gold
hoop earrings, three–strand pearl
necklace, Japan **30.00**

Cowboy, 6" h, brown hair, blue eyes, yellow hat and neckerchief, white shirt, yellow star badge, unmarked **30.00**

Geisha Girl, 4¹/₂" h, short black hair, white
skin, downcast eyes, gold eyebrows and
eyelashes, holding white and gold fan in
raised left hand, white and gold
hairpiece with yellow tassel, pink ki-
mono, painted fingernails, Irice, Japan
.... **25.00**

Girl

5¹/₄" h, long blond hair, straight bangs,
blue flowers at ponytail on top of
head, eyes looking right, raised hand,
slender neck, blue dress, Parma by
AAI, Japan, A–222 .... **12.50**

6" h, blond hair, blue eyes looking right,
open–mouth smile, rosy cheeks,
large red hat tied with red bow under
chin, holly leaves dec, red and white
candy–striped mittens, red coat with
white fur cuffs and gold button, Reliable Glassware and Pottery, 3088
.... **22.00**

Girl with large sunbonnet, downcast eyes,
flower on jacket, white collar, Norcrest Fine
China, Japan, 6" h, $15.00.

Graduate, 5" h, blond shoulder–length
straight hair, open eyes, pink cap and
tassel, pink and white gown with gold
accents, unmarked **25.00**

Island Girl, 6" h, wearing hibiscus in black
hair, downcast eyes, green sarong, carrying basket on head, Shawnee Pottery,
896 .... **25.00**

Lady

5" h, young, wearing Christmas outfit,
hp, blond wavy hair, downcast eyes,
red stocking cap with white ribbed
band and tassel, poinsettia on band,
red neckerchief with white polka
dots, white dress with raised collar,
gold accents, Napco, Japan, CX5409
.... **17.50**

5¹/₂" h, young, black hat with white and
gold ribbon tied in large bow under
chin, black and white dress, bare
shoulders, Relpo, Sampson Import
Co, Chicago, IL, Relpo, Japan, 2031
.... **15.00**

5³/₄" h

Blond hair, downcast eyes, raised
arms, chin resting on intertwined
fingers, white hat with gold trim,
brown dress with white raised
collar, white gloves, pearl drop
earrings and necklace, white and
gold flower brooch, Rubens Originals Los Angeles, Japan, 495
.... **15.00**

White hair with gold accents, up-
swept hair style, white skin,
downcast eyes, gold arched eyebrows and eyelashes, pink
flounced hat with yellow rose
dec, matching dress, Lefton,
PY641 .... **15.00**

Lady, black hat, gray bow and dress, blond hair, pearl drop earrings, pearl necklace, Napcoware, C7494, orig silver foil label, $22.50

7" h, brown hair, downcast eyes, raised right hand, black hat with white and gold ribbon, black dress, white glove with gold accents, pearl drop earrings and necklace, Inarco, C-2322 . . . . **18.00**

7½" h, young, blond hair, downcast eyes, white bonnet with blue ribbons, white ruffled dress, gold accents, Norleans, Japan **25.00**

Malaysian Princess, 5¼" h, gold skin, closed eyes, arms crossed in front of chest, white headdress with gold dec, pearl drop earrings, Royal Sealy, Japan **30.00**

Nurse, 5¼" h, short blond hair, downcast eyes, raised right hand, white cap with Red Cross insignia, white uniform with gold accents, painted fingernails, unmarked **25.00**

Spanish Dona, 6½" h, black hair, white skin, blue eyes, tilted head, white and gold dress, tiara, and mantilla, gold necklace, Stanfordware, Sterling, OH **28.00**

LAMPS

Collecting lamps can be considered an illuminating hobby. Not only is the collection practical, versatile, and decorative, but it keeps you out of the dark. Whether you prefer a particular lamp style, color, or theme, you will find a wonderful and enlightening assortment at any flea market.

Banquet
Figural glass font, Jenny Lind, black iron pedestal and base **255.00**
Miniature, 17" h, bronze pedestal, brass font, base with four ornate feet, milk glass globe **220.00**

Betty, tin, simple design, hook hanger **60.00**
Boudoir
Art Deco Style, ribbed cone-shaped green Depression Era Glass shade flanked by pair of metal stylized rearing horses, stepped black glass base, 1930s **125.00**
Art Nouveau Style, tall tubular octagon-shaped pink Depression Era Glass shade with emb nudes on four sides, square black metal base **85.00**
Character
Popeye, spinach can with raised figures, ceramic, 1975 King Features **150.00**
Strawberry Shortcake **65.00**
Country Store, 29" h, 20" d, nickel plated brass font, wire frame, orig waffle tin shade, Aladdin **395.00**
Desk, Sheaffer pen, adv **250.00**
Figural
Cockatoo, glass, red, US Glass **750.00**
Draped Maiden, leaning against lamppost, bronzed white metal, white glass globe, rectangular stepped base **95.00**
Fish, ceramic, brown, leaping out of waves, brown and ivory circular paper shade **25.00**
Flowers, stylized, three flaring wrought iron stems with curlicue leaves, plastic globular shades, circular brass base, 1930s **45.00**
Hula Girl, white metal, wearing grass skirt, motorized hip movement, circular base, late 1940s **75.00**
Native Man, ceramic, two bulbs, Shawnee Pottery **42.00**
Oriental Figures, ceramic, two figures each lamp, Shawnee Pottery, pr **20.00**
Rooster, ceramic, red, black, and white, crowing, circular paper shade with hex sign dec, 1950s **12.00**
Saturn, blue Depression Era Glass, circular stepped base, 1930s **60.00**

Battery Operated, camping type, Glo-Globe, round ball, plastic, half white, half orange, base marked "Eveready No. 2350," gives required battery sizes and types, Made in Hong Kong, white push button, 5" d, $10.00.

Telephone, plaster, turquoise, black and white speckled, desk-type phone with clock face replacing dial, removable receiver with built-in cigarette lighter, matching rectangular venetian blind shade **35.00**
Western Theme, ceramic, cowboy and cowgirl flanking inverted horseshoe surrounding clock face, white, gold trim, rect white plastic venetian blind shade, 1950s **25.00**
Hanging, brass **95.00**
Miner's
Candlestick type, unmarked **150.00**
George Anton, brass, teapot type **145.00**
Justrite, nickel plated, 1913 . . . . . . **70.00**
Wolf, safety, miniature **400.00**
Miniature, milk glass, shade, marked "Improved Banner" **85.00**
Novelty
Artillery Shell, brass, metal dome shade **40.00**
Deer Trophy, tripod base made from three deer legs, photo transfer shade with grazing animals dec **30.00**
Fish Bowl Stand, ceramic, green double tree stump base, black cat sitting on one stump, glass fish bowl on other **35.00**
Lava, bottle-shaped, Lava Simplex Corp, Chicago, IL **50.00**
Motion, illustrated plastic cylinder, Econolite, 11" h
Niagara Falls, 1957 . . . . **35.00**
Vintage Cars, some damage to inside **90.00**
Water-skiers, 1958 . . . . **55.00**
Silhouette
Harem Girl, plaster, green, red and gold accents, circular frame with central harem girl carrying lantern, blue glass panel, PGH Statuary Co **50.00**
Nude, figural, pot metal, painted green, standing before shield-shaped frosted glass panel, 1930s **110.00**
Sparking, 3½" h, camphene, pewter, single tube, cap burner, side handle . . . **150.00**
Table
Candlestick Type, brass, ribbed and fluted column, circular dished base, orange paper shade **15.00**
Painted, glass dome-shaped shade with mountain landscape, bronzed metal vasiform column, circular base **325.00**
Tiffany Type, six caramel slag glass panels in dome-shaped shade, floral and foliate dec framework, cylindrical illuminated base with caramel slag glass panels, three bulbs **325.00**

LAW ENFORCEMENT COLLECTIBLES

Do not sell this category short. Collecting is largely confined to the law enforcement community, but within that group collecting badges, patches, and other police paraphernalia is big. Most collections are based upon items from a specific locality. As a result, prices are regionalized.

There are some crooks afoot. Reproduction and fake badges, especially railroad police badges, are prevalent. Blow the whistle on them when you see them.

Newsletter: *Police Collectors News,* RR1, Box 14, Baldwin, WI 54002.

Badge
Deputy Sheriff, Juneau County, 2½" h, shield shape, metal, gold finish, blue inscription, raised seal design, c1940 . . . . **40.00**
Police, Chanute, KS, "2," shield shape **275.00**
Special Police
1922, Kansas City, Hallmark   **75.00**
1930s, 2½ h, sunburst shape, silvered brass, black inscription **25.00**
Trenton Police, 2¼ × 2½", star shape, silvered brass, black inscription, raised "70" in center, 1930s   **25.00**
Billy Club, wooden **20.00**
Booklet, *The ABC of Practical Pistol Instruction For Home Guards,* Police Auxiliary, c1920, 27 pgs, NRA of America . . . **4.25**
Brochure, *The New 1953 Ford Police Car,* police badge shape outline, policemen riding in police car on front cov   **12.00**
Buckle, New York City, c1900 . . . . . . **75.00**
Cigar Box, Yellow Cab, policeman and yellow taxi cab, 2 × 5½" **5.00**

Badge, Fire Police, Southeastern Vol. Fire Co, silvered metal, 3" l, $25.00.

Cracker Jack Prize, 1½" l, ½" h, litho tin paddy wagon, blue, white, and yellow **12.00**
Game, Rival Policeman, McLoughlin Bros, 1896, policeman chasing man on box cov **275.00**
Helmet, New York City, riot type, leather **200.00**
Magazine, *Police Gazette,* January, 1959 . . . . **40.00**
Mirror, San Diego Police Dept, framed with badge and legend "To Protect & To Serve," wood frame, 16 × 28" . . . **65.00**
Patch
Maricopa County Deputy Sheriff, star center **2.00**
San Francisco, eagle **3.00**
Photograph, Detroit, MI, parade, six policemen riding in open patrol wagon, 1917 . . . . **12.00**
Sheet Music, *Police Parade March,* c1917 . . . . **25.00**
Toy, windup, litho tin, policeman on motorcycle, Unique Art **150.00**

LENOX

Johnathan Cox and Walter Scott Lenox founded the Ceramic Art Company, Trenton, New Jersey, in 1889. In 1906 Lenox established his own company. Much of Lenox's products resemble Belleek, not unexpectedly since Lenox lured several Belleek potters to New Jersey.

Lenox has an upscale reputation. China service sets sell, but within a narrow price range, e.g., $600 to $1,200 for an ordinary service of eight. The key is Lenox gift and accessory items. Prices are still reasonable. The category has not yet been truly "discovered."

Bowl
Art Deco, SS overlay, blue glazed ground, ftd **115.00**
Shell, 9" d, pink and gold, green mark **86.00**
Chocolate Set, cov chocolate pot, six cups and saucers, Golden Wheat pattern, cobalt blue ground, 13 pcs . . . **275.00**
Christmas Ornament, snowflake, porcelain, 24K gold finials, 1982 . . . . **45.00**
Cup and Saucer, Golden Wreath pattern **20.00**
Figure
Carousel Horse, 1987 . . . . **150.00**
Centennial Bride, 1987 . . . . **90.00**
Goose Girl, 1991 . . . . **65.00**
Jug, 4" h, hp, grapes and leaves, shaded brown ground, sgd "G Morley"   **240.00**
Limited Edition Collector Plate, 10½" d, Edward Marshall Boehm artist, MIB
1970, Wood Thrush **225.00**

Salt, cream, green wreath mark, 3 × 2 × 1", $35.00.

1979, Golden Crowned Kinglet   **65.00**
Nappy, 4½ × 7", ftd, shell shape, pink tinged beige **35.00**
Nativity Figure
Holy Family **135.00**
Shepherds **150.00**
Three Kings **150.00**
Plate, Tuxedo pattern, gold mark **10.00**
Platter, 13" d, Temple Blossom pattern **90.00**
Sculpture
American Goldfinch, 1987 . . . . . . **45.00**
Blue Jay, 1986 . . . . **45.00**
Peace Rose, 1988 . . . . **125.00**
Wood Duck, 1991 . . . . **45.00**
Shoe, white, bow trim **185.00**
Vase, 6" h, roses dec, sgd "W Morley" **165.00**

LETTER OPENERS

Isn't it amazing what can be done to a basic form? I have seen letter openers that are so large that one does not have a ghost's chance in hell of slipping them under the flap of a No. 10 envelope. As they say in eastern Pennsylvania, these letter openers are "just for nice."

Advertising letter openers are the crowd pleaser in this category. However, you can build an equally great collection based on material (brass, plastic, wood, etc.) or theme (animal shapes, swords, etc.)

Advertising
Donegal & Conoy Mutual Fire Insurance Co, brass, 9" l, c1920 . . . . . . **35.00**
Fuller Brush Man **10.00**
Purity Brand Salt, International Salt Co of NY, celluloid, made by Whitehead and Hoag, Newark, NJ, 7¾" l   **20.00**
Alligator, beige, black and white eyes, marked "Germany," c1900 . . . . . . **75.00**
Art Deco, rooster **25.00**
Dragon, brass **40.00**
Elephant, ivory **30.00**
Horse, rearing, brass, cutout floral blade, 7¼" l **18.00**

Sterling silver, intaglio top, iron blade, 5⅜" l, $12.00.

Indian, beige, black accents **60.00**
Ivory, three layer handle, mother–of–pearl
    insets, ornate **125.00**
Owl, celluloid **65.00**
Tennis Racquet, bronze **14.00**

LICENSE PLATES

They are mounted row after row on walls in a garage, den, and even living room. License plate collectors are truly among the possessed.

Collectors specialize. The most obvious approach is by state. But this just scratches the surface. Government plates, vanity plates, law enforcement plates, and special-issue plates are just a few of the other potential collecting categories.

License plates are found most frequently at automobile flea markets. When they are found at general flea markets, they are usually encountered in large groups. Be prepared to buy the lot. Most sellers do not want them picked over. They know they can never sell the junk.

Club: Automobile License Plate Collectors Association, Inc, Box 712, Weston, WV 26452.

Periodicals: *PL8S, The License Plate Collector's Hobby Paper,* PO Box 222, East Texas, PA 18046; *The Plate Trader,* 1–M Ridge Run, Marietta, GA 30067.

Batmobile, 4 × 7", emb litho tin, black,
    white, red, and blue, copyright 1966
    National Periodical Publications, Inc
    . . . . **12.00**
Boy Scout, 1957 National Jamboree, Michi-
    gan, No 30, Valley Forge, Water Won-
    derland **28.00**
Chicago, 1924, round, raised letters
    . . . . **30.00**
District of Columbia, Inauguration 1977,
    metal, beige background, red and dark
    blue design **20.00**
Napoleon Solo, The Man from UNCLE, red,
    emb name and logo, Marx, 1967 Metro–
    Goldwyn–Mayer, Inc **25.00**

Top: Philippines, 1953, $1.00; bottom: Canadian, Saskatchewan, Wheat Province, 1953, $1.00.

Peace, 6 × 12", thin metal, blue and white,
    peace symbol, 1970s **25.00**
Political
    Eisenhower, In 1954 Give Ike A Republi-
        can Congress, 6 × 12", metal, dark
        blue, white lettering **55.00**
    Harrisburg Republican Club with
        Dewey–Bricker, fiberboard, dark
        blue background, yellow inscription,
        1944 . . . . **25.00**
    Jimmy Carter/A New Beginning, 6 ×
        12", plastic, red, white, blue, and
        green design, c1976 . . . . **15.00**
    John F Kennedy, 2 × 4", black, yellow
        California and JFK 464 . . . . **35.00**
Souvenir, 6 × 12", New York World's Fair,
    emb tin, orange, blue, and gold, black
    lettering, Unisphere image, 1964–65
    . . . . **25.00**
State
    Arizona, motorcycle, 1971 . . . . **5.00**
    Connecticut, 1911–12 . . . . **150.00**
    Delaware, four digit, 1913 . . . . . **175.00**
    Iowa, antique automobile, 1964 . . . **6.00**
    Massachusetts, four digit, 1911 . . . **75.00**
    Michigan, 1923 . . . . **15.00**
    Nebraska, 1930, enamel **15.00**
    Ohio, 1910 . . . . **175.00**
    Pennsylvania, school bus, 1969   **12.00**

LIMITED EDITION COLLECTIBLES

Collect limited edition collectibles because you love them, not because you want to invest in them. While a few items sell well above their initial retail price, the vast majority sell between 25¢ and 50¢ on the original retail dollar. The one consistent winner is the first issue in any series.

Whenever possible, buy items with their original box and inserts. The box adds another ten to twenty percent to the value of the item. Also, buy only items in excellent or better condition. Very good is not good enough. So many of each issue survive that market price holds only for the top condition grades.

Clubs: Enesco Precious Moments Collectors' Club, One Enesco Plaza, PO Box 1466, Elk Grove Village, IL 60009; Gorham Collectors Guild, PO Box 6150, Providence, RI 02940; Lowell Davis Farm Club, 55 Pacella Park Drive, Randolph, MA 02368.

Periodicals: *Collector Editions,* 170 Fifth Ave, 12th Floor, New York, NY 10010; *Collectors' Bulletin,* RR #1, Canton, IL 61520; *Collector's Mart Magazine,* PO Box 12830, Wichita, KS 67277; *Collectors News,* 506 Second St, PO Box 156, Grundy Center, IA 50638; *Plate World,* 9200 North Maryland Ave, Niles, IL 60648.

Berlin Design, Christmas Plate
    1975, Christmas in Dortland **20.00**
    1976, Christmas in Augsburg **45.00**
    1978, Christmas in Berlin **55.00**
    1981, Christmas Eve in Hahnenklee
        . . . . **30.00**
Bing & Grondahl
    Buffalo Bill's Wild West Series Plate,
        Jack Woodson
        1984, Congress of Rough Riders
            . . . . **35.00**
        1984, Pony Express **45.00**
    Christmas in America Series Plate
        1987, Christmas Eve at the White
            House **20.00**
        1988, Christmas Eve at Rockfeller
            Center **45.00**
    Christmas Series Plate
        1962, Winter Night **30.00**
        1964, The Fir Tree and Hare   **20.00**
        1970, Pheasants in the Snow   **12.00**
        1978, Christmas Tale **17.00**
        1982, Christmas Tree **35.00**
    Figurine, Peter, #1696 . . . . **145.00**
    Jubilee 5-Year Christmas Series Plate
        1950, Eskimos **120.00**
        1955, Dybol Mill **130.00**
        1970, Amalienborg Castle **20.00**
        1980, Yule Tree **35.00**
    Mother's Day Plate
        1971, Cat and Kitten **10.00**
        1975, Doe and Fawns **15.00**
        1976, Swan Family **20.00**
        1978, Heron **17.00**

Crown Staffordshire
  Christmas Series Plate, 1979, Monarch
    of The Glen **25.00**
  Stained Glass Series Plate
    Holy Stephanius **25.00**
    Visitation **25.00**
  St. Patrick's Day, 1979 .... **35.00**
Cybis, figurine
  1964, Rebecca **215.00**
  1966, First in Flight **285.00**
  1975, Wendy with Doll **225.00**
Edwin Knowles
  Annie Series Plate
    1983, Annie and Grace **20.00**
    1983, Daddy Warbucks **15.00**
  Frances Hook Legacy Series Plate
    1985, Fascination **20.00**
    1986, Discovery **20.00**
  Hibel Christmas Series Plate
    1985, The Angel's Message ... **25.00**
    1989, Peaceful Kingdom **30.00**
  Oklahoma Series Plate, Oh What a
    Beautiful Mornin' **15.00**
  The King & I Series Plate
    1985, Getting to Know You ... **15.00**
    1985, Shall We Dance? **25.00**
Hackett
  Impressions Series Plate, Jo Anne Mix,
    1982, Windy Day **25.00**
  Special Moments Series Plate, R Es-
    calera, 1982, April **25.00**
  Wondrous Years Series Plate, R Escalera,
    1981, After The Rains **25.00**
Hamilton Collection
  Honeymooners Series Plates, D Kilmer,
    1987, The Honeymooners **35.00**
  Little Ladies Series Plates, Maude
    Humphrey Bogart, 1989, Playing
    Bridesmaid **35.00**

Figurine, Mallard, base marked "Special Edition, Birds In Flight Collection, Limited Series, Flight of the Mallard, Taiwan," 4½ × 3" base, 9" h, $15.00.

Haviland, Twelve Days of Christmas Plate
  1970, Partridge **35.00**
  1971, Two Turtle Doves **15.00**
  1972, Three French Hens **25.00**
  1973, Four Calling Birds **20.00**
Haviland & Parion
  Christmas Madonnas Series Plate
    1972, By Raphael **25.00**
    1973, By Feruzzi **50.00**
    1977, By Bellini **30.00**
  Tapestry I Series Plate
    1972, Start of the Hunt **30.00**
    1975, Unicorn Surrounded ... **45.00**
  Tapestry II, The Lady and the Unicorn
    Series Plate
    1977, To My Desire **25.00**
    1982, Tase **35.00**
Kirk, Stieff, Christmas Ornament, Twelve
  Days of Christmas
    1987, Six Geese A–Laying **10.00**
    1988, Eight Maids A–Milking **10.00**
Lenox, Boehm Bird Series Plate
  1971, Goldfinch **90.00**
  1978, Mockingbirds **95.00**
Lladro
  Annual Ornament, 1989 .... **35.00**
  Christmas Bell
    1988 .... **45.00**
    1992 .... **25.00**
  Christmas Ornament, miniature
    1989, Holy Family **60.00**
    1990, Three Knights **65.00**
Noritake, Easter Eggs
  1975 .... **18.00**
  1982 .... **18.00**
Porsgrund
  Father's Day Plate
    1971, Fishing **10.00**
    1972, Cookout **8.00**
  Mother's Day Plate
    1970, Mare & Foal **8.00**
    1976, Girl & Calf **8.00**
Rosenthal, Christmas Plate
  1910, Winter Peace **370.00**
  1915, Walking to Church **120.00**
  1916, Christmas During War ... **160.00**
  1931, Path of the Magi **135.00**
  1945, Christmas Peace **240.00**
  1957, Christmas by the Sea **115.00**
  1971, Christmas in Garmisch **60.00**
Royal Copenhagen
  Christmas Plate
    1977, Immervad Bridge **18.00**
    1980, Bringing Home the Tree **25.00**
  Figurine
    Boy with Gourd, #4539 .... **225.00**
    Two Children, #1761 ...... **625.00**
    Milkmaid, #899 .... **425.00**
Royal Doulton
  Christmas Plate, Beswick
    1972, Christmas in England ... **40.00**
    1976, Christmas in Holland ... **25.00**
    1978, Christmas in America **45.00**
  Victorian Christmas Series Plate
    1977, Skaters **30.00**
    1979, Sleigh Ride **15.00**

Victorian Valentine Series Plate
  1976, Victorian Boy and Girl **25.00**
  1980, On a Swing **25.00**
Schmid
  Christmas Plate, Lowell Davis
    1983, Country Christmas **50.00**
    1987, Blossom's Gift **45.00**
    1990, Wintering Deer **30.00**
  Country Pride Series Plate, Lowell Davis,
    1981, Plum Tuckered Out ... **100.00**
Spode, Christmas Plate
  1970, Partridge **25.00**
  1973, We Three Kings of Orient **35.00**
Towle, Master Engravers, Railroad Ballad
  Series Sterling Plate, Ballad of Casey
  Jones **45.00**
Wedgwood
  Christmas Plate, Jasperware
    1970, Trafalgar Square **20.00**
    1971, Piccadilly Circus **25.00**
    1973, Tower of London **55.00**
    1979, Buckingham Palace **40.00**
  Mother's Day Plate
    1971, The Baptism of Achilles **15.00**
    1974, Domestic Employment **25.00**
W S George, Gone With The Wind, Golden
  Anniversary Plate, 1989, Frankly My
  Dear **30.00**

LINENS

Carefully examine linens for signs of wear, patching, and stains. Be cautious of estate linens that are unwashed and unironed. Question why the dealer has not prepared them for sale. Remember, you have no knowledge that the stains will come out. Also check all sets to make certain the pieces match.

Caring for Linens: If you are not planning to use your linens, store them unpressed, rolled, covered with an old pillow case, and out of bright sunlight. Rinse linens and the storage pillow case several times to make certain all detergent residue is removed.

If you are going to use your linens on a regular basis, wrap them in acid–free white tissue or muslin folders. Whenever possible, store linens on rollers to prevent creasing. You can get acid–free storage materials from Talas, 104 Fifth Avenue, New York, NY 10011.

Club: International Old Lacers, PO Box 481223, Denver, CO 80248.

Antimacassar, crocheted, fancy "F" in center, basket of flowers on each side, beige, 10 × 17" **30.00**
Apron, crocheted, pale pink, blue stripes at bottom and down sides, 13 × 17"
  .... **23.00**

Dresser Scarf, linen, cross–stitch embroidered baskets of flowers, $15.00.

Bedspread
  Batiste, white on white embroidery, 70
    × 106" **60.00**
  Chenille, double size
    Bright pink flowers, white ground
      .... **35.00**
    Green flowers, white ground   **25.00**
  Crocheted
    Child Size, child's prayer, "Now I
      Lay Me" alternating with squares
      of girl with candle, children skip-
      ping, bed, teddy bear, toys, cream
      colored, 52 × 96" **195.00**
    Full Size, ecru cotton, wide strips of
      hand crocheted popcorn stitch
      panel, gathered drop **125.00**
    Embroidered, figural lady and gentle-
      man, 1930s **35.00**
    Organdy, pastel, matching shams, Royal
      Society Kit #565, 1930–40 ... **45.00**
  Bread Tray Liner, crocheted, "Bread" in
    center, 6½ × 13" **20.00**
  Bridge Cloth, cross–stitch dec, Quimper
    pattern, green, blue, rose, and yellow,
    c1920 .... **100.00**
  Coverlet, white cotton, hand embroidered
    flowers, hand crocheted trim and fringe
    .... **75.00**
  Crib Blanket, pink bunnies and balloon dec,
    1930s **38.00**
  Dish Towel
    Embroidered, white textile bag, designs
      and days of week, 7 pc set, 38 ×
      18" **25.00**
    Printed cotton, strawberries design, blue
      border **8.00**

Doily, 18" d, crocheted twine cotton thread,
  pineapple pattern **12.00**
Dresser Set, cotton, white, embroidered la-
  dies and flowers, blue, pink, yellow, and
  green, crocheted edge **35.00**
Pillow Case, cotton, hand embroidered,
  crocheted trim, pr **10.00**
Pillow Cover, embroidered in red
  Collie center, 15" sq **30.00**
  Deer, antlers, 16" sq **30.00**
  Good Night Mama & Papa Dear, child's
    .... **20.00**
  I Slept & Dreamed/I Woke & Found,
    early 1900s **85.00**
Shawl, mauve and gold flowers, fringe dec,
  early 1900s **110.00**
Sheet, linen, finely embroidered panel, un-
  usual hemstitching, 69 × 98" **95.00**
Tablecloth
  Embroidered map of Florida, 48 × 50"
    .... **40.00**
  Tuscany Lace, beige, 56 × 84"   **275.00**
Tablecloth Set, tablecloth, 8 matching nap-
  kins, ecru, pull work, brown tones,
  cross–stitch deer pattern, paper label
  "Moravian Art Linen, Made In Czecho-
  slovakia" never used, 50 × 70"   **125.00**
Table Runner, Battenburg Lace, lacy 5" to
  7" wide Battenburg border all around,
  18 × 54" **168.00**
Wall Hanging, crocheted, The Spirit of St
  Louis, airplane in center, 17½ × 25"
  .... **95.00**

LITTLE GOLDEN BOOKS

Read me a story! For millions of children that story came from a Little Golden Book. Colorful, inexpensive, and readily available, these wonderful books are a hot collectible. You see them everywhere.

Be careful, you may be subject to a nostalgia attack because sooner or later you are going to spot your favorite. Relive your childhood. Buy the book. You won't be sorry.

Club: Golden Book Club, 19626 Ricardo Ave, Hayward, CA 94541.

Steve Canyon, *Milton Caniff, #356, c1959, $5.50.*

Bedtime Stories **9.00**
Buffalo Bill Jr, Gladys Wyatt, c1956 ... **5.50**
Captain Kangaroo and Panda, 1st ed, aver-
  age condition **9.00**
Dinosaurs, 1978 .... **6.00**
Doctor Dan at the Circus, Pauline Wilkins,
  c1960 .... **17.50**
Grandpa Bunny, Jane Werner, illus Walt
  Disney Studios, c1951 .... **15.00**
Heidi **8.00**
Huckleberry Hound Safety Signs, Ann
  McGovern, c1961 .... **7.00**
I'm An Indian Today, 1st ed **9.00**
It's Howdy Doody Time, 1st ed **20.00**
Lassie Shows The Way, fair **9.00**
Little Red Riding Hood, illus Sharon
  Koester, with paper dolls **25.00**
Ludwig Von Drake, 1st ed **14.00**
Mickey Mouse Club Stamp Book, Kathleen
  N Daily, c1956, orig stamps **20.00**
101 Dalmatians, near mint **6.00**
Our Puppy, Elsa Ruth Nast, c1948 ... **10.00**
Rusty Goes to School, Pierre Probst, c1962
  .... **5.00**
Saggy Baggy Elephant **9.00**
Santa's Toy Shop, 1950, 1st ed, very good
  condition **20.00**
Snow White **9.00**
The Aristocats, excellent condition **4.00**
The Black Hole, 1979 .... **6.00**
The Bunny Book **9.00**
The Christmas ABC, 1st ed **9.00**
Tiger's Adventure, William P Gottlieb,
  c1954 .... **5.50**
Zorro **14.00**

LITTLE ORPHAN ANNIE COLLECTIBLES

Little Orphan Annie is one of those characters that pops up everywhere—

Doily, peacock feather pattern, white cotton, 10" d, $10.00.

radio, newspapers, movies, etc. In the early 1930s "Radio Orphan Annie" was syndicated regionally. It went network in 1933. The show's only sponsor was Ovaltine. Many Little Orphan Annie collectibles were Ovaltine premiums.

Actually, Little Orphan Annie resulted from a sex–change operation. Harold Gray, an assistant on the "Gumps" strip, changed the sex of the leading character and submitted the same basic strip concept as a proposal to the *New York News.* The 1924 operation was a success.

Annie's early companions were Sandy, her dog, and Emily Marie, her doll. "Daddy" Warbucks replaced the doll, and the strip went big time. After Gray died in 1968, the strip was farmed out to a succession of artists and writers. The result was disastrous.

Radio and cartoon strip Little Orphan Annie material is becoming expensive. Try the more recent movie– and stage–related items if you are looking for something a bit more affordable.

Bank, circular, Famous Artists Syndicate, 1936 . . . . **225.00**
Big Little Book, *Little Orphan Annie in the Thieves' Den,* Helen Berke, Harold Gray artist, 1948 . . . . **20.00**
Book, *The Little Orphan Annie Book,* James Whitcomb Riley, color illus by Ethel Betts, 1908 . . . . **25.00**
Bracelet, identification disc, 1934 . . . **20.00**
Clicker, red, white, and black, Mysto members, 1941 . . . . **35.00**
Compass/Sundial, 1½" d, brass, silvery frosted finish, reverse with stamped Egyptian symbols, 1938 . . . . **75.00**

Mug, ceramic, "Didja Ever Taste Anything So Good As Ovaltine? And It's Good For Yuh, Too," Orphan Annie holding up identical mug, Sandy running for his Ovaltine on back, Harold Gray illus, c1932, $32.00.

Puzzle, Famous Comics Jig Saw No. 1, Stephens Kindred & Co, distributed by Novelty Distributing Co, 255 diecut cardboard pieces, comic sheet, 7¼ × 7¼" cardboard box, 12¼ × 13", $45.00.

Decoder, brass, dark luster, 1935 . . . . **25.00**
Gravy Boat, lusterware, white, orange, yellow, and black **175.00**
Handbook, *Secret Guard,* paper sheet, decoder, and clicker, orig mailing envelope, Quaker Puffed Wheat Sparkies and Rice Sparkies premium, 1941 . . . . **90.00**
Manual, *Radio Orphan Annie's Secret Society,* 1937 . . . . **30.00**
Mask, Annie, 1933 . . . . **30.00**
Medal, 1⅛" d, "Good Luck," brass, portrait under wishbone, Ovaltine adv, 1934 . . . . **25.00**
Mug, ceramic, 1932 . . . . **20.00**
Nodder, 3½" h, painted bisque, stamped on back "Orphan Annie," 1930s . . . **150.00**
Pastry Set, child's, baking utensils, Transogram "Gold Medal" Toy, 1930s **75.00**
Pendant, 2½" h, brass and plastic, figural, glossy paint, c1977 . . . . **10.00**
Photo, 8 × 10", black and white, glossy, Shirley Bell, sgd "To My Friend/Radio's Little Orphan Annie/Shirley Bell," 1932 . . . . **40.00**
Pinback Button, 1¼" d, "Little Orphan Annie/Some Swell Sweater," color portrait, white, black print **50.00**
Premium, talking stationery, 12 sheets and envelopes, 4 pg folder, orig mailing envelope, Ovaltine, 1937 . . . . **100.00**
Ring, brass, portrait on top, orig luster, 1934 . . . . **75.00**
Salt and Pepper Shakers, pr, 3" h, plaster, Annie and Sandy, 1940s **25.00**
Sheet Music, *Little Orphan Annie* . . . **15.00**
Snowdome, 3⅝ × 2⅞ × 2¾", plastic, Annie and Sandy, 1970s **10.00**
Stove, child's, metal` **35.00**
Tab, "Orphan Annie's Parents Smoked," blue and white, 1968 copyright **15.00**
Whistle, tin, signal, three tones **30.00**

LITTLE RED RIDING HOOD

On June 29, 1943, the United States Patent Office issued design patent #135,889 to Louise Elizabeth Bauer, Zanesville, Ohio, assignor to the A. E. Hull Pottery Company, Incorporated, Crooksville, Ohio, for a "Design for a Cookie Jar." Thus was born Hull's Little Red Riding Hood line. It was produced and distributed between 1943 and 1957.

Early cookie jars and the dresser jars with a large bow in the front can be identified by their creamy off–white color. The majority of the later pieces have very white pottery, a body attributed to The Royal China and Novelty Company, a division of Regal China. Given the similarity in form to items in Royal China and Novelty Company's "Old McDonald's Farm" line, Hull possibly contracted with Royal China and Novelty for production as well as decoration.

Great hand-painted and decal variation is encountered in pieces, e.g., the wolf jar is found with bases in black, brown, red, or yellow.

Prices for many pieces are in the hundreds of dollars. Prices for the advertising plaque and baby dish are in the thousands.

Attempts at determining production levels have been unsuccessful. This category has the potential for an eventual market flooding, especially for the most commonly found pieces. New collectors are advised to proceed with caution.

Undecorated blanks are commonly found. Value them between 25 and 50 percent less than decorated examples.

REPRODUCTION ALERT: Be alert for a Mexican produced cookie jar that closely resembles Hull's Little Red Riding Hood piece. The Mexican example is slightly shorter. Hull's examples measure 13" high.

Bank, standing **575.00**
Basket, open, large floral decal **275.00**
Batter Pitcher **400.00**
Butter Dish, cov **350.00**
Canister
    Coffee **590.00**
    Salt **850.00**
    Sugar **590.00**
Cookie Jar, red shoes, open basket, gold star apron **275.00**

Cookie Jar, red hood, floral decal on skirt, $275.00.

Dog, white and tan, 4" h, $195.00.

Fraim, 2¾" l, $5.00.

Cracker Jar, cov, 8½" h	500.00
Creamer	
Pantaloons	400.00
Side pour	115.00
Tab handle	275.00
Lamp	2,150.00
Milk Pitcher, standing, 8" h	275.00
Mustard, cov, orig spoon, 5½" h	325.00
Salt and Pepper Shakers, pr	
Large	125.00
Small	50.00
Spice Jar, allspice, cinnamon, cloves, nutmeg, or pepper, price each	625.00
String Holder	1,850.00
Sugar, cov, standing	400.00
Teapot, cov	285.00
Wall Pocket	500.00

LLADRO PORCELAINS

Lladro porcelains are Spain's contribution to the world of collectible figures. Some figures are released on a limited edition basis; others remain in production for an extended period of time. Learn what kinds of production numbers are involved.

Lladro porcelains are sold through jewelry and "upscale" gift shops. However, they are the type of item you either love or hate. As a result, Lladro porcelains from estates or from individuals tired of dusting that thing that Aunt Millie gave for Christmas in 1985 do show up at flea markets.

Club: Lladro Collectors Society, 43 West 57th St, New York, NY 10019.

Beagle Puppy, L–1071–G/M	125.00
Bride's Maid, L–5598	160.00
Curiosity, L–5393	40.00
Dog playing bongo drums, L–1156	500.00
Dog Singing, L–1155	500.00
Ducklings, L–1307	130.00
Girl with Calla Lillies, L–4650	120.00
Girl with Mandolin, 8" h	75.00
Heavenly Sounds, l–2195–M	170.00
Japanese Camelia, L–5181	90.00
Pastorial Couple, flower basket, L–4669	850.00
Picture Perfect	350.00
Rag Doll, L–1501	195.00
Sharpening the Cutlery, L–5204	450.00
Spring Flowers, L–1509	175.00

LOCKS

Padlocks are the most desirable lock collectible. While examples date back to the 1600s, the mass production of identifiable padlocks was pioneered in America in the mid–1800s.

Padlocks are categorized primarily according to tradition or use: Combination, Pin Tumbler, Scandinavian, etc. Cast, brass, and iron are among the more sought–after types.

Reproductions, copycats, and fakes are a big problem. Among the trouble spots are screw key, trick, iron lever, and brass lever locks from the Middle East, railroad switch locks from Taiwan, and switch lock keys from the U.S. Midwest. All components of an old lock must have exactly the same color and finish. Authentic railroad, express, and logo locks will have only one user name or set of initials.

Club: American Lock Collectors Association, 36076 Grennada, Livonia, MI 48154.

Newsletter: *Padlock Quarterly*, PO Box 9397, Phoenix, AZ 85068.

Eight Lever, 2½" h, iron, Samson, Corbin	15.00
Four Lever, 2" h, iron, Ajax, Corbin	12.00

Master Secret Service, No. 7, Laminated Padlock, orig 1¼ × 2¼" box with lion illus, $10.00.

Safe, 2³⁄₄" l, $7.50.

Gate Lock, 10" h, iron and brass, manufacturer's name **70.00**
Lever
  2" h
    Brass, Corbin **18.00**
    Iron
      Master, No. 41 . . . . **15.00**
      Sargent **12.00**
  2¹⁄₄" h, iron, Jupiter, Corbin **12.00**
  2⁵⁄₈" h, brass, Yale **30.00**
Money Bag Lock, 3" l, brass **35.00**
Pin Tumbler
  1¹⁄₂" h, brass, Best, Phil Fuels Co, logo
    lock, keyhole cov **18.00**
  1³⁄₄" h, brass, Reese US **5.00**
  2" h
    Brass
      USA Ordinance Dept, Corbin,
        logo lock **18.00**
      Yale, push key **15.00**
    Iron, push key, brass hasp
      Eagle **30.00**
      Yale **10.00**
Railroad
  C & EL RR, 2" h, signal, brass, XLCR,
    Corbin **28.00**
  C & NW RY, 2¹⁄₂" h, steel, Eagle **25.00**
  CMSTP & P, 3¹⁄₈" h, iron, brass hasp,
    Adlake **32.00**
  CSTPM & O, 2¹⁄₄" h, iron, Fraim **20.00**
  L & N RR, 2¹⁄₂" h, switch, steel,
    Slaymaker **40.00**
  MSTP & SSM RY, 2³⁄₄" h, switch, brass,
    Adlake **125.00**
  Pennsylvania RR, 2¹⁄₄" h, switch, steel,
    Slaymaker **25.00**
Shackle, 2⁷⁄₈" h, rotating, iron, Sterling
  . . . . **28.00**
Six Lever
  2" h
    Brass, Yale **15.00**
    Iron
      Fraim, brass levers **12.00**

O M Edwards Company . . . **12.00**
Reese, bronze plated **10.00**
Secure, Excelsior **5.00**
Steinke **38.00**
Winchester, brass plated **85.00**
2¹⁄₄" h, brass, push key, Harvard **24.00**
Trunk Latch Lock, Eagle Lock Co **5.00**

LUGGAGE

Until recently luggage collectors focused primarily on old steamship and railroad trunks. Unrestored, they sell in the $50 to $150 range. Dealers have the exterior refinished and the interior relined with new paper and then promptly sell them to decorators who charge up to $400. A restored trunk works well in both a Country or Victorian bedroom. This is why decorators love them so much.

Within the past three years, there has been a growing collector interest in old leather luggage. It is not uncommon to find early twentieth-century leather overnight bags priced at $150 to $300 in good condition. Leather suitcases sell in the $75 to $150 range.

LUNCH KITS

Lunch kits, consisting of a lunch box and matching thermos, were the most price-manipulated collectibles category of the 1980s. Prices in excess of $2,500 were achieved for some of the early Disney examples. What everyone seemed to forget is that lunch boxes were mass-produced.

The lunch kit bubble is in the process of bursting. Price are dropping for the commonly found examples. A few dealers and collectors are attempting to prop up the market, but their efforts are failing. If you are buying, it will pay to shop around for the best price.

Buy lunch kits. Resist the temptation to buy the lunch box and thermos separately.

I know this is a flea market price guide, but lunch kits can get pricy by the time they arrive at a flea market. The best buys remain at garage sales where the kits first hit the market and sellers are glad to get rid of them at any price.

Newsletter: *Hot Boxing*, PO Box 87, Somerville, MA 02143.

Periodical: *Paileontologist's Retort*, PO Box 3255, Burbank, CA 91508.

Alvin and the Chipmunks, 7 × 9 × 4", vinyl, King–Seeley, copyright 1963
. . . . **200.00**
A–Team, steel, plastic thermos, King–Seeley, 1985 . . . . **25.00**
Battle of the Planets, 7 × 9 × 4", metal, blue plastic thermos, King–Seeley, copyright 1979 . . . . **45.00**
Bionic Woman, 7 × 8 × 4", emb metal, plastic thermos, Aladdin, copyright 1977
. . . . **50.00**
Bobby Soxer, 7 × 8¹⁄₂ × 4", vinyl, Aladdin, c1959 . . . . **400.00**
Captain Kangaroo, vinyl, thermos, King–Seeley, 1964–66 . . . . **95.00**
Circus Wagon, 7 × 9 × 4¹⁄₂", metal, dome shape, American Thermos, c1958 **225.00**
Close Encounters Of The Third Kind, 7 × 8 × 4", metal, color illus, King–Seeley, copyright 1977–78 . . . . **45.00**
Corsage, 7 × 9 × 4", vinyl, color illus, King–Seeley, c1970 . . . . **75.00**
Daniel Boone, 7 × 8¹⁄₂ × 4", steel, King–Seeley, 1965 copyright **125.00**
Disneyland, 7 × 8 × 4", metal, color illus, park attractions, Aladdin, c1957 **75.00**
18 Wheeler, 7 × 8 × 4", emb metal, color illus, Aladdin, c1978 . . . . **125.00**
Family Affair, 7 × 8 × 4", metal, color illus, King–Seeley, copyright 1969 **75.00**
Flying Nun, 7 × 8 × 4", emb metal, color illus, Aladdin, copyright 1968 . . . . **75.00**
Fraggle Rock, 7 × 9 × 4", metal, color photos, plastic thermos, King–Seeley, copyright 1984 . . . . **25.00**
Freihofer's Chocolate Chip Cookies, 7 × 8 × 4", vinyl, brown, color photo, unused, 1960s **125.00**
Gene Autry/Melody Ranch, 6¹⁄₂ × 9 × 3¹⁄₂", Universal, 1954–55 . . . . . . **175.00**
Gone With The Wind, 1940 . . . . **450.00**
Holly Hobbie, steel, Aladdin, 1973–74
. . . . **16.00**
Julia, 7 × 9 × 4", metal, color illus, King–Seeley copyright 1969 . . . . **75.00**
Laugh–In, steel, plastic thermos, Aladdin, 1970 . . . . **70.00**
Lawman, 6¹⁄₂ × 8¹⁄₂ × 4", steel, American Thermos, c1961 . . . . **150.00**
Ludwig Von Drake in Disneyland, 7 × 8 × 4", emb metal, color illus, 1962 **55.00**
Mam'Zelle, 7 × 9 × 3¹⁄₂", vinyl, blue, illus, Aladdin, c1971 . . . . **110.00**
Mary Poppins, 7 × 9 × 4", vinyl, white, color illus, Aladdin, c1973 . . . . . **125.00**
Munsters, 7 × 9 × 4", metal, color illus, King–Seeley, copyright 1965 . . . **125.00**
New Zoo Review, vinyl, plastic thermos, Aladdin, 1975 . . . . **65.00**
Orbit, 7 × 9 × 4", metal, American Thermos, c1963 . . . . **125.00**
Osmonds, 7 × 8 × 4", emb metal, color illus, Aladdin, copyright 1973 . . . . **50.00**
Peanuts, 5 × 7¹⁄₂ × 9", vinyl, full color Lucy and Snoopy illus, King–Seeley, c1965 copyright **25.00**

Plaid, 7 × 9 × 3½", metal, metal thermos, Universal, c1959 . . . . **100.00**

Return of the Jedi, 7 × 9 × 4", metal, color illus, red plastic thermos, King–Seeley, copyright 1983 . . . . **50.00**

Road Tote, 6½ × 9 × 4½", vinyl, red, traffic signs illus, unmarked, 1970s **200.00**

Satellite, 7 × 9 × 4", metal, American Thermos, c1958 . . . . **75.00**

Shari Lewis And Her Friends, 7 × 9 × 3½", vinyl, black, color illus, Aladdin, copyright 1963 . . . . **200.00**

Sport Skwirts, metal, color illus, Ohio Art copyright 1972 . . . . **25.00**

Star Trek, 7 × 9 × 4", metal, dome shape, emb, Aladdin, copyright 1968 **400.00**

Street Hawk, 7 × 8 × 4", emb metal, color illus, thermos, Aladdin, copyright 1984 . . . . **200.00**

Take A Ham to Lunch, 7 × 8 × 4½", triangular shape, yellow vinyl, yellow handle, marked "Product of Hong Kong," c1970 . . . . **100.00**

Tarzan, 7 × 8 × 4", emb metal, color illus, Aladdin, copyright 1966 . . . . **555.00**

The Fox and the Hound, 7 × 8 × 4", emb metal, plastic thermos, Aladdin, c1981 . . . . **45.00**

The Guns of Will Sonnet, 7 × 8½ × 4", steel, King–Seeley, copyright 1968 . . . . **125.00**

The Life And Times Of Grizzly Adams, 7 × 9 × 4", metal, dome shape, color illus, Aladdin, copyright 1977 . . . . **75.00**

The Monroes, 7 × 8 × 4", emb steel, Aladdin, copyright 1967 . . . . **110.00**

Track King, 7 × 9 × 3½", metal, color illus, Okay Industries, c1975 . . . **200.00**

Twiggy, vinyl, thermos, King–Seeley, 1967–68 . . . . **190.00**

VW Bus, 6½ × 10½ × 4½", metal, Omni Graphics, 1960s **200.00**

Wagon Train, steel, thermos, King–Seeley, 1964 . . . . **140.00**

Walt Disney Character Firefighters, 7 × 9 × 4½", metal, dome shape, color illus, Aladdin, c1969 . . . . **125.00**

Walt Disney School Bus, 7 × 9 × 4½", metal, dome shape, plastic thermos, color illus, Aladdin, 1960s **75.00**

Wild Bill Hickock and Jingles, 7 × 8 × 4", steel, color illus, Aladdin, copyright 1955 . . . . **125.00**

MAGAZINES

The vast majority of magazines, especially if they are less than thirty years old, are worth between 10¢ and 25¢. A fair number of pre–1960 magazines fall within this price range as well.

There are three ways in which a magazine can have value: (1) the cover artist, (2) the cover personality, and (3) framable interior advertising. In three instances, value rests not with the magazine collector, but with the speciality collectors.

At almost any flea market, you will find a seller of matted magazine advertisements. Remember that the value being asked almost always rests in the matting and not the individual magazine page.

Periodical: *PCM (Paper Collectors' Marketplace)*, PO Box 127, Scandinavia, WI 54977.

American Golfer, December, 1932 **18.00**

American Home **2.00**

American Photography, 1932 . . . . **8.00**

Art and Beauty, 1926 . . . . **4.00**

Atlantic Monthly
1914 . . . . **4.00**
1929 . . . . **1.50**

Better Homes and Gardens, 1933 . . . . **1.50**

Boy's Life, August 1957 . . . . **15.00**

Business Week, 1935 . . . . **5.00**

Capper's Farmer, illus cov, Twelvetrees **12.00**

Collier's, June 9, 1938 . . . . **7.00**

Cosmopolitan, 1942 . . . . **2.00**

Country Home . . . . **.75**

Delineator, 1918 . . . . **25.00**

Democrat Press, The Great Flood Disaster of 1955, pictorial, black and white, 60 pgs **20.00**

Ebony, 1958 . . . . **5.00**

Esquire, September 1934 . . . . **12.00**

Farm & Fireside, November 1920 . . . . **4.00**

Farm Mechanics, 1928 . . . . **8.00**

Field and Stream **3.00**

Fortune, 1937 . . . . **12.00**

Good Housekeeping, 1942 . . . . **2.00**

Harper's Bazaar, illus cov **10.00**

Harper's Monthly, 1922 . . . . **4.00**

Harper's Weekly, December 1900 . . . **15.00**

Hobbies, August 1942 . . . . **2.00**

House Beautiful, illus cov **12.00**

Junior Home **1.00**

Ladies' Home Journal, 1925 . . . . **5.00**

Leica & Ziess, 1938 . . . . **10.00**

Life
Beatles, 1960s **25.00**
Eisenhower cov, April 16, 1945 . . . . **10.00**
Fred Astaire and son cov, Aug 25, 1941 . . . . **9.00**
Illustrated cover, artist sgd **20.00**
Jimmy Stewart cov, Sept 24, 1945 **10.00**

Literary Digest, 1924 . . . . **1.00**

Look, James Dean cov, 1956 . . . . **18.00**

Mattel Barbie Magazine, Nov–Dec 1963 . . . . **10.00**

McCall's, 1932 . . . . **10.00**

Mechanics Illustrated **1.00**

Modern Art, 1927, nude poses **30.00**

Modern Screen, 1940, Jeannette MacDonald cov **30.00**

Movie & Theatre News, 1933 . . . . **7.00**

Movie Star Parade, January 1947 . . . . **22.00**

Nature, March 1925 . . . . **5.00**

Newsweek, Hitler cov **12.00**

Outdoor Life 1932 . . . . **12.00**

People's Home Journal, 1918 . . . . **8.00**

Pictorial Review, March 1915 . . . . . . **12.50**

Picture Play, 1932, Carol Lombard cov **40.00**

Playboy, 1958 . . . . **10.00**

Popular Science, 1935 . . . . **1.00**

Puck, January 30, 1889 . . . . **10.00**

Radio Mirror, 1936, Fred Astaire cov **30.00**

Reader's Digest, 1940 . . . . **1.00**

Saturday Evening Post
1917, cov with children running from baseball game in rain, Rockwell **42.00**
1923, Pearl Harbor **10.00**
1953, boy in bed with dog and doctor holding needle on cov, Rockwell **36.00**

Train, oval, silver and red, 8½" × 3½", $25.00.

TV Guide, *Johnny Carson and his bride cover, June 27 to July 3, $5.00.*

Screen Stories, 1949, "Take Me Out To The
    Ball Game" cov **25.00**
S E P, January 3, 1920, Lyendecker cov
    . . . . **25.00**
Sports Illustrated, 1961, Roger Maris cov
    . . . . **30.00**
Sunbathing For Health, December 1951
    . . . . **2.50**
The Theater Magazine, 1908 . . . . **5.00**
Time
    1940, Mussolini and Bodoglio cov
    . . . . **25.00**
    1969, August 8, John Wayne cov **17.50**
Town and Country, July 1948, Dali cov
    . . . . **35.00**
TV Guide
    Elvis cov **30.00**
    NYC–TeleVision Guide, 1948–53 **40.00**
    Superman **30.00**
Vanity Fair **4.00**
Vogue, 1928, Lepape illus cov **40.00**
Who's Who In Sports, 1st issue, 1950 **35.00**
Woman's Home Companion, 1916   **20.00**
Woman's World, February 1936 . . . . . **5.00**

MAGIC

Presto, chango—the world of magic
has fascinated collectors for centuries.
The category is broad; it pays to specialize. Possible approaches include children's magic sets, posters about magicians, or sleight–of–hand tricks.

When buying a trick, make certain
to get instructions—if possible, the original. Without them, you need to be a
mystic, rather than a magician, to figure
out how the trick works.

Magic catalogs are treasure chests of
information. Look for company names
such as Abbott's, Brema, Douglas Ma-
gicland, Felsman, U. F. Grant, Magic
Inc., Martinka, National Magic, Nelson
Enterprises, Owen Magic Supreme, Petrie–Lewis, D. Robbins, Tannen, Thayer,
and Willmann. Petrie–Lewis is a favorite
among collectors. Look for the interwoven "P & L" on magic props.

Magicians of note include: Alexander, Blackstone, Carter The Great,
Germain The Wizard, Houdini, Kar–I,
Kellar, Stock, and Thornston. Anything
associated with these magicians has potentially strong market value.

Club: Magic Collectors Assoc, 19 Logan
St, New Britain, CT 06051.

Book
    *Fred Keating/Magic's Greatest Enter-
        tainer,* 16 pgs, c1950 . . . . **25.00**
    Gilbert Knots & Splices, rope tying
        tricks, 66 pgs, 1909 . . . . **40.00**
    Magic Made Easy, 28 pgs, 1930 copy-
        right **20.00**

Magicdotes, Robert Orben, 44 pgs, 1948
    copyright **15.00**
Transcendental Magic, Eliphas Levi
    . . . . **85.00**
Booklet
    Mysto Magic, 5½ × 7", 48 pgs, A C Gil-
        bert kit, copyright 1922 . . . . . . **25.00**
    Nicola Magician–Illusionist, 8 × 11", 20
        pgs, 1915 . . . . **75.00**
    Thurston's Book of Magic, 3½ × 6", 8
        pgs, 1920–30 . . . . **15.00**
Broadside, 5 × 24", De La Mano, magic
    acts vignettes, c1880 . . . . **85.00**
Catalog
    Heaney Company, 1924 . . . . **20.00**
    *Learn to Entertain with Super Magic
        Tricks & Puzzles* **20.00**
Flyer, De La Mano's, double sided, c1880
    5 × 14", Magic Show adv **60.00**
    6 × 10", blue stock **25.00**
Magazine, *Linking Ring, Magicians of the
    World,* 1939 . . . . **15.00**
Magic Box, 5½" sq, orig sealed carton,
    1960s **18.00**
Magic Kit
    PF Fliers Blackstone Magic Wedge Kit,
        sealed bag with Balance Magic, Dis-
        appearing Coin Trick, and Defy
        Gravity, box with Blackstone Jr illus,
        1970s **15.00**
    Scarecrow Magic Kit, Ralston Purina Co
        premium, 1960s **25.00**
Magic Trick, Fun, Magic, and Mystery, 4 ×
    9" red and white envelope with Phantom
    Card Trick and Pick–It–Out Card Trick,
    1930s **20.00**
Pinback Button
    14th Annual International Brotherhood
        of Magicians Convention, Battle
        Creek, Michigan, blue and white,
        1939 . . . . **6.00**
    Houdini Convention Club of Wisconsin,
        blue and white, 1930s **8.00**
    The International Brotherhood of Magi-
        cians, orange, 1930s **12.00**

MAGNIFYING GLASSES

The vast majority of magnifying
glasses that are offered for sale at flea
markets are made–up examples. Their
handles come from old umbrellas,
dresser sets, and even knives. They look
old and are highly decorative—a deadly
combination for someone who thinks
they are getting a one–hundred–year–
old plus example.

There are few collectors of magnifying glasses. Therefore, prices are low,
often a few dollars or less, even for some
unusual examples. The most collectible
magnifying glasses are the Sherlock
Holmes type and examples from upscale
desk accessory sets. These often exceed
$25.00.

MARBLES

Marbles divide into handmade glass
marbles and machine–made glass, clay,
and mineral marbles. Marble identification is serious business. Read and re-
read these books before buying your first
marble: Paul Baumann, *Collecting Antique Marbles, Second Edition* (Wallace–
Homestead, 1991); and Mark E. Randall
and Dennis Webb, *Greenberg's Guide to
Marbles* (Greenberg Publishing, 1988).

Children played with marbles. A
large number are found in a damaged
state. Avoid these. There are plenty of
examples in excellent condition.

Beware of reproductions and modern copycats and fakes. Comic marbles
are just one of the types that is currently
being reproduced.

Clubs: Marble Collectors' Unlimited, PO
Box 206, Northboro, MA 01532; Marble
Collectors Society of America, PO Box
222, Trumbull, CT 06611; National Mar-
ble Club of America, 440 Eaton Rd,
Drexel Hill, PA 19026.

Akro Agate
    ½" d, bull's eye **20.00**
    ⅝" d, contemporary **3.00**
Bennington Type
    ⅝" d, mottled blue **25.00**
    ⅞" d, mottled brown **30.00**
Cat's Eyes, Vitro–Agate, bag of 100, c1950
    . . . . **35.00**
Comic Strip, glass
    Emma **60.00**
    Koko **30.00**
    Skeezix **45.00**
    Tom Mix **55.00**
Onionskin
    ½" d, blue and white swirls **25.00**
    2" d, red and yellow swirls **275.00**
Opaque Swirl, ⅝" d **35.00**
Sulphide
    1¼" d, pig **60.00**
    1⅝" d, woman **150.00**
    1¾" d, Chow dog **75.00**
Swirl, 1" d, blue, orange, and green   **55.00**
Transparent Swirl, ⅝" d
    Divided Core Swirl **15.00**
    Latticino Core Swirl **10.00**
    Solid Core Swirl **20.00**

MARILYN MONROE COLLECTIBLES

In the 1940s a blonde bombshell
exploded across the American movie
screen. Born Norma Jean Mortonson in
1926, she made her debut in several
magazines in the mid-1940s and appeared in the Twentieth Century Fox

movie *Scudda Hoo! Scudda Hey!* in 1948.

Now known as Marilyn Monroe, she captured the public eye with her flamboyant nature and hourglass figure. Her roles in such films as *The Dangerous Years* in 1948, *Bus Stop* in 1956, *Some Like It Hot* in 1959, and *The Misfits* in 1961 brought much attention to this glamour queen.

Her marriages to baseball hero Joe DiMaggio and famous playright Arthur Miller, not to mention her assorted illicit affairs with other famous gentlemen, served to keep Marilyn's personal life on the front burner. It is commonly believed that the pressures of her personal life contributed to her untimely death on August 5, 1962.

Clubs: All About Marilyn, PO Box 291176, Los Angeles, CA 90029; Marilyn Forever, PO Box 638, Swayzee, IN 46986-0638.

Autograph, on white paper **150.00**
Bank, 7" h, battery operated, insert coin and her dress blows up **55.00**
Blotter, 3¾ × 9", cardboard, full color Earl Moran art **65.00**
Book
   Norma Jean, The Life of Marilyn Monroe, dj, 1969 . . . . **25.00**
   Marilyn, Norman Mailer, hard cov, dj, 270 glossy pgs, black and white and color photos, library copy **10.00**
Calendar
   1953 . . . . **10.00**
   1954, "Golden Dreams," nude on red background portrait, glossy, full pad, 11 × 24" **175.00**
   1955 . . . . **25.00**
Change Tray, 4⅛" d, litho metal, round, color portrait on red ground, mahogany frame, 1950s **40.00**
Lobby Card, *The Seven Year Itch*, No. 8, 11 × 14", 1955 . . . . **35.00**
Magazine
   Life
      April 7, 1952, cover article, 172 pgs, 10½ × 14" **25.00**
      August 17, 1962, framed **50.00**
   Marilyn Monroe Pin–Ups, 32 pgs, black and white and color photos, 8½ × 11", 1953 . . . . **70.00**
   Modern Man, nude photos, 1956 **35.00**
   Rave, 8 × 10¼", August 1956, 64 pgs, full color front cov, 28 page article and photos **50.00**
   That Girl Marilyn!, 56 pgs, black and white photos, 4 × 6", c1955 **18.00**
   TV Guide, volume 6, #4, January 23–29, 1953 . . . . **35.00**
Magazine Cover, *Screen Annual*, 1953 . . . . **100.00**

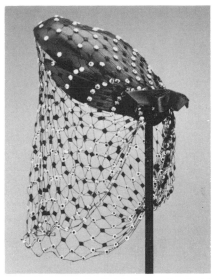

Evening Hat, black silk, black netted veil with rhinestones, letter of authenticity accompanies hat, $1650.00.

Movie Poster
   Home Town Story, MGM, 1951   **200.00**
   Let's Make It Legal, Twentieth Century Fox, 1951 . . . . **150.00**
   O. Henry's Full House, Fox, 1952 . . . . **135.00**
   Some Like It Hot, United Artists, 1959 . . . . **300.00**
Necktie, *The Seven Year Itch*, black, colorful stitched image, Made in England, mid–1950s **75.00**
Paper Dolls, Saalfield, No. 158610, uncut, 10¾ × 12½", 1953 . . . . **145.00**
Playing Cards, nude, sealed, complete set **32.00**
Script, *Bus Stop*, 123 pgs, 1956 . . . . **120.00**
Sheet Music, *Bus Stop*, Monroe cov, 1956 . . . . **25.00**
Snowdome, red plastic, marked "Koziol" **35.00**
Statue, 4" h, porcelain **8.00**
Title Card, *We're Not Married*, Twentieth Century Fox, Marilyn with Ginger Rogers, Fred Allen, and Victor Moore, 1952 . . . . **35.00**

MARX TOYS

My favorite days as a child were filled with the adventures of cowboys and Indians in their constant struggle for control of Fort Apache. I have only Louis Marx to thank for those hours of imagination and adventure for I was a proud owner of a Marx playset.

The Marx Toy Company was founded after World War I when Louis and David Marx purchased a series of dies and molds from the bankrupt Strauss Toy Company. In the following years the Marx Toy Company produced a huge assortment of tin and plastic toys, including 60 to 80 playsets with hundreds of variations. These playsets, some with lithographed tin structures, are very collectible if complete. Marx also manufactured a number of windup and action toys like Rock–em Sock–em Robots and the very popular Big Wheel tricycle.

The Marx Toy Company was bought and sold a number of times before finally filing for bankruptcy in 1980. The Quaker Oats Company owned Marx from the late 1950s until 1978, at which time it was sold to its final owner, the British toy company Dunbee–Combex.

Ambulance, 13½" l, litho tin, windup, brake, siren, red and black trim on ivory ground, 1937 . . . . **450.00**
American Trucking Co Moving Van, 5" l, tin, friction, green lettering on blue ground, rear door opens **175.00**
Army Playset **30.00**
Army Truck, 12" l, plastic, steel frame, rubber tires, tailgate opens, olive drab, c1950 . . . . **75.00**
Auto Transport, 30½" l, tin, carries coupe, roadster, and dump truck, eight wheels and spare, 1938 . . . . **500.00**
Bagatelle Game **28.00**
Brewster Rooster **100.00**
Cadillac Coupe, 11" l, litho tin, windup, orange body, black trim, trunk rack, 1931 . . . . **375.00**
Circle X Ranch, 21 × 15 × 5", diecut cardboard, punch–out pieces, MIB   **150.00**
City Airport, 17 × 11" red steel base, battery operated lights, two monoplanes, litho tin control tower and two hangars, c1935 . . . . **125.00**
City Delivery Van, 11" l, steel, yellow, red fenders, tin grille **200.00**
City Hospital Ambulance, litho tin, windup, red trim on blue ground, rear opens, c1930 . . . . **350.00**
Climbing Tractor, 8¼" l, litho tin, windup, 1930 . . . . **175.00**
Convertible, 11" l, steel, blue top, red body, white tires, 1930s **325.00**
Coo Coo Car, crazy car, 8" l, litho tin, windup, 1931 . . . . **750.00**
Dial Typewriter, 11" l, 5¾" w, black, red, and gold, flat keyboard, 1930s   **125.00**
Dick Tracy Squad Car, 11¼" l, litho tin, windup, siren, flashing red spotlight, two rubber and two wooden wheels, 1949 . . . . **300.00**
Dippy Dumper, crazy car, 8¾" l, litho tin, windup, celluloid Popeye and Brutus figures, movable dump cart, 1940 . . . . **650.00**
Doughboy Tank, 10" l, litho tin, windup, tan ground, 1942 . . . . **250.00**

Toy, Mystery Space Ship, plastic, space ship, rockets, figures, orig booklet, $65.00.

Dump Truck, #1013, 18" l, plastic, c1950 .... **150.00**

Eagle Air Scout, 26" l, 26½" wingspan, litho tin, windup, silver body, blue trim, revolving propeller, 1929 .... **350.00**

Fighter Plane, 5" wingspan, litho tin, windup, two engines, wooden wheels, stars and bars decal on wings and fuselage, 1940s **75.00**

Fire Chief Car, 8" l, steel, friction, red body, black fenders and bumper, black and white wheels, siren, 1936 ...... **250.00**

Fire Truck, 14½" l, steel, windup, baked enamel finish, two ladders, two fire extinguishers, cranking fire tower, tin fireman, 1948 .... **225.00**

Flash Gordon Signal Pistol, 6¾" l, steel, enameled, green, sparking mechanism, siren, 1936 .... **95.00**

Flying Fortress, 13½" l, 18" wingspan, litho tin, windup, red and silver, four engines, silver propellers, white balloon wheels, sparking machine guns **325.00**

G–Man Pursuit Car, #7000, 14½" l, litho tin, windup, sparking mechanism, red and navy blue body, cream trim, aluminum rear bumper, 1935 .... **500.00**

Greyhound Bus Terminal, 16" l, 11" w, litho tin, two pumps, two sign boards, two garage entrances, drugstore, waiting room, c1938 .... **300.00**

Hey Hey the Chicken Snatcher, 8½" h, litho tin, windup, 1926 .... **250.00**

Hill Climbing Dump Truck, 13½" l, litho tin, windup, rubber treads, 1932 **150.00**

Honeymoon Special, 6" d, litho tin, windup, train with engine and three cars, 1927 .... **150.00**

Joy Rider, crazy car, 8" l, litho tin, windup, 1928 .... **650.00**

Lazy Day Farms Playset **95.00**

Liberty Bus, 5" l, litho tin, windup, 1931 .... **125.00**

Lone Ranger Adventure Set, 1973, MIB
   Blizzard Adventure **15.00**
   Canoe **30.00**
   Hidden Silvermine Adventure **15.00**

   Landslide Adventure **15.00**
   Lost Cavalry Pass **20.00**
   Missing Mountain Climber **15.00**
   Mysterious Prospector **40.00**
   Tribal Pow Pow **15.00**

Mammy's Boy, 11" h, litho tin, windup, walking, changeable expression, holding cane, 1929 .... **200.00**

Meadow Brook Dairy Truck, 10" l, tin, carries milk bottles, 1940 .... **300.00**

Midget Tractor, 5¼" l, litho tin, red, green, yellow, and black, curved radiator, 1940 .... **65.00**

Mortimer Snerd's Tricky Auto, 7½" l, litho tin, windup, crazy car, 1939 .... **800.00**

Mystery Car, 9" l, steel, tin radiator, red, 1936 .... **175.00**

Mystic Motorcycle, 4¼" l, litho tin, windup, blue, yellow, and white, 1936 **175.00**

New Sky Bird Flyer, litho tin, 9½" h control tower, 24" l crossbar, two planes, one motor, 1947 .... **450.00**

North American Van Lines Tractor Trailer, 13" l, litho tin, windup **200.00**

Old Jalopy, 5¾" l, litho tin, windup, crazy car, driver wearing glasses, 1950 **250.00**

Peter Rabbit, 5½" l, plastic, windup, crazy car, 1950s **450.00**

Pinocchio the Acrobat, 16" h, 11" w, litho tin, windup, composition, jointed, cardboard legs, 1939 .... **250.00**

Playset, MIB
   Captain Blood & The Buccaneers **50.00**
   Desert Storm Air Wars LTD **55.00**
   Gold Rush **85.00**
   Prehistoric Times
     #1000 .... **155.00**
     #3398, orig booklet, animals, men, trees, mountains, 1961 ... **135.00**
   Superior Barn, livestock **30.00**
   Superior Gas Station, tin **75.00**

Popeye Pirate Click Pistol, 10" l, litho tin, 1930s **115.00**

Racer, windup **35.00**

Road Grader **40.00**

Roadside Rest Service Station, 13½" l, 10" w, battery operated, 1935 **500.00**

Rocket Racer, 16" l, litho tin, windup, litho tin driver, red body, blue backrest, green, yellow, blue, and black trim, green and black wheels, 1935 **500.00**

School Bus, 11½" l, steel, wood wheels, pull toy, 1930s **225.00**

Service Station, metal, missing gas pump and two light poles, minor scratches, 1948–53 .... **225.00**

Smoky Sam, 6½" l, plastic hat, body, and car, litho tin head and wheels, windup, crazy car, 1950 .... **200.00**

Sparks Racer, 8¼" l, litho tin, windup, yellow body, red and black trim, sparking mechanism, 1928 .... **300.00**

Speed Racer, tin **225.00**

Stake–body Truck, 13½" l, metal, gold and white **85.00**

Tractor, tin litho, orig male figure **130.00**

Trans–Atlantic Zeppelin, 10" l, litho tin, windup, striped rudder, c1930 **400.00**

Tricky Taxi, 4½" l, litho steel, clockwork motor, 1935 .... **75.00**

Trunk, holds Royal Bus **125.00**

Tumbling Monkey, 4½" h, litho tin, windup, 1942 .... **110.00**

Turnover Tank, 9" l, litho tin, windup, 1930 .... **250.00**

Typewriter, tin, 1930s **110.00**

Uncle Wiggily Car, 7½" l, litho tin, windup, crazy car, 1935 .... **850.00**

Volunteer Fire Department Car **75.00**

MARY GREGORY GLASS

Who was Mary Gregory anyway? Her stuff certainly is expensive. Beware of objects that seem like too much of a bargain. They may have been painted by Mary Gregory's great–great granddaughter in the 1950s rather than in the 1880s. Also, watch the eyes. The original Mary Gregory did not paint children with slanted eyes. Guess who did?

Box, cov
   3⅛" d, cranberry, girl and floral sprays, hinged lid **265.00**
   4½" d, cranberry, white enameled young girl on cov **275.00**

Cruet, green, young girl carrying flowers, applied clear handle and stopper **90.00**

Liqueur Glass, 3⅜" h, lime green, little girl **50.00**

Match Holder, 2¼" h, cranberry, young boy **90.00**

Miniature, pitcher, 2" h, sapphire blue, white enameled dec **225.00**

Mug, 4½ h, amber, ribbed, girl praying **55.00**

Perfume Bottle, 4⅝" h, cranberry, little girl, clear ball stopper **165.00**

Pitcher
   9½" h, medium green, boy and girl dec **250.00**

10" h, sapphire blue, child dec
.... **345.00**
10½" h, clear, man in sailboat, ruffled
top **125.00**
Plate
6¼" d, cobalt blue, white enamel girl
with butterfly net **125.00**
11" d, black amethyst, stag running
.... **285.00**
Saltshaker, 5" h, paneled, blue, girl in garden dec, brass top **175.00**
Toothpick Holder, cranberry, girl and floral
sprays **55.00**
Tumbler
2¼" h, pr, cranberry, boy on one, girl on
other **100.00**
5¾" h, blue, white enameled boy, gold
bands, pedestal foot **140.00**
Vase
4" h, cranberry, boy and girl reading
books, pr **110.00**
5" h, robin's–egg blue, girl running
through flower field dec **125.00**
9" h, emerald green, frosted, girl holding
flowers in apron and hand
.... **150.00**

MATCHBOOKS

Don't play with matches. Save their covers instead. A great collection can be built for a relatively small sum of money. Matchcover collectors gain a fair amount of their new material through swapping.

A few collectors specialize in covers that include figural shaped or decorated matches. If you get into this, make certain you keep them stored in a covered tin container and in a cool location. If you don't, your collection may catch fire and go up in smoke.

Clubs: Rathkamp Matchcover Society, 1359 Surrey Road, Vandalia, OH 43577; The American Matchcover Collecting Club, 16 Forest View Dr, Asheville, NC 28804.

Note: There are over thirty regional clubs throughout the United States and Canada.

Newsletters: *Matchcover Classified,* 16425 Dam Rd #31, Clearlake, CA 95422; *The Match Hunter,* 740 Poplar, Boulder, CO 80304.

ABC Coach Lines, Fort Wayne, IN **2.00**
Albert Sheetz Mission Candies/Ice Cream,
diamond quality **2.00**
American Ace, boxes .... **.12**
Banks .... **.02**
Big Joe Sells Best Because It Is Best, dia-
mond quality **2.00**
Billiards .... **.05**

Pin–Up, Butch's Tavern, Terre Haute, IN, Superior Match Co, Chicago, artist, double size, $1.50.

Bob's Tavern, Brewster, NE **2.00**
Casinos .... **.05**
Chevrolet, 1952 .... **3.00**
City Club Beer **2.50**
Delta Airlines, 50th Year, 1929–79 ... **2.50**
Ehlers Coffee, 1930s **1.50**
Fairs .... **.15**
Feuer's Restaurant, Chicago, IL, diamond
quality **2.00**
Foreign .... **.05**
Girlies, non stock .... **.40**
Griffith's Sinclair Station, Danielsville, GA
.... **2.00**
Holiday Inns, stock design .... **.10**
Hygrade Frankfurters and Honey Band
Ham, diamond quality **2.25**
JFG Coffee, 1930s **1.50**
Joe Louis & Max Schmeling Championship
Fight, Giant **18.00**
Krasdale Coffee, 1930s **1.50**
Lone Star Beer, stock cov **2.50**
Lou's Diner, Mill Plain, CT **3.00**
Matchtones, Universal trademark ..... **.10**
Medford Cafe, Mystic 6010, diamond qual-
ity **2.25**
Motel Washington, Fairfax, VA **3.00**
Old Master Coffee, 1930s **1.75**
Patriotic .... **.05**
Playboy Club, Atlanta **2.00**
Pontiac Motor Division **3.50**
Presidential Yacht, "Patricia" **10.00**
Pull for Willkie, Pullquick Match **28.00**
Remember Pearl Harbor, red, white, and
blue, anti–Japan slogan on cover, Uncle
Sam on back, early 1940s **10.00**
Revelation Tooth Powder, 1930s **6.00**
San Diego Zoo, c1970 .... **1.00**
Shurfire Coffee, 1930s **1.50**
Stoeckle Select Beer, Stoeckle Brewery **6.00**
Taxi Cabs, assorted companies **4.00**
Texas Centennial, Dallas, 1936 ..... **2.50**
TWA Airline **5.00**
Vote For Governor Brown, photo **2.00**
Wrigley's Chewing Gum **3.00**

MATCHBOX TOYS

Leslie and Rodney Smith founded Lesney Products, an English company, in 1947. They produced the first Matchbox toys. In 1953 the trade name "Match-box" was registered and the first diecast cars were made on a 1:75 scale. In 1979 Lesney produced over 5.5 million cars per week. In 1982 Universal International bought Lesney.

Newsletter: *Matchbox USA,* 62 Saw Mill Rd, Durham, CT 06422.

Clubs: American–International Matchbox Collectors & Exchange Club, 532 Chestnut Street, Lynn, MA 01904; Matchbox Collectors Club, PO Box 278, Durham, CT 06422; The Matchbox International Collectors Assoc, 574 Canewood Crescent, Waterloo, Ontario N2L 5P6 Canada.

Ambulance, Lomas, #41, white **30.00**
Benz Limousine, 1910, 1966 Models of Yes-
teryear Series, MIB **40.00**
Boat and Trailer, #48, red, white, and blue
.... **35.00**
Bomag Road Roller, 1979, yellow, Superfast
Series, MOC **10.00**
Cadillac, 1913, 1967 Models of Yesteryear
Series, MIB **40.00**
Cattle Truck and Trailer, MBP **20.00**
Coca–Cola Lorry, #37, yellow **55.00**
DAF Girder Truck, 1968, light cream, MIB
.... **35.00**
Daimier, 1911, dark yellow, black fenders,
1966 Models of Yesteryear Series, MIB
.... **12.00**
Datsun 260Z and Speed Boat, MBP
.... **20.00**
Faun Dump Truck, yellow, 1976, Superfast
Series, MOC **8.00**
Ford GT, #41, white **30.00**
Fowler Big Lion Showmans Engine, 1958
Models of Yesteryear Series, MIB
.... **45.00**
Galaxie Police Car, #55, white, orig box
.... **25.00**
Ice Cream Truck, Lyons Maid, #37, blue
.... **45.00**
Impala Taxi, #20, yellow, red int, orig box
.... **20.00**
Jeep, glider, white base, MBP **25.00**
Lagonda Coupe, 1938, beige and black,
1973 Models of Yesteryear Series, MIB
.... **9.00**
Lamborghini Miura, red, 1969 King Size se-
ries, MIB **45.00**
Leyland Tipper, red, Le Transport labels,
1969 King Size series, MIB **45.00**
Lincoln Continental, #31, orig box
Dark blue **35.00**
Light green **20.00**
Low Loader with bulldozer, light green,
1967 King Size series, MIB **45.00**
Matchbox City Case, playset, 1972, MIB
.... **35.00**
Maxwell Roadster, 1911, 1965 Models of
Yesteryear Series, MIB **40.00**

Land Rover Fire Truck, red, #57, MOC, $5.00.

Mercedes Benz, 220 SE, dark red **35.00**
Mercury Cougar, metallic gold, 1968 King
    Size series, MIB **45.00**
Mercury Police Car, #55, white, orig box
    .... **30.00**
Military Ambulance and Staff Car, MBP
    .... **25.00**
Military Dumper and Dozer, olive, MBP
    .... **30.00**
Model A Truck, Matchbox adv on truck
    panel, MOC **5.00**
Packard Landolet, 1912, 1964 Models of
    Yesteryear Series, MIB **40.00**
Peugeot, 1907, 1969 Models of Yesteryear
    Series, MIB **40.00**
Pipe Truck, yellow cab, MBP **75.00**
Pontiac Convertible, #39, yellow, orig box
    .... **45.00**
Racing Car Transporter, 1965, light green,
    missing one tire **20.00**
Ready Mix Concrete Truck, orange, 1963
    King Size series, MIB **45.00**
Renault, 1911 two seater, 1963 Models of
    Yesteryear Series, MIB **40.00**
Skip Truck, 1976, red, yellow load bucket,
    Superfast Series, MOC **8.00**
Snow Trac, 1964, red, MIB **30.00**
Spyker, 1904, 1961 Models of Yesteryear
    Series, MIB **40.00**
Taylor Jumbo Crane, yellow and red boom
    box, 1964 King Size series, MIB
    .... **50.00**
Transcontinental Truck and Trailer, MBP
    .... **25.00**

McCOY POTTERY

Like Abingdon Pottery, this attractive pottery is sought by those no longer able to afford Roseville and Weller pottery. Commemorative cookie jars and planters seem to be rapidly increasing in price, like the Apollo Spaceship cookie jar at $45.00. These specialty items bring more from secondary collectors than from McCoy collectors who realize the vast quantity of material available in the market.

Beware of reproductions. The Nelson McCoy Pottery Company is making modern copies of their period pieces. New collectors are often confused by them.

Newsletter: *Our McCoy Matters,* PO Box 14255, Parkville, MO 64152.

Ball Jug, yellow **25.00**
Bank, Seaman's Savings, sailor with sea bag
    .... **50.00**
Basket, basketweave design, green and
    white ext, white int, 1957 .... **25.00**
Bookends, pr, jumping horses, marked
    "Nu–Art" **18.50**
Bowl, 6" d, matte green **25.00**
Bud Vase, 8" h, matte green **5.00**
Console Bowl, 8¾" d, blue, tulip dec **7.50**
Cookie Jar
    Coffee Cup **37.00**
    Fireplace **95.00**
    Raggedy Ann **95.00**
    Tugboat **30.00**
    W C Fields **150.00**
    Woodsy Owl **250.00**
Creamer, sitting dog, green, 1950s ... **25.00**
Decanter, Apollo **195.00**
Flower Frog, 2½" d, heart shape, blue onyx
    .... **30.00**
Jardiniere, 9" h, brown **50.00**
Mug, Suburbia pattern, yellow **7.50**
Pitcher, elephant, white, 1940s **45.00**
Planter
    Dog, light green and white **12.00**
    Frog, green **8.50**
    Sprinkling Can, white, rose decal **6.50**
Salt and Pepper Shakers, pr, cabbage **10.00**
Soap Dish, Lucile **100.00**
Spittoon, frog dec **125.00**
Tankard Set, Buccaneer, green, two mugs
    .... **50.00**

Pitcher, turtle, green, yellow eyes, mouth, and floral buds, 9½" l, $20.00.

Teapot
    Grecian pattern **25.00**
    Pine Cone **75.00**
Vase, 7½" h, mottled green, marked "Brush,
    #709" **18.00**

MEDICAL ITEMS

Anything medical is collectible. Doctors often discard instruments, never realizing that the minute an object becomes obsolete, it also becomes collectible. Many a flea market treasure begins life in a garbage can behind the doctor's office.

Stress condition and completeness. Specialize in one area. Remember, some instruments do not display well. Dad's wife will not let him keep his collection of rectal examiners in the living room.

Club: Medical Collectors Assoc, 1300 Morris Park Ave, Bronx, NY 10461.

Periodical: *Scientific, Medical & Mechanical Antiques,* 11824 Taneytown Pike, Taneytown, MD 21787.

Apothecary Beaker, Whitall–Tatum Co, 500
    cc **25.00**
Apothecary Bottle, Sunnybrook Medicinal
    Whiskey, apothecary, sealed, orig box
    with prescription storage window, color
    graphics **85.00**
Artificial Eye, 25 in fitted box **150.00**
Book
    Medical, Practical Hematological Diag-
      nosis, 1933 .... **18.00**
    Surgical Emergencies In Children, 1936
      .... **25.00**
    System of Medicine: Nose, Throat, and
      Ear, 1910 .... **35.00**
Bottle, glass
    Allens Lung Balsam, clear, applied top,
      6½" h **25.00**
    Chlorate Potassique, clear, pontil,
      painted brown, 6½" h **20.00**
    Granular Citrate of Magnesia, cobalt,
      kite with letter inside, ring top, 8" h
      .... **30.00**
Broadside, paper, Oxygenated Bitters, "A
    Sure Remedy for Dyspepsia," black and
    white, 17½ × 23" **100.00**
Dental Cabinet, three drawers on top, bev-
    eled mirror, drawers on bottom, orig in-
    struments, 1926 .... **575.00**
Display, Kickapoo Indian Medicine, diecut
    cardboard, Indian brave presenting prod-
    uct package, wearing tribal buckskins,
    beads, and moccasins, 40" w, 69" h
    .... **3,000.00**
Drill, Electro Dental Mfg Co, foot control
    .... **50.00**

Reward Pin, Miller Memorial Blood Center, 1 Gallon, gold toned, red and white enameled dec, orig plastic sleeve, ³⁄₄" l, $3.50.

Glass Eye, human size **20.00**
Lens Kit, Fits–U–Eyeglasses Kit, velvet lined case **12.00**
Pencil, King's Puremalt Tonic adv, brass holder, black and white celluloid wrapper with text, one end holds pencil, other end with eraser, 3½" l **18.00**
Poster, Hygienic Water Cure Sanitorium, "Our Home on the Hillside," Dansville, NY, building and horse–drawn carriages illus, Sage, Sons & Co litho, 36 × 24" **100.00**
Puzzle Card, Dr S A Richmond's Epileptine, The Only Cure For Epilepsy, c1890 **5.00**
Quack Gadget
    Electro–Violet Ray Machine, "The Scientific Healing Method," orig instruction books, carrying case **80.00**
    Myofasciatrom Model RV3, electrical, walnut case **75.00**
Restraints, leather cuffs, heavy canvas belt, key, Atlas Safety **85.00**
Sign
    Dr McMunn's Kinate of Quinine and Cinchone, bedridden woman using medicine, gazing outside, paper, printed by Thomas & Eno, 10 × 14" **400.00**
    Henry, Johnson & Lord, various products listed and illus, tin, 14 × 20" **500.00**
    Kickapoo Indian Remedies, Chief Red Spear portrait, paper, J Ottmann Lith Co, 17½ × 23½" **2,400.00**
String Holder, SSS For The Blood, caldron shape, orig cast iron int four "S" ball retainer, 5" d, 5" h **175.00**
Tin, Jim Dandy Veterinary Product, colorful animal illus **70.00**
Trade Sign, figural mortar and pestle, zinc, maroon glass bulls–eye at center, 23" d, 36" h **650.00**

MEGO ACTION FIGURES

Mego action figures were made from 1972 to 1982. Ranging in size from 3³⁄₄" to 12¹⁄₂" tall, they were characterizations of Marvel and DC comic book heroes. Later runs were characters from popular TV shows and movies.

There can be a number of variations to individual figures, as well as packaging techniques—boxes or blister packs. Mego action series include: The Mad Monster Series, 1974; The Official Greatest Super Heroes, 1972–78; The Wizard of Oz, 1974; Star Trek (television) 1974–76; and Star Trek: The Motion Picture, 1979.

Amazing Spiderman
    8" h, orig box **100.00**
    12½" h
        Fly Away Action **125.00**
        Poseable **70.00**
        Web Spinning **150.00**
Aquaman, 8" h, unpackaged **30.00**
Batman
    Batman, 8" h, unpackaged **35.00**
    Joker, 8" h
        Mint on Kresge card **195.00**
        Unpackaged **40.00**
    Penguin, 8" h
        Mint on Kresge card **195.00**
        Unpackaged **35.00**
Black Hole, 1979
    3³⁄₄" h
        Dr Durant **10.00**
        Humanoid **30.00**
        Kate McCrae **20.00**
        Maximillian **20.00**
        Old Bob **35.00**
        Pizer **10.00**
    12" h
        Captain Hollard **40.00**
        Dr Reinhardt **40.00**
Buck Rogers
    3³⁄₄" h
        Ardella **8.00**
        Buck **15.00**
        Draconian Guard **15.00**
        Draconian Marauder **35.00**
        Twiki **10.00**
    12" h
        Dr Huer **40.00**
        Killer Kane **40.00**
        Wilma **30.00**
Captain America, 12" h, MIB **175.00**
CHiPs, Jimmy Squeeks, 3³⁄₄" h **5.00**
Comic Action Heroes, 3³⁄₄" h, 1975–78
    Aquaman **50.00**
    Fortress of Solitude **22.00**
    Green Goblin **45.00**
    Hulk **35.00**

Joker, unpackaged **20.00**
Penguin
    Mint **60.00**
    Unpackaged **20.00**
Shazam **60.00**
Spiderman **40.00**
Superman **50.00**
Wonder Woman **40.00**
Conan, 8" h, orig box, mid 1970s   **425.00**
Dukes of Hazzard
    3³⁄₄" h
        Boss Hogg **6.00**
        Cletus **30.00**
        Daisy **6.00**
        Uncle Jessie **25.00**
    8" h
        Bo **20.00**
        Boss Hogg **20.00**
Falcon, 8" h, MIB **125.00**
Fantastic Four, 8" h
    Human Torch, blister pack **40.00**
    Invisible Girl, orig box **90.00**
    Thing, blister pack **40.00**
Flash Gordon
    Dr Zarkov **50.00**
    Ming **70.00**
General Zod, 12" h, MIB **125.00**
Green Arrow, 8", orig box **175.00**
Green Goblin, 8" h, carded **375.00**
Happy Days
    Chachi **30.00**
    Potsie **30.00**

Action Figure, Broadway Joe Namath, 12" l, football uniform, green and white, Mego Corp, MCMLXX 14³⁄₄" l orig box, $30.00.

Incredible Hulk, flyaway action **90.00**
Iron Man, 8" h, orig box **150.00**
Jor–El, 12" h, MIB **95.00**
Lizard, 8" h, unpackaged **55.00**
Kiss, Gene, 12" h **75.00**
Knights
    King Arthur **250.00**
    Sir Galahad **200.00**
Laverne and Shirley **50.00**
Love Boat, Gopher **8.00**
Mad Monster Series, 8" h
    Dracula **175.00**
    Mummy **95.00**
    Wolfman **150.00**
Micronauts
    Acroyear II **15.00**
    Baron Karza **20.00**
    Biotherm **30.00**
    Galactic Defender **10.00**
    Rhodim Orbitor **15.00**
Moonraker, 12" h, 1979
    Drax **150.00**
    Holly Goodhead **150.00**
    James Bond **100.00**
    Jaws **500.00**
One Million Years BC, Trog **35.00**
Our Gang, Buckwheat **60.00**
Planet of the Apes, 8" h
    Astronaut **25.00**
    Burke **50.00**
    Cornelius **25.00**
    Dr Zaius, Bend 'n' Flex **20.00**
    Soldier Ape **25.00**
    Zira, unpackaged **25.00**
Pocket Super Heroes, 3¾" h, 1979
    Aquaman **50.00**
    Captain Marvel **20.00**
    General Zod **15.00**
    Jor–El **15.00**
    Wonder Woman **20.00**
Robin Hood
    Friar Tuck **75.00**
    Maid Marian **100.00**
    Robin **100.00**
    Sheriff of Nottingham **75.00**
Shazam, 8" h, unpackaged **40.00**
Sonny and Cher
    Cher **45.00**
    Sonny Bono **40.00**
Spider Man
    8" h
        MOC **35.00**
        Unpackaged **18.00**
    12" h
        MIB **125.00**
        Unpackaged **25.00**
Star Trek, 8" h, 1974
    Andorian **150.00**
    Cheron **100.00**
    Kirk **30.00**
    McCoy **30.00**
    Mugato **175.00**
    Romulan **150.00**
    The Gorn **120.00**
    The Keeper **120.00**
    Uhura **35.00**

Star Trek: The Motion Picture, 1979
    3¾" h
        Betelgeusian **25.00**
        Decker **15.00**
        Megarite **25.00**
        Scotty **15.00**
    12" h
        Arcturian **50.00**
        Illia **30.00**
        Klingon **50.00**
        Spock **30.00**
Steve Trevor, 12" h, MIB **75.00**
Superhero Bendables, 5" h, 1972–74
    Batgirl **120.00**
    Catwoman **175.00**
    Mr Mxyzptik **125.00**
    Robin **75.00**
    Shazam **125.00**
    Tarzan **75.00**
    Wonder Woman **100.00**
Superman
    8" h, MOC **75.00**
    12" h, 1967 . . . . **100.00**
Superman the Movie, 12" h
    Lex Luthor, MIB **95.00**
    Superman **50.00**
Tarzan
    5" h, bendie **60.00**
    8" h, MIB, mid 1970s **85.00**
Teen Titans, 7" h, 1977
    Kid Flash, carded **300.00**
    Speedy, carded **350.00**
Thor, 8" h, orig box **400.00**
Western Heroes
    Buffalo Bill Cody **150.00**
    Cochise **150.00**
    Davy Crockett **200.00**
Wizard of Oz, Munchkin Flower Girl **40.00**
Wonder Woman
    Nubia, 12" h, MIB **125.00**
    Queen Hippolite, 12" h, MIB **95.00**
    Steve Trevor, 12" h, 1976 . . . . . . **75.00**
    Wonder Woman
        8" h, orig box, 1974 . . . . . . **300.00**
        12" h
            MIB **125.00**
            Unpackaged **45.00**
World's Greatest Super Heroes, 8" h,
    1972–78
    Aqualad, carded **325.00**
    Batman, removable cowl, orig box
    . . . . **350.00**
    Conan, carded **350.00**
    Falcon, carded **200.00**
    Green Arrow, orig box **175.00**
    Human Torch, carded **40.00**
    Invisible Girl, orig box **90.00**
    Iron Man, carded **200.00**
    Joker, fist fighting, orig box **450.00**
    Kid Flash, carded **350.00**
    Mr Fantastic, carded **40.00**
    Robin, removable mask, orig box
    . . . . **350.00**
    Supergirl, orig box **420.00**
    Thing, carded **40.00**
    Wonder Girl, carded **300.00**

METLOX POTTERY

In 1921 T. C. Prouty and Willis, his son, founded Proutyline Products, a company designed to develop Prouty's various inventions.

Metlox (a contraction of metallic oxide) was established in 1927. When T. C. Prouty died in 1931, Willis reorganized the company and began to produce a line of solid-color dinnerware similar to that produced by Bauer. In 1934 the line was fully developed and sold under the Poppytrail trademark. Fifteen different colors were produced over an eight-year period.

Other dinnerware lines produced in the 1930s include Mission Bell (sold exclusively by Sears & Roebuck), Pintoria (based on an English Staffordshire line), and Yorkshire (patterned after Gladding McBean's Coronado line). Most of these lines did not survive World War II.

In the late 1930s Metlox employed the services of Carl Romanelli, a designer whose work appeared as figurines, miniatures, and Zodiac vases. A line called Modern Masterpieces featured bookends, busts, figural vases, figures, and wall pockets.

In 1946 Evan K. Shaw, whose American Pottery in Los Angeles had been destroyed by fire, purchased Metlox. The California Ivy pattern was introduced in 1946, California Provincial and Homestead Provincial in 1950, Red Rooster in 1955, California Strawberry in 1961, Sculptured Grape in 1963, and Della Robbia in 1965. Bob Allen and Mel Shaw, art directors, introduced a number of new shapes and lines in the 1950s, among which are Aztec, California Contempora, California Free Form, California Mobile, and Navajo.

When Vernon Kilns ceased operation in 1958, Metlox bought the trade name and select dinnerware molds. A separate Vernon Ware branch was established. Under the direction of Doug Bothwell the line soon rivaled the Poppytrail patterns.

Between 1946 and 1956 Metlox made a series of ceramic cartoon characters under license from Walt Disney. A line of planters designed by Helen Slater and Poppets (doll–like stoneware flower holders) were marketed in the 1960s and 1970s. Recent production includes novelty cookie jars and Colorstax, a revival solid-color dinnerware pattern.

The company ceased operations in 1989.

The recent cookie jar craze has attracted a number of collectors to Metlox's cookie jar line. Most examples sell within a narrow range. The Little Red Riding Hood jar is an exception, often selling at two to three times the price of other cookie jars.

Brown–Eyed Susan, Coupe Shape, Vernon Ware
Bowl
    5" d, 2³/₄" h **15.00**
    5⁵/₈" d **8.00**
    6¹/₈" d, tab handle **10.00**
    9" d **18.00**
Carafe, cov, 8¹/₈" h **35.00**
Chop Plate, 12³/₈" d **20.00**
Creamer and Sugar, cov **35.00**
Cup **7.00**
Cup and Saucer **10.00**
Plate
    6" d **5.00**
    9³/₄" d **10.00**
Salt and Pepper Shakers, pr **15.00**
California Ivy
Bowl
    5¹/₄" d **6.00**
    6³/₄" d **8.00**
Casserole, cov **42.00**
Chop Plate, 13" d **12.00**
Creamer and Sugar, cov **15.00**
Cup and Saucer **8.00**
Plate
    6¹/₄" d **4.00**
    10¹/₄" d **10.00**
Platter, oval, 13" l **24.00**
Vegetable, 9" d **20.00**
California Provincial
Ashtray, 6" **45.00**
Berry Bowl **8.00**
Bread Tray **45.00**
Cigarette Box **95.00**
Coaster **10.00**
Coffeepot **60.00**
Cream Soup **8.00**
Creamer and Sugar **35.00**
Gravy **20.00**
Lug Soup **10.00**
Marmalade Jug **45.00**
Mug, tankard **25.00**
Mustard, no lid **15.00**
Plate
    Bread and Butter **6.00**
    Dinner **12.00**
    Salad **10.00**
Salad Bowl, 11" d **35.00**
Soup, flat **15.00**
Vegetable, cov **42.00**
Green Rooster
Batter Bowl, two spout, 6¹/₄" d . . . **27.00**
Bowl, large **45.00**
Canister
    Coffee **75.00**
    Flour **125.00**

Sugar **90.00**
Tea **65.00**
Cocoa Mug **25.00**
Coffeepot **85.00**
Creamer and Sugar **19.00**
Jam Jar **35.00**
Plate, 10" d **9.00**
Salt and Pepper Shakers, pr, handled
    . . . . **27.00**
Stein **50.00**
Teapot **110.00**
Tumbler, 5" h **20.00**
Homestead Provincial
Casserole, open **8.00**
Creamer **7.00**
Cup and Saucer **6.50**
Plate, 6" d **3.50**
Lotus
Butter Dish **40.00**
Gravy Boat **28.00**
Provincial, blue and white
Coffeepot **95.00**
Cup and Saucer **10.00**
Mug **45.00**
Plate
    6" d, bread and butter **5.00**
    7" d, salad **10.00**
    9¹/₂" d, dinner **15.00**
Red Rooster
Bowl, oatmeal **18.00**
Canister Set, four canisters **275.00**
Coffeepot **70.00**
Cruet Set **165.00**
Mug, small **22.00**
Pitcher, milk **45.00**
Salad Bowl, large **95.00**
Teapot **75.00**

MILITARIA

Soldiers have returned home with the spoils of war as long as there have been soldiers and wars. Look at the Desert Storm material that is starting to arrive on the market. Many collectors tend to collect material relating to wars from their young adulthood or related to reenactment groups to which they belong.

It pays to specialize. The two obvious choices are a specific war or piece of equipment. Never underestimate the enemy. Nazi material remains the strongest segment of the market.

Reproductions abound. Be especially careful of any Civil War and Nazi material.

Clubs: American Society of Military Insignia Collectors, 526 Lafayette Ave, Palmerton, PA 18071; Assoc of American Military Uniform Collectors, PO Box 1876, Elyria, OH 44036; Company of Military Historians, North Main St, Westbrook, CT 06498; Imperial German Military Collectors Association, 82 Atlantic St, Keyport, NJ 07735.

Magazines: *Military Collectors' News,* PO Box 702073, Tulsa, OK 74170; *North South Trader,* PO Drawer 631, Orange, VA 22960; *Military Trader,* PO Box 1050, Dubuque, IA 20004.

CIVIL WAR
Autograph, 4 × 3" card, Confederate, A H Garland, dated **60.00**
Belt, Union infantry soldier, 1863   **150.00**
Book, *Pictorial History of Civil War of Union,* Stevens **90.00**
Bullet Mold, picket pattern bullet **45.00**
Cartridge Box, Weston **300.00**
Dental Chest, dovetail construction, six drawers, lift top, brass plaque with name
    . . . . **950.00**
Field Glasses, 7¹/₂" l, brass, Lemaire Fabt, Paris **125.00**
Helmet Badge, brass shield and eagle, company number in center **45.00**
Insignia, brass, lieutenant **25.00**
Leg Irons, old barrel key **85.00**
Mess Kit, bone handles, orig leather case
    . . . . **175.00**
Muster Roll, 20th Regt Illinois, August to October 1863, folds out to 20 × 30", document entries **100.00**
Plate, 8" d, 50th Anniversary Battle of Gettysburg, W Adams & Co **50.00**
Ribbon, blue–gray, Lincoln's head surrounded by "With Malice Toward None, With Charity For All," 1861–65
    . . . . **90.00**
Shell Jacket, Union cavalry, buttons, lining, and inspector's marks **425.00**
Sword, NCO, dated 1863 . . . . **275.00**
Tintype, full length, unidentified Confederate cavalry man, gear, sword, and carbine **450.00**

WORLD WAR I
Badge, Tank Corps, British cap, 8th Churka
    . . . . **20.00**
Belt, web **15.00**
Document, 16¹/₈ × 20¹/₈", US Army, photograph and discharge paper, Warren Bennethum, reverse painted flag, framed, 1919 . . . . **65.00**
Gas Mask, carrying can, shoulder strap, canister attached to bottom, German
    . . . . **75.00**
Helmet
    Army **50.00**
    Doughboy, mini, Nashville, 1934   **59.00**
Medal, Iron Cross **35.00**
Periscope, wood, used in trench warfare
    . . . . **75.00**
Pinback Button
    ⁷/₈" d, Western Electric Soldier's Comfort Club, black and white **8.00**
    1¹/₄" d, Welcome Home Soldiers of York County, PA **20.00**

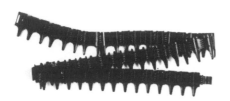

Ammunition Belt, German, WWII, MG34, 50 round links, ¼" w, 32½" l, 1½"h, $6.00.

Poster, "Lend the Way They Fight, Buy Bonds to Your Utmost," full color action scene, red and black lettering, green border 50.00
Uniform, US Army, engineer, coat, belt, pants, cap, canvas leggings, wood puttees, leather gaiters, canteen 300.00
Watch Fob, brass, US soldier and sailor 20.00

WORLD WAR II
Arm Band, 4" w, Civilian Defense Air Raid Warden, white, blue circle, red and white diagonal stripes within triangle 12.00
Badge, Nazi, General Assault, silver, c1940 .... 30.00
Binoculars, Army, M–17, field type, 7½" l, olive drab, 7 × 50 power, fixed optics 100.00
Book, A. Hitler, *Mein Kampf*, 1933, 407 pgs, dust jacket 15.00
Cap, AAF Officer's, 50–Mission, gabardine, gilded eagle, marked "Flighter by Bancroft, O D" 120.00
Envelope, Iwo Jima flag raising, 8/29/45, artist G F Hadley 15.00
Flag, 2 × 3", Nazi 40.00
Hat, Nazi SS, rabbit fur, quilted int, black ties at ear flaps, olive green wool body, RZM/SS, skull and eagle devices 325.00
Knife, black finish blade, "USN" and "Mark S Sheath" marked on guard, gray web belt, gray fiber scabbard 50.00
Magazine, *Time,* 1942, Nazi cov, Gen Field Marshall Fedor Von Bock 34.00

Machine Gun Cloth Belt, British, WWII, 250 round, 1⅛" w, 14' 6¼" l, $12.00.

Map Case, leather, German, WWII, officer's, pebble finish, 7¼" w, 10½" l, 12" h, $60.00.

Manual, *Recognition Pictorial Manual*, Bureau of Aeronautics, Navy Department, Washington, DC, June 1943, contains silhouettes and technical information on Allied and Axis aircraft, 6 × 10", 80 pgs, black and white 45.00
Patch, pilot's wings, leather, AAF, emb, standard design, flying jacket attachment type 30.00
Pencil Holder, 3½" h, plastic, red, white, and blue, marked "Victory" 10.00
Pin, Maritime Commission Award of Merit, sterling, raised eagle with inscribed chest "Ships For Victory" in front of red enamel "M," blue enamel ground 18.00
Poster, 22 × 28", "Fill It! Harvest War Crops," full color 45.00
Ring, Nazi, silver, crossed swords, helmet, and swastika 50.00
Shirt, Nazi, brown, SA, black collar tabs and piping, eagle buttons, c1933 150.00
Sweater, sleeveless, olive drab, "V" neck 25.00
Victory Pin, 1" d, diecut, plastic, gold, white and red British lion and US eagle, blue letter "V" behind figures 22.00
Wallet, Japanese, woven and leather, Rising Sun 45.00

VIETNAM
Book, *Frontline–The Commands of Wm Chase,* 1975, autographed 1st edition, 228 pgs 38.00
Bracelet, POW, names 25.00
Helmet, US tanker, Fiberglas, dark green, intercom system on side 50.00
Medal
  Air Force Commendation, parade ribbon and lapel bar, orig case 20.00
  Vietnam Service 15.00
Uniform Tunic, US Army, sergeant, 5th Division, green, red diamonds insignia, gold stripes 40.00

MILK BOTTLES

There is an entire generation of young adults to whom the concept of milk in a bottle is a foreign idea. In another fifteen years a book like this will have to contain a chapter on plastic milk cartons. I hope you are saving some.

When buying a bottle, make certain the glass is clear of defects from manufacture and wear and the label and/or wording is in fine or better condition. Buy odd-sized bottles and bottles with special features. Don't forget the caps. They are collectible too.

Newsletter: *The Milk Route,* 4 Ox Bow Rd, Westport, CT 06880.

Alex Bolin & Son, Bradford, PA, pt, round, emb, orig cap 6.00
Andersons Creamery, emb, 7 oz 4.00
Ausable Dairy Corp, NY, pt, round, emb 5.00
Borden's Golden Crest, amber 18.00
Brookfield Dairy, Hellertown, PA, ½ pt, emb, baby face 20.00
Calhoun County Creamery, AL, qt, emb 12.00
Clinton Milk Co, qt, smoky beige 15.00
Dairylee Milk, sq, double baby face, red and yellow pyro, qt 50.00
E F Mayer, qt, amber 40.00
Erdman & Sons, Lykens, PA, pyroglazed, pt 34.00
Flanders Dairy, qt, pyroglazed 45.00
Franklin Dairy, Tupperlake, NY, qt, round, red pyro 6.00
George Signor, Keeseville, NY, pt, round, emb 4.00
Good Rich Dairy Products, Mt Carmel, PA, pt, emb, baby face 30.00
Grasslands Dairy 10.00
Hidden Acres Farms, Washington, NJ, qt, sq, clear, baby face, four leaf clover 30.00
Hursts Dairy, VA, qt, round, emb 8.00
Jolly Dairy Ice Cream Co, GA, qt, round, emb 5.00
Langs Creamery, qt, amber 40.00
Margrove Inc Cream Craft Products, NY, qt, sq, red pyro 5.00
North Hampton Dairy, MA, qt, emb, baby face 30.00
Old Home Milk Co, ½ pt, round, orange pyro 8.00
Polly Meadows, round, blue pyro, girl's head illus 8.00
Rosedale Dairy, qt, round, green pyro 12.00
Sanitary Dairy, sq, orange 8.00

Garners Dairy Co, Uniontown, PA, qt size, $5.00.

Solomons Dairy, qt, sq, black pyro . . . **5.00**
Sunny Dale Dairy, IN, qt, round, pyro
. . . . **10.00**
Weber Dairy Co, ¼ pt, round, emb   **14.00**
Willow Springs Farm, WI, pt, round, emb
. . . . **7.00**

MILK GLASS

Milk glass is an opaque white glass that became popular during the Victorian era. A scientist will tell you that it is made by adding oxide of tin to a batch of clear glass. Most collect it because it's pretty.

Companies like Atterbury, McKee, and Westmoreland have all produced fine examples in novelties, often of the souvenir variety, as well as household items. Old-timers focus heavily on milk glass made before 1920. However, there are some great pieces from the post–1920 period that you would be wise not to overlook.

Milk glass has remained in continuous production since it was first invented. Many firms reproduce old patterns. Be careful. Old-timers will tell you that if a piece has straw marks, it is probably correct. Some modern manufacturers who want to fool you might have also added them in the mold. Watch out for a "K" in a diamond. This is the mark on milk glass reproductions from the 1960s made by the Kemple Glass Company.

Milk glass is practical. A glass sitting beside a plate of cookies gives others in the room the impression that you are drinking milk. Hint, hint!

Club: National Milk Glass Collectors Society, 46 Almond Dr, Hershey, PA 17033.

Animal Dish, cov
    Duck, wavy base, glass eyes, painted
        beak **125.00**
    Fox, Atterbury **170.00**
    Hen, 6⅞" l, red glass eyes **50.00**
    Lamb, picket base, Atterbury **75.00**
    Lion, picket base, Atterbury **65.00**
    Rabbit, domed, split rib base **65.00**
    Robin, nest base, Atterbury **150.00**
    Squirrel, acorn base **125.00**
    Swan, arched neck, raised wings, lattice
        base, McKee **220.00**
    Turkey, nest base **85.00**
Ashtray, Westmoreland
    5¼" sq, English Hobnail pattern   **22.50**
    6½" sq, Beaded Grape **15.00**
Bottle, 10¾" h, figural, bear, sitting, forelegs
    folded across chest **120.00**
Bowl
    6" d, Paneled Grape, ruffled, ftd, West-
        moreland **40.00**
    7" d, H pattern, Atterbury **55.00**
    8" d, Ball and Chain pattern, openwork
        rim **45.00**
    9" d, Old Quilt pattern, ftd, Westmore-
        land **40.00**
    9½" d, Rock Crystal, orig label, McKee
        . . . . **55.00**
Butter Dish, cov
    4⅞" l, Roman Cross pattern, sq ftd base,
        cube shape finial **50.00**
    9" d, Paneled Grape, Westmoreland
        . . . . **50.00**
Candlestick
    4" h, Beaded Grape, Westmoreland,
        price for pair **20.00**
    7¾" h, swirled, ribbing twists counter–
        clockwise from base, wax guard
        . . . . **35.00**
Compote, 8½" d, Lattice Edge pattern, floral
    dec, Daisy and Button–type pattern ped-
    estal base, Challinor, Taylor **75.00**
Creamer
    Forget–Me–Not pattern **35.00**
    Paneled Wheat pattern **30.00**
Match Holder
    4½" h, Jolly Jester, patent date on bot-
        tom **85.00**
    5" l, wall type, Indian head **65.00**
Mayonnaise, Beaded Grape, crimped, West-
    moreland **15.00**
Mug, 3" h, Ivy in Snow pattern **32.00**
Mustard, 5" h, owl, glass insert, orig
    threaded top, Atterbury **150.00**
Perfume Bottle, figural, Gibson girl   **100.00**
Pitcher
    7½" h, owl, glass eyes **150.00**

8" h, Dart and Bar pattern, blue, rect
    handle, ftd **95.00**
Plate
    4⅛" d, Rising Sun **65.00**
    6" d, three owl heads, fluted openwork
        rim, gold paint **50.00**
    7½" d, Blackberries pattern, beaded rim,
        Westmoreland **12.00**
    8" d, Eagle pattern, star rim, Fenton
        . . . . **40.00**
    8¼" d, Ring & Petal, Westmoreland, No
        1875 . . . . **12.50**
    9" d, Wicket, Atterbury **40.00**
Platter, 13¼" l, retriever swimming through
    cattails, lily pad border **70.00**
Relish, 4½ × 11", figural, fish, emb "Pat
    June 4, 1872" **40.00**
Salt and Pepper Shakers, Paneled Grape
    pattern, Westmoreland, pr **24.00**
Souvenir
    Figure, 5½" h, owl, glass eyes, Hot
        Springs, SD **100.00**
    Hatchet, 6½" l, pr **25.00**
Spooner, Melon with Leaf and Net, deco-
    rated, patent date **85.00**
Sugar, cov
    Basketweave pattern, dated 1874 **100.00**
    Sunflower pattern **50.00**
Vase, 9" h, Old Quilt, fan, Westmoreland
    . . . . **22.00**

MINIATURES

If you want to find miniatures at flea markets, look in the cases because the size that you are most likely to find is "doll house." The other two sizes are child's and salesman's sample. These rarely show up at flea markets.

Beware. Miniatures have been sold for years. Modern craftspeople continue to make great examples. Alas, their handiwork can be easily aged so that it will fool most buyers. Also, Cracker Jack giveaways, charms, etc. should not be confused with miniatures.

Clubs: International Guild of Miniature Artisans, PO Box 71, Bridgeport, NY 18080; National Assoc of Miniature Enthusiasts, PO Box 69, Carmel, IN 46032.

Periodicals: *Miniature Collector*, 30595 Eight Mile Rd, Livonia, MI 48152; *Nutshell News*, 21027 Crossroads Cir, PO Box 1612, Waukesha, WI 53187.

Child's
    Bed, 21¾" h, 28¾" l, 18" w, brass, early
        20th C **195.00**
    Carriage, 34" l, wicker, open, parasol,
        brocade upholstery, early 20th C
        . . . . **385.00**
    Chair, wood, seat with Kutztown adv
        . . . . **175.00**

Cradle, 37" l, walnut, dovetailed, shaped
sides, hand holds, cutout rockers
.................................**225.00**
Measuring Cup, Pyrex **10.00**
Rocker, 9¼" h, arms, painted blue
.................................**165.00**
Wash Bowl, Dutch children dec   **60.00**
Doll House
Bed, Petite Princess **18.00**
Candelabra, Petite Princess **20.00**
Cradle, wood **25.00**
Desk, 5½" h, lady's, chair, c1875   **90.00**
Dining Room Set, table, two benches,
cast iron, white lacquer finish, Ar-
cade, price for three piece set   **50.00**
Floor Lamp, 4" h, metal, black, gilded
frame, glass beaded shade ...**100.00**
Ironing Board, cast iron, folding, Kilgore,
c1930 ....**20.00**
Patio Set, litho tin, round table, four
chairs, floral design **35.00**
Piano, matching bench, Renwal   **30.00**
Refrigerator, metal, Tootsietoy, c1920
.................................**25.00**
Stool, metal, Tootsietoy **12.00**
Stove, metal, Tootsietoy, c1920   **25.00**
Tea Set, porcelain, cov teapot, creamer,
cov sugar, and tray **50.00**
Vanity, Renwal **8.00**
Salesman's Samples
Boots, 4½" h, leather **100.00**
Cash Register, R C Allen, dated 1958
.................................**25.00**
Food Grinder, 3" h, J P Co **35.00**
Gate, 18" l, 10½" h, wood and metal
.................................**200.00**
Harrow, 7½" l, iron and wood, horse-
drawn **95.00**
Loom, 9½" w, 15½" d, 12½" h, "Minia-
ture Loom" paper label, NRA ink
stamp **25.00**
Porch Swing, 16" l, wood **125.00**
Screen Door Set, 8¾" w, 12½" h, Griffin
Perfection **20.00**
Stove, 10½" w, 5" h, Royal **60.00**
Wringer, 7¼" w, 8" h, Lovell Manufac-
turing Co, Erie, PA **30.00**

MODEL KITS

A plastic model kit is a world of fun
and fantasy for people of all ages. Model
kit manufacturers such as Revell/Mono-
gram, Aurora, and Horizon create and
produce detailed kits that let the builders
imagination run wild. Creative kits give
movie monsters a creepy stare, F16
fighter planes a sense of movement, and
hot-rod roadsters that race on a drag strip
across a table top.

Most model kits were packed in a
decorated cardboard box with an image
of the model on the surface. It contained
the requisite pieces and a set of assembly
instructions. Model kits are snapped together or glued together. Painting and
decoration is up to the assembler. Model
kits are produced from plastic, resin, or
vinyl, requiring a bit of dexterity and pa-
tience to assemble.

Buying model kits at flea markets
should be done with a degree of caution.
An open box spells trouble. Look for
missing pieces or loss of the instructions.
Sealed boxes are your best bet, but even
these should be questioned because of
the availablity of home shrink-wrap kits.
Don't be afraid—inquire about a
model's completeness before purchasing
it.

Clubs: Kit Builders International, PO Box
38, Stanton, CA 90680; Society for the
Preservation and Encouragement of
Scale Model Kit Collecting, 3213 Hardy
Dr, Edmond, OK 73013.

Periodicals: *Kit Builders and Glue
Sniffers,* PO Box 201, Sharon Center, OH
44274; *Model and Toy Collector,* 137
Casterton Ave, Akron, OH 44303.

Addams Family House, Aurora, 1965
.................................**850.00**
Alfred E Neuman, Aurora, 1965 ....**325.00**
AMI, 1966 T-Bird **20.00**
Archie's Car, Aurora, 1969 ....**120.00**
Armored Dinosaur, Prehistoric Scenes, Au-
rora, 1972 ....**40.00**
A-Team Van, AMT, 1983 ....**20.00**
Attack Trak, Masters of the Universe, Mono-
gram, 1984 ....**15.00**

*Robotech 2-in-1 Kit, Revell, copyright 1984,
4½ × 7¼" box, $20.00.*

Autogyro, James Bond, Airfix, 1969   **300.00**
Banana Splits Banana Buggy, Aurora, 1969
.................................**325.00**
Barnabas Collins, Dark Shadows, MPC,
1968 ....**275.00**
Batmobile, Imai, 1983 ....**45.00**
Black Hole, Vincent, MPC, 1979, complete,
unsealed **12.00**
Black Knight of Milan, Aurora, 1961, MISB
.................................**125.00**
Black Knight of Nuremberg, Aurora, 1956
.................................**120.00**
Bonanza, Revell, 1965 ....**150.00**
Captain Kidd, Bloodthirsty Pirates, Aurora,
1965 ....**120.00**
Charlie's Angels Van, Revell, 1977   **30.00**
Compact Pussycat, Wacky Racers, MPC,
1969 ....**175.00**
Cornfield Roundup Diorama, Planet of the
Apes, Addar, 1975 ....**45.00**
Creature From the Black Lagoon, Glow Kit,
Aurora, 1972 ....**140.00**
Cyclops and Robinson Family, Lost in
Space, Aurora, 1965 ....**1,200.00**
Daddy the Suburbanite, Weird-Ohs, Hawk,
1963 ....**75.00**
Dempsey vs Firpo, Great Moments in
Sports, Aurora, 1965 ....**100.00**
Draconian Marauder, Buck Rogers, Mono-
gram, 1979 ....**20.00**
Dragnut, Ed "Big Daddy" Roth, Revell,
1963 ....**60.00**
Dragula, Blueprinters series, AMT/ERTL,
1991 ....**20.00**
Dr Deadly's Daughter, Monster Scenes, Au-
rora, 1971 ....**120.00**
Dr Jekyll as Mr Hyde, Monsters of the Mov-
ies, Aurora, 1974 ....**90.00**
Duke's Digger, Dukes of Hazzard, MPC,
1980 ....**25.00**
Escape From the Crypt, Haunted Mansion,
Disney, MPC, 1974 ....**45.00**
Esmerelda Whoozis, Aurora, 1968   **120.00**
Evil Kneivel's Sky Cycle X2, Addar, 1974
.................................**25.00**
First Lunar Landing 25th Anniversary,
Monogram, ¹⁄₄₈ scale, MISB **25.00**
Flag Raising at Iwo Jima, Aurora, 1968
.................................**150.00**
Flipper and Sandy, Revell, 1968 ...**100.00**
Fonz Dream Rod, Happy Days, AMT, 1976
.................................**35.00**
Frankenstein, long box, Canadian issue, Au-
rora, 1961, MISB **150.00**
Galaxy Convertible, T-Jet, HO Scale, red,
Aurora, 1963, MIB **125.00**
Galaxy Runner, Message from Space, Entex,
1978 ....**20.00**
George Harrison, Revell, 1965 .....**140.00**
George Washington, Aurora, 1967   **125.00**
Ghost of the Treasure Guard, Pirates of the
Caribbean, Disney, MPC, 1972   **45.00**
Giant Wasp, Gigantics, MPC, 1975   **50.00**
Godzilla's Go-Kart, Aurora, 1966   **1,500.00**
Good Ship Flounder, Dr Doolittle, Aurora,
1967 ....**140.00**

Star Wars, The Empire Strikes Back, Luke Skywalker's Snowspeeder, 8" l scale model, copyright Lucasfilm Ltd, 1980 Trademark, 10 × 7½ × 3¾", $30.00.

Gowdy the Dowdy Grackle, Dr Seuss, Revell, 1960 . . . . **120.00**
Guillotine, Aurora, 1964 . . . . **225.00**
Hercules and the Lion, Aurora, 1966 . . . . **425.00**
Hitler, Born Losers, Parks, 1965 . . . . **150.00**
H M S Bounty, Mutiny on the Bounty, Revell, 1961 . . . . **100.00**
Hot Dogger Hangin' Ten, Silly Surfers, Hawk, 1964 . . . . **45.00**
Indian Warrior, Pyro, 1960 . . . . **60.00**
Invaders Flying Saucer, Monogram . . . **45.00**
Invisible Man, Horizon, 1988 . . . . **45.00**
Jaguar XJS, Return of the Saint, Revell, 1979 . . . . **45.00**
Jaws of Doom, Six Million Dollar Man, MPC, 1975 . . . . **30.00**
Jekyl as Hyde, Aurora Glow, orig box **50.00**
Joker's Goon Car/Gotham City Police Car, AMT/ERTL, 1990 . . . . **15.00**
John F Kennedy, Aurora, 1965 . . . . . **125.00**
King Arthur, Camelot Scenes, Aurora, 1968 . . . . **150.00**
Lone Ranger, Aurora, 1972, MIB **60.00**
Ma Barker's Getaway Car, Bloody Mama, MPC, 1970 . . . . **65.00**
Mars Probe Landing Module, Lindberg, 1969 . . . . **90.00**
Mazinga, Shogun Warriors, Monogram, 1977 . . . . **30.00**
Metaluna Mutant, Jumbo Kit, Tskuda, 1986 . . . . **80.00**
Mexican Senorita, Aurora, 1957 . . . . . **45.00**
Mod Squad Woody Surf Wagon, Aurora, 1969 . . . . **150.00**
Monkeemobile, Airfix, 1967 . . . . **375.00**
Moonbus, 2001, Aurora, 1969 . . . . . **350.00**
Mummy, Aurora, 1972, England, MISB **50.00**
Munster's Koach, AMT, 1964 . . . . . . **275.00**
My Mother the Car, AMT, 1965 . . . . . **75.00**
1914 Stutz Bearcat, Bearcats, MPC, 1971 . . . . **55.00**
Nutty Nose Nipper, Aurora, 1965 **165.00**
Paddy Wagon, Remco, 1961, unassembled, orig box **295.00**
Phantom of the Opera, Horizon, 1988 . . . . **45.00**

Pilgrim Space Station Model, #9001, MPC, 1970, sealed, slight box warp **25.00**
Pink Panther Custom Car, Eldon, 1969 . . . . **90.00**
Rawhide, Gil Favor, Pyro, 1958 . . . . . **60.00**
Red Knight of Vienna, Aurora, 1961, MISB **25.00**
Road Hog, Lindy Loonys, Lindberg, 1964 . . . . **145.00**
Roadster, Mannix, MPC, 1968 . . . . . . **75.00**
Robin, Comic Scenes, Aurora, 1974 **35.00**
Roman Gladiator with Trident, Aurora, 1959 . . . . **325.00**
Roto the Assault Vehicle, Masters of the Universe, Monogram, 1984 . . . . . . **15.00**
Sand Worm, Dune, Revell, 1985 . . . . **20.00**
Seaview, Voyage to the Bottom of the Sea, Aurora, 1966 . . . . **250.00**
Signaling Device for Shipwrecked Sailors, Multiple Toymakers, 1965 . . . . **50.00**
Simple Simon Pie Wagon, Revell, 1966 . . . . **75.00**
Snoopy and His Motorcycle, Monogram, 1971 . . . . **40.00**
Speed Shift Fred Flypogger, Monogram, 1965 . . . . **250.00**
Spindrift, Land of the Giants, Aurora, 1968 . . . . **200.00**
SS United States, World's Fastest Liner, Revell Authentic Kit, 1953, no instructions **45.00**
Sta-Puft Marshmallow Man, Jumbo Kit, Tskuda, 1986 . . . . **45.00**
Steel Plunkers, Frantics, Hawk, 1965 **45.00**
Strange Change Time Machine, MPC, 1974 . . . . **65.00**
Stroker McGurk and His Surf/Rod, MPC, 1964 . . . . **125.00**
SWAT Command Van, Revell, 1976 **25.00**
Sweathogs Car, Welcome Back Kotter, MPC, 1976 . . . . **40.00**
Tarpit, Prehistoric Scenes, Aurora, 1972 . . . . **45.00**
Tarzan, Aurora, 1972, MISB **45.00**
The Bride of Frankenstein, Horizon, 1988 . . . . **45.00**
The Frog, Castle Creatures, Aurora, 1966 . . . . **90.00**
The Mummy, Luminators Series, Monogram, 1991 . . . . **7.00**
The Phantom and the Voodoo Witch Doctor, Revell, 1965 . . . . **175.00**
Three Musketeers, Athos, Porthos, and Aramis, Aurora, 1959 . . . . **375.00**
T J Hooker Police Car, MPC, 1982 **15.00**
Totally Fab, Frantics, Hawk, 1965 . . . **45.00**
Toyota Mark II 2000 GSS, 1:24 scale, By Grip, made in Japan, motorized, MISB **40.00**
Tree House Diorama, Planet of the Apes, Addar, 1975 . . . . **45.00**
20 Mule Team, Death Valley Days, Borax premium **45.00**
United States Infantryman, Aurora, 1956 . . . . **90.00**
Vampire Glow Heads, MPC, 1975 . . . **35.00**

The Visible V8 Engine, Renwal Blueprint Models, #802, 16 × 22 × 3", $35.00.

Va-Va-Vette, Krazy Kar Kustom Kit, AMT, 1968 . . . . **90.00**
Vincent, Black Hole, MPC, 1982 . . . . **25.00**
Voyager, Fantastic Voyage, Aurora, 1969 . . . . **325.00**
Wacky Back Whacker, Aurora, 1965 . . . . **165.00**
Weird-Ohs, reissues, Testors, MISB, complete set of 8 . . . . **60.00**
Witch, Glow in the Dark, Aurora, 1972 . . . . **100.00**
Wolfman, Aurora, 1972, England, MISB **30.00**
Wyatt Earp, Pyro, 1958 . . . . **60.00**
Yacht Sphinx, Entex, 1:32 scale, 16 × 19 × 4" **40.00**
Yellow Submarine, MPC, 1968 . . . . **200.00**
Zorro, Aurora, 1965 . . . . **275.00**

MONSTERS

Collecting monster-related material began in the late 1980s as a generation looked back nostalgically on the monster television shows of the 1960s, e.g., *Addams Family, Dark Shadows,* and *The Munsters,* and the spectacular monster and horror movies of the 1960s and 1970s. Fueling the fire was a group of Japanese collectors who were raiding the American market for material relating to Japanese monster epics featuring reptile monsters such as Godzilla, Rodan, and Mothra.

It did not take long for collectors to seek the historic roots for their post-World War II monsters. A collecting revival started for Frankenstein, King Kong, and Mummy material. Contemporary items featuring these characters also appeared.

This is a category rampant with speculative fever. Prices rise and fall rapidly depending on the momentary popularity of a figure or family group. Study the market and its prices carefully before becoming a participant.

Stress condition and completeness. Do not buy any item in less than fine condition. Check carefully to make certain that all parts or elements are present for whatever you buy.

Since the material in this category is of recent origin, no one is certain how much has survived. Hoards are not uncommon. It is possible to find examples at garage sales. It pays to shop around before paying a high price.

While an excellent collection of two-dimensional material, e.g., comic books, magazines, posters, etc., can be assembled, stress three-dimensional material. Several other crazes, e.g., model kit collecting, cross over into monster collecting, thus adding to price confusion.

Clubs: Count Dracula Fan Club, 29 Washington Sq West, New York, NY 10011; Dark Shadows Fan Club, PO Box 69A04 West Hollywood, CA 90069; Munsters & The Addams Family Fan Club, PO Box 69A04, West Hollywood, CA 90069.

Newletter: *Shadow Gram,* PO Box 92, Maplewood, NJ 07040.

Periodical: *Dark Shadows Collectables Classifieds,* 6173 Iroquois Trail, Mentor, OH 44060.

Annual, *Castle Of Frankenstein 1967 Monster Annual,* 8$\frac{1}{2}$ x 11", 66 pgs, Warren Publishing, c1974 . . . . **15.00**
Bank, King Kong
    12" h, windup, plastic, Empire State Building, King Kong climbs building, Japan **75.00**
    12$\frac{1}{2}$" h, hard vinyl, Relic Art Ltd, copyright 1977 RKO General Inc, missing trap **50.00**
Book
    The Addams Family, Pyramid Publications Inc, paperback, 4 x 7" . . . **20.00**
    The Munsters and the Great Camera Caper, Whitman, 1965, 212 pgs, hard cov, 5$\frac{1}{2}$ × 8" **15.00**
Booklet, *Munsters Official Ghoul Guide,* 1989 . . . . **30.00**
Box, model, Graveyard Ghoul, instruction sheet **20.00**
Calendar, 1966, 9 × 12", full color Don Post Monster masks, each month with different monster illus **75.00**
Coloring Book
    Godzilla, 8$\frac{1}{2}$ × 11", Resource Publishers Inc, copyright 1977 . . . . . . **25.00**
    The Cool Ghoul Monster Coloring Book, 15 × 9", 32 pgs, Wanamaker, 1964, unused **20.00**

Comic Book, *Dark Shadows,* Barnabus Collins cov, Gold Key, 1969 . . . . **15.00**
Costume
    Dracula, orig box, Ben Cooper, copyright UP Co, 1960s **75.00**
    King Kong, orig box **20.00**
    Lily Munster, orig box **75.00**
Doll
    King Kong
        13" h, stuffed corduroy body, soft vinyl head, talking mechanism, Mattel, copyright 1966 . . . . **50.00**
        15" h, King Kong, vinyl head, hands, and feet, holding Fay Raye figure **35.00**
    Munsters, Grandpa, 5" h, Remco, 1964 . . . . **175.00**
Figure
    Addams Family, Lurch, 5$\frac{1}{2}$" h, hard plastic, soft molded vinyl head, Remco, copyright 1964 . . . . **75.00**
    Creature From The Black Lagoon, Mego **200.00**
    Frankenstein, Marx **15.00**
    Vampire, 5" h, pop–up, hard plastic, Multiple Products Corp, 1964 . . . . **15.00**
Game
    Dark Shadows Game, fold–out paper playing board, four standup figures, and playing cards, orig box, Milton Bradley, 1968 . . . . **40.00**
    Dracula Mystery Game, Hasbro, orig box, copyright 1963 Universal Pictures Corp **125.00**
    King Kong Game, Dino de Laurentis Corp, copyright 1976 . . . . **25.00**
    Phantom of the Opera Mystery Game, orig box, Hasbro, 1963 . . . . . **150.00**
Gum Card Wrapper
    King Kong, Donruss, 1965 . . . . . . **55.00**
    Son Of Spook Theater, Leaf, 1963 **50.00**
Iron–On Transfer
    Creature, swimming scene **20.00**
    Phantom of the Opera, 9 × 12", pr, Kaumagraph Toy Division, copyright 1964 . . . . **50.00**
Jewelry Box, Munsters, musical, MIB **35.00**
Lobby Card, 11 × 14", *Rodan The Flying Monster,* full color image, copyright 1957 . . . . **50.00**
Magazine
    Fangoria, 1979 . . . . **100.00**
    Life, Vol 64, #11, March 15, 1968, 10 page article on Frankenstein **15.00**
    Monster World, Munsters feature **45.00**
    3–D Monsters, Vol 1, #1, Fair Publishing Ltd, copyright 1964 . . . . . **25.00**
Magic Drawing Slate, 8 × 14", Horrorscope, cardboard, five Universal monsters illus, unused **50.00**
Model Kit
    Dark Shadows, Barnabus Collins, 1/2 scale, MPC, 1968 . . . . **325.00**

Gigantic Tarantula, plastic, orig box, unassembled, Fundimensions, 1975 . . . . **25.00**
Godzilla, assembled, Aurora **80.00**
Hunchback of Notre Dame, orig box, Aurora, 1973 . . . . **100.00**
Monster Scenes
    Dr Deadly, orig box with sealed contents **140.00**
    Gruesome Goodies, MIB, Aurora **85.00**
    Mummy, assembled, Aurora **30.00**
    Phantom of the Opera, assembled, missing cape cord, Aurora **35.00**
Movie Poster, one sheet
    Die Monster Die **50.00**
    Munster Go Home **50.00**
    The Mummy **150.00**
Photo
    Dark Shadows, three 5 × 7" full color photos of Quentin, one black and white post card, unopened, Philadelphia Chewing Gum Corp, copyright 1969 . . . . **50.00**
    Ghost of Frankenstein, 8$\frac{1}{2}$ × 11", black and white glossy, 1970s **18.00**
Pinback Button
    Creature of the Black Lagoon, 3$\frac{1}{2}$" d, litho metal, color illus, Elwar Ltd, 1963 . . . . **35.00**
    Creepy Magazine Fan Club, 2$\frac{1}{2}$" d, litho metal, color illus of Uncle Creepy, Warren Publishing Co, 1968 **15.00**
Puppet
    Herman Munster, talking mechanism **150.00**
    Lily Munster, fabric body, vinyl head, Ideal, c1965 . . . . **75.00**
Puzzle
    Addams Family Mystery, 14 × 24", orig box, Milton Bradley, copyright 1965 . . . . **75.00**
    Dracula
        APC Puzzle, orig cardboard canister, copyright 1974 . . . . **25.00**
        Jaymar, dungeon scene, orig box, 1963 . . . . **75.00**
    Frankenstein, Frankenstein fighting with Wolfman scene, orig box, Jaymar, 1963 . . . . **125.00**
    Mummy, Mummy carrying screaming victim, orig box, Jaymar, 1963 . . . . **100.00**
    Wolfman, orig box, Hasbro, 1963 . . . . **150.00**
Shopping Bag, 15 × 15", Famous Monsters 1974 Convention, plastic, red, yellow, white, and black **20.00**
Snowdome, Creature of the Black Lagoon, MIB **15.00**
Soaky Bottle, 10" h, Wolfman, soft plastic, hard plastic head, 1960s **75.00**
Target, Frankenstein Horror Target, inlaid figural target, two styrofoam balls, orig box, Hasbro, 1963 . . . . **500.00**

Toy, Flying Eyeball Ghost from Ghost Busters, plastic, purple, removable eyeball, base marked "copyright 1984 Columbia Pictures, Made in China, 25B," 7" w, 3" h, $5.00.

Trading Cards
　Famous Monsters, complete set　**250.00**
　Monster Laffs, complete set **35.00**
　Terror Monsters, purple, 38 of 66 cards
　　........................... **180.00**
　View–Master Reels, Dracula, set of 3, orig
　　story booklet, copyright 1976 .... **15.00**

MORTON POTTERIES

　　Morton is an example of a regional pottery that has a national collecting base. Actually, there were several potteries in Morton, Illinois: Morton Pottery Works and Morton Earthenware Company, 1877–1917; Cliftwood Art Potteries, Inc., 1920–1940; Midwest Potteries, Inc., 1940–1944; Morton Pottery Company, 1922–1976; and, American Art Potteries, 1947–1961.

　　Prior to 1940 local clay was used and fired to a golden ecru. After 1940 clay was imported and fired white. Few pieces are marked. The key to identifying Morton pieces is through the companies' catalogs and Doris and Burdell Hall's book, *Morton's Potteries: 99 Years*, (published by the authors, 1982).

American Art Potteries, 1947–1961
　Bowl, 10" d, elongated octagonal, green,
　　yellow int **8.00**
　Creamer and Sugar, 3" h, stylized flow-
　　ers, blue, peach spray glaze
　　........................ **18.00**
　Demitasse Cup and Saucer, stylized
　　flower dec on cup, gray, pink spray
　　glaze **14.00**
　Planter, 6" h, cowboy boot, blue, pink
　　spray glaze **12.00**
　Television Lamp, 7 × 10", conch shell,
　　purple, pink spray glaze **18.00**
　Vase, 10½" h, cornucopia, gold, white
　　int **10.00**

Cliftwood Art Potteries, Inc, 1920–1940
　Bookends, pr, 6 × 5 × 3½", elephant
　　shape, blue mulberry drip glaze
　　....................... **85.00**
　Candlesticks, pr, 11" h, sq base, choco-
　　late drip glaze **50.00**
　Creamer, 4" h, chocolate drip glaze
　　....................... **35.00**
　Figure, 4½" l, reclining cat, cobalt blue
　　glaze **25.00**
　Lamp, 7½" h, owl on log, yellow　**35.00**
Midwest Potteries, Inc, 1940–1944
　Figure
　　6" w, 10" l, bear, brown spray glaze
　　　.................... **30.00**
　　8½" h, female dancer, stylized,
　　　white, gold dec **25.00**
　Flower Bowl, 10" d, 5½" h, circular,
　　brown, yellow drip glaze, 2 pcs
　　....................... **16.00**
　Miniature, 2" h, goose, white, gold dec
　　....................... **6.00**
　Wall Mask, 5 × 3¼", smiling, curly hair
　　....................... **16.00**
Morton Pottery Company, 1922–1976
　Bank, 5½ × 7", pig, black **25.00**
　Pie Bird, 5" h, white, multicolored wings
　　and back **22.00**
　Planter
　　7" h, cowboy and cactus, natural
　　　colors **12.00**
　　9½" h, rabbit, female holding um-
　　　brella, egg shape planter　**12.00**
　Vase, 8½" h, cornucopia, shell base,
　　blue **14.00**
　Wall Pocket, 6½" h, teapot shape, white,
　　red apple dec **12.00**
Morton Pottery Works and Morton Earthen-
　ware Co, 1877–1917
　Baker, 5½" d, brown Rockingham mot-
　　tled glaze **35.00**
　Coffeepot, 5 pt, brown Rockingham
　　glaze, ornate emb dec **90.00**

Planter, woman, wide brimmed hat, matt white, 7½" h, $30.00.

Mixing Bowl, 12½" d, yellowware, white
　band, narrow blue stripes top and
　bottom **45.00**
Pitcher, 1¼" h, miniature, bulbous body,
　green glaze **25.00**
Teapot, 4½" h, acorn shape, brown
　Rockingham glaze **30.00**

MOTORCYCLES

　　Some of these beauties are getting as expensive as classic and antique cars.

　　Motorcycles are generational. My grandfather would identify with an Indian, my dad with a BMW or Harley Davidson, and I with the Japanese imports. I suspect that most users of this book are not likely to buy an older motorcycle. However, just in case you see a 1916 Indian Power Plus with sidecar for a thousand or less, pick it up. Its book value is $15,000.00.

Club: Antique Motorcycle Club of America, 14943 York Rd, Sparks, MD 21152.

Periodicals: *Bike Journal International,* 6 Prowitt St, Norwalk, CT 06855; *Hemmings Motor News,* PO Box 100, Bennington, VT 05201.

MOVIE MEMORABILIA

　　The stars of the silver screen have fascinated audiences for over three–quarters of a century. In many cases, this fascination had as much to do with their private lives as their on–screen performances.

　　This is a category where individuals focus on their favorites. There are superstars in the collectibles area. Two examples are Charlie Chaplin and Marilyn Monroe.

　　Posters are expensive. However, there are plenty of other categories where a major collection can be built for under $25.00 per object. Also, do not overlook the present–day material. If it's cheap, pick it up. Movie material will always be collectible.

Club: Hollywood Studio Collectors Club, Suite 450, 3960 Laurel Canyon Blvd, Studio City, CA 91604.

Periodicals: *Big Reel,* PO Box 83, Madison, NC 27025; *Classic Images,* PO Box 809, Muscotine, IA 52761; *Hollywood Collectibles,* 2900 N Meade St, Suite 4, Appleton, WI 54911; *Movie Advertising*

Collector, PO Box 28587, Philadelphia, PA 19149; *Movie Collectors' World,* PO Box 309, Fraser, MI 48026; *Nostalgia World,* PO Box 231, North Haven, CT 06473.

Activity Book, *Planet of the Apes,* 10¹/₂ × 12¹/₂", Saalfield Publishing Co, copyright 1974 .... **25.00**

Almanac, 6¹/₂ × 9", 1947–48 Motion Picture, hard cover, over 1,000 pgs **55.00**

Ashtray, 2¹/₂ × 4 × 3¹/₂", china, figural image of Mae West reclining on chaise lounge, "Come Up And See Me Sometime" slogan, Made in Japan, 1930s **125.00**

Blotter, *Hunchback of Notre Dame,* Lon Chaney, pictorial scene **40.00**

Bottle, 5" h, figural, Scarlett O'Hara, glass, clear, brass cap **75.00**

Coloring Book, *Chitty Chitty Bang Bang,* Whitman, copyright 1968, 128 pgs **15.00**

Game, Hangman with Vincent Price, plastic playing pieces, orig box, Milton Bradley, 1976 .... **20.00**

Handbill, 5¹/₂ × 8", Marvelous Motion Pictures, lists hourly showing of *In The Black Tent,* c1901 .... **75.00**

Lobby Card, 11 × 14"
  Blazing Frontier, color photo, PRC Picture, 1940s **50.00**
  Gang Busters, color photo, Visual Drama Inc, 1950s **25.00**
  Gang War, color scene, 20th Century Fox, 1958 .... **20.00**
  Gun Brothers, color photo, United Artists, 1956 .... **15.00**
  Hot Rod Rumble, color photo, Allied Artists, 1950s **25.00**

Singing In The Rain, full color photo of Gene Kelly, Donald O'Connor, and Debbie Reynolds **75.00**

The Hot Angel, color photo, Paramount Pictures, 1958 .... **45.00**

The Kidnappers, black and white, Manson, 1964 .... **20.00**

The Top Secret Master Plan, color photo, Astor Pictures, c1950 .... **45.00**

Magazine
  Life, April 26, 1954, black and white photo of Grace Kelly **18.00**
  Modern Screen, 8¹/₂ × 11¹/₂", June 1935, 124 pgs, full color cover of Mae West **35.00**
  Modern Times, Charlie Chaplin, French, 1930s **55.00**
  Motion Picture, 8¹/₂ × 11¹/₂", December 1927, 120 pgs, full color art **25.00**
  Screen Album, 8¹/₂ × 11¹/₃", Spring, 1947, 28 pgs, full color photo of Betty Grable **25.00**

Movie Poster
  One Sheet, 27 × 41", *Loves Of Carmen,* William Fox film, 1927 ..... **400.00**
  Six sheet, 12 × 15" folded
    Bomba And The Jungle Girl, Monogram Picture, 1952 ..... **200.00**
    Drums of Fu Manchu, Republic Pictures, 1940 .... **225.00**
    Raiders of the Seven Seas, United Artists, 1953 .... **125.00**
    Sea of Sand, British, The Rank Organization, 1958 .... **100.00**
    The Farmers Daughter, RKO Radio Pictures, 1947 .... **150.00**
    Untamed Women, United Artists, 1952 .... **175.00**

Paperback Book
  A Hard Day's Night, Dell, 1964, 156 pgs **20.00**
  Cool Hand Luke, Fawcett, 1965, cover photo of Paul Newman **8.00**
  Enter The Dragon, Award Books, 1973, Bruce Lee cov **12.00**
  The Desperate Hours, Perma Books, 1955, cover photo with Humphrey Bogart and Fredric March **10.00**

Paperweight, 3¹/₂" h, MGM lion, copper, marked "Metro–Goldwyn–Mayer Lion, the Greatest Star on the Screen," 1940s **150.00**

Pencil Box, 1 × 2¹/₃ × 8", Charlie Chaplin, litho tin, hinged, c1920 .... **50.00**

Photograph
  Rudolph Valentino with Sheik, framed **45.00**
  Shirley Temple, *Captain January,* Wheaties premium, 1930s **35.00**

Pinback Button, *The Red Ace,* Marie Walcamp photo, 1920s **22.00**

Post Card, *Little Colonel,* Shirley Temple, England **20.00**

Program, 9 × 12", *Wings,* Clara Bow and Gary Cooper, Paramount Picture, 1927 .... **50.00**

Sheet Music
  Some Sunday Morning, 9 × 12", Warner Bros, copyright 1945, black and white photo of Flynn and Alexis Smith **40.00**
  Those Charlie Chaplin Feet, 11 × 13¹/₂", black and white cov photo with blue accents, 1915 copyright **25.00**

Souvenir Book, *My Fair Lady,* hardbound, 1964 .... **35.00**

Tablet, Rock Hudson, 8 × 10", color photo, 1950s **15.00**

Toy, mechanical, Charlie Chaplin, wood, England, 1920s **245.00**

Window Card, 14 × 22", *The Rare Breed,* Jimmy Stewart and Maureen O'Hara, full color, sgd by Stewart, Universal Picture, 1966 .... **75.00**

MUGS

The problem with every general price guide is that they do not cover the broad sweeping form categories, e.g., wash pitchers and bowls, any longer. A surprising number of individuals still collect this way.

If you stay away from beer mugs, you can find a lot of examples in this category for under $10.00. Look for the unusual, either in form or labeling. Don't forget to fill one now and then and toast your cleverness in collecting these treasures.

Club: Advertising Cup and Mug Collectors of America, PO Box 680, Solon, IA 52333.

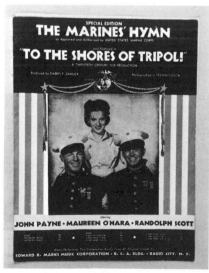

Magazine Tear Sheet, The Marx Bros, A Night In Casablanca, 1946, 8 × 11", $10.00.

Sheet Music, The Marines' Hymn, Special Edition, Featured in "To The Shores of Tripoli," Twentieth Century Fox Production, John Payne, Maureen O'Hara, and Randolph Scott on cov, $4.00.

Advertising

A & W Root Beer, clear glass, logo **5.00**

Big Boy Restaurant, clear glass **3.00**

Carter Carburetor, stoneware **15.00**

Choo Choo Cherry, 3" h, plastic, red, blue and white accents, orig mailing box, copyright 1969 The Pillsbury Co **25.00**

Frosty Root Beer, clear glass, set of 6 .... **30.00**

Lefty Lemon, 3½" h, plastic, Funny Face series, Pillsbury Co, copyright 1969 .... **25.00**

Nestle's Quik, 4" h, plastic, figural, bunny head, ear handles, back with raised "Quik," marked "The Nestle Co Inc," 1970s **20.00**

Ovaltine, 3¼" h, plastic, red, full color decal **25.00**

Rudy Tootie Frutti, 3" h, hard plastic, Funny Face series, Pillsbury Co, copyright 1974 .... **25.00**

Whitetower Restaurant **22.00**

Batman and Robin, pr, 3" h, milk glass, black Batman illus on one, other with orange Robin illus, Westfield copyright 1966, National Periodical Publications Inc **25.00**

Beatles, 3" h, white glass, black images, text "Yea!, Yea!, Yea!, Yea!," unauthorized, 1960s **25.00**

Care Bear, days of week, American Greeting Corp **2.00**

Davy Crockett, 3" h, plastic, red, tan lid, relief portrait image, mid 1950s **75.00**

Dukes of Hazzard, 3½" h, plastic, white, red, white, and blue design, color photos, Irwin copyright 1981 .... **15.00**

Grog, BC Comics **3.00**

Gulliver's Travels, 3¼" h, china, gold accent, Hammersley & Co, England, c1939 .... **125.00**

Disney, Jungle Book, characters dancing around base, white ground, gold trim, marked "Designed and Made for Disneyland, Walt Disney World, Made in Japan," 3½" h, $5.00.

Fire King, fired–on orange, white int, glass, marked "Anchor Hocking Fire King Ware, Made in USA," 3½" h, $.50.

Hopalong Cassidy, 3" h, milk glass, red Hoppy illus and name on front, western scene on back **25.00**

Howdy Doody, 3¼", h, plastic, red, full color decal, Ovaltine premium, 1948–51 .... **50.00**

Jiggs, 5" h, ceramic, yellow cane handle, marked "Jiggs" and "Puck" on back, 1960s **125.00**

Joe 90, 3" h, china, white, color illus, ATV copyright 1968, Washington Pottery Ltd **25.00**

Little Orphan Annie, 3¾" h, plastic, brown, full color decal, Ovaltine premium, c1939 .... **30.00**

Mickey Mouse, 2¾" h, china, color image of Mickey and dog, orange rim and handle, marked "Made In Japan," 1930 .... **100.00**

Minnie Mouse, 3" h, china, color transfer, Bavaria China **175.00**

Pan–American Exposition, 2" h, glass, clear handle, scalloped edge, inscribed with red script **35.00**

Pogo Possum and Beauregard Hound, pr, 4¼" h, plastic, blue, full color decals, Walt Kelly copyright, 1960s **25.00**

Snuffy Smith, 5" h, ceramic, gray finish, marked "Snuffy" and "Puck" on back, 1950s **125.00**

Winnie The Pooh Friends, 3¾" h, set of 4, ceramic, painted and glazed, Enesco sticker, 1964 copyright **55.00**

MUSICAL INSTRUMENTS

Didn't you just love music lessons? Still play your clarinet or trumpet? Probably not! Yet, I bet you still have the instrument. Why is it that you can never seem to throw it out?

The number of antique and classic musical instrument collectors is small, but growing. Actually, most instruments are sold for reuse. As a result, the key is playability. Check out the cost of renting an instrument or purchasing one new. Now you known why prices on "used" instruments are so high. Fifty dollars for a playable instrument of any quality is a bargain price. Of course, it's a bargain only if someone needs and wants to play it. Otherwise, it is fifty dollars ill–spent.

Do not overlook music related items.

Club: The American Musical Instrument Society, 414 East Clark St, Vermillion, SD 57069.

Periodicals: *Concertina & Squeezebox,* PO Box 6706, Ithaca, NY 14851; *Strings,* PO Box 767, San Anselmo, CA 94960.

INSTRUMENTS AND ACCESSORIES

Accordion, 12 × 6", Concertone, two stops, two sets of reeds, 10 keys, gilt valves, ebonized panels and frame **125.00**

Banjo

Unknown Maker, American, 10" d, calfskin head, nickel band on maple shell, faux cherry finish on neck, c1900 .... **225.00**

Wondertone, S S Steward, walnut, marquetry inlay, 1920s **185.00**

Banjo Bag, cloth, green, button closure **10.00**

Bugle, officer's, c1900 .... **100.00**

Castinets, pr, early 20th C **38.00**

Cello, Sears Roebuck, inlaid edges, c1900 .... **475.00**

Clarinet, Laube, thirteen keys, two rings, Grenadilla wood, C, low pitch **350.00**

Cymbals, 13" d, pr, leather handles, c1900 .... **140.00**

Drum

Bass, German, foot pedal, c1860 **550.00**

Snare, 14" d, Acme Professional, c1900 .... **175.00**

Glockenspiel, carrying strap and case **65.00**

Guitar

Cambridge, rosewood and spruce, ebony fingerboard, nickel plated head, 1905–10 .... **145.00**

The Marlowe, c1900 .... **160.00**

Guitar Case, canvas, brown, leather bound edges, strap, buckle, and handles, late 1800s **15.00**

Harmonica

Hohner Marine Band, ten single holes, twenty reeds, brass plates, nickel covers, gilt lettering on red hinged case, c1903 .... **30.00**

Rol–Monica Player, Bakelite, 1900s **165.00**

Ocarina, F, soprano, European, c1900 .... **25.00**

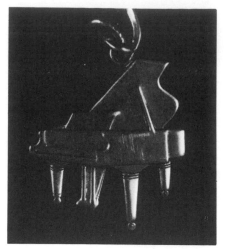

Charm, piano, silver, c1965, $8.00.

Organ Stool, orig needlepoint upholstery
...........................**75.00**
Piano Stool
   Metal, circular seat, ornate design, ad-
     justable height, claw and glass ball
     feet, 1880–1915 ....**125.00**
   Wood, circular seat, plain design, adjust-
     able height, 1880–1915 .....**75.00**
Pick, oval, gutta percha **4.00**
Saxophone
   Marceau, B–flat, tenor, brass, polished
     ....**150.00**
   Tourville & Co, tenor, silver **350.00**
Tambourine, Mexican, c1900 ....**80.00**
Trombone, Marceau, B–flat, bass, brass
........................**250.00**
Violin, Otto Hoyer, round stick with ivory
   face, silver and ebony frog, plain sides,
   silver–sheathed adjuster **300.00**
Violin Case, wood, flannel lining, varnished,
   nickel plated lock **40.00**
Zither Tuning Hammer, ivory handle, early
   1900s **8.00**

MUSIC RELATED

Book, *History of English Music,* Davey, Lon-
   don, 1895 ....**12.00**
Booklet, *How Music Is Made,* C G Conn
   Co, 1927 56 pgs, illus **5.00**
Catalog
   Carl Fischer, Inc, c1929, 48 pgs, 4$\frac{1}{2}$ ×
     7$\frac{1}{2}$" **40.00**
   Needham Organ & Piano Co, 1900, 16
     pgs, 7 × 9$\frac{1}{4}$" **30.00**
   Rudolph Wurlitzer Co, 1920, 176 pgs, 8
     × 10$\frac{1}{4}$" **95.00**
   Simplex School Of Music, 1910, 32 pgs,
     5$\frac{3}{4}$ × 8$\frac{3}{4}$" **14.00**
   Thomas A Edison, Inc, 1919, 12 pgs, 5
     × 8" **20.00**
Cigar Label, 5 × 5", Huyler Cigars, musi-
   cian image **4.00**
Post Card, Battle Creek military band, Battle
   Creek, IA, black and white **10.00**

Poster
   Roca, 36 × 56", Roca posed with
     squeeze–box illus, c1900 ...**200.00**
   Woody Herman, 14 × 22", "America's
     New Sensation!," Herman with clari-
     net illus, c1951 ....**185.00**
Program, 10 × 13", Johnny Mathis, 1970
........................**10.00**
Songbook, *Songs Scouts Sing,* 4$\frac{1}{4}$ × 6$\frac{3}{4}$",
   musical note cov **25.00**
Toy
   Guitar, Tom and Jerry, hard plastic,
     black, full color paper illus, Mattel
     Toys, copyright 1965 ....**30.00**
   Microphone, Michael Jackson Cordless
     Electronic Microphone, orig box, MJJ
     Productions Inc, copyright 1984
........................**25.00**

NAPKIN RINGS

If you get lucky, you may find a great Victorian silver-plated figural napkin ring at a flea market. Chances are that you are going to find napkin rings used by the common man. But do not look down your nose at them. Some are pretty spectacular.

If you do not specialize from the beginning, you are going to find yourself going around in circles. Animal–shaped rings are a favorite.

Advertising
   Union Theatres, tin **12.00**
   Worcester Salt, salt sack illus, pr **15.00**
Bakelite, red, carved **35.00**
Bisque, 2" d, sailboat, yellow **60.00**
Brass, two elves, dogs, and dragon **25.00**

Monkey, dressed, Derby Silver Co, #828, oval base, $225.00.

Celluloid, figural
   Grapes, emb **12.00**
   Tiger **36.00**
China
   Egyptian scene, Nippon **75.00**
   Flowers and butterfly, Noritake ...**15.00**
   Owl, seated on ring **25.00**
Cloisonne, white flowers, dark blue ground
........................**45.00**
Cut Glass, hobstars and diamonds ...**85.00**
Metal, lady holding stick, c1942 ....**15.00**
Silver Plated
   Brownie, Palmer Cox **75.00**
   Parrot, rect base, Rogers Mfg Co **50.00**
   Ring, floral band, 2" w **20.00**
   Turtle **30.00**
Sterling Silver
   Butterfly and reed design, anchor mark
........................**50.00**
   Eagle, figural **85.00**
   Knight, standing alongside ring, round
     base, Babcock & Co **40.00**
   Peacock, standing **75.00**
World's Fair, Chicago, Hall of Science,
   1933 ....**35.00**

NAUTICAL COLLECTIBLES

There is magic in the sea, whether one is reading the novels of Melville, watching Popeye cartoons, or standing on a beach staring at the vast expanse of ocean. Anyone who loves water has something nautical around the house.

This is one case where the weathered look is a plus. No one wants a piece of nautical material that appears to have never left the dock.

Club: Nautical Research Guild, 62 Marlboro St, Newburyport, MA 01950.

Periodicals: *Nautical Brass*, PO Box 3966, North Ft Myers, FL 33918; *Nautical Collector,* PO Box 16734, Alexandria, VA 22302.

Almanac, Nautical Almanac, Riggs &
   Brother, Philadelphia, PA, 1910, 154
   pgs, nautical instruments, partially used
   ship's log **125.00**
Book
   *Masting, Mast–making and Rigging of
     Ships,* Robert Kipping, 1877, orig cov
........................**90.00**
   *The Galley Guide: A Purely Humanitar-
     ian Work, Planned Out of Consider-
     ation For The Digestive Apparatus of
     Those Who Cruise–The Thing, After
     All, Upon Which Success Or Failure
     Largely Depends,* Alex W Moffat,
     Motor Boat Publishing, NY, 1923,
     145 pgs **20.00**

Diving Helmet, homemade, $135.00.

Brochure, *Cruising With Safety,* 1947, 76
   pgs, sailboat and motorboat photos,
   glossy stiff covs **10.00**
Cigar Label, 5" sq, Cutter Cigars, sailing
   yacht flying US flag, 1887 . . . . **32.00**
Crew List, whale ship *Montpelier,* Sept 6,
   1853, names, positions, number of
   shares in voyages to be received
   . . . . **125.00**
Fog Horn, 30" l, brass, 19th C **85.00**
Harpoon Head, 3⅛" l, whale ivory, incised
   designs **100.00**

Puzzle, **The Werra,** *McLoughlin, c1895–
1905, 48 hand–cut pressboard pieces, wood
frame, 12 × 9" cardboard box, guide picture,
23½" × 17½", $60.00.*

Log Book, bark *Manchester,* voyage between Boston and New Orleans, c1884
   . . . . **125.00**
Magazine Tear Sheet, Sterling Engine Co,
   "The New Models for 1935," multicolored Donald Douglas yacht paintings,
   1935 . . . . **15.00**
Navigation Scale, 24" l, boxwood, B Dodd,
   19th C **210.00**
Quarterboard, *Edith Nute,* traces of black
   paint, orig gold lettering **200.00**
Rudder, 59" l, orig white paint traces,
   19th C **50.00**
Sea Chart, 23 × 19", Chart of the North
   and Baltic Seas, J Thompson, outline
   colored, 1816 . . . . **35.00**
Signal Horn, 15" l, foot operated, "E A Gill,
   Gloucester, MA" **110.00**

NEWSPAPERS

"Read All About It" is the cry of
corner newspaper vendors across the
country. Maybe these vendors should be
collected. They appear to be a vanishing
breed.

Some newspapers are collected for
their headlines, others because they represent a special day, birthday, or anniversary. Many people saved the newspaper announcing that JFK was shot. Did
you save a paper from the day war was
declared against Iraq? I did.

Club: Newspaper Collectors Society of
America, Box 19134, Lansing, MI
48901.

Periodical: *PCM (Paper Collectors' Marketplace),* PO Box 128, Scandinavia, WI
54977.

1836, April 23, The Fall of the Alamo, *The
   New Yorker* **100.00**
1860, Lincoln/Douglas Election **42.00**
1863, Battle of Gettysburg **175.00**
1871, Oct 28, Great Chicago Fire, *Leslie's
   Illustrated* **150.00**
1898, Feb 15, sinking of the *Maine*   **40.00**
1903, Dec 17, Wright Bros Fly **220.00**
1906, April 18, San Francisco earthquake,
   Chicago Daily News **110.00**
1917, Oct 6, White Sox win opener   **55.00**
1926, Sept 23, Tunney defeats Jack
   Dempsey **25.00**
1927, Babe Ruth's 60th Homerun,
   Galveston Daily News **82.00**
1929, Oct 28, stock market crash . . . **65.00**
1934, May 23, Bonnie and Clyde killed
   . . . . **70.00**
1937, May 6, Hindenburg crash **40.00**
1941, Dec 7, Pearl Harbor attacked   **45.00**
1944, Nov 8, Roosevelt Elected **20.00**
1945, Aug 6, First Atomic Bomb Dropped
   On Japan **24.00**

*1836, Sept 5, Daily National Intelligencer,
Washington, 18 × 20½" folded, $15.00.*

1954, May 17, school segregation decision
   . . . . **10.00**
1962, Feb 20, John Glenn's space flight
   . . . . **15.00**
1963, Nov 22, Kennedy assassination **30.00**
1973, Oct 11, Agnew resignation . . . **10.00**
1974, Aug 9, Nixon resignation **25.00**
1977, Aug 17, Elvis Dies, *Los Angeles
   Times* **27.00**
1980, Reagan/Carter Election **4.00**

NILOAK POTTERY

When you mention Niloak, most
people immediately think of swirled
brown, red, and tan pottery, formally
known as Mission Ware. However,
Niloak also made items in a host of other
designs through 1946. These included
utilitarian wares and ceramics used by
florists that can be bought for a reasonable price. If Niloak prices follow the
trend established by Roseville prices,

*Vase, Mission Ware, cream, blue, and brown
swirls, imp "Niloak" on bottom, 9¼" h,
$195.00.*

now is the time to stash some of these later pieces away.

Club: Arkansas Pottery Collectors Society, 12 Normandy Rd, Little Rock, AR 72207.

Ashtray, hat shape, blue, glossy finish **7.50**
Bowl, 5" d, red, cream, blue, and green
.... **35.00**
Bud Vase, 4" h, blue and pink, matte finish
.... **22.00**
Candlesticks, pr, Mission Ware
   2" h, brown, blue, and cream **65.00**
   8½" h, blue, brown, and cream marbleized swirls **125.00**
Cornucopia, light pink **5.00**
Ewer, 11" h, turquoise shading to pink, matte finish, relief floral dec **65.00**
Match Holder, figural, duck, brown and white swirls **15.00**
Paperweight, rabbit, paper label **35.00**
Pitcher
   7" h, pink, glossy finish **25.00**
   10" h, eagle **30.00**
Planter
   Camel, Hywood Line **20.00**
   Frog, rose glaze, Hywood Line ... **27.50**
   Swan, pink, small **5.00**
   Wishing Well, 7¼" h, dusty rose **12.00**
Urn, 4½" h, brown and blue marbleized swirls, Mission Ware **35.00**
Vase
   3⅞" h, brown, green, blue, and cream marbleized swirls, wide neck, paper label, Mission Ware **65.00**
   6" h, green, wing handles **25.00**
   6½" h, blue, glossy finish, wing handles
.... **25.00**
   8" h, marbleized swirls, corset top, bulbous bottom, Mission Ware **125.00**
Wall Pocket, 6" h, brown, blue, and tan, Mission Ware **75.00**

NIPPON

Nippon is handpainted Japanese porcelain made between 1891 and 1921. The McKinley tariff of 1891 required goods imported into the United States to be marked with their country of origin. Until 1921, goods from Japan were marked "Made in Nippon."

Over two hundred different manufacturer's marks have been discovered for Nippon. The three most popular are the wreath, maple leaf, and rising sun. While marks are important, the key is the theme and quality of the decoration.

Nippon has become quite expensive. Rumors in the field indicate that Japanese buyers are now actively competing with American buyers.

Clubs: International Nippon Collectors Club, 112 Ascot Dr, Southlake, TX 76092; Lakes & Plains Nippon Collectors Club, PO Box 230, Peotone, IL 60468; Long Island Nippon Collectors Club, 145 Andover Pl, West Hampstead, NY 11552; New England Nippon Collectors Club, 64 Burt Rd, Springfield, MA 01118.

Ashtray, 6½" d, molded in relief, cigar and matchbox, green mark **345.00**
Basket, large, heavy white moriage, green ground **175.00**
Berry Set, 7 pcs, master and six serving bowls, bisque, pastel orange flowers outlined in gold, RC mark **98.00**
Biscuit Jar, ruffled, narrow center, pink and red roses, white ground, TEOH mark
.... **125.00**
Bowl
   5½" d, bisque, forest scene, Maple Leaf mark **48.00**
   8¾" d, gold leaves, blue mark ... **90.00**
Cake Set, 10½" d cake platter, six 6¼" d plates, pink roses, green mark ... **200.00**
Calling Card Tray, 7½" l, floral dec, cobalt blue, green "M" in Wreath mark
.... **200.00**
Candlesticks, pr, 9" h, white, column shape, gold dragon dec **195.00**
Candy Dish, oblong, ftd, pink and white rosebuds on gold medallions, multicolored jewels, gold beaded trim, dark green ground, Maple Leaf mark **65.00**

Vase, high glaze, pink, lavender, and yellow flowers, green leaves, gold trim, 9¼" h, $150.00.

Celery Dish, 11½" l, bisque, scenic, Wreath mark **50.00**
Chocolate Set, 10 pcs, 11" h cov pot, four cups and saucers, hp roses, gold leaves, blue Maple Leaf mark **800.00**
Cigar Holder, oval tray, sailboat design, green mark **135.00**
Cinnamon Stick Holder, 4½" h, cylinder shape, ftd, blue mark **200.00**
Coaster, 3¾" d, floral, blue mark **28.00**
Cup and Saucer, bisque, forest scene, Wreath mark **48.00**
Demitasse Set, 10 pcs, 6" h cov pot, four cups and saucers, silver overlay, white ground, RC Noritake Nippon mark
.... **275.00**
Dish, 7½" w, divided, three sections, green mark **90.00**
Doll, 4¾" h, girl, pink bow in hair, incised mark **110.00**
Feeding Dish, child's, 8" d, girl and dog illus, blue mark **75.00**
Hatpin Holder, 4½" h, WW I airplane illus, green mark **175.00**
Ink Blotter, 4¼" h, gold sticker, red mark
.... **140.00**
Inkwell, 3" sq, int well, horse and rider, green mark **165.00**
Lemonade Set, 5 pcs, pitcher and four tumblers, hp purple grapes, Art Deco border dec, Apple Blossom mark **175.00**
Milk Pitcher, 10½" h, stylized flowers, yellow and brown **150.00**
Mug, 5½" h, moriage, sailboat scene
.... **100.00**
Nappy, 6" w, white floral dec, Wedgwood blue, eight sided, two handles, green "M" in Wreath mark **125.00**
Nut Cup, set of 6, hp roses, gold accents
.... **110.00**
Plaque, pierced to hang
   8" d, hp sunset with sailboat scene, blue Maple Leaf mark **95.00**
   9⅝" sq, hp landscape, houses, mountains, water, boats, geese, and man carrying water vessel, gold rim
.... **135.00**
   11" d, basket with nuts, green mark **275.00**
Plate, 10½" d, floral dec, heavy gold beading and designs, scalloped rim, green "M" in Wreath mark **80.00**
Relish Dish, 8½" l, landscape scene, green mark **125.00**
Rose Bowl, 5¾" h, hp floral dec, lavender, Wedgwood, green "M" in Wreath mark
.... **500.00**
Shaving Mug, 3¾" h, yellow mark ... **85.00**
Sugar Shaker
   Cobalt blue and floral, 4½" h, blue Maple Leaf mark **175.00**
   White, grape design, gold leaves, blue mark **55.00**
Syrup, underplate, 3½" h, hp floral dec, Wedgwood, green "M" in Wreath mark
.... **225.00**

Tankard, 12" h, hp iris dec, Royal Nippon mark **295.00**

Tea Set, 17 pcs, 9" h cov teapot, six cups, five saucers, four tall cups, paneled hexagonal form, white chrysanthemum blossoms and colored leaves, white ground **75.00**

Tea Strainer, 6" l, floral dec, cobalt blue ground, lug handle, blue Maple Leaf mark **125.00**

Tidbit Plate, rose panels and Greek Key design **30.00**

Urn, 10" h, cov, floral dec, green mark **195.00**

Vase
6" h, pink thorny roses, hexagonal body, handled, six legs **65.00**

9" h, Egyptian scene, gold trim, hexagonal body, wide shoulder, green "M" in Wreath mark **210.00**

Whiskey Jug, 7½" h, large pinecone and pine tree, glossy finish, Wreath mark **400.00**

NORITAKE CHINA

Noritake is quality Japanese china imported to the United States by the Noritake China company. The company, founded by the Morimura Brothers in Nagoya in 1904, is best known for its dinnerware lines. Over one hundred different marks were used, which are helpful in dating pieces.

The Larkin Company of Buffalo, New York, issued several patterns as premiums, including the Azalea, Briarcliff, Linden, Savory, Sheridan, and Tree in the Meadow patterns, which are found in quantity.

Be careful. Not all Noritake china is what it seems. The company also sold blanks to home decorators. Check the artwork before deciding that a piece is genuine.

Newsletter: *Noritake News,* 1237 Federal Ave East, Seattle, WA 98102.

Bowl
6" d, floral dec, gold accent, handled **55.00**

8" d, hp pink, yellow, and white roses int, gilt dec ext, scalloped edge, artist sgd **145.00**

Bread Plate, 14" l, 6¼" w, white, pale green and gold floral border, open handles **24.00**

Calling Card Tray, adv, Morimura Brothers, NY, Geisha artists painting ceramics dec, dated 1907 . . . . **335.00**

Candy Dish, cov, multicolored, stylized floral dec **95.00**

Children's Dishes, six plates, cups, and saucers, teapot, creamer and sugar, cookie plate, platter, and cov casserole, white, gold trim, orig box, 1922 . . . . . . **250.00**

Coffeepot, cov, Scheherazade pattern **48.00**

Condiment Tray, 7" l, rect, gilt dec, white ground **25.00**

Creamer and Sugar, cov, Scheherazade pattern **30.00**

Demitasse Cup and Saucer, orange and blue flowers **18.00**

Dinner Service, Vintage pattern, 90 pcs, 7 pc place settings for 12, plus serving pcs **500.00**

Dish, 8" w, relief molded, nut dec, handled, green mark **120.00**

Dresser Doll, figural, gold lustre **185.00**

Humidor, cov
6" h, stylized floral and dotted panels and white bands, compressed ball finial **225.00**

7" h, figural, owl, red head and wings, yellow around eyes, tan chest, luster finish **300.00**

Napkin Rings, pr, Art Deco style, portrait dec, one with girl wearing red fur–trimmed cloak, other with man wearing top hat and cape **100.00**

Night Light, 13" h, figural, Egyptian and owl **350.00**

Nut Set, 7 pcs, figural, peanut, 7¼" d master bowl, six 3" d individual bowls **175.00**

Plaque
6" d, three relief–molded dog heads, brown and white **600.00**

8½" d, silhouette of girl in bouffant dress, looking into hand mirror, green "M" in Wreath mark **100.00**

Powder Box, desert scene, Arab on camel, cobalt blue ground, ornate gold beading **300.00**

Punch Bowl Set, 9 pcs, banquet size bowl, eight cups, swans, cottage, island, and trees landscape, heavy raised gold dec, green "M" in Wreath mark **675.00**

Shaving Mug, 3¾" h, hp stalking tiger scene, green "M" in Wreath mark **200.00**

Bowl, chestnut dec in browns, orange, and yellow, 7¾" d, 2⅛" h, $95.00.

Tobacco Jar, 6½" h, hp golfer wearing red jacket and cap and black and white checkerboard knickers, green "M" in Wreath mark **190.00**

Vase
5" h, oval medallions with scarlet birds and flowers, gold lustre ground, 1930s **35.00**

5½" h, relief molded, squirrel on berried leafy branch, shaded brown ground **150.00**

Wall Pocket
8" h, wooded landscape, house near water, blue lustre ground **75.00**

8½" h, red flower dec, red mark **95.00**

8¾" h, floral dec, orange and gold lustre ground **65.00**

NORITAKE CHINA, AZALEA

Noritake china in the Azalea pattern was first produced in the early 1900s. Several backstamps were used. You will find them listed in *Warman's Americana and Collectibles* (Wallace-Homestead). They will help date your piece.

Azalea pattern wares were distributed as a premium by the Larkin Company of Buffalo and sold by Sears, Roebuck and Company. As a result, it is the most commonly found pattern of Noritake china.

Each piece is handpainted, adding individuality. Hard-to-find examples include children's tea sets and salesmen's samples. Do not ignore the handpainted glassware in the Azalea pattern that was manufactured to accompany the china service.

Berry Set **160.00**
Bonbon, 6¼" w **50.00**
Bread Tray, 12" l **110.00**
Butter Dish **125.00**
Cake Plate, two handled **35.00**
Casserole, cov, gold finial **500.00**
Celery, 10" l, closed handle **360.00**
Cheese Dish **145.00**
Condiment Set **75.00**
Cup and Saucer **15.00**
Egg cup **70.00**
Gravy Boat **50.00**
Jam Jar, spoon, liner **175.00**
Jug, 1 quart **220.00**
Mustard, handle, no spoon **50.00**
Plate
Child's **100.00**
Dinner **20.00**
Salad **10.00**
Square **50.00**

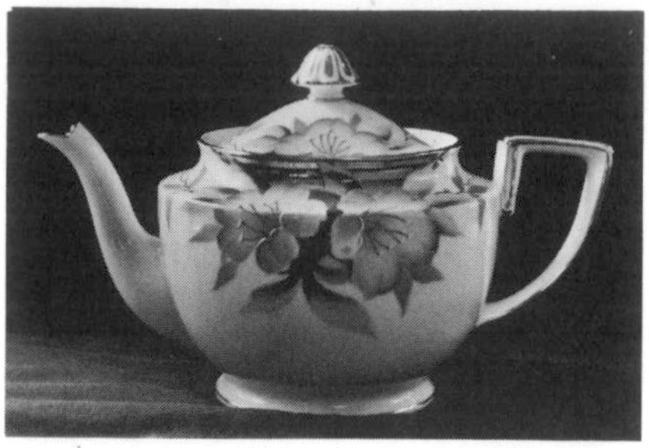

Teapot, gold finial, marked "Handpainted Japan," $5\frac{1}{2}$" h, $395.00

Saltshaker	**30.00**
Soup, flat	**28.00**
Syrup	**110.00**
Teapot, cov, gold finial	**475.00**
Vegetable Bowl, round, large	**50.00**
Whipped Cream Set	**45.00**

NORITAKE CHINA, TREE IN THE MEADOW

If you ever want to see variation in a pattern, collect Tree in the Meadow. You will go nuts trying to match pieces. In the end you will do what everyone else does—learn to live with the differences. Is there a lesson here?

Tree in the Meadow was distributed by the Larkin Company of Buffalo, New York. Importation began in the 1920s, almost twenty years after the arrival of Azalea pattern wares. Check the backstamp to identify the date of the piece.

Berry Set, large bowl, open handles, six small bowls **70.00**
Bowl, $6\frac{1}{2}$" d, green mark **28.00**
Butter Tub **58.00**
Cake Plate **32.00**
Celery Tray **40.00**
Compote, $6\frac{1}{2}$" d, $2\frac{3}{4}$" h **185.00**
Condiment Set, 5 pcs, mustard pot, ladle, salt and pepper shakers, and tray **40.00**
Creamer **25.00**
Cup and Saucer **12.00**
Demitasse Coffeepot **375.00**
Dinner Service, six tea plates, bread and butter plates, breakfast plates, dinner plates, and fruit bowls, four cups and saucers, cake plate, compote, divided relish, 12" l platter, 14" l platter, pr salt and pepper shakers, cov butter dish with drain insert, double cruet set, gravy boat with underplate, cov vegetable bowl, creamer, and sugar bowl **650.00**
Dish, pierced handles, blue lustre border, 6" l **40.00**
Fruit Bowl, $7\frac{3}{4}$" l, shell shaped **275.00**
Gravy Boat, attached underplate **70.00**
Jam Jar, underplate, spoon **65.00**

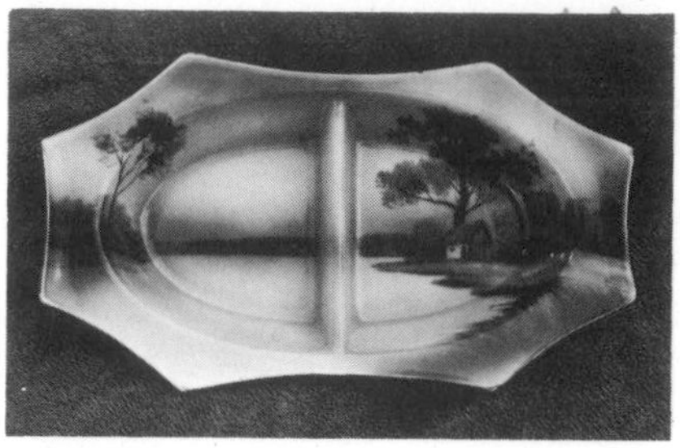

Relish Dish, divided, $45.00.

Lemon Dish, center ring handle, $5\frac{1}{2}$" d **15.00**
Plate
- 6" d **10.00**
- $7\frac{1}{2}$" d **12.00**
- $8\frac{1}{2}$" d **15.00**

Platter, 12" l **32.00**
Salad Bowl, $8\frac{1}{2}$" d **55.00**
Salt and Pepper Shakers, pr **30.00**
Sauce Dish, underplate, spoon, green mark **50.00**
Shaving Mug, $3\frac{3}{4}$" h, green mark **85.00**
Snack Set, tray and cup **25.00**
Sugar, cov **25.00**
Teapot, cov **90.00**
Tea Set, teapot, creamer, and cov sugar, six cups and saucers **135.00**
Tile, chamfered corners, 5" w, green mark **25.00**
Toothpick Holder **65.00**
Vase, 7" h, fan shape **150.00**
Vegetable Dish, $9\frac{3}{4}$" l, oval, Noritake mark **30.00**
Waffle Set, sugar shaker and syrup jug **70.00**
Wall Plaque, $8\frac{1}{2}$" l, green mark **75.00**

NUDES

Mom, Dad made me put this category in. Honest, Mom! He really did!

Ashtray
- Bronze, figural, Gendarme **25.00**
- Tin, litho, 4" d, Marilyn Monroe, red ground, dark brown border, name in bottom margin **30.00**

Bookends, pr, figural, cast iron, woman kneeling, leg extended forward, bronze finish **70.00**

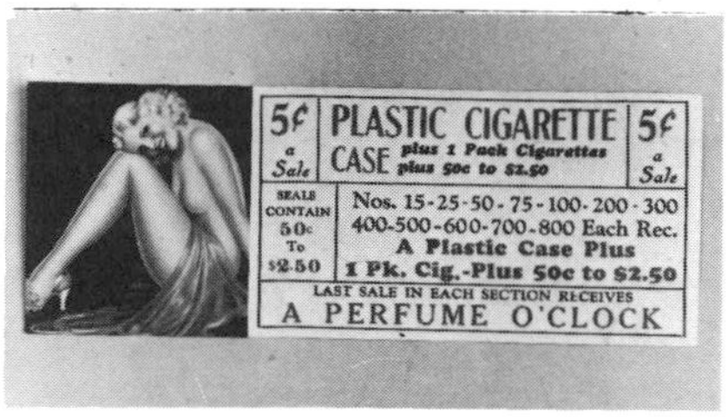

Punchboard Label, 5¢, litho paper, 8 × 3", $15.00.

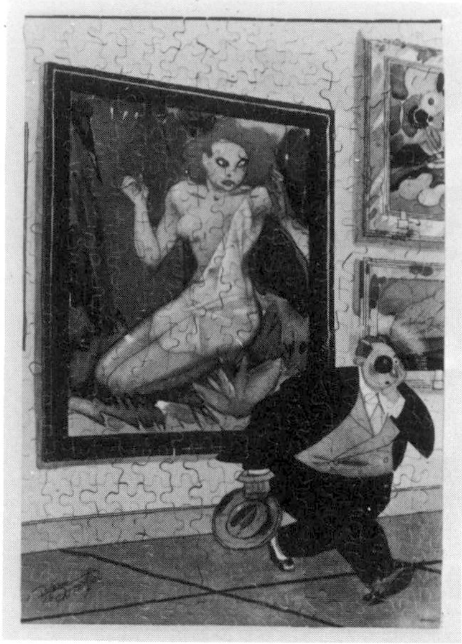

Puzzle, No Nudes Is Bad Nudes, Ballyhoo series, Dell Publishing, 333 diecut cardboard pieces, 9 × 7" cardboard box, $15\frac{1}{4}$ × $10\frac{1}{2}$", $30.00.

CD Set, book, Madonna, *Sex,* explicit photo and text, orig 12 × $15\frac{1}{2}$" bright foil package **70.00**
Figure, $9\frac{1}{2}$ × $10\frac{1}{2}$", female, Sanzio **25.00**
Hood Ornament, 10" l, woman, c1940 ..... **55.00**
Knife, $3\frac{1}{4}$" l, silvered metal, black and white female portrait, dark red glitter accents, c1920 ..... **25.00**
Lamp, 9" h, nude sitting atop ribbed column, arms support crackle glass globe **370.00**
Magazine, *Playgirl,* 1976 ..... **10.00**
Pin, $\frac{7}{8}$" d, female standing, brass frame, early 1900s **20.00**
Pipe, carved nude on bowl, orig case, Meerschaum **190.00**
Playing Cards
- Gaiety, 1954 ..... **25.00**
- Royal Flushes, nudes, king size, boxed **14.00**

Print, woman, orig frame and matting, Earl Moran **150.00**
Program, Dutch Treat Club, 1937, "To The Pure" theme **65.00**
Record Album, The Cars, reclining Vargas lady on cov, 1979 ..... **27.00**

NUTCRACKERS

Fast food and time did in the nutcracking community. From the mid-nineteenth through the mid-twentieth century it was not uncommon to find a bowl of nuts awaiting cracking in the kitchen, living room, or dining room.

Cast Iron, parrot, painted green, red, and gold, 10" l, $275.00.

Just as there is a never–ending search for a better mousetrap, so was man never content with his nutcracker design. The variety is endless, from cast iron dogs of the turn–of–the–century to brass legs from the Art Deco period.

Many modern collectors like the wooden military and civilian figures that come from Germany. Have you ever tried cracking a nut in them? Useless, utterly useless.

Bear, wood, glass eyes **100.00**
Bird, wood, curved neck, long tail, worn finish **100.00**
Dog, cast iron
    Bronze finish **45.00**
    Nickel finish, 11" l, marked "The LA Althoff Mfg Co, Chicago" **45.00**
Eagle, brass **25.00**
Elephant, cast iron, painted **145.00**
Jester, brass **75.00**
Monk, head, hand carved face, Germany, 12" h **18.00**
Parrot, cast iron, painted green, red, and gold, 10" l **30.00**
Rooster, brass **25.00**
Squirrel, cast iron **20.00**
Toy Soldier, wood, red, black, and white paint, furry beard, Germany **75.00**

OCCUPIED JAPAN

America occupied Japan from 1945 to 1952. Not all objects made during this period are marked "Occupied Japan." Some were simply marked "Japan" or "Made in Japan." Occupied Japan collectors ignore these two groups. They want to see their two favorite little words.

Beware of falsely labeled pieces. Rubber–stamp marked pieces have appeared on the market. Apply a little fingernail polish remover. Fake marks will disappear. True marks are under glaze. Of course, if the piece is unglazed to begin with, ignore this test.

Club: The Occupied Japan Club, 29 Freeborn Street, Newport, RI 02840.

Ashtray
    4" d, sq, porcelain, green floral . . . **12.00**
    6¾" d, chrome plated, pierced floral rim **10.00**
Cigarette Box, 3¾" × 4 × 5", multicolored, gold floral and scroll **10.00**
Demitasse Cup and Saucer, floral, pink and lavender **8.00**
Figure
    2½" × 2¼", three monkeys, see no evil, hear no evil, speak no evil . . . **18.00**
    3½" h, couple, man wearing red coat, yellow pants, holding hat, woman wearing blue, green, and purple dress, pedestal base **17.00**
    3¾" h, swan, wings spread **10.00**
    4" h, Dickens Character
        Mrs Gamp **35.00**
        Sidney Croton **30.00**
    4½" × 4¾", bird, pink body, gray wings, yellow beak **20.00**
    6¼" h, colonial girl holding skirt, orange and blue dress, pink bow, gold trim **18.00**
    10" h, Oriental girl, blue and green outfit, gold trim **28.00**
Gravy Boat, Royal Oak pattern, Meilo Norleans **18.00**
Jewelry Box, 1" h, metal, twelve drawers **12.00**
Nodder, donkey, celluloid **40.00**
Pencil Sharpener, painted cast metal, boxer **85.00**
Pin, bird, celluloid **8.50**
Planter
    2½" h, dog **8.00**
    4¾" l, donkey, pulling wagon **10.00**
Reamer, 3¾" h, 2 pcs, strawberry shape, red, green leaves and handle **65.00**
Sugar, cov, Royal Oak pattern, Meilo Norleans **22.00**
Teapot, 6½" h, floral dec on brown ground **22.00**

Teapot, bisque, pink rose, green leaves, blue flowers, white ground, gold trim, red "Made in Occupied Japan" mark, 2¾" w, 2¾" h, $8.00.

Toby Mug, 2½" h, black hat, blue collar **15.00**
Toy, windup
    Dancer, 3½ × 4½ × 8½", litho tin and celluloid, man standing by black and white tin street sign "Hollywood" and "Vine" **165.00**
    Lion, MIB **90.00**
Vase, head, Oriental woman, marked "Occupied Japan" **40.00**

OCEAN LINER COLLECTIBLES

Although the age of the clipper ships technically fits into this category, the period that you are most likely to uncover at flea markets is that of the ocean liner. Don't focus solely on American ships. England, Germany, France, and many other foreign countries had transoceanic liners that competed with and bested American vessels.

Today is the age of the cruise ship. This aspect of the category is being largely ignored. Climb aboard and sail into the sunset.

Clubs: Steamship Historical Society of America, Inc, Suite #4, 300 Ray Drive, Providence, RI 02906; Titanic Historical Society, PO Box 51053, Indian Orchard, MA 01151–0053.

Ashtray, *Princess*, glass, Sweden **8.00**
Booklet, *White Star Line Sailing List*, 1933 . . . . **38.00**
Cabinet Card, 1890s steamboat **36.00**
Candy Container, litho tin, full color *Queen Mary* illus on lid, 1930s **40.00**
Creamer, 3" h, Cunard *White Star*, white, tan and light gray striping, logo on bottom, 1930s **50.00**
Cup, *Lattorff Ocean Liner* **20.00**
Deck Plan
    Normandie, unfolds to 43 × 8½", c1935 . . . . **95.00**
    SS *Manhattan*, 10 pgs, unfolds to 28 × 9", 1936 . . . . **50.00**
    SS *Paris*, 16 pgs, unfolds to 43 × 8½", decks, cabins, and int views, c1934 . . . . **75.00**
Lapel Stud, *Normandie*, enameled brass, shield shape, 1930s **20.00**
Menu
    Johnson Line **10.00**
    Liberte, 9 × 11½", December 10, 1956, 4 pgs **75.00**
    Matson Line **7.00**
    SS *City of Omaha*, Christmas 1940 **5.00**
    SS *Oakwood*, American Export Lines, Christmas 1939 . . . . **5.00**

Reverse Painting on Glass, **Titanic,** *oval wood frame, 25 × 18½", $125.00.*

Sun Line cruise ship, titled *Stella Solaris,*
  1930s, set of 7 . . . . **18.00**
Mirror, pocket, Steamship *Augustus,* emb
  . . . . **52.00**
Passenger List
  SS *Leviathan,* 1924 . . . . **15.00**
  Transylvania II, Anchor Line, June 22,
  1938 . . . . **18.00**
Pin, USS *Constellation,* metal, diecut, fig-
  ural, masted ship, pewter finish, 1930s
  . . . . **18.00**
Pinback Button
  Lusitania, multicolored illus **25.00**
  North West, sepia photo, early 1900s
  . . . . **18.00**
Poster
  18 × 22", Cunard Line, RMS *Caronia,*
  ship in exotic Mediterranean setting,
  Anon, c1948 . . . . **150.00**
  28 × 17", SS *United States,* full color
  scene, T C Skinner, 1952 . . . **200.00**
Sheet Music
  *The Band Played "Nearer My God To
  Thee" As The Ship Went Down,*
  Morris Music Co, NY, 1912   **60.00**
  Wreck of the Titanic, A. Stauffer Publishing, 1912 . . . . **125.00**
Sign
  25¾ × 29", Cunard steamship, paper litho, front view of ship *Aurania* leaving New York pier, Major & Knapp
  Litho Co, c1872, pair of uncut prints
  . . . . **3,350.00**
  32 × 29½", *Kaiserin Victoria*
  oceanliner, tin, steamship sailing
  from New York harbor image, Statue
  of Liberty background, Fred Pansing
  illus **800.00**
  37 × 25", French Line, tin, oceanliner
  under steam illus, self framed
  . . . . **300.00**
Stock Certificate, Cunard Steamship Co, Ltd
  . . . . **7.50**
Tin, Bremen Coffee, *Bremen* at sea on front
  panel, litho tin, 1930s **50.00**

OLD SLEEPY EYE

The Old Sleepy Eye Flour Company
of Sleepy Eye, Minnesota, offered Sleepy
Eye premiums in the early 1900s. Many

of the early stoneware products were
made by the Weir Pottery Company,
which eventually became the Monmouth Pottery Company.

The company's advertising is just as
popular as its giveaway premiums. Beware of fantasy items, e.g., pocket mirrors, glass plates, and toothpick holders,
as well as reproduction stoneware
pitchers (marked "Ironstone" on the bottom) being imported from Taiwan.

Club: Old Sleepy Eye Collectors Club of
America, PO Box 12, Monmouth, IL
61462.

Advertising Premium Card, 5½ × 9", full
  color, Indian lore illus and text, Old
  Sleepy Eye trademark **80.00**
Calendar, 1904 . . . . **200.00**
Cookbook, bread loaf shape, portrait of
  Chief **125.00**
Mug, 4¼" h, cobalt blue dec, gray ground,
  small Indian head on handle, Western
  Stoneware Co, 1914–1918 . . . . . **325.00**
Pillow Cover, Before The Great Father,
  unused **350.00**
Pitcher, 6¼" h, cobalt blue dec, white
  ground, small Indian head on handle,
  Western Stoneware Co, 1906–1937
  . . . . **200.00**
Post Card, mill scene **20.00**
Salt Bowl, 6½" d, 4" h, Flemish blue dec,
  gray ground, stoneware, Weir Pottery
  Co, 1903 . . . . **450.00**
Stein, chestnut brown, 40 oz, 1952
  . . . . **450.00**
Teaspoon, SP, marked "Unity" **90.00**
Vase, 9" h, brown dec, yellow ground,
  molded cattails and dragonflies, Western
  Stoneware Co **850.00**

Vase, blue and gray rushes, 9" h, $265.00.

OLYMPIC COLLECTIBLES

Gallantly marching behind their
flags, the best athletes from nations
around the world enter the Olympic Col-
iseum. Whether the first modern Olympic games in 1896 or the recent 1994
Winter Games, the spirit of competition
remains the same. The Olympic collector shares this feeling.

It's a contest to see who can garner
the most and have the scarcest items.
Olympic collectors are adept at leaping
hurdles and running miles in pursuit of
their oft-elusive gold medal collectibles.

A few select collectors focus on objects picturing the games of ancient
Greece. Bronze and ceramic figures,
decorated pottery, and jewelry with an
Olympic motif do surface occasionally.

Olympic collectibles run hot and
cold. They are more popular in Olympic
years than in years when there are no
games. American collectors concentrate
on the Olympic games held in the
United States. The one exception is the
1936 Olympics, a game popular with
collectors worldwide.

Club: Olympin Collector's Club (Olympic Pins), 1386 5th St, Schenectady, NY
12303.

Badge
  Competitor's, XV, Helsinki, Finland,
  bronze colored, Helsinki skyline,
  multicolored Olympic rings, yellow
  ribbon, gold lettering, "Yoeosurheilu
  Athletisme," 1952 . . . . **75.00**
  Guest, XX, Munich, Germany, 1972 sun-
  burst, gold, white lettering, "Gast"
  . . . . **90.00**
  Guest of Honor, XVI, Melbourne, Austra-
  lia, 1956, gold, white outline, map of
  Australia, white ribbon, red lettering,
  "Guest of Honor" **85.00**
  Judge's, bronze, Olympic rings above
  Brandenburg Gate, "XI Olympiade
  Berlin 1936" **75.00**
  Official's, Big Ben above multicolored
  Olympic rings, "XIV Olympiad Lon-
  don 1948," hanging multicolored
  ribbon with "Official" tag, white rib-
  bon with gold "International Federa-
  tion" **100.00**
  Security, XIX, Mexico City, Mexico,
  1968 white metal, rect, enameled
  . . . . **100.00**
Book, *1936 Olympic Games,* photos of
  Sonja Henie and other world athletes
  . . . . **450.00**
Coaster, XX, Munich, Germany, 1972, pa-
  per, "Munscher Bier," double sided
  . . . . **25.00**

Ewer, 12" h, ceramic, nude athlete stringing bow, Olympic logo, and "1960"   **33.00**

Figurine, 11" h, porcelain, nude male shot-putter, white, holding gold ball, XI, Berlin, Germany, 1936 Hutschenreuther **275.00**

Frisbee, 9½" d, Olympic illus and inscriptions in silver and gold, orig box, 1979 copyright **25.00**

Mascot Pin, white figure standing behind sign with Rising Sun, Olympic rings, and "Tokyo," 1964 ....**100.00**

Medallion, participant's medal, bronze, Red Square on obverse, Olympic rings and logo, Cyrillic lettering, "XXII Mockba 1980" on reverse **225.00**

Media Pin
   XXIII, Los Angeles, USA, 1984 cloisonne, "ABC" and stars **55.00**
   XXIV, *Sports Illustrated*, cloisonne, rect, white ground, Seoul, South Korea, 1988, "Seoul 88" **25.00**
   XXV, NBC, domed, gold colored, multicolored peacock, Olympic rings, "Barcelona 92" **10.00**

Pin
   XIV, London, Great Britain, Olympic rings, 1948 ....**35.00**
   XV, Helsinki, Finland, Russian team, Soviet flag, red enamel, gold mast, 1952 ....**125.00**
   XVI, Melbourne, Australia, Romanian, gold, torch shape, multicolored Olympic rings on white enamel flame, "Romania" on torch, 1956 ....**30.00**
   XIX, enameled, basketball and hoop, "CCCP" on basketball, "Mexiko–65 XIX" and Olympic rings on hoop **30.00**
   XX, oval, gold, enameled, Olympic rings on white ground, "Munich 1972" **20.00**

Plate, XX, Munich, Germany, porcelain, Bing & Grondahl, 1972 ....**45.00**

Press Pin, white, gold outline, radio tower with Rising Sun at apex, emitting radio waves, Olympic rings, black lettering, "UER–EBU Tokyo 1964" **150.00**

Program
   XIV, 8 × 10½", weight lifting trials, 20 pgs, 1948 ....**15.00**
   XV, Helsinki, Finland, rowing tryouts, July 3–5, 72 pgs, 1952 ......**20.00**

Sign, 16½ × 18", 1980 Winter Olympics, Campbell's Soup adv **40.00**

Souvenir Pin, XXII, Moscow, USSR, 1980, Misha the bear standing on winner's block **10.00**

Sponsor Pin
   XXIII, Los Angeles, USA, Olympic rings and snowflake, Campbell's Soup adv, 1984 ....**10.00**
   XXV, Barcelona, Spain, multicolored Barcelona logo above red Coca–Cola logo, 1992 ....**5.00**

Staff Pin, XXIII, Los Angeles, USA, stars in motion logo over Olympic rings, "Staff," 1984 ....**25.00**

Stickpin, Poland, gold, enameled, white eagle on red ground **25.00**

Tickets, pr, XXII, Moscow, USSR, unused, 1980 ....**8.00**

Tie Tack, diecut, Montreal's Olympic logo, gold plated, 1976 ....**15.00**

Visor, 1980 Olympics, fabric, elastic headband, full color Winter Games symbol **25.00**

Wristwatch, 1984 Olympics, digital, orig unopened blister card **35.00**

OWL COLLECTIBLES

Most people do not give a hoot about this category, but those who do are serious birds. Like all animal collectors, the only thing owl collectors care about is that their bird is represented.

Newsletter: *The Owl's Nest*, Howard Alphanumeric, PO Box 5491, Fresno, CA 93755.

Advertising Trade Card, Liebig's Extract of Meat Co Ltd, 1961, set of six cards **15.00**

Avon Bottle, sachet, gold foil eyes, frosted white glass, $5.00.

Bank, brass, glass eyes **65.00**

Cheese Dish, cov, glass, Owl and Pussy Cat, clear **195.00**

Cigar Tin, White Owl **20.00**

Clock, 9" h, adv for Wise Potato Chips, figural, wood composition, electric, Lux, detailed molded feathers, inset domed glass eyes, c1930 ....**250.00**

Cookie Jar, Woodsy Owl **95.00**

Creamer, Sugar, and Shaker Set, gold, green trim **20.00**

Dakin Figure, 7" h, Woodsy Owl, vinyl, red plastic hat, orig sign, orig stitched tag on trousers, c1960 ....**35.00**

Doll, 6½" h, Woodsey Owl, plush, "Give A Hoot, Don't Pollute" **10.00**

Figurine, ceramic, glass eyes **15.00**

Letter Opener, bronze **30.00**

Pin, 1½" h, diecut, white celluloid, blue accents, tiny mounted thermometer, early 1900s **30.00**

Plate, 7½" d, milk glass **35.00**

Salt and Pepper Shakers, pr, china, brown and white, scholarly expression, horn rim glasses **6.50**

Toy, 6" h, Musician The Owl, windup, brown plush body, litho tin eyes, beak, and sheet music, rubber feet, built–in key, orig box, T N, Japan, 1960s   **65.00**

Watch Fob, 1 × 1¾", silvered brass, owl perched on roost, inscribed "Be Wise" on chest, worn luster, early 1900s **20.00**

PADEN CITY GLASS

The Paden City Glass Manufacturing Company, Paden City, West Virginia, was founded in 1916. The plant closed

Puzzle, 1932 Olympic Games, Toddy premium, color litho, orig envelope, 13 × 10", $30.00.

Candlesticks, pr, white owls, gold stripes, blue ground, handpainted by M Hooker, 1914, 8¼" h, $95.00.

in 1951, two years after acquiring the American Glass Company.

Paden City glass was handmade in molds. There are no known free-blown examples. Most pieces were unmarked. The key is color. Among the most popular are opal (opaque white), dark green (forest), and red. The company did not produce opalescent glass.

Bowl, Peacock and Rose, pink, 9" d, ftd **50.00**
Cake Plate, Black Forest, pink **35.00**
Candlesticks, pr, Crow's Foot, red ... **35.00**
Candy Dish, Mrs B, three sections, red, gold trim **50.00**
Cheese and Cracker Server, Glades, cobalt blue **45.00**
Cocktail Shaker, Utopia, 3 pc, crystal **165.00**
Compote
    Gazebo, clear, 8" d **40.00**
    Gothic Garden, yellow, 7" d **35.00**
Console Bowl, Peacock and Rose, green, 11" sq **55.00**
Creamer and Sugar, cov, Cupid, green **24.00**
Cup and Saucer, Crow's Foot, amber   **7.00**
Figure, rooster **70.00**
Finger Bowl, Black Forest, green **15.00**
Goblet, Georgian Line 69, red, 9 oz, 5$^{13}/_{16}$" h **18.00**
Ice Bucket, Black Forest, pink **75.00**
Ice Cream Soda, Party Line, 7" h, ftd
    Amber **18.50**
    Pink **25.00**
Iced Tea Tumbler, Georgian Line 69, red, 11 oz, 5$^5/_8$" h **15.00**
Mayonnaise Dish, Nora Bird, pink, ftd **40.00**

Candy Dish, amethyst, etched dots and floral vine dec, stepped dome lid, button finial, 6⅝" h, $59.00.

Old Fashioned Tumbler, Georgian Line 69, red, 3½" h **15.00**
Pitcher, cov, Party, green **60.00**
Plate
    Cupid, 10" d, dinner **15.00**
    Largo, blue, ftd **18.00**
    Popeye and Olive, 10" d, dinner, red **18.50**
Salt and Pepper Shakers, pr, Party Line, orig tops, red **45.00**
Server, Black Forest, green, center handle **35.00**
Sherbet, Georgian Line 69, red **12.50**
Tray, Cupid, pink, oval, ftd, 11" l ... **150.00**
Tumbler
    Georgian Line 69, red, 3½" h, ftd, "V" shape **10.00**
    Penny Line, red, 6" h **12.00**
Vase, California Poppy, 12" h **125.00**

PAPER DOLLS

Paper dolls have already been through one craze cycle and appear to be in the midst of another. The recent publication of Mary Young's *A Collector's Guide To Magazine Paper Dolls: An Identification & Value Guide* (Collector Books, 1990) is one indication of the craze. It also introduces a slightly different approach to the subject than the traditional paper doll book.

The best way to collect paper dolls is in uncut books, sheets, and boxed sets. Dolls that have been cut out, but still have all their clothing and accessories, sell for fifty percent or less of their uncut value.

Paper doll collectors have no desire to play with their dolls. They just want to admire them and enjoy the satisfaction of owning them.

Club: The Original Paper Doll Artists Guild, PO Box 176, Skandia, MI 49885.

Periodicals: *Doll Reader*, 6405 Flank Dr, Harrisburg, PA 17112; *Loretta's Place Paper Doll Newsletter*, 808 Lee Ave, Tifton, GA 31794; *Paper Doll Gazette*, Rte 2, Box 52, Princeton, IN 47670; *Paper Doll News*, PO Box 807, Vivian, LA 71082; *Paperdoll Review*, PO Box 584, Princeton, IN 47670; *P D Pal*, 5341 Gawain #883, San Antonio, TX 78218.

Book
    Annette, Walt Disney, uncut, 1962 .... **20.00**
    Ann Sheridan, Whitman, #986, copyright 1944, 10½ × 13" **125.00**
    Ann Southern, Saalfield, #2437, copyright 1943, 11 × 12½" **150.00**

Betsy McCall, Biggest Paper Doll, Gabriel & Sons, 1955 .... **20.00**
Doris Day, Whitman, #1952, copyright 1955, 10½ × 12" **25.00**
First Family Paperdoll & Cut–Out Book, Ronald and Nancy Reagan on cover, Patti and Ronald Jr on back, 16 pgs, 9 × 12" **15.00**
Janet Leigh Cutouts & Coloring, two dolls, Merrill Publishing Co ... **45.00**
Let's Play Paper Dolls, McLoughlin, 1938 .... **20.00**
Mary Martin, Saalfield, #2425, 1942 copyright, 11 × 12½", uncut **150.00**
Miss America Magic Doll, Parker Bros, 1953 .... **18.00**
Patty's Party, Stephens Publishing Co, c1950 .... **8.00**
Shari Lewis, five pgs, Treasure Books **32.00**
Shirley Temple, Saalfield, Christmas, uncut **60.00**
Sleeping Beauty, Whitman, copyright 1970, 10 × 13" **80.00**
Swing Your Partners, Abbott, 1940s, 11 × 13" **40.00**
Folder
    Dinah Shore, Whitman, copyright 1958, 10½ × 12" **80.00**
    Dolly's Wardrobe, chromolitho, Dean & Son, c1910 .... **75.00**
    Lennon Sisters, Whitman, copyright 1958, 9 × 12", unpunched ... **60.00**
Uncut Sheets
    Betsy McCall, Dress 'n' Play, McCall's Magazine, 1963 .... **12.00**
    Dolly Dingle **30.00**
    Enameline Flower Girls, adv, set of three **25.00**

Uncle Sam's Heroes, WWI Army and Navy uniforms, uncut sheet, $10.00.

PAPER MONEY

People hide money in the strangest places. Occasionally it turns up at flea markets. Likewise early paper money came in a variety of forms and sizes quite different from modern paper currency.

Essentially, paper money breaks down into three groups—money issued by the federal government, by individual states, and by private banks, businesses, or individuals. Money from the last group is designated as obsolete bank notes.

As with coins, condition is everything. Paper money that has been heavily circulated has only a small fraction of the value of a bill in excellent condition. Proper grading rests in the hands of coin dealers.

Krause Publications (700 East State Street, Iola, WI 54990) is a leading publisher in the area of coinage and currency. Among Krause's books are *Standard Catalog of World Paper Money*, 2 vol; *Standard Catalog of United States Obsolete Bank Notes, 1782-1866*, 4 vol; *Standard Catalog of United States Paper Money*, ninth edition; *Standard Catalog of National Bank Notes*, second edition; and *Early Paper Money of America*. Recently Krause published the *Standard Catalog of Depression Scrip of the United States*. As you can see, there is a wealth of information available to identify and price any bill that you find. *Bank Note Reporter*, a Krause newspaper, keeps collectors up-to-date on current developments in the currency field.

Before you sell or turn in that old bill for face value, do your homework. It may be worth more than a Continental, which by the way, continues to be a real "dog" in the paper money field.

PAPERBACK BOOKS

This is a category with millions of titles and billions of copies. Keep this in mind before paying a high price for anything.

A great deal of the value of paperbacks rests in the cover art. A risqué lady can raise prices as well as blood pressure. Great art can make up for a lousy story by an insignificant author. However, nothing can make up for a book's being in poor condition, a fate which has befallen a large number of paperbacks.

Catch-22, *Joseph Heller, Dell, $5.00.*

For a detailed listing, I recommend that you consult Kevin Hancer's *Hancer's Price Guide To Paperback Books, Third Edition* (Wallace-Homestead, 1990) and Jon Warren's *The Official Price Guide to Paperbacks* (House of Collectibles, 1991). Both are organized by company first and then issue number. Hence, when trying to locate a book, publisher and code number are more important than author and title.

The vast majority of paperbacks sell in the 50¢ to $2.50 range.

Periodical: *Paperback Parade*, PO Box 209, Brooklyn, NY 11228.

PAPERWEIGHTS

This is a tough category. Learning to tell the difference between modern and antique paperweights takes years. Your best approach at a flea market is to treat each weight as modern. If you get lucky and pay modern paperweight prices for an antique weight, you are ahead. If you pay antique prices for a modern paper weight, you lose and lose big.

Paperweights divide into antique (prior to 1945) and modern. Modern breaks down into early modern (1945 to 1980) and contemporary (1980 and later). There is a great deal of speculation going on in the area of contemporary paperweights. It is not a place for amateurs or those with money they can ill afford to lose. If you are not certain, do not buy.

Clubs: Caithness Collectors Club, Bldg #12, 141 Lanza Ave, Garfield, NJ 07026; International Paperweight Society, 761 Chestnut St, Santa Cruz, CA 95060; Paperweight Collectors, Inc, PO Box 1059, East Hampton, MA 01027.

Newsletters: *Paperweight Gaffer*, 35 Williamstown Cir, York, PA 17404; *Paperweight News*, 761 Chestnut St, Santa Cruz, CA 95060.

Advertising

Bell System, glass, bell shape, blue 95.00

Best Pig Forceps, compliments J Reimers, Davenport, IA, glass, pig shape, 6" d **100.00**

Chelton Trust Co, 2½" d, celluloid over metal, bright green, red, and white design, diecut celluloid perpetual calendar disk wheel on bottom, orig box, early 1900s 40.00

Chisholm Steel Shovel Works, Cleveland, OH, glass 65.00

Columbia National Bank, glass . . . 10.00

Consolidated Ice Co, 3 × 5½ × 3½" h, white metal, figural, polar bear sitting on block of ice, inscribed "Pure Ice" and "Distilled Water," company name on sides of base, early 1900s 65.00

Eagle Electric, 2½" d, celluloid over metal, revolving celluloid disk wheel mounted on top, diecut opening reveals fuse adv, 1920s 35.00

El Roco Gas, iron, figural 25.00

Hoover Ball & Bearing Co, 1¾" d, 2" h, chromed steel, eight ball bearings in channel around one large bearing 35.00

Laco Drawn Wire Quality, ceramic, white ground, black letters, half-lightbulb shape, backstamped "Rosenthal" 60.00

Lehigh Sewer Pipe & Tile Co, Ft Dodge, IA, glass 12.00

National Surety Co, bronze, eagle on world globe 45.00

Parke-Davis, pewter, baby in womb 25.00

Pike Sharpening Stones, ½ × 2 × 3", glass, whetstone block, fused glass cov on oil-stone base, multicolored paper label pictures pike and sharpening tools, c1900s 65.00

Purdue Foundry, cast iron, Kewpie 35.00

Speyer Building, 2¾" d, celluloid, black and white, tin band, detailed drawing of building 30.00

St John Mill, $\frac{1}{2} \times 1\frac{1}{2} \times 3\frac{1}{2}''$, brass, figural, inscribed "Extra," issued by Furber, Stockford & Co, Boston, MA, early 1900s **30.00**

Star Line Goods, $1\frac{3}{4} \times 2\frac{1}{4} \times \frac{1}{2}''$ h, cast iron, brass colored, figural, turtle, 1" oval celluloid shell, inscription in center of shell, 1904 copyright **80.00**

The Ransbottom Bros Pottery Co, Roseville, OH, glass, dome type, illus of brothers **70.00**

Universal Block **18.00**

Black Organization, glass **40.00**

Cartoon Character, Woodstock, $2\frac{1}{2} \times 3''$, glass, stippled, Determined, #8576, late 1970s **15.00**

Commemorative

Crane Co, Chicago, 75th Anniversary, brass, $2\frac{3}{8}''$ d, round **30.00**

Prince Charles and Lady Diana Spencer, 3" d, etched portraits, purple ground, Caithness **175.00**

Confederate Monument, Montgomery, AL, glass **30.00**

Franklin Mint, Baccarat **75.00**

Political

John F Kennedy, $2\frac{7}{8}''$ d, sulfide, bust, black amethyst ground, Baccarat **90.00**

McKinley, $1 \times 2\frac{1}{2} \times 4''$, glass, rect, sepia photo, inscribed "Pres McKinley, Wife and Home, Canton, O," marked "Cent Glass & Nov Co" on reverse, 1900s **50.00**

Souvenir, Mt St Helens, iridized, dated 1988 . . . . **25.00**

World's Fair

Chicago World's Fair, Hall of Science, $1 \times 2\frac{1}{2} \times 4''$, glass, rect, full color image **30.00**

Pan–American Expo, Temple of Music, $1 \times 2\frac{1}{2} \times 4''$, glass, rect, small caption, 1901 . . . . **35.00**

Uzi–Submachine Gun, lucite **16.00**

Horse motif, high relief, $2\frac{3}{8}''$ d, $155.00.

PARKING METERS

I have seen them for sale. I have even been tempted to buy one. The meter was a lamp base, complete with new lamp wiring and an attractive shade. To make the light work, you put a coin in the meter. Can you imagine my date's face when I ran out of quarters? I'm not sure why, but they are rather pricey, usually in the $50 to $100 range. Maybe it has something to do with the fine that you will pay if you obtain one illegally.

Might be a good idea to stash a few coin–operated meters away. Have you experienced one of the new electronic meters? Isn't progress wonderful?

PATRIOTIC COLLECTIBLES

Americans love symbols. We express our patriotism through eagles, flags and shield, the Liberty Bell, Statue of Liberty, and Uncle Sam. We even throw in a few patriots, such as George Washington. It was great to see the American symbols proudly displayed across the country due to the success of Operation Desert Storm.

Advertising

Bookmark, $2 \times 2\frac{1}{4}''$, diecut, celluloid, shield shape, red, white, and blue,

Flag, Washington Bicentennial, 1932, orange top and bottom, blue center, $17 \times 23\frac{1}{2}''$, $12.00.

bronze colored Liberty Bell, bank name on back, c1920 . . . . . . **40.00**

Tray, Cascade Beer, Uncle Sam and five ethnic people illus, San Francisco **650.00**

Bank, Dime Register, Uncle Sam, 1941 . . . . **38.00**

Bookmark, Star Spangled Banner, embroidered **25.00**

Cigar Cutter, silvered metal case, red, white, and blue accent enamel of flag being raised behind raised image of Liberty Bell, slogan "Let's Keep It Ringing," metal loop for watch chain, bright chrome cutter blade, marked "Hickok" **40.00**

Clock, mantel, God Bless America, American flag second hand waves back and forth, Howard Miller Mfg **125.00**

Figure, 16" h, Uncle Sam rolling up sleeves, plaster **30.00**

Milk Bottle, $9\frac{1}{2}''$ h, clear glass, quart, emb "Augusta Dairies, Augusta, GA," orange lettering, Statue of Liberty flanked by company name, "God Bless America" and "The Land of The Free" slogans **85.00**

Paint Book, $10 \times 13\frac{1}{2}''$, Old Glory, 20 pgs, war scenes, Saalfield, 1917 . . . . . . **30.00**

Pin, diecut silvered metal eagle with shield symbol on chest, holding miniature replica brass alarm clock, c1890 . . . . **30.00**

Pinback Button

Abraham Lincoln, black and white, slogan "Be Your Own Lincoln," 1920s **20.00**

All American Shoe, red, white, and blue, brown eagle against cloudy sky, red inscription, orig back paper ad **18.00**

Cherry Smash, multicolored, portrait of George Washington **18.00**

George Washington, colorful portrait, gold ground, blue border, gold lettered name and "Memorial Building," c1920 . . . . **12.00**

National IB of EW Defense, civilian worker shaking hands with Uncle Sam, industrial background . . . **15.00**

The Spirit of '76, red, white, and blue, slightly yellowed, c1912 . . . . . **35.00**

Uncle Sam, multicolored, back paper for "Play Button Gum" series, c1920 . . . . **15.00**

Plate, bread and butter, clear glass, Constitution signer's names, emb 1776–1876 . . . . **80.00**

Seal, "Patriotic Decorations," diecut gummed seals, red, white, and blue, ten of orig 25, Dennison, c1925 . . . . . . **15.00**

Sheet Music, *America Forever March,* John Philip Sousa **30.00**

Watch, Uncle Sam holding shirt open, "Vote" across chest, red, white, and blue band **25.00**

PEANUTS COLLECTIBLES

Peanuts is a newspaper cartoon strip written and illustrated by Charles M. Schulz. The strip started about 1950 and starred a boy named Charlie Brown and his dog, Snoopy. Its popularity grew slowly. In 1955, merchandising was begun with the hope of expanding the strip's popularity. By the 1970s Charlie Brown and the gang were more than just cartoon strip characters. They greeted every holiday with T.V. specials; their images adorned lunch boxes, pencils, pins, T–shirts, and stuffed toys. Macy's Thanksgiving Day Parade wouldn't be complete without a huge Snoopy floating down Seventh Avenue.

Club: Peanuts Collector Club, 539 Sudden Valley, Bellingham, WA 98226.

Apron, Snoopy on doghouse design, "Home is where the supper dish is!" **12.50**
Bank
    Linus, figural, ceramic, hp, Determined, 8½" h, 1969 .... **50.00**
    Peppermint Patty, baseball series, papier–mache, Determined, 1973 .... **45.00**
    Snoopy, ceramic, lying on flowered egg, Determined, #1551, late 1970s **25.00**
    Woodstock, standing, papier–mache, Determined, #1503, 1970s ... **12.00**
Banner, Lucy in psychiatrist booth, "For a Nickel I Can Cure Anything," Determined, 1971 .... **8.00**
Bell
    Schroeder, Schmid, #278 419, 6" h, 1974 .... **50.00**
    Snoopy and the Beaglescouts, Schmid, orig box, 1984 .... **25.00**

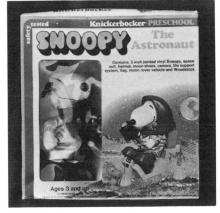

Doll, Snoopy The Astronaut, Knickerbocker, 1958, vinyl, $25.00.

Book
    Charlie Brown Christmas, 1965, first edition, dj **25.00**
    Happiness Is a Warm Puppy, Charles M Schulz, Determined, hard cov, Lucy hugging Snoopy cov illus, 1962 .... **3.00**
    Peanuts Treasury, Charles M Schulz, Holt, Rinehart & Winston, first edition, cartoon anthology, 1968 **15.00**
Bookends, pr, figural, one with Charlie Brown leaning against door, other with Snoopy holding food dish in mouth and kicking door, Butterfly, 1970s ... **75.00**
Box, cov, porcelain, heart shape, Snoopy finial **25.00**
Child's Tea Set, Snoopy, metal, J Chein & Co, #276, orig box, 1970s **100.00**
Comic Book, *Peanuts,* Dell, #878, Charlie Brown and Snoopy watching TV cov illus, 1958 .... **20.00**
Cookie Jar, Snoopy, standing **30.00**
Doll
    Lucy, plastic, jointed, red dress, saddle shoes, Determined, #378, orig box, 1970s **35.00**
    Peppermint Patty, rag, removable outfit, green and white shirt, black pants, Ideal, #1413–4, 1976 .... **15.00**
    Pigpen, 8½" h, blue overalls, Hungerford, orig pkg **100.00**
    Snoopy, 12" h, sitting, plush, felt eyes, eyebrows, and nose, red paper tag, Determined, #835, 1971 ..... **15.00**
Earring Tree, Snoopy **12.50**
Figure, porcelain Snoopy laying in food dish, Willits, MIB **15.00**
Frame, desk top **20.00**
Game, Peanuts, Selchow & Righter, 1959 .... **45.00**
Ice Bucket, vinyl, white, dancing Snoopy and Woodstock on rainbow illus, Shelton Ware, #9002, 1979 ..... **50.00**
Iron–On Transfer, Snoopy, fabric, Interstate Brands premium, 1972 presidential election themes, set of six **15.00**
Lunch Box, vinyl, white, Schroeder playing piano surrounded by Peanuts gang one side, baseball illus other side, Charlie Brown swinging bat illus on plastic thermos, King Seeley, #6168/3, 1973 **30.00**
Mirror, 8 × 10½", Snoopy in hot–air balloon surrounded by flying Woodstocks illus, Determined, 1970s **20.00**
Mug, milk glass, yellow metal lid, Lucy holding balloon illus, Avon Shampoo, orig box, 1969 .... **12.00**
Music Box, Snoopy on top of doghouse, wood, Schmid
    Astronaut, orig tag **95.00**
    Flying Ace **85.00**
Night Light, Snoopy, WWI flying ace **10.00**
Nodder
    Charlie Brown, 5½" h, Japan, 1960s **50.00**

Lucy, wearing red dress **90.00**
Snoopy, dogfighter pilot **35.00**
Paper Dolls, Snoopy, ten outfits, Determined, #274, 1976 .... **25.00**
Patch, fabric, Frieda, "I'm in Love," Butternut premium, 1970s **4.00**
Pinback Button, 2¼" d, Lucy, dressed as Halloween witch, carrying broom, cloth front, metal back, 1980s **8.00**
Plate
    Mother's Day, Linus holding rose, Schmid, orig box, 1972 ...... **20.00**
    Woodstock's Christmas, Schmid, orig box, 1976 .... **25.00**
Playing Cards, Linus holding security blanket, "Security," Hallmark, #125BC98–1, 1975 .... **15.00**
Pop–Up Book, *It's Good to Have a Friend,* Charles M Schulz, Hallmark, #400HFC 36, dancing Snoopy and Woodstock cov illus, 1972 .... **35.00**
Poster, Pigpen, "If You're Going to Be an Ecologist, You've Got to Stir Things Up a Little," Springbok, #PTR 302–3, 1971 .... **12.00**
Punching Bag, inflatable, Charlie Brown, "I Need All the Friends I Can Get," Determined, 1970s **35.00**
Radio, Snoopy, figural, plastic, Determined, #351, 1975 .... **15.00**
Record, *Oh Good Grief,* Vince Guaraldi, Warner Bros, #1747, 1968 ...... **10.00**
Rug, latch hook, "Buddies," Snoopy hugging Woodstock illus, Malina, #26/13, 20 × 27", 1970s **35.00**
Scissors, plastic, red, Joe Cool figure on front **9.50**

Music Box, wood, Snoopy on doghouse roof, plays "Over There," base marked "copyright United Features Syndicate, 1968," 5" d base, 8" h, $40.00.

Snowdome, musical, porcelain base, Willits
.............................**50.00**
Telephone, Snoopy, touchtone, orig box,
Bell **110.00**
Toothbrush, plastic, battery operated,
Snoopy on doghouse stand, Kenner,
#30301, 1972 ....**40.00**
Toy
Battery Operated, rowing Snoopy, orig
box, 1965 ....**35.00**
Pull, Snoopy **12.00**
Windup, Snoopy Chef, flips food, orig
box, 1958 ....**45.00**
Wallet, Snoopy dressed as cowboy design
............................**15.00**
Wastebasket, metal, Charlie Brown and
Snoopy illus, Chein Co, 13" h, 1970s
............................**20.00**
Wind Chimes, plastic, figural Woodstock
and Snoopy on doghouse, metal chimes,
Aviva, orig box, 1973 ....**30.00**

PENCIL CLIPS AND PAPER CLIPS

Paper clips clip pieces of paper together. Pencil clips hold pencils in one's pocket. Both were popular; both were used to advertise products. Neither form is used much today. Too bad, these little giveways must have been handy reminders and some of the graphics can be great.

The listings below are for paper clips with celluloid buttons and metal spring clips, all dating from the early 1900s. Pencil clips have celluloid buttons with metal pencil holders.

PAPER CLIP
Bissel Company, 1" l, multicolored, red inscription **30.00**
Boston Varnish Co, 1¼" l, multicolored,
gold inscription **30.00**
Edison Portland Cement Co, 1¾" d, celluloid, yellow and black design, Thomas A
Edison Trademark, 1920s **25.00**
Lane Mfg Co, Montpelier, VT, 2½" l, black
and white sawmill illus, c1900 ...**25.00**
McKibbin Hat, 1¾" l, brown portrait of gentleman, tinted flesh–tone face, light
blue–green ground **45.00**
Peacock Condoms, 2 × 2", litho metal, yellow, green and red design, c1940 **35.00**
Star Egg Carriers and Trays, 1¾" l, multicolored, dark olive green ground, red,
yellow, and white inscription **60.00**

PENCIL CLIP
Advertising
Bull Brand Feeds, yellow and red,
black–spotted steer in center, c1930
............................**20.00**

Canada General Insurance, blue and
white, 1930s **15.00**
Ebner Coal Co, blue and white, 1930s
............................**15.00**
Hammer Mill, black and white,
Gruendler Crusher & Pulverizer Co,
silvered clip, c1920 ....**30.00**
Hatfield, red, white, and blue, 1950s
............................**12.50**
Linco Bleach, red and white, 1930s
............................**10.00**
Ritz Crackers, litho tin, yellow, blue, and
red, Nabisco logo, c1930 ....**10.00**
7Up, black, white, and red, 1930s
............................**25.00**
Solarine, bright yellow and black sun
face logo, red ground, white letters
"The Face That Sets The Pace In The
Metal Polish Race," c1920 ...**40.00**
Squirt, white, full color illus, 1950s
............................**50.00**
Strongharts Rations, tinted color portrait
of German Shepherd, black and
white rim, c1930 ....**35.00**
Tuxedo Feeds, black, white, and red,
c1930 ....**15.00**
Viking Snuff, blue and white, 1930s
............................**18.00**
Wonder Feeds, red, white, and blue, red
lettering, c1930 ....**35.00**
Baseball, celluloid, black and white photo
portrait, silvered metal clip, c1950,
Thurman Tucker, Cleveland Indians
............................**20.00**
Character, Captain Marvel **12.00**
Patriotic, God Bless America, red, white,
and blue **12.00**

PENNSBURY POTTERY

Henry and Lee Below established Pennsbury Pottery, named for its close proximity to William Penn's estate "Pennsbury", three miles west of Morrisville, Pennsylvania, in 1950. Henry, a ceramic engineer and mold maker, and Lee, a designer and modeler, had previously worked for Stangl Pottery in Trenton, New Jersey.

Henry Below died on December 21, 1959, leaving the pottery in trust for his wife and three children with instructions that it be sold upon the death of his wife. Lee Below died on December 12, 1968. In October 1970 the Pennsbury Pottery filed for bankruptcy. The contents of the company were auctioned off on December 18, 1970. On May 18, 1971, a fire destroyed the pottery and support buildings.

Many of Pennsbury's forms, motifs, and manufacturing techniques have

Stangl roots. A line of birds similar to those produced by Stangl were among the earliest Pennsbury products. While the carved design technique originated at Stangl, high bas–relief molds did not.

Pennsbury products are easily identified by their brown wash background. The company also made pieces featuring other background colors. Do not make the mistake of assuming that a piece is not Pennsbury because it does not have a brown wash.

Pennsbury motifs are heavily nostalgic, farm, and Pennsylvania German oriented. The pottery made a large number of commemorative, novelty, and special-order pieces.

Marks differ from piece to piece depending on the person who signed the piece or the artist who sculptured the mold.

Concentrate on one pattern or type. Since the pieces were hand carved, aesthetic quality differs from piece to piece. Look for pieces with a strong design sense and a high quality of execution. Buy only clearly marked pieces. Look for decorator and designer initials that can be easily identified.

Many of the company's commemorative and novelty pieces relate to businesses and events in the Middle Atlantic States, thus commanding their highest price within that region.

Look-Alike Alert: The Lewis Brothers Pottery, Trenton, New Jersey, purchased fifty of the lesser Pennsbury molds. Although they were supposed to remove the Pennsbury name from the molds, some molds were overlooked. Further, two Pennsbury employees moved to Lewis Brothers when Pennsbury closed. Many pieces similar in feel and design to Pennsbury were produced. Many of Pennsbury's major lines, including the Harvest and Rooster patterns, plaques, birds, and highly unusual molds, were not reproduced.

Amish
Ashtray **15.00**
Beer Stein **18.00**
Cake Stand **75.00**
Creamer **13.00**
Cruet Set, vinegar and oil jars, jug
shape, pr **135.00**
Pitcher, miniature, 2" h **12.00**
Salt and Pepper Shakers, pr **55.00**
Red Rooster
Bowl, 5½" d **14.00**

Pie Plate, PA German motif, double eagle, 9½" d, $50.00.

Butter Dish, cov **25.00**
Creamer, 2" h **15.00**
Cup and Saucer **18.00**
Pitcher
    4" h **28.00**
    7¼" h **42.00**
Plaque, 7 × 5" **18.00**
Plate, 10" d, dinner **14.00**
Platter, 13½" l **70.00**
Snack Tray and Cup **20.00**
Sugar, cov **18.00**
Vegetable Bowl, divided **30.00**

PENS AND PENCILS

Forget the ordinary and look for the unusual. The more special the object or set is, the more likely it is that it will have a high value. Defects of any kind drop value dramatically.

When buying a set, try to get the original box along with any instruction sheets and guarantee cards (you will be amazed at how many people actually save them).

Clubs: American Pencil Collectors Society, 2222 S Millwood, Wichita, KS 67213; Pen Collectors of America, PO Box 821449, Houston, TX 77282; Pen Fancier's Club, 1169 Overcash Drive, Dunedin, FL 34698.

Periodicals: *Pens,* PO Box 64, Teaneck, NJ 07666; *Pen World Magazine,* PO Box 6007, Kingwood, TX 77325.

Advertising
    Bookmark, diecut celluloid, C Howard Hunt Pen Co adv, 1 × 2" **30.00**
    Cabinet, Esterbrook Pens, tin, rotating cylinder holds pen nibs, orig boxes with nibs, 10½" d, 14" h **195.00**

Display, Sheaffer, large figural fountain pen, plastic and brass, c1970, 6" d, 60" l **425.00**
Sign, Dixon's American Graphite Pencils, paper, woman in Victorian parlor sketching child, 13 × 29" **300.00**
Thermometer, Waterman's Ideal Fountain Pen, diecut tin, pen shape, 3¾" w, 19½" h **700.00**
Pen
  Advertising
    Bell Telephone, Waterbury, ballpoint, MIB **25.00**
    Blue Diamond Vacumatic, gold pearl stripes, 1940 . . . . **90.00**
  Character
    Hopalong Cassidy, 6" l, black plastic and silvered metal, 3–D plastic portrait, Parker Pen Co, c1950 . . . . **50.00**
    Tom Mix, 4¾", marbleized, rope script, 14K, gold plated, Southern Pen Co, c1920 . . . . **75.00**
  Jefferson, fountain, red and orange marbleized Catalin, brass clip, 5¼" l **20.00**
  Parker
    Blue Diamond Vacumatic, gold pearl stripes, 1940 . . . . **90.00**
    Maroon, stainless steel cap, chrome–plated trim, 1950 . . . . **30.00**
    Regal, fountain, olive green, tan, and black marbleized Catalin, 5¼" l **25.00**
  Sheaffer
    Lifetime
      Black, brown stripe **50.00**
      Emerald pearl stripes, 1939 . . . . **60.00**
    White Dot Triumph Snorkel, maroon palladium silver rib, 1953 **40.00**
  Waterman, Ideal #452, SS, 1925 . . . . **150.00**
Pencil
  Advertising
    American Foundry and Mfg Co, St Louis, MO, mechanical, red, white and blue, 1950s **50.00**
    Bell Telephone, Duro Lite, lead, spinner for dial **35.00**

Sheaffer's, pen and pencil set, White Dot, Triumph pen, 14K point, $75.00.

    Hudson–Essex, PA dealership, metal bullet shape, "Shoot Straight For Triangle Motor Co," 1930s, 4" l **30.00**
    Kendall Oil, "The 2000 Mile Oil," mechanical, metal, and plastic, late 1930s, 5½" l **15.00**
    Livestock Commission, silvered metal holder, celluloid wrapper with Clay, Robinson & Co adv, metal tip one end holds sharpened pencil, other end with small inset red glass stone, 3¼" l **20.00**
    Missouri Pacific Lines, mechanical, yellow marbleized plastic and metal, railway pictorial logo, "Sunshine Special, The Scenic Limited, Air Conditioned, A Service Institution," 5½" l **30.00**
  Character
    Elsie, 5" l, mechanical, Secretary Pen Co, Borden Co copyright, 1930–1940 . . . . **60.00**
    Popeye, 10½" l, metal, mechanical, silver–gray, black and dark red illus and text, Eagle Pencil Co, 1930–40 . . . . **25.00**
  Commemorative, "Remember Pearl Harbor, United We Stand, We Will Win," red, white, and blue plastic, local business sponsor adv, 5" l **65.00**
  Parker Duofold, marbleized green **170.00**
  Personality, Lindbergh, wood, lead, gold colored, blue "Plucky Lindy" portrait, red "Spirit of St. Louis," 7½" l, unsharpened **28.00**

PERFUME BOTTLES

Perfume bottles come in all shapes and sizes. In addition to perfume bottles, there are atomizers (a bottle with a spray mechanism), colognes (large bottles whose stoppers often have an application device), scents (small bottles used to hold a scent or smelling salts), and vinaigrettes (an ornamental box or bottle with a perforated top). The stopper of a perfume is used for application and is very elongated.

Perfume bottles were one of the hottest collectibles of the 1980s. As a result of market manipulation and speculative buying, prices soared. The wind started to blow in the wrong direction. The field began to stink. Many prices collapsed.

Whew, the wind is changing again as new collectors follow the scent. Today's collectors are also interested in commercial bottles They enjoy their

Atomizer, light green glass, cut leaf and stem design, light green cord, silver plated top, 3¹/₂" w, 4" h, $25.00.

pretty shapes and colors as well as those sexy names.

Clubs: International Perfume & Scent Bottle Collectors, 310 Maple Ave, Vienna, VA 22180; Perfume and Scent Bottle Collectors, 2022 East Charleston Blvd, Las Vegas, NV 89104.

Atomizer, 3¹/₂" h, octagonal, dark amethyst, cone finial, SP neck, rubber bulb   **38.00**
Blown Three Mold, glass, pale aqua, Gothic Arch, cork stopper, c1825 ...... **110.00**
Commercial
  Ambergris, US Treasury, sample   **10.00**
  Avon, 3¹/₄" h, California Perfume Co, glass, violet sachet, half full, violet paper label, 1912 .... **125.00**
  Black Satin **8.00**
  Coty, set, perfume, lipstick, and compact, MIB **200.00**
  D'orsy Intoxication **85.00**
  Fragonard, miniature bottles, set of 3
  .... **48.00**
  Givenchy, orig red silk box **45.00**
  Jovan Sculptura, gold torso stopper
  .... **68.00**
  Joy Poudre, orig packaging and carton
  .... **55.00**
  Lucien Long, 3 pc set **95.00**
  Lunvin, 4¹/₂" h **20.00**
  Saxony **5.00**
  Schiaparelli Shocking, 3" h, orig leather case **245.00**

Scottish Heather **45.00**
Siarda, sculpture of David's head   **75.00**
Valdome LaMarquis **65.00**
White Shoulders, lipstick type **10.00**
Cranberry Glass
  3³/₄" h, bulbous, enameled blue and gray flowers, blue, orange, and white leaves, clear flattened ball stopper
  .... **90.00**
  5¹/₄" h, gold bands, blue and white florals, gold ball stopper **120.00**
  5¹/₂" h, beveled, clear cut faceted bubble stopper **110.00**
Cut Glass, 6¹/₂" h, Button and Star pattern, rayed base, faceted stopper, Brilliant period **100.00**
Czechoslovakian, glass
  3¹/₂" h, clear and frosted **100.00**
  3⁵/₈" h, opaque black, clear stopper
  .... **85.00**
Fenton, Hobnail, cranberry opalescent, flat stopper **90.00**
Figural
  Dog, glass, clown collar, gray, c1890
  .... **40.00**
  Heart Shape, 5¹/₂" h, glass, cut flowers on front and back, clear cut faceted stopper **75.00**
  Lady and Parrot, 3³/₈" h, china, blue, white, black, yellow, green, and orange, metal and cork stopper   **70.00**
Moser Glass, blue, white enamel and gold trim, gilded metal rose shaker stopper, c1900 .... **110.00**
Pairpoint, 5¹/₂" h, heavy crystal, controlled bubbles **60.00**

Perfume Bottles, left: silver overlay, opaque body, crown finial, $90.00; right: silver overlay, clear glass body, blue enamel dec, $100.00.

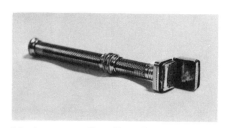

Vinaigrette, sterling silver, box top, etched diamonds on top, writing device in handle, 3³/₈" l, $350.00.

Scent
  Glass, hobnail **35.00**
  Prince of Wales Feathers Scent, 2¹/₄" h, deep blue, raised feather pattern, open pontil **110.00**
  Sea Horse, 2¹/₂" h, clear, rigaree dec, open pontil **60.00**
  Steuben, 4¹/₂" h, amber, eight ribs, orig hand blown stopper, marked "Steuben, 2183"
  .... **235.00**
  Sunburst, 1⁷/₈" h, oval, clear, open pontil
  .... **150.00**

PEZ DISPENSERS

The Pez dispenser originated in Germany and was invented by Edvard Haas in 1927. The name "Pez" is an abbreviation of the German word for peppermint—"pfefferminz." The peppermint candy was touted as an alternative to smoking.

The first Pez container was shaped like a disposable cigarette lighter and is referred to by collectors as the non-headed or regular dispenser.

By 1952 Pez arrived in the United States. New fruit-flavored candy and novelty dispensers were also introduced. Early containers were designed to commemorate holidays or favorite children's characters including Bozo the Clown, Mickey Mouse, and other popular Disney, Warner Brothers, and Universal personalities.

Collecting Pez containers at flea markets must be done with care. Inspect each dispenser to guarantee it is intact and free from cracks and chips. Also, familiarize yourself with proper color and marking characteristics.

Periodicals: *Optimistic Pezzimist*, PO Box 606, Dripping Springs, TX 78620; *Plastic Candy Dispenser*, 3851 Gable Lane Dr #513, Indianapolis, IN 46208.

Angel, Christmas, 1960s **5.00**
Annie, licensed character, 1970s **20.00**
Baloo, Disney, 1980s **10.00**
Barney Bear, MGM cartoon characters, 1980s **10.00**
Baseball Glove, 1960s **100.00**
Batman **15.00**
Blob Octopus, Halloween, 1960s ... **70.00**
Boy with Hat, Pez Pal, 1960–79 .... **10.00**
Bozo, diecut, 1960s **100.00**
Bride, Pez Pal, 1960–79 .... **250.00**
Bugs Bunny, 1979, with feet **6.00**
Bullwinkle, licensed character, 1960s
.... **150.00**
Bunny, fat ears, Easter, 1960s **1.00**

Captain America, black, visor **50.00**
Captain PEZ **85.00**
Casper, diecut, 1960s **100.00**
Cat, derby **40.00**
Charlie Brown, frown, MIP **6.00**
Cockatoo, Kooky Zoo, 1970s **10.00**
Cocoa Marsh, premium, 1960s **100.00**
Cool Cat, Warner Brothers cartoon charac-
     ters, 1970–89 . . . . **20.00**
Creature from the Black Lagoon, movie
     monster, 1960s **175.00**
Creature, Halloween, 1960s **75.00**
Crocodile, Kooky Zoo, 1970s **30.00**
Dalmatian **20.00**
Dead Head Dr Skull, Halloween, 1960s
     . . . . **1.00**
Diabolic, Eerie Spectres, 1960s **50.00**
Donkey Kong, Jr, premium, 1980s   **200.00**
Dumbo, Disney, 1960s **5.00**
Elephant, orange body, green head, red hat,
     diecut red tongue, marked "Made in
     Austria," 4½" h **35.00**
Engineer, Pez Pal, 1960–79 . . . . **30.00**
Foghorn Leghorn, Warner Brothers cartoon
     characters, 1970–89 . . . . **20.00**
Football Player, 1960s **50.00**
Fozzie Bear, licensed character, Sesame
     Street, 1991 . . . . **1.00**
Goofy, MIP **8.00**
Gorilla, circus, 1970s **10.00**
Green Hornet, licensed character, 1960s
     . . . . **300.00**
Happy Bear, circus, 1970s **10.00**
Incredible Hulk, Super Heroes, 1970s   **5.00**
Indian Chief **150.00**
Jiminy Cricket, Disney, 1960s **15.00**
Lamb, Easter, 1960s **1.00**
Li'l Bad Wolf, Disney, 1960s **5.00**
Maharaja, Pez pal, 1960–79 . . . . **60.00**
Mama Giraffe, circus, 1970s **20.00**
Mary Poppins, Disney, 1960s **200.00**
Merry Melody Maker
     Clown **6.00**
     Dog **20.00**
     Frog **15.00**
     Koala **20.00**
     Lamb **15.00**
     Monkey **20.00**
     Panda **6.00**
Mickey Mouse, diecut, 1960s **90.00**
Mimic the Monkey, circus, 1970s . . . **40.00**
Monkey, light blue body, dark brown and
     tan head, white cap, 4" h **30.00**
Moo Moo Cow, Kooky Zoo, 1960s   **20.00**
Mopsy, Beatrix Potter, Eden, 1972 . . . **30.00**
Mr Ugly Scrooge, Halloween, 1960s   **1.00**
Olive Oyl, licensed character, 1960s
     . . . . **125.00**
Orange, crazy fruit, 1970s **40.00**
Panther, Kooky Zoo, 1970s **40.00**
Penguin, Super Friends, soft head, 1970s
     . . . . **35.00**
Peter Pez, MOC **6.00**
Pineapple, crazy fruit, 1970s **200.00**
Pinocchio, Disney, 1950s **10.00**
Pirate, Pez Pal, 1960–79 . . . . **25.00**

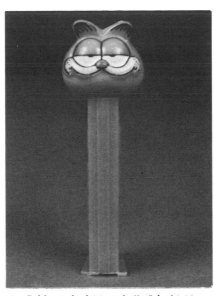

Garfield, marked "Austria," 4" h, $6.00.

Policeman, Pez Pal, 1960–79 . . . . . . **15.00**
Practical Pig, Disney, 1960s **10.00**
Psychedelic Eye, 1960s **200.00**
Pumpkin, sgd "Jamie Lee Curtis," sold with
     autographed 4 × 5" black and white
     photograph of Jamie, sgd in black felt tip
     pen **75.00**
Raven, Kooky Zoo, 1970s **10.00**
Ringmaster, circus, 1970s **25.00**
Road Runner, MOC **6.00**
Robot, blue, 3½" h, c1950 . . . . **75.00**
Rooster **35.00**
Rudolph the Red–Nosed Reindeer, Christ-
     mas, 1960s **5.00**
Santa Claus, painted eyes **5.00**
Sheik, Pez pal, 1960–79 . . . . **75.00**
Silly Clown, 1970s **25.00**
Silver Glow, MOC **10.00**
Snow White, Disney, 1960s **60.00**
Space Gun **150.00**
Spaceman, full body, 1950s **90.00**
Speedy Gonzales, Warner Brothers cartoon
     characters, 1970–89 . . . . **10.00**
Spike, MGM cartoon characters, 1980s
     . . . . **10.00**
Stewardess, Pez Pal, 1960–79 . . . . . **40.00**
Thor, Super Heroes, 1970s **60.00**
Thumper **20.00**
Truck, Cab #1, single rear axle, 1960s
     . . . . **10.00**
Whistle, 1980s **2.00**
Wile E Coyote, Warner Brothers cartoon
     characters, 1970–89 . . . . **5.00**
Winnie the Pooh **20.00**
Wonder Woman, Super Friends, hard head,
     1970s **5.00**
Woodstock, licensed character, 1991   **1.00**
Wounded Soldier, Bicentennial, 1976
     . . . . **75.00**
Yappy Dog, Kooky Zoo, 1970s **80.00**
Zorro, Disney, 1960s **75.00**

PICKLE CASTORS

Imagine a matched table setting elaborate enough to include a pickle castor. When was the last time that you were served pickles with your evening meal? What's wrong with the pickle lobbyists?

Almost all the emphasis is on the Victorian pieces, i.e., castors from the 1870 to 1915 period.

Deduct twenty-five percent if the pickle fork is missing, even more if the lid is missing. No one wants a fly in his pickles anymore than he does in his soup.

Amethyst, applied floral dec, SP frame and
     lid **275.00**
Blue
     Currier and Ives pattern, SP frame
          . . . . **165.00**
     Sprig pattern, ornate frame marked
          "Reed and Barton", orig fork and
          fancy lid **175.00**
Cranberry, barrel shaped cranberry glass in-
     sert, multicolored enamel floral dec, fig-
     ural frame with acorns and dog's feet
     . . . . **400.00**
Crystal
     10" h, Swirl pattern insert, begging dog
          finial, orig tongs, marked "Hartford
          Quadplate" **200.00**
     11¾" h, acid etched octagonal insert
          with floral and bird medallion, orig
          tongs, frame marked "Meriden Co.
          182" **245.00**
Emerald Green, paneled insert with enam-
     eled florals, ornate SP frame **225.00**

Clear, swirled pressed glass insert, begging dog finial, Hartford Quadplate 718, 10" h, $125.00.

Opalescent, Daisy and Fern pattern, blue, ornate ftd SP frame, orig tongs   **275.00**

Pigeon Blood, Bulging Loops pattern, 8" h ftd SP frame marked "Empire Mfg Co" **285.00**

Satin, pink, swirled insert, ornate ftd Pairpoint frame **235.00**

Yellow, barrel shaped yellow glass insert, butterfly and flowers dec, lid slides on handle, cherubs on front and back corners of frame, marked "Rogers"   **745.00**

PICTURE FRAMES

We have reached the point where the frame is often worth more than the picture in it. Decorators have fallen in love with old frames. If you find one with character and pizzazz at a flea market for a few dollars, pick it up. It will not be hard to resell it.

Who said picture frames have to be used for pictures? They make great frames for mirrors. Use your imagination.

Brass
2¾ × 3½", plain **10.00**
7 × 12", Art Nouveau style, two oval openings, easel back **125.00**

Curly Maple, 16¾ × 20½", refinished **90.00**

Gesso, pine framework, oval, acorns and leaves dec, gilded inner edge, beaded outer edge, mahogany stained . . . **48.00**

Golden Oak, 14¼ × 17½", molded   **20.00**

Mahogany
9 × 12¾", laminated, folk art pyramid dec, old varnish finish **45.00**
12½ × 15", deep well, black inner edge, pr **80.00**

Rosewood Veneer, 7⅝ × 8¾", beveled **50.00**

Silver Plated, 9¾ × 17½", 2" wide border, rough textured finish **100.00**

Tramp Art, 17¼ × 19½", rect, chip carved, diamond shape projections on each corner, 1915 . . . . **45.00**

Walnut, 16 × 19½", chip carved edge, applied hearts **50.00**

PIE BIRDS

They were never meant to whistle, although they look like they could. Pie birds were inserted in the middle of pies when baking them to stop the contents from overflowing.

They come in a variety of shapes and are usually made of porcelain. Many are collected as secondary objects by collectors from other categories.

Bird
Black
Royal Worcester **38.00**
White base **22.00**

Ceramic, yellow, green, red, and white, $18.00.

Blue Willow **18.00**
Crow, black **40.00**
White, big mouth **30.00**
Shawnee **25.00**
Black Chef, holding rolling pin **55.00**
Black Man, holding pie, blackbird flying out of pie depicted on shirt **55.00**
Chicken **48.00**
Dog, baying, white with black spots   **50.00**
Duck, blue **20.00**
Elephant, standing on hind legs, white, England **50.00**
Frog on reeds **55.00**
Funnel, white
Inscribed "Nut Brown Pie Funnel" **50.00**
Yellow top, pie man followed by three children and dog **50.00**
Mermaid, black face and arms, white hair, green tail **52.00**
Minstrel, wearing black suit and hat, white face with black features **52.00**
Owl, white, sitting on stump, English   **45.00**
Penguin, wearing green scarf and hat   **55.00**
Rooster, Pearl China Co, instruction leaflet **18.00**

PIG COLLECTIBLES

This is one animal that does better as a collectible than in real life. Pig collectibles have never been oinkers.

Established pig collectors focus on the bisque and porcelain pigs of the late nineteenth and early twentieth centuries. This is a limited view. Try banks in the shape of a pig as a specialized collecting

area. If not appealing, look at the use of pigs in advertising. If neither pleases you, there is always Porky. "That's All, Folks!"

Baggage Tag, 2⅛" d, celluloid, black and white, farmer riding large ear of corn pulled by two hogs, inscribed "Canaan Land For Grapes" and "Wine, Iowa Land For Corn and Swine," unused, 1913 . . . . **22.00**

Bank
Advertising
A & P, 2 × 3 × 5", red vinyl, logo on each side, early 1970s   **15.00**
Harley–Davidson, black **20.00**
China, Royal Copley **65.00**
Delft, one pig sitting on the other, Made in Holland **150.00**
Porky Pig, plastic **25.00**
White clay, seated, clear glaze . . . **30.00**

Bottle, 6½" h, figural, ceramic, tan glaze, blue eyes **150.00**

Chocolate Mold, figural, tin, two parts **65.00**

Comic Book, Porky Pig, Whitman, #1408, 1942 . . . . **25.00**

Cookie Jar
Harley–Davidson Hog, copyright 1984 HD, McCoy **300.00**
Pig sitting on stack of chocolate chip cookies, Doug Anderson Pottery **395.00**

Cutting Board, 19½ × 9½", pig shape, black edge within red outer edge   **40.00**

Figure
10 × 16", Kay Finch **32.00**
11" h, Porky Pig, carnival chalk, painted, 1940s **35.00**

Gravy Boat, porcelain, two pink pigs swinging **45.00**

Matchsafe, pink pig poking head through fence **60.00**

Pail, 6½" d, 3" h, litho tin, Three Little Pigs illus, 1930s **75.00**

Paperweight, figural, glass, Best Pig Forceps, compliments J Reimers, Davenport, IA **100.00**

Pillow, figural **15.00**

Figurine, china, high glaze, European, 7¼" l, 5½" w, 2½" h, $75.00.

Pinback Button, 1¼″ d, Weilands/The Finest Pork Products, dancing yellow pig named Willie, light blue ground, 1930s **25.00**

Playing Cards, Three Little Pigs, complete deck, orig box marked "By Special Permission Walt Disney Enterprises," 1930s **50.00**

Salt and Pepper Shakers, pr, 4″ h, figural, one playing accordion, other playing saxophone, glazed and painted, marked "Japan," c1930 .... **45.00**

Squeaker Toy, 6½″ h, Porky Pig, soft rubber, painted, Sun Rubber Co   **50.00**

Statue, 7″ h, Porky Pig, plaster, painted, 1940–1950 .... **50.00**

Stuffed Toy, velvet, Steiff **60.00**

Tape Measure, figural, celluloid **25.00**

PIN–UP ART

The stuff looks so innocent, one has to wonder what all the fuss was about when it first arrived upon the scene. Personally, I like it when a little is left to the imagination.

George Petty and Alberto Vargas (the "s" was dropped at *Esquire's* request) have received far more attention than they deserve. You would be smart to focus on artwork by Gillete Elvgren, Billy DeVorss, Joyce Ballantyne, and Earl Moran. While Charles Dana Gibson's girls are also pinups, they are far too respectable to be considered here.

Book, *Art of Steve Woron,* autographed **15.00**

Box, candy, Billy DeVorss, 11 × 16″, color image, 1930s **150.00**

Calendar

  Armstrong, Rolf

    1930s, 12 × 18″, color artwork, Nehi adv **150.00**

    1947, "See You Soon," 11 × 23″, salesman's sample, Sept pad **45.00**

  "Chippendale Revue," 1988 ...... **8.00**

  Elvgren, Gillete

    1952, 8½ × 13″, glossy, spiral bound, full color art, Brown & Bigelow **90.00**

    1955, "Stepping Out," 16 × 33″, December pad **85.00**

  Moran, Earl

    1939, 15 × 33″, litho **175.00**

    1944, desk **50.00**

    1946, "Evening Star," 16 × 33″, unused **175.00**

  Munson, 1947, twelve cheesecake poses, orig envelope **95.00**

  Petty, George

    1949, "Come On Along," 7½ × 16″, full color art, unused   **65.00**

    1955, *Esquire,* twelve poses   **95.00**

Varga

  1944, 12 poses, orig envelope   **165.00**

  1946, pocket folder, 3 × 4½″ closed, opens to 4½ × 21½″ strip, Vargas and *Esquire* copyrights **60.00**

Calendar Top, Jayne Mansfield, 1950s **45.00**

Christmas Card, 5½ × 8″, multicolored, MacPherson **22.00**

Cigarette Lighter, George Petty, chrome, 1950s **45.00**

Date Book, 1945 *Esquire,* 5 × 7″, spiral bound, subtitled "G I Edition, pinup art by Vargas," movie star photos ... **60.00**

Exhibit Cards, set of 10, 1930–40 ... **60.00**

Fan, adv, flapper, color, 1920s **55.00**

Folder, Sally of Hollywood & Vine, cardboard, sliding insert changes dress to underwear to nude **22.00**

Gatefold

  Esquire, Dorothy Dandridge **15.00**

  Moore, Al **10.00**

Hairpin, George Petty, orig 4 × 5½″ yellow, red, black, and white card, artist sgd, 1948 .... **20.00**

Illusion Glass, 5″ h, full color decal of pinup wearing sheer clothing, clothing disappears when glass sweats, set of 5, c1938 .... **100.00**

Letter Opener, 8½″ h, plastic, figural, flat back, standing nude holding adv disk overhead, designed by Gillete Elvgren, 1940–1950 .... **18.00**

Magazine

  Hollywood Tales, Vol 1, #36, full color art, 24 pgs, 1930s **30.00**

  Life, Aug 11, 1941, Rita Hayworth in swimming suit on cov **10.00**

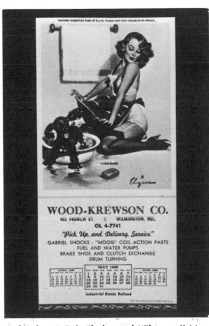

Calendar, A Fair Shake, sgd "Elvgren," May, 1966, orig envelope, 5 × 10″, $25.00.

Matchbook Cover, Petty girl, "Snug As A Bug," Martins Tavern, Chicago, late 1940s **3.00**

Notebook, Earl Moran, 1945 ...... **45.00**

Note Pad, 3 × 4½″, pastel, 1944 calendar on back **6.00**

Photocard, *Esquire,* Hurrell Girl, set of six in orig envelope, 1940 .... **95.00**

Playing Cards

  Elvgrin, 1950s, MIB **65.00**

  Vargas, *Esquire,* double deck, alligator case **95.00**

Poster, 17 × 33″, full color, woman in shorts walking wire–haired terrier, Walt Otto, c1951 .... **50.00**

Program, Ice Capades, *Esquire,* Petty illus **32.00**

Puzzle, 10¼ × 15½″, Perfect Double, Winter Queen skier and All American Girl ice skater, 5¼ × 7¼″ black, white, and yellow box, cov with half of completed puzzle, Buell, c1942 .... **20.00**

Sample, Calendar, 1941, 16 × 33½″ stiff paper, wall type, full color portrait art by Rolf Armstrong, brunette model, clinging red dress, black bodice, white fur stole **150.00**

Sketch Book, Fritz Willis, 1966 ..... **85.00**

Yearbook, 10½ × 14″, spiral bound, wall calendar with cardboard cov and backing sheet, 1947, *Esquire,* Vargas   **60.00**

PLANTERS

No, I am not talking about Planter's Peanuts. I am chronicling those strange and decorative containers that people seem intent to force vegetation to grow from. If I had a "You Have To Be Nuts To Own It" category in this book, I might have been tempted to include planters in it. Don't you find it just a bit strange to see English ivy growing out of the top of a ceramic pig's head?

A planter is any container suitable for growing vegetation. It may be constructed of any number of materials ranging from wooden fruit crates and painted tires found on suburban front lawns to ceramic panthers stalking 1950s television sets. If you thought all those planters you got from the florist were junk, read on. Too bad you threw them out or sold them for a dime each at your last garage sale.

This category deals with the figural ceramic variety found in abundance at all flea markets.

Astronaut and Space Shuttle, Inarco   **75.00**

Basket, black and white, marked "McCoy USA" **12.00**

Bear, brown, glossy, Brush–McCoy, 5″ h **18.00**

Birds on Perch, four white, yellow, and black birds on brown tree branch, glossy, marked "Shawnee 502"... **30.00**

Blackamoor, heavy gold trim **25.00**

Butterfly on Log, brown and white, glossy, marked "Shawnee USA 524" **3.00**

Cart, blue ext, yellow int, glossy, Shawnee, marked "USA 775" **6.00**

Cat, pink, green eyes and bow, glossy, McCoy, unmarked **12.00**

Clock, Metlox, California Provincial **95.00**

Conch Shell, yellow and green, glossy, Hull **35.00**

Cowboy and Cactus, natural colors, Morton, 7" h **12.00**

Cradle, blue, semi gloss, emb basketweave design with flowers and swags dec, marked "McCoy" **8.00**

Cucumber, natural color, Mother Earth Line, Morton, #395 .... **3.00**

Dachshund, brown, glossy, Hull, #119, 15" l **70.00**

Dog at Mailbox **24.00**

Duck, swimming, white, orange beak and feet, Brush–McCoy, #133 .... **45.00**

Dutch Children at Well, Shawnee ... **13.00**

Elf, sitting on large elf shoe, multicolored, glossy, marked "Shawnee 765" ... **6.00**

Frog on Lily Pad, green and brown, glossy, marked "Shawnee 726" **18.00**

Giraffe, green, glossy, Hull, #115, 9" h **30.00**

Globe, blue and green globe on yellow stand, glossy, marked "Shawnee USA" **12.00**

Golf Ball and Bag, Conrad Ceramics, 1957 .... **30.00**

Gondolier, black, glossy, marked "Royal Haeger by Royal Hickman 657," 19½" l **20.00**

Goose, #80, Hull **30.00**

Gourd, red, Abingdon, #667, 5½" h **25.00**

Guitar, black, semi gloss, marked "Red Wing USA #M–1484" **15.00**

Hat, inverted, flared brim, pink, matte, Red Wing, marked "Rum Rill #H–36 USA" **10.00**

Lady, with two wolfhounds, Brayton Laguna, 11" h, 7½" w **175.00**

Lamb, white, pink ears, blue ribbon, matte, Hull, #965 .... **45.00**

Log, applied squirrel figure, gray spray glaze, American Art Potteries, 7" h **15.00**

Mallard, head down, Royal Copley **18.00**

Mouse, leaning on cheese wedge, multicolored, glossy, Shawnee, marked "USA 705" **12.00**

Oriental Man, Shawnee, #539 ..... **25.00**

Panther, stalking, black, glossy, McCoy, unmarked, 1950s **18.00**

Parrot, Hull **25.00**

Pelican, turquoise, matte, McCoy, marked "NM USA" **10.00**

Pheasant, gold trim, Hull **58.00**

Piano, upright, green, glossy, Shawnee, marked "USA 528" **15.00**

Pigeon, turquoise, black spatter and shading, Royal, Hull, #91 .... **20.00**

Poodle Head, wearing hat and bow, white, matte, Hull, #114 .... **40.00**

Quail, natural color spray glaze, American Art Potteries, 9½" h **22.00**

Rolling Pin, marked "Camark N1–51" **8.00**

Rooster, gray feathers, red comb, green grassy base, glossy, marked "McCoy USA" **15.00**

Santa Claus, natural colors, Morton **25.00**

Scottie Dog, Royal Copley **15.00**

Siamese Cat, Hull, #63 .... **60.00**

Skunk, black and white, pastel pink and blue basket, airbrushed, Brush–McCoy, #249, 6½" h **30.00**

Swan, pink, matte, marked "Red Wing USA #259" **12.00**

Turkey, brown, red wattle, Morton ... **10.00**

Water Trough, gold trim, Shawnee ... **17.00**

Whale, black, Freeman McFarlin, 10" l **45.00**

Club: Peanut Pals, 804 Hickory Grade Rd, Bridgeville, PA 15017.

Bank, figural Mr Peanut, cast iron, 5 × 11½ × 3½" **25.00**

Canister, figural peanut, plastic, reissue, 11 × 5 × 5" **5.00**

Clock, wall, 12" h, Mr Peanut, plastic, red **125.00**

Commemorative Coin, silver, emb Mr Peanut, dated "1916–1991," #2322 of 2720 .... **55.00**

Cookie Jar, Mr Peanut, ceramic, MIB **25.00**

Costume, Mr Peanut, fiberglass, wearing monocle and top hat, costume shell extends to waist, 20" d, 50" h **475.00**

Display, tin, diecut figural peanuts on flange front, holds one glass jar, 7½" w, 4½" h **1,500.00**

Doll, Mr Peanut

  Cloth, stuffed, orig clear plastic mailer, unopened, 1960s, 20" h **20.00**

  Wood, jointed, yellow body, white hands, black legs and arms, blue hat, 9" h **155.00**

Figure, Mr Peanut, blinks right eye, electric, 8" w, 24" h **4,500.00**

Garden Ornament, post sitter, Mr Peanut, cast iron **27.50**

Glass, Mr Peanut, black and tan **20.00**

Jar, cov, glass

  Barrel shaped, emb running peanut on sides, peanut finial, 8" d, 13" h **150.00**

  Football shaped, flattened front and back emb "Planter's Salted Peanuts," peanut finial, 7" w, 8¼" h **195.00**

  Octagonal, emb Mr Peanut and lettering, peanut finial, 8" w, 12" h **150.00**

  Peanut shaped, large emb vertical peanut shell at each corner, vertically lettered "Planters" between each peanut, peanut finial, 8½" w, 13¾" h **150.00**

  Round, red stenciled applique of Mr Peanut and Planter's product names, 10" h **40.00**

  Square, Mr Peanut decal front, threaded lid, 8¼" h **20.00**

Dog, white, gray spots, black eyes and nose, pink tongue, 6" w, 6¾" h, $15.00.

PLANTER'S PEANUTS COLLECTIBLES

Amedeo Obici and Mario Peruzzi organized the Planter's Nut and Chocolate Company in Wilkes–Barre, Pennsylvania, in 1906. The monocled Mr Peanut resulted from a trademark contest in 1916. Standard Brands bought Planters only to be bought themselves by Nabisco.

Planter's developed a wide range of premiums and promotional items. Beware of reproductions.

Peanut Chopper, mail order premium, blue and gold with white letters, chopper with key to turn blades, orig cap and mailing box, unused, $20.00.

Serving spoon, 5¼" l, silver plated, Carlton, c1930, $25.00.

Letter Opener, brass, Mr Peanut **150.00**
Pail, one pound, Mr Peanut playing instruments and flying through air illus, bail handle, 3½" d, 4" h **600.00**
Paint Book
   Colorful Story of Peanuts as Told by Mr Peanut, soft cov, 28 pgs, copyright 1957, 7½ × 10½" **30.00**
   Planters Peanuts Paint Book No. 2, 1929 .... **120.00**
Paperweight, metal, Mr Peanut figure, "Mr Peanut" and "Compliments Planter's Nut & Chocolate Company" emb on base, 3" w, 7" h **575.00**
Peanut Butter Maker, Mr Peanut, MIB **35.00**
Pencil, Mr Peanut, mechanical **20.00**
Platform Scale, figural Mr Peanut standing on scale, 20" w, 45" h, 22" d **16,250.00**
Punchboard, "Planters Salted Peanuts," Mr Peanut and product tin illus, 5¢ punch, 10 × 12" **38.00**
Salt and Pepper Shakers, pr, ceramic, faceted monocle, 4½" h **55.00**
Snap Gun, heavy paper, Mr Peanut in oval on grip, c1940, 8¾" l **200.00**
Thermometer, diecut tin, Mr Peanut, 16" h **55.00**
Toy Car, figural peanut, plastic, Mr Peanut driver, 5" l, 2½" h **500.00**
Wristwatch, presented to salesman, recent issue
   Mr Peanut on dial **20.00**
   Planter's pennant on dial **25.00**

PLAYBOY COLLECTIBLES

The Playboy empire of the 1960s and 1970s is dead. The clubs and casino are closed. Hugh got married. Is there no God?

Playboy was promotion-minded. Anything associated with it is collectible. Most *Playboy* magazines sell in the $1.00 to $3.00 range except for very early (1953 to 1960) issues. The key magazine to own is Volume One, Number One, but isn't this always the case?

Ashtray, 1960 .... **15.00**
Book
   Playboy Jazz Festival, hardcover, 1959 .... **12.00**
   Twelfth Anniversary Playboy Reader, 874 pgs, hardcover, 1966 .... **25.00**
Cake Pan, bunny logo shape, Wilton Enterprises **10.00**
Calendar
   1961, 5½ × 6½", desk, MIB **45.00**
   1962, nude Stella Stevens with dog **85.00**
   1968, 8½ × 13" envelope, wall calendar, Playmate DeDe Lind on January and envelope **60.00**
Car Freshener, Playboy logo, black and white **2.00**
Cigarette Lighter, ½ × 2 × 2½" h, chromed metal, black enameled side panels, white Playboy rabbit symbol, worn from use **45.00**

Cake Pan, Wilton, Stock No. 2105–3025, aluminum, full color orig paper label, 10¼" w, 15" l, $10.00.

Magazine
   1955, January, loose centerfold of Miss January, 48 pages **225.00**
   1956, July, Alice Denham, Miss July, 72 pages **40.00**
   1961, full year, set of 12 .... **75.00**
   1966 .... **3.00**
Mug, black, white Playboy logo **4.00**
Printers Plate, Playboy Club Hotel ... **30.00**
Puppet, hand, Playboy Rabbit, plush **150.00**
Puzzle, 1967, Miss October, Majken Haugedal, cardboard canister **40.00**
Shot Glass, 2¾ h, weighted bottom, single Playboy image, name repeated in black, c1960 .... **40.00**

PLAYING CARDS

The key is not the deck, but the design on the deck surface. Souvenir decks are especially desirable. Look for special decks such as Tarot and other fortune-telling items.

Always buy complete decks. There are individuals who just collect Jokers and have a bad habit of removing them from a deck and then reselling it. Also, if you are buying a playing card game, make certain that the instruction card is included. Prices listed are for complete decks.

Clubs: Chicago Playing Card Collectors, Inc, 1559 West Platt Blvd, Chicago, IL 60626; 52 Plus Joker, 204 Gorham Ave, Hamden, CT 06514; International Playing Card Society, 3570 Delaware Common, Indianapolis, IN 46220; Playing Card Collectors Assoc, Inc, 3621 Douglas Ave, Racine, WI 53404.

Advertising
   Avis, Avis Features GM Cars **5.00**
   Bumble Bee Tuna **6.00**
   Champion Spark Plugs, red and black logos, white border **8.00**
   Diamond Salt, orig box **18.00**
   Hertz Rent A Car, dark green **8.00**
   United Founders Life Insurance Co, blue and white **7.50**
Airline
   American Airlines, DH-4 .... **10.00**
   Ozark Airlines, 1984 World's Fair, sealed deck **2.00**
   Pan American, white logo, light blue ground **10.00**
Hotel Fremont and Casino, Las Vegas, NV, red and white, diamond design ... **5.00**
Marilyn Monroe, nude, sealed **32.00**
Ocean Liner, Holland/America, orig box **25.00**
Poker Taurino, Mexican, Spanish inscription on box, c1950 .... **12.00**

Adv, Bud Light, Anheuser–Busch, Spuds MacKenzie image, plastic coated, United States Playing Card Co, 1987, 2³⁄₈ × 3¼",
$5.00.

Railroad

    C & O, Peake Chessie's Old Man   **5.00**
    New York, New Haven & Hartford, orig
      wrapper and box **40.00**
Tee–Up, golf cartoon on each card, orig
    box, c1950 .... **10.00**
Souvenir
    Pro Football Hall of Fame, Canton, OH
    .... **7.50**
    The Vista Dome, 1950–60 ...... **15.00**
    Wild Animal Park, San Diego **6.50**
World's Fair
    1933 Chicago World's Fair, Walgreen
      building, two complete decks, un-
      opened box **45.00**
    1939 New York World's Fair, double
      deck **135.00**

POLITICAL ITEMS

Collect the winners. For whatever reason, time has not treated the losers well, with the exception of the famous Cox–Roosevelt pinback button.

This is a good category to apply my Dad's Thirty Year Rule—"For the first thirty years of anything's life, all its value is speculative." Do not pay much for items less than thirty years old. But do remember that time flies. The Nixon–JFK election was over thirty years ago.

Also concentrate on the nontraditional categories. Many people collect pinbacks and posters. Try something unusual. How about political ties, mugs, or license plates?

Club: American Political Items Collectors, PO Box 134, Monmouth Junction, NJ 08852.

Periodicals: *The Political Bandwagon,* PO Box 348, Leola, PA 17540; *The Political Collector,* PO Box 5171, York, PA 17405.

Ashtray, 4½" d, Nixon, blue, raised white
    portrait and border, Wedgwood/England,
    1970 .... **15.00**
Bandanna, 26" sq, red, white, and blue,
    blue–tone photo of Eisenhower **85.00**
Book, *Theodore Roosevelt's Letters To His*
    Children, 6 × 8", 240 pages, 1919
    .... **15.00**
Bumper Stickers, Wallace for President
    .... **5.00**
Bust, 9½" h, John F Kennedy, plaster **45.00**
Convention Badge, National
    1948, Democrat, Philadelphia, 1½ ×
      5½", brass hanger with Betsy Ross
      house, fob with City Hall and Wm
      Penn statue, blue enameled "Press"
      bar, white fabric ribbons **18.00**
    1968, Republican, Miami, brass, state-
      shaped top hanger, PA/Press, lower
      hanger keystone shaped, raised state
      seal, white fabric ribbon **20.00**
Eraser, 1¼" h, rubber, figural, Stevenson,
    painted black accents, pipe cleaner to
    fasten to pencil, unused **20.00**
Hat, 6" h, 12" d brim, "Nixon Now," soft
    cloth, red, white, and blue, 1968 **10.00**
License Plate, 4 × 13½", Willkie, orange,
    gold letters outlined in dark blue, blue
    edge **20.00**

Button, flasher type, LBJ for the USA, Johnson's face, dark blue plastic ribbon marked "MNPL," copyright 1964 Democratic National Committee, IAM insignia on back, $15.00.

Match Book, Willkie, black and white die-
    cut, "America Needs Him" slogan
    .... **15.00**
Medal, Harry Truman, commemorative, MIB
    .... **35.00**
Mirror, pocket, 2", red, white, and blue,
    "I'm For Ike" **15.00**
Necktie, 47" l, Wilson/Marshall, black,
    white embroidered names, red, white,
    and blue flag **50.00**
Needle Book, 2¾ × 4¾", Hoover, black
    and white photos, red, white, and blue
    cardboard, lists Ohio state candidates on
    inside, 1928 .... **18.00**
Paperweight, 2½ × 4 × 1", Grant's Tomb
    Dedication, clear glass, sepia paper illus
    of Washington, Lincoln, and Grant
    affixed to back, 1897 .... **20.00**
Pen, 5" l, Eisenhower, brass, black and
    white plastic, slogan "For The Love Of
    Ike–Vote Republican" **25.00**
Pennant, GOP Republican National Con-
    vention, elephant head and building,
    Chicago, 1952 .... **25.00**
Pin, 2 × 3½", Willkie, red, white, and blue
    enameled white metal, ribbon–like de-
    sign, ten inset rhinestones and center
    Willkie button **35.00**
Pinback Button
    Abraham Lincoln, celluloid, 1809–1909
    .... **30.00**
    Johnson and Humphrey, 4" d, jugate, in-
      auguration, black, white, red, and
      blue, gold seal, light blue portrait of
      Kennedy between black and white
      portraits of Johnson and Humphrey,
      1965 .... **40.00**
Plate, 12" d, Franklin D Roosevelt, cobalt
    border **30.00**
Post Card, "The Nation Needs Nixon and
    Lodge," black and white, Oregon for
    Nixon Comm, unused **15.00**
Poster, 14 × 22", Nixon Rally, black and
    white, heavy cardboard, Levittown, PA,
    1968 .... **40.00**

Pinback Button, George Wallace campaign, blue letters, white ground, red border, 3½" d, $15.00.

Puzzle Card, 2¾ × 4", green and white, two hidden images of McKinley and Tom Reed, adv on back for Barber's Magic Liniment **18.00**

Record, 7" sq, Stevenson Speaks, black and white photo overlaid with thin plastic 78 rpm record, issued by AFL–CIO, Philadelphia address on back **25.00**

Ribbon, 3 × 5¾", For President Gen. W. S. Hancock, dark pink ribbon, gold design, 1" sepia paper photo of Hancock   **81.00**

Sheet Music

 Anchors Aweigh, President F D Roosevelt portrait cov, 1935 . . . . **20.00**

 Dedicated To The GOP/A Victory Is Ours/A Rousing Republican Campaign Song, 1904 copyright, blue and white, 7 × 11" **15.00**

Tab, 2" d, Humphrey, blue, green, red, white, and black, "Labor for Humphrey" **4.50**

Watch Fob, 1¼" d, "Taft for President," black and white celluloid, black leather fob, orig strap **65.00**

Wristwatch, 1½" d watch, black and white portraits of Bush and Gorbachev, white shaded to blue ground, silver metal casing, orig box, Russian paper slip, late 1980s **85.00**

POST CARDS

This is a category where the average golden age card has gone from 50¢ to several dollars in the last decade. Post cards' golden age is between 1898 and 1918. As the cards have become expensive, new collectors are discovering the white-border cards of the 1920s and 30s, the linens of the 1940s, and the early glossy photograph cards of the 1950s and 1960s.

It pays to specialize. This is the only way that you can build a meaningful collection. The literature is extensive and can be very helpful.

Clubs: *Barr's* and *Postcard Collector* list over fifty regional clubs scattered across the United States.

Periodicals: *Barr's Post Card News,* 70 S 6th St, Lansing, IA 52151; *Gloria's Corner,* PO Box 507, Denison, TX 75021; *Postcard Collector,* Joe Jones Publishing, PO Box 337, Iola, WI 54945.

Advertising

 Atles Beer, truck, multicolored, divided back **30.00**

 Bull Durham, "Trip Around the World" **30.00**

 Bulova Watch, government postal back **6.00**

 Campbell's Soup, horizontal format **30.00**

 Livermore & Knight Publishing . . . **10.00**

 Pontiac for 1948 . . . . **8.00**

 Zeno Gum, mechanical **25.00**

Holiday

 Christmas, Santa, red suit **8.00**

 Fourth of July, red, white, and blue, gold ground, Germany, 1910 . . . . **2.00**

 Halloween, orange pumpkin, artist sgd "Ellen Clapsaddle" **8.00**

 New Year, multicolored, 1907 . . . . **8.00**

 Valentine, children and women . . . **4.00**

Political

 Eisenhower/Nixon, full color, "Vote for Your Future, Vote Republican," unused, 1956 . . . . **10.00**

 Hitler, glossy black and white cartoon picture, penciled note, May 15, 1943 postmark **15.00**

 William Howard Taft, cartoon type **12.00**

Railroad

 Burlington Zephyr, stationed at 1934 Century of Progress Exposition, unused **12.00**

 Depot Scene, photographic **8.00**

State

 Alabama **1.00**

 Idaho . . . . **.50**

 South Carolina . . . . **.75**

Scenic, Delaware Water Gap, PA, No. 121, Moore & Gibson Co, New York, Germany, inked message on front, $15.00.

World's Fair

 Columbian Expo, Chicago, 1893   **25.00**

 Pan–American Expo, Buffalo, 1901, color **10.00**

POSTERS

Want a great way to decorate? Use posters. Buy ones you like. This can get a bit expensive if your tastes run to old movie or advertising posters. Prices in the hundreds of dollars are not uncommon. When you get to the great lithographed posters of the late nineteenth and early twentieth centuries, prices in the thousands are possible.

Concentrate on one subject, manufacturer, illustrator, or period. Remember that print runs of two million copies and more are not unheard of. Many collectors have struck deals with their local video store and movie theater to get their posters when they are ready to throw them out. Not a bad idea. But why not carry it a step further? Talk with your local merchants about their advertising posters. These are going to be far harder to find in the future than movie posters.

Because so many people save modern posters, never pay more than a few dollars for any copy below fine condition. A modern poster in very good condition is unlikely to have long-term value. Its condition will simply not be acceptable to the serious collector of the future.

Advertising

 Bob Hoffman's Simplified System of Body Building, 14 × 22", cardboard, 1930s **30.00**

 Raleigh Cigarettes, 12 × 18", high gloss paper, full color, WWII era, urging redemption of B & W (Brown & Williamson) coupons for war stamps **50.00**

Cause

 Hippie Love, Groovie, Flower Power, 17 × 22", stiff paper, Sparta Poster #2, Dave Schiller copyright, 1967, stylistic text, Snoopy in balloon, many characters on bottom half . . . **100.00**

 NRA/We Do Our Part, 21 × 27", red, white, and blue, orig folds **90.00**

Concert

 Family Dog, 13½ × 20", stiff paper, May 3, 1968, Avalon Ballroom **75.00**

 GD On The Road, 18½ × 28", stiff paper, color illus of skeleton and roses in black, dark purple trim, 1968 . . . . **80.00**

Miller High Life Racing, facsimile signatures of Bobby Allison and Bobby Hillin Jr, bios and driver and car specifications on back, Miller Brewing Company, Milwaukee, WI, 8 × 10", $3.00.

Disneyland, 18 × 24", Insurance By North America, large color photo, titled "Happiness Afloat At Disneyland," Mark Twain riverboat, c1957 . . . . **150.00**

Movie

Four Boys and A Gun, 27 × 41", United Artists, red, white, sepia photos, scattered tack holes, 1956 . . . . **45.00**

Satellite in the Sky, three sheets   **50.00**

Day Mars Invaded Earth, three sheets **75.00**

The Glory Stompers, 27 × 41", American International Picture, black, white, and red, 1967 . . . . **50.00**

Voyage to Bottom of the Sea, one sheet **50.00**

Political

Alfred E Neuman For President, 21 × 30", glossy, full color, MAD Party mascot in lower corner, pronounced fold creases, c1968 . . . . **20.00**

Ford/Dole, 15 × 24", full color glossy, statesmen–like image **35.00**

Kennedy for President/Leadership For The 60s, 13 × 21", red, white, and blue, black and white photo, rolled **125.00**

Mondale/Ferraro, 13½ × 12", stiff cardboard, red, white, and blue . . . **15.00**

Students for Reagan, 22 × 28", cardboard, blue–tone photo of Reagan and students, red, white, and blue type, white ground, "Paid For By Citizens For Reagan '80, A Special Project Of The Fund For A Conservative Majority" **20.00**

Promotional

Captain Charles A Lindbergh, Fearless Pilot, Successful New York To Paris Non–Stop Flier, Graduate of US Army Flying Schools, The Army Trained Him, 13 × 15", black and white, paper, #6 of 1927 series **90.00**

Elton John, 22 × 35", stiff glossy paper, large colorful caricature illus of John and band, c1970 . . . . **25.00**

Jefferson Airplane/Spitfire, 46 × 46", paper, record store type, full color, Grunt Records, RCA Records copyright, 1976 . . . . **65.00**

Louis–Schmeling Fight, 14 × 22", cardboard, black and white, cartoon illus **125.00**

Saturday Evening Post, 28 × 41", promoting David O Selznick's *Gone With The Wind* article, 1942   **85.00**

The Steve Miller Band, Book of Dreams, 36 × 36", thick stiff cardboard, Kelly & Mouse artists, 1976 copyright, small Capitol Records logo . . . **60.00**

The Supremes, 21½ × 27", *Philadelphia Inquirer,* 1968, comic section on back **12.00**

World War I, 11 × 14", paper

Cheer Up, Let The Hun Have The Grouch, He Has Good Reason For It, Gordon Grant artist, black, white, and orange **40.00**

Letter Home, letter writer and text of letter, unidentified artist, black, white, and green **30.00**

My Boy, That's The Finest Recommendation You Can Have, unidentified artist, black, white, and green, Civil War veteran holding Honorable Discharge certificate **35.00**

The Watch On The Rhine, unidentified artist, black, white, two shades of orange **30.00**

World War II

Remember Dec 7th!, 22 × 28", paper, full color, tattered US flag at half mast . . . . : **90.00**

Someone Talked, 14 × 22", paper, full color, drowning serviceman, Siebel artist, OWI Poster #18, 1942 printing number **75.00**

United Nations For Freedom, 28½ × 40", paper, black and white Statue of Liberty, Broder artist, thirty bright full color flags on black ground, OWI Poster #19, 1942 printing number **60.00**

Waste Fats, 20 × 28", paper, full color art, H Koerner artist, OWI Poster #63, 1943 printing number . . . **65.00**

Political, Richard Nixon, 1968, 21 × 13½", $20.00.

PUPPETS

No, somebody is not pulling your strings, there really is a category on puppets. This category covers marionettes and related jointed play toys, as well as finger and paper puppets. There is bound to be a few of your favorite character collectibles hanging around this new category.

Periodical: *Puppetry Journal,* 8005 Swallow Dr, Macedonia, OH 44056

Finger, Monkees, Davy Jones, 5" h, vinyl, sticker with 1970 Columbia Pictures Inc copyright **25.00**

Hand

Barney Google **50.00**

Dick Tracy, 1961 . . . . **75.00**

Dopey, 9" h, soft vinyl head, fabric body, Gund, 1950s **30.00**

Gumby, 9" h, fabric and vinyl, Lakeside Toys, copyright 1965 . . . . **55.00**

Joker, 12" h, Ideal, 1966 . . . . **100.00**

Lady Elaine Fairchild, 12" h, vinyl head, stuffed cloth body, Ideal, copyright 1977 Fred Rogers **25.00**

Lucy, Peanuts Magic Catch Puppets, blue dress, Synergistics, 1978   **15.00**

Morticia, 10" h, vinyl head, fabric body, Ideal, 1964 copyright **150.00**

Peter Pan, 10½" h, set of four, Peter Pan, Tinkerbell, Wendy, and Captain Hook, soft vinyl head, fabric body, orig tags, Gund, 1950s **125.00**

Playboy Bunny **150.00**

Pokey, 9" h, fabric and vinyl, Lakeside Toys, copyright 1965 . . . . **55.00**

Popeye, 8" h, blue plush fabric, soft vinyl head, tag "Hygienic Toys Made In England By The Chad Valley Co Ltd," 1960s **25.00**

Raggedy Ann & Andy, Knickerbocker, pr **20.00**

Robin, 10" h, vinyl, Ideal, 1966   **80.00**

Three Stooges, Curly, 9" h, fabric body, vinyl head, 1960s **50.00**

Uncle Fester, 9½" h, vinyl head, fabric body, orig package, Ideal, copyright 1964 Filmways TV Productions Inc **200.00**

Yosemite Sam, 1960s **25.00**

Marionette

Baker Clown, orig box **85.00**

Batman, 15" h, composition head and hands, wood body and feet, wood control handle, unmarked, 1966 . . . . **50.00**

Bozo, Knickerbocker, 1960s, mint puppet, poor box **130.00**

Chipmunks, Theodore, 11" h, stuffed fabric body, soft vinyl head, plastic hand control, unmarked, 1970s **45.00**

Fred Flintstone, 1960s **75.00**

Monkey, long brown fur, hand type, long legs and arms, 43" l, $7.50.

Marie Osmond, plastic, orig box, Madison Ltd, copyright 1978 Osbro Productions Inc **50.00**
Mickey Mouse, 4½" h, composition, black string, 1970s **25.00**
Marionette Theater, Saalfield, punched–out characters, 1930s **35.00**
Push–Up, Batman, 8" h, plastic, Kohner, 1966 .... **65.00**

PURINTON POTTERY

Bernard Purinton founded Purinton Pottery in 1936 in Wellsville, Ohio. In 1941 the pottery relocated to a newly built plant in Shippenville, Pennsylvania. The company's first product at the new plant, a two-cup premium teapot for Mc-Cormick Tea Company, rolled off the line on December 7, 1941.

Maywood, Plaid, and several Pennsylvania German designs are patterns attributed to designer Dorothy Purinton. William Blair designed the Apple and Intaglio patterns.

Purinton Pottery did not use decals, as did many of its competitors. Greenware was hand painted by locally trained decorators who then dipped the decorated pieces into glaze. Hand painting also allowed for some of the variations in technique and colors found on Purinton ware today.

The plant ceased operations in 1958, reopened briefly, and finally closed for good in 1959. Cheap foreign imports were cited as the cause of the company's decline.

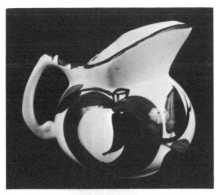

Apple, creamer, green rim, red apple, green leaves, cream ground, ink stamped "Purinton Slip Ware," 6" w, 4½" h, $10.00.

Purinton made a complete dinnerware line for each pattern plus a host of accessory pieces ranging from candleholders to vases. A number of kitchenware and specialty pieces were also produced. These should not be overlooked. Among the harder-to-find items are animal figurines, tea tiles, and a Tom and Jerry bowl and mug set.

Apple
  Cereal Bowl **28.00**
  Coffeepot, cov **25.00**
  Creamer, double spout, 1½" h ... **10.00**
  Grease Jar **20.00**
  Kent Jug, pint **15.00**
  Plate
    9" d, luncheon **14.00**
    12" d, grill **20.00**
  Salt and Pepper Shakers, pr, range
    .... **25.00**
Fruit
  Pitcher, large **30.00**
  Plate, 9¾" d, dinner **12.00**
Plaid
  Coffee Mug, 8 oz **15.00**
  Grease Jar, cov **20.00**
  Plate, 9¾" d, dinner **12.00**
  Salt and Pepper Shakers, pr, jug shape
    .... **6.00**

Apple, teapot, 6¼" h, 7½" w, $25.00.

PUZZLES

The keys to jigsaw puzzle value in order of importance are: (1) completeness (once two or more pieces are missing, especially if they are in the center, forget value); (2) picture (no one is turned on by old mills and mountain scenery); (3) surface condition (missing tabs or paper or silverfish damage causes value to drop dramatically); (4) age (1945 is a major cutoff point); (5) number of pieces (the more the better for wood); and (6) original box and label (especially important for wooden puzzles). Because of the limitless number of themes, jigsaw puzzle collectors compete with collectors from virtually every other category.

Jigsaw puzzle collectors want an assurance of completeness, either a photograph or a statement by the seller that they actually put the puzzle together. "I bought it as complete" carries no weight whatsoever. Unassembled cardboard puzzles with no guarantees sell for $1.00 or less, wooden puzzles for $3.00 or less. One missing piece lowers price by thirty percent, two missing pieces by fifty percent, and three missing pieces by seventy-five percent or more. Missing packaging (a box or envelope) deducts twenty-five percent from the price.

Club: American Game Collectors Assoc, 49 Brooks Ave, Lewiston, ME 04240.

Note: The following retail prices are for puzzles that are complete, in very good condition, and have their original box.

ADULT PUZZLES
Cardboard
  Depression Era, late 1920s through 1940
    Milton Bradley, Movieland, four puzzle set **75.00**
    Movie stars and movie–related
      .... **20.00**
    Nonweeklies
      Guide Picture **2.00**
      No Guide Picture **4.00**
    Perfect Picture Puzzles
      Guide Picture **2.00**
      No Guide Picture **4.00**
    Tuco
      Guide Picture **3.00**
      No Guide Picture **5.00**
    Weeklies **10.00**
  World War II theme **12.50**
  Post World War II
    Up to 500 pieces **1.00**
    500 to 1,000 pieces **2.00**
    Over 1,000 pieces **3.00**

Springbok
Circular box **4.00**
Square box **1.50**
Wood
1908–1910 craze
Up to 200 pieces **25.00**
200 to 500 pieces **30.00**
Over 500 pieces **40.00**
Mid–1920s to mid–1930s craze
Up to 200 pieces **20.00**
200 to 500 pieces **30.00**
500 to 1,000 pieces **40.00**
Over 1,000 pieces **65.00**
Post–1945
Up to 500 pieces **15.00**
Over 500 pieces **20.00**
Par Co.
Up to 500 pieces **100.00**
Over 500 pieces **200.00**

CHILDREN'S PUZZLES

Cardboard
Pre–1945
Less than 20 pieces **5.00**
Over 20 pieces **10.00**
Puzzle set, three to four puzzles
. . . . **15.00**
Post–1945
Less than 20 pieces **1.00**
20 to 200 pieces
Cartoon Character **3.00**
Super Hero **4.00**
Television, pre–1980 . . . . . . **5.00**
Over 200 pieces **2.00**
Frame Tray, cartoon **12.00**
Frame Tray, cowboy **17.50**
Frame Tray, general **4.00**

Adult, America's Cup Yacht Race, Travel series, Toddy, Inc, copyright 1933, 50 diecut cardboard pieces, figural pieces, spinner to play race game on assembled puzzle, 13¼ × 10" cardboard box, 13 × 9¾", $40.00.

Adv, Dixies Nature Series No 9, Baltimore Oriole, 125 pgs, premium, orig print and mailing envelope, 1933, 8¾ × 10", $5.00.

Composition, 1880s to 1920s
McLoughlin Brothers
General scene **75.00**
Transportation theme **150.00**
Other Manufacturers
Fairy tale **25.00**
General scene **50.00**
Transportation scene **100.00**
Wood
Madmar
General scene **15.00**
Patriotic scene **20.00**
Map
Pre–1880 . . . . **75.00**
1880 to 1915 . . . . **50.00**
1915 to 1940 . . . . **20.00**
Others
General scene **12.50**
Transportation scene **17.50**
Parker Brothers
Dolly Danty series **35.00**
General scene **20.00**

ADVERTISING & NOVELTY PUZZLES

Cardboard
1930s **15.00**
Post–1945 . . . . **5.00**
Wood
Pre–1945 . . . . **50.00**
Pseudo **25.00**

RADIO CHARACTERS AND PERSONALITIES

Radio dominated American life between the 1920s and the early 1950s. Radio characters and personalities enjoyed the same star status as their movie counterparts. Phrases such as "The Shadow Knows" or "Welcome Breakfast Clubbers" quickly date an individual.

Many collectors focus on radio premiums, objects offered during the course of a radio show and usually received by sending in proof of purchase of the sponsor's product. Make certain an object is a premium before paying extra for it as part of this classification.

Many radio characters also found their way into movies and television.

Trying to separate the products related to each medium is time consuming. Why bother? If you enjoyed the character or personality, collect everything that is related to him or her.

Clubs: Old Time Radio Club, 56 Christen Ct, Lancaster, NY 14086; Oldtime Radio–Show Collectors Assoc, 45 Barry St, Sudbury, Ontario P3B 3H6 Canada; Radio Collectors of America, Ardsley Cir, Brockton, MA 02402.

Periodicals: *Friends of Old–Time Radio,* PO Box 4321, Hamden, CT 06514; *Old Time Radio Digest,* 4114 Montgomery Rd, Cincinnati, OH 45212.

Amos 'n' Andy
Ashtray, 5½ × 6 × 7½", plaster, Amos and Andy standing on each side of barrel, rim reads "I'se Regusted," professionally repaired break, restored airbrush paint, 1930s **80.00**
Map, 5 × 8" orig envelope, Pepsodent Co premium, 1935 copyright, 1947 . . . . **85.00**
Paperback Book, *Amos & Andy,* 4 × 6" vertical format, 16 pgs, dusty, heavily soiled covers, extensive wear, c1930s **150.00**
Toy, Amos 'N' Andy Fresh Air Taxicab, 3½ × 8 × 5" h, litho tin windup, built-in key, Marx, missing celluloid windshield and hood ornament, Andy neatly reattached to back seat, scattered paint wear, c1930 **425.00**
Archie
Booklet, *Duffy's First Reader by Archie,* 5 × 7", 49 pgs, softcover, published by Bristol–Myers, c1943 . . . . . **50.00**
Pinback Button, "Meet 'Archie' Thursday Night," 2¾" l, white lettering, dark red ground, c1940 . . . . **45.00**
Captain Midnight, record, "The Years to Remember," 7" d, flexible vinyl, punch out decoder, Longines Symphonette Society, #6 from "The Silver Dagger Strikes" series, 1960s **35.00**
Charlie McCarthy
Carnival Chalkware, 15½" h, milticolored, glitter accents, 1930–1940 . . . . **85.00**
Dummy, 8 × 18½", cardboard, diecut, multicolored, movable lever controls mouth and eyes, 1930–40 . . . . **58.00**
Perfume Bottle, 3½" h, clear glass, removable black plastic hat, late 1930s **40.00**
David Harding Counterspy, matchbook, 1½ × 2", red, white, blue, and orange, matches removed, adv for Old Nick candy bars, reverse lists times of Counterspy Radio Show, ABC network, c1940 . . . . **15.00**

Eddie Cantor

Record Set, 10 × 12" stiff cardboard cov, set of four 78 rpm records, 1947 copyright, distributed by Monitor, minor damage, inked inscription, one record broken **30.00**

Transcription Disk, 16" d disk, marked in pen on each side, "NBC Symphony Pines of Rome, 3/22/52," and "NBC Cantor Show Biz, 12/15/51," orig plain green sleeve **40.00**

Fibber McGee and Molly

Fan Card, 8 × 12", glossy black and white photo neatly mounted on cardboard, 1930s **50.00**

Game, The Amazing Adventures of Fibber McGee, Milton Bradley, 1936 .... **35.00**

Gang Busters, badge, Official Phillips H Lord's Gang Busters, two shades of brass luster, blue accent paint, light overall wear **60.00**

G–Men Club, Special Agent Membership Card, 2½ × 4¼", stiff green cardboard card, black printing, inked name, 1930s **60.00**

Green Hornet

Better Little Book, *The Green Hornet Strikes,* Whitman #1453, 1940 copyright **150.00**

Fan Card, 3½ × 5½", color photos, back with brown and white facsimile signature **60.00**

Jack Armstrong, Hike O Meter **20.00**

Jimmie Allen, Model, 19" l, 24" wingspan, Thunderbolt, orig box, unused, 1930s **100.00**

Little Orphan Annie

Bracelet, Radio Orphan Annie's Identification Disc, silvered brass bracelet, metal links, "S" initial on metal plate, serial no. on reverse, 1934 .... **40.00**

Manual, *Secret Society,* 6 × 8½", 8 pgs, 1937 .... **55.00**

Ring, Secret Message, silvered brass, "ROA" symbol on each side, 1937 message decoder **200.00**

Soakie, 10½" h, vinyl, figural Annie holding bouquet, removable molded hair cap, paper sticker on base, 1977 copyright **20.00**

Lone Ranger

Badge, horseshoe shaped, brass, 1930s **20.00**

Bolo Tie, gold colored six–point star slide **12.00**

Figure, 1½" h, Lone Ranger riding Silver, TLR Inc, 1941 .... **25.00**

Mitzi Green, pinback button, 1¼" d, photo and "I'm on the Air, Mitzi Green, in Happy Landings" in center, "Ward's Soft Bun Bread, WKAN, Tues & Thurs, 6:00 pm" in white lettering on rim, 1930s **5.00**

Radio Stars of Today, log book, 9 × 12½", *Radio Stars of Today and Radio Log,* 32 pgs, issued by National Union Radio Corp, stiff green cov, large sepia photos of stars, late 1920s **85.00**

Red Skelton, post card, 3½ × 5½", radio show cast photo, matte finish, postmarked 1948 .... **20.00**

Sergeant Preston

Distance Finder, 2½ × 3½", diecut, silver, Quaker Cereal premium, 1955 .... **35.00**

Dog Whistle, gold colored **45.00**

The Gumps, book, *The Gumps in Radio Land,* 3½ × 5½", soft cov, Pebeco Toothpaste premium, 96 pgs, 1937 copyright **35.00**

The Shadow

Blotter, 4 × 9", Blue Coal, red, white, blue, and yellow, 1940s, unused pair **75.00**

Pinback Button, 1¼" d, celluloid, yellow and green, "The Shadow of Fu Manchu," 1930s **75.00**

Premium Photo, 8 × 10" glossy black and white, "Compliments of Blue Coal, America's Finest Anthracite," facsimile signature, 1930s ... **100.00**

Uncle Don, pinback button, 1¼" d

Uncle Don Good Humor–GHHC, Uncle Don in uniform, blue letters **25.00**

Uncle Don's Boscoe Club, black and dark brown image, bright yellow ground, holding jar, 1930s ... **30.00**

RADIOS

If a radio does not work, do not buy it unless you need it for parts. If you do, do not pay more than $10.00. A radio that does not work and is expensive to repair is a useless radio.

The radio market has gone through a number of collecting crazes in the 1980s and 1990s. It began with Bakelite radios, moved on to figural and novelty radios, and now is centered on early transistors and 1940s plastic case radios. These crazes are often created by manipulative dealers. Be suspicious of the prices in any specialized price guide focusing on these limited topics. There are several general guides that do a good job of keeping prices in perspective.

Clubs: Antique Radio Club of America, 300 Washington Trails, Washington, PA 15301; Antique Wireless Assoc, 59 Main St, Bloomfield, NY 14469.

Periodicals: *Antique Radio Classified,* PO Box 2, Carlisle, MA 01741; *Radio Age,* 636 Cambridge Road, Augusta, GA 30909; *The Horn Speaker,* PO Box 1193, Mabank, TX 75147; *Transistor Network,* RR1 Box 36, Bradford, NH 03221.

Adler, Model 201–A Royal, table, rect wood case, three front dials, five tubes, battery, 1924 .... **125.00**

Admiral

Model 4W19, portable, plastic, raised front dial, lattice grill, flex handle, right button, broadcast, AC/DC, battery, 1951 .... **40.00**

Model 7T10E–N, table, plastic, right front square dial, left horizontal louvers, two knobs, broadcast, AC/DC, 1947 .... **35.00**

Advertising

Avon, Skin So Soft, AM, MIB **35.00**

Coke Bottle **18.00**

Dr Pepper, can shape **25.00**

Fire Chief **25.00**

Air Castle, model 606–400WB, table, wood, right rect dial, left cloth grill with fretwork, two knobs, broadcast, battery, 1951 .... **35.00**

Airline, Model 14BR–514B, table, plastic, ivory painted, Art Deco style, right slide rule dial, push–button, left horizontal louvers, two knobs, 1946 ...... **100.00**

Atwater Kent, Model 165Q, cathedral, wood, right window dial, cloth grill with scrolled fretwork, three knobs, broadcast, short wave, battery, 1933 **225.00**

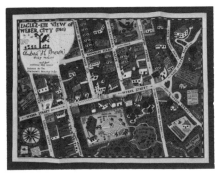

Amos 'n' Andy, Eagle's View of Weber City map, orig Pepsodent mailer, 5½ × 8¼" envelope, $45.00.

Artone, gray sandstone case, restored, 12¼ × 5 x 6½", $150.00.

Bendix, Model 55P2, table, plastic, imitation walnut, slide rule dial, vertical grill bars, rear handle, two knobs, broadcast, AC/DC, 1949 . . . . **40.00**

Bulova, Model 270, portable, transistor, leatherette, right round dial knob, plastic grill with crest, broadcast, battery, 1957 . . . . **35.00**

Character

Dick Tracy, 1¼ × 2½ × 4" h, plastic and metal, 2–transistor portable, silver and black face, silvered metal sound screen marked "Police," black vinyl shoulder holster, carrying strap, earplug, orig box, marked "Made in Japan," 1961 US copyright **165.00**

He–Man/Skeletor, 2½ × 4 × 5" h, hard plastic, two dimensional image of He–Man on one side, Skeletor on back, blue, yellow, and flesh–tone, red raised names, copyright 1985 Mattel **20.00**

John Lennon, 4 × 5 × 1½" h, black, raised gold lettering "John Lennon 1940–1980," 8½" hard plastic figure wearing glasses, jean jacket and pants, pink shirt, figure in orig cellophane bag, 4 × 4 × 8" orig box **175.00**

Mark Twain Riverboat, 2½ × 12 × 7¼" h, detailed replica, hard plastic, diecast metal paddlewheel, stamped brass railings, steel rods, pewter trim, marked "Made in Japan," 1960s **300.00**

Continental, Model TR–208, portable, transistor, diagonally divided front, window dial, checkered grill, AM, battery, 1959 . . . . **25.00**

Crosley

Model 11–1204, white **135.00**

Model E15TN, table, plastic, upper front dial, perforated grill with horizontal bar, two knobs, broadcast, AC/DC, 1953 . . . . **75.00**

Emerson

Model 69, console, walnut, round dial, lower cloth grill with three vertical bars, step–down top, AC, 1934 . . . . **120.00**

Model 343, table, plastic, right dial, left horizontal grill bars, center vertical bars, broadcast, short wave, AC, 1940 . . . . **50.00**

Model 511, marbleized plastic **150.00**

Model 561, black, 1949 . . . . **55.00**

Model 883, series B, table, blue, sleep timer **35.00**

Model CX–284, portable, cloth covered, inner right dial, left louvers, slide–in door, handle, two knobs, battery, 1939 . . . . **30.00**

Fada, Model 260B, table, black Bakelite and chrome, right front dial, left cloth grill with Art Deco style bars, two knobs, broadcast, AC/DC, 1936 . . . . **85.00**

Farnsworth, Model ET–061, table, plastic, upper front slide rule dial, lower checkered grill, two knobs, broadcast, short wave, AC/DC, 1946 . . . . **60.00**

Firestone, Model 4–A–78, table, plastic, oblong panel, right semi–circular dial, left grill, two knobs, broadcast, AC/DC, 1950 . . . . **45.00**

General Electric

Model 62, table, clock, plastic, ivory, upper thumb–wheel dial, left clock, horizontal grill bars, broadcast, AC, 1948 . . . . **45.00**

Model P776A, portable, transistor, leather case, right round dial, horizontal grill bars, handle, AM, battery, 1959 . . . . **25.00**

Howard, Model 307, table, wood, two-tone, lower front rect slide rule dial, upper grill, broadcast, short wave, AC, 1940 . . . . **55.00**

Majestic, Model 5T, table, clock, plastic, Art Deco style, center round dial surrounds clock, rear grill, two knobs, broadcast, AC/DC, 1939 . . . . **100.00**

Motorola

Model 5X11U, table, plastic, center round dial with inner perforated grill, stand, two knobs, broadcast, AC/DC, 1950 . . . . **40.00**

Model L14E, portable, transistor, plastic, right dial knob, lower horizontal bars, left knob, handle, AM, battery, 1960 . . . . **25.00**

Olympic, Model LP–163, table, plastic, right front slanted round dial, horizontal wrap–around louvers, two knobs **65.00**

Philco

Model 37–640, console, wood, upper round dial, lower grill with vertical fretwork, seven tubes, broadcast, short wave, AC, 1937 . . . . . . **135.00**

Model 42–KR5, refrigerator, wood, rounded sides, right dial, left clock, curved base to fit top of refrigerator, 1942 . . . . **60.00**

Little Wonder Microphone, Wonder Specialities, Inc, Cleveland, OH, yellow and black box, orig price sticker, 4½" h brown metal microphone, frayed electrical cord, orig instructions, 4⁹/₁₆" h, 3¼" w, 2½" d box, $30.00.

RCA

Model 9TX23, Little Nipper, table, wood, Art Deco style, right front vertical slide rule "V" dial, left grill, two knobs, AC/DC, 1939 . . . . **75.00**

Model 56X, plastic, brown, Art Deco dial **45.00**

Model 87K–1, console, wood, slanted slide rule dial, vertical grill bars, push–button, tuning eye, broadcast, short wave, 1938 . . . . **145.00**

Realtone, Model TR–970, transistor **35.00**

Sparton, Model 309, portable, plastic, left front dial, center lattice grill, handle, broadcast, AC/DC, battery, 1953 **35.00**

Stromberg–Carlson, Model 56, console, wood, hinged front door hides controls, Art Deco style fretwork, eight tubes, AC, 1933 . . . . **225.00**

Westinghouse

Model H–397T5, table, clock, plastic, maroon, small tombstone style, slide rule dial, upper alarm clock, lower grill, broadcast, AC, 1953 . . . . **45.00**

Model 637T6, coral **35.00**

Zenith, Model 4–T–26, tombstone, wood, lower black dial, upper cloth grill with Art Deco style fretwork, four tubes, broadcast, short wave, AC, 1935 **125.00**

RAILROADIANA

Most individuals collect by railroad, either one near where they live or one near where they grew up. Collectors are split about evenly between steam and diesel. Everyone is saddened by the current state of America's railroads. There are Amtrak collectors, but their numbers are small.

Railroad collectors have been conducting their own specialized shows and swap meets for decades. Railroad material that does show up at flea markets is quickly bought and sent into that market. Collectors use flea markets primarily to make dealer contacts, not for purchasing.

Railroad paper from timetables to menus is gaining in popularity as railroad china, silver-plated flat and hollow wares, and lanterns rise to higher and higher price levels. The key to paper ephemera is that it bear the company logo and have a nice displayable presence.

Clubs: Railroad Enthusiasts, 456 Main Street, West Townsend, MA 01474; Railroadiana Collectors Association, Inc., 795 Aspen, Buffalo Grove, IL 60089; The Twentieth Century Railroad Club, 329

West 18th St, Suite 902, Chicago, IL 60616.

Newsletters: *Key, Lock and Lantern,* 3 Berkeley Heights Park, Bloomfield, NJ 07003; *The Main Line Journal,* PO Box 121, Streamwood, IL 60107.

Ashtray, Baltimore & Ohio Railroad, clear glass, round **25.00**
Badge
    American Electric Railway Association Convention, 1926 .... **18.00**
    Railway Express Agency, #19789, brass, red enamel **45.00**
Blanket, Canadian Pacific **85.00**
Broadside
    Central Vermont Railroad, Rand Avery & Company, 14 × 22″ **250.00**
    Lehigh Valley Railroad, promotes excursion tickets for celebration welcoming Admiral Dewey, red and blue lettering, 1899, 19½″ × 24″ **300.00**
Calendar
    Chicago, Milwaukee, St Paul Railway, pretty girl illus, Sep/Oct 1903, 10 × 14″ **75.00**
    Union Pacific Railroad, 1958 .... **10.00**
China
    Baltimore & Ohio Railroad
        Berry Bowl **50.00**
        Butter Pat **55.00**
        Cereal Bowl, 6½″ d **60.00**
        Cream Soup **75.00**
        Cup **55.00**
        Plate
            8″ d, lunch **85.00**
            10″ d, dinner **120.00**
        Soup, flat **85.00**
    Missouri Pacific, plate, 10½″ d, dinner, states and wildflowers illus, Syracuse China **55.00**
    Union Pacific, children's set, circus motif
        Cereal Bowl, full figured clown **135.00**
        Plate
            Dinner, clown **175.00**
            Salad, dog balancing ball **135.00**
Conductor's Suit, CB & Q, three pieces, dark blue, brass emb buttons **95.00**
Creamer, PRR, International Silver Co, soldered, seamless, PRR on bottom **100.00**
Folder, Burlington Zephyr, streamline train, layout diagram and illus, c1933 **35.00**
Lamp, wall, pullman type, brass, early electric, white bakelite shades, heavy wall brackets, 7 ½″ h, pr **135.00**
Lantern
    Adams & Westlake, conductor's, carbide, nickel over brass **195.00**
    Adlake Non Sweating Lamp, Chicago, yellow, red, blue, and clear lights, 17½″ h **150.00**
    D & H, clear globe **250.00**

Puzzle, King George V Engine, Great Western Railway series, Chad Valley Co, Harborne, England, 1930s, 207 hand–cut plywood pieces, irregular edge, 9½ × 6¼″ cardboard book type box, 8½ × 22″, $75.00.

    L & N Hanlan, clear short globe **50.00**
    Missouri Pacific Railroad, hand, 4″ clear globe **75.00**
    New York Central, bell bottom, red globe, 6″ h, Dietz, No. 6, raised letters **100.00**
    NYNH & H RR, two color globe, Adams & Westlake, c1887 .... **150.00**
Oil Can, Missouri Pacific **34.00**
Padlock, Rock Island Railroad, orig key **30.00**
Playing Cards
    California Zephyr, 1950–1960 ... **15.00**
    Denver & Rio Grande Railways, complete deck **35.00**
Post Card, Washington Virginia Railway Co, scenic, pack **12.00**
Poster, paper
    Black Valley Railroad, "Great Central Fast Route," temperance adv with volcanoes and devils around trains in background, stagecoach and ambulance in foreground, 23 × 16½″ **900.00**
    Great Northern & Northern Pacific Railroad, black and white, pioneers crossing prairie, "The Path of Empire," 38¼ × 27″ **95.00**
    Ohio Valley Scenic Railroad, "Take The Yellow Car, To Niagara Falls, Round Trip 50¢" conductor pointing to yellow trolley car, 21 × 28″ ... **275.00**
    Toledo & Ann Arbor Railroad, timetable, train crossing trellised bridge to Michigan via Hoosac tunnel, vignettes of Chief Pontiac, Miss Ann Arbor, and Uncle Remis, 32 × 22″ **2,000.00**

Tool, hammer, 25¾″ l, $20.00.

Print, Indian Chief, copyright Great Northern Railroad **55.00**
Sign
    Atlantic Coast Line, metal, round, stenciled black lettering, reflective gold ground, 29½″ d **85.00**
    Illinois Central RR, promotes trips to Mardi Gras and 1885 New Orlean's World Expo, woman sitting below arch, holding mask and fan, overlooking fountain and Expo building, paper, 10½ × 30″ **650.00**
Step, from Pullman Railroad Station, wood, handle cutout in top, 21″ w, 10″ h, 17½″ d **25.00**
Sugar Bowl, PRR, International Silver Co, soldered, keystone mark on bottom **100.00**
Tablecloth, Illinois Central Railroad, banquet size **65.00**
Timetable
    Erie Railroad, illus, 1907 .... **30.00**
    Hoosier Tunnel Route, 1895 ..... **50.00**
    L & N Kansas City Southern, Passenger train, 1955–56 .... **5.00**
Towel, pullman, blue stripe, dated 1925 .... **15.00**

RECORDS

Most records are worth between 25¢ and $1.00. A good rule to follow is the more popular the record, the less likely it is to have value. Who does not have a copy of Bing Crosby singing "White Christmas?"

Until the mid–1980s the principal emphasis was on 78 rpm records. As the decade ended, 45 rpm records became increasingly collectible. By 1990 33⅓ rpm albums, especially Broadway show related, were gaining in favor.

To find out what records do have value, check L. R. Dock's *1900–1965 American Premium Record Guide, Fourth Edition* (Books Americana, 1992) and Jerry Osborne's *The Official Price Guide To Records, Tenth Edition* (House of Collectibles, 1993).

By the way, maybe you had better buy a few old record players. You could still play the 78s and 45s on a 33¹/₃ machine. You cannot play any of them on a compact disc player.

Periodicals: *DISCoveries*, PO Box 309, Fraser, MI 48026; *Goldmine*, 700 E State St, Iola, WI 54990; *Record Collectors Monthly*, PO Box 75, Mendham, NJ 07945.

Adult
    Jayne Mansfield, 12¹/₂ × 12¹/₂" cardboard dj, full color photo, single 33¹/₃ record, c1956 . . . . **20.00**
    The Untouchables, 12¹/₄ × 12¹/₄" cardboard cov, 33¹/₃ rpm, Capitol label, early 1960s **15.00**

Children's
    Barbie Sings, 45 rpm, Mattel Stock No. 840, copyright 1961 . . . . **35.00**
    Bugs Bunny in Storyland, 78 rpm, Capitol Records, two records, copyright 1949 . . . . **35.00**
    Daffy Duck Meets Yosemite Sam, 10 × 10" stiff paper, 78 rpm, Capitol, early 1950s **30.00**
    Donald Duck Golden Record, 7 × 8" colorful paper sleeve, 45 rpm **25.00**
    Dorothy and The Wizard of Oz, 12¹/₂ × 14" rigid cardboard cov, three 12" d 78 rpm records, Capitol Records, 1949, worn cov **150.00**
    Felix Talking Movie Wheels, 11¹/₂ × 11¹/₂" thin cardboard cov, brightly colored, 33¹/₃ rpm thin vinyl record, thin paper disc with picture image, 1960 . . . . **55.00**
    Songs Girl Scouts Sing Album, 10¹/₄ × 10¹/₄" cov, two 78 rpm records, 12 scouting songs, c1940, worn covs, used records **15.00**
    Super Heroes Christmas Album, 33¹/₃ rpm, Peter Pan Label, copyright DC Comics, 1977 . . . . **35.00**
    The Song Hits From Pinocchio, 10 × 10" stiff cardboard, 33¹/₃ rpm, Decca, 1949 copyright **90.00**
    Walt Disney's So Dear To My Heart, 10¹/₂ × 12" thick cardboard cov, four records, Capitol label, 1949 copyright **85.00**
    Walt Disney's Song of Tomorrowland Golden Record, 6³/₄ × 7¹/₂" colorful sleeve, yellow vinyl 78 rpm, 1950s **30.00**

Comedy
    Here's Johnny Magic Moments From The Tonight Show, 12¹/₄ × 12¹/₄" cardboard cov, two 33¹/₃ rpm records, Casablanca label **20.00**
    Laugh In '69 Cast Album, 12¹/₄ × 12¹/₄" cardboard cov, 33¹/₃ rpm, Reprise label, 1969 . . . . **10.00**
    Phil Silvers, 7 × 7" cardboard cov, 45 rpm, Columbia label, 1950s **20.00**

Cowboy
    Gene Autry, two 10" d 78 rpm records, Okeh label, late 1930s **20.00**

Firestone Presents Your Christmas Favorites, FTP Records, NY, Vol 3, 33¹/₃ rpm, 1964, $5.00.

    Lone Ranger, 7 × 8" cardboard dust cov, 45 rpm Little Golden Record, 1958 copyright **40.00**
    Roy Rogers, Pecos Bill, 10¹/₂ × 12" rigid cardboard, three 78 rpm records **75.00**
    The Restless Gun, 7 × 7" glossy paper slip case, 45 rpm, title song from 1957 TV show **25.00**

Movie, 45 rpm
    East of Eden, Columbia, 1957 . . . . **30.00**
    It's A Mad, Mad, Mad, Mad World, United Artists, 1963 . . . . **18.00**
    Lady Sings The Blues, Motown, 1972 . . . . **10.00**
    To Kill A Mockingbird, Ava, 1962 . . . . **30.00**

Political, Spiro T Agnew Speaks Out, Collector's Edition, orig shrink wrap, 1972 campaign, black and white Agnew photo on cov **15.00**

Rock 'N' Roll, 45 rpm
    Beatles, All You Need Is Love, Capitol, 5964 . . . . **18.00**
    Jerry Lee Lewis, Great Balls Of Fire, Sun, 281 . . . . **20.00**
    Three Dog Night, Mama Told Me Not To Come, Dunhill, 1970 . . . . . . **5.00**

Sports Champions, 6³/₄" sq cardboard dust jacket, 33¹/₃ rpm record, Columbia Records, 1962 copyright, full color cov player photo, facsimile signature, biography, statistics
    Don Drysdale, Los Angeles Dodgers **60.00**
    Mickey Mantle, New York Yankees **60.00**
    Willie Mays, San Francisco Giants **60.00**

RED WING POTTERY

Red Wing, Minnesota, was home to several potteries. Among them were Red Wing Stoneware Company, Minnesota Stoneware Company, and The North Star Stoneware Company. All are equally collectible.

Red Wing has a strong regional base. The best buys are generally found at flea markets far removed from Minnesota. Look for pieces with advertising. Red Wing pottery was a popular giveaway product.

Club: Red Wing Collectors Society, Inc, PO Box 124, Neosho, WI 53059.

Blossomtime, Concord Shape
    Berry Bowl **3.00**
    Cup and Saucer **4.50**
    Plate
        6" d **2.00**
        10¹/₂" d **5.00**
    Platter, 13¹/₂" l **10.00**
    Vegetable Bowl, 8¹/₂" d **9.00**
Bobwhite
    Centerpiece, figural quail on tray **95.00**
    Pitcher, large **70.00**
    Water Cooler, orig spigot and base **525.00**
Cookie Jar
    Chef, yellow **80.00**
    Dutch Girl, tan **110.00**
    Pierre, blue **100.00**
Jug, brown, wide mouth, 1¹/₂ gal **30.00**
Round–Up
    Berry Bowl **35.00**
    Casserole, large **70.00**
    Cereal Bowl **35.00**
    Creamer and Sugar **165.00**
    Cup and Saucer **40.00**
    Gravy, cov **125.00**
    Plate, bread and butter **30.00**
    Platter
        13" l **135.00**
        20" l **395.00**
    Relish **95.00**
    Salad Bowl, large **300.00**
    Salt and Pepper Shakers, pr **150.00**
    Serving Bowl **75.00**
    Vegetable Bowl, divided **70.00**
Vase, blue and white stoneware, lion dec, marked "Red Wing Union" **350.00**

Mark, Red Wing, USA, 946.

Village Green
Casserole, cov **24.00**
Dinner Service, four each 10" plates, 6"
plates, cups and saucers **75.00**
Pitcher, 4¼" h **15.00**

ROBOTS

This category covers the friction, windup, and battery operated robots made after World War II. The robot concept is much older, but generated few collectibles. The grandfather of all modern robot toys is Atomic Robot Man, made in Japan between 1948 and 1949.

Robots became battery operated by the 1950s. Movies of that era fueled interest in robots. R2D2 and C3PO from *Star Wars* are the modern contemporaries of Roby and his cousins.

Robots are collected internationally. You will be competing with the Japanese for examples.

When buying at a flea market, take time to make certain the robot is complete, operates (carry at least two batteries of different sizes with you for testing), and has the original box. The box is critical.

Periodical: *Robot World & Price Guide*, PO Box 184, Lenox Hill Station, New York, NY 10021.

Atlas, 2 × 6 × 3¾" h, built-in key, litho tin, plastic feet, soft plastic rocket attached to back, orig box, marked "Industria Argentia" in English and Spanish on toy and box, 1960s **325.00**
Battery Operated Action Robot, 4 × 6 × 10½" h, hard plastic, orig box, colorful lid, bump and go action, lights, machine gun sound, turn around body, fires missiles from spring loaded launchers on top of head, 1970s **65.00**
Ding–A–Lings, Claw, 3 × 3 × 5½" h, plastic, red, blue, yellow, and green, Topper Corp, 1970s **40.00**
Dr Who Talking K–9, 6" h, battery operated, plastic, gray, BBC, Palitoy, 1978 .... **100.00**
Extracter, 9½" h, plastic, blue, litho tin chest plate, silver accents, marked "Made In Japan," c1970 .... **50.00**
Lost In Space, 12" h, plastic, red, metallic blue arms and legs, clear dome head, claw hands, Remco, copyright 1966 Space Productions **400.00**
Mr Robot, 11" h, litho tin, silver, red arms, clear plastic head, Cragstan **400.00**
Oz Tin Man, 21½" h, battery operated, forward and backward walking action, arms swing, Remco, copyright 1969, orig colorful box **320.00**

Rock'em – Sock'em Robots, World's Only Fighting Robots, Marx, plastic, moved by hand lever controls, one red and one blue-green robot, yellow boxing ring, white rubber ropes, orig box, #5015MO, 21" l extended, 14" w, 13" h, $150.00.

Raid Robot, 6 × 8 × 12" h, hard plastic, remote control, dark green Raid bug, bright yellow on face, black back spots, flexible rubber antenna, red dot eyes light up, forward and backward movement, speaks, 1980s **300.00**
Robert The Robot, 14" h, battery–operated, eyes light, orig box, Ideal, 1950s **200.00**
Rocky, 4" h, Fred Flintstone type painted soft vinyl head, 3" d litho metal body, diecut tin arms, bump and go action, orig 3½ × 3½ × 4½" colorful box, unauthorized Japanese **325.00**
The Great Garloo, 18" h, battery–operated, green plastic, black, white, and tan tiger skin waist cloth, medallion, serving tray, Marx, 1960s **350.00**
Toto, 8" h, plastic and litho tin, dark gray, orange feet and accents, marked "Made In Japan," c1960 .... **120.00**
Walking Twiki, 7" h, built–in key, plastic, walks forward, grip lock hands, Mego copyright 1979 Robert C Dille ... **45.00**
Wind–Up Radar Hunter Robot, 2½ × 4 × 6½" h, hard plastic, built–in key, colorful box with display window, walks forward as antenna spins, Busy Bee, Hong Kong, 1970s **65.00**

ROCK 'N' ROLL COLLECTIBLES

My Dad ought to be forced to do this category. He grew up in the Rock 'n' Roll era, but tuned it out. He claims this is why he can hear and I cannot. I have heard rumors that he actually went to Bandstand in Philly, but he refuses to confirm them.

Most collectors focus on individual singers and groups. The two largest sources of collectibles are items associated with Elvis and the Beatles. As revivals occur, e.g., the Doors, new interest is drawn to older collectibles. The market has gotten so big that Sotheby's and Christie's hold Rock 'n' Roll sales annually.

Periodicals: *Kissaholics Magazine*, PO Box 22334, Nashville, TN 37202; *The New England KISS Collectors' Network*, 168 Oakland Ave, Providence, RI 02908; *Tune Talk*, PO Box 851, Marshalltown, IA 50158.

Autograph
Chubby Checker, 8 × 10", glossy black and white photo, black felt tip "It Ain't Over Till It's Over, Keep It Up, Love Chubby Checker 86" **30.00**
Fats Domino, 8 × 10", full color photo, sgd "God Bless And Rock Around The Clock" **20.00**
Belt Buckle, 2½ × 3", Kiss, cast metal, gold finish, center color illus, 1976 copyright **45.00**
Book, *Woodstock 69*, Joseph J Sia, Scholastic Book Services, copyright 1970, 124 pgs **25.00**
Costume, girl's, Davy Jones, molded thin plastic mask, one piece rayon mini dress with Monkees logo, orig box, Bland Charnas Co Inc, copyright 1967 Rayburt Productions Inc **60.00**
Diary, 4 × 5½", Dick Clark American Bandstand Secret Diary, vinyl cov cardboard, gold colored metal lock, clear, orig price sticker, 1950s **60.00**
Doll
Diana Ross, 19" h, molded hard plastic body, vinyl face and arms, gold glitter dress, orig box with Supremes picture, Ideal, copyright 1969 Motown Inc **100.00**
Dick Clark, 25" h, plush stuffed body, molded vinyl head and hands, marked "Juro" on back of neck, c1950 .... **150.00**

Album Cover, Santana, $8.00.

Hat, 9" l, Rock Around The Clock, blue felt, removable cardboard record on top, marked "Manufactured by Bing Crosby Phonocards Inc," c1950 .... **60.00**

Jacket, tour, silver/gray satin, yellow and white embroidered couple dancing, black "Rock and Roll" above, embroidered 1963, back with gold, black, and white "The Drifters On Broadway," tag inside marked "Ragtime Collection" **150.00**

Magazine

Dick Clark Official American Bandstand Yearbook, 9 × 12", 40 pgs, color and black and white photos, c1950 .... **25.00**

Rock and Roll Songs, 8½ × 11", Vol 3, #11, Dec 1957 .... **15.00**

Post Card, Rolling Stones, 4½ × 6½", two, perforated, "The Rolling Stones Exile On Main Street" in red, marked "Scene 1" and "Scene 2," c1972 .... **15.00**

Poster

Doors, 24 × 36", full color, green bottom border, white Doors logo, copyright 1968 Doors Production Corp **20.00**

Moody Blues, 18½ × 25½", stiff paper, April 1, 1970, concert, Terrace Ballroom, Salt Lake City, UT **50.00**

Program

Freddie and the Dreamers, 10 × 13", 20 pgs, late 1960s **25.00**

The Dave Clark 5, 10 × 13", 24 pgs, c1965 .... **45.00**

The Temptations, 9 × 12", 16 pgs, black and white photos and text, Program Publishing, 1966 copyright ... **30.00**

Record, Buddy Holly, Peggy Sue/Every Day, 78 rpm, Coral label, 1957 .... **25.00**

Record Case, 7½ × 9", Tune Tote, vinyl cov cardboard, blue design, black, white, blue, and flesh tone, black plastic carrying handles, paper sleeves for records, Ponytail, 1950s **25.00**

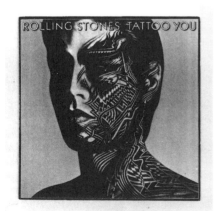

Record Album, Rolling Stones Tattoo You, $15.00.

Sheet Music, 9 × 12", Bill Haley and His Comets, *Rock Around the Clock,* 2 pgs, copyright 1953 Myers Music **18.00**

Ticket

Eric Clapton, 2¼ × 3", 1975 Tampa, FL, concert, black and white, blue-tone photo, stub **15.00**

Woodstock, 1969, three day ticket, letter of authenticity **125.00**

Tour Book, Rod Stewart, 9½ × 13½", 1978–79 World Tour, 96 pgs **15.00**

View–Master Reel, 4½" sq envelope, Monkees, three reels, booklet and orig catalog, Rayburt Productions, 1967 copyright **30.00**

NORMAN ROCKWELL

The prices in this listing are retail prices from a dealer specializing in Rockwell and/or limited edition collectibles. Rockwell items are one of those categories for which it really pays to shop around at a flea market. Finding an example in a general booth at 10¢ on the dollar is not impossible or uncommon.

When buying any Rockwell item, keep asking yourself how many examples were manufactured. In many cases, the answer is tens to hundreds of thousands. Because of this, never settle for any item in less than fine condition.

Club: Rockwell Society of America, 587 Saw Mill River Rd, Ardsley, NY 10502.

Bell

Chilling Chore, 1977 .... **45.00**

Garden Girl, 1978 .... **40.00**

Book, *My Adventures As An Illustrator,* Rockwell, 1960 .... **20.00**

Calendar, 1946, Tom Sawyer, John Morrel & Co **60.00**

Catalog, Winchester Western Sporting Arms, 1966 .... **35.00**

Figurine

Day In The Life Of A Boy, Gorham, 1980 .... **65.00**

Little Mother, Rockwell Museum, 1981 .... **50.00**

The Graduate, Dave Grossman, 1983 .... **30.00**

Toy Maker, Rockwell Museum, 1979 .... **75.00**

Ingot, Santa Planning A Visit, gold plated silver, Hamilton Mint, 1975 ..... **45.00**

Magazine Cover

Boy's Life, 1951 .... **20.00**

Saturday Evening Post, 1940 ..... **20.00**

TV Guide, 1970 .... **5.00**

Magazine Tear Sheet, black and white, average price **6.00**

Plate, First Day of School, Rockwell Museum, 6½" d, $17.50.

Music Box, Between The Acts, Schmid **125.00**

Plate

Campfire Story, Boy Scout Series, Gorham, 1978 .... **20.00**

Christmas, Bringing Home the Tree, orig mailing envelope, Franklin Mint, 1971 .... **250.00**

Cradle of Love, Mother's Day, Lynell Studios, 1980 .... **20.00**

Leapfrog, Dave Grossman, 1979 **35.00**

Somebody's Up There, Christmas Series, Rockwell Society, 1979 .... **30.00**

While The Audience Waits, Rockwell Museum, 1982 .... **15.00**

Stein, Braving The Storm, Rockwell Museum **60.00**

ROSEVILLE POTTERY

Roseville rose from the ashes of the J. B. Owen Company when a group of investors bought Owen's pottery in the late 1880s. In 1892 George F. Young became the first of four succeeding generations of Youngs to manage the plant.

Roseville grew through acquisitions of another Roseville firm and two in Zanesville. By 1898 the company's offices were located in Zanesville. Roseville art pottery was first produced in 1900. The trade name Rozane was applied to many lines. During the 1930s Roseville looked for new product lines. Utilizing several high-gloss glazes in the 1940s, Roseville revived its art pottery line. Success was limited. In 1954 the Mosaic Tile Company bought Roseville.

Pieces are identified as early, middle (Depression era), and late pieces. Because of limited production, middle period pieces are the hardest to find. They also were marked with paper labels that have become lost over time. Some key patterns to watch for are Blackberry, Cherry Blossom, Faline, Ferella, Futura, Jonquil, Morning Glory, Sunflower, and Windsor.

Clubs: American Art Pottery Association, 125 E Rose Ave, St Louis, Mo 63119; Roseville's of the Past Pottery Club, PO Box 681117, Orlando, FL 32868.

Basket
    Foxglove, blue **245.00**
    Freesia, green, 391–8 . . . . **140.00**
    Gardenia, gray, 608–8 . . . . **165.00**
    Iris, blue, 30–4 . . . . **68.00**
    Magnolia, brown, 384–8 . . . . **105.00**
    Peony, 10″ d, yellow **65.00**
    Pine Cone, brown, 410–10 . . . . . **295.00**
    Poppy, pink, hanging **45.00**
    Zephyr Lily, green, 395–10 . . . . . **120.00**
Bookends, pr
    Bittersweet, green **125.00**
    Snowberry, blue, 18–E **85.00**
Bowl
    Bushberry, brown, 415–10 . . . . . **125.00**
    Clematis, blue **50.00**
    Columbine, 6″ d, blue **60.00**
    Fuchsia, 8½″ d, blue **100.00**
    Laurel, 9″ l, oval, gold **60.00**
    Snowberry, pink **50.00**
    Wincraft, blue, 228–12 . . . . **85.00**
Candleholder, pr
    Gardenia, gray, 652–4 . . . . **120.00**
    Magnolia, green **35.00**
    Panel, 2½″ h, brown **75.00**
    White Rose, 2¼″ h **30.00**
Compote
    Donatello, 5 × 6½″ **95.00**
    Florentine **40.00**
Console Bowl, Zephyr Lily, 10″ d, brown
    . . . . **125.00**
Console Set, Foxglove, 12″ d bowl, pr
    1½″ h candlesticks, 423 bowl, 1149
    candlesticks, red **175.00**
Ewer
    Bushberry, 6″ d, blue **65.00**
    Dawn, pink, 834–15 . . . . **450.00**
    Freesia, 6″ d, green **35.00**
Flower Frog
    Clematis, brown **55.00**
    Ixia, pink **60.00**
    Peony, pink **70.00**
    Pine Cone, 5″ h, green, 21 . . . . . **200.00**
    Poppy, brown, 35 . . . . **105.00**
Jardiniere
    Baneda, 7″ h, green **400.00**
    Cherry Blossom, 7″ h **465.00**
    Donatello, 5″ h, ivory **70.00**
    Foxglove, blue, 659–5 . . . . **60.00**
    Pine Cone, 3″ h, brown **58.00**
    Poppy, 3″ h, green **25.00**

Flower Frog, Cremona, orig sticker, $30.00.

Jug
    Cherry Blossom, 4″ h, brown . . . **180.00**
    Wisteria, 4″ h, brown, 629–4 . . . **225.00**
Pillow Vase
    Futura, 81 . . . . **395.00**
    Panel, 6″ h, brown **120.00**
Planter, Velmoss, 16″ d **35.00**
Sugar, Snowberry, pink **20.00**
Teapot, Peony, green **85.00**
Tea Set, Peony **195.00**
Urn, Wincraft, blue, 256–5 . . . . **60.00**
Vase
    Apple Blossom, 10″ h **135.00**
    Baneda, 6¼″ h, pink **225.00**
    Clematis, green **65.00**
    Columbine, 8″ h, brown **120.00**
    Cosmos, 7″ h, blue **100.00**
    Dahlrose, 8″ h **85.00**

Vase, Rozanne, Woodland, beige ground, brown tiger lily, marked "EE" on base, 9¾″ h, $750.00.

    Donatello, 4″ h **45.00**
    Ferella, 10½″ h, brown **295.00**
    Freesia, tangerine, 123–9 . . . . **95.00**
    Fuchsia, 6″ h, blue, 893–6 . . . . . **195.00**
    Futura, 7″ h, pink **325.00**
    Magnolia, 8″ h, tan **100.00**
    Moss, 6½″ h, ftd, two handles   **125.00**
    Mostique, 10½″ h **60.00**
    Pine Cone II, 8″ h, brown **75.00**
    Russco, 9″ h, blue, double bud . . . **50.00**
    Snowberry, 9″ h, blue **90.00**
    Thorn Apple, 304 . . . . **50.00**
    Tuscany, 5″ h, urn shape, pink . . . **60.00**
    Velmoss, 8″ h, blue **90.00**
    Wincraft, apricot, 275–12 . . . . . . **160.00**
    Zephyr Lily, blue, 133–8 . . . . **135.00**
Wall Pocket
    Florentine 7″ h **150.00**
    Snowberry, pink **110.00**
    Tuscany, pink **65.00**
Window Box
    Apple Blossom, pink, 369–12 . . . **100.00**
    Gardenia, 9″ l, green **65.00**
    Magnolia, brown **45.00**
    Wincraft, 13 × 4″, blue **55.00**

ROYAL CHINA

The Royal China Company, located in Sebring, Ohio, utilized remodeled facilities that originally housed the Oliver China Company and later the E. H. Sebring Company. Royal China began operations in 1934.

The company produced an enormous number of dinnerware patterns. The backs of pieces usually contain the names of the shape, line, and decoration. In addition to many variations of company backstamps, Royal China also produced objects with private backstamps. All records of these markings were lost in a fire in 1970.

In 1964 Royal China purchased the French–Saxon China Company, Sebring, Ohio, which it operated as a wholly owned subsidiary. On December 31, 1969, Royal China was acquired by the Jeannette Corporation. When fire struck the Royal China Sebring plant in 1970, Royal moved its operations to the French–Saxon plant.

The company changed hands several times, until operations ceased in August 1986.

Collectors tend to concentrate on specific patterns. Among the most favored are Bluebell (1940s), Currier and Ives (designed by Gordon Parker and introduced 1949–50), Colonial Homestead (1951–52), Old Curiosity Shop (early 1950s), Regal (1937) Royalty (1936), and blue and pink Willow Ware (1940s).

Because of easy accessibility, only purchase pieces in fine to excellent condition. Do not buy pieces whose surface is marked or marred in any way.

Colonial Homestead
Cake Plate, tab handles, 10" d ... **12.00**
Cereal Bowl, 6¼" d **5.00**
Creamer and Sugar, cov **12.00**
Cup and Saucer **4.00**
Plate
  6" d, bread and butter **1.50**
  10" d, dinner **3.50**
Salt and Pepper Shakers, pr **10.00**
Currier & Ives, blue and white
Ashtray **12.50**
Bowl
  Berry **4.00**
  Cereal, 6¼" d **12.00**
Butter Dish **25.00**
Casserole **65.00**
Creamer **5.00**
Cup and Saucer **3.00**
Gravy Underplate **2.00**
Pie Plate
  10" d **15.00**
  11" d **10.00**
Pie Server **12.00**
Plate
  5" d, bread and butter **1.00**
  6" d, salad **2.50**
  9" d, lunch **8.50**
  10" d, dinner **5.00**
Salt and Pepper Shakers, pr **15.00**
Sugar, cov **12.00**
Teapot, cov **75.00**
Trivet, 7¾" d **14.00**
Vegetable Bowl
  8½" d, rimmed **7.00**
  9" d, rimmed **9.00**
  10" d, rimmed **10.00**

Pie Plate, marked "Royal China Jeannette Corp, Conventional and Microwave Oven Approved, Dishwasher Safe, USA," skating scene, 10" d, $12.00.

Old Curiosity Shop
Bowl, 9" d **12.00**
Casserole, cov **45.00**
Cup and Saucer **4.00**
Gravy **10.00**
Plate, 10" d, dinner **4.00**
Soup, flat, 8½" d **6.00**

ROYAL DOULTON

Chances of finding Royal Doulton at flea markets are better than you think. It often is given as gifts. Since the recipients did not pay for it, they often have no idea of its initial value. The same holds true when children have to break up their parent's household. As a result, it is sold for a fraction of its value at garage sales and to dealers.

Check out any piece of Royal Doulton that you find. There are specialized price guides for character jugs, figures, and toby jugs. A great introduction to Royal Doulton is the two–volume videocassette entitled *The Magic of a Name*, produced by Quill Productions, Birmingham, England.

Clubs: Heartland Doulton Collectors, PO Box 2434, Joliet, IL 60434; Mid–America Doulton Collectors, PO Box 483, McHenry, IL 60050; Royal Doulton International Collectors Club, PO Box 1815, Somerset, NJ 08873; Royal Doulton International Collectors Club (Canadian Branch), 850 Progress Ave, Scarborough, Ontario M1H 3C4 Canada.

Periodicals: *Collecting Doulton*, 2 Strafford Ave, Elsecar, Barnsley, S Yorkshire S74 8AA England; *Doulton Divvy*, PO Box 2434, Joilet, IL 60434.

Animal Figure, 5" h, cat, white **135.00**
Ashtray, John Barleycorn **90.00**
Bowl, 9¼" d, Rosalind **70.00**
Candlesticks, 10¼" h, floral, blue ground, pr
.... **150.00**
Character Jug
Large, 5¼ to 7" h
  Pied Piper **60.00**
  Tony Weller **150.00**
Miniature, 2¼ to 2½" h
  Granny **50.00**
  Sancho Panza **60.00**
Small, 3½ to 4" h
  Arriet **100.00**
  Mr Micawber **85.00**
  St George **65.00**
Tiny, 1¼" h
  Gardener **40.00**
  Paddy **100.00**

Plate, Gibson Girl, They Take A Morning Run, copyright 1901 by Life Publishing Co, $95.00.

Cup and Saucer, Sandhurst **30.00**
Dickens Ware
Ashtray, Tony Weller **35.00**
Demitasse Cup and Saucer, Mr Pickwick
  on cup, Sam Weller on saucer **55.00**
Sauce Dish, 5¼" d, Fat Boy **45.00**
Tray, 4 × 5⅜", Barnaby Rudge **50.00**
Figurine
Afternoon Tea, HN1747 .... **250.00**
Artful Dodger, HN546 .... **55.00**
Beachcomber, HN2487 .... **165.00**
Bedtime, HN1978 .... **80.00**
Boatman, HN2417 .... **165.00**
Bride, HN2873 .... **150.00**
Buttercup, HN2309 .... **155.00**
Charlotte, HN2423 .... **165.00**
Coachman, HN2282 .... **400.00**
Cup of Tea, HN2322 .... **135.00**
Dreamweaver, HN2283 ...... **175.00**
Elegance, HN2264 .... **175.00**
Faith, HN3082 .... **125.00**
Innocence, HN2842 .... **155.00**
Janet, HN1537 .... **155.00**
Lori, HN2801 .... **115.00**
Mandy, HN2476 .... **95.00**
Michelle, HN2234 .... **155.00**
Sam Weller, D2973, bottom rim chip
.... **95.00**
Stiggins, HN536 .... **55.00**
Jug
Rip Van Winkle **250.00**
Sairey Gamp, small A mark **65.00**
Mug
Granny **55.00**
Old Salt **60.00**
Pitcher, 8" h, Old Bob Ye Guard, pinch–in
type **95.00**
Plaque, 14" d, Long John Silver **125.00**
Plate
6¾" d, Coaching Days **60.00**
10" d, Shakespeare Plays **45.00**
Tankard, 6" h, Queen Elizabeth at Old
Moreton Hall, c1920 .... **20.00**
Tile, Shakespeare Ware, Much Ado About
Nothing **60.00**

Toby Jug
Beefeater, D6233 . . . . **45.00**
Happy John, 5½" h, #6070, c1939
. . . . **45.00**

RUGS

You have to cover your floors with something. Until we have antique linoleum, the name of the game is rugs. If you have to own a rug, own one with some age and character.

Do not buy any rug without unrolling it. Hold it up in the air in such a way that there is a strong light behind it. This will allow you to spot any holes or areas of heavy wear.

Chain Stitch
Floral and diamond design, blues and pinks, black ground, 8' × 10' **55.00**
Floral design, blue, green, and red, 4' × 6' **27.50**
Character, Donald Duck and Nephews, cotton, marked "Made in Belgium" **35.00**
Hooked
Abstract, cross in center, colorful, 29" × 41" **27.50**
Cat, folksy
Lying on pillow, blue, black, and white cat, salmon red and green pillow, dark gray and pink ground, salmon border, loosely hooked, fading, repair, 25½" × 35½" **225.00**
Lying on rect platform, two shades of olive, red, and white, gray–beige ground, multicolored foliage, wear, fading, some repair, 20" x 38" **275.00**
Eagle, red, white, and blue **100.00**
Floral, red roses, black ground, leaf scroll border, rag and yarn, damage to border, 27" × 46" **82.50**
Floral, unfinished, orig frame, browns, gray, and faded pink, 26½" × 33"
. . . . **55.00**
Little Bo Peep, three sheep, faded colors, some wear, 18½" × 37" **220.00**
Morning Glories, pastel shades, ivory ground, deep purple border, slight color bleeding, 26" × 38" **27.50**
Peacock, primitive, folksy, red, blue, yellow, and green, black ground, edge wear and damage, 32" × 38" **55.00**
Swan, cattails, water lilies, blues, greens, brown, black, and white, braided border, modern, mounted on frame, 20" × 36" **70.00**
Winter Landscape, house and trees, faded pink, blue, green, brown, white, and black, 16½" × 26" **72.00**
Oriental, contemporary
Heriz pattern, red ground, 3'3" × 5'6"
. . . . **195.00**

Sarouk pattern, red ground, 3'1" × 5'5"
. . . . **125.00**
Rag, Pennsylvania, strip
Bluish gray and white, blue warp, 3' × 15' **90.00**
Green and white, colorful string warp, one end frayed, partial orig factory label "Hollinger Mills Co, Carlisle, PA" **440.00**
Woven, ingrain, small floral design, red, greens, and ivory, wear and damage, 3' × 22' **50.00**

SALT AND PEPPER SHAKERS

Hang on to your hats. Those great figural salt and pepper shaker sets from the 1920s through the 1960s have been discovered by the New York art and decorator crowd. Prices have started to jump. What does this say about taste in America?

When buying a set, make certain it is a set. Check motif, base, and quality of workmanship. China shakers should have no cracks or signs of cracking. Original paint and decoration should be present on china and metal figures. Make certain each shaker has the right closure.

Salt and pepper shaker collectors must compete with specialized collectors from other fields, e.g., advertising and black memorabilia. Dad keeps after me to find him a pair shaped like jigsaw puzzle pieces. I have not seen a pair yet nor found a dealer who has seen one. Do you think Dad will relent in his quest? Forget it.

Club: Novelty Salt & Pepper Shakers Club, 581 Joy Road, Battle Creek, MI 49017.

Advertising
Ken–L–Ration, Fifi and Fido **15.00**
Kool Cigarettes, Willie and Millie Penguin, 1940s, 3½" h **65.00**
Pachmayr Gun Works, LA, shotgun shells, red, orig box **45.00**
Texaco, gas pumps, plastic, decal dec
. . . . **18.00**
Amish Couple, cast metal, painted, 3½" h
. . . . **10.00**
Bananas, ceramic, yellow and tan **6.50**
Black Children, 3 pc set, 3" high figures in 4" h yellow and pink nursery basket, sgd "Betson's Handpainted," Japan, 1930s
. . . . **30.00**
Cactus, china, Rosemeade **25.00**
Cake and Cut Slice, miniature **15.00**

Character
Aunt Jemima, Uncle Moses, 3½" h, plastic, yellow, black, and white accents on red ground, F & F Works, c1950
. . . . **35.00**
Campbell Kids, plastic, 1950s, 4½" h
. . . . **35.00**
Captain Midnight and Joyce Ryan, plaster, painted, 1940s **100.00**
Chilly Willy and Charlie Chicken, 4" h, china, 1958 Walter Lantz copyright
. . . . **80.00**
Dick Tracy and Tess Trueheart, 3" h, plaster, painted, Famous Features copyright, 1942 . . . . **65.00**
Donald Duck, 3" h, china, white glaze, blue, black, red, and yellow, Leeds, 1940s **25.00**
Christmas Trees, ceramic **20.00**
Cocker Spaniels, china **12.00**
Depression Glass
Banded Rings **40.00**
English Hobnail, pink **70.00**
Hazel Atlas, cobalt blue **24.00**
Starlight, clear **18.00**
Duck, stylized, blue glossy finish **35.00**
Dutch Boy and Girl, large, Shawnee **40.00**
Gay 90's Hat Rack, 6½" h, plastic and metal rack, yellow straw boater hat salt, black derby pepper, hats hang on rack, base holds toothpicks, orig box, 1954
. . . . **15.00**
Hammer and Nail, ceramic, gray nail, brown and black hammer **12.00**
Huggems, china
Bears
Tan **20.00**
Yellow **20.00**

Pattern Glass, Daisy & Cube, sapphire blue, orig top, $27.50.

Ducks, yellow and black **45.00**
Dutch Boy and Girl **35.00**
Rabbits
    White, ear mold flaw **20.00**
    Yellow **20.00**
Indian and Squaw, 3" h, composition wood, yellow and green accents on natural brown ground, copyright 1947 . . . **28.00**
Lawnmowers, plastic, 1950s **20.00**
Lobster, red on green base, claws held above head, attached by springs, Japan **24.00**
Pixies, ceramic, blue outfit, yellow hair **10.00**
Souvenir
    1939 New York World's Fair, 4" h, Perisphere and Trylon, hard plastic, one piece, orange, dark blue base **30.00**
    Florida, pink flamingos, hp, 3" h . . . **6.50**
    Mexico, man and woman nodders **30.00**
    New York, Empire State Building, Statue of Liberty, silvered cast metal   **8.00**
    State of Maryland, Parkcraft, 48 state series, figural state and blue clamshell, manufactured by Taneycomo Ceramic Factory, c1957 . . . . **20.00**
    Washington, DC, Washington Monument and White House, silvered cast metal **5.00**
Telephone and Directory, ceramic, black phone, white book with black lettering **8.00**
Thimble and Spool, miniature **15.00**
Turkeys, ceramic, multicolored **15.00**

SCHOOL MEMORABILIA

"School Days, School Days, good old golden rule days." Dad's been singing this refrain since he moved his operation into the former Vera Cruz elementary school in Pennsylvania. If you can't beat 'em, join 'em. Dad, this category is for you.

Advertising Trade Card, Henderson's Red School House Shoes **20.00**
Bell, No. 7, brass, turned wood handle **40.00**
Book, *School Memories,* 1920s, unused **18.00**
Calendar
    1915, "School Days," Hood's Sarsaparilla adv **70.00**
    1960, The Travelers Co, hanging   **11.00**
Catalog, JB Clow & Sons, *Modern Plumbing for Schools,* 1916, 88 slick pgs, photos and names of schools as nationwide clients, 9½ × 12" **45.00**
Certificate
    Indiana Young People's Reading Circle, 1896, organized by the State Teachers' Association, 5¼ × 3¼"   **10.00**

Teacher's Elementary School Certificate, Perry County, OH, 1905, sunrise over mountain vignette, 9¼ × 13" **15.00**
Clock, Seth Thomas, oak case, 8 day **150.00**
Cookie Jar, figural, bell, marked "ABC" **50.00**
Desk, student's
    Cherry, top folds up, cast iron scrolled sides **125.00**
    Formica, metal legs, rect top, c1950 . . . . **10.00**
    Oak, 18 × 22 × 20", drawer under seat with pencil tray **75.00**
Diploma, 19½ × 17¼", framed, PA, 1915 . . . . **50.00**
Game
    College Football, Milton Bradley, c1930 . . . . **45.00**
    Pinky Lee's Alphabet Game, 1950s **7.00**
Magazine, *Collier's,* "School Days" cov, Maxfield Parrish, 1908 . . . . **85.00**
Map, wall mount type, United States, orig wood case, varnished **45.00**
Penmanship Book, *Palmer Penmanship,* 135 pgs, 1908 . . . . **28.00**
Photograph, black and white, school children standing in front of school, oak leaves cover bare feet, c1935, 8 × 9½" **15.00**
Pin, horseshoe shape, "East Side School, Elk Rapids, Michigan" **25.00**
Pinback Button
    Bowdoin College, 1¼" d, Elijah Kellogg portrait, "Commencement of 1940," black and white, 1940s **3.00**
    Gaston Grammar School, 1" d, multicolored, c1915 . . . . **2.00**
    Yale College, 1¼" d, campus and founder illus, "150 Years Ago," black, white, and blue, 1896–1900 . . . . **5.00**
Pointer, wooden **18.50**
Post Card, Lincoln Building, Quakertown Schools, PA, black and white **5.00**
Program, Michigan vs Ohio, homecoming, football player illus cov, 36 pgs, 7 × 10", Nov 6, 1920 . . . . **40.00**
Report Card, Pupil's Report, neatly filled in, 1900 . . . . **3.00**
Reward of Merit
    Card of Approbation, 1871, 50 tokens of merit, Swiss landscape litho on back **5.00**
    Card of Honor, 1879, Diligency–One Hundred Tokens of Merit, multicolored chromolithograph **15.00**
    Card of Merit, Model Scholar, attached cut girl scrap, 1889 . . . . **10.00**
    Certificate Of Honor, 60 Merits, printed, red and white, 1877 . . . . **20.00**
    Excelsior, Fifty Merits, white and blue, gold trim, 1866 . . . . **10.00**
    Reward of Merit, schoolhouse illus, hp, reverse with student list, 1862   **6.00**

Pencil Case, Ronald McDonald, white plastic, red and yellow Ronald and character, 5" w, 10" h, unused, $4.50.

Testimonial of Approbation, 1872, black and white, 8½ × 10¼" **12.00**
Toledo Public Schools Grade One Card of Worth, 1876, blue and red   **8.00**
School Kit, Devoe Water Colors, Devoe & Raynolds Co **3.50**
Sheet Music
    Everybody Loves A College Girl, Kerry Mills, 1911 . . . . **5.00**
    Little Old Red Schoolhouse, Wheeler & Durham, 1890 . . . . **12.00**
    School Bells, Harris, Pfeiffer cov artist **10.00**
    School Day Sweethearts, Glen Edwards, 1923 . . . . **5.00**

Picture, The Little Red Schoolhouse, schoolroom scene, dunce in corner, little girl with red dress in center with dress up in back hooked to pigtails, multicolored, marked "Chesterfield Picture," 11 × 14", $5.00.

School Life, Charles L Johnson, Respectfully Dedicated to All Schools, 1912 ....**15.00**

The Schoolhouse Blues, Irving Berlin, 1921 ....**10.00**

Teacher's Pet, Allan Roberts and Jerome Brainin, 1937 ....**5.00**

You Don't Learn That In School, Nat King Cole, 1947 ....**4.00**

Slate, wood frame, felt bound **22.00**

SEBASTIAN MINIATURES

Prescott Baston, the originator and first designer of Sebastian figures, began production in 1938 in a plant located in Marblehead, Massachusetts. The handpainted, lightly glazed figures, ranging in size from three to four inches, were usually based on characters from literature and history.

Club: Sebastian Collector's Society, 321 Central Street, Hudson, MA 01749.

Abraham Lincoln, seated **125.00**
Barkis, 1946 ....**55.00**
Betsy Ross, #129 ....**85.00**
Evangeline, #12 ....**125.00**
Gabriel #11 ....**135.00**
Henry Hudson, #311 ....**175.00**

John Alden, $200.00.

Kennel Fresh, ashtray, #239 ....**300.00**
Mark Twain, #315 ....**100.00**
Parade Rest, #216 ....**100.00**
Peggotty, #52–A **85.00**
Santa Girl, lamppost, sgd **67.00**
Shaker Man, #1 ....**150.00**
St Joan of Arc, bronzed **275.00**
The Doctor, green, Marblehead label **110.00**
The Pilgrims, 1947 ....**65.00**
Thomas Jefferson, #124 ....**85.00**

SECONDHAND ROSES

This is a catchall category—designed specifically for those items which are bought solely for their utilitarian use. Anyone who regularly attends country auctions, flea markets, or garage sales has undoubtedly seen his fair share of "recycled" household goods. Ranging from wringer washers to electronic video games, these products and appliances are neither decorative nor financially lucrative. They are strictly secondhand merchandise.

There is not much reason to focus on brand names, with two exceptions—Maytag and Craftsman. First, Maytag, widely regarded as the Cadillac of washers and dryers, consistently realizes higher prices than any other brand. Second, Craftsman hand tools, distributed by Sears, generally bring higher prices due to the company's generous replacement policy.

As a result of advances in technology and space constraints in modern homes, several larger-sized appliances have little or no value on today's market. For example, console stereos and large chest freezers can often be had free for the hauling.

All items listed below are in good, clean condition. All parts are intact and appliances are in working order. The prices are designed to get you in the ballpark. Good luck in getting a hit.

APPLIANCES
Air Conditioner
    Purchased in Spring or Summer **75–100.00**
    Purchased in Fall or Winter **50–75.00**
    Purchased during heatwave, double the Spring/Summer price
Dehumidifier **20–30.00**
Dishwasher, portable
    1–5 years old **50–75.00**

    Over 5 years old **25–50.00**
Dryer
    Maytag
        1–5 years old **125–175.00**
        Over 5 years old **75–100.00**
    Other Brands
        1–5 years old **100.00**
        Over 5 years old **50–75.00**
Fan
    Oscillating
        Purchased in Summer **15–25.00**
        Purchased any other time **10–15.00**
    Window
        Purchased in Summer **10–20.00**
        Purchased any other time **5–15.00**
Floor Polisher **5–20.00**
Freezer
    Chest
        Large Size, less than 5 years old **5–10.00**
        Small Size, less than 5 years old **50.00**
        Over 5 years old, large or small **0–5.00**
    Upright
        Apartment Size
            1–5 years old **85–100.00**
            Over 5 years old **25–75.00**
        Full Size
            1–5 years old **125–175.00**
            Over 5 years old **50–100.00**
Humidifier **10–20.00**
Iron **2–5.00**
Microwave Oven
    Large, 1–5 years old **75–85.00**
    Small, 1–5 years old **50–60.00**
    With electronic controls or built–in turntable, add **5–10.00**
Mixer, countertop, two bowls ...**10–12.00**
Refrigerator
    Apartment Size
        1–5 years old **85–100.00**
        Over 5 years old **50–75.00**
    Dormitory or Bar Size **25–50.00**
    Full Size
        1–5 years old **150–200.00**
        Over 5 years old **100–125.00**
    Side–by–Side Model, deduct **10–20.00**
    With Ice Maker, add **20.00**
Rug Shampooer **10–20.00**
Sewing Machine, modern, electric
    Cabinet Model
        Standard, no frills **25–50.00**
        Assorted attachments and stitching variations **50–75.00**
    Portable **25–30.00**
Small Kitchen Appliances (blender, corn popper, electric knife, hand–held mixer, toaster) **2–10.00**
Space Heater **5–15.00**
Toaster Oven **10–20.00**
Vacuum Cleaner, canister or upright **15–35.00**

Washer
  Apartment Size, 1–5 years old
  ....**75–150.00**
  Full Size
    Maytag
      1–5 years old **200–250.00**
      Over 5 years old ...**150–175.00**
    Other Brands
      1–5 years old **150–200.00**
      Over 5 years old ...**100–150.00**
  Wringer Washer
    Maytag
      Square aluminum tub
      ....**200–250.00**
      Other models **50–60.00**
    Other Brands **25–35.00**

CHILDREN'S ITEMS
Car Seat **5–10.00**
Crib, wood **20–30.00**
Highchair, metal, plastic, and vinyl
  ....**10–15.00**
Playpen, tubular steel frame, mesh sides
  ....**10–15.00**
Stroller **10–15.00**

ENTERTAINMENT & RECREATION
Card Table, four chairs **20–25.00**
Entertainment Center, adjustable shelves
  ....**25–50.00**
Exercise Equipment
  Bicycle, stationary **10–25.00**
  Rowing Machine **20–30.00**
  Stepper **25–50.00**
  Weight Lifting Bench **5–15.00**
  Weights, barbell, two dumbbells, and
    110 lbs weights **25–30.00**
Movie Projector, 8mm or Super 8
  ....**5–20.00**
Projection Screen **10–15.00**
Slide Projector **15–25.00**
Stereo
  Console, wood cabinet, record player
    and radio combination **0–25.00**
  Turntable, two speakers, name brand
    ....**10–25.00**
Television
  Black and White, console or portable,
    any age **0–10.00**
  Color
    Console
      1–5 years old, remote control
      ....**75–150.00**
      Over 5 years old **35–50.00**
    Portable
      1–5 years old, remote control
      ....**75–150.00**
      Over 5 years old **50–75.00**
Television Snack Tables, set of four, rack
  ....**2–5.00**
Television Stand, casters **5–10.00**
VCR
  Beta **0.00**
  VHS
    1–5 years old **100–125.00**
    Over 5 years old **75–85.00**

Video Game System
  Full Size
    Nintendo **20–30.00**
    Sega Genesis, Super Nintendo (en-
      hanced graphics) **75–100.00**
  Hand Held, with power pack
    Atari Lynx **20–40.00**
    Nintendo Game Boy **25–50.00**
    Sega Game Gear **50–65.00**
  Video Games, any size, any brand
    ....**5–25.00**

MISCELLANEOUS HOUSEHOLD GOODS
Dinnerware, service for eight **25–50.00**
Flatware, service for eight, stainless steel
  ....**15–20.00**
Kerosene Heater **35–50.00**
Linens (afghans, bedspreads, blankets) like–
  new condition **5–10.00**
Pots and Pans, 8 pc set
  Aluminum **25–30.00**
  Copper Bottom **50–75.00**
  Stainless Steel **35–50.00**
Stemware, three sizes, 24 pcs ...**35–45.00**
Wardrobe, metal **15–20.00**
Water Glasses, set of eight **2–5.00**

OFFICE EQUIPMENT
Answering Machine **10–15.00**
Computer, monitor, more than 2 years old
  ....**10–50.00**
Computer Desk **15–30.00**
Desk, steel, gray, industrial **5–10.00**
Filing Cabinet, metal
  Two Drawer **20–25.00**
  Four Drawer **40–45.00**
Metal Shelving **5–10.00**
Telephone **5–10.00**
Typewriter
  Electric **15–20.00**
  Electronic **25–40.00**
  Manual **5–10.00**

TOOLS AND GARDENING EQUIPMENT
Garden Tools
  Electric Hedge Trimmer, edger, leaf
    blower **8–15.00**
  Hoe, rake, shovel **2–5.00**

Teapot, yellow and pink roses, small white flower, green leaves, white ground, gold trim, imp "Made In England," "A. W. Wood, England" mark, $10.00.

Hand Tools (hammer, pliers, saw, screw-
  driver, wrench)
  Craftsman **5–8.00**
  Other Brands **2–5.00**
Ladder
  Extension
    Aluminum **45–50.00**
    Wooden **25–30.00**
  Step
    4' **8–10.00**
    6' **12–15.00**
Lawn Mower
  Electric **15–25.00**
  Gas
    Purchased in Spring or Summer
    ....**35–50.00**
    Purchased in Fall or Winter
    ....**25–40.00**
  Rotary **0–5.00**
Lawn Sweeper **5–10.00**
Power Tools (drill, grinder, saber saw,
  sander) **10–20.00**
Snowblower
  Purchased in Spring or Summer
    ....**35–50.00**
  Purchased in Fall or Winter
    ....**50–75.00**
  Purchased during or after major snow-
    storm, double the Fall/Winter price
Weed Wacker
  Electric **15–20.00**
  Gas **20–30.00**
Wheelbarrow **10–20.00**

SEWING ITEMS

This is a wide-open area. While many favor sterling silver items, only fools overlook objects made of celluloid, ivory, other metals, plastic, and wood. An ideal special collection would be sewing items that contain advertising.

Collecting sewing items has received a big boost as a result of the Victorian craze. During the Victorian era a vast assortment of practical and whimsical sewing devices were marketed. Look for items such as tape measures, pincushions, stilettos for punchwork, crochet hooks, and sewing birds (beware of reproductions).

Modern sewing collectors are focusing on needle threaders, needle holders, and sewing kits from hotels and motels. The general term for this material is "Twenty Pocket" because pieces fit neatly into twenty-pocket plastic notebook sleeves.

Advertising Trade Card
  Clarks, ONT Thread, boy fishing   **8.00**
  Domestic Sewing Machine Co, "Prize
    Lincoln Buck Wilton," **8.00**

J P Coats, black boy sitting on spool of
thread, "We Never Fade" **5.00**
The New Home Sewing Machine, child
with book **18.00**
Singer Sewing Machine, opens, "The
Tea Party, Mothers Helper," 1899
.... **20.00**
Booklet, *How To Make Children's Clothes*,
Singer, 1930 .... **8.00**
Bookmark, Merrick Spool Cotton **10.00**
Buttonhole Scissors, Germany **12.00**
Catalog
Davis Sewing Machine Co, Watertown,
NY, 1895, 18 pgs **25.00**
Domestic Sewing Machine, New York,
NY, 1883, 26 pgs **32.00**
M J Cunning Co, Cincinnati, OH, 1909,
20 pgs, needlework and embroidery
supplies **16.00**
New Home Sewing Machine, New York,
NY, 1900, 12 pgs **12.00**
Ormond Manufacturing Co, Baltimore,
MD, 1878, 96 pgs, various sewing
machines and accessories **75.00**
Singer Manufacturing Co, NJ, 1900, 8
pgs **24.00**
Wilson Sewing Machine Co, Chicago,
IL, 26 pgs **38.00**
Chatelaine, silver, three love tokens, 1880s
.... **100.00**
Darner
Egg, black **4.00**
Slipper shape, maple wood base, 5½" l
.... **8.00**
Darning Kit, folder, leather, dog on cov
.... **12.00**
Doll, 12" h, Simplicity, complete with pat-
tern book and tape measure **70.00**
Embroidery Tufting Machine, Perfection,
orig box, dated 1800s **85.00**
Manual
Butterick, needle art, color illus, 1922
.... **20.00**
Singer, #221 .... **35.00**
Mending Kit
Bakelite, red and ivory **20.00**
Enameled, green, tape measure in base
.... **20.00**
Needle and Shuttle Case, 16" d, metal, ap-
prox 100 wood containers, Boye **165.00**
Needle Book, A Century of Progress, com-
plete **6.00**
Needle Case
Bone, turned, awl tip **60.00**
Sterling Silver **40.00**
Pincushion
Advertising, Traveler's Insurance ... **8.00**
Doll, arms at head **10.00**
Open flower, linen **15.00**
Persian Cat, Victorian, figural, pot metal
.... **52.00**
Pin Tray, Columbian Stoves adv **10.00**
Sewing Box, 10¾" d, 6½" h, wicker, pink
.... **75.00**
Sewing Machine
Household, treadle, walnut **165.00**

Singer
221 Featherweight, black, orig case
.... **200.00**
Featherweight, century medallion, at-
tachments, orig case **350.00**
Sewing Scissors, Oriental silk case ... **20.00**
Tape Measure
Advertising
Arrowhead Co–Op Creamery   **15.00**
Colman's Mustard, celluloid, white,
yellow illus, black lettering   **25.00**
Hoover Vacuum Cleaner, figural,
canister type **75.00**
Illinois Surgical Supply Co, black,
white, and orange **30.00**
Miami Laundry/Fancy Dry Cleaners
.... **22.00**
Figural, Indian, marked "Japan"   **20.00**
Plastic, apple shape **30.00**
Walnut, squirrel charm pull **40.00**
Thimble
Advertising, Hoover–Home–Happiness
.... **10.00**
Sterling Silver, figural
Kitten with ball **45.00**
Teddy Bear **75.00**

SHAWNEE POTTERY

The Shawnee Pottery company was
founded in Zanesville, Ohio, in 1937.
The plant, formerly home to the American Encaustic Tiling Company, produced approximately 100,000 pieces of
pottery per working day. Shawnee produced a large selection of kitchenware,
dinnerware, and decorative art pottery.
The company ceased operations in
1961.

Club: Shawnee Pottery Collectors Club,
PO Box 713, New Smyrna Beach, FL
32170.

Bowl
Corn King, #6, 6½" d **30.00**
Corn Queen, #5 .... **25.00**
Casserole, cov
Corn King, #74, large **50.00**
Lobster, French style, 2 quart **30.00**
Cookie Jar
Dutch Girl, gold trim **225.00**
Lucky Elephant, gold trim **595.00**
Mugsey **425.00**
Puss 'N Boots **160.00**
Smiley Pig
Chrysanthemum **325.00**
Gold Trim, blue bib, black hooves,
decals **375.00**
Shamrocks **245.00**
Winking Owl **165.00**
Winnie Pig
Blue Collar **325.00**
Green Collar **325.00**
Corn Dish, Corn King, oval **25.00**

Planter, Wishing Well, green, marked "710,"
8½ x 5¼", $18.00.

Creamer
Cat, yellow and green **55.00**
Corn King **22.00**
Elephant **35.00**
Puss 'N Boots **35.00**
Cup, Corn King, #90 .... **28.00**
Figurine, Pekingese **50.00**
Grease Jar, no lid, Pennsylvania Dutch
.... **25.00**
Incense Burner, Chinaman, blue base,
marked "USA," 5" h **30.00**
Lamp, Oriental figures, tall, pr **20.00**
Marmalade, cov, Fruits **37.00**
Pitcher
Boy Blue, decals, gold trim **250.00**
Charlie Chicken **80.00**
Fruits, juice **50.00**
Gray, dolphin handle, 1 quart ... **15.00**
Smiley Pig
Clover Bud **250.00**
Red Flower **145.00**
Red Scarf **135.00**
Planter
Antique Car, gold trim **20.00**
Doe, pr, yellow and maroon **14.00**
Flying Goose **13.00**
Oriental Man, #537 .... **25.00**
Pixie Boot, green, gold trim **14.00**
Plate
Corn King, dinner, #68 .... **15.00**
Corn Queen, #69 .... **15.00**
Platter, Corn King, #96 .... **40.00**
Salt and Pepper Shakers, pr
Corn King, range **20.00**
Dutch Boy and Girl, large **60.00**
Fruits **27.00**
Milk Can **20.00**
Mugsey, large **145.00**
Pennsylvania Dutch, #210 ...... **25.00**
Puss 'N Boots, small **25.00**
Smiley Pig
Large, green bib **135.00**
Small, clover bud **75.00**
Smiley Pig and Winnie Pig, green, small
.... **55.00**
Sprinkling Cans, small **15.00**
Winking Owls, small **15.00**
Sugar Shaker, White Corn **55.00**
Teapot
#309 .... **50.00**
Corn King, #65, individual **100.00**

Granny Anne, peach apron **150.00**
Tom the Piper's Son **95.00**
White Corn, 30 oz **75.00**
Vase, Bowknot, green **13.00**

SHEET MUSIC

Just like post cards, this is a category whose ten cent and quarter days are a thing of the past. Decorators and dealers have discovered the cover value of sheet music. The high-ticket sheets are sold to specialized collectors, not sheet music collectors.

You can put a sheet music collection together covering almost any topic imaginable. Be careful about stacking your sheets on top of one another. The ink on the covers tends to bleed. If you can afford the expense, put a sheet of acid-free paper between each sheet. Do not, repeat do not, repair any tears with Scotch or similar brand tape. It discolors over time. When removed, it often leaves a gummy residue behind.

Clubs: City of Roses Sheet Music Collectors Club, 13447 Bush St SE, Portland, OR 97236; National Sheet Music Society, 1597 Fair Park Ave, Los Angeles, CA 90041; New York Sheet Music Society, PO Box 1214, Great Neck, NY 11023; Ragtime Society, PO Box 520, Station A, Weston, Ontario, Canada M9N 3N3; Remember That Song, 5623 N 64th Ave, Glendale, AZ 85301.

Periodical: *Sheet Music Magazine,* 352 Evelyn St, Paramus, NJ 07653.

All Bound Round With A Woolen String, Charles Seamon, 1898 . . . . **15.00**
America I Love You, Edgar Leslie and Archie Gottler, Sophie Tucker cov photo, 1915 . . . . **25.00**
Anything You Can Do, Irving Berlin, from movie *Annie Get Your Gun,* 1946 **5.00**
Beatrice Fairfax, Grant Clark, Joseph Mc-Carthy and James V Monaco, 1915 **5.00**
Beautiful Isle of Somewhere, "As Sung At Funeral Of Our Martyred President William McKinley," Jessie Brown Pounds and John S Fearis, 1923 . . . . **25.00**
By The Time I Get To Phoenix, Jim Webb, Glen Campbell cov photo, 1967 **3.00**
Chicken Chowder, Irene Giblin, 1905 **15.00**
Daddy Has A Sweetheart And Mother Is Her Name, Gene Buck and Dave Stamper, 1912 . . . . **10.00**
Dance Of The Fireflies, E T Paull and Sentenis **35.00**
Don't Take My Darling Boy Away, Will Dillon and Albert Von Tilzer, 1915 . . . . **15.00**

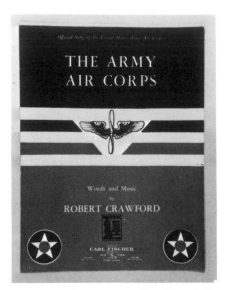

The Army Air Corps, *words and music by Robert Crawford, "Official Song of the United States Army Air Corps," $3.00.*

Everybody Loves A College Girl, Kerry Mills, 1911 . . . . **10.00**
For The First Time, I've Fallen In Love, Charles Tobias and David Kapp, Kay Kyser photo, 1943 . . . . **5.00**
Ghost of John James Christopher Benjamin Bings, 1887 . . . . **15.00**
Good For Nothin' But Love, William Kernell and Harlan Thompson, from movie *The Big Party,* Sue Carol and Dixie Lee photo, 1930 . . . . **10.00**
Have A Smile For Everyone You Meet, J Keirn Brennan, Paul Cunningham, and Bert Rule, Corinne Griffith photo, 1918 . . . . **5.00**
High & Mighty, John Wayne, 1954 **20.00**
I Got Rhythm, Ira and George Gershwin, 1930 . . . . **5.00**
I'll Be In My Dixie Home Again To-Morrow, Roy Turk and J Russell Robinson, 1922 . . . . **10.00**
In My Canoe, Isham Jones and O E Story, 1913 . . . . **3.00**
I've Got The Profiteering Blues, Al Wilson and Irving Bibo, 1920 . . . . **10.00**
Let's Sail To Dreamland, Harry Kogen, Henry Busse, and Lou Holzer, 1938 . . . . **3.00**
Love Among The Whispering Pines, Charles B Weston, 1913 . . . . **10.00**
Mikado, Gilbert and Sullivan, Pfeiffer cover artist **10.00**
My Wubba Dolly, Kay and Sue Werner, 1939 . . . . **5.00**
Nothing Lives Longer Than Love, Sam M Lewis and Pete Wendling, Wayne King photo, 1935 . . . . **3.00**
Pickles & Peppers, Adaline Sheperd, 1907 . . . . **20.00**
Russian Rag, Cobb, 1918 . . . . **10.00**

She Is More To Be Pitied Than Censored, W B Grey, 1898 . . . . **10.00**
Silver Sleigh Bells, E T Paull, large folio **50.00**
Some Enchanted Evening, Richard Rodgers and Oscar Hammerstein II, from musical *South Pacific,* signed Ezzio Pinza cov, 1949 . . . . **10.00**
Song of the Alumnaie/Albany Female Academy, 1850s **40.00**
Sunflower Tickle, Benjamin Richmond, 1908 . . . . **10.00**
That's What Makes A Wild Cat Wild, Norton, 1908 . . . . **25.00**
Umbrella Man, James Cavanaugh, Larry Stock, and Vincent Rose, Kay Kyser photo, 1938 . . . . **3.00**
Way Up Yonder, James Bland **15.00**
Where The Butterflies Kiss The Buttercups Good-Night, Harry Pease, Charles O'Flynn, and Ed G Nelson, 1929 **5.00**

SHOE-RELATED COLLECTIBLES

This is a category with sole. Nothing more needs to be said.

Advertising Trade Card
A S T Co. Shoe Tips, Father Time, Donaldson Bros **9.00**
Bixby & Co Shoe Polish, Lady Liberty holding shoe polish **8.00**
Herrods $5.00 Shoes, drum shape, Bufford Litho **7.50**
Alarm Clock, Star Brand Shoes, Gilbert **50.00**
Bag, paper, Red Goose Shoes, 25 pcs **15.00**
Cabinet, Shoe Lace Service Station, tin, Woodlawn Mills Shoe Laces, orig marquee, 11½" w, 14" h **1,250.00**
Charm, miner's knee boots, made from compressed anthracite coal, pr attached to orig card, c1930 . . . . **50.00**
Clicker, Peters Weatherbird Shoes, litho tin, multicolored, trademark bird, 1930s **30.00**
Comic Book, premium, PF Magic Shoe Adventure Book, *Rocket Kids Moon Story,* BF Goodrich, 1962 . . . . **22.00**
Display
Red Goose Shoes, papier mache goose with nodding head and glass eyes, 13" w, 24" h **1,000.00**
US Rubber Boot, large buckled rubber boot made from Froyal tempered rubber, working brass buckles, 28" h **150.00**
Flyswatter, wire, wood handle, Blount's Shoes Are Better on one side, other with Scripps-Reno Co, Dry Goods, Cloaks and Suits **4.00**
Key Tag, Armour Leather Company, shoe sole shape, brown leather, inscribed "Leather—Key To Foot Health," c1930 . . . . **15.00**

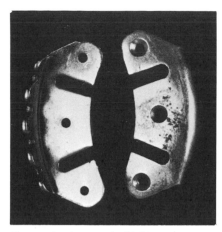

German toe taps, each, $8.00.

Mask, premium, Weatherbird Shoes, set of
three **75.00**
Miniature, cast lead, replica man's wing–tip
oxford shoe, bottom inscribed "Walk–
Over, 90th Anniversary," c1940 **12.00**
Mirror, pocket, adv
Brown Shoe Co, White House **150.00**
Cherry Blossom Boot Polish, product tin
illus, 1920s **60.00**
Penknife
Advertising, Kinney Shoes, colonial style
blade and bottle opener **45.00**
Figural Shoe, low cut button shoe, black
celluloid, single steel blade marked
"Wadsworth, Germany" and in-
scribed "Atlantic City" and "Mary"
. . . . **32.00**
Pinback Button, adv
All America Shoe, eagle over inscription,
white ground, blue and red lettering
. . . . **15.00**

*Puzzle, The Whole Family Saves at Thom
McAn's, Thom McAn, 1932, 100 diecut cardboard pieces, double sided, Gambling's Gang
scene on reverse, 10¼ × 13", $35.00.*

Hanover Shoe, red and black high button shoe and inscription, white
ground, dated 1905 . . . . **25.00**
Kirkendall Shoes, black and white high
button shoe illus, blue and white
border inscription **18.00**
Tess and Ted School Shoes, multi-
colored, well dressed boy and girl
illus, white ground **30.00**
Plaque, hanging, two sided, copper clad
over plaster, three dimensional figure
and high button shoe mounted on ornate
shelf bracket each side, female one side,
well–dressed gentleman other side
. . . . **650.00**
Salesman Sample, shoe, Thom McAn, com-
position, orig shoe box **85.00**
Shoe Buttonhook, The Savings Store, Kalamazoo, MI **12.50**
Shoehorn
A S Beck Shoes, metal, 1940s **5.00**
Queen Quality, 2 × 6", celluloid, curled
handle, color portrait of lady, c1900,
pr **35.00**
Shoe Shine Kit, child's, Shinola, 1953, MIB
. . . . **20.00**
Sign, Selz Royal Blue Shoe, Chicago, glass,
acid etched and reverse painted, blue,
white, and silver, 20 × 16" **200.00**
String Holder, Red Goose Shoes, hanging,
diecut tin goose above holder, 14" w,
27" h **825.00**
Tin, Shinola Shoe Polish, round, flat, litho,
2" d **18.00**
Toy Top, Peters Weatherbird, litho tin, blue,
yellow, and red, inscription "Peters
Weatherbird, Solid Leather Shoes,"
wood dowel, 1930s **25.00**

SILVER FLATWARE

Popularity of a pattern, not necessarily age, is the key to pricing silver
flatware. Since most individuals buy by
pattern, buy only from dealers who have
done the research and properly identified each piece that they are selling. Deduct fifty percent from the value if a
piece has a monogram.

If you are planning to buy a set, expect to pay considerably less than if you
were buying the pieces individually. Set
prices should be bargain prices.

Alaska Silver, German Silver, Lashar
Silver, and Nickel Silver are alloys designed to imitate silver plate. Do not be
fooled.

Asparagus Tongs, Buttercup, Gorham
. . . . **120.00**
Beef Fork, Hanover, Gorham **65.00**
Berry Fork, Hanover, Gorham **30.00**
Berry Spoon
Buttercup, Gorham **85.00**
Isis, Gorham **400.00**

Bonbon Spoon, Celeste, Gorham **15.00**
Cheese Knife, Hanover, Gorham **70.00**
Citrus Spoon, Beaumont, Gorham . . . **13.00**
Coffee Spoon, Chantilly, Gorham **15.00**
Cream Soup
Champlain, Amston **15.00**
Chapel Bells, Alvin **15.00**
Chateau Rose, Alvin **14.00**
Southern Grandeur, Easterling **14.00**
Dessert Spoon, Medici Old, Gorham **32.00**
Dinner Fork, Bridal Bouquet, Alvin **23.00**
Egg Spoon, Ivy, Gorham **32.00**
Fish Fork, Hanover, Gorham **35.00**
Fork, Poppy, Gorham **75.00**
Gravy Ladle
Grecian, Gorham **95.00**
Southern Grandeur, Easterling **30.00**
Individual Butter
Camelia, flat handle, Gorham **11.00**
Celeste, hollow handle, Gorham **13.00**
Champlain, flat handle, Amston **14.00**
Chapel Bells, flat handle, Alvin . . . **12.00**
Lasagna Server
Chantilly, Gorham **26.00**
Dauphin, Durgin **25.00**
Lemon Fork, Bridal Bouquet, Alvin **14.00**
Lunch Fork
Bridal Bouquet, Alvin **21.00**
Buttercup, Gorham **17.00**
Camelia, Gorham **19.00**
Chantilly, Gorham **17.00**
Chateau Rose, Alvin **19.00**
Medici Old, Gorham **30.00**
Master Butter
Celeste, hollow handle, Gorham **14.00**
Chapel Bells, flat handle, Alvin . . . **13.00**
Southern Grandeur, flat handle, Eas-
terling **12.00**
Olive Spoon, Hanover, Gorham **28.00**
Oval Soup, Celeste, Gorham **17.00**
Pasta Scoop
Buttercup, Gorham **25.00**
Chantilly, Gorham **25.00**
Pickle Fork, Chantilly, Gorham **16.00**
Pie Knife, Isis, Gorham **500.00**
Pierced Tablespoon, Marie Louise,
Blackinton **49.00**
Place Spoon, Buttercup, Gorham **28.00**
Preserve Spoon, Ivy, Gorham **110.00**
Pudding Spoon, Grecian, Gorham **150.00**
Punch Ladle, Buttercup, hollow handle,
Gorham **27.00**

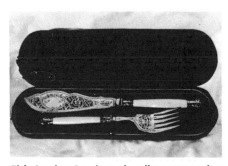

*Fish Serving Set, ivory handles, ornate dec,
fitted case, $95.00.*

Salad Fork, Bridal Bouquet, Alvin ... **20.00**
Salt Spoon, Grecian, Gorham **35.00**
Seafood Fork, Medici Old, Gorham **22.00**
Soup Ladle
    Buttercup, Gorham **155.00**
    Chantilly, Gorham **155.00**
Sugar Spoon
    Bridal Bouquet, Alvin **15.00**
    Camelia, Gorham **13.00**
    Celeste, Gorham **16.00**
    Chapel Bells, Alvin **14.00**
    Chateau Rose, Alvin **13.00**
    Marie Louise, Blackinton **35.00**
Tablespoon, Southern Grandeur, Easterling
    .... **28.00**

Teaspoon
    Bridal Bouquet, Alvin **13.00**
    Camelia, Gorham **10.00**
    Celeste, Gorham **12.00**
    Champlain, Amston **13.00**
    Chapel Bells, Alvin **11.00**
    Chateau Rose, Alvin **12.00**
    Marie Louise, Blackinton **45.00**
    Poppy, Gorham **22.00**
    Southern Grandeur, Easterling **11.00**

SILVER, PLATED

G. R. and H. Ekington of England are credited with inventing the electrolytic method of plating silver in 1838. In late nineteenth-century pieces, the base metal was often Britannia, an alloy of tin, copper, and antimony. Copper and brass also were used as bases. Today the base is usually nickel silver.

Rogers Bros., Hartford, Connecticut, introduced the silver plating process to the United States in 1847. By 1855 a large number of silver plating firms were established.

Extensive polishing will eventually remove silver plating. However, today's replating process is so well developed that you can have a piece replated in such a manner that the full detail of the original is preserved.

Identifying companies and company marks is difficult. Fortunately there is Dorothy Rainwater's *Encyclopedia of American Silver Manufacturers, 3rd Edition* (Schiffer Publishing, 1986).

Bowl, Derby Silver Company, foliate
    repousse, figure of squirrel on oak
    branch, 9" h **325.00**
Bread Tray, Daffodil **95.00**
Butter Dish, three pcs, base, lid, and insert,
    delicate double rows of tiny beading, cut
    glass drip trap, Meriden Silver Plate Co
    .... **50.00**
Cake Basket, swing handle, Tufts **55.00**
Cheese Ball Frame, 5" d, mechanical, elabo-
    rate border, E G Webster & Sons **75.00**

Cigar Case, 5" l, scrollwork and leaf dec,
    holds three cigars **35.00**
Cigar Holder, 10½" h, champagne bottle,
    beaded trim, engraved "CIGARS,"
    Graham Silver marks **75.00**
Cigarette Lighter, Ronson, oval, Art Nou-
    veau design, ftd **18.00**
Compact, triangular, hand mirror shape, lip-
    stick concealed in handle, int and ext
    mirrors, turquoise cabochon thumbpiece
    .... **135.00**
Creamer and Sugar, marked "Meriden"
    .... **100.00**
Cruet Set, Victorian, cut glass bottles, minor
    nicks, 19th C, 10¾" h **350.00**
Cup, baby's, two handles, monogrammed
    .... **20.00**
Flask, pocket, emb, cup lid **75.00**
Flatware Service, luncheon set, twelve
    knives and forks, two crumbers, serving
    knife and fork, engraved blades, ivory
    handles **125.00**
Ice Bucket, Baroque pattern, thermos lined,
    Wallace **225.00**
Knife Rest, dolphin, marked "Pairpoint"
    .... **35.00**
Matchsafe, dog and quail dec **25.00**
Napkin Ring
    Dog, pulling sled, emb greyhounds on
        sides, engraved "Sara," Meriden
        .... **165.00**
    Floral Bouquets, Victorian **15.00**
Salt, ornate, blue ruffled top, liner ... **25.00**
Sugar Spoon, ornate **8.00**
Syrup, geometric and floral strap work
    body, figural finial, Meriden, 1865, re-
    plated **85.00**
Tatting Shuttle **25.00**
Tea Strainer, wood handle, Hallmark, 1917
    .... **30.00**

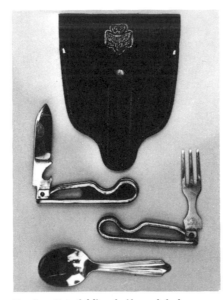

Feeding Set, folding knife and fork, spoon, leather case with gold Girl Scout emblem, $12.00.

Toothpick Holder
    Colonial Lady **65.00**
    Rooster, engraved "Picks," 2" h **48.00**
Umbrella Stand, elongated trumpet shape,
    interlaced flowering branches, H Wilkin-
    son & Co, copper showing, 20½" h
    .... **225.00**
Wick Trimmer, floral dec, tray, Hallmark
    .... **85.00**

SMOKEY BEAR COLLECTIBLES

It is hard to believe that Smokey Bear has been around for fifty years, but on August 9th, 1994, the National Forest Service's Number One Celebrity became half a century old. The popularity of Smokey started during the Second World War as part of a national-awareness campaign for the prevention of forest fires. The National Forest Service ran slogans like "Keep 'Em Green; Forests are Vital to National Defense" in an attempt to keep the public's attentions on the war effort.

From then to now Smokey has been more the just a crusader for fire awareness and prevention; he has been a collectible character and a source of enjoyment to many admirers. There were a wide variety of Smokey collectibles produced: watches, radios, toys, posters, coloring books, and many games and books. Most had short production runs and were used as Forest Service giveaways or were sold by a select number of department store chains.

Good luck in your collecting, and remember, only you can prevent forest fires.

Activity Book **20.00**
Ashtray, figural
    Log shape, ceramic, raised Smokey head
        on one end, other with "Prevent For-
        est Fires," 1950s, 3½ × 4½ × 6"
        .... **50.00**
    Smokey Bear, trees and sign on tray, foil
        label "Reg Pat Off Norcrest Japan"
        .... **95.00**
Bank, figural, white, gold trim **65.00**
Bookmark, ruler on reverse, 1961, 8" l
    .... **5.00**
Board Game, Smokey Bear Game, Milton
    Bradley, 1968 .... **18.00**
Candy Container, figural **350.00**
Coloring Sheet, pr, 8½ × 11" **5.00**
Comic Book, No. 1016, four color, 1959
    .... **15.00**
Cracker Jack Premium, storybook, card-
    board cov, 2½ × 3¾" **18.00**
Fan, adv, 1950s **45.00**

Children's Book, **The Smokey Bear Book,** *Golden Shape Book, Mel Crawford, Western Publishing Co, 24 pgs, 1970, 8 x 8", $10.00.*

Figure, cigarette, "Snuffit" **12.00**
Flyer, colorful, 1959, 3½ × 6" **5.00**
Lunch Box, black vinyl, King–Seely Thermos Co, c1965, 7 × 9½ × 4" . . . **85.00**
Music Box, chipped **25.00**
Pinback Button
  "Join Smokey's Campaign, Prevent Forest Fires!," yellow and brown, 1970s, 1½" d **12.00**
  "Keep America Green/Save A Tree," light green, black Smokey illus and lettering, 1½" d **10.00**
  "Smokey Bear Is Alive & Well!, Prevent Forest Fires," yellow, brown lettering, 1980s **8.00**
Ring, brass, expandable, figural Smokey with raised hand and shovel, 1970s
  . . . . **25.00**
Salt and Pepper Shakers, china, yellow muzzle and hat, blue trousers, brown body, salt holding shovel, pepper holding bucket, 1960s, 4" h **20.00**
Sheet Music **5.00**
Sign, cardboard, hanging, "Smokey Time," clock face with movable hands, Virginia Division of Forestry, c1960, 18 × 24"
  . . . . **45.00**
Soaky Bottle, figural **17.00**
Tab **5.00**

SOAKIES

Soaky bottles are plastic bubble bath containers molded in the shape of popular children's characters. The first Soakies were marketed by the Colgate–Palmolive Company in the 1960s and were an innovative marketing tool designed to convince kids (especially boys) that "Bathtime is Funtime."

As with any profitable idea, copycats soon appeared. One successful line produced by the Purex Company was called the Bubble Club. These containers were fashioned after Hanna–Barbera characters.

The bottles included in this category are all plastic figural containers and range in size from 6" to 11" high.

Colgate–Palmolive, Soaky
  Alvin Chipmunk, holding harmonica behind back, baseball cap lid, 1963, 8" h **20.00**
  Bambi, removable head, 1963, 9" h
    . . . . **20.00**
  Bozo the Clown, Bozo name on each wrist, "Bozo The Clown" and "Capitol Records" on bottom, removable head, mid 1960s, 10" h **25.00**
  Brutus, wearing red and white striped shirt, red pants, 1964, 10" h   **18.00**
  Bugs Bunny
    8½" h, soft vinyl cylinder figure fits over bottle, 1960s, 8½" h   **35.00**
    10½" h, removable head, hard plastic, mid 1960s **30.00**
  Bullwinkle Moose, removable head, stiff brown inserted antlers, mid 1960s, 11" h **35.00**
  Casper, removable head, Harvey Cartoons copyright, mid 1960s, 10" h
    . . . . **37.00**
  Creature From The Black Lagoon, metallic green, removable head, 1963, 10" h **60.00**
  Deputy Dawg, removable red hat, undated Terrytoons copyright, mid 1960s, 8½" h **23.00**
  Elmer Fudd, removable head, 1963, 9" h
    . . . . **20.00**
  Frankenstein, removable head airbrushed in peach flesh tones, early prototype, 1963, 10" h **125.00**
  Jiminy Cricket, removable head, 1963, 10" h **20.00**
  Mighty Mouse,
    8½" h, arms folded across chest, plain cap, 1963 copyright   **10.00**
    10" h, removable head, arms at sides, 1965 copyright **35.00**
  Mr Magoo, removable head, 1963, 10" h
    . . . . **24.00**
  Mummy, white body, green removable head, 1963, 10" h **65.00**
  Muskie, removable head, 1965, 10" h
    . . . . **12.00**
  Pinocchio, Disney, 1960s, 9½" h   **25.00**
  Pluto, removable head, 1963, 10" h
    . . . . **17.00**
  Popeye, holding anchor, standing on rope spool, removable head, 1964, 10" h **20.00**
  Rocky Squirrel, removable head, mid 1960s, 9" h **22.00**
  Simon Chipmunk, holding book behind back, removable head, 1963, 10" h
    . . . . **20.00**
  Smokey Bear, removable yellow hat lid, 1963, 9" h **25.00**
  Speedy Gonzales, 10" h **20.00**
  Sylvester Cat, 1960s, 10" h **15.00**
  Tennessee Tuxedo, removable head, eating ice cream, orig box, 10" h
    . . . . **25.00**
  Theodore Chipmunk, standing on bucket, holding sandwich behind back, removable head, 1963, 10" h
    . . . . **22.00**
  Top Cat, removable head, 1963, 10" h
    . . . . **18.00**
  Tweety Bird, 1960s, 10" h **18.00**
  Wendy, removable head, Harvey Cartoons copyright, mid 1960s, 10¼" h
    . . . . **18.00**
  Wolfman, metallic copper colored figure, removable head, painted pants, wearing tattered V–neck shirt, early prototype, 1963, 10" h **125.00**
  Woody Woodpecker, removable red topknot, 1960s, 9" h **12.00**
Purex
  Atom Ant, removable head, 9" h   **30.00**
  Bamm–Bamm, green and white outfit, black club, 1960s, 8½" h **26.00**
  Dino, purple body with black spots, tan muzzle and hair, trap in underside, 1960s, 10¾" h **20.00**
  Huckleberry Hound, Bubble Club Fun Bath, bank, hard plastic removable head, marked "Knickerbocker" on bottom, 1960s, 10" h **18.00**
  Pebbles
    8½" h, removable cap, 1960s
      Brown and black outfit, red–brown hair **18.00**

Mr Jinks with Pixie and Dixie, Hanna Barbera Productions, Inc, Purex Corp, Ltd, early 1960s, 10" h, $15.00.

Green and yellow outfit, red–
orange hair **21.00**
10" h, three–dimensional figure,
white outfit with blue buttons,
small flesh–tone cap on head,
1960s **60.00**
Peter Potamus, Bubble Club Fun Bath,
bank, unopened, uncut coin slot,
1967, 10½" h, orig box **98.00**
Punkin Puss, removable head, orig cardboard label around base, 1960s,
11½" h **72.00**
Snagglepuss, mid 1960s, 9" h **50.00**
Spouty Whale, Bubble Club Fun Bath,
unopened, orig cardboard wrap-
around tag, 1966, 4" h, 10" l   **36.00**
Touche Turtle
4" h, 10" l, plastic trap in belly,
"Touche Away" on shell, 1960s
. . . . **50.00**
10½" h, standing upright, Bubble
Club Fun Bath, removable hard
plastic head, 1960s **75.00**
Yakky Doodle, Bubble Club Fun Bath,
squatting duck figure, orig cardboard
tag, 1960s, 6" h, 7½" l **25.00**
Yogi Bear, Bubble Club Fun Bath, hard
plastic removable head, orig cardboard tag, 1961, 9½" h **72.00**
Roclar Distributors, Cecil, hard vinyl, clear
stopper in bottom early 1960s, 8" h
. . . . **35.00**

SOAP COLLECTIBLES

At first you would not think that a lot
of soap collectibles would survive. However, once you start to look around,
you'll see no end to the survivors. Many
Americans are not as clean as we think.

There is no hotel soap listed. Most
survivors sell for 50¢ to $2.00 per bar.
Think of all the hotels and motels that
you have stayed at that have gone out of
business. Don't you wish you had saved
one of the soap packets? You don't?
What are you—normal or something?

Advertising Trade Card
Calkins Champion Washer, red ground
. . . . **28.00**
Doty's Washer, folder type, red, black,
and buff, 1873 price list **15.00**
Gold Dust Washing Powder, diecut, full
color, c1890, 3 × 3½" **35.00**
Higgins Soap, afternoon in Central Park,
horse and carriage, color **6.00**
Lenox Soap, diecut, standup **10.00**
New Process Soap, multicolored   **15.00**
Wool Soap, diecut, "My Mamma used
Wool Soap" **14.00**
Blotter, American Family Soap, Uncle Sam
illus, c1910 . . . . **15.00**
Bookmark, Dingman's Soap, illus of baby
. . . . **8.75**

Box
Fairbank's Santa Claus Soap, wood, 14
× 10 × 20½" **250.00**
Fun–To–Wash Soap, black Mammy
wearing red bandanna illus, early
1900s, 3¼" h **25.00**
Larkin Sweet Home Soap, wood   **45.00**
Brochure
Colgate/Fab Laundering, 1921 . . . **20.00**
Drey Doppel Soap, daguerreotype,
1893, color **25.00**
Clicker, Sapolio, litho tin, red, white, and
blue background, yellow product name,
1930s, 1¼" d **30.00**
Magazine Tear Sheet, Sapolio Soap, framed
. . . . **125.00**
Mirror, adv, pocket size, celluloid, round
Lava Chemical Resolvant Soap, c1910,
2½" d **35.00**
Reuter's Soap, mother and child, green
ground, 1910 copyright, 2⅛" d
. . . . **45.00**
Pinback Button, Gold Dust Washing Pow-
der, multicolored, late 1890s, 1¼" d
. . . . **75.00**
Playing Cards, adv, Best Grand Laundry,
"We wash everything with Ivory Soap"
. . . . **5.00**
Poster, Old Dutch Cleanser, fabric, can
illus, blue and white ground, red border,
1930s, 15 × 20" **75.00**
Pot Scraper, Babitts Cleanser **225.00**
Ruler, Glory Soap Chips, celluloid, folding,
blue and orange Swift & Co trademark,
1919 calendar, 5½" l **20.00**
Sign
Ivory Soap, cardboard, little girl washing
doll's clothing, Maud Humphrey
illus, 17 × 24½" **450.00**
Lautz Soap, paper, laughing man holding soap bar, 21 × 17½" . . . **225.00**
Lava Soap, cardboard, full color, c1910,
8 × 8" **20.00**
Palmolive Soap, green, black, and white,
1930s, 14 × 22" **20.00**
Tulip Soap, paper, woman surrounded
by tulips and various other vignette
scenes, framed, 21½ × 27½"   **55.00**
Soap
Castile Soap, Oletyme Products, Indianapolis, IN, "Made in Accordance
with the Fair Labor Standards Act of
1933," three bars, orig 7¼ × 3½ ×
1" box with castle illus **7.00**
Hanna–Barbera Bath Soap, Roclar,
1976, Yogi Bear, Yakky Doodle, and
Chopper on wrapper, 3 × 2 × 1"
bar **8.00**
Sinclair Oil, dinosaur shape, MIB   **15.00**
Soap Dish
Graniteware, hanging, cobalt blue swirl
. . . . **110.00**
Porcelain, Blue Onion, drain **58.00**
Soap Saver, tin frame, twisted wire handle,
hanging loop, wire mesh container, 3½
× 2½", 7" l handle **20.00**

Stickpin, Gold Dust Washing Powder, celluloid, multicolored, brass rim, c1896
. . . . **75.00**
Store Display, Ivory Soap, inflatable   **25.00**
Tape Measure, Fab Detergent, celluloid
. . . . **27.50**
Thermometer, Lincoln Laundry, wood, early
1900s, 12 × 3" **25.00**
Tip Tray, Fairy Soap, girl sitting on soap bar,
holding flowers, orange center, brown
rim, c1936, 4¼" d **75.00**

SODA FOUNTAIN AND ICE CREAM COLLECTIBLES

The local soda fountain and/or ice
cream parlor was the social center of
small-town America between the late
1880s and the 1960s. Ice cream items
appeared as early as the 1870s.

This is a category filled with nostalgia—banana splits and dates with
friends. Some concentrate on the advertising, some on the implements. It is all
terrific.

Clubs: National Association of Soda
Jerks, PO Box 115, Omaha, NE 68101;
The Ice Screamer, PO Box 465,
Warrington, PA 18976.

ICE CREAM
Ashtray, Breyers Ice Cream, Hall China
. . . . **22.50**
Cone Dispenser, glass jar, nickel plated insert holds stacked cones upright, metal
lid, 6½" d, 14" h **300.00**
Dipper, Eric Spec Co, cone shape   **220.00**
Fudge Warmer, Howell's Hot Fudge   **48.00**
Ice Cream Maker, Whirl–A–Whip, soft ice
cream, nickel plated brass dome top,
yellow porcelain over cast iron base
. . . . **400.00**

*Scoop, Gilchrist's No 31, wood handle,
bronze plated mechanism, stainless steel
bowl and dislodger, 11" l, $110.00.*

Sign, Walgreen's Malted Milk 25¢, brown, yellow, red, and cream, wood frame, 47 × 25", $400.00.

Light Fixtures, pr, figural, ice cream cones, painted metal, 10" d, 15" h **110.00**
Mold, metal, Sealtest Ice Cream, pt **17.00**
Serving Tray, Benham's Ice Cream, tin, Palmer Cox brownies surround large dish of ice cream, 10½ × 13¼" **150.00**
Sign
    "Ice Cream," Wrigley's Spearmint adv, hanging, two sided, diecut porcelain, 30" w, 9" h **1,450.00**
    Peter Pan Ice Cream, tin, character illus **115.00**
    Polar Ice Cream, 18 × 24", polar bear illus **495.00**
    Regal Ice Cream, tin, flange, strawberry cone illus **165.00**
    Rich Valley Ice Cream, 9" d, yellow and red, 1940s **40.00**
Tip Tray, Binghamton Ice Cream, pretty girl wearing red scarf and hat, "Everybody's Favorite," oval, 4¼ × 6¼" **195.00**

SODA FOUNTAIN

Bottle, Henri's Ice Cream and Soda Shop adv, Las Vegas **10.00**
Cup Holder, SP, lily form, set of 6 . . . **30.00**
Display, Vin Fiz Sparkling Grape Drink, diecut cardboard, four women and caricatured boy drinking soda, 38 × 25 × 7½" **2,000.00**
Door Push, Coca–Cola, porcelain, red and white, orig metal mounting bracket, 26" w, 4" h **400.00**
Glass, Modox, emb Indian Chief image, 5" h, 3" d **50.00**
Ice Cream Soda Glass, emb copper, attached straw, 5¾" d, 16" h **295.00**
Sign
    Golden Cola, chalkboard **38.00**
    Multiple Flavors, tin, white lettering, blue ground, interlocking clips for added flavors, flavors inclue tutti–frutti, peach, pineapple, and butterscotch, 11" w, 22" h **220.00**
    Orange Crush, tin with blackboard **65.00**
Straw Holder, glass
    Clear, pressed design, four sided, orig lid, 12½" h **100.00**
    Green, pressed design, four sided, no lid, 9½" h **100.00**
    Mottled Peach, plain cylinder, ftd, orig lid, 4" d, 12" h **170.00**

Syrup Bottle, grapefruit, glass, red script lettering on white enamel label, gold border, plated metal measure cap, FM Williams, 1913 copyright **70.00**
Syrup Dispenser
    Hires, hourglass shape, metal dispenser top, 7½" d, 14" h **325.00**
    Orange Crush, brown glass body, metal dispenser top, orig carrying case, 7" d, 13" h **130.00**
    Ward's Lemon–Crush, figural lemon shaped dispenser **450.00**

SOFT DRINK COLLECTIBLES

National brands such as Coca–Cola, Canada Dry, Dr Pepper, and Pepsi–Cola dominate the field. However, there were thousands of regional and local soda bottling plants. Their advertising, bottles, and giveaways are every bit as exciting as those of the national companies. Do not ignore them.

Clubs: Dr Pepper 10–2–4 Collector's Club, 1529 John Smith, Irving, TX 75061; Pepsi–Cola Collectors Club, PO Box 1275, Covina, CA 91722.

Booklet, Hires Condensed Milk, 1898 . . . . **22.00**
Bottle
    Dr Pepper, Waco, TX, bottler, slight purplish hue, 8½" h **35.00**
    Smile Soda, concentrate, 1922, 6" h **30.00**
Bottle Stopper, Hires Root Beer, metal and rubber **12.00**
Bottle Topper, Squirt, cardboard **18.00**
Calendar
    Orange Crush, 1941, full pad . . . **325.00**
    Royal Crown Cola, Wanda Hendrix pictures, 1950 . . . . **35.00**
Case, Grapette Soda, thirty bottles in orig carrier
Certificate, Pepsi–Cola, sponsoring Rogers Silverware, 1917 . . . . **12.00**
Checkerboard, Hires Root Beer, adv back flaps with pointing boy and text "Exhilarating and Appetizing," 12 × 12" open size **350.00**

Drinking Cup, Pepsi, racing car theme, Pepsi 89 car, "Pepsi, Official Soft Drink of the Daytona 500," red plastic cap, reverse side with facing flags and their meanings, 4¼" d, 6½" h, $1.00.

Cigarette Lighter, Royal Crown Cola, bottle shape **45.00**
Clock
    Frostie Root Beer, cuckoo, Frostie swinging on pendulum **125.00**
    Kist Beverages, round, light–up **215.00**
    Sundrop Cola, pin–up girl, light–up **245.00**
    Teem **45.00**
Cooler, 7Up, aluminum **50.00**
Door Push
    Grapette, aluminum **110.00**
    Pepsi–Cola, wrought iron, 1960s **95.00**
    White Rock Sparkling Water **100.00**
Glass
    Dr Pepper, flared, script "Dr Pepper," first issued, 6" h **1,700.00**
    Moonshine Soda, flared, syrup line **45.00**
Ice Cream Scoop, Hires, plastic **10.00**
Match Holder, Moxie, diecut tin, bottle shaped, "Moxie, Very Healthful," 2¾" w, 7" h **275.00**
Mileage Chart, Pepsi–Cola, tin, framed **45.00**
Mug, Hires Root Beer, "Join Health and Cheer," boy holding mug, 5" h **225.00**
Poster, Orange Crush, colorful, 1940s **65.00**
Puzzle, Hood's Sarsaparilla, cardboard, double horse–drawn buggy carrying doctor away from laboratory and factory building, 15 × 10" **95.00**
Radio, Dr Pepper, wood case, soda cooler shape, working, 12" w, 8½" h **1,200.00**
Sign
    Buckeye Root Beer, emb tin, diecut **65.00**

Hazel Club, cream soda, celluloid
.... **65.00**
Hires
 Paper, ''Drink Hires,'' 9 × 21''
 .... **38.00**
 Tin, emb, ''Ask For Hires In Bottles,''
 beige lettering, brown ground,
 white highlights, 27¾ x 9¾''
 .... **310.00**
Julep, emb tin, ''Drink Julep, Six Deli-
 cious Flavors,'' bottle illus, 27¼'' w,
 19'' h **105.00**
Moxie, emb tin, ''Drink Moxie,'' red,
 black, and yellow, 27 × 19'' **200.00**
Nesbitt's Orange Soda, cardboard, orange Grinch Monster, 1950s, 5 × 6''
 .... **8.00**
Pepsi–Cola, porcelain, red, white, and
 blue banner, double dotted logo,
 ''America's Biggest Nickel's Worth,''
 18 × 6'' **300.00**
Squirt, tin, bottle illus, chalkboard ...**75.00**
Thermometer
 A–Treat Ginger Ale, porcelain and tin
 .... **85.00**
 Double Cola, turquoise, 5'' w, 16'' h
 .... **95.00**
Dr Pepper
 17'' h, emb tin, ''Drink Dr Pepper,
 Good For Life at 10, 2 and 4,''
 bottle with clock illus **275.00**
 20'' h, tin, 1960s logo **50.00**

Dr Well's—the Cooler Doctor, tin
 .... **45.00**
Mason Root Beer, tin **65.00**
Mission Orange, bottle shape, 5'' w,
 16'' h **95.00**
Moxie, tin, Archie pointing, 9¾'' w,
 25¼'' h **95.00**
Royal Crown Cola, 25'' h **60.00**
Tray
 Frank's Pale Dry Ginger Ale, color litho
 of bottle, 1930s **50.00**
 Pepsi–Cola, round, bottle cap shape,
 1940 .... **325.00**
Walkie–Talkie, Pepsi–Cola, bottle shaped
 .... **25.00**
Water Set, Dr Pepper, pitcher and eight
 glasses, iron anvil and wheat shafts
 trademark illus, 8½'' h pitcher, 6'' h
 glasses **45.00**

SOUTH OF THE BORDER COLLECTIBLES

When you live on the East Coast and do not roam west of Chicago, you are not going to see South of the Border collectibles except for the tourist souvenirs brought home by visitors to Central and South America. However, the growing Hispanic population is beginning to look back to its roots and starting to proudly display family and other items acquired south of the border.

Over the past several years there has been a growing interest in Mexican jewelry. In fact, several new books have been published about the subject. Mexican pottery and textiles are also attracting collector attention.

At the moment, buy only high–quality, handmade products. Because of their brilliant colors, South of the Border collectibles accent almost any room setting. This is an area to watch.

SPACE ADVENTURERS COLLECTIBLES

This category deals only with fictional space heroes. My grandfather followed Buck Rogers in the Sunday funnies. Dad saw Buster Crabbe as Flash Gordon in the movies and cut his teeth on early television with Captain Video. I am from the Star Trek generation.

Do not overlook the real live space heroes, like the astronauts and cosmonauts who venture out into space. Material relating to these pioneers is going to be very collectible in the year 2091. Refer to the next category: ''Space Exploration Collectibles.''

Club: Galaxy Patrol, 22 Cotton St, Worcester, MA 01610.

Periodical: *Strange New Worlds,* Box 223, Tallevast, FL 34270.

Buck Rogers
 Badge, Chief Explorer, Cream of Wheat
 premium, 1933–35 .... **150.00**
 Big Little Book, *Buck Rogers 25th Century AD,* Whitman, #742, 1932
 .... **100.00**
 Disintegrator Pistol, Cream of Wheat
 premium **150.00**
 Handkerchief, Wilma, Cream of Wheat
 premium, 1933–35 .... **300.00**
 Holster, leather, brown, metal buckle
 and rivets, 1930s, 9'' h **75.00**
 Mask, Wilma, paper, 8 × 11'' ...**65.00**
 Rubber Stamp, set of 11, yellow, wood
 back, Wilma, Buddy, Alura, and two
 different Buck Rogers, c1930 **90.00**
Captain Meteor, holster and belt, leather,
 black lettering, atomic symbol, stars, and
 planets on silver ground, 1950s, 5 ×
 8½'' holster **35.00**
Captain Video
 Game, Captain Video Space Game, Milton Bradley, early 1950s **75.00**

Soda Bottle, RC Cola, red, white, and blue labels, 11'' h, $2.00.

Change Purse, leather, emb figures, 5'' l, $1.00.

Pencil Box, Buck Rogers, American Lead Pencil Co, John F Dille Co, 1936, 8⅜ × 4⅞'', $37.50.

Goggles **95.00**
Ring, photo **100.00**
Watch, orig card **40.00**
Flash Gordon
Comic Book, King Comics #1, 1966
. . . . **10.00**
Costume, space outfit, c1950 . . . **135.00**
Game, orig box **25.00**
Glass, Flash **25.00**
Lobby Card, ''Flash Gordon Conquers
the Universe,'' Universal Pictures, 11
× 14'' **50.00**
Lunch Box, plastic, color decals, Alad-
din, copyright 1979 King Features
Syndicate, 7 × 10 × 5'' **65.00**
Paint Book, Whitman, 32 pgs, copyright
1936 King Features Syndicate, 11 ×
14'' **100.00**
Pocket Watch, Ingersoll, c1939 **350.00**
Toy
Spaceship, diecast metal, blue, white
accents, orig display card, LJN
Toys, copyright 1975, 3'' l **20.00**
Starship, diecast metal and plastic,
sticker on each wing, Tootsietoy,
copyright 1978 King Features
Syndicate, 5'' l **25.00**
Wallet, faux leather, zipper, 1949 KFS
copyright **75.00**
Lost In Space, The Robinson Family
Comic Book, Gold Key, #8, 1968
. . . . **25.00**
Halloween Costume, Ben Cooper, 1965
. . . . **175.00**
Writing Tablet, cov with June Lockhart
in silver flight uniform holding futuristic telephone, 1965, 8 × 10''
. . . . **24.00**
Rex Mars, Planet Patrol Atomic Pistol
Flashlight, battery operated, hard plastic,
red gun, blue trigger, clear front piece,
incised name and logo on gold grip,
1950s, 7¾'' l, orig box **50.00**
Space 1999
Board Game, Milton Bradley, 1975
. . . . **25.00**
Coloring Book, Saalfield, 1975, 8½ ×
11'', unused **10.00**
Gum Card Wrapper, 1975, unopened
pack **10.00**
Moon Car, MIP **70.00**
Space Patrol
Belt Buckle, decoder **110.00**
Binoculars, black **80.00**
Cosmic Smoke Gun, red, short barrel
. . . . **150.00**
Microscope, orig slides **175.00**
Projector, Terra V, rocket shape, plastic,
blue and yellow, orig mailing box,
Ralston Co premium, early 1950s,
5½'' h **150.00**
Ring, hydrogen ray gun **200.00**
Walkie–Talkie Space–A–Phones, plastic,
red and white, 1952, orig mailing
box **95.00**

Puzzle, Flash Gordon, Attack Scene, Milton Bradley Co, copyright 1951, one of set of 3 puzzles, 30 pieces, figural pieces, cardboard box, guide, 12¼ × 9½'', $75.00.

Wristwatch, silvered metal case, black
and red numerals, gray leather straps,
US Time, early 1950s **60.00**
Tom Corbett
Belt Buckle, ''Space Patrol Cadet,'' silver
finish, raised logo and designs in-
cluding Saturn, stars, and lightning
bolt, 1950s, 2½ × 3'' d **40.00**
Book, *Wonder Book of Space*, Rockhill
Radio Recording, hard cov, 24 pgs,
color illus, 1953, 5½ × 8'' . . . **12.00**
Coloring Book, unused, 1952 . . . . **95.00**
Flashlight, orig box, 1952 . . . . **95.00**
Lunch Box, 1952 . . . . **120.00**
Patch, ''Space Cadet,'' cloth, red, yel-
low, and blue, Kellogg's premium,
2 × 4'' **25.00**
Picture, Space Patrol Magic Space Pic-
ture, Chex cereal premium, ''#20
Planetoid Prospector,'' stiff paper,
3 × 4'' **15.00**
Thermos, metal, yellow plastic cup,
Aladdin Industries, copyright 1952
Rockhill Radio, 6'' h **45.00**
Wristwatch, ''Tom Corbett Space Ca-
det,'' Ingraham, silvered metal, black
leather band, c1951, not running
. . . . **65.00**

SPACE EXPLORATION COLLECTIBLES

The use of rockets at the end of World War II and the beginnings of the space research program gave reality to future space travel. In the 1950s, real life

space pioneers and explorers replaced the fictional characters as the center of the public's attention. The entire world watched on July 23, 1969, as man first walked on the moon. Although space exploration has suffered occasional setbacks, the public remains fascinated with its findings and potential.

The American and Russian space programs produced a wealth of souvenir and related material. Beware of astronaut–signed material that may contain printed or autopen signatures. Reproduction patches and decals have flooded the market. Be aware of these items and shop with care.

Ashtray, clear glass, turquoise and black
illus, astronaut scooping moon rock
sample, ''Apollo 11, 1969,'', 5½'' d
. . . . **12.00**
Badge, commemorative, ''US First Man On
The Moon,'' celluloid badge, black and
white portraits, 3½'' d **15.00**
Cereal Premium, Cheerios, ''Space Shuttle
Adventure Kit,'' sponsored by General
Mills and Rockwell International, 24 pg
booklet, pre–cut shuttle model with assembly instructions, 4½'' h color peel–
off sticker on card, 8¼ × 10'' black and
white iron–on transfer, and orig mailing
envelope, mid 1981 . . . . **15.00**

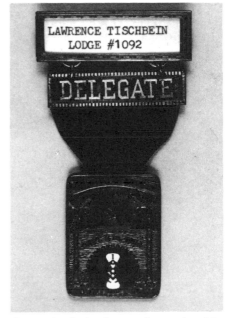

Convention Badge, bronze, International Association of Machinists and Aerospace Workers, 26th Convention, blue ribbon, delegate bar, Sept 1964, Miami Beach, space capsule in front of moon, ocean scene with palm trees, 4'' l, $20.00.

Charm Bracelet, silvered metal, space capsule, moon orbiter craft, moon landing craft, astronaut, and moon charms, each charm ¾" h **25.00**

Coloring Book, *Apollo, Man On The Moon,* Saalfield, 80 pgs, based on actual NASA program, 1969, 8¼ × 11", unused **18.00**

First Day Cover, envelope issued and postmarked April 27, 1963, red "Men in space" photo, sgd by Gus Grissom, J H Glenn Jr, and Alan B Shepard Jr, 3¾ × 6½" **75.00**

Glass, clear glass, moon landing commemorative, red, white, and blue bands, illus, and inscriptions, "One Small Step . . . ," 3¼" h **10.00**

Gum Cards, set of three, Topps, #13, #25, and #32, full color NASA photos, back with orange and green 3–D sketch, 1963, 2½ × 3½" **18.00**

Keychain Tag, Freedom 7, metal, gold color, space capsule and "May 5, 1961," reverse with Pledge of Allegiance **15.00**

Medal, Apollo XII, gold colored metal, Nov 19–20, 1969, raised astronauts' portraits **15.00**

Mug, white china, replica reprint of July 21, 1969, *New York Times* headline, green lettering, sponsor text on back, 6½" h **24.00**

Newspaper, *Baltimore Sun,* Feb 21, 1962, front page photo and wire reports of Glenn's first US orbital flight, 12 × 15½" folded **8.00**

Pin, moon orbiter, gold colored metal, detailed relief image, late 1960s **18.00**

Pinback Button
  Apollo II, 1969 . . . . **10.00**
  Astronaut Glenn, blue and white   **25.00**

Jigsaw Puzzle, Life *magazine cov,* Journey to the Moon, Apollo Mission *poster, 500 pcs, 8½ × 11" box, copyright 1969 Schisgall Enterprises, and Time, Inc, $20.00.*

Columbia Space Shuttle, full color photo, late 1980s, 2¼" d **12.50**

Sputnick Commemorative, "You Are Out Of This World, Sputnik!," white continents background and red ocean, black lettering, late 1950s **18.00**

Plaque, Moon Landing, ceramic, Delft, limited edition, 8½" d, orig box **35.00**

View–Master Reels, set of three, America's Men In Space, Project Mercury, 1962, booklet **20.00**

SPORTS COLLECTIBLES

There has been so much written about sports cards that equipment and other sport–related material has become lost in the shuffle. A number of recent crazes, such as passion for old baseball gloves, indicates that this is about to change.

Decorators have discovered that hanging old sporting equipment on walls makes a great decorative motif. This certainly helps call attention to the collectibility of the material.

Since little has been written outside of baseball and golf collectibles, it is hard to determine what exactly are the best pieces. A good philosophy is to keep expenditures at a minimum until this and other questions are sorted out by collectors and dealers.

Clubs: Boxiana & Pugilistica Collectors International, PO Box 83135, Portland, OR 97203; Golf Collectors Society, PO Box 491, Shawnee Mission, KS 66201; The Golf Club Collectors Association, 640 E Liberty St, Girard, OH 44420.

Periodicals: *Boxing Collectors Newsletter,* 59 Bosson St, Revere, MA 02151; *Malloy's Sports Cards and Collectibles,* 15 Danbury Rd, Ridgefield, CT 06877; *Sports Collectors Digest,* 700 East State St, Iola, WI 54990.

Annual, *Boxing Annual for 1953,* Rocky Marciano cov **30.00**

Autograph, Jack Dempsey, miniature boxing gloves, c1920 . . . . **65.00**

Badge, copper plated white metal, engraved front "1 Mile Run 1st Prize," reverse "St Patrick's Field Day May 30, 1910" **15.00**

Book , *The Spectacle of Sports from Sports Illustrated,* 1957, 320 pgs, dj **25.00**

Booklet, *Keds Handbook of Sports,* 1926 . . . . **20.00**

Boxing Gloves, child's, red, white wristbands with Ali signature and slogans, 1976 copyright Herbert Muhammad Enterprises **18.00**

Wrestling, poster, Pat "Crusher" O'Hara vs Luke Graham and midget Diamond Jim Brady vs Vincent Garabaldi, cardboard, black and white, 14 × 22", $25.00.

Charge Coin, brass, emb, "Horace Partridge Co/Athletic & Sporting Goods" on one side, other with "Discount & Charge Coin," 1890s, 1¼" d **18.00**

Clock, Joe Lewis souvenir, white metal, figural boxer, "Joe Lewis, World Champion," 9" w, 13" h **100.00**

Dispenser, marbleized plastic bowling ball, chrome push top, six glasses, figural bowler handle **60.00**

Yacht Racing, program, America'a Cup, Festival of Sport, Official Souvenir Magazine, Sept 1986, multicolored cov, real photos, 24 pgs, 8¼ × 11½", $10.00.

Display, Holmes/Ali, Caesar's Palace, oilcloth, 17 × 17" **20.00**

Fan, cardboard, toddler wearing diaper and oversized boxing gloves, entitled "I Ain't Bluffin," Hiebel illus, Gerlach–Barklow Co pub, car adv text on back, wood handle, c1940 . . . . **25.00**

Glass, Wilson Tennis Balls, set of six **25.00**

Handbook, women's, *Handbook of Light Gymnastics*, Lucy B Hunt, 1887, 92 pgs, hardcover **50.00**

Hockey Stick, autographed, Bobby Hull **75.00**

Lamp, figural, cast metal woman bowler, alley, and pins, wood stand, painted fiber shade, 16" w, 9½" h base **25.00**

Lapel Stud, multicolored James J Corbett portrait, heavyweight boxing champion, white ground, red lettering, c1896 . . . . **50.00**

Newspaper Adv, Max Baer, 1934 world heavyweight champion, endorsing premium physical development set from Quaker Wheat Crackels, from lower half of Sunday comic strip page, 10½ x 15½" **12.00**

Nodder, San Diego Gulls hockey player, composition, caricature sea gull head, Sports Specialties sticker on bottom **150.00**

Pass, Sportsman's Park, 1943 . . . . **15.00**

Photograph
    Canadian athlete wearing medals, standing on snowshoes, hand colorized **60.00**
    Montreal Canadians, team photo, 1937, 5 × 9" **120.00**
    Rocky Graziano, black and white, glossy, bold black marker autograph, 1947–48, 8 × 10" **30.00**
    Yale, Hockey and Baseball teams, 1900 . . . . **90.00**

Poster, Radio Returns of the Louis–Schmeling Fight, Martin's Scotch Whiskey adv, O Soglow illus, 14 × 22" **100.00**

Sign, flange, porcelain, Spalding Athletic Goods For Sale Here, 20 × 18¾" **1,200.00**

Tin, League Cigarettes, soccer motif **20.00**

STANGL POTTERY

Stangl manufactured dinnerware between 1930 and 1978 in Trenton, New Jersey. The dinnerware featured bold floral and fruit designs on a brilliant white or off–white ground.

The company also produced a series of three–dimensional bird figurines that are eagerly sought by collectors. The bird figurines were cast in Trenton and finished at a second company plant in Flemington. During World War II the demand for the birds was so great that over 60 decorators were employed to paint them. Some of the birds were reissued between 1972 and 1977. They are dated on the bottom.

Club: Stangl Bird Collectors Association, PO Box 419, Ringoes, NJ 08551.

BIRDS

3250D, Gazing Duck, 3¾" h **65.00**
3276S, Bluebird, 5" h **90.00**
3404D, Lovebirds, pr, kissing, 4½" h **115.00**
3405D, Cockatoo, pr, 9½" h **125.00**
3408, Bird of Paradise, 5½" h **95.00**
3431, Duck, running, 5" h **350.00**
3448, Blue–Headed Vireo, 4¼" h . . **65.00**
3449, Paroquet, 5½" h **100.00**
3452, Painted Bunting, 5" h **90.00**
3456, Cerulean Warbler, 4¼" h **60.00**
3491, Hen Pheasant, 6¼ × 11" **175.00**
3503, Parula Warbler **40.00**
3518D, White–Headed Pigeon, pr, 7½ × 12½" **550.00**
3581, Chickadees, group of three, 5½ × 8½" **175.00**
3582, Parakeets, pair, blue–green, 7" h **185.00**
3589, Indigo Bunting, 3¼" h **60.00**
3591, Brewer's Blackbird, 3½" h **95.00**
3592, Titmouse, 2½" h **55.00**
3595, Bobolink, 4¾" h **115.00**
3596, Gray Cardinal, 4¾" h **75.00**
3626, Broadtail Hummingbird, blue flower, 6" h **100.00**
3627, Rivoli Hummingbird, pink flower, 6" h **100.00**
3635, Goldfinches, group of four, 4 × 11½" **200.00**
3715, Blue Jay, 10¼" h **525.00**
3722, European Finch, 4½" h **125.00**
3747, Canary, left, blue flower, 6¼" h **175.00**
3750, Scarlet Tanager, pink body, pr, 8" h **275.00**
3756D, Audubon Warbler, pr, 7¾" h **275.00**
3758, Magpie–Jay, 10¾" h **525.00**
3811, Chestnut–backed Chickadee, 5" h **85.00**
3814, Black–throated Green Warbler, 3⅛" h **125.00**
3848, Golden–crowned Kinglet, 4⅛" h **80.00**
3852, Cliff Swallow, 3¾" h **110.00**
3923, Vermillion Flycatcher, 5¾" h **500.00**
3924, Yellow throated Warbler, 5½" h **60.00**

DINNERWARE

Country Garden
    Butter Dish **35.00**
    Cake Stand **30.00**
    Casserole, 8" d **50.00**
    Coffeepot, 4 cup **50.00**
    Creamer, individual **12.00**
    Cup and Saucer **15.00**
    Egg cup **12.00**
    Gravy Boat **20.00**
    Plate
        7" d **8.00**
        11" d **35.00**
    Sauce Boat **20.00**
    Shaker **10.00**
Daisy, #1870, 1935
    Candleholder, pr, blue **50.00**
    Creamer and Sugar, green **20.00**
    Cup and Saucer, green **18.00**
    Plate
        6" d, bread and butter, blue . . . **8.00**
        8" d, salad, red **10.00**
        10" d, dinner, yellow **20.00**
    Salad Bowl, red, 10½" d **30.00**
    Vegetable Bowl, oval, blue, 10" l **25.00**
Harvest
    Carafe, wood handle **60.00**
    Cup and Saucer **20.00**
    Fruit Dish, 6" d **10.00**
    Plate
        7" d, salad **10.00**
        9" d, luncheon **15.00**
        10" d, dinner **20.00**
        14" d, chop **40.00**
    Salad Bowl, shallow, 10" d **40.00**
    Teapot, cov **70.00**
    Vegetable Bowl, oval, 10" l **34.00**
Terra Rose
    Ashtray, #3242 . . . . **35.00**
    Butter, cov **20.00**
    Cake Stand **20.00**
    Casserole, 6" d **12.00**
    Cereal Bowl, 5½" d **10.00**
    Creamer and Sugar **20.00**
    Gravy and liner **18.00**
    Plate
        8" d, salad **9.00**
        9" d, luncheon **10.00**
        10" d, dinner **12.00**
    Salt and Pepper Shakers, pr **12.50**

Vase, rose and blue, #3732, 11" h, $27.50.

Server, center handle, green speckled,
10" d **20.00**
Teapot, 6 cup **35.00**
Thistle
Casserole, individual, stick handle **25.00**
Coffeepot, cov **25.00**
Cup and Saucer **10.00**
Egg cup **12.00**
Fruit Dish, 5½" d **12.00**
Gravy Boat **20.00**
Pitcher, 1 quart **35.00**
Plate
6" d, bread and butter **6.00**
10" d **15.00**
Platter, oval, 14¾" l **40.00**

STAR TREK COLLECTIBLES

In 1966, a new science fiction television show introduced America to a galaxy of strange new worlds filled with new life forms. The voyages of author Gene Roddenberry's starship *Enterprise* enabled the viewing audience to boldly go where no man had gone before.

These adventures created a new generation of collectors: "Trekkies." From posters, costumes, and props to pins, comic books, and model kits, there in no limit to the number of Star Trek collectibles that can be found.

With the release of Paramounts' *Star Trek: The Motion Picture* in 1979, the Star Trek cult grew. The *Enterprise's* new devotees inspired the inevitable new sequels: *Star Trek II: The Wrath of Khan, Star Trek III: The Search for Spock, Star Trek IV: The Voyage Home, Star Trek V: The Final Frontier,* and *Star Trek VI: The Undiscovered Country.*

In 1987, Trekkies demanded the return of the *Enterprise* to television and were rewarded with *Star Trek: The Next Generation. Deep Space Nine* and *Voyager* soon followed. These television series have generated their own followings as well as merchandise.

Whether you are an old Trekkie or a Next Generation Trekkie, keep seeking out those collectibles. May your collection live long and prosper.

Club: International Federation of Trekkers, PO Box 3123, Lorain, OH 44052.

Periodicals: *Starlog Magazine,* 475 Park Ave South, New York, NY 10016; *Trek Collector,* 1324 Palms Blvd, Dept 17, Los Angeles, Ca 90291.

TELEVISION SERIES (1966)

Action Figure, Mego, 1974–76
Klingon **30.00**
McCoy **20.00**
Romulan **100.00**
The Keeper **50.00**
Activity Book, Punch Out and Play Album, Saalfield, 1975 . . . . **45.00**
Belt Buckle, brass, Lee Belts **10.00**
Binoculars, Larami **60.00**
Board Game, Hasbro, 1974 . . . . . . **30.00**
Book
Mudd's Angels, Bantam **2.50**
Star Fleet Technical Manual, Ballantine **15.00**
The Making of Star Trek, Ballantine, 1968 . . . . **3.00**
The Trouble with Tribbles, Ballantine, 1973 . . . . **2.00**
Bop Bag, Spock, inflatable, AHI, 1975 . . . . **32.00**
Bottle, Saurian Brandy **100.00**
Calculator, Star Trekulator, Mego, c1975 . . . . **40.00**
Colorforms **28.00**
Coloring Book, Planet Ecnal's Dilemma, Whitman, 1978, 8 × 11", unused **18.00**
Comic Book
Gold Key Enterprise Logs, Gold Key Comics, Vol 1 . . . . **6.00**
Star Trek, Gold Key Comics
#5 . . . . **50.00**
#44 . . . . **13.00**
Commemorative Coin, Enterprise, 1974 . . . . **35.00**
Costume
Klingon, 1976 . . . . **50.00**
Mr Spock, Ben Cooper, 1967 . . . . **90.00**
Freezicle Set, 1975 . . . . **30.00**
Game, Star Trek Phaser II Target Game, orig box **50.00**
Glass, Enterprise, Dr Pepper, 1978 . . . **40.00**
Greeting Card, cardboard, Spock photo on front, diecut punch–out Vulcan ears, "I Must Be Hard Of Hearing . . . I Haven't Heard From You Lately," orig envelope, Random House Greetings, copyright 1976 Paramount Pictures Corp, 18" l open size **12.00**
Lunch Box, Aladdin, 1968 . . . . **200.00**

Birthday Card, punch–out Captain Kirk figure, tri–fold, Random House Greetings, 1976, 5 × 10" folded, $15.00.

Model Kit, Klingon Battle Cruiser, lights, AMT, 1967 . . . . **60.00**
Movie Viewer, 1967 . . . . **15.00**
Paint Set, 12 × 16" canvas portrait, boxed, slightly used, Hasbro, 1974 copyright **50.00**
Phaser Ray Gun **25.00**
Plate, Ernst Enterprises, crew on transporter illus **25.00**
Playset
Enterprise Bridge, vinyl, Mego, 1974 . . . . **85.00**
Mission to Gamma VI, Mego, 1976 . . . . **225.00**
Poster Kit, "Color Yourself," two 14" un-colored posters, Enterprise scenes, 1976 . . . . **55.00**
Record
Cryer in Emptiness, record and book, record with heat damage **85.00**
Passage to Moauv, record and book, 1975, Paramount **125.00**
The Time Stealer, Power Records, Peter Pan, 1975 . . . . **5.00**
Thermos, metal, color illus, white plastic cup, Aladdin Industries, copyright 1968 Paramount Pictures Corp, 6½" h **60.00**
Tracer Gun, 1966 . . . . **30.00**
Trading Cards, Topps, set of 88, 1976 . . . . **30.00**
Tribble, stuffed, Mego **65.00**
Tricorder, cassette player, Mego, 1976 . . . . **75.00**

CARTOON SERIES (1973)

Paper Napkins, Party Creations/Tuttle Press, unopened pkg, 1976 . . . . **3.50**
Patch, fabric, Federation emblem, 1975 . . . . **20.00**

THE NEXT GENERATION (1987)

Action Figure, Lewis Galoob Toy Co, 1988
Data, blue skin **30.00**
Ferengi **9.00**
Picard **4.00**
Q **12.00**
Book
The Children of Hamlin, No. 3 . . . . **2.50**
Metamorphosis **3.00**
Costume, Ferengi **8.00**
Lunch Box, Halsey Taylor/Thermos . . . **8.00**
Model Kit, Enterprise, AMT **10.00**
Pattern, crew jumpsuit, Simplicity **6.00**
Phaser, Lewis Galoob Toy Co **18.00**
Vehicle
Ferengi Fighter, Lewis Galoob Toy Co **12.00**
Shuttlecraft Galileo, Lewis Galoob Toy Co **15.00**

THE MOTION PICTURE (1979)

Action Figure, Mego, 1979
3¾" h
Decker **15.00**
Scotty **10.00**
Spock **10.00**

12" h
    Arcturian **50.00**
    Decker **75.00**
    Spock **30.00**
Activity Book, *Make Your Own Costume,*
    Wallaby, 1979 . . . . **10.00**
Beanbag Chair **25.00**
Board Game, Milton Bradley, 1979   **25.00**
Bumper Sticker **2.00**
Coloring Book, Giant Story **12.00**
Comic Book, *Motion Picture Magazine,*
    Marvel Comics, 1979 . . . . **3.00**
Costume, Ilia **15.00**
Doll, Kirk, cloth, Knickerbocker **25.00**
Dual Phaser II, South Bend, 1979 . . . **35.00**
First Aid Kit **10.00**
Glass, Kirk, Spock, and McCoy, Coca–Cola,
    1980 . . . . **15.00**
Keychain, Spock, lucite **2.00**
Playset, Command Bridge **30.00**
Pocket Book, *The Entropy Effect,* No. 2, Si-
    mon and Schuster **2.50**
Pop–Up Book, Wanderer Books **10.00**
Putty, Larami **10.00**
Puzzle, jigsaw, sick bay, Milton Bradley
    . . . . **10.00**
Rubber Stamp **4.00**
Trading Cards, Topps, set of 88, 1979   **8.00**
Tumbler, plastic, Coca–Cola, 1980   **12.00**
Wallet **5.00**
Wastebasket **20.00**
Water Pistol **30.00**

THE WRATH OF KHAN (1982)
Game Watch **75.00**
Model Kit, Enterprise, AMT **15.00**
Mug, Khan **4.00**
Photocards, FTCC, 5 × 7", set of 30   **25.00**
Pinback Button, Enterprise crew, Image
    Products **2.00**
Playing Cards, photo illus backs **8.00**
Pocket Book, *The Trellisane Confrontation,*
    No 14, Simon and Schuster **2.50**
Poster **25.00**

THE SEARCH FOR SPOCK (1984)
Action Figure, ERTL, Spock, 1984 . . . . **8.00**
Comic Book, *Star Trek III Movie Special,*
    DC Comics, 1984 . . . . **3.50**
Eraser, Excelsior, Diener Enterprises . . . **5.00**
Glass, Fal–Tor–Pan, Taco Bell, 1984   **5.00**
Kite **15.00**
Pinback Button, Chekov, Button–Up Co
    . . . . **2.00**
Pocket Book, *The Vulcan Academy Mur-*
    ders, No 20, Simon and Schuster   **3.00**
Post Card Book **4.00**
Trading Cards, ship cards, laminated, FTCC,
    set of 20 . . . . **8.00**

THE VOYAGE HOME (1986)
Comic Book, *Star Trek IV Movie Special,*
    DC Comics, 1987 . . . . **2.50**
Pocket Book, *Star Trek IV: The Voyage*
    Home, Simon and Schuster **2.50**

Poster **20.00**
Program **12.00**
Trading Cards, set of 60 . . . . **8.00**

THE FINAL FRONTIER (1989)
Action Figure, Lewis Galoob Toy Co, Kirk
    . . . . **30.00**
Comic Book, *Star Trek V Movie Special,* DC
    Comics, 1989 . . . . **3.00**
Logbook, *Captain's Log: William Shatner's*
    Personal Account of the Making of Star
    Trek V: The Final Frontier **3.50**
Model Kit, *Enterprise* and shuttle, AMT
    . . . . **10.00**
Pin, *Enterprise* in triangle, Collectors Clas-
    sics **6.00**

STAR WARS COLLECTIBLES

It was in a galaxy not so long ago that author and director George Lucas put into motion events that would change the way we think of space. In 1977 a movie was produced that told the story of an evil Empire's tyrannical rule over the galaxy and of the adventures of a young man from a distant world to end this tyranny. Luke Skywalker's aventures became the Star Wars saga and spanned six years and three separate movies: *Star Wars,* *The Empire Strikes Back,* and *Return of the Jedi.*

The enormous success of the Star Wars movies inspired the release of a wide range of movie–related products including toys, games, costumes, records, and comic books. As you travel through the flea market aisles in search of *Star Wars* treasure, "May the Force Be With You."

Periodical: *The Star Wars Collection Trading Post,* 6030 Magnolia, PO Box 29396, St Louis, MO 63139.

STAR WARS (1977)
Action Figure, Kenner, 1977–1979
    Blue Snaggletooth, Sears **42.00**
    Boba Fett, rocket launcher, mail offer
    . . . . **150.00**
    Chewbacca **20.00**
    Princess Leia Organa **25.00**
Activity Book, *Artoo Detoo's Activity Book,*
    Random House, 1979 . . . . **8.00**
Alarm Clock, C–3PO and R2–D2, talking,
    Bradley, 1980 . . . . **20.00**
Bank
    Chewbacca, Sigma, MIB **45.00**
    Darth Vader, ceramic, Roman Ceramics
    . . . . **28.00**
Beach Towel, Darth Vader **4.00**

Belt Buckle, logo, Leather Shop Inc   **15.00**
Birthday Candle, Chewbacca, Wilton   **5.00**
Board Game, Adventures of R2–D2, Kenner
    . . . . **12.00**
Book, pop–up **15.00**
Bop Bag, Jawa, inflatable, Kenner . . . **40.00**
Cake Decorating Kit, R2–D2, Wilton   **15.00**
Carrying Case, vinyl **20.00**
Coloring Set, Star Wars Poster Art, Craft
    Master, 1978 . . . . **15.00**
Comic Book, Marvel Comics Group
    No. 1 . . . . **8.00**
    No. 7 . . . . **2.00**
Cookie Jar, C–3PO, ceramic, Roman Ce-
    ramics Corp **75.00**
Costume, Darth Vadar, orig box, Ben Coo-
    per, copyright 1977 20th Century Fox
    Film Corp **30.00**
Game **15.00**
Glass, Chewbacca, Burger King, Coca–Cola
    . . . . **8.00**
Han Solo Laser Pistol, *Star Wars* sticker,
    Kenner **35.00**
Helmet, Darth Vader, plastic, Don Post Stu-
    dios **100.00**
Jigsaw Puzzle, Luke, Kenner, #40110, 500
    pcs, purple box **5.00**
Keychain, Millennium Falcon, metal, Adam
    Joseph Industries **6.00**
Lightsaber, inflatable, Kenner **65.00**
Lunch Box, King Seeley Thermos, 1978
    . . . . **15.00**
Model Kit, Millennium Falcon, lights, Mod-
    ern Plastics Co, 1977 . . . . **55.00**
Movie Viewer, Kenner, 1978 . . . . **25.00**
Night Light, Yoda, Adam Joseph Industries
    . . . . **5.00**
Pencil Tray, C–3PO **30.00**
Picture Frame, Darth Vader **35.00**
Playset, Land of the Jawas **100.00**
Robot, R2–D2, radio controlled, Kenner
    . . . . **50.00**
Rocket Kit, X–Wing with Maxi–Brutel, Estes
    . . . . **20.00**
Roller Skates, Darth Vader and Imperial
    Guard **18.00**
Sketch Book, *The Star Wars Sketchbook,*
    Balantine Books, 1977, 98 pgs, orig
    drawings **38.00**
Stickpin, Darth Vader **5.00**
String Holder, R2–D2, scissors **25.00**

Creature Cantina Action Playset, No. 39120,
Kenner, 14¼" l, 8" w, 3½" h, MIB, $50.00.

Stuffed Toy
Chewbacca, dark brown, plastic eyes and nose, brown vinyl cartridge belt, gray plastic cartridges, orig Kenner tag, 1977 20th Century Fox Film Corp, 18" h **40.00**
R2–D2, jointed legs, orig Kenner tag, copyright 1977 20th Century Fox Film Corp **25.00**
Tankard, Obi–Wan Kenobi, ceramic, California Originals **35.00**
Trading Cards, Topps, first series, blue, set of 66 .... **18.00**
Vehicle
Death Star Space Station **75.00**
Millennium Falcon Spaceship **80.00**

THE EMPIRE STRIKES BACK (1980)
Action Figure, Kenner, 1980–82
Imperial TIE Fighter Pilot **15.00**
Luke Skywalker, Hoth battle gear **18.00**
Arcade Game **500.00**
Bulletin Board, glow–in–the–dark, 11 × 17" **10.00**
Centerpiece, Designware **8.00**
Clock, wall, Bradley **20.00**
Coloring Book, Chewbacca, Han, Leia, and Lando on cov, Kenner **4.00**
Comic Book, Marvel Special Edition **3.00**
Dinnerware Set **18.00**
Glass, Lando Calrissian, Burger King, Coca–Cola **5.00**
Han Solo Laser Pistol, *Empire Strikes Back* sticker, Kenner **20.00**
Iron–On Transfer, Darth Vader and Storm Troopers **8.00**
Medal, X–Wing, W Berrie & Co, Inc **6.00**
Mug, robots, ceramic **8.00**
Notebook **4.00**
Paint Set, glow–in–the–dark, Darth Vader **12.00**
Patch, crew, "Vader in Flames" **7.50**
Place mats, set **15.00**
Playset
Ice Planet Hoth **80.00**
Turret and Probot, J C Penney **90.00**
Sketchbook, Ballantine, 1980 .... **12.00**
Sleeping Bag **20.00**
Toothbrush Holder, Snowspeeder **30.00**
Trading Cards, Topps, first series, red, set of 132 .... **10.00**
Vehicle, Rebel Armored Snowspeeder **25.00**

RETURN OF THE JEDI (1983)
Action Figure, Kenner, 1983
Gamorrean Guard **15.00**
Han Solo, Carbonite Chamber **50.00**
Lando Calrissian, Skiff Guard disguise **12.00**
Paploo **10.00**
R2–D2, pop–up lightsaber **25.00**
Sy Snootles and the Rebo Band, boxed set **28.00**
Weequay **15.00**
Yak Face, with coin **100.00**

Activity Book, picture puzzles **3.50**
Bank, Emperor's Royal Guard, Adam Joseph Industries **15.00**
Belt **2.00**
Biker Scout Laser Pistol, Kenner **20.00**
Bookmark, Admiral Ackbar, Random House **3.50**
Candy Container, Jabba the Hutt, figural, Topps **1.50**
Card Game, Play–for–Power **7.00**
Comic Book, Marvel Super Special ... **3.00**
Costume, Klaatu, Ben Cooper, "Revenge of the Jedi" on chestplate **25.00**
Curtains **12.00**
Doll, Chewbacca, stuffed **10.00**
Glass, Emperor's Throne Room, Burger King, Coca–Cola **3.50**
Lightsaber, Droid, battery operated **30.00**
Mask, Gamorrean Guard, soft rubber, Ben Cooper **10.00**
Paint Set, figurine, C–3PO, Craft Master **8.00**
Patch, crew, "Revenge of the Jedi" **20.00**
Pencil, character head **1.00**
Picnic Table **55.00**
Pinback Button, Heroes in Forest, 2¼" d **2.00**
Playset
Ewok Village **40.00**
Jabba the Hutt **45.00**
Puzzle, frame tray, Leia and Wicket, Craft Master **3.00**
Shoelaces, Stride Rite **1.00**
Sit 'n Spin, Wicket **12.00**
Stickpin, Princess Kneesa, Adam Joseph Industries **5.00**
Toothbrush, Jedi Masters, Oral–B **3.00**
Toy Chest, bookcase **50.00**
Trading Cards, Topps, first series, red, set of 132 .... **8.00**
Vehicle, Speeder Bike **15.00**

"STRADIVARIUS" VIOLINS

In the late nineteenth century inexpensive violins were made for sale to students, amateur musicians, and others who could not afford an older, quality instrument. Numerous models, many named after famous makers, were sold by department stores, music shops, and by mail. Sears, Roebuck sold "Stradivarius" models. Other famous violin makers whose names appear on paper labels inside these instruments include Amati, Caspar DaSolo, Guarnerius, Maggini, and Stainer. Lowendall of Germany made a Paganini model.

All these violins were sold through advertisements that claimed that the owner could have a violin nearly equal to that of an antique instrument for a modest cost; one "Stradivarius" sold for $2.45. The most expensive model cost less than $15.00. The violins were handmade, but by a factory assembly line process.

If well cared for, these pseudo antique violins often develop a nice tone. The average price for an instrument in playable condition is between $100.00 and $200.00.

SUGAR PACKETS

Do not judge sugar packets of the 1940s and 1950s by those you encounter today. There is no comparison. Early sugar packets were colorful and often contained full-color scenic views.

Many of the packets were issued as sets, with a variety of scenic views. They were gathered as souvenirs during vacation travels.

There is a large number of closet sugar packet collectors. They do not write much about their hobby because they are afraid that the minute they draw attention to it, prices will rise. Most sugar packets sell for less than $1.00.

Its time to let the sugar out of the bag. Get them cheap while you can.

Clubs: Sugar Packet Clubs International, 15601 Burkhart Rd, Orville, OH 44667; Sugar Packet Collectors Society, 105 Ridge Road, Perkasie, PA 18944.

SUPER HEROES COLLECTIBLES

Super heroes and comic books go hand in hand. Superman first appeared in *Action Comics* in 1939. He was followed by Batman, Captain Marvel, Captain Midnight, The Green Hornet, The Green Lantern, The Shadow, Wonder Woman, and a host of others.

The traditional Super Hero was transformed with the appearance of The Fantastic Four—Mr. Fantastic, The Human Torch, The Invisible Girl, and The Thing. The mutant hero lives today with Teenage Mutant Ninja Turtles.

It pays to focus on one hero or a related family of heroes. Go after the three–dimensional material. This is the hardest to find.

Captain Marvel
Glass, "Shazam" **25.00**

Iron–on Transfer, Captain Marvel with hands on hips, cape flying, saying "Shazam!," full color, 1972–73, 8 × 10" sheet, unused **12.00**

Jigsaw Puzzle, Captain Marvel, Fawcett Publications, Rides The Engine Of Doom, 1941, 13 x 18" **150.00**

Little Golden Book, *A Circus Adventure,* Western Publishing, 1977 ..... **5.00**

Post Card, Captain Marvel's Secret Message, blue, dip in water to reveal message, 1940s, 3 × 5½" **75.00**

Captain Midnight

Decoder, illus, premium **85.00**

Stamp Album, Air Heroes, Skelly Oil **22.00**

Green Hornet

Book, *Case of the Disappearing Doctor,* Whitman, TV Edition series, 225 pgs, 1966 .... **10.00**

Coloring Book, Watkins–Strathmore, copyright 1966, 8 × 11", unused **30.00**

Gum Card Wrapper, Donruss, Green Hornet insect logo, 1966 ..... **60.00**

Model Kit, Aurora, 1966 Chrysler Imperial "Black Beauty" car, 1/32 scale, plastic, 1966, unassembled in sealed box **700.00**

Pinback Button, black, red, green, and blue illus, 1966 Greenway Productions Inc copyright on rim, 4" d **50.00**

Poster, Black Beauty automobile image, from orig Aurora model kit box artwork, limited edition, 1990, 14 × 22" **15.00**

Secret Print Putty, secret print book, magic print paper, Colorforms Toy, unopened blister pack, copyright 1966 .... **65.00**

Sticker Card Wrapper, Topps, color Green Hornet illus, 1966 ..... **40.00**

Wallet, vinyl, green, Green Hornet on front, Kato on back, Green Hornet insect and logo on both sides, magic slate, pencil, and black and white photo of Kato inside, Mattel, copyright Greenway Productions, 1966, 3½ × 4½" **60.00**

Green Lantern, magazine, *Comic Crusader,* #10, Green Lantern cov, 1970 ... **30.00**

Incredible Hulk

Action Figure, Mego, 1979 ...... **30.00**

Gum Card Pack, Topps, seven photo cards, one sticker, one piece bubble gum, Lou Ferrigno color photo on wrapper, 1979, unopened **8.00**

Model Kit, Aurora, 1/12 scale, plastic, raging Hulk bending steel girder, 1966, orig box **350.00**

Paperback Book, black and white reprints of early Hulk comics, illus, 1966, 5 × 7" **18.00**

Poster, Marvel Comics, color, Jack Kirby drawing, 1966, 28 × 42" **50.00**

Record Album, Peter Pan, four stories, Neal Adams cover art, 1978 ... **8.00**

Stickers Wrapper, Philadelphia Gum Corp, color Hulk illus, 1966 **20.00**

Spiderman

Bicycle Siren, Empire Toys, plastic, red and yellow, decals, copyright Marvel Comics Group, orig box and attachments, unused, 1978, 4" h **40.00**

Doll, Knickerbocker, plush, red, white, and black outfit, orig tag, copyright Marvel Comics Group, 1978, 20" h **20.00**

Model Kit, Aurora, 1/12 scale, plastic, Spiderman shooting webbing over Kraven the Hunter, 1966, assembled, unpainted **190.00**

Paperback Book, Lancer, black and white reprints of early Spiderman comics, illus, 1966, 5 × 7" ... **18.00**

Party Masks, Reed, four 8 × 10" masks, 9 × 12" cardboard display card, 1978, sealed pkg **12.00**

Wristwatch, Dabs & Co, 1977 ... **75.00**

Superman

Drink Carton, cardboard, orange drink, 1972, unused **15.00**

Glass, Superman in Action, clear, blue illus, peach color inscriptions, copyright National Periodical Publications Inc, 1964, 4¼" h **50.00**

Greeting Card, Superman & Friends, set of 48, 1978 .... **50.00**

Gym Bag, DC Comics, vinyl, yellow and blue, red Superman and logo, 1971 .... **50.00**

Hairbrush, wood, red, white, and blue decal, 1940s, 2½ × 4½" **75.00**

Jigsaw Puzzle, Whitman, Superman surrounded by Brainiacs, 1964 **30.00**

Model Kit, Aurora, 1/8 scale, Superman smashing through brick wall, 1963, unassembled in box **300.00**

Movie Viewer, Acme, plastic viewer, two boxes film, 1965, unused on card **30.00**

Paint Book, *Superman To The Rescue,* Western Publishing Co Inc, 24 pgs, copyright 1980 DC Comics Inc, unused **15.00**

Pencil Case, vinyl, zippered, red and blue illus and logo on yellow ground, Standard Plastic Products, copyright National Periodical Publications Inc, 1966, 3½ × 8" **58.00**

Pennant, felt, red, white logo, white, pink, and yellow Superman illus, copyright National Periodical Publications Inc, 1966, 11 × 29" **60.00**

Puzzle, sliding squares, black and white, Superman flying over buildings, orig display card, 5 x 6" **70.00**

Record and Storybook Set, Musette Records, #1, "The Flying Train," 1947 .... **50.00**

Record Player, 1978 .... **65.00**

Comic Book, DC National Comics, Wonder Woman, #124, $1.50.

Tattoo, Topps, Superman snapping chains off chest illus on wrapper, various Superman scene tattoos, 1962 .... **50.00**

Wonder Woman

Doll, Mego, 1976, 12" h, unused in box Queen Hippolyte, jointed, fabric costume **80.00**

Steve Trevor, wearing pilot uniform **70.00**

Glass, clear, illus on front, logo and name on back, Pepsi issue, copyright DC Comics, 1978, 6¼" h **18.00**

Model Kit, 1/12 scale, plastic, Wonder Woman lassoing octopus, 1965, unassembled in box **650.00**

Record and Storybook Set, 33⅓ rpm record, 16 pg comic book, cardboard record sleeve, "Wonder Woman vs the War God" and "Amazons from Space," Neal Adams artwork, 1977 .... **15.00**

Wristwatch, gold case, color illus of Wonder Woman, Dabs, copyright DC Comics, 1977 .... **75.00**

SWANKYSWIGS

Swankyswigs are decorated glass containers that were filled with Kraft Cheese Spreads. They date from the early 1930s. See D. M. Fountain's *Swankyswig Price Guide* (published by author in 1979) to identify pieces by pattern.

Most Swankyswigs still sell for under $5.00. If a glass still has its original label, add $5.00 to the price.

Woman on telephone, another woman listening in, brown, 3³/₄" h, $3.00.

Club: Swankyswigs Unlimited, 201 Alvena, Wichita, KS 67203.

Atlantic City, cobalt glass, 5" h **25.00**
Bands, black and red **3.00**
Bicentennial, yellow, Coin Dot design, 1975
. . . . **10.00**
Bustling Betsy, blue, 3³/₄" h **3.00**
Carnival, fired–on dark blue **7.50**
Checkerboard, red **25.00**
Cornflower, 3¹/₂" h
  Dark Blue, #2 . . . . **3.00**
  Light Blue
    #1 . . . . **3.00**
    #2 . . . . **3.00**
Daisy, red, green, white, 3³/₄" h **3.00**
Dots and Circles, green **3.75**
Forget–Me–Not, 3¹/₂" h
  Dark Blue **3.00**
  Red **3.00**
Jonquil, yellow, 3¹/₂" h **3.00**
Kiddie Kup
  Bird and Elephant, red **2.00**
  Pig and Bear, blue **2.00**
Lily of the Valley, red and black, 4³/₄" h
. . . . **10.00**
Posy, light blue **3.00**
Sailboat
  Cobalt, red dec, 4¹/₂" h **15.00**
  Crystal, white dec, 4³/₄" h **6.50**
  Red, white sailboats and stars, 4³/₄" h
. . . . **18.00**
Star, black **5.00**
Tavern, silver, 4³/₄" h **15.00**
Tulip, black, 3¹/₂" h, #1 . . . . **3.00**

SWIZZLE STICKS

They just do not make swizzle sticks like they used to. There is no end of the ways to collect them—color, motif, region, time period, and so on.

Souvenir, plastic, Cortina Restaurant, skier; La Rond, Fountainbleau, carousel; Salon Isabeau Chateau Roberval, beaver; Poodle Room, Fountainbleau, Poodle, $.50 each.

You can usually find them for less than $1.00. In fact, you can often buy a box or glass full of them for just a few dollars. Sets bring more, but they have to be unusual.

Club: International Swizzle Stick Collectors Association, PO Box 1117, Bellingham, WA 98227–1117.

Bird, Chez **10.00**
Fruit, glass, set of 12, includes stand   **55.00**
Glass Marble, set of 3, figural horse int
. . . . **35.00**
Jack Dempsey Restaurant, green and orange
. . . . **18.00**
Penthouse, set of 8 . . . . **20.00**
Piccadilly Circus Bar **2.00**
Pitchfork, American Export Lines adv   **4.00**
Zulu, MOC, 1950s **16.00**

TAYLOR, SMITH, and TAYLOR DINNERWARE

W. L. Smith, John N. Taylor, W. L. Taylor, Homer J. Taylor, and Joseph G. Lee founded Taylor, Smith, and Taylor in Chester, West Virginia. In 1903 the firm reorganized and the Taylors bought Lee's interest. In 1906 Smith bought out the Taylors. The firm remained in the family's control until it was purchased by Anchor Hocking in 1973. The tableware division closed in 1981.

One of Taylor, Smith, and Taylor's most popular lines was LuRay, produced

from the 1930s through the early 1950s. Designed to compete with Russel Wright's American Modern, it was produced in Windsor Blue, Persian Cream, Sharon Pink, Surf Green, and Chatham Gray. Coordinating colors encourage collectors to mix and match sets.

Taylor, Smith, and Taylor used several different backstamps and marks. Many contain the company name as well as the pattern and shape names.

A dating system was used on some dinnerware lines. The three-number code included month, year, and crew number. This system was discontinued in the 1950s.

Autumn Harvest
  Casserole Lid **20.00**
  Cup **3.00**
  Plate
    6³/₄" d **2.00**
    10" d **3.00**
  Saucer **1.00**
  Sugar **5.00**
Boutonniere
  Casserole Lid **20.00**
  Creamer and Sugar **10.00**
  Cup **3.00**
  Plate
    6³/₄" d **2.00**
    10" d **3.00**
  Platter
    Oval **8.00**
    Round **12.00**
  Salt and Pepper Shakers, pr **10.00**
  Saucer **1.00**
LuRay
  Berry Bowl, 5¹/₂" d, pink **3.50**
  Bowl, tab handle, blue **12.00**
  Creamer and Sugar, cov, pink **20.00**
  Cup and Saucer, pink **7.50**
  Demitasse Cup and Saucer, pink   **25.00**
  Demitasse Sugar, blue **45.00**
  Epergne, yellow **75.00**
  Mixing Bowl, 5¹/₂" d, pink **40.00**
  Nappy, pink **14.00**
  Pitcher, water, pink **48.00**
  Plate
    Bread and Butter, pink, 6" d . . . **3.00**
    Chop, yellow **25.00**
    Dinner, blue **13.00**
    Grill, yellow **25.00**
    Lunch, blue **7.00**
    Salad, 7" d, pink **4.00**
  Platter
    9" l, yellow **15.00**
    13¹/₂", green **18.00**
  Relish, green **25.00**
  Salt and Pepper Shakers, pr, blue   **20.00**
  Soup, tab handle, green **15.00**
  Vegetable
    Oval, yellow **16.00**
    Round, 8" d, gray **28.00**
Taverne
  Berry Bowl, 5¹/₄" d **8.00**

Butter Dish, cov **225.00**
Casserole, cov, ftd **75.00**
Creamer and Sugar, cov **30.00**
Cup and Saucer **13.00**
Plate
   6" d **5.00**
   7¼" d **10.00**
   9" d **12.00**
Vegetable
   Oval, 9¼" l **22.00**
   Round, 8¾" d **22.00**

TEDDY BEARS

Teddy bear collectors are fanatics. Never tell them their market is going soft. They will club you to death with their bears. Do not tell anyone that you heard it here, but the Teddy Bear craze of the 1980s has ended. The market is flooded with old and contemporary bears.

The name "Teddy" Bear originated with Theodore Roosevelt. The accepted date for their birth is 1902–1903. Early bears had humped backs, elongated muzzles, and jointed limbs. The fabric was usually mohair; the eyes were either glass with pin backs or black shoe buttons.

The contemporary Teddy Bear market is as big or bigger than the market for antique and collectible bears. Many of these bears are quite expensive. Collectors who are speculating in them will find that getting their money out of them in ten to fifteen years is going to be a bearish proposition.

Clubs: Collectors Club for Classic Winnie the Pooh, 468 W Alpine #10, Upland, CA 91786; Good Bears of the World, PO Box 13097, Toledo, OH 43613.

Periodicals: *National Doll & Teddy Bear Collector,* PO Box 4032, Portland, OR 97208; *Teddy Bear & Friends,* 6405 Flank Dr, Harrisburg, PA 17112; *Teddy Bear Review,* 170 Fifth Ave, New York, NY 10010.

Bear Related Items
  Book
    Book of Bears, Frank Ver Beck, J B Lippincott Co, 1906, 96 pgs
    . . . . **45.00**
    Little Bears Ups & Downs,, Rand McNally, 1936 . . . . **15.00**
    Paddy Paws, Four Adventures, Grace Coolidge, Rand McNally, 1937
    . . . . **20.00**
    The Teddy Bears, Bray illustrator, Judge, 1907, set of 8 . . . . **160.00**

Brochure, *Teddy Bear's Baking School,* teddy bear illus, 1906 . . . . **50.00**
Dish, 6" d, china, full color illus, youngster bear finishing picture on blackboard, early 1900s **50.00**
Spoon, 5½" l, SP, figural handle, enamel dec, Russia **50.00**
Teddy Bear
  Character Novelty Co, 15" h, synthetic plush, cinnamon, plastic eyes, label sewn in ear, c1960 . . . . **60.00**
  Clemens, 16" h, mohair, beige, short mohair inset snout, glass eyes, metal tag, c1950 . . . . **275.00**
  Gund, 13" h, Cubbie Bear, acrylic plush, dark brown, soft vinyl molded face, painted eyes, wearing dress and shoes, removable apron, label sewn in leg seam, c1950 . . . . **85.00**
  Ideal Toy Co, 15" h, Musical Clown Bear, synthetic plush, cinnamon colored body, white pants with brown and yellow spots, paw pads, and ear linings, yellow felt hat, molded soft vinyl face, plastic eyes, label sewn in shoulder seam, c1950 . . . . . . **135.00**
  . . . . **135.00**
  Knickerbocker
    14" h, mohair, brown, jointed, inset snout, floss nose and mouth, felt pads, windup music box, 1950s
    . . . . **175.00**
    20" h, mohair, brown, jointed, flat face **100.00**
  North American Bear Co
    Vanderbear Family, 12" h, Fluffy, 1983 . . . . **28.00**
    Very Important Bear, William Shakesbear, 1981–88 . . . . **400.00**

Post Card, emb, color, International Art Publishing Co, New York–Berlin, Series 791, printed in Germany, divided back, 1907, 3½ × 5½", $30.00.

Steiff, 17" h, Teddy Baby **875.00**
Unidentified Maker
  8" h, short mohair, gold, glass eyes, black fabric nose, no paw pads, c1910 . . . . **600.00**
  15" h, short mohair, rust, shoe button eyes, sliced–in ears, c1915
  . . . . **350.00**
  19" h, long mohair, gold, short gold mohair inset snout, wide set glass eyes, American, c1930 . . . **325.00**
  21" h, long mohair, gold, velveteen paw pads, glass eyes, British, c1930 . . . . **500.00**

TEENAGE MUTANT NINJA TURTLES

It's hard to believe that an independent black-and-white illustrated comic by Eastman and Laird could cause such a craze. But it's true and they're out there.

Teenage Mutant Ninja Turtles are everywhere and kids love them. Toys, clothes, movies, daily television cartoon shows and even T.M.N.T. cereal are available across the country.

Merchandising of T.M.N.T. began in 1988. The Turtles' popularity demanded a live-action movie in 1990. Since then Teenage Mutant Ninja Turtles have mutated into one of the most popular kids' collectibles of the late twentieth century.

Collecting Turtle items isn't difficult, just take a peek under any plastic manhole cover and you're sure to find Michaelangelo, Donatello, Leonardo, or Raphael staring back at you. Cowabunga, Dude!

Action Figures, Playmates, 4½" h
  April O'Neil, #5055, 1989, blue stripe
  . . . . **12.00**
  Baxter Stockman, 1988 . . . . **9.00**
  Bebop, Turtle Force Fan Club Flyer, 1988 . . . . **20.00**
  Donatello, #5612, Sewer–swimmin', Wacky Action windup, Quiz Joke Book, 1989 . . . . **6.00**
  Foot Soldier, #5008, 1988 . . . . **7.50**
  Genghis Frog, #5051, 1989 . . . . . . **7.50**
  Krang, #5056, 1989 . . . . **12.50**
  Leonardo, #5001, 1988 . . . . **6.00**
  Metalhead, #5053, 1990 . . . . **5.00**
  Michaelangelo, #5150, Midshipman Mike, 1991 . . . . **5.00**
  Mutagen Man, 1990 . . . . **6.00**
  Pizzaface, 1990 . . . . **6.00**
  Raphael, #5144, Grand Slammin' Raph, Sewer Sports All–Stars, 1991 . . . **5.00**
  Rat King, 1989 . . . . **7.50**
  Ray Filet, #5110, yellow and blue, 1990–91 . . . . **15.00**

Action Figure, Michaelangelo, Weapon: Nunchukus, Playmates, unopened, 7³/₄ × 10¹/₂", $30.00.

Rocksteady, #5009, 1988 . . . . **7.50**
Shredder, #5617, Slice 'n Dice Shredder, Wacky Action windup, with joke book, 1990 . . . . **6.00**
Splinter, 1988 . . . . **8.00**
Tokka, #5130, 1991 . . . . **5.00**
Usagi Yojimbo, #5054, 1989 . . . . . **8.00**
Walkabout, #5139, 1991 . . . . **5.00**
Comic Book
  Teenage Mutant Ninja Turtles Adventures, second series
    No. 1, Shredder, Bebop, and Rocksteady return to Earth **9.00**
    No. 6, introduction to Leatherhead and Mary Bones **3.50**
Mutant Maker Crazy Character Creation Kit, #5695, Playmates, 1990 . . . . **12.00**
Stuffed Toy, Raphael, plush, 13" h . . . **20.00**
Training Manual, No. 3 . . . . **5.00**
Vehicles & Accessories
  Don's Sewer Squirter, #5681, 1991
    . . . . **8.00**

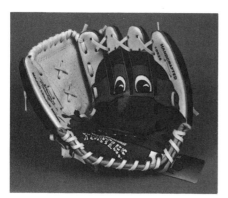

Baseball Glove, green, yellow, red mask, purple trim, orig paper tag, #18535, Endorsed by Raphael, Major League Model, Remco, 9" h, $20.00.

Foot Cruiser **35.00**
Mega Mutant Killer Bee, #5635, 1990
  . . . . **6.00**
Pizza Thrower, 1989 . . . . **35.00**
Psycho Cycle, #5691, 1990 . . . . . **25.00**
Retrocatapult, #5663, 1990 . . . . . **11.00**
Sewer Playset, #5685, 1990 . . . . . **50.00**
Technodrome, 22" h, 1988 . . . . . . **60.00**
Toilet Taxi, #5552, 1990 . . . . **7.00**
Turtle Blimp, green vinyl, 30" l, 1988
  . . . . **30.00**
Video Game, talking, hand held, Konami, 1990 . . . . **30.00**
Wristwatch, LCD digital, plastic strap, flip–up figure, Hope, 1991 . . . . **12.00**

TELEPHONES AND TELEPHONE–RELATED ITEMS

If you ask a number of people when they think the telephone was invented, most will give you a date in the early twentieth century. The accepted answer is 1876, when Alexander Graham Bell filed his patent. However, crude telegraph and sound–operated devices existed prior to that date.

Beware of reproduction phones or phones made from married parts. Buy only telephones that have the proper period parts, a minimum of restoration, and are in working order. No mass–produced telephone in the United States made prior to 1950 was manufactured with a shiny brass finish.

Concentrating on telephones is only half the story. Telephone companies generated a wealth of secondary material from books to giveaway premiums. Dig around for examples from local companies that eventually were merged into the Bell system.

Clubs: Antique Telephone Collectors Association, Box 94, Abilene, KS 67410; Telephone Collectors International, Inc, 19 North Cherry Dr, Oswego, IL 60543.

Avon Bottle, candlestick telephone shape
  . . . . **5.00**
Booth, wood, no doors **125.00**
Keychain, princess phone, pink **5.00**
Lapel Stud, SS, enameled, "V" symbol with office worker, switchboard operator, and line repairman below inscription **15.00**
Magazine, *Telephony*, 1955 . . . . **.50**
Mirror, pocket, adv, Missouri and Kansas Telephone Co, Bell System, American Telephone & Telegraph, celluloid, blue and white, early 1900s, 2¹/₂" l **65.00**

Notepad, Southern New England Telephone Co, simulated leather, red good luck stamp on cov, black inscription, blue Bell System logo on back **20.00**
Paperweight, Bell System, New York Telephone Co, figural, bell, glass, dark blue, gold lettering, c1920, 3¹/₄" h **70.00**
Pay Phone, 1950s **165.00**
Pen, Bell Telephone, Esterbrook **45.00**
Pencil, lead, Bell Telephone, Auto Point
  . . . . **25.00**
Pin
  Bell System, hanger, celluloid, diecut, bell shape, blue, white lettering, "Local Long Distance Telephone" on front, reverse with "When in Doubt, Telephone and Find Out, Use the Bell," Whitehead & Hoag patent, 1905, 1" l **12.00**
  New England Telephone & Telegraph, service award, octagonal, 10K gold, raised Bell System logo above faux ruby, 1930s, ¹/₂" d **15.00**
Pinback Button
  Bell Telephone System, blue lettering and logo, white ground, "3 Sale Club" on center bell logo, "Plant Employee Sales, Go Get 'Em, Eastern Division" on rim, 1906–1907, ⁷/₈" d
    . . . . **25.00**
  Chicago Telephones, red ground, white slogan lettering, 2¹/₄" d **25.00**
  New England Telephone & Telegraph Co, Bell System, blue and white
    . . . . **25.00**
  Kansas Independent Telephone Ass'n, black and white candlestick telephone standing on brown and yellow sunflower, early 1900s, 1¹/₂" d **45.00**

Candlestick, brass, Western Electric, 1904 patent, 11¹/₄" h, $55.00.

Sign

Indiana Telephone Co, 18 × 18", two sided, porcelain enamel, black and white, "Indiana Telephone Corporation, Local & Long Distance Service," late 1940s **65.00**

New England Telephone & Telegraph System, square, early roped "Local and Long Distance Telephone" bell in center of Bell Systems circle, blue and white, 11" sq **80.00**

Stand, gossip bench, mahogany, 1940s **75.00**

Stickpin, Bell System, diecut celluloid hanger, blue and white, reverse inscribed "When In Doubt Telephone And Find Out/Use The Bell," c1905, 1 × 1" **42.00**

Switchboard, transmitter broom, pre–1935 . . . . **400.00**

Telephone

Advertising, Sparkle, Crest Toothpaste, 10½" h **40.00**

Candlestick, straight pipe, dial   **185.00**

Desk

American Electric, rotary **15.00**

Kellogg **15.00**

Leich, hand crank **35.00**

Stromberg–Carlson, black, rotary **20.00**

US Army, marked "Connecticut" **40.00**

Western Electric, cradle **50.00**

Double Box, oak, Stromberg–Carlson type **350.00**

Single Box, wood, plain front, 1915–1920 . . . . **200.00**

Wall, American Electric

Pre–Rotary **25.00**

Rotary **27.50**

TELEPHONE CARDS

One of the latest collecting crazes is telephone cards, commonly known as telecards. They have been big in Europe for years. Look for an explosion in the U. S. during the last half of the 1990s.

Telecards are actually credit cards issued by all the major telephone companies as well as many private companies. You purchase a card and then use up the credit each time you place a call. After the credit value of the card is exhausted, you have an instant collectible.

Some telecards are produced as part of a series, some are limited editions. Most stand alone. The cards are issued in quantities that start in the hundreds and continue into the tens of thousands.

Collector value rests in a card's graphics, issuing telephone company, and the number issued. Prices are highly speculative. Only time will tell how this new collectible will "reach out and touch" collectors.

Prices listed here are from current sales lists issued by several individuals selling directly to collectors. The market has yet to determine if a premium is to be paid for cards with an unexpended credit balance.

Advantage Com & Marketing, Inc (ACMI), remote types, unknown values, unknown quantities issued

Endangered Series, Humpback Whale **15.00**

Green Bay Packers, Hall of Fame, Bart Star **12.00**

Jerry Lee Lewis, Great Balls of Fire **9.00**

Ameritech, Baby Bell Co, remote memory type card

CoinSaver Edition, set of 4, $1, $2, $5, $10 value, unknown quantity issued **31.00**

Internal Christmas/Greeting Telecard, $5 value, 5,000 issued **20.00**

Mackinac Island, set of 3, $2, $5, $10 value, 13,600 issued **24.00**

Amerivox, remote type card

Eagle, charter member, uncut corners, $250 value, $1,000 value, 100? issued **1,200.00**

Elvis

ID, $10 value, 23,000 issued   **21.00**

White suit, Cowan painting, test card, $7 value, unknown issue **160.00**

Lovers, Perillo, test card, $2.50 value, 100 issued **175.00**

New York Skyline, $10, $100, 2,000 issued **100.00**

Ocean Sunset, folder, cranberry flag, $10, $100 value, 1,000 issued **120.00**

Patsy Cline, proof card, $10 value, unknown issue **200.00**

Seattle Skyline, folder, $10, $100, 2,000 issued **100.00**

St Louis Arches, cranberry flag, $10, $100, 1,000 issued **110.00**

AT & T, remote type card, known as teletickets, issued in units rather than dollar amounts

Aeroplan, Dusseldorf Am Rhein, German, 10 units, 6,000 issued   **25.00**

Best Western, Statue of Liberty, 10 units, 666 issued **390.00**

Democratic National Convention Set, 10, 25, 50 units, estimated 250 issued **950.00**

Peace Card, 10 units, 10,000 issued **70.00**

Rolls–Royce, German, folder, 10 units, 999 issued **275.00**

Statue of Liberty, convention update on reverse, 25 units, 500 issued   **885.00**

Comdez, remove type card

Alison, $6 value, 2,500 issue **9.50**

Andrea, $12, 2,500 issue **15.50**

Global Telecommunications Solutions, remote type card

AIDS Awareness, 17 units value, 5,000 issued **13.00**

Love Stamp, red rose heart, 16 units value, 1,000 issued **12.50**

Smithsonian Postal Service, 16 units value, 5,000 issued **12.00**

GTE Hawaiian Tel, magnetic type cards

Aloha State Games, surfer, 3 units value, 3,000 issued **15.00**

Diamond Head, Waikiki Beach, 10 units value, 90,000 issued **21.00**

Hawaiian Open 25th Anniversary Ed, 10 units value, 750 issued **900.00**

Hawaiian Sunset, 10 units, 10,000 issued **17.00**

Hula Bowl, 48th Annual, Hula Girl, 3 units value, 6,000 issued **10.00**

Sun and Fun, 3 units value, 1,000 issued **65.00**

GTI Telecom, remote type cards, unknown quantities issued

Florida Attractions, 15 units **9.00**

GTI Soccer, 120 units **60.00**

Medieval Times, 40 units **21.00**

Space Shuttle, Spanish, 20 units   **13.00**

International Telecom, Inc (Alaska), Schlumberger chip type

Artic Visions Series

Dog Musing, $10.50 value, 5,000 issued **14.50**

Northern Lights, $52.50 value, 5,000 issued **57.00**

Denali National Park

Bull Caribou, $10.50 value, 4,000 issued **14.50**

Mt McKinley, $52.50 value, 2,000 issued **57.00**

MCI, remote type cards, no information on quantities issued

Phone Cash, first issue, 15 units

American **40.00**

Spanish **45.00**

Nynex, New York Telephone, Baby Bell Co, optical type card

Democratic National Convention

$1 value, complimentary, 20,000 issued **1,000.00**

$5.25 value, 16,000 issued   **275.00**

English, Phonecard, 40 units, BT and drum major figure, green, $25.00.

Ellis Island Series, $5.25 value, 50,000 issued

 #1, building **13.00**
 #2, Statue of Liberty **13.00**
 #3, Ellis Island **13.00**
 #4, John E Moore Paddleboat **13.00**
Empire State Building, night scene, Christmas folder, $5.25 value, estimated at 25,000 issued **33.00**
Lillihammer 1994 Luge, $5.25, 25,000 issued **29.00**
Wish You Were Here, $5.25 value, 70,000 issued
 Lake George **8.00**
 Niagara Falls **8.00**
Yellow Telephone/Skyline, complimentary, $1 value, 100,000 issued
 . . . . **65.00**
Phoneline USA, remote type card
American Flag, $20 value, unknown quantity, inactive **10.00**
Hawaiian Flag
 Local Access Number, $5 value, unknown quantity, active **7.25**
 Local Access Number, $20 value, unknown quantity, Japanese, inactive **11.00**
 1-800 Access Number, $5 value, unknown quantity, inactive . . . **2.75**
 1-800 Access Number, $10 value, unknown quantity, Chinese, active **13.50**
Misty's Hula 1993, $10 value, 20,000 issued, active **13.50**
Phantom of the Great Warrior, international calls, $20 value, 5,000 issued, active **26.00**
Queen Elizabeth II, 1993, $10, 2,500 issued, inactive **5.50**
Save the Whales, domestic calls, $5 value, 10,000 issued, inactive **2.75**
Statue of Liberty, $10 value, unknown quantity, inactive **5.00**
PTI, Prepaid Telecomm Intn'l, Inc, remote type card, donates 10% to Wetlands Habitat Development fund, cards reproduce revenue stamps issued by US Dept of Interior
1934 Mallards Alighting, $5 value, 31,000 issued **7.50**

French, Pour Telephoner Choisissez Votre Heure, 50 units, remote type chip. $65.00.

1936 Canada Geese, gold star, $5 value, 1,000 issued **9.50**
1939 Green Winged Teal, $5 value, 31,000 issued **7.00**
1941 Ruddy Ducks, gold star, $5 value, 1,000 issued **9.50**
1943 Wood Ducks, $5 value, 31,000 issued **7.00**
Sprint, remote type card
Corvette, 1960 model, 10 units, 4,000 issued **8.50**
Flamingo, 20 units, 3,000 issued **20.00**
Great Danes, 20 units, 4,000 issued
 . . . . **14.00**
Hallmark, 1993 market test, Moon Doggie, 10 units value **16.00**
Horses on the Range, 10 units, 9,000 + issued **8.00**
Lady Liberty, $10 value, 46,000 issued
 . . . . **20.00**
Las Vegas, $10 value, 10,000 + issued
 . . . . **8.00**
Mt Rushmore, International, 10 units, 37,000 + issued **8.00**
Red Roses, 20 units, 4,000 issued **14.00**
Teletrading Cards Inc, remote type card
Baseball's Greatest Set, four cards each with $5 value, 5,000 issued **38.00**
Wizard of Oz Set, six cards each with $5 value, 5,000 issued **55.00**
US West, Baby Bell Co, gemplus chip type card
Bowl and Pestle, $5.25 value, 30,000 issued **9.00**
Huckleberry Basket, $3 value, 10,000 issued **6.00**
Storage Bags, $11 value, 10,000 issued
 . . . . **26.00**
Worldlink, remote type card
Desert Cowboy, English and Spanish, 25 unit value, unknown quantity **48.00**
Exxon Tiger, 5 units, 5,000 + issued
 . . . . **6.00**
Marilyn Monroe, laughing smile, $10 value, 1,500 issued **13.00**
Statue of Liberty, 3 units value, 2,050 issued **7.00**

TELEVISION CHARACTERS AND PERSONALITIES

The golden age of television varies depending on the period in which you grew up. Each generation thinks the television of their childhood is the best there ever was.

TV collectibles are one category in which new products quickly establish themselves as collectible. The minute a show is canceled, something that happens rather rapidly today, anything associated with it is viewed as collectible.

The golden age of TV star endorsements was the 1950s through the 1960s. For whatever reason, toy, game, and other manufacturers are not convinced that TV stars sell products. As a result, many shows have no licensed products associated with them. Because of the absence of three-dimensional material, collectors must content themselves with paper, such as *TV Guide* and magazines.

Periodicals: *Big Reel,* PO Box 83, Madison, NC 27025; *Television History Magazine,* 700 E Macoupin St, Staunton, IL 62088; *The TV Collector,* PO Box 1088, Easton, MA 02334.

Addams Family
Board Game, Milton Bradley, based on 1973–75 cartoon series, 1974 **30.00**
Halloween Costume, Ben Cooper, 1965
 Lurch, black one-piece body suit with silver glitter Lurch and Thing illus, no mask, unused in poly bag **120.00**
 Morticia, purple one-piece body suit with dress illus adorned with small creatures, plastic mask, unused in box **240.00**
Ben Casey
Board Game, Transogram, 1961 **30.00**
Comic Book, Dell #3, 1962 . . . . . . **5.00**
Jigsaw Puzzle, "The Ordeal Is Over," Milton Bradley, 1962 . . . . **40.00**
Bewitched
Book, *The Opposite Uncle,* Whitman, TV Edition series, 200 pgs, 1968
 . . . . **8.00**
Card Game, Stymie, Ideal, vinyl playing board with cast photos, playing cards, 1965 . . . . **32.00**
Comic Book, Dell #7, 1966 . . . . . **15.00**
Writing Tablet, cast photo on cov, 1964, 8 × 10" **15.00**
Big Valley, comic book, Dell #3, 1967
 . . . . **10.00**
Bonanza
Book, *Killer Lion,* Whitman, TV Edition series, color photo cov, 1966 **15.00**
Comic Book, Gold Key #14, 1960s
 . . . . **4.00**
Cup, litho tin, Ben, Hoss, and Little Joe one side, Ponderosa ranch illus other side, 1960s, 3" h **20.00**
Captain Kangaroo
Chenille-Kraft Fun Kit, Barry Products, kit includes chenille pom-poms, bendable wire stems, soft vinyl animal heads, and straws, 1956, unused on card **30.00**
Coloring Book, dot-to-dot, Whitman, 150 pgs, 1959, 8 × 11", partially colored **10.00**

Jigsaw Puzzle, Fairchild, 1950s, 75 pcs, 9 × 11″ box **30.00**
Party Napkins, paper, Futura, 1956, 7 × 7″, pkg of sixteen **22.00**
View–Master Reel Set, Sawyer, 16 pg booklet, 1950s **30.00**

Charlie's Angels
Board Game, Milton Bradley, 1977, sealed **30.00**
Custom Van, Corgi, diecast metal, rear doors open, cast photo on box, 1978, 5″ l, unused **35.00**
Gum Card Wrapper, Topps, 1977   **8.00**

Combat
Board Game, Ideal, Vic Morrow and Rick Jason on box, 1963 . . . . . **55.00**
Book, Whitman, TV Edition series, 200 pgs, 1964 . . . . **10.00**
Card Game, Milton Bradley, 1964 . . . . **32.00**

Daniel Boone, canoe, inflatable, unopened, 1965 . . . . **20.00**

Dark Shadows
Board Game, Whitman, 1968 . . . . **42.00**
Comic Book, Gold Key, #9, 1971 . . . . **10.00**
Model Kit, Barnabas Collins, MPC, plastic, 1/12 scale, glow–in–the–dark pcs, orig box, 1968 . . . . **350.00**

Dragnet
Book, Whitman, hard cov, TV adventure series, 1968 . . . . **7.00**
Target Game, Transogram, tin target stand, four plastic tip–over criminals, 1955 . . . . **30.00**

Dr Kildare
Board Game, Perilous Night, Ideal, 1963 . . . . **30.00**

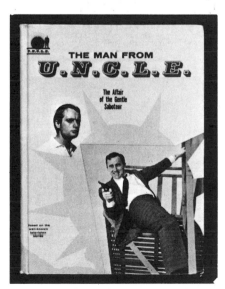

Book, The Man From UNCLE, The Affair of The Gentle Saboteur, by Brandon Keith, Whitman Publishing Co, 1966, illus by Tom Gill, hard cover, 210 pages, 5¾ × 7¾″, $10.00.

Color Set, Pencil–By–Number, Standard Toykraft, six pre–numbered pictures, six colored pencils, 1962, orig box **40.00**
Doctor's Kit, Hasbro, stethoscope, germ slides, Smith Brothers cough drops, hypodermic needle, hospital guide, medical bag, and other accessories, 1963, sealed in orig box **120.00**
Jigsaw Puzzle, Emergency, Milton Bradley, 600 pcs, 1962 . . . . **40.00**
Record, 45 rpm, *Theme From Dr Kildare*, MGM, Chamberlain photo sleeve, 1962 . . . . **10.00**

Dukes of Hazzard, cereal bowl, Deka Plastic, hard plastic, cast and car color photos around outside, 1981, 6″ d . . . **10.00**

Ed Sullivan Show, bank, Topo Gigo, figural, mouse **12.00**

Emergency!
Board Game, Milton Bradley, 1974 . . . . **24.00**
Survival Kit, Fleetwood, plastic hatchet, vinyl case, knife, sheath, and compass, Kevin Tighe photo on pkg, 1975, MOC **15.00**

Get Smart
Comic Book, Dell #1 . . . . **20.00**
Jigsaw Puzzle, Jaymar, Maxwell Smart and Agent 99, orig box, copyright 1966 Talent Associates, 14 × 19″ **25.00**

Gilligan's Island, writing tablet, color Gilligan and Skipper photo on cov, 1965, 8 × 10″ **18.00**

Grizzly Adams
Book, Harry C James, sgd **12.00**
Stuffed Toy, bear **13.00**

High Chaparral
Book, *Apache Way,* Whitman, 1969, hard cov, 5 × 8″ **9.00**
Comic Book, Gold Key #1, 1968   **7.00**

Hogan's Heroes
TV Guide, November 27, 1965, Bob Crane and Cynthia Lynn cov photo **12.00**
Writing Tablet, Bob Crane photo cov, 1965, 8 × 10″ **20.00**

Hopalong Cassidy, mug, milk glass, green Hoppy on Topper illus, 1950s, 3″ h **18.00**

I Love Lucy, comic book, Dell #9, 1955 . . . . **20.00**

Laugh–In
Electric Drawing Set, Lakeside, 1968, unused **60.00**
Magazine, #4, 66 pgs, Arte Johnson color photo cov, 1969 . . . . **10.00**
Record Album, 33⅓ rpm, Columbia, Rowan and Martin photo cov, 1969 . . . . **10.00**

Lone Ranger
Pencil Box, heavy cardboard, faux black leather, Lone Ranger on Silver on lid, American Pencil Co, 1949, 5 × 9″ **80.00**

Tattoos, Philadelphia Gum Corp, Lone Ranger fighting Indian, 1966   **32.00**

Man From UNCLE
Card Game, Illya Kuryakin Card Game, Milton Bradley, 1966 . . . . **24.00**
Oldsmobile Super 88 Car, Corgi, diecast metal, blue, 1966, 5″ l **70.00**
Pop Gun, plastic, luger style, Illya and Napoleon on pkg, 1965, unused **15.00**
Poster, Napoleon Solo, black and white, 24 × 36″, unused in orig shrink wrap **25.00**

MASH, gum card pack, Topps, six photo cards and gum, 1982, unopened   **8.00**

Mod Squad
Figure, Pete Cochran, hard plastic, Aurora, 1969, 3″ h **20.00**
Model Kit, station wagon, Aurora, 1/25 scale, plastic, includes Linc, Pete, and Julie figures, 1970, unassembled in box **180.00**

Munsters
Book, *The Great Camera Caper,* Whitman, TV Edition series, 225 pgs, 1964 . . . . **10.00**
Doll, Remco, vinyl head with synthetic hair, hard plastic body, 1964, 5″ h
Grandpa **215.00**
Lily **200.00**
Halloween Bag, A & W Rootbeer premium, plastic, Munster family holding mugs illus, 1988, unused   **20.00**
Lunch Box, thermos, 1964 . . . . . **190.00**

Roy Rogers, coloring book, *Rodeo Days,* Whitman, 50 pgs, 1962, 8 × 11″, partially colored **15.00**

Sea Hunt, 1987 series starring Ron Ely
Divers' Knife, Ja–Ru, MOC **12.00**

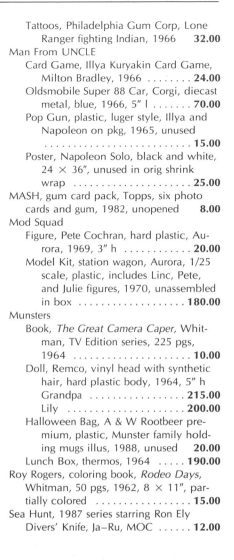

Topo Gigio, figure, Ed Sullivan Show, gray felt, blue and white striped nightshirt and cap, holding candle, $12.00.

Divers' Watch and Sunglasses, Ja–Ru,
MOC **10.00**
Starsky & Hutch, jigsaw puzzle, orig un-
opened, 1976 . . . . **8.00**
The Untouchables
Board Game, Transogram, Robert Stack
photo on board and box, 1961
. . . . **26.00**
Gum Card Wrapper, Leaf, Robert Stack
photo illus, 1961 . . . . **42.00**
Three Stooges, gum card wrapper, Fleer,
Larry, Moe, and Joe photo wrapper,
1965 . . . . **24.00**
Voyage to The Bottom Of The Sea
Book, TV Edition series, Whitman, 1966
. . . . **10.00**
Gum Card Wrapper, Donruss, *Seaview*
illus, 1964 . . . . **42.00**
Welcome Back Kotter
Halloween Costume, Mr Kotter, Col-
legeville, 1976, vinyl suit and mask
. . . . **30.00**
Wastebasket, tin, cast photo illus, 1975,
22" h **24.00**

TELEVISION LAMPS

No 1950s living room would be complete without a black ceramic gondola slowly meandering across the top of the television set. Long before the arrival of VCRs, descramblers, and Nintendo systems, figural lamps dominated the top of televisions. The lamps were made of colorful high gloss ceramics and the subject matter ranged from the relatively mundane dog statue to the more exotic (tasteless?) hula dancer.

A collection of ten or more of these beauties will certainly lighten up the conversation at your next party. On second thought, it does not take ten. The pink poodle lamp on my television is more than enough to do the job.

Ceramic
Accordion, translucent, ivory colored,
"Lawrence Welk," gold trim and let-
tering **65.00**
Buffalo, brown, standing on rocks
. . . . **32.00**
Butterfly, green, yellow, and black, leafy
base **30.00**
Fish, white, round metal base **18.00**
Flamingos, pink, black, and white, one
with wings spread, planter base, Lane
& Co, Van Nuys, CA, dated 1957
. . . . **50.00**
Gazelle, black, jumping over palm
fronds **35.00**
Hearth, green, yellow/orange screen
. . . . **28.00**
Horses, pair of black racing horses,
green foliate base **38.00**

Island Girl, green, leaning against palm
tree, screen background **40.00**
Lighthouse and Cottage, multicolored
. . . . **32.00**
Mallard, airbrushed, green and brown,
wings spread, planter base . . . **35.00**
Mallards in Flight, Maddux **45.00**
Owl, brown, green interior, sgd "Kron"
. . . . **20.00**
Panther, black, stalking, white screen
background, green oval base   **25.00**
Poodles, pr, pink and black, black oval
planter base **30.00**
Rooster, crowing, multicolored, standing
on brown fence, Lane & Co, Van
Nuys, CA, 13" h **45.00**
Sampan, ivory colored boat **20.00**
Scottie Dog, pouncing, gold **18.00**
Siamese Cats, 13" h **35.00**
Plaster, dying stag, brown stag, yellow
flower and base, gold trim **25.00**
Plastic, Niagara Falls, motion lamp   **85.00**
Seashells, seashell grouping **15.00**

TELEVISIONS

Old television sets are becoming highly collectible. It is not unusual to see a dozen or more at a flea market. Do not believe a tag that says they work. Insist that the seller find a place to plug it in and show you.

A good general rule is the smaller the picture tube, the earlier the set. Pre–1946 televisions usually have a maximum of five stations, 1 through 5. Channels 7 through 13 were added in 1947. In 1949 Channel 1 was dropped. UHF appeared in 1953.

In order to determine the value of a television, you need to identify the brand and model number. See *Warman's Antiques And Their Prices* for a more detailed list.

Club: Antique Wireless Association, 59 Main St, Bloomfield, NY 14469.

Console
Admiral, Model 20X1, Bakelite, 10"
screen, 1947–1948 . . . . **300.00**
Air King, Model A–1001, 10" screen,
twenty tubes, flat front, 1950   **85.00**
Bendix, Model 3051, square, 16" screen
. . . . **35.00**
DuMont, Model RA–101, Revere, 15"
screen, double doors, 1946   **125.00**
Magnifier, Pilot, Model TV–37, plastic, tabs
attach to grill, marked "Pilot TV"
. . . . **175.00**
Portable
Motorola, Model 7–TV5, leatherette cabinet, 7" screen, lid, handle . . . **150.00**

Tele–Tone, Model TV–208, 7" porthole
screen, handle, 1948 . . . . **150.00**
Zenith, metal, light–weight, 1950s
. . . . **35.00**
Table Model
Admiral, Model 19A11, black Bakelite,
7" screen, 1948–1949 . . . . . . **150.00**
Automatic, Model TV–707, blonde
wood, 7" screen, 1948 . . . . . . **150.00**
Fada, Model S–1015, wood, Bakelite
mask, square lines, 12" screen, 1949
. . . . **75.00**
General Electric, Model 805, Bakelite,
10" screen, streamlined, 1948
. . . . **175.00**
Philco, Model 50–701, Bakelite, 7"
screen, 1950 . . . . **200.00**
Westinghouse, Model H–196, rounded
top, 10" screen, 1949 . . . . **125.00**

THERMOMETERS

The thermometer was a popular advertising giveaway and promotional item. Buy only thermometers in very good or better condition which have a minimum of wear on the visible surface. Remember, thermometers had large production runs. If the first example that you see does not please you, shop around.

Club: Thermometer Collectors Club of America, 6130 Rampart Dr, Carmichael, CA 95608.

Advertising
Arbuckle's Coffee, colorful **250.00**
Bailey's Beverages, wood **30.00**
Borden Feed, orig box, 1952 . . . . **25.00**
Cash Value Tobacco, tin **22.50**
Champion Spark Plugs **20.00**
Chesterfield Cigarettes, 13" l, porcelain
. . . . **40.00**
Doan's Pills, wood **175.00**
Dr Pepper, 20" h, tin, 1960s logo
. . . . **50.00**
Dr Pierce's Chemical Co, Bakelite, 1931
. . . . **18.00**
Dunham's Shred Coconut, circular, brass
. . . . **300.00**
First National Bank, Fremont, OH,
wood, orig box **30.00**
Georgia Real Estate Co, wood, 21" h,
1915 . . . . **70.00**
Happy Jim Chewing Tobacco, 35" h
. . . . **75.00**
Hill's Brothers Coffee, little man drinking
coffee **450.00**
Keen Kutter **25.00**
Kendall Oil, round **25.00**
Lake Contrary Park, St Joseph, MO, "Big
Free Show Every Night" **375.00**
Lincoln Laundry, 12 × 3", wood, early
1900s **25.00**
Lone Star Beer, round, 1958 . . . . **125.00**

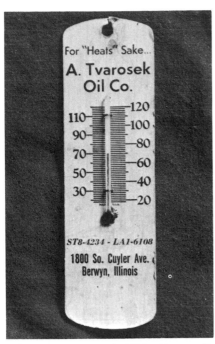

Advertising, A Tvarosek Oil Co, Berwyn, IL, cardboard, black letters, 1⁷⁄₈ × 6¹⁄₈" h, $4.00.

Moxie, "Old Fashion Moxie," metal
.... 20.00
Naco Fertilizer Co, Charleston, SC
.... 22.00
Natures Remedy, porcelain 250.00
Nyal Drugstore Service, 38" h 28.00
Old Dutch Root Beer, 27" h, 1940
.... 65.00
Pal Orange Ade, 26" h 40.00
Raymon's Brownie Kidney Pills, little
     doctor and roll of pills illus   350.00
Reuter & Co, Highland Spring Brewery,
     Boston, patented 1885, brass
.... 175.00
Rochester American Insurance Co, NY,
     porcelain 27.00
Royal Crown Cola, 20 × 10", card-
     board, Santa Claus and bottle, 1950s
.... 35.00
Sauer's Vanilla, wood, 1919 ..... 68.00
Snow Goose Flour, 39" h, blue trim,
     white ground 50.00
Standard Home Heating Oils, tin, torch
     logo 35.00
Sun Crest, bottle shape 65.00
Switch and Manufacturing Co, Carlisle,
     PA, 36" h, frog, dark blue trim, white
     ground 45.00
Tracto Weather Station, tin, orig box
.... 75.00
Washer Hardware, Sheldon, IA, wood
     frame 24.00
Figural
     Black man, 1949 .... 25.00
     Cat, 7¹⁄₂" h, bisque, Bradly label, Japan
.... 22.00

Owl, 6" h, plaster body 75.00
World's Fair
     1934 Chicago World's Fair, 2¹⁄₂ × 2¹⁄₂",
          octagonal shape, silver and blue dial
          symbol and lettering, brass rim, black
          metal back and hanging 50.00
     1964 New York World's Fair, 6 × 6",
          diamond shape, metal and plastic,
          full color illus 25.00

THINGS TOURISTS BUY

This category demonstrates that, given time, even the tacky can become collectible. Many tourist souvenirs offer a challenge to one's aesthetics. But they are bought anyway.

Tourist china plates and glass novelties from the 1900 to 1940 period are one of the true remaining bargains left. Most of the items sell for under $25.00. If you really want to have some fun, pick one form and see how many different places you can find from which it was sold.

Clubs: American Spoon Collectors, 4922 State Line, Westwood Hills, KS 66205; The Scoop Club, 84 Oak Ave, Shelton, CT 06484.

Periodical: *Antique Souvenir Collectors News,* PO Box 562, Great Barrington, MA 01230.

Album, souvenir, Haynes Yellowstone, 1940
.... 15.00
Ashtray, Memphis, TN, black boy, dog, and
     dice 95.00
Bookmark, Washington, DC, Capitol, brass,
     pinned 28.00
Bottle Opener, Brown Palace Hotel   24.00
Canoe, glass, flower dec, "Souvenir of
     Youngstown, OH" 30.00
Change Tray, Hotel Coronado, china   8.00
Compact, Hawaii, Elgin 30.00
Creamer, St James, MN 25.00
Dish, Atlantic City, china, puppy dec, Ger-
     many 50.00
Fan, Niagara Falls, silk 8.50
Hatchet, Hazelton, PA, white milk glass, red
     lettering, 6" l 25.00
Honey Pot, Belleville, KS 10.00
Mug, Jackson Courthouse, Kansas City, MO,
     china 10.00
Paperweight, New Salem State Park, glass,
     round, 2³⁄₄" d 30.00
Pennant, Kennedy Space Center, red felt,
     white lettering and Saturn V, 1966–67,
     26" l 18.00
Pin, enameled dec, Rockefeller Center, NY
.... 20.00
Pinback Button, Asbury Park, NJ, black and
     gray, beach scene 15.00

Charm, Washington DC, silver, c1960, $5.00.

Plate, Carnegie Library, Chickasha, OK,
     china, 7" d 12.00
Post Card, Main Street, large city 4.00
Salt and Pepper Shakers, pr, The Baker Ho-
     tel, Mineral Wells, TX, hp 18.00
Shot Glass, Berlin, Germany, clear, multi-
     colored city illus 5.00
Shovel, Kearney, NE, glass, gold scoop and
     lettering, clear handle, 6¹⁄₂" l 20.00
Snowdome
     Dewey Beach, plastic dome, sea gull
          and sea shells, 1960s, 2³⁄₄ × 2¹⁄₄ ×
          2" 8.00
     Long Beach Island, NJ, lighthouse shape
.... 30.00
Spoon
     Fairmount, MN, Opera House, SS
.... 45.00
     Los Angeles, CA, Mt Lowe Incline Rail-
          road, rose handle 30.00
Tin, Bunker Hill Monument, color litho
.... 35.00
Tumbler, Souvenir Hemingford, NE, ruby
     stained, 1912 calendar 30.00
View Book, *Photostint Views of Picturesque
     Detroit, The Convention City,* 16 color
     plates, 9 × 6" 8.00

TINS

The advertising tin has always been at the forefront of advertising collectibles. Look for examples that show no deterioration to the decorated surface and which have little or no signs of rust on the inside or bottom.

The theme sells the tin. Other collectors, especially individuals from the transportation fields, have long had their eyes on the tin market. Tins also play a major part in the Country Store decorating look.

Prices for pre–1940 tins are still escalating. Before you pay a high price for a tin, do your homework and make certain it is difficult to find.

Club: Tin Container Collectors Association, PO Box 440101, Aurora, CO 80014.

Angela Mia Cottonseed Oil **45.00**
April Showers Talc **10.00**
Bagley's Old Colony, pocket **95.00**
Bickmore Gall Salve **15.00**
Big Buster Popcorn, 10 oz, colorful, unopened **85.00**
Cadet Condom, round **46.00**
Calumet Baking Powder, 10 lbs **40.00**
Cambridge Blend Coffee **80.00**
Carter's Ideal Typewriter Ribbon, flower dec **5.00**
Champion & Staudinger Choice Tea, orange and black **125.00**
Chesterfield Cigarette, cat on lid **38.00**
Cleveland's Superior Baking Powder, lid, label **25.00**
Coast Pact Oysters, gal **20.00**
Cuticura Ointment **8.00**
CW & Co Cough Drops, canister **65.00**
Darma Tea, trunk shape **35.00**
Davis Baking Powder, sample **25.00**
Dewitts Hygenic Power **10.00**
Dining Car Coffee, 1 lb, key wind ... **58.00**
Douglass & Sons Capsicum Cough Drops, Ginna **75.00**
Educator Cakelets, made in Krackerland, hinged lid, multicolored animal illus, 1920s **145.00**
Educator Crackers **45.00**
Epicure Tobacco, pocket **90.00**
ESL Condom **45.00**
Farmer Peet Lard **12.00**
Father Christmas Candy, 1930s **55.00**

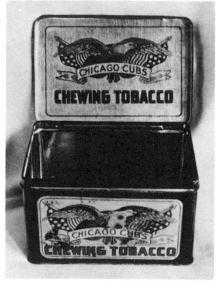

Tin, Chicago Cubs Chewing Tobacco, Rock City Tobacco Co, Quebec, blue border, gold ground, 6³/₈ × 4³/₈ × 4", $125.00.

Fitch Talc, c1930 .... **10.00**
George Washington Instant Coffee ... **30.00**
Golden Pheasant Prophylactics **68.00**
Heide's Almond Paste, workers and improved factory scene **70.00**
Herald Square Typewriter Ribbon ... **15.00**
Hersh's Best Coffee, 1 lb **80.00**
Huyler's Cocoa **35.00**
Improved Trojans Prophylactics **28.00**
In-B-Tween Cigarritos, large **30.00**
Instant Postum **22.00**
John Orderleys, Owl Drug Co **25.00**
Johnson's Waxed Floor Cleaner, 1940 .... **15.00**
Keebler Saltines, 1940s **22.00**
Lighthouse Cleanzer **8.00**
Little Chief Shortening, pail, Indian Chief illus **60.00**
Lucky Strike, flat **8.00**
Maxwell House Coffee, 1 lb, 1909 **20.00**
Mennen Talc, sample, Art Deco design **18.00**
Monarch Teenie Weenie Popcorn, pail, 1920 .... **225.00**
Mrs. Tucker's Shortening, pail, 1914, missing lid **30.00**
New Bachelor Cigar, man playing cards and dreaming of woman **100.00**
Noonan's Cleansing Cream, 1½" d, woman holding mirror **25.00**
Ojibwa Tobacco **125.00**
Old Colony Tobacco, pocket **95.00**
Old English Curve Cut **15.00**
Park & Tilman Talcum Powder **10.00**
Petersons Ointment **8.00**
Philip Morris **22.50**
Polly Peachtree Hair Straight **10.00**
Postmaster Cigar, "2 for 5¢ smokers" **75.00**
Pure Indian Tea, sample size **35.00**
Ramon's The Little Doctor **20.00**
Rapid Harness Menders **15.00**
Rawleigh's Phosphate Baking Powder **30.00**
Red Belt, pocket **75.00**
Red Seal Marshmallow **30.00**
Regulax **15.00**
Richelieu Tea **12.00**
Riley Toffee **15.00**
Secretarial Deluxe Typewriter Ribbon, gold **4.00**
Shedd's Peanut Butter, 5# pail **15.00**
Sheik Condom, 1931 .... **40.00**
Snow Flake Crackers, hinged, 9 × 9" **49.00**
Squadron Leader Tobacco **50.00**
Star Brand Typewriter Ribbon **7.00**
Sunshine Biscuit **12.00**
Swee-Touch-Nee tea, trunk style, red, gold and black **18.00**
Sylae Tooth Powder, sample size **6.00**
Tiger Tobacco, 4 × 6" **58.00**
Type Bar Typewriter Ribbon, sq, blue and white **5.00**
Union Leader, 4 × 6" **28.00**
US Marine, pocket **140.00**

Vasoline Camphor Ice **8.00**
Velvet Night Talcum **24.00**
Vogue Roytype Typewriter Ribbon, flower dec **6.00**
Walter's Palm Toffee **100.00**
Wedding Breakfast Maple/Cane Sugar Syrup, red and gold, stenciled **100.00**
Worlds Champion Polish **15.00**
Yellow Bonnet, 1 lb, key wind, unopened **25.00**
Youngs Victoria Cream **10.00**
ZBT Baby Powder **10.00**

TOBACCO–RELATED COLLECTIBLES

The tobacco industry is under siege in the 1990s. Fortunately, they have new frontiers to conquer in Russia, Eastern Europe, Asia, and Africa. The relics of America's smoking past, from ashtrays to humidors, are extremely collectible.

Many individuals are not able to identify a smoking stand or a pocket cigar cutter. I grew up in York County, Pennsylvania, which along with Lancaster County was the tobacco center of the East. Today, tobacco growing and manufacturing have virtually disappeared. Is it possible that there will be a time when smoking disappears as well?

Clubs: International Seal, Label, and Cigar Band Society, 8915 East Bellevue Street, Tuscon, AZ 85715; Society of Tobacco Jar Collectors, 3021 Courtland Blvd, Shaker Heights, OH 44122.

Banner, 36 × 72", King Pin Tobacco, cloth, full color, Liggett & Myers **125.00**
Box
    Old Plug Tobacco, Irvin & Leedys, Henry Country, VA, walnut, 4 × 7 × 12" **20.00**
    Tinsley's Natural Leaf Tobacco, wood **18.00**
Case, Liggett & Myers Chewing Tobacco, pocket **10.00**
Clock, Mayo's Tobacco adv, figure–eight regulator, composition, 30½" h **900.00**
Display, tobacco store
    Indian bust, plaster, wearing headdress, holding tomahawk, 21" h ... **175.00**
    Turkish bust, plaster, 20" h **100.00**
Needle Book, Society Snuff Tobacco, diecut **20.00**
Plug Cutter, The Standard Tobacco Knife, cast iron **55.00**
Post Card, Happy Thought **10.00**
Sign
    Bull Durham Tobacco, 12 × 20", paper **40.00**
    Hiplane Tobacco, tin, horizontal **95.00**

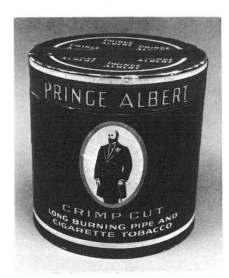

Prince Albert, Crimp Cut, round, $40.00.

Redford's Celebrated Tobaccos, paper, blacks growing and picking tobacco on plantation, 25½ × 20″ ... **175.00**

Velvet Tobacco, porcelain, pipes and tobacco tin on tray, "Velvet, The Smoothest Smoking Tobacco, Sold Here," 39 × 12″ **85.00**

Spittoon, brass, Redskin Brand Chewing Tobacco **115.00**

Store Bin, Sweet Cuba Tobacco, litho tin, slant top, yellow, black, and red, 8 × 8 × 11″ **105.00**

Tax Stamp, 6 × 7″, 1870 .... **12.50**

Thermometer
    Cash Value Tobacco, tin **22.50**
    Happy Jim Chewing Tobacco, 35″ h
    .... **75.00**
    Mail Pouch Tobacco **65.00**

Tin, upright pocket type
    Bond Street **37.88**
    Half & Half **5.00**
    Kite, paper **10.00**
    Monte Cristo, pencil box shape ... **85.00**
    Palmy Days **125.00**
    Red Jacket **50.00**
    Tuxedo **10.00**

Tobacco Bag, Bull Durham, orig box of 24, sealed **35.00**

Tobacco Cutter, counter style
    Brown's Mule, cast iron, marked "R. J. Reynolds Tobacco Co" **75.00**
    Enterprise Mfg, The Champion Knife Improved **65.00**
    SCWW & Co, Triumph **45.00**

Tobacco Rugs
    Dartmouth, football player **18.00**
    Tufts, hockey player **18.00**

TOKENS

Token collecting is an extremely diverse field. The listing below barely scratches the surface with respect to the types of tokens one might find.

The wonderful thing about tokens is that, on the whole, they are very inexpensive. You can build an impressive collection on a small budget.

Like matchcover and sugar packet collectors, token collectors have kept their objects outside the main collecting stream. This has resulted in stable, low prices over a long period of time in spite of an extensive literature base. There is no indication that this is going to change in the near future.

Club: Token and Medal Society, Inc, PO Box 951988, Lake Mary, FL 32795.

ACME, Saloon, El Paso, TX, copper–nickel alloy, "N F Newland Prop" in oval on front, reverse with "Good For 1 ACME Drink" **12.50**

Applegates Palace of Flying Animals, brass, two donkeys, "Then Shall We Three Meet Again" **12.00**

Baltimore Oriole Celebration, white metal, memorial statue on front, reverse with oriole, inscription, and date "Sep 12, 13, 14, 1882" **5.00**

Fada Radio **15.00**

Fred Biffar & Co, Chicago, "Firearms, Ammunition, Pocket Cutlery, Sporting Goods" on front, reverse with good luck symbols, "Good Luck," and "Membership Emblem of the Don't Worry Club," c1930 .... **10.00**

Garden City Billiard Table Co, Chicago, IL, brass, inscription on front, reverse with "Palace/Good For 5¢ in Trade," 1880s **15.00**

Globe Fire Insurance Company, NY, copper, eagle holding Liberty Bell and "Centennial 1776 1876" on front, reverse with world globe and company name and address **4.00**

Horace Greeley, campaign, brass, portrait and "Sage of Chappaqua" on front, reverse with eagle and "Greeley, Brown, and Amnesty 1872," ⅞″ d **30.00**

Knights of the Golden Eagle, Washington, D C, brass, capitol building and "Annual Convocation of Supreme Castle, Knights of the Golden Eagle, Washington, May 22, 1888" on front, reverse with laurel wreath around rim and blank center **20.00**

Knights Templars, Easton, PA, gilt brass, maltese cross and crossed swords on front, reverse with "36th Annual Conclave of the Grand Commandery of KT of Pennsylvania Easton May 28, 1889" **15.00**

Lion Buggy Co, Cincinnati, OH, brass, lion's head and company name on front, reverse with anchor and rope **5.00**

Michigan Central Railroad, brass, "MCRR 50" on front, reverse with "½ CORD," milled border **75.00**

Palmer House Barber Shop, copper–nickel alloy, name and "10¢ 66" on front, blank reverse **15.00**

Pennsylvania State Agricultural Fair, Philadelphia, PA, gilt brass, sheep and inscription on front, reverse with cow and calf above masonry capital and Philadelphia coat of arms, 1880 .... **25.00**

Pony House Saloon, Dayton, OH, brass, name and address on front, reverse with "Good For 5¢ In Trade," c1900 ... **4.00**

Remington, brass, "Shot With A Kleanbore Remington Cartridge" on front, reverse with "Shot With A Remington Rifle," 1¼″ d **8.00**

Scranton Stove Works, Scranton, PA, brass, gear inscribed with company name and scroll with "Dockash Medal" on front, reverse with world globe and "Dockash Range World Hunt Souvenir 1886" **3.00**

22 Nord–Amer Sangerfest, Chicago, IL, woman holding lyre and German inscription on front, reverse with inscription and date within wreath, 1881 **5.00**

Vaughan's Seed Store, Chicago, copper–nickel alloy, six story building on front, reverse with inscription and date "1887" **5.00**

Women's Relief Corps Convention, Columbus, OH, bronze, female bust portrait and signature "Kate B Kenwood" on front, reverse with inscription and date "Sept 1888" **12.00**

TOOTHPICK HOLDERS

During the Victorian era, the toothpick holder was an important table accessory. It is found in a wide range of materials and was manufactured by American and European firms. Toothpick holders also were popular souvenir objects in the 1880 to 1920 period.

Do not confuse toothpick holders with match holders, shot glasses, miniature spoon holders in a child's dish set, mustard pots without lids, rose or violet bowls, individual open salts, or vases. A toothpick holder allows ample room for the toothpick and enough of an extension of the toothpick to allow easy access.

Club: National Toothpick Holder Collectors Society, 1224 Spring Valley Lane, West Chester, PA 19380.

Figural
    Barrel, white milk glass, metal hoops **25.00**
    Beaver, wood, painted features, broad tail, hollowed out trunk **5.00**

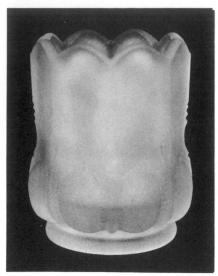

Toothpick Holder, Degenhart Glass, Michigan type pattern, heavily frosted white, heart with "D" mark, $5.00.

Boot, purple slag glass **50.00**
Cat, bisque, wearing coachman's outfit, barrel holder **55.00**
Cat and Bucket, SP **65.00**
Clown, brass, marked "Jenning Bros" **30.00**
Donkey, pulling cart, china, Occupied Japan **8.00**
Dwarf, bisque, 4½" h **25.00**
Egg, chick emerging, feet on branch, SP, sq base, Hartford **70.00**
Rooster, SP, engraved "Picks," 2" h **48.00**
Top Hat and Umbrella, brass **20.00**
Pattern Glass
Colonial, cobalt, Cambridge **25.00**
Feather, clear **65.00**
Heart, pink opaque **60.00**
Hobb's Hobnail, vaseline **20.00**
Iowa, clear **24.00**
King's Crown, ruby stained **38.00**
Paddlewheel and Star, clear **25.00**
Royal Oak, frosted rubina **125.00**
Three Dolphins, amber **45.00**
Souvenir
Custard Glass, Belvedere, IL **35.00**
Ruby Stained, Button Arches pattern, "Mother 1947" **20.00**

TORTOISE SHELL ITEMS

It is possible to find tortoise shell items in a variety of forms ranging from boxes to trinkets. Tortoise shell items experienced several crazes in the nineteenth and early twentieth centuries, the last occurring in the 1920s when tortoise shell jewelry was especially popular.

Anyone selling tortoise shell objects

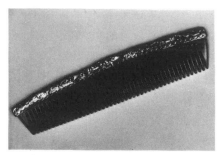

Comb, Amerith, removable sterling silver back, emb floral design, 8¼" l, $5.00.

is subject to the Endangered Species Act and its amendments. Tortoise shell objects can be imported and sold, but only after adhering to a number of strict requirements.

Box, rect, mid 19th C, 5 × 3½" . . . **175.00**
Bracelet, bangle, silver inlay, 3" d . . . **35.00**
Calling Card Case, mother-of-pearl and ivory inlaid design, c1825, 4 × 3" **225.00**
Cigar Box, rect, rounded corners, gold inlaid dec **250.00**
Coin Purse, silver inlaid dec, 3 × 2" **150.00**
Comb
Side, applied metallic dec, simulated gemstones **65.00**
Spanish, ornate design, 5½" l **45.00**
Eyeglass Case, rounded corners, eyeglasses, 5" l **165.00**
Hairpin, carved poppy blossoms . . . **140.00**
Hand Mirror, oval **110.00**
Humidor, rect, hinged lid, 4½" h . . . **150.00**
Letter Opener, silver fox head handle, 12" l **225.00**
Match Safe, pocket, emb sides **65.00**
Pill Box, small ivory feet, 2½" l **80.00**
Shaving Brush, inlaid mother-of-pearl dec handle **40.00**
Snuff Box, pique dec, ½ × 2 × 1¼" **110.00**
Stickpin, carved fly perched on coral branch, gold filled pin **75.00**
Straight Razor, Landers **30.00**

TOY TRAINS

Toy train collectors and dealers exist in a world unto themselves. They have their own shows, trade publications, and price guides. The name that you need to know is Greenberg Book Div., Kalmbach Publishing Co., 21027 Crossroads Circle, Waukesha, WI 53187. Their mail order catalog contains an exhaustive list of their own publications as well as those by others. If you decide to get involved with toy trains, write for a copy.

The two most recognized names are American Flyer and Lionel, and the two most popular gauges are S and O. Do not overlook other manufacturers and gauges.

The toy train market has gone through a number of crazes—first Lionel, then American Flyer. The current craze is boxed sets. Fortunately, the market is so broad that there will never be an end to subcategories to collect.

Clubs: American Flyer Collectors Club, PO Box 13269, Pittsburgh, PA 15243; Lionel Collectors Club of America, PO Box 479, La Salle, IL 61301; The National Model Railroad Association, Inc, 4121 Cromwell Rd, Chattanooga, TN 37421; Toy Train Operating Society, Inc, Suite 308, 25 West Walnut Street, Pasadena, CA 91103; Train Collectors Association, PO Box 248, Strasburg, PA 17579.

Periodical: *Classic Toy Trains,* 21027 Crossroads Circle, PO Box 1612, Waukesha, WI 53187.

Note: The following prices are for equipment in good condition.

AMERICAN FLYER, POSTWAR, S GAUGE

303, Atlantic, steam locomotive, 4-4-2, 1954–56 . . . . **20.00**
322AC, New York Central, steam locomotive, 4-6-4, black, white lettering, 1950 . . . . **45.00**
405, Silver Streak, Alco, Pa, engine, 1952 . . . . **80.00**
632, Lehigh New England, hopper, gray, red dot in logo, white lettering, 1946–53 . . . . **2.00**
734, Missouri Pacific, box car, 1954 **12.00**
743, track maintenance car, motorized **24.00**
940, Wabash, hopper and dump car, 1953–56 . . . . **12.00**
941, Frisco Lines, gondola, 1953–56 **7.50**

American Flyer, A C Gilbert Co, New Haven, CT, engine, diesel switcher, #370, silver, blue and yellow decals, orig box, 10" l, $95.00.

24310, Gulf, tank car, silver, orange logo, 1958–60 ....**8.00**

24330, Baker's Chocolate, tank car, 1961–72 ....**25.00**

24516, New Haven, flat car, 1957–59 ....**10.00**

24526, caboose, 1957 ....**12.00**

24773, Columbus, passenger car, 1957–58 ....**45.00**

LIONEL, POSTWAR (1945–69)

60, Lionelville, trolley type engine, aluminized paper reflector, 1955–58 **175.00**

85, telegraph pole **12.00**

120, tunnel **35.00**

145, automatic gateman, 1950–66 **15.00**

167, whistle controller, 1945–46 .....**1.00**

212T, US Marine Corps, dummy locomotive, blue, white stripes and lettering, 1958–59 ....**175.00**

419, heliport control tower, 1962 ...**75.00**

614, Alaska, NW–2 Switcher, 1959–60 ....**100.00**

625, Lehigh Valley, GE 44–ton switcher, red, white stripe and lettering, 1956–57 ....**75.00**

665, steam locomotive, 4–6–4, 1954–59 ....**75.00**

1007, Lionel Lines, caboose, SP Die 3, 1948–52 ....**1.50**

1062, steam locomotive, 2–4–2, 1963–64 ....**18.00**

1063, transformer, 75 watts, 1960–64 **9.00**

1866, West & Atlantic, baggage, passenger car, 1959–62 ....**24.00**

2257, Lionel, offset–cupola caboose, red, illuminated, extra details, 1948 ....**10.00**

2401, Hillside, pullman car, 1948–49 ....**24.00**

2431, observation car, metal, blue, silver roof, 1946–47 ....**12.00**

2465, Sunoco, tank car, 1946 ....**8.00**

2522, President Harrison, passenger car, 1962–66 ....**60.00**

2560, Lionel Lines, crane, eight–wheel, black boom, 1946–47 ....**20.00**

3330, flat car, operating submarine kit, 1960–61 ....**50.00**

3356, Santa Fe Railway Express, box car, 1956–60 ....**35.00**

3366, circus car, white, nine white rubber horses, 1959–62 ....**45.00**

3444, Erie, gondola, 1957–59 ......**30.00**

3461, flat car, logs, dump, 1949–55 **25.00**

3494–275, State of Maine, box car, 1956–58 ....**55.00**

3530, searchlight car, pole and base **25.00**

3662 1, automatic milk car, white, brown roof, 1955–60 and 1964–66 ....**30.00**

3927, Lionel Lines, engine, 1956–60 ....**60.00**

4452, Pennsylvania, gondola, 1946–48 ....**48.00**

6017, Lionel Lines caboose, SP dies, 1951–61 ....**15.00**

6025, Gulf, tank car, 1956–57 ....**8.00**

6414, Evans Auto Loader, red, black superstructure, four autos with windows, bumpers, and rubber tires, red, yellow, blue, and white cars, 1955–57 ...**20.00**

6417–50, Lehigh Valley, caboose, N5C, gray, 1954 ....**32.00**

6445, Fort Knox Gold Reserve, silver, clear windows, coin slot, 1961–63 ....**40.00**

6446–1, N & W, hopper and dump car, marked "546446," 1954–55 ....**25.00**

6461, transformer car, 1949–50 .....**25.00**

6465, Lionel Lines, tank car, 1958–59 ....**5.00**

6480, Explosives, box car **4.00**

6482, refrigerator car, white, black lettering, 1957 ....**20.00**

6819, flat car, helicopter, 1959–60 **25.00**

8403, Jesse James Train Set, MIB ...**250.00**

MARX

112, Lehigh Valley, diesel switcher locomotive, plastic, red, 1974–76 .....**15.00**

251, Canadian Pacific, Vancouver, maroon, gold lettering, black frame, four wheel, 6" l **60.00**

396, Canadian Pacific, steam locomotive, streamlined, sheet metal, electric motor, black cab, copper boiler and sideboards, 1941 ....**20.00**

548, Guernsey Milk, gondola, blue, cream int, four silver milk cans, eight wheel, 6" l **35.00**

551, New York Central, tender for steam locomotive, four wheel, blue, 1934–41 and 1950–55 ....**20.00**

554, Northern Pacific, high side gondola, red, yellow int, silver frame, four wheel, 6", 1938–40 ....**7.00**

567, New York Central, dump car, yellow, brown interior, red and white frame, four wheel, 6" l **18.00**

1235, Southern Pacific, caboose, red and silver, 7" l, 1952–55 ....**5.00**

1998, Rock Island, S–3 diesel, dummy, red and gray, 1962 ....**40.00**

3824, Union Pacific, caboose, yellow and brown, black frame, four wheel, 6" l **3.00**

5532, Allstate, tank car, plastic, turquoise, eight wheel, 1962 ....**5.00**

86000, Lackawanna, hopper, blue, red int, four wheel, 6" l, 1953 ....**3.00**

131000, Seaboard Coast Line, gondola, yellow, four wheel, 1973 ....**2.00**

TOYS

The difference between a man and a boy is the price of his toys. At thirty, one's childhood is affordable, at forty expensive, and at fifty out of reach. Check the following list for toys that you may have played with. You will see what I mean.

Clubs: Antique Toy Collectors of America, Two Wall Street, New York, NY 10005; Diecast Exchange Club Newsletter, PO Box 1066, Pinellas Park, FL 34665.

Periodicals: *Antique Toy World*, PO Box 34509, Chicago, IL 60634; *Collectible Toys & Values*, 15 Danbury Rd, Ridgefield, CT 06877; *Die Cast Digest*, PO Box 12510, Knoxville, TN 37912; *Die Cast and Tin Toy Report*, PO Box 501, Williamsburg, VA 23187; *Plastic Figure & Playset Collector*, PO Box 1355, La Crosse, WI 54602; *Toy Trader*, PO Box 1050, Dubuque, IA 52004; *Toy Shop*, 700 East State St, Iola, WI 54990.

Bandai, Japan
    '63 Corvair, friction, tin, litho tin int, tin bumpers, headlamps, and grill, celluloid windows, 8½" l **75.00**
    Cadillac Sedan, friction, tin, litho tin int, tin bumper, grill, and headlamps, diecast mirror, 17" l **425.00**
    Police Motorcycle with rider, tin **125.00**

Buddy L, car, wood **65.00**

Chein
    Bunny and Cart, windup, litho tin **45.00**
    Pelican, windup, litho tin, hops, early Chein logo, 5" h **265.00**

CK, Japan, Artillery Tank, pre–war Japanese tank, windup, litho tin, moves in circles, 4" l **45.00**

Como Plastics, All Star Dairy Foods Superman Saving Van, truck, Superman and logo decal on roof, 6" l **60.00**

Corgi, Chitty Chitty Bang Bang Vehicle, diecast, with accessories and figures, 6" l **90.00**

Cragstan, Remote Control Car, Cadillac style car, battery operated, litho tin, electric headlamps, forward and reverse action, orig box, 9" l **85.00**

Daisy, pop gun, wood stock, double barrel **65.00**

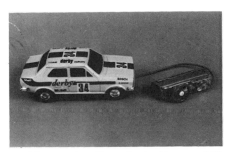

Asahi, Race Car, Team Derby Europe, #34, yellow, blue stripes, white and black trim, Mobile, Dunlop, Shell, Bosch, blue plastic battery control, Made in Japan, 3½" h, 8½" l, $85.00.

GW, Japan, Bar–Bee–Q, battery operated, combination grill and rotisserie, metal, orig instructions and 9" w, 4¾" d, 9" h box, $165.00.

Daiya, Japan, Bonnet Style School Bus, battery operated, litho tin, tin bumpers, grill, headlamps, and hubcaps, forward and reverse action, flashing lights, 13½" l **410.00**

Dinky Toys, Pullmor Car Transporter, diecast transport truck, orig loading ramp and inserts, orig box, 9½" l **195.00**

Germany, car, 4" l, bump–and–go action **1,175.00**

Gilbert
    Experimental Lab, 1950s **45.00**
    Microscope Set, 1938 .... **35.00**

Glendale, Railroad Station Playset, tin **110.00**

Griswold, Kwik–Bake Electric Oven, orig instructions and booklet **70.00**

Haji, Japan, Select A Matic 100 Juke Box, windup, litho tin, plays music from revolving record, 4½" h **150.00**

Hasbro, Transformers Radios, AM ... **30.00**

Home Foundry Mfg Co, Home Foundry Metal Casting Set, casting kit makes toy soldiers, molds, material, lead, 9 × 15" box **120.00**

Hubley, fire truck, 5" l, wood wheels **50.00**

Micromatic Tool & Mfg Co, Milwaukee, MI, Micro–Mix Mixer, battery operated, tin, plastic, aluminum bowl, cupcake tin, and cookie sheet, 7¾" w, 10¼" h orig box, $150.00.

Ideal
    Motorific Torture Tract Set, 1965, 20 × 11 × 2½", MISB **40.00**
    Skyport Building Set, over 475 pcs, 1968, 27 × 18 × 3" **100.00**

Irwin Toys, Walt Disney Dancing Cinderella, windup, plastic, Cinderella and Prince Charming waltz in circles, orig box, 5" h **195.00**

Jakel, Airomatic Glider Gun, tin, 1945 style pistol with three balsa wood gliders, 9" l **70.00**

Japan
    Buick Convertible, friction, tin, 9" l **100.00**
    Cat, windup, plush body, metal wheels **95.00**
    Model T Coupe, friction, litho tin, 9" l **45.00**
    Model T Roadster, 1917 Model T, friction, litho tin, plastic trim, 9" l **40.00**
    Vacuum Cleaning Mama Bear, windup, tin, cloth, and plush bear, forward and reverse action, 7" h **120.00**
    Volkswagen, friction, tin **150.00**

JE Stevens Co, Stevens Bang–O 50 Shot Repeater, diecast repeating cap pistol, Tenite grips with emb horse one side, cowboy other side, 7" l **90.00**

Kenner
    Burger Grill and Shake Set, orig food mixes, 1968, 22 × 14 × 11" **100.00**
    Easy Bake Oven Set, tin, orig box **42.00**
    Electric Mold Master, Make and Mold Your Own Army, 1963, 22 × 16 × 5", MIB **100.00**
    See–Action Football Game, battery operated slide projector, 288 different plays, 1973, 22 × 16 × 4½", MIB **65.00**

Keystone, Ride–Em Shovel **135.00**

Kingsbury, fire pumper **750.00**

Linemar, Japan
    Army Radio Jeep, battery operated, remote control, litho tin, rolls forward, driver signals left turn, orig box, 7½" l **55.00**
    Suzette The Eating Monkey, battery operated, litho tin, rolls eyes, cuts steak, lifts to mouth, chews, and repeats action, orig box, 8½" h **495.00**

Lumar, A & P Supermarkets truck, heavy tin, 19½" l **135.00**

Marx
    Bear Cat Racer #4, windup, litho tin car and driver, black tin wheels, 5" l **185.00**
    Dick Tracy Squad Car #1, windup, litho tin, tin bumpers, grill, and headlamps, siren, 11" l **200.00**
    Disneyland Casey Junior Express, windup, plastic locomotive, litho tin cars, 12½" l **60.00**

Funny Indian, windup, cloth, tin, and vinyl, rocks back and forth while beating drums, orig box, 7" h **120.00**

Siren Fire Chief Car, windup, pressed steel, electric headlamps, 15½" l **215.00**

Maxx Steele, Robo Force, robot telephone, MIB **150.00**

Nichols
    Stallion "22" pistol, diecast, oval style barrel, 5 shot cylinder, cap loading bullets, 7" l **80.00**
    Stallion 38 Six Shooter, cap pistol, diecast, plastic bone grips, six cap-shooting bullets, 10" l **165.00**

Nylint
    Econoline Van **65.00**
    Pepsi Truck **60.00**

Playtime Industries, Knight Rider Walkie Talkies, Universal Studios, 1982, 13 × 9 × 2", MIB **60.00**

Ralston Toys, Allied Van Lines truck, diecast, black plastic wheels, decals, orig box, 8½" l **50.00**

Remco, The Flintstones Motorized Paddy Wagon, dinosaur with paddy wagon cage on back, battery operated, plastic, orig box **195.00**

Rolly Toys, Germany, Rolly Poly Clown, very colorful, moving eyes, musical action, 15½" h **475.00**

Structo, Army Convoy Set, #521, two trucks, searchlight, missile launcher **785.00**

Sutcliffe, Jupiter Ocean Pilot Cruiser, windup, tin boat, orig box, 9" l ... **100.00**

TN, Japan, VW Sedan, tin, litho tin int, oval rear window, tin bumpers, grill, and headlamps, colored plastic inserts in engine cover, 7½" l **160.00**

Tonka
    Cement Truck **40.00**
    Pound Puppy **70.00**
    VW Beetle, missing one headlight and some paint **25.00**
    Wrecker **75.00**

Tootsie Toy
    Greyhound Bus, diecast, worn paint, 8" l **15.00**

Unknown Japanese Maker, Army Jeep, friction, litho tin, 3¾" l, 2" h, $10.00.

Triumph Spitfire, plastic, green convertible, 3" l **8.00**

Topper

Ding–A–Ling Space Skyway, Rocky the Robot, battery operated, 1971, 14 × 19 × 4", MIB **100.00**

Suzy Homemaker, washer and dryer, battery operated **95.00**

TPS, Japan, Pool Shooting Monkey, litho tin windup, MIB **400.00**

Unknown Origin, Fire Department Playset, tin building **250.00**

Wyandotte

City Service, wrecker **75.00**

Gamble Truck, semi **95.00**

Highway Freight, truck, 1940s ... **65.00**

Ice Cream Truck, hard plastic, 1950s, MIB **85.00**

Woody, car **40.00**

Y, Japan

Rolls–Royce Silvercloud Saloon, friction, litho tin, tin bumpers, grill, headlamps, and trim, orig box, 8" l **250.00**

Surprise Santa Claus, windup, vinyl Santa, tin base, rings bell, pulls package out of sack, orig box, 9" h **130.00**

TRAMP ART

Tramp art refers to items made by itinerant artists, most of whom are unknown, who made objects out of old cigar boxes or fruit and vegetable crates. Edges of pieces are often chip–carved and layered. When an object was completed, it was often stained.

Tramp art received a boost when it was taken under the wing of the Folk Art groupies. You know what has happened to the Folk Art market.

Box

10" l, white porcelain buttons, worn finish **110.00**

14½" l, chip carved, multi–layered lid, paneled sides, secret compartment in lid, old label reads "Made by Gus C Leyerle 10–30–57," minor edge damage **65.00**

Box, mirror inside, red lining, 10½ × 6 × 4", $75.00.

Chest of Drawers, miniature, three drawers, porcelain pulls, old alligatored finish, back label reads "I bought this July 2, 1955," old repairs to crest, 13" h **140.00**

Cuckoo Clock, polychrome dec, birds perched on arched crest inscribed and cutout to read "Made in Brookfield, Mass, Aderlarl Courville," losses and repairs, early 20th C, 21" h **925.00**

Desk, miniature, pine, multi–layered chip carved stars, compasses, circles, and geometric shapes, slant front hinged lid, blue paper lined int, six drawers, c1930, 21 × 15" **1,000.00**

Jewelry Box

12¼" h, poplar, bird finial, floral dec, carved name "Addie," four swing out trays, center compartment, scrolled feet, old dark finish   **200.00**

14" l, burgundy velvet panels, gilded tin trim, lid mirror, velvet lining   **150.00**

Magazine Rack, hanging, brass tack dec, dark finish, 15" w **75.00**

Mirror, pine, chip carved, multi–layered moons, circles, hearts, and geometric designs, c1930, 12¼" w, 20½" h **925.00**

Picture Frame, chip carved, floral design, four rect slats overlapping at corners, early 20th C, 8½ × 10" opening **110.00**

Sewing Box, pincushion frame top, single drawer, dark finish, 9½" l **30.00**

TRAPS

When the animal rights activists of the 1960s surfaced, trap collectors crawled back into their dens. You will find trap collectors at flea markets, but they are quiet types.

Avoid traps that show excessive wear and pitting. In order to be collectible a trap should be in good working order. Careful when testing one. You may get trapped yourself.

Club: North American Trap Collectors Association, PO Box 94, Galloway, OH 43119.

Bear, Newhouse, hand forged teeth, early model **900.00**

Coyote and Fox, Verbail **100.00**

Fly

Glass, aqua colored **32.00**

Sears Farm Master **50.00**

Wee Stinky, fruit jar **10.00**

Gopher

JVJ, Crete, NE **30.00**

Renkens **10.00**

Hawk, Gibbs **125.00**

Kodiak Bear, Herter's #6, chain and swivel **425.00**

Minnow

Handmade, metal and mesh, hinged door, 12" l **32.00**

Shakespeare, glass, pale green, metal lid, emb name, 1 gal **85.00**

Mole

Nash, Kalamazoo, MI **15.00**

Rittenhouse, spear type **15.00**

Mouse

Catchemalive, wood and tin **45.00**

Chasse, 3 hose choker **35.00**

CM Coghill, attaches to Mason jar **15.00**

Last Word, wood snap **8.00**

Schyler, folding killer, metal **18.00**

Wiggington, glass **20.00**

Wire mesh, 9" l **40.00**

Muskrat, Funsten Brothers, floating   **500.00**

Partridge, Davenport **110.00**

Rat

Fut Set, metal **18.00**

Little Jimmy, wood and tin, live trap **20.00**

Little Samson, iron, teeth **150.00**

Weasel, Official Weasel, wood, snap type, Animal Trap Co **8.00**

Wolf, Newhouse #4½, chain and swivel **160.00**

TRAYS

Tin lithographed advertising trays date back to the last quarter of the nineteenth century. They were popular at any location where beverages, alcoholic and nonalcoholic, were served.

Because they were heavily used, it is not unusual to find dents and scratches. Check carefully for rust. Once the lithographed surface was broken, rust developed easily.

Smaller trays are generally tip trays. Novice collectors often confuse them with advertising coasters. Tip trays are rather expensive. Ordinary examples sell in the $50.00 to $75.00 range.

Advertising

Aunt Lydia's 6 Cents Per Spool, Button & Carpet Thread, 9½ × 11", oak, open design **110.00**

Baker Cocoa, tip **125.00**

Billy Baxter Ginger Ale, tin **35.00**

Christian Feigenspan, woman illus **40.00**

Columbus Brewing Co, 4¼" d, tip, early 1900s **75.00**

Cottolene Shortening, 4½" d, litho tin, multicolored illus, black ground, NK Fairbank Co **40.00**

Evervess Sparkling Water, 10½ × 14" **35.00**

Falls City Brewing Co, 13" d, topless girl on horse **250.00**
Fitzgerald Ale Beer **18.00**
Franklin Life Insurance, tip **30.00**
Geo Ehret's Hellgate Brewery, NY, 13½ × 16¾", oval, tin **25.00**
Greater NY, tavern scene **50.00**
Hampdan's Ale, handsome waiter **165.00**
Hanley's Ale, Connoisseur **165.00**
Hebburn House Coal, 4" l, eagle in center, holding banner, wood grain ground **42.50**
Hopski Soda, litho tin, frog pouring drinks **50.00**
Incandescent Light & Stove Co, tip **75.00**
King's Pure malt, tip **35.00**
Miller High Life, girl sitting on moon **25.00**
Molson, porcelain **60.00**
Moxie Centennial, 1984 . . . . **35.00**
New England Brewing, stag illus **65.00**
Old Reading Beer, white lettering, blue ground, red border **50.00**
Peerless Ice Cream **85.00**
Rockford Watches, 3½ × 5", tin, girl wearing green dress **115.00**
Stollwerck Chocolate, tip **25.00**
Ubero Coffee, Boston **60.00**
Character, Pinocchio and Gepetto, 8 × 10", litho tin, 1940 copyright **20.00**
Commemorative
    Gettysburg Battlefield, 16½" l, oval, 1863 . . . . **45.00**
    Lindbergh Commemorative, 3¼ × 5", china, white, hp, plane, US and French flags on continents illus and "May 21, 1927," Moisy & LeRoi **70.00**
    Queen Elizabeth II Coronation, June 2, 1953, 4¾" d, pin tray, coat of arms, gold trim, Paragon **31.00**
Political
    North Dakota Governor, Gov Sarles 10¢ Cigar, 4" l, litho tin, black, gold, brown **50.00**
    Taft and Sherman, 4½" d, tip, litho tin, jugate portraits, rim caption "Grand Old Party/1856 To 1908," black and gold border **125.00**

William McKinley, 13 × 16", oval, litho tin, color portrait, green ground, signature, c1900 . . . . **100.00**
Souvenir
    Firestone Carriage Convention, 6½" l, brass, 1914 . . . . **20.00**
    Rochester, MN, 2½ × 6", ruby stained glass, gold trim **10.00**
    Valley Forge, Washington's Headquarters **40.00**
    Washington's Home, Mt Vernon, VA, 7½ × 11", porcelain, portraits of George and Martha Washington and Mt Vernon, multicolored, sq corners, gold trim, marked "Germany" **75.00**
    Yellowstone Park, 4" l, oval, copper, silver wash **12.00**
World's Fair
    1933 Chicago World's Fair, Century of Progress, 4¾" d, brass, emb, raised detailed exhibit buildings **25.00**
    1964 New York World's Fair, 8 × 11", litho tin, Unisphere and Avenue of Flags, eggshell white rim, gold inscription **15.00**

TROPHIES

There are trophies for virtually everything. Ever wonder what happens to them when the receiver grows up or dies? Most wind up in landfills. It is time to do something about this injustice.

Dad has begun collecting them. He is focusing on particular shapes and awards of unusual nature. He has set a $5.00 limit, which is not much of a handicap when it comes to trophy collecting. In fact, most of his trophies have been donated by individuals who no longer want them.

Always check the metal content of trophies. A number of turn-of-the-century trophies are sterling silver. These obviously have weight as well as historic value. Also suspect sterling silver when the trophy is shaped like a plate.

TURTLE COLLECTIBLES

Turtle collectors are a slow and steady group who are patient about expanding their collection of objects relating to these funny little reptiles. Don't you believe it! I am one of those collectors; and, I'm not at all slow about the expansion of my collection.

I find turtle collectibles everywhere. Like all animal collectibles, they come in all shapes and sizes. Candles, toys, storybooks, jewelry, and ornaments fea-

turing turtles can be found at almost any flea market.

Watch out for tortoise shell items. This material is subject to the provisions of the Federal Endangered Species Act.

Club: National Turtle and Tortoise Society, PO Box 66935, Phoenix, AZ 85282.

Bottle, figural turtle, clear glass, inscribed "Merry Xmas," tin cap, 5¼" h . . . **30.00**
Cookie Jar
    California Originals, upside down turtle **48.00**
    McCoy, Timmy Turtle **40.00**
Dish, cov, figural turtle, amber glass, removable shell lid **95.00**
Doorstop, figural turtle, painted green, 8" l **85.00**
Earrings, pr, aqua colored paste stone shells, screw posts **20.00**
Figure
    Japan, earthenware, brown, 2⅞" h **1.00**
    Weller, Coppertone, 5½" h **85.00**
Flower Insert, figural turtle, dark green glaze, Cliftwood Potteries, #2, 5½" l **12.00**
Paperweight, figural turtle, cast iron, Fire Insurance adv on celluloid insert in hinged shell lid, int mirror, early 1900s, 4" l **150.00**
Pin, wood body, carved clear lucite shell **50.00**
Pincushion, figural, cast iron body, stuffed velvet shell cushion **25.00**
Planter, figural, white matte glaze, McCoy **5.00**

Charm, silver, green scarab body, c1965, $10.00.

Biltmore Ice Cream, 15¼ × 10¼", $24.00.

Shell, Green Sea, bleached white, minor crack, 10" l, 8½" w, $5.00.

Salt and Pepper Shakers, pr, figural, ceramic, walking upright, dark green shells, brown bodies **6.00**
Stuffed Toy, plush, felt trim, Steiff, 5½" l **45.00**
Toothpick Holder, figural, child holding umbrella seated on turtle, SP, Pairpoint **175.00**

TYPEWRITERS

The first commercially produced typewriter in America was the 1874 Shoels and Gliden machine produced by E. Remington & Sons. The last quarter of the nineteenth century was spent largely in experimentation and attempting to make the typewriter an integral part of every office environment, something that was achieved by 1910. Although there were early examples, the arrival of a universally acceptable electric typewriter dates from the 1950s.

The number of typewriter collectors is small, but growing. Machines made after 1915 have little value, largely because they do not interest collectors. Do not use the patent date on a machine to date its manufacture. Many models were produced for decades. Do not overlook typewriter ephemera. Early catalogs are quite helpful in identifying and dating machines.

Clubs: Early Typewriter Collectors Association, 2591 Military Ave, Los Angeles, CA 90064. Internationales Forum Historishe Burowelt, Postfach 500 11 68, D–5000 Koln–50, Germany;

Newsletters: *The Typewriter*, 1216 Garden St, Hoboken, NJ 07030; *The Typewriter Exchange*, 2125 Mt Vernon Street, Philadelphia, PA 19130.

Advertising
    Erasure Template, celluloid
        Munson Pneumatic Speed Keys, keyboard illus, 1920s **20.00**
        Remington, typist and typewriter image, c1920 . . . . **25.00**
    Pinback Button, Oliver Typewriter Co, black and white, early typewriter image, red border, white lettering **25.00**
Typewriter
    Adler **125.00**
    Bing **130.00**
    Corona Folding **60.00**
    Demountable **80.00**
    Fox, No 23 . . . . **140.00**
    Hammond, Multiplex **225.00**
    Harris Visible, No 4 . . . . **90.00**
    L C Smith, No 3 . . . . **25.00**
    Mignon, No 4 . . . . **150.00**
    National, No 2 . . . . **100.00**
    Noiseless **175.00**
    Oliver, No 8 . . . . **100.00**
    Remington, portable, c1929 . . . . . **25.00**
    Royal, No 10 . . . . **25.00**
    Smith Premier, No 2 . . . . **50.00**
    Standard Folding **250.00**
    Underwood, portable **25.00**
    Wellington **150.00**
Typewriter Ribbon Tin
    Codo Super Fiber **7.00**
    Hallmark **5.00**
    Herald Square **6.00**
    Kleanwrite **7.00**
    Madame Butterfly **8.00**
    Midnight **5.00**
    Panama **8.00**
    Secretarial **5.00**
    Sun Strand **6.00**
    Thoroughbred **5.00**
    Twins **8.00**

1939 New York, adv post card, "The 14–Ton Giant Underwood Master Operating Daily At The New York World's Fair, 1939," giant typewriter, Fair symbols, $5.00.

UMBRELLAS

Umbrellas suffer a sorry fate. They are generally forgotten and discarded. Their handles are removed and collected as separate entities or attached to magnifying glasses. Given the protection they have provided, they deserve better.

Look for umbrellas that have advertising on the fabric. Political candidates often gave away umbrellas to win votes. Today baseball teams have umbrella days to win fans.

Seek out unusual umbrellas in terms of action or shape. A collection of folding umbrellas, especially those from the 1950s, is worth considering.

Umbrellas are generally priced low because sellers feel that they are going to have difficulty getting rid of them. They probably will. Buy them and put a silver lining on their rainy cloud.

Advertising
    Coca–Cola **25.00**
    Japan Tea, floral designs and mastiff dog medallion, "Mastiff Extra Chop, Choicest Japan Tea, Abbott Grocery," 65" d open size, 40" h **100.00**
    The Morning Call, Allentown, PA, newspaper, comic strip characters, unused **25.00**

UNIVERSAL POTTERY

Universal Potteries of Cambridge, Ohio, was organized in 1934 by The Oxford Pottery Company. It purchased the Atlas–Globe plant properties. The Atlas–Globe operation was a merger of the Atlas China Company (formerly Crescent China Company in 1921, Tritt in 1912, and Bradshaw in 1902) and the Globe China Company.

Even after the purchase, Universal retained the Oxford ware, made in Oxford, Ohio, as part of their dinnerware line. Another Oxford plant was used to manufacture tiles. The plant at Niles, Ohio, was dismantled.

Three of Universal's most popular lines were Ballerina, Calico Fruit, and Cattail. Both Calico Fruit and Cattail had many accessory pieces. The 1940 and 1941 Sears catalogs listed an oval wastebasket, breakfast set, kitchen scale, linens and bread box in the Cattail pattern. Unfortunately, the Calico Fruit decal has not held up well over time. Collectors may have to settle for less than perfect pieces.

Not all Universal pottery carried the Universal name as part of the backstamp. Wares marked "Harmony House," "Sweet William/Sears Roebuck and Co.," and "Wheelock Peoria" are part of the Universal production line. Wheelock was a department store in Peoria, Illinois, that controlled the Cattail pattern on the Old Holland shape.

Periodical: *The Daze,* PO Box 57, 10271 State Rd, Otisville, MI 48463.

Ballerina
    Salt and Pepper Shakers, pr, burgundy
    . . . . **16.00**
    Tray, 13" d, yellow **10.00**
Calico Fruit
    Custard Cup, 5 oz **4.00**
    Jug, cov **40.00**
    Plate, 6" d, bread and butter **4.00**
    Refrigerator Set, three round jars, 4", 5",
    and 6" **45.00**
    Salt and Pepper Shakers, pr, range
    . . . . **18.00**
    Soup Bowl, tab handle **6.00**
Cattail
    Bowl **15.00**
    Casserole, cov, 8¼" d **15.00**
    Cookie Jar, cov **45.00**
    Gravy Boat **20.00**
    Milk Jug, 1 quart **20.00**
    Platter, oval **20.00**

URINALS

When you have to go, you have to go—any port in a storm. You have been in enough bathrooms to know that all plumbing fixtures are not equal.

The human mind has just begun to explore the recycling potential of hospital bedpans. Among the uses noted are flower planters, food serving utensils, and dispersal units at the bottom of down spouts. How have you used them? Send your ideas and pictures of them in action to the Bedpan Recycling Project, 5093 Vera Cruz Road, Emmaus, PA 18049.

VALENTINES

There is far too much emphasis placed on adult valentines from the nineteenth century through the 1930s. It's true they are lacy and loaded with romantic sentiment. But, are they fun? No!

Fun is in children's valentines, a much neglected segment of the valentine market. If you decide to collect them, focus on penny valentines from the 1920 through 1960 period. The artwork is bold, vibrant, exciting, and a tad corny. This is what makes them fun.

There is another good reason to collect twentieth-century children's valen-

tines. They are affordable. Most sell for less than $2.00, with many good examples in the 50¢ range. They often show up at flea markets as a hoard. When you find them, make an offer for the whole lot. You won't regret it.

Club: National Valentine Collectors Association, PO Box 1404, Santa Ana, CA 92702.

Art Nouveau, heart shaped, folding . . . **5.00**
Comical
    Boy wearing sailor suit, duck, "Will You
    Be My Valentine," c1920 . . . . . **2.00**
    Lady Killer, A J Fisher, NY, c1850
    . . . . **30.00**
Diecut
    Girl, emb, silver and gold paper lace,
    folding, greeting inside **15.00**
    Two girls, "Valentine's Greetings," Ger-
    many **7.00**
Foldout, standup
    Boy and girl holding flowers, walking
    through forest, four tiers, Germany,
    c1910 . . . . **28.00**
    Boy and girl sitting on chaise lounge,
    diecut, emb, Germany **15.00**
    Boy painting girl's portrait, "I'd Love To
    Paint You My Valentine," USA **3.00**
    Cupid holding gift, "To My Sweetheart,"
    red tissue paper, USA **7.00**
Honeycomb, Cupid's Temple of Love,
    c1928 . . . . **15.00**
Mechanical, Such Is Married Life, c1950
    . . . . **45.00**

Post Card, With Love's Fond Greeting, heart with child in red suit, plumed hat, divided back, Series No. 942, International Art Publishing Co, $5.00.

Valentine, three dimensional, diecut, 3⅞ × 6⅞" h, $8.50.

Post Card
    Boy and girl, "Love's Greeting," Ellen H
    Clapsaddle, 1922 . . . . **5.00**
    Cupid on swing of roses, red hearts and
    gold scrollwork border, E Nash **1.50**
    Cupid shooting hearts and arrows at lov-
    ers, heart background, "February
    14th," green ivy trim, Germany,
    1910 . . . . **1.50**
    Gibson Girl on swing, gilded back-
    ground, "To My Valentine" **2.00**
    Pumpkin man and woman, sitting on
    bench, "To My Valentine" **5.00**
    Woman with valentine, red hearts, "A
    Valentine Reminder," John Winsch
    . . . . **18.00**
Pullout, religious sentiment, flowers, five
    layers, Germany **50.00**
Standup
    Little Lulu and Tubby **15.00**
    Parrot, "I'd Make a Bird of a Valentine,"
    Germany **4.00**

VERNON KILNS

Founded in Vernon, California, in 1912, Poxon China was one of the many small potteries flourishing in southern California. By 1931 it was sold to Faye G. Bennison and renamed Vernon Kilns, but it was also known as Vernon Potteries Ltd. Under Bennison's direction, the company became a leader in the pottery industry.

The high quality and versatility of its wares made it very popular. Besides a varied dinnerware line, Vernon Kilns also produced Walt Disney figurines and advertising, political, and fraternal items. One popular line was historical and commemorative plates, which included several plate series, featuring scenes from England, California missions, and the West.

Surviving the Depression, fires, earthquakes, and wars, Vernon Kilns could not compete with the influx of imports. In January 1958, the factory was closed. Metlox Potteries of Manhattan Beach, California, bought the trade name and molds along with the remaining stock.

Newsletter: *Vernon View*, PO Box 945, Scottsdale, AZ 85252.

Anytime, Platter, 13½" l **22.00**
Casual California
   Plate
      Bread and Butter, lime **20.00**
      Dinner, 10" d, pine **15.00**
   Saucer, pine **2.50**
   Tumbler, mocha **22.00**
Early California, chowder bowl, lug handle,
   blue **10.00**
Gingham
   Bowl, 5½" d, berry **4.00**
   Butter Dish, cov **50.00**
   Cup and Saucer **7.00**
   Mixing Bowl
      7" d **20.00**
      8" d **22.00**
   Pitcher, 2 quart **45.00**
   Plate
      6¼" d **2.00**
      9½" d **7.00**
   Salt and Pepper Shakers, pr **10.00**
   Teapot, cov **55.00**
Hawaiian Coral
   Creamer **15.00**
   Cup **10.00**
   Plate
      Bread and Butter **7.00**
      Dinner **15.00**
   Saucer **2.50**
   Sugar
      Covered **20.00**
      Open **10.00**
Hawaiian Flowers, Don Blanding, maroon
   Chop Plate
      12" d **100.00**
      14" d **150.00**
   Creamer **36.00**
   Cup **30.00**
   Plate
      Bread and Butter **20.00**
      Lunch, 9½" d **40.00**
   Saucer **6.00**
   Sugar, cov **50.00**
Homespun
   Mixing Bowl, 7" d **42.00**
   Pitcher, 2 quart **45.00**

Moby Dick
   Chop Plate, 13" d, pink **195.00**
   Plate
      6" d, blue **18.00**
      9" d
         Blue **60.00**
         Brown **50.00**
Modern California
   Berry Bowl, sand **5.00**
   Carafe, orchid **65.00**
   Chop Plate, 12" d, sand **30.00**
   Creamer, azure **18.00**
   Cup and Saucer, sand **10.00**
   Gravy, straw **25.00**
   Muffin Tray, cov, azure **100.00**
   Plate
      6¼" d, bread and butter, straw   **8.00**
      7½" d, azure **5.00**
      9½" d, lunch, pistachio **15.00**
      10½" d, dinner, straw **20.00**
   Platter, 12" l, orchid **25.00**
   Salt and Pepper Shakers, pr, orchid
      .... **20.00**
   Saucer, pistachio **3.00**
   Sugar, cov, orchid **25.00**
   Vegetable
      Oval, 10" l, azure **22.00**
      Round, 9" d, orchid **22.00**
Organdie
   Butter Dish, cov **50.00**
   Carafe, stopper **45.00**
   Casserole, tab handles, 4" l, no lid
      .... **25.00**
   Chop Plate, 14" d **55.00**
   Coffee Server **40.00**
   Gravy **25.00**
   Pitcher
      ½ Pint
      2 quart **45.00**
   Tumbler, 14 oz **28.00**

Gingham, tid–bit server, two tiers, green, yellow, and rust, gold colored metal handle, 6½" d, 9½" d, 10" h, $30.00.

Rose–a–Day
   Pitcher, 1 quart **25.00**
   Tumbler **22.00**
Sherwood
   Casserole **40.00**
   Coffeepot **45.00**
   Teapot **45.00**
Tickled Pink
   Salt and Pepper Shakers, pr **20.00**
   Serving Tray, center wooden handle
      .... **25.00**
Tradewinds
   Carafe **65.00**
   Chop Plate, 13" d **35.00**
   Pitcher
      ½ pint **20.00**
      1 pint **25.00**
   Plate
      7½" d, salad **10.00**
      10" d, dinner **15.00**
   Platter, 9½" l **20.00**
   Salad Bowl, 10½" d **55.00**
   Salt and Pepper Shakers, pr **20.00**
   Sauceboat **25.00**
   Sugar, cov **20.00**
   Tea cup **10.00**
   Tumbler **25.00**
   Vegetable Bowl, 7½" d **20.00**

VIDEO GAMES

At the moment, most video games sold at a flea market are being purchased for reuse. There are a few collectors, but their number is small.

It might be interesting to speculate at this point on the long–term collecting potential of electronic children's games, especially since the Atari system has come and gone. The key to any toy is playability. A video game cartridge has little collecting value unless it can be put into a machine and played. As a result, the long–term value of video games will rest on collectors' ability to keep the machines that use them in running order. Given today's tendency to scrap rather than repair a malfunctioning machine, one wonders if there will be any individuals in 2041 that will understand how video game machines work and, if so, be able to get the parts required to play them.

Next to playability, displayability is important to any collector. How do you display video games? Is the answer to leave the TV screen on 24 hours a day?

Video games are a fad waiting to be replaced by the next fad. There will always be a small cadre of players who will keep video games alive, just as there is a devoted group of adventure game

Pong, Atari, orig box, $20.00.

players. But given the number of video game cartridges sold, they should be able to fill their collecting urges relatively easily.

What this means is that if you are going to buy video game cartridges at a flea market, buy them for reuse and do not pay more than a few dollars. The closer to its release you try to buy a game, the more you pay. Just wait. Once a few years have passed, the sellers will just be glad to get rid of them.

VIEW-MASTER

William Gruber invented and Sawyer's Inc., of Portland, Oregon, manufactured and marketed the first View-Master viewers and reels in 1939. The company survived the shortages of World War II by supplying training materials in the View-Master format to the army and navy.

Immediately following World War II a 1,000-dealer network taxed the capacity of the Sawyer plant. In 1946 the Model C, the most common of the viewers, was introduced. Sawyer was purchased by General Aniline & Film Corporation in 1966. After passing through other hands, View-Master wound up as part of Ideal Toys.

Do not settle for any viewer or reel in less than near-mint condition. Original packaging, especially reel envelopes, is very important. The category is still in the process of defining which reels are valuable and which are not.

Club: National Stereoscopic Association, PO Box 14801, Columbus, OH 43214.

Projector
    S–1, metal, brown, single lens, carrying case **50.00**
    Sawyer's, plastic, single lens **10.00**
Reel, single
    51, Garden of the Gods, CO, white reel, printed title, blue and white envelope **1.00**
    62, Hawaiian Hula Dancers, white reel, hand lettered, blue and white envelope **3.00**
    86, Franklin D Roosevelt's Home, Hyde Park, NY, white reel, printed title, blue and white envelope, 1950 . . . . **2.00**
    92, Oregon Caves National Monument, white reel, hand lettered, blue and white envelope **2.00**
    181, Colonial Williamsburg, VA, white reel, hand lettered, blue and white envelope **10.00**
    222, Tournament of Roses, Pasadena, CA, white reel, printed title, blue and white envelope, 1953 . . . . **10.00**
    253, Carlsbad Caverns National Park, white reel, hand lettered, blue and white envelope **4.00**
    342, Race Horses of the Bluegrass Country, KY, white reel, printed title, blue and white envelope, 1952 . . . . . **3.00**
    510, Lake Patzcuaro and Paricutin Volcano, white reel, hand lettered, blue and white envelope **6.00**
    623, Ruins of Pachacamac, near Lima, Peru, white reel, hand lettered, blue and white envelope **20.00**
    742, Movie Stars, Hollywood III, white reel, printed title, blue and white envelope **15.00**
    942, Life with the Cowboys, white reel, printed title, blue and white envelope, 1951 . . . . **2.00**
    4300, The Taj Mahal and Red Fort, Agra, India, white reel, printed title, blue and white envelope, 1949 **3.00**
    9055, Prehistoric Cliff Dwellers of Mesa Verde, CO, white reel, printed title, blue and white envelope, 1950 **5.00**
    SAM–1, Adventures of Sam Sawyer, Sam Flies to the Moon, booklet, white reel, printed title, blue and white envelope **4.00**
    SP–9039, San Diego, CA, white reel, printed title, blue and white envelope, 1949 . . . . **1.00**
Reel, three–pack
    965–A, B, and C, Buffalo Bill, Jr **25.00**
    A–102, Eskimos of Alaska **8.00**
    A–163, Yosemite National Park, Packet No 2 . . . . **9.00**
    A–635, Historic Philadelphia, edition A **12.00**

    A–949, Walt Disney World, Adventureland **6.00**
    B–343, Mark Twain's Huckleberry Finn **30.00**
    B–503, Dark Shadows, edition A, 1968 . . . . **20.00**
    B–811, Forging A Nation, America's Bicentennial Celebration **8.00**
    CH–6A, B, and C, Birth of Jesus, booklet **3.00**
    J–32, Thailand, GAF **6.00**
Viewer
    Mickey Look Viewer Gift Set, plastic, six story reels, 1989 . . . . **8.00**
    Model F, lighted, dark brown plastic, pressure bar on top **18.00**
    Modern Viewer **1.50**

WADE CERAMICS

Dad has a Wade animal collection because he drinks quantities of Red Rose Tea. Red Rose Tea issued several series of small animals. Like many of his other collections, Dad is not happy until he has multiple sets. "Drink more tea" is the order of the year at his office. How much simpler it would be just to make a list of the missing Wades and pick them up at flea markets.

Ashtray
    Camel, Whimtray **18.00**
    Tortoise in center **30.00**
Bank
    Pig wearing suit, Westminster Piggy Bank Family **40.00**
    Thomas the Tank Engine, blue . . . **60.00**
Basket, Gothic **95.00**
Butter Dish, cov, Basket Ware **38.00**
Creamer and Sugar, Copper Lustre . . . **32.00**
Figure
    Elephant, Happy Families **5.00**
    Humpty Dumpty, Nursery Favourites **20.00**
    Pelican, Whimsies **15.00**
    Squirrel, Red Rose Tea premium . . . **5.00**
    St Bernard, St Bruno Tobacco premium **20.00**
    Windmill, Whimsey–On–Why . . . **40.00**
Pipe Rest, German Shepherd **25.00**
Pitcher
    Advertising, White Label Dewar's Scotch Whiskey **28.00**
    Embossed rabbit and trees, Heath, green **80.00**
Plate, Grape dec **18.00**
Puppy Dish **15.00**
Shaving Mug, biplane **18.00**
Tankard
    1925 MG **12.00**
    Barrel **15.00**
    Irish Porcelain, hunt scene **28.00**
Teapot, cov, Bramble Ware **90.00**

Vase, Charles and Diana, Royal Commemoratives **55.00**

WALGREENS COLLECTIBLES

What was your favorite drugstore? My dad has fond memories of hanging out at the local soda fountain—he says nothing can compare to the malted milk and ice cream concoctions of his youth. I wouldn't know. Unfortunately, the soda fountain counters were dismantled long before my time. In the old days a trip to Walgreens meant not only filling a prescription and picking up health and beauty care staples, it also meant taking a seat and ordering up your favorite soda fountain treat. Nowadays, when you take a trip to the drugstore, chances are you're sick, and the trip is a necessity. It certainly doesn't conjure up the pleasant memories it used to.

Walgreens is a new listing in *Flea Market*. Drugstore memorabilia has been a popular collectibles category for some time and many collectors specialize in a particular brand. Walgreen Drug Stores provide a vast range of items from which to choose.

Walgreen's has been in business since 1901. The first store was founded in Chicago, Illinois, by Charles R. Walgreen, Sr. A Walgreen has been in charge ever since. Today there are 1,800 stores coast to coast and by the year 2000 there will be over 3,000 in operation.

There are many different Walgreen brand products, i.e., soda fountain accessories, drugs, toys, cosmetics, and items from its exhibit at the 1933 Chicago World's Fair, just to name a few. In the 1950s, Walgreen's was the largest drugstore operation with soda fountains in the United States. They sold more ice cream, malts, and sundaes than any other retailer. For more information about Walgreen Drug Stores, refer to Herman Kogan and Rick Kogan's *Pharmacist To The Nation, A History of Walgreen Company* (Walgreen Co, 1989).

The creation of fast food franchises meant the demise of soda fountains. Today, they no longer exist.

Bottle, paper label
   Child's Witch Hazel, 1928, 16 oz, 8" h **17.00**

Tins, left: Peau–Doux Talc, vertical rect, litho tin, 4 oz, 1938, 4½" h, $35.00; center: Carrel Tidy Dainty Deodorant, vertical round, litho tin, 2 oz, 5¼" h, $25.00; right: Carrel Paisley's Lavender Scented Talcum Powder, vertical round, litho tin, 3 oz, 1940, 4¾" h, $30.00.

Gay Cologne, Leon Laraine, green and white Art Deco style bottle, 1941, 6 oz, 6" h **22.00**
Olafin Cod Liver Oil, 1935, 16 oz, 8" h **12.00**
Union Drug Alcohol, 1930, 16 oz, 7" h **12.00**
Walgreen Lilac Bouquet Beard Gloss, blue and cream label, barber screw cap, 1918, 4 oz, 6" h **40.00**
Walgreen Tar Soap Shampoo, barber screw cap, 1920, 12 oz, 7½" h **15.00**
Box, Peau–Doux Shaving Cream, yellow, red, and black, 1938, orig 4 oz tube, 7½" h **12.00**
Bracelet, copper, Walgreen building, souvenir Chicago World's Fair, 1933–34 .... **45.00**
Canister, cardboard
   Calonite Powder, Research Labs, vertical round, orange and blue, 1920, 3 oz, 4" h **22.00**
   Powdered Alum, Walgreen Labs, vertical round, yellow and brown, 1925, 3" h **15.00**
   Triomphe Bath Powder, Carrel, cream and pink, 1940, 6 oz, 14" d **20.00**
Coin, copper colored, Walgreen building, souvenir Chicago World's Fair, 1933–34, 2½" d **40.00**
Dosage Glass, white letters, 1930, 4 oz **25.00**
Drink Shaker, Art Deco style, aluminum, black letters, souvenir Chicago World's Fair, 1933–34, 11" h **75.00**
Golf Balls, Peau–Doux brand, green box, 1938, sleeve of three **75.00**
Jar, ointment, Union Drug, white glass, paper label, orange and blue, 1935, 3 oz, 2½" h **16.00**
Malt Glass, clear, 1940, 16 oz, 8½" h **40.00**
Menu Holder, black, 1935, 1½ × 3½" **75.00**
Playing Cards, Peau–Doux brand adv, green and black, 1935, two deck pack **20.00**
Pocket Mirror, Green Bay store opening, 1938 .... **60.00**

Sign
   Malted Milk, back board type, 1938, 45 × 25 × 3" **400.00**
   Stained glass, back boards, 1935, 113 × 25", pr **450.00**
Straw Holder, white china, 4" w base, 3½" h **50.00**
Tin
   All Purpose Talc, vertical oval, litho, blue and cream, 1934, 6" h ... **18.00**
   Carrel Paislay's Talcum Powder, vertical rect oval, litho, 1940, 3 oz, 4¾" h **30.00**
   Coffee, orange and black, screw top, 1 lb, 1927 .... **350.00**
   Golden Crown Tennis Balls, cylinder, 1938, 8" h, sleeve of three ... **75.00**
   Lady Charlotte Chocolates, colonial scenes, cream ground, 1940, 2½ × 4 × 7½" **25.00**
   Malted Milk, litho, 1935, 25 lb, 13 × 9½ × 9½" **125.00**
   Peau–Doux Brand
      Styptic Powder, vertical oval, litho, yellow and red, 1938, 1½ oz, 2¾" h **45.00**

Tin, malted milk can, litho tin, 25–pound size, 1935, 13 × 9½ × 9½", $125.00.

Talc, vertical rect, litho, yellow and
red, 1938, 4 oz, 4½" h **35.00**
Walgreen Brand
Aspirin, rect flat, orange and brown,
24 tablets, 1938 . . . . **22.00**
Hygienic Baby Talc, vertical oval, litho, white, black, and red, 1932,
4 oz **75.00**
Salted Peanuts, vertical round, or-
ange, cream, and black, 1935, 16
oz, 4½" h **35.00**
Toiletry Kit, Peau–Doux brand, includes
talc, styptic powder, and shaving cream,
red box, 1938 . . . . **125.00**
Toy, litho tin, Linemar
Walgreen Cash Register Bank, red, gray,
and blue, 2½" h **40.00**
Walgreen Delivery Truck, white and red,
7" l, 2½" h **75.00**
Walgreen Ice Cream Truck, white, blue
letters, 1950, 20½ × 7 × 4" **200.00**

WALL POCKETS

The wall pocket, what can be said?
O.K., what the hell is a wall pocket? My
grandmother used them for plants—a
"rooter" she called them or something
like that. But now they are used as match
holders and little places to put little
things.

Most of the common wall pockets
were produced between the 1930s and
1960s; though there are some that date
to the Victorian era. Wall pockets can be
made of wood, tin, glass, or ceramic.
Ceramic examples have been produced
both domestically and abroad. Wall
pockets come in all shapes and sizes, but
all have a small hole on the back side for
the insertion of the wall hook.

Dirt build–up and staining is very
common, though most collectors prefer
them to be neat and clean. Carefully
check any wall pocket prior to purchase.
Dirt can hide cracked or broken areas as
well as common household repairs.

Acorn, figural, light brown, marked
"Frankoma 190" **20.00**
Apple Blossom, blue, 8½" h, marked "Rose-
ville" **150.00**
Baby and Diaper, figural, marked "4921, Ja-
pan" **12.00**
Bird at Well, figural, marked "Made in
Czechoslovakia 5676 A" **48.00**
Broom, inverted, figural, marked "L & F Ce-
ramics © Hollywood, Hand Made"
. . . . **20.00**
Cockateel, figural, light coloring, Morton
Potteries, #578 . . . . **18.00**
Cocker Spaniel head, figural, marked
"Royal Copley" **15.00**

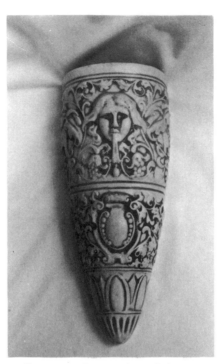

Weller Pottery, ivory, sgd, 10" l, $95.00.

Cornucopia, figural, pink, marked "Red
Wing 441" **30.00**
Cowboy Boot, figural, blue and white
speckled, marked "Frankoma 133"
. . . . **24.00**
Dust Pan, inverted, figural, marked "Califor-
nia" **12.00**
Fish, figural, yellow stripes, marked "Gilner
Calif C" **18.00**
Fruit Basket, figural, marked "Japan" **18.00**
Geese, basketweave and palm tree back-
ground, marked "Made In Japan" **25.00**
Geisha, figural **70.00**
Glendale, Weller, 23" h **575.00**
Grape Cluster, figural, marked "Royal
Haeger R–745 USA" **20.00**
Horseshoe, figural, horsehead center, green
. . . . **20.00**
House and Tree, blue lusterware, marked
"Noritake (M) Hand Painted Made In Ja-
pan" **95.00**
Parrot and Pink Flowers, Japanese lus-
terware, marked "Hand Painted (H) Ja-
pan" **40.00**
Peacock, figural, marked "West Coast Pot-
tery, California USA–441" **45.00**
Seashell, figural, Hull, Royal Woodland,
pink and gray, marked "W13 7½ Hull
USA" **65.00**
Straw Hat, figural, marked "Stewart G Mc-
Cullock © Calif" **10.00**
Sunflower, figural **10.00**
Teapot, figural, pink apple dec, Shawnee
. . . . **25.00**
Umbrella, figural, black, white handle,
marked "McCoy USA" **30.00**

WASH DAY COLLECTIBLES

I keep telling my mother that
women's liberation has taken all the fun
out of washing and ironing. She quickly
informs me that it was never fun to begin
with. The large piles of unironed clothes
she keeps around the house are ample
proof of that.

Wash day material is a favorite of
advertising collectors. Decorators have a
habit of using it in bathroom decor. Is
there a message here?

Advertising Trade Card
Conqueror Clothes Wringer, fold up
. . . . **12.00**
Larkin, Ottumwa Starch **3.00**
Sapolio, Enoch Morgan & Sons, boy
wearing fancy clothes **2.50**
Box
Fun–To–Wash Soap, black Mammy
wearing red bandanna illus . . . **25.00**
Gold Dust Washing Powder, Fairbanks,
Gold Dust Twins, full **30.00**
Brochure, 3⅞ × 6", Gold Dust, Brite Spots,
black lettering, yellow ground, 16 pgs
. . . . **25.00**
Brush, horsehair, wood handle **20.00**
Calendar, 1929, Clothesline, full pad **60.00**
Carpet Beater, wire, braided loop, wood
handle **25.00**
Catalog, Holland–Rieger Wringer Washing
Machines, 12 pgs **8.00**
Clothes Dasher, Ward Vacuum Washer
. . . . **35.00**
Clothes Dryer, wood, Empress Horseshoe
. . . . **100.00**
Clothespin, carved, late 19th C **10.00**
Iron
Blue Enamel, gas **42.00**
Enterprise, straight back edge, removable
handle **15.00**
Ober, open handle holes, emb, marked
"#12 Ober Pat Pend" **15.00**

*Toy, battery operated, tin and plastic, rubber
hose, tag reads "Wash–O–Matic," TN, Japan, orig box, 4¼" d, 5¾" h, $55.00.*

Ironing Board, wood, folding, turned legs, painted green **125.00**
Laundry Basket, woven splint, oval, rim handles **35.00**
Pinback Button, Gold Dust Washing Powder, multicolored illus, twins in tub, c1896 .... **50.00**
Sample, Gold Dust Twins Scouring Powder **125.00**
Scrub Board, wooden, handmade, some orig white paint **110.00**
Sign
    Borax Dry Soap, metal, red and white **45.00**
    Flame Proof Wax, women ironing clothes, 1890s **875.00**
Sock Stretcher, wood **30.00**
Sprinkler Bottle, clear glass **15.00**
Washboard
    Midget–Washer, wood frame, glass insert **12.00**
    The Zinc King, wood frame, zinc insert **15.00**

WATCH FOBS

A watch fob is a useful and decorative item attached to a man's pocket watch by a strap. It assists him in removing the watch from his pocket. Fobs became popular during the last quarter of the nineteenth century. Companies such as The Greenduck Co. in Chicago, Schwabb in Milwaukee, and Metal Arts in Rochester produced fobs for companies who wished to advertise their products or to commemorate an event, individual, or group.

Most fobs are made of metal and are struck from a steel die. Enameled fobs are scarce and sought after by collectors. If a fob was popular, a company would order restrikes. As a result, some fobs were issued for a period of twenty–five years or more. Watch fobs still are used today in promoting heavy industrial equipment.

The most popular fobs are those relating to old machinery, either farm, construction, or industrial. Advertising fobs are the next most popular group.

Looking at the back of a fob is helpful in identifying a genuine fob from a reproduction or restrike. Genuine fobs frequently have advertising or a union trademark on the back. Some genuine fobs do have blank backs; but a blank back should be a warning to be cautious.

Club: International Watch Fob Association, Inc, 6613 Elmer Dr, Toledo, OH 43615.

Advertising
    American Snow Plows & Wings   **25.00**
    Bronco Brand Overalls **125.00**
    Butler M C, Kansas City, scales, pumps, and water supplies **30.00**
    Caterpillar, strap **24.00**
    Chicago Business Men's Association Insurance **15.00**
    Clarke's Pure Rye **50.00**
    DOKK, Chattanooga, TN, strap, moons and stars **50.00**
    Dr Pepper Billiken **85.00**
    Duenning Construction Co, Slinger, WI, enameled **10.00**
    E C Atkins Silver Steel Saws, saw dec **38.00**
    Fidelity Flour, porcelain **75.00**
    Fordson Tractor **40.00**
    Galion Iron Works, three machines dec **28.00**
    Germer Stove, diecut **50.00**
    Gold Dust Twins **225.00**
    Hampshire Swine, porcelain **50.00**
    Ingersoll–Rand, brass, man with jackhammer **25.00**
    Manitowoc Speed Shovel, nickel and enamel **28.00**
    Miller Brothers 1010 Ranch, ornate **190.00**
    National Fidelity & Casualty Co, Omaha, emb eagle **65.00**
    Old Dutch Cleanser, strap **48.00**
    Oshkosh Beer, porcelain **150.00**
    Phoenix Glass Co, SP brass, phoenix, sun, and sunrays, ornate border, leather strap, 1900–24 .... **95.00**

Advertising, Lorain, Thew Shovel Co of Lorain, OH, plated brass, $20.00.

    Richards Wilcox Hardware Specialist, Aurora **28.00**
    Savage Pistol **125.00**
    South Western Concrete Association **17.50**
    Texas Portland Cement **50.00**
Art Nouveau, SS **25.00**
Automobile
    Ford, The Universal Car, silvered and enameled brass, blue and white accents, Ford emblem, c1920   **100.00**
    Studebaker, tire design, enameled   **38.00**
Fraternal
    Independent Order of Odd Fellows, 94th Anniversary, April 12, 1913   **25.00**
    Knights of Pythias, bronze, 1906   **10.00**
Holiday, Labor Day, 1913 .... **55.00**
Political
    Bryan–Kern, nickel plated, red and blue enameled details, eagles and flags center, strap **30.00**
    Charles Evans Hughes, celluloid, sepia bust portrait over name, 1$\frac{1}{2}$" d **60.00**
    Roosevelt–Fairbanks, brass, figural elephant **30.00**
    William Howard Taft, diecut brass, black details **20.00**

WATT POTTERY

Watt Pottery, located in Crooksville, Ohio, was founded in 1922. The company began producing kitchenware in 1935. Most Watt pottery is easily recognized by its simple underglaze decoration on a light tan base. The most commonly found pattern is the Red Apple pattern, introduced in 1950. Other patterns include Cherry, Pennsylvania Dutch Tulip, Rooster, and Star Flower.

Club: Watt Pottery Collectors USA, Box 26067, Fairview Park, OH 44126.

Periodical: *Watt's News,* PO Box 708, Mason City, IA 50501.

Apple
    Bean Pot
        #75, individual **300.00**
        #76 .... **200.00**
    Bowl, #73, green band **80.00**
    Casserole, cov
        #18, individual, handled **275.00**
        #601 .... **175.00**
    Cereal Bowl, 5$\frac{1}{4}$" d **35.00**
    Coffee Cup, #121 .... **275.00**
    Creamer, #62 .... **130.00**
    Mixing Bowl, ribbed, #04 ..... **125.00**
    Pie Baker
        #33 .... **175.00**
        Adv **150.00**
    Pitcher, #15 .... **60.00**

Mixing Bowl, Apple pattern, #7, 7" d, $100.00.

Salt and Pepper Shakers, pr, hourglass **195.00**
Autumn Foliage
Coffee Server, #115 .... **525.00**
Pitcher, #16 .... **60.00**
Cherry
Bowl, #52 .... **55.00**
Pitcher **85.00**
Double Leaf
Mixing Bowl, #5 .... **85.00**
Pitcher, #16 .... **145.00**
Morning Glory, pitcher, #96 ...... **625.00**
Open Apple, creamer, #62 ...... **1,200.00**
Pansy, plate, 8½" d **80.00**
Peedeeco
Casserole, stick handle **75.00**
Cookie Jar, bean pot shape **85.00**
Raised Pansy, casserole, individual, handled **45.00**
Rooster
Bowl, cov, #67 .... **250.00**
Creamer, #62 .... **175.00**
Ice Tub, cov, #76, hairline in lid **300.00**
Pitcher, #15 .... **150.00**
Starflower
Bowl, #39 .... **25.00**
Casserole, cov, #54 .... **675.00**
Mug, #501 .... **120.00**
Pitcher, #15 .... **75.00**
Platter, round, green and brown **150.00**
Saltshaker **85.00**
Teardrop
Creamer, #62 .... **130.00**
Pitcher **75.00**
Tulip
Bowl, #75 .... **85.00**
Bowl, #600 cov, ... **300.00**
Cookie Jar **285.00**

WEDGWOOD

It is highly unlikely that you are going to find eighteenth, nineteenth, or even early twentieth century Wedgwood at a flea market. However, you will find plenty of Wedgwood pieces made between 1920 and the present. The wonderful and confusing aspect is that many Wedgwood pieces are made the same way today as they were hundreds of years ago.

Unfortunately, Wedgwood never developed a series of backstamps to help identify a piece's age. As a result, the only safe assumption by which to buy is that the piece is relatively new. The next time you are shopping in a mall or jewelry store, check out modern Wedgwood prices. Pay fifty percent or less for a similar piece at a flea market.

Club: The Wedgwood Society, The Roman Villa, Rockbourne, Fordingbridge, Hents, SP6 3PG, England.

Newsletter: *American Wedgwoodian*, 55 Vandam Street, New York, NY 10013.

Basalt
Bowl, classical scenes, imp mark, 4⅜" d, 2⅜" h **50.00**
Box, cov, round, black, white cameo design, 3½" d, 4" h **75.00**
Creamer, black, classic figural scene of old man with serpent and young man with dish in his hand on one side, other side with classical figure of old woman washing young woman's feet, 2¾" h **130.00**
Jar, cov, classical figures, imp mark, 4¼" d, 3" h **80.00**
Vase, putti and garlands design, imp mark, 7½" h **130.00**
Drabware
Bowl, basketweave pattern, flared lip, imp "Wedgwood," 7" d, 3⅝" h **200.00**
Plate, glazed, gold lines, c1830, 7" d **70.00**
Jasperware
Biscuit Jar, cov, white classical cameos, dark blue ground, SP cov, rim, handle, and ftd base, marked "Wedgwood," 4¾" d, 5¾" h **150.00**

Pitcher, jasper, blue, white classical figures, marked "Wedgwood," c1940, 14" h, $95.00.

Chocolate Pot, white classical cameos, dark blue ground, 6" h **135.00**
Hair Receiver, white classical cameos on cov, dark blue ground, marked "Wedgwood," 3½" h **145.00**
Milk Pitcher, Grecian garden scene and floral bands, light olive green ground, marked "Wedgwood/England," 6¼" h, 4½" d **150.00**
Pin Tray, lavender, relief flowers, Cupids, and chariot design, 1½" w **40.00**
Teapot, white classical cameos, dark olive ground, 7½" w, 4½" h **150.00**
Vase, beaker shape, white classical figures in landscape, black ground, marked "Wedgwood, Made in England," 3½" h **75.00**
Stoneware, white
Honey Pot, beehive shape, attached underplate, 4" h **130.00**
Teapot, white glazed stoneware, floral design, gold trim, dog finial, c1820, 10⅜" w **130.00**

WELLER POTTERY

Weller's origin dates back to 1872 when Samuel Weller opened a factory in Fultonham, near Zanesville, Ohio. Eventually, he built a new pottery in Zanesville along the tracks of the Cincinnati and Muskingum Railway. Louwelsa, Weller's art pottery line, was introduced in 1894. Among the famous art pottery designers employed by Weller are Charles Babcock Upjohn, Jacques Sicard, Frederick Rhead, and Gazo Fudji.

Weller survived on production of utilitarian wares, but always managed some art pottery production until cheap Japanese imports captured its market immediately following World War II. Operations at Weller ceased in 1948.

Basket
Coppertone, 8½" h **175.00**
Louella, 6½" h **90.00**
Melrose, 10" h **175.00**
Bowl
Fairfield, 4½" h **80.00**
Flemish, 8½" d, daisies, ftd **165.00**
Tivoli, 2½" h **75.00**
Bud Vase
Glendale, double, 7" h **225.00**
Woodcraft, 6½" h **35.00**
Candleholders, pr,
Florala, 5" h **50.00**
Paragon, 2" h **35.00**
Comport
Creamware, two handles, ftd **85.00**
Monochrome, 10" h **60.00**
Console Bowl, Malverne, 14½" l, 2" h, 6" h frog **100.00**

Console Set, Blossom, bowl and two candlesticks **50.00**
Ewer, Sabrinian, 10½" h **225.00**
Hair Receiver, Louella, 3" h **50.00**
Hanging Basket
  Candis, 5½" h **90.00**
  Woodcraft, 6" h **125.00**
Jardiniere
  Claywood, 8" d, cherries and trees
   . . . . **75.00**
  Marbleized, 10" d **250.00**
  Rosemont, 8" d **160.00**
  Woodcraft, 9½' h, woodpecker and
   squirrel dec **300.00**
Oil Jar, Barcelona, 25½" h **850.00**
Pitcher
  Ivoris, 6" h **40.00**
  Zona, 7½" h **135.00**
Planter
  Blue Drapery, 4" h **65.00**
  Warwick, 3½" h **70.00**
Plate, Zona dinnerware, 10" d **20.00**
Tankard, Floretta, 15" h, standard glaze, sgd
  on base **75.00**
Vase
  Fleron, 19½" h **450.00**
  Hudson, 7¼" h, berries and leaves dec,
   pink and light green ground   **375.00**
  Lavonia, 10" h **130.00**
  Marbleized, 4½" h **50.00**
  Marvo, 10" h **70.00**
  Silvertone, 11½" h **160.00**
  Tutone, 4" h **35.00**
Wall Pocket
  Pearl, 7" h **175.00**
  Pumilla, 7" h **75.00**
Window Box
  Classic, 4" h **65.00**
  Forest, 14½" l **325.00**

WESTERN COLLECTIBLES

Yippy Kiyay partner, it's time to get a move on and lasso up some of those Western goodies. Western yuck has become Western kitsch.

Western collectibles are objects decorated with a Western theme. Some of these "Western" collectibles began life on the range in the plants of Eastern manufacturers. Only the truly dedicated have lamps with dried cactus standards.

Actually, Western material can be divided into five groups—American Indian material, cowboy items (boots, saddles, etc.), Mexican collectibles, cowboy kitsch, and movie and T.V. cowboy hero collectibles. Include dude ranch Western under cowboy kitsch.

You will not find Country Western items listed here. There is a big difference between Miss Kitty and Miss Dolly,

if you get my drift, partner. Due to its enormous popularity, Country Western collectibles are listed in their own category.

Meanwhile, happy trails to you and I hope that you'll be back in the saddle again before too long.

Clubs: National Bit, Spur & Saddle Collectors Association, PO Box 3098, Colorado Springs, CO 80934; Western Americana Collectors Society, PO Box 620417, Woodside, CA 94062.

Periodicals: *Cowboy Guide,* PO Box 47, Millwood, NY 10546; *Wild West,* 6405 Flank Dr, Harrisburg, PA 17112; *Yippy Yi Yea Magazine,* 8393 East Holly Rd, Holly, MI 48442.

Badge
  Deputy Marshall, Tombstone, AZ, 1960s
   . . . . **395.00**
  Deputy Sheriff, Pinal County, AZ
   . . . . **165.00**
  Tucson Police Department **165.00**
Bag, Indian Territory, gold **145.00**
Basket, Papogo, urn shape, step design,
  8½" l **135.00**
Book, *Wild Life On The Plains, Horrors of Indian Warfare,* W L Holloway, 1891, leather bound, illus **95.00**
Bootjack, Naughty Nellie, gold paint
  . . . . **125.00**

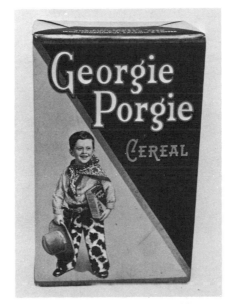

Georgie Porgie Cereal, recipes on side, manufacturing and nutritional information on back, black, yellow, and white box, red, black, and gold letters, boy wearing blue checkered shirt, red kerchief, black and white chaps, tan cowboy hat, 4¾" w, 7¾" h, $125.00.

Bottle Opener, cast iron, horse rear, MIB
  . . . . **48.00**
Bridle Rosettes, Anti Horse Thief Association, pr **250.00**
Catalog
  Kauffman Saddlery Co, 19 pgs . . . **18.00**
  Visalia Saddle Company, 1935, 128 pgs
   . . . . **75.00**
Certificate, Cherokee Strip Cow Punchers
  Association **50.00**
Check, signed "Pawnee Bill" **250.00**
Display Rack, saddle, A & W Co Horseshoes adv, cast iron and wood   **750.00**
Hotel Registration Card, Dodge City, KS,
  Wyatt Earp **10.00**
License, chauffeur's, Oklahoma, 1940
  . . . . **55.00**
Milk Bottle, Plains Dairy, WY, Cheyenne
  Frontier Days **20.00**
Pencil Sharpener, painted cast metal
  Cowboy **45.00**
  Gun **42.00**
Pin
  Figural, Texas, Sam Houston, ribbon,
   1936 . . . . **90.00**
  Texas Cousins Farm and Ranch   **30.00**
Pitcher, pottery, brown and tan, chuck
  wagon scene **25.00**
Poster, Yakima Canutt Rodeo **40.00**
Print
  Northern Pacific North Coast, *Montana Roundup,* orig shipping tube   **100.00**
  Thoroughbred Horse, set of 4, framed
   . . . . **100.00**
Record, Chevrolet adv, 1964, Ben
  Cartwright **32.00**
Riata, rawhide **165.00**
Rope, horsehair **40.00**
Rope Maker, patent 11/12/1907 . . . . **15.00**
Salt and Pepper Shakers, pr
  Advertising, Rod's Steak House, Williams, AZ **35.00**
  Figural, cactus, tray with figural cowboy,
   California **25.00**
Scarf Holder, SS, saddle shape **15.00**

Ceiling Fixture, glass shade, brown on white western motif, orig light fixture, 12" sq, $75.00.

Shaving Mug
   Leather Tanner's Tools **200.00**
   Wild Horse **250.00**
Sign, Rainbow Bread, cowboy motif **75.00**
Silhouette, pr, metal, cowboy **50.00**
Songbook, Bob Baker, western theme
. . . . **20.00**
Spurs
   Buermann
      Cowpunchers Favorites, double but-
      ton **125.00**
      Silver mounted, drop shank **650.00**
   Cates, silver mounted, eagle **450.00**
   Garcia, silver, fancy **325.00**
   Kelly, bull **140.00**
   North & Judd **125.00**
Spur Straps **30.00**
Ticket, Wild West Show, 1905 . . . . . **300.00**
Tin, Hazard Double No Trouble
   Gunpowder, 1 lb **550.00**
Wall Decoration
   Covered wagon, singing cowboy playing
   guitar, howling dog, campfire scene,
   pressed cardboard, 1950s, 4 pcs
   . . . . **50.00**
   Water Buffalo Horns, mounted **100.00**
Watch Fob
   Gallup Saddlery, saddle shape, Pueblo
   . . . . **150.00**
   Star Brand Saddles, saddle shape, Oak-
   land **125.00**

WESTMORELAND GLASS

Westmoreland Glass Company made a large assortment of glass. Some early pieces were actually reproductions of earlier glass, but have now become legit!

Westmoreland made clear glass in many patterns, some nicely decorated. Its milk glass patterns are becoming quite popular at flea markets.

Be on the lookout for discontinued pieces. They add variety to any Westmoreland setting. Also keep alert at flea markets for pieces that are still in production. Many patterns have remained popular for decades. Flea market prices are generally much lower than contemporary department store prices.

Clubs: National Westmoreland Glass Collectors Club, PO Box 372, Westmoreland City, PA 15692; Westmoreland Glass Collectors Club, 2712 Glenwood, Independence, MO 64052.

Appetizer Set, Paneled Grape, white milk
   glass with dec, 3 pc set **65.00**

Ashtray, English Hobnail, amber, 4½" sq
. . . . **7.50**
Basket
   Della Robbia, 9" **175.00**
   English Hobnail, 5" **15.00**
   Paneled Grape, white milk glass, 8",
      ruffled **65.00**
Butter Dish, cov, Old Quilt, white milk
   glass, ¼ lb **35.00**
Cake Salver
   Della Robbia **125.00**
   Paneled Grape, white milk glass **65.00**
Candlesticks, pr, Della Robbia, 2 light, 4" h
. . . . **120.00**
Candy Container, Santa on sleigh, milk glass
. . . . **85.00**
Candy Dish, cov
   Della Robbia, scalloped edge **75.00**
   Old Quilt, white milk glass, sq, ftd
   . . . . **32.00**
Celery
   English Hobnail, 9" l **15.00**
   Old Quilt, white milk glass, 6" l, ftd
   . . . . **35.00**
Cheese Dish, cov, Old Quilt, white milk
   glass **52.00**
Chocolate Box, cov, Paneled Grape, white
   milk glass with dec, 6½" **55.00**
Cigarette Jar, cov, English Hobnail, amber
. . . . **12.50**
Cocktail
   Della Robbia **20.00**
   English Hobnail **8.00**
Creamer, English Hobnail, sq, ftd **8.50**
Cream Soup, English Hobnail, amber
. . . . **10.00**
Cup and Saucer
   Della Robbia **27.00**
   English Hobnail **8.00**
Decanter, English Hobnail **45.00**
Egg Plate, Paneled Grape, white milk glass
. . . . **75.00**

Candy Dish, cov, Bramble, milk glass, 1955, 5¾" h, $10.00.

Epergne Set, Paneled Grape, white milk
   glass **110.00**
Finger Bowl, Della Robbia, 5" d **30.00**
Fruit Cocktail, Paneled Grape, white milk
   glass, 3½" bell shaped bowl, 6" sauce
   plate **24.00**
Goblet, Della Robbia, price for set of six
. . . . **20.00**
Hat, English Hobnail **12.50**
Ivy Ball, Paneled Grape, white milk glass
   with dec **48.00**
Marmalade, cov, English Hobnail . . . **15.00**
Mayonnaise Set, Paneled Grape, white milk
   glass **35.00**
Nappy
   Della Robbia, 4½" **30.00**
   English Hobnail, amber, 5" d, round
   . . . . **9.50**
Oyster Cocktail, English Hobnail, amber
. . . . **10.00**
Parfait, English Hobnail, amber **15.00**
Pitcher
   Della Robbia, 32 oz **200.00**
   English Hobnail, 38 oz, rounded **60.00**
Planter, Paneled Grape, white milk glass,
   4½" sq **40.00**
Plate
   Della Robbia, 9" d **30.00**
   English Hobnail, 8" d **7.50**
   Panel & Grape, white milk glass, 6¼" d
   . . . . **15.00**
Puff Box, cov, English Hobnail, amber, 6" d
. . . . **18.00**
Relish, 3 part
   English Hobnail, 8" d **15.00**
   Paneled Grape, white milk glass, 9" d
   . . . . **40.00**
Rose Bowl, English Hobnail, 4" d **15.00**
Salt and Pepper Shakers, pr
   Della Robbia **50.00**
   Paneled Grape, white milk glass, small
   . . . . **24.00**
Sauce Boat, Paneled Grape, white milk
   glass **30.00**
Sherbet
   Della Robia **16.00**
   English Hobnail **9.00**
Spooner, Paneled Grape, white milk glass
. . . . **40.00**
Straw Jar, English Hobnail, 10" h **55.00**
Sugar, Paneled Grape, white milk glass
. . . . **18.00**
Torte Plate, Della Robbia, 14" d **80.00**
Tumbler
   Della Robbia, 8 oz **20.00**
   English Hobnail, 5 oz, sq ftd **8.00**
Vase, 10" h, bud, black milk glass, hex base
. . . . **15.00**
Water Goblet, English Hobnail **10.00**
Water Set, Old Quilt, white milk glass,
   pitcher and six ftd tumblers **90.00**
Whiskey, English Hobnail, 3 oz **9.00**
Wine
   Della Robbia **24.00**
   English Hobnail, amber, sq ftd . . . **10.00**
   Paneled Grape, white milk glass **30.00**

WHAT'S IN THE CASE?

After years of wandering around the country visiting flea markets of every shape and size, there is one phrase I hear over and over again, "What's in the case?"

This question has inspired a new category. "What's in the case?" deals with items found in glass–covered tabletop showcases. Their numbers are infinite. Their variety limitless. They are in the case because they are the smallest of the small, too delicate, or expensive. Showcases have also helped to discourage the unfortunate but all–too-common disappearing act performed with many pocket–size collectibles.

Items under glass are generally valuable and to handle them without a dealer's permission is practically a sacrilege. Arrangement in the case may be haphazard or organized, depending on the dealer's selling methods. Don't be surprised if you find a number of cases packed to overflowing.

WHISKEY BOTTLES, COLLECTORS' EDITIONS

The Jim Beam Distillery issued its first novelty bottle for the 1953 Christmas market. By the 1960s the limited edition whiskey bottle craze was full blown. It was dying by the mid-1970s and was buried sometime around 1982 or 1983. Oversaturation by manufacturers and speculation by non–collectors killed the market.

Limited edition whiskey bottle collecting now rests in the hands of serious collectors. Their Bible is H. F. Montague's *Montague's Modern Bottle Identification and Price Guide* (published by author, 1980). The book used to be revised frequently. Now more than five years pass between editions. The market is so stable that few prices change from one year to the next.

Before you buy or sell a full limited edition whiskey bottle, check state laws. Most states require a license to sell liquor and impose substantial penalties if you sell without one.

Clubs: Hoffman National Collectors Club, PO Box 37341, Cincinnati, OH 45222; International Association of Jim Beam Bottle & Specialties Club, 5013 Chase Ave., Downers Grove, IL 60515; Michter's National Collectors Society, PO Box 481, Schaefferstown, PA 17088; National Ski Country Bottle Club, 1224 Washington Ave, Golden, CO 80401.

Ballantine
　　Fisherman **8.00**
　　Silver Knight **15.00**
Jim Beam
　　Beam Club and Convention
　　　　Blue Hen Club, 1982 . . . . **25.00**
　　　　Camellia City Club, 1979, State Capitol building **20.00**
　　　　Convention, ten, Norfolk, 1980
　　　　　　. . . . . **20.00**
　　　　Fox Uncle Sam, 1971 . . . . **12.00**
　　　　Twin Bridge Club, 1971 . . . . . **55.00**
　　Beam on Wheels
　　　　Chevrolet, Camaro, 1969, orange
　　　　　　. . . . . **55.00**
　　　　Ernie's Flower Car, 1976 . . . . . **25.00**
　　　　Mercedes, 1974, white **40.00**
　　　　Model T Ford, 1913, black . . . **35.00**
　　　　Train Baggage Car **50.00**
　　Casino Series
　　　　Golden Nugget, 12½" h, 1969 **35.00**
　　　　Harolds Club, covered wagon, green 1969 . . . . **5.00**
　　Centennial Series
　　　　Antioch, arrow, 1967 . . . . **7.00**
　　　　Colorado Centennial, Pike's Peak, 1976 . . . . **10.00**
　　　　St Louis Arch, 1966 . . . . **18.00**
　　Executive Series
　　　　Cobalt, 1981 . . . . **18.00**

Jim Beam, The Honorable Order of Kentucky Colonels, 1970, $10.00.

　　　　Italian Marble Urn, 1985 . . . . . **15.00**
　　　　McShane, Titans, 1980 . . . . . . **85.00**
　　　　Texas Rose, 1978 . . . . **15.00**
　　Foreign Countries, Australia, Kangaroo, 1978 . . . . **15.00**
　　People Series
　　　　Hank Williams Jr **45.00**
　　　　Mortimer Snerd, 1976 . . . . **30.00**
　　　　Paul Bunyan **6.00**
　　Regal China Series, Franklin Mint, 1970
　　　　. . . . . **8.00**
　　Sport Series
　　　　Bob Hope Desert Classic, 1974
　　　　　　. . . . . **10.00**
　　　　Chicago Cubs **35.00**
　　　　Football Hall of Fame, 1972 . . . **8.00**
　　　　Kentucky Derby 97th, 1971 . . . **7.00**
　　States Series
　　　　Hawaii, 1971 . . . . **7.00**
　　　　Nevada, 1963 . . . . **35.00**
　　　　South Dakota, Mt Rushmore, 1969
　　　　　　. . . . . **6.00**
　　Trophy Series, Rabbit, 1971 . . . . . **12.00**
Ezra Brooks
　　Animal Series
　　　　Moose, 1973 . . . . **20.00**
　　　　Penguin, 1973 . . . . **10.00**
　　Fish Series
　　　　Sailfish, 1971 . . . . **10.00**
　　　　Trout and Fly, 1970 . . . . **10.00**
　　Heritage China Series, Telephone, 1971
　　　　. . . . . **12.00**
　　People Series
　　　　Betsy Ross, 1975 . . . . **12.00**
　　　　Dakota Cowgirl, 1976 . . . . **30.00**
　　　　Oliver Hardy, bust **15.00**
　　　　Winston Churchill, 1969 . . . . . **10.00**
　　Sports Series
　　　　Baseball Player, 1974 . . . . **15.00**
　　　　Minnesota Hockey Player, 1975
　　　　　　. . . . . **20.00**
J W Dant
　　Atlantic City **5.00**
　　Wrong–Way Charlie **18.00**
Garnier
　　Alfa Romeo Racer, 1969 . . . . **25.00**
　　Pheasant, 1969 . . . . **30.00**
　　Valley Quail, 1969 . . . . **10.00**
Grenadier
　　American Revolution Series, Third New York, 1970 . . . . **20.00**
　　Moose Lodge, 1970 . . . . **14.00**
　　Napoleonic Series, Eugene, 1970 **20.00**
Hoffman
　　Bird Series, Blue Jays, 1979, pr . . . **35.00**
　　Occupation Series, music box
　　　　Mr Bartender, "He's a Jolly Good Fellow" **25.00**
　　　　Mr Shoe Cobbler, "Danny Boy"
　　　　　　. . . . . **18.00**
　　　　Mrs Lucky, "The Kerry Dancer"
　　　　　　. . . . . **12.00**
　　School Series, Kentucky Wildcats, basketball **30.00**
　　Wildlife Series, Falcon & Rabbit, miniature, 1978 . . . . **10.00**

Lionstone
  Bicentennial Series
    Molly Pitcher **10.00**
    Sons of Freedom **30.00**
  Bird Series
    Bluejay **22.00**
    Mourning Doves **55.00**
  Circus Series
    Fire–Eater **12.00**
    Snake Charmer **15.00**
    Tatooed Lady **12.00**
  Oriental Worker Series, Egg Merchant
    . . . . **30.00**
  Sports Series, football **25.00**
Luxardo
  Cocktail Shaker, 1957 . . . . **15.00**
  Duck, green **30.00**
  Gondola, 1960 . . . . **15.00**
  Tower of Fruit **20.00**
McCormick
  Bird Series, Ring–neck Pheasant, 1982
    . . . . **50.00**
  Confederate Series, Robert E Lee   **30.00**
  Country Western Series, Hank Williams
    Jr, 1980 . . . . **75.00**
  Elvis Series, black, #3, 1980 . . . . . **50.00**
  Football Mascots
    Arizona Wildcats **25.00**
    Georgia Bulldogs, black helmet, red
      jersey **15.00**
    Purdue Boilermaker, 1974 . . . . **20.00**
    Wisconsin Badgers, 1974 . . . . **18.00**
  Great American Series, Charles Lind-
    bergh, 1977 . . . . **30.00**

Whiskey Bottle, Cabin Still, 1969, matte finish, $12.00.

Sports Series
  Air Race Pylon, 1970 . . . . **12.00**
  Muhammad Ali, 1980 . . . . **25.00**
Cyrus Noble
  Animal Series, Mountain Lion & Cubs,
    miniature, 1979 . . . . **15.00**
  Mine Series, Landlady, 1977 . . . . **30.00**
  Sea Animals, Seal Family, 1978   **40.00**
Old Commonwealth
  Fireman, Fallen Comrade, #4, 1983
    . . . . **65.00**
  Golden Retriever, 1979 . . . . **25.00**
  Rip Van Winkle, 1970 . . . . **35.00**
  Yankee Doodle **25.00**
Old Fitzgerald
  California Bicentennial, 1970 . . . . **20.00**
  Memphis Commemorative, 1969   **10.00**
  Nebraska, 1972 . . . . **25.00**
Ski Country
  Birds
    Condor **45.00**
    Peacock **80.00**
  Circus
    Clown **45.00**
    Ringmaster **25.00**
  Domestic Animal Series, basset, minia-
    ture, 1978 . . . . **20.00**
  Indian Series
    Ceremonial Deer Dancer **85.00**
    End of Trail, miniature, 1976   **65.00**
  Waterfowl Series, Pelican, brown, 1976
    . . . . **40.00**
  Wildlife Series
    Bobcat Family **50.00**
    Skunk Family, 1978 . . . . **45.00**
    Snow Leopard **40.00**

WHISKEY–RELATED COLLECTIBLES

Whiskey and whiskey–related items are centuries old. Normally, the words conjure up images of the Western saloon and dance hall. Since the taste of similar whiskeys varies little, manufacturers relied on advertising and promotions to create customer loyalty.

Ashtray, Canadian Club **20.00**
Bottle, I W Harper's Whiskey, ovoid flask
  with reverse glass label, Grand Army of
  the Republic medal image on label com-
  memorates 29th National Encampment,
  6" h **150.00**
Fan, Four Roses Whiskey **15.00**
Key Chain
  Calvert Reserved Blended Whiskey, plas-
    tic, bottle replica, 1940s **8.00**
  Hunter Blended Whiskey, metal tag with
    horse jumping fence, "First Over The
    Bars," horseshoe key ring, 1940s
    . . . . **10.00**
Lamp, oil, Seagrams Whiskey **20.00**
Matchsafe, Old Judson Whiskey **120.00**

Whiskey Pitcher, Four Roses, white ground, $8.50.

Mirror, adv, Garrett's Baker Rye, celluloid,
  oval, nude lounging by stream, $1\frac{3}{4}$ ×
  $2\frac{3}{4}$" **300.00**
Panorama, Early Times Whiskey, plaster,
  painted, log still with oxen–drawn
  wagon laden with barrels from the
  Brown Forman Distillery Co, $22\frac{3}{4}$ ×
  $27\frac{3}{4}$" **100.00**
Pinback Button
  Duffy's Pure Malt Whiskey, trademark
    slogan **28.00**
  Gallagher & Burton, Philadelphia Distill-
    ery, logo trademark, early 1900s
    . . . . **10.00**
  Grandpa's Rye Whiskey, lady offering
    shot glass to gentleman **85.00**
  Old Crow Whiskey, General Sam Hous-
    ton portrait, "Vote For The Whiskey
    Of Famous Men," 1930s **5.00**
Pitcher
  G W Seven Star Whiskey, aluminum
    . . . . **5.00**
  Meredith's Diamond Club Whiskey
    . . . . **45.00**
Shot Glass
  Bottoms Up, cobalt **8.50**
  Peoria Co Club Whiskey, Peoria, IL,
    etched **25.00**
Sign
  Paul Jones Four Roses Whiskey, tin, wild
    game illus, 36 × 25" **125.00**
  Sam Clay Whiskey, tin, monogrammed
    center, black, white, and gold, $18\frac{1}{2}$
    × $26\frac{1}{2}$" **200.00**
Token, Green River Whiskey **65.00**
Trade Card, Old Kentucky Distillery, mon-
  keys shortening cat's tail, whiskey box
  chopping block, 1898 . . . . **20.00**
Tray
  Fulton Whiskey, silver plate **30.00**
  Green River Whiskey, black man and
    horse **75.00**

WHISTLES

Webster defines a whistle as an instrument for making a clear, shrill sound. No wonder children love them.

Collectors can whistle a happy tune at virtually every flea market. The most desirable whistles are those associated with well–known characters and personalities. They can command prices that are hardly child's play.

Advertising
B F Goodrich, bird **15.00**
Buster Brown Shoes, 1 × 1½", litho tin, Buster and Tige portrait illus, brown ground, yellow border, green lettering, "With The Tread Straight Feature That Helps You Walk 'Toes Straight Ahead' To Health," 1930s **40.00**
Butter Nut Bread, 1920s **20.00**
Endicott Johnson Shoes
Airplane shaped, litho tin, green, red lettering, 1930s **32.00**
Rect, litho tin, yellow, black lettering, 1930s **25.00**
Keds, Supersonic Space Whistle, 2 × 2¼", plastic, figural, flat, dark blue space capsule against white cratered moon, secret compartment in back, c1962 . . . . **12.00**
Oscar Meyer, Weinermobile, plastic, 2" l **8.00**
Peters Weatherbird Shoes, litho tin, yellow, red and green lettering, 1930s **19.00**
Weatherbird Shoes, litho tin, weather vane illus, "All Leather Best for Boys Girls," 1930s **20.00**

Safety Guard Member, tin, red, white, blue, and yellow, Kirchnof, Newark, NJ, 1942, 2½" l, $10.00.

Character and Personality
Cracker Jack
Stiff Paper, red and white, 1940s **15.00**
Tin, silvered, 1930s **18.00**
Jack Armstrong, ring, brass, Egyptian symbols on sides, built–in siren top, 1938 . . . . **70.00**
Little Orphan Annie, 3¼" l, brass tube, "Orphan Annie's Sandy Dog Whistle," telescopes to 5¼" l, flat diecut dog head on end, Ovaltine premium, 1940 . . . . **65.00**
Man's Face, emb tin, gold finish **12.00**
Wristwatch shape, litho tin, rect yellow face, red, white, and blue bands, Japan **15.00**

WICKER

Wicker or rattan furniture enjoyed its first American craze during the late Victorian era. It was found on porches and summer cottages across America. It realized a second period of popularity in the 1920s and '30s and a third period in the 1950s. In truth, wicker has been available continuously since the 1870s.

Early wicker has a lighter, more airy feel than its later counterparts. Look for unusual forms, e.g., corner chairs or sewing stands. Most wicker was sold unpainted. However, it was common practice to paint it in order to preserve it, especially if it was going to be kept outside. Too many layers of paint decreases the value of a piece.

Bookcase, stick and ball dec, four shelves, ball feet, 42" h **350.00**
Chair
Funeral Parlor, woven triangle design in upper back, openwork on lower half, painted white, 36" h **150.00**
Photographer's, woven oval panel and openwork back, curlicue dec, rolled arms, round seat, long skirt with diamond design, painted white, 42" h **450.00**
Chaise Lounge, double row of X's on back, lidded magazine pocket arms, serpentine footrest, ball feet, painted white, 54" l **750.00**
Creel Basket, center lid hole, early 1900s **55.00**
Fernery, square well, diamond design in side panels, natural color, 12" sq, 32" h **125.00**
Footstool, rect upholstered top, woven sides, wrapped legs, painted white, 16" w **150.00**
High Chair, barrel shaped, wooden seat and footrest, painted white, 32½" h **225.00**

Shopping Basket, two handles, woven diamond design, 6½ × 13½ × 9", $5.00.

Parlor Set, Bar Harbor, armchair, rocker, and sofa, removable cushions, tight weave and openwork, Ypsilanti Reed Furniture Co, painted white . . . **1,250.00**
Parlor Table, 27½" d, 30¼" h, circular top with basketweave pattern, curlicue trim, circular base shelf with cane insert, white **125.00**
Rocker, child's, rolled arms and back **125.00**
Settee, rect back with inverted triangle design, diamond herringbone patterned seat, braided edging, 43" l **450.00**

WILLOW WARE

The traditional willow pattern, developed by Josiah Spode in 1810, is the most universally recognized china pattern. A typical piece contains the following elements in its motif: willow tree, "apple" tree, two pagodas, fence, two birds, and three figures crossing a bridge.

Willow pattern china was made in almost every country that produces ceramics. In the 1830s over two hundred English companies offered Willow pattern china. Buffalo China was one of the first American companies to offer the pattern. Japanese production started about 1902, around the same time Buffalo made its first pieces.

Since the Willow pattern has been in continuous production, the term reproduction has little meaning. However, the Scio Pottery, Scio, Ohio, is currently producing an unmarked set that is being sold in variety stores. Because it lacks marks collectors should beware!

Clubs: International Willow Collectors, 2903 Blackbird Rd, Petoskey, MI 49770;

Willow Society, 39 Medhurst Rd, Toronto, Ontario M4B 1B2 Canada.

Newsletters: *American Willow Report*, PO Box 900, Oakridge, OR 97463; *The Willow Word,* PO Box 13382, Arlington, TX 76094.

Bowl, blue
    4¾" d, berry, Royal Pottery, Stafford-shire, Burslem **8.00**
    6" d, Johnson Bros **5.00**
    Creamer, 3½" h, blue, Ridgway **12.00**
    Cream Soup, Buffalo **10.00**
    Cup and Saucer, oversized, brown, Two Temples II pattern, England **48.00**
    Demitasse Set, coffeepot, creamer, six cups and saucers, Occupied Japan . . . **100.00**
    Dish, 9" d, pea green, Imperial Royal Nimy, Belgium, c1920 . . . . **45.00**
    Egg Cup, 5½" h, pink, England **22.00**
    Gravy Boat, blue, Ridgway, England **35.00**
    Kerosene Lamp, 8" h, blue, wall mount, re-flector, Japan **85.00**
    Mug, 3½" h, blue, straight sides **15.00**
Pitcher, blue
    6½" h, Japan **35.00**
    11" h, octagonal, Mason's Ironstone **450.00**
Plate, blue
    3¼" d, child's **8.00**
    5¾" d, Stevenson & Sons, England **30.00**
    6" d, Allerton, England **15.00**
    8½" d, Occupied Japan **25.00**
    9" d, lunch, Homer Laughlin **10.00**
    10" d, dinner, Barker Bros, England **10.00**
    10¼" d, grill, Japan **15.00**
    11" d, grill, blue, Maastricht **10.00**
Platter, blue
    6¼" l, child's, Japan **20.00**
    13½" l, Homer Laughlin **20.00**
    17½" l, Ridgway, England **175.00**
Salt and Pepper Shakers, pr, 4⅝" h, blue, England **60.00**

Soup Bowl, 6½" d, blue, underplate   **85.00**
Sugar Bowl, cov, blue
    2¼" h, child's **10.00**
    5" h, Ridgway, England **45.00**
Teapot, cov, Allerton, England **125.00**
Vase, 2¼" h, bud, blue **25.00**
Vegetable Bowl, blue
    8½" l, Meakin **35.00**
    9" l, Royal China, E Hughes & Co **15.00**
Wash Bowl, 16" d, blue **325.00**

WOOD

There is just something great about the grain, patina, and aging qualities of wood. This is a catch–all category for wooden objects that otherwise would not have appeared. The objects are utili-tarian, yet classic for their type.

Ballot Box, dovetailed, slot in lid, orig lock, red stained int, refinished ext, 14½" l **125.00**
Barber Pole, painted black, red, and white, iron brackets, 31" l **350.00**
Barrel, stave constructed, wood bands, 20" h **125.00**
Bar Vent, cutout nine point star in triangle, traces of red, white, and blue paint, 42" h **700.00**
Bowl, oblong, burl, end handles, 20" l **175.00**
Bucket, cov, iron–bound, locking peg, painted red, 10½" d **60.00**
Butter Churn, barrel shaped, round top door, wrought iron fittings, metal bands, hand crank, dasher, sawbuck base, 39" h **75.00**
Candle Box, birch, dovetailed, finger grips on beveled sliding lid, stained red, 9" l **175.00**
Candle Drying Rack, eight removable disks with wire hooks, 40" h **575.00**
Grain Measure, nesting set of four, sizes graduated from 8¾" d to 15" d, painted gray **150.00**
Inkwell, gold and black, glass liner, paper label reads "S Silliman & Co Chester, Conn," 2½" d **25.00**

Jar, cov, turned finial, 6¾" h **200.00**
Keg, stave constructed, split sapling bands, worn paper label reads "Rifle Powder, Rustin Powder Co, Cleveland, Ohio," 13" h **125.00**
Knife Box, bentwood, cutout handle, square nail construction, 15" ! **50.00**
Match Holder, beehive shaped, tartan de-coupage, ivory top socket, 3" h   **80.00**
Medicine Chest, mirrored door, towel bar, early 1900s **95.00**
Mortar and Pestle, turned, age cracks, 7" h **35.00**
Pipe Box, hanging, scalloped edge, dove-tailed drawer, square nail construction, 12" h **150.00**
Plate, deep, 9" d **200.00**
Salt Box, hanging, chip carved dec, wire nail construction, 10" h **150.00**
Sock Stretcher, 16" l **15.00**
Spoon, rope twist handle, turned ivory fin-ial, 8¼" l **45.00**
Sugar Bucket, miniature, stave constructed, tin bands, wire bail and wood handle, painted red, 4½" h **250.00**

WORLD'S FAIRS COLLECTIBLES

It says a lot about the status of world's fairs when Americans cannot stage a fair in 1993–1994 that is even half as good as the 1893 Columbian Ex-position in Chicago. Was the last great world's fair held in New York in 1964? Judging from recent fairs, the answer is an unqualified yes.

Although it is important to stress three–dimensional objects for display purposes, do not overlook the wealth of paper that was given away to promote fairs and their participants.

Clubs: World's Fair Collectors' Society, Inc, PO Box 20806, Sarasota, FL 34276; World's Fair Society, 529 Barcia Dr, St Louis, MO 63119.

Magazine: *World's Fair*, PO Box 339, Corte Madera, CA 94976.

1888 Cincinnati Centennial, ribbon, silk, brass hanger bar, issued by Centennial Pageant Association, 3 × 7" **60.00**
1893 Columbian Exposition, Chicago
    Medal, white metal, bust portrait and in-scriptions, 2" d **20.00**
    Paperweight, ferris wheel **75.00**
    Photo Engravings, *The Vanished City*, pen and pictures, hard cov, 15 × 11" **100.00**
    Sheet Music, *World's Columbian Exposi-tion Waltz*, color cover illus   **100.00**
    Spoon, set of six, orig box **125.00**

Butter Pat, Shenango, colorful Indian mark, 3½" d, $3.00.

Snake, wood, articulated, pink eyes, 6" h, 37" l, $10.00.

Tickets, pr, May 1–Oct 30 admittance, George Washington and Abraham Lincoln images, American Bank Note Co, 2¼ × 4" **24.00**

1898 Trans–Mississippi Exposition, Omaha
Handkerchief, silk, tattered edge **10.00**
Napkin Ring, engraved **10.00**

1901 Pan–American Exposition, Buffalo
Change Purse **15.00**
Change Tray, Kings Pure Malt adv **50.00**
Letter Opener, brass, figural, buffalo **35.00**
Pin, brass, 1½" w hanger bar, 1½" d brass mechanical skillet **50.00**
View Book, photo and artwork illus, glossy paper pages, captions, 80 pgs, 6½ × 9" **25.00**

1904 Louisiana Purchase Exposition, St Louis
Cup, Palace of Manufacturers decal, Germany **25.00**
Egg, tin **65.00**
Inkwell, porcelain **45.00**
Post Card, Cascade Gardens and Grand Basin, color, hold–to–light, Nov 12, 1904 postmark, 3½ × 5½" . . . **20.00**
Souvenir Spoon **26.00**
View Book, Sights, Scenes and Wonders of the World's Fair, photo and artwork illus, captions, 128 pgs, 5 × 6¾" **35.00**

1915 Panama–Pacific International Exposition, San Francisco, change purse, suede, silvered brass closure, 2½ × 3½" **25.00**

1926 Philadelphia Sesquicentennial, bank, Liberty Bell replica, cast iron, 3½" h, 4" d **60.00**

1933–34 Century of Progress, Chicago
Ashtray, tire, Firestone **55.00**
Atlas, *Century of Progress, Atlas of the World* **30.00**
Book, *Chicago 1833–1933 A Century of Progress*, hard cov, pictorial **45.00**
Booklet, *Chinese Lama Temple*, textured paper, photos and text of Chinese artifacts, 64 pgs, 6¼ × 9¼" **20.00**
Bookmark, etched metal, set of ten **150.00**
Bottle Opener, pocket, collapsible, black enameling **22.00**
Cigarette Case, lady's **35.00**
Coasters, set of four **20.00**
Commemorative Coin, Kelvinator **25.00**
Compact, enameled cov **30.00**
Folder, Blatz Old Heidelberg Beer, die-cut, stein shape, color cov, 5½ × 13" **24.00**
Game, Game of Nations, 48 playing cards, instruction cards, orig box **75.00**
Guide Book, attraction listings, photos, foldout grounds map, 4 pg Firestone exhibition adv, 194 pgs, copyright 1933 Cuneo Press, 6 × 9¼" **25.00**

Handkerchief, Japanese silk, set of three **50.00**
Key, oversized, silvered brass, Travel and Transport Building one side, Hall of Science other side, 8½" l . . . **28.00**
Photograph, panoramic view of grounds, identification legend for major exhibits, 10 × 60" **50.00**
Pinback Button, "I'm From New York–Visitor–A Century of Progress" **25.00**
Pocket Watch, chrome, black and white Fort Dearborn exhibit on dial, Chicago skyscrapers and Fort Dearborn engraved on back, 1⅞" d, orig box **200.00**
Thermometer, Havoline Tower replica, cast iron, inscribed "Havoline Thermometer Tower, Chicago's World's Fair 1933–1934," 4½" h **75.00**
Vase, blue matte, 3½" h **45.00**
View Book, Color Beauties, exhibit buildings, full color and monochrome, grounds map, 32 pgs, 6½ × 8¼" **30.00**

1939 New York World's Fair
Bowl, white china, full color montage design, Paden City Pottery, 10" d **80.00**
Chair, Kan–O–Seat, tripod seat, collapses to walking cane, blonde wood, 35" l **85.00**
Clock, electric, wood case, ship's tiller wheel shape, brass trim, Trylon, Perisphere, and inscription on 4½" d dial, not working **100.00**
Doll, boy porter, stuffed velveteen, celluloid head, Trylon and Perisphere illus on hat, Japan, 9" h **100.00**
Dresser Scarf, felt, multicolored inked artwork, purple ground, 8½ × 11½" **50.00**
Fan, diecut cardboard, five sepia building photos, 10 × 10½" **75.00**
Glass, set of four, each with different exhibit building, Business Administration, Food, Medicine and Public Health, and Textile Buildings, 4¾" h **125.00**
Guide Book, exhibits listing, illus, fold-out aerial view grounds map, 256 pgs, 5 × 8" **20.00**
Hot Pads, litho paper over asbestos, Administration building, set of three **75.00**
Scrapbook, Kork–Craft, brown paper pages, cloth and cork over cardboard covers, 11 × 14", unused . . . **100.00**
Snowdome, black plastic base, Trylon and Perisphere figures inside, 3" d, 4" h **250.00**
Tablecloth, linen, multicolored aerial view of grounds, East River, Hudson River, and Statue of Liberty illus, visiting nations flags border, 52 × 52" **150.00**

Telephone File, World's Fair List Finder, litho tin, mechanical, Trylon and Perisphere on cov, 3¾ × 7¼" **95.00**
Toy, souvenir, Billy Rose's Aquacade airship, cardboard and balloon, orig mailing envelope **50.00**
View Book, glossy photos with captions, 48 pgs, 9½ × 12" **25.00**

1939 Golden Gate Exposition, San Francisco
Filmstrip, for use in Pathegrams Cine Vue viewer, black and white, #5, #6, and #7, set of three, orig box **115.00**
Pillow Cover, textured fabric, blue fringe, blue flocked artwork and inscription "Golden Gate International Exposition, San Francisco Bay," 15 × 16½" **65.00**

1962 Century 21 Exposition, Seattle
Glass, white logo and inscription, clear glass, 4¼" h **12.00**
Program, *King and His Court*, four–man softball team, 12 pgs, 7 × 10" **24.00**

1964 New York World's Fair
Ashtray, china, exhibit buildings, 7½" d **20.00**
Bank, Unisphere replica, ceramic, brown, gold orbit bands and trim, 4" d, 5" h **25.00**
Box, cedar, paper fair scene on lid, varnished, 3 × 3½ × 5½" . . . **20.00**
Folder, Hall of Magic, entertainment attractions sponsored by General Cigar Co, 16 × 19" open size **15.00**
Mirror, purse, acetate cov, 2¼ × 3½" **25.00**
Plate, white china, major exhibits illus in center, gold brocade border, 10" d **18.00**
Puzzle, jigsaw, Vatican Pavilion, color, 19 × 20½" assembled size, orig box **25.00**
Slides, color, 35mm, Transportation and International Areas, set of ten, orig envelope **18.00**

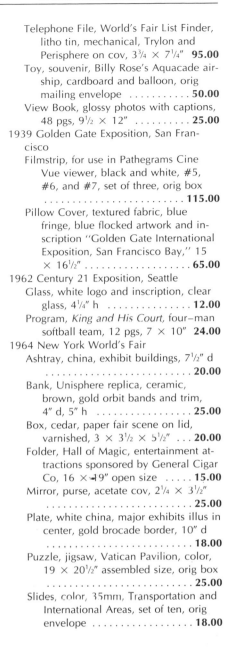

Ashtray, Seattle World's Fair, 1962, orange, brown back, back marked "Made in Seattle Wash, House of Porcelain," 5 × 4½", $8.00.

Combination bottle opener, shot glass, and stirring spoon, The Mad Hatter from Alice in Wonderland, 1933 Century of Progress, Chicago, 9¹⁄₂" l, $45.00.

Starr Bus Tours Kit, guide book, discount tickets, coupon book, brochures, leaflets, and newsletter folder, 9 × 12" envelope **40.00**

RUSSEL WRIGHT

Russel Wright was an American industrial engineer with a design passion for domestic efficiency through simple lines. Wright and his wife, Mary Small Einstein, wrote *A Guide To Easier Living* to explain the concepts.

Some of his earliest designs were executed in polished spun aluminum. These pieces, designed in the mid-1930s, included trays, vases, and teapots.

Russel Wright worked for many different companies in addition to creating material under his own label, American Way. Wright's contracts with firms often called for the redesign of pieces which did not produce or sell well. As a result, several lines have the same item in more than one shape. Among the companies for which Wright did design work are Chase Brass and Copper, General Electric, Imperial Glass, National Silver Com-

pany, and the Shenango and Steubenville Pottery Companies.

Though most collectors focus on Wright's dinnerware, he also designed glassware, plastic items, textiles, furniture, and metal objects. His early work in spun aluminum often is overlooked as is his later work in plastic for the Northern Industrial Chemical Company.

American Modern
  Casserole, handled
    Bean Brown **75.00**
    Chartreuse **45.00**
  Celery, chartreuse **22.50**
  Chop Plate, chartreuse **25.00**
  Demitasse Coffeepot
    Chartreuse **68.00**
    Seafoam **75.00**
  Gravy Underplate
    Chartreuse **35.00**
    Gray **38.00**
  Pitcher, 1¹⁄₂" quart
    Chartreuse **65.00**
    Coral **85.00**
  Sugar, cov, gray **10.00**
  Teapot
    Chartreuse **45.00**
    Coral **85.00**
Iroquois
  Berry Bowl, 5¹⁄₂" d
    Charcoal **8.00**
    Ice Blue **6.00**
    Pink **6.00**
  Butter Dish, ¹⁄₂ lb
    Charcoal **45.00**
    Ice Blue **45.00**
  Carafe
    Ice Blue **140.00**
    Pink **125.00**

Pitcher, American Modern, granite gray, 10³⁄₄" h, $45.00.

Casserole, 4 quart, Ice Blue **75.00**
Casserole Lid, 8" d, white **35.00**
Cereal Bowl, 5" d
    Charcoal **8.00**
    Lemon Yellow **7.00**
    Nutmeg **7.00**
Chop Plate, Ripe Apricot **25.00**
Creamer and Sugar, stacking, nutmeg
  . . . . **20.00**
Cup and Saucer, coffee
    Nutmeg **12.00**
    Pink **12.00**
Demitasse Coffeepot, nutmeg . . . **150.00**
Gumbo
    Ice Blue **47.00**
    Ripe Apricot **22.00**
Mug, Ice Blue **47.00**
Plate
  6¹⁄₂" d, bread and butter, nutmeg
  . . . . **3.00**
  7¹⁄₂" d, salad, pink **6.00**
  10" d, dinner
    Nutmeg **8.00**
    Pink **8.00**
Platter, oval, 12³⁄₄" l
    Apricot **50.00**
    Lettuce Green **50.00**
    Nutmeg **20.00**
Tea cup, charcoal **10.00**
Teapot, white **140.00**
Vegetable
    Covered, Ripe Apricot **35.00**
    Open, charcoal **20.00**

WRISTWATCHES

The pocket watch generations have been replaced by the wristwatch generations. This category became hot in the late 1980s and still is going strong. There is a great deal of speculation occurring, especially in the area of character and personality watches.

Since the category is relatively new as a collectible, no one is certain exactly how many watches have survived. Dad has almost a dozen that were handed down from his parents. If he is typical, the potential market supply is far greater than anyone realizes. Beware before paying big prices. Many wristwatches are going to be sold five years from now at far less than their 1991 price.

Clubs: National Association of Watch & Clock Collectors, Inc, 514 Poplar St, Columbia, PA 17512; The Swatch Collectors Club, PO Box 7400, Melville, NY 11747.

Periodicals: *Comic Watch Times,* 106 Woodgate Terrace, Rochester, NY

14625; *International Wrist Watch,* 242 West Ave, Darien, CT 06820.

Advertising
  Apple Cinnamon Cheerios **25.00**
  Big Boy, Windert **85.00**
  Coke, Walt Disney World 15 Year Anniversary **45.00**
  Fruit Stripe Gum **50.00**
  Fruit Wrinkles, digital **12.00**
  Moonstones Cereal **125.00**
  Nabisco Ritz Crackers **60.00**
  Red Goose Shoes, 1½" d, silvered brass case, inscribed "Friedman Shelby/All Leather Shoes," orig brown leather bands, c1930 ....**125.00**
Character and Personality
  Care Bears, Bradley, 1983, not working **25.00**
  Chipmunks, Bradley, 1984, not working **25.00**
  Cinderella, Timex, no band **15.00**
  Gene Autry, Six Shooter, animated gun, illus box, 1951 ....**475.00**
  Hollie Hobbie, Bradley, 1972, not working **40.00**
  Hopalong Cassidy, Good Luck From Hoppy, not working **125.00**
  Lone Ranger, Hi Yo Silver, new band **225.00**
  Mary Marvel, 1948, new band, not working **155.00**
  Mickey Mouse
    Bradley **25.00**
    Ingersoll, no picture **90.00**
    US Time, polka dot face, gilt ground **175.00**
  Minnie Mouse, 1973, not working **85.00**
  Orphan Annie, Bobs Merrill, 1971 ....**95.00**
  Shirt Tales, Timex, 1981 ....**40.00**
  Snoopy, United Features/Swiss ...**85.00**
  Superman
    Dabs, 1977 ....**95.00**
    DC Comics, 1976 ....**165.00**
  Wonder Woman, DC Comics, 1975 ....**150.00**
  Zorro, US Time **50.00**
Lady's
  Bulova, Accutron, 14K case, leather bands **125.00**

Ebel, 17j, 14K case and band, c1948 ....**225.00**
Girod, 14K yg case **150.00**
Illinois
  Antoinette, 15j, gold filled, c1929 ....**60.00**
  Mary Todd, 16j, 18K, c1929 **175.00**
Longines, 14K yg case, orig box **250.00**
Nicolet, 17j, flexible band, cabochon crystal, small diamond on each side of square face **95.00**
Omega, 17j, silver, wire lugs, c1925 ....**85.00**
Rolex, 17j, gold filled, c1945 ....**60.00**
Man's
  Angelus, 17j, day, date, and moon phase, steel, c1949 ....**150.00**
  Bueche–Girod, 17j, date, month, and moon phase, steel **150.00**
  Bulova, Sky Chief, 17j, steel, c1940 ....**225.00**
  Elgin
    Lord Elgin 680, 21j, 14K gold **100.00**
    Sportsman, 17j **25.00**
  Hamilton, 17j, gold filled case, stem wind, leather band, orig box **150.00**
  Illinois, Aviator, 17j, gold filled **175.00**
  Jules Jergensen, quartz, day and date, leather band **150.00**
  Omega, Constellation, 24j, auto–wind, steel, c1962 ....**125.00**

ZOO COLLECTIBLES

Dad has been trying for years to find a "Z" category to end *Warman's Americana and Collectibles.* His trouble is he spent too much of his childhood at the circus and not enough at the zoo. It's tough to beat the old man. Gotcha Pop!

Ashtray, Denver Zoo, glass, decal center **4.50**
Box, popcorn, Cretors Westview Park, children eating popcorn illus, animal background, unused, 1929 ....**45.00**
Door Hanger, City Zoo, white and yellow, "Do Not Disturb" on back **1.00**
Game, Fun At The Zoo Game, 1960s **15.00**

Puzzle, Ding Dong School, National Mask & Records, 1950s, frame tray, 10 hand–cut plywood pieces, Zoo Keeper, monkey on shoulder, 11½ × 8½", $15.00.

Medal, Philadelphia Zoo, silver finish, c1960 ....**10.00**
Pennant, San Francisco Zoo **5.00**
Pinback Button
  American Eagle/Philadelphia Zoo, 1¼" d, black and white, c1930 ....**10.00**
  Benson's Wild Animal Farm, Nashua, NH, Safari, black and white tiger illus and lettering, 1930s **5.00**
  Columbus Zoo, multicolored, monkeys in three evils pose, 1950s **4.00**
  Junior Naturalist, ⅞" d, black and white photo of Uncle John, early 1900s **10.00**
  The Zoo Babies, black and white tiger cubs illus, 1896–1900 ....**5.00**
  The Zoo Nursery, black and white tiger cub illus, "We Love to Be Fondled," 1930s **8.00**
  The Zoo, Prince, "King of Them All," black and white lion head, 1901–10 ....**8.00**

PART THREE

Reference Sources

Flea Marketeer's Annotated Reference Library

You Cannot Tell the Players Without a Scorecard

A typical flea market contains hundreds of thousands of objects. You cannot be expected to identify and know the correct price for everything off the top of your head. You need a good, basic reference library.

As a flea marketeer, there are two questions about every object that you want to know: What is it? and How much is it worth? A book that answers only the first question has little use in the field. Titles in the "Books about Objects" list contain both types of information.

The basic reference library consists of fifty titles. I admit the number is arbitrary. However, some limit was necessary. Acquiring all the titles on the list will not be cheap. Expect to pay somewhere between $1,000 and $1,250.

The list contains a few books that are out of print. You will have to pursue their purchase through used-book sources. Many antiques and collectibles book dealers conduct book searches and maintain "wants" lists. It is not uncommon to find one or more of these specialized dealers set up at a flea market. Most advertise in the trade papers, especially *The Antique Trader Weekly*, PO Box 1050, Dubuque, Iowa 52001 and "Books For Sale" in the classified section of *Antique Week, Central Edition*, PO Box 90, Knightstown, IN 46148. One dealer that I have found particularly helpful in locating out-of-print books is

Joslin Hall Rare Books, PO Box 516, Concord, MA 01742.

Many reference books are revised every year or every other year. The editions listed are those as of Spring 1995. When you buy them, make certain that you get the most recent edition.

One final factor that I used in preparing this list was a desire to introduce you to the major publishers and imprints in the antiques and collectibles field. It is important that you become familiar with Antique Publications, Avon Books Americana, Collector Books, House of Collectibles, L-W Books, Schiffer Publishing, Wallace-Homestead, and Warman.

General Price Guides

Husfloen, Kyle, ed. 1995. *The Antique Trader Antiques and Collectibles Price Guide*, 11th ed. Dubuque, IA: The Antique Trader, 1995.

There are over a dozen general price guides to antiques and collectibles. Of course, I think my dad's are the best. However, when I want a second opinion or cannot find a specific item in Dad's guides, I use the *Trader's* guide. The descriptions are great and prices are accurate. Most importantly, it is a price guide that focuses on the heartland of America.

Rinker, Harry L., ed. *Warman's Americana and Collectibles*, 7th ed. Radnor, PA: Wallace-Homestead, 1995.

This contains the stuff with which your parents, you, and your children grew up and played. More than any other modern price guide it is a record of what is found in the attics, closets, basements, garages, and

sheds of America. It will make you regret everything you ever threw out. It has gone twelve years without a rival, which says a great deal about the Warman format that Dad developed for it.

Rinker, Harry L., ed. *Warman's Antiques and Collectibles Price Guide*, 29th ed. Radnor, PA: Wallace-Homestead, 1995.

This book is more than just a list of objects with prices. It is a user's guide. The introduction to each category contains a brief history, list of reference books, names and addresses of periodicals and collectors' clubs, museums to visit, and information on reproductions. It is the first place to start whenever you need information.

Identification of Reproductions and Fakes

Hammond, Dorothy. *Confusing Collectibles: A Guide to the Identification of Contemporary Objects*, rev. ed. Radnor, PA: Wallace-Homestead, 1979. Out of print.

This book provides information about reproductions, copycats, fantasy items, contemporary crafts, and fakes from the late 1950s through the 1960s. Much of this material appears in today's flea markets. Some is collectible in its own right. The best defense against being taken is to know what was produced.

Hammond, Dorothy. *More Confusing Collectibles*, Vol. II. Wichita, KS: C. B. P. Publishing Company, 1972. Out of print.

Confusing Collectibles took a broad approach to the market. *More Confusing Collectibles* focuses primarily on glass. It contains all new information, so you really do need both volumes.

Lee, Ruth Webb. *Antiques Fakes and Reproductions, Enlarged and Revised.* Published by author: 1938, 1950. Out of print. Note: This book went through eight editions. The later editions contain more information. A good rule is to buy only the fourth through eighth editions.

Dorothy Hammond followed in Ruth Webb Lee's footsteps. Lee's book chronicles the reproductions, copycats, fantasy items, and fakes manufactured between 1920 and 1950. While heavily oriented toward glass, it contains an excellent chapter on metals, discussing and picturing in detail the products of Virginia Metalcrafters.

Books About Objects

Barlow, Ronald S. *The Antique Tool Collector's Guide to Value,* 3rd edition. El Cajon, CA: Windmill Publishing Company, 1991.

This is *the* book for tools. Barlow has compiled auction and market prices from across the United States. Since this book is organized by tool type, you need to identify the type of tool that you have before you can look it up. There are plenty of illustrations to help.

Bunis, Marty and Sue. *Collector's Guide to Antique Radios,* 3rd ed. Paducah, KY: Collector Books, 1994.

There are a wealth of radio books in the market place. This one is tuned in to a wide band of radios. Organization is by manufacturer and model number. Although heavily illustrated, the book does not picture the majority of the models listed. The book also covers radio parts and accessories.

Cunningham, Jo. *The Collector's Encyclopedia of American Dinnerware.* Paducah, KY: Collector Books, 1982, 1992 price update.

This is a profusely illustrated guide to identifying twentieth-century American dinnerware. In spite of the fact that many new companies and patterns have been discovered since Cunningham prepared her book, it remains a valuable identification tool, especially since its pricing is updated periodically.

Docks, L. R. *American Premium Record Guide: Identification and Value Guide to 1915–1965 78s, 45s, and LPs,* 4th ed. Florence, AL: Books Americana, 1992.

This is an excellent testament to the variety of record-collecting interest in the marketplace. While Docks' remains the best general record price guide in the market, his supremacy is under challenge by Jerry Osborne's *The Official Price Guide to Records,* 10th edition (House of Collectibles, 1993) and numerous specialized record price guides being published by Krause Publications under the Goldmine banner, e.g., Neal Umphred's *Goldmine's Rock 'n Roll 45 RPM Record Price Guide* (Krause Publications, 1992).

Duke, Harvey. *The Official Identification and Price Guide to Pottery and Porcelain,* 7th ed. New York, NY: House of Collectibles, 1989.

This is the perfect companion to Cunningham. Duke covers many of the companies and lines of which Cunningham was unaware when she first published her book in the early 1980s. Illustrations are minimal, making it necessary to know the name of your pattern before looking anything up. The book is well-balanced regionally. Many West Coast pottery manufacturers finally receive their due.

Florence, Gene. *The Collector's Encyclopedia of Depression Glass,* 11th ed. Paducah, KY: Collector Books, 1994.

This is the Depression glass collector's bible. Among its important features are a full listing of pieces found in each pattern and an extensive section on reproductions, copycats, and fakes. One difficulty is that there are hundreds of glass patterns manufactured between 1920 and 1940 that are not found in this book because they do not have the Depression Glass label. Supplement the book with Gene Florence's *Kitchen Glassware of the Depression Years,* also published by Collector Books.

Foulke, Jan. *11th Blue Book Dolls and Values.* Cumberland, MD: Hobby House Press, Inc., 1993.

Foulke is the first place doll collectors turn for information. The book is high-end, turning its back on many of the post-World War II and contemporary dolls. Within the doll field, it sets prices more than it reports them. Crosscheck Foulke's prices in Julie Collier's *The Official Identification and Price Guide to Antique and Modern Dolls,* 4th edition (House of Collectibles, 1989).

Franklin, Linda Campbell. *300 Years of Housekeeping Collectibles.* Florence, AL: Books Americana, 1992.

Books Americana split the second edition of *300 Years of Kitchen Collectibles* into two separate volumes, albeit retaining the edition number for one of the spinoffs. Now, instead of paying $10.95 for a handy-to-use single source, you have to pay $45.90 for two volumes at $22.95 each. Hopefully a publisher will see an opportunity and once again put this information in a single volume. Until such time, it makes sense to buy the two Franklin volumes.

Franklin, Linda Campbell. *300 Years of Kitchen Collectibles,* 3rd ed. Florence, AL: Books Americana, 1991.

The second edition of this book was well organized, had a readable format, and was easy to use. The recently released third edition provides ample proof that bigger is not necessarily better. The new format is incredibly awkward. The wealth of secondary material may be great for the researcher and specialized collector, but it is a pain to wade through for the generalist. Franklin joins the Coca-

Cola Company as someone who failed to recognize that they had created a classic. For now this is better than nothing, but it provides a real opportunity for a challenger.

Gibbs, P. J. *Black Collectibles Sold in America.* Paducah, KY: Collector Books, 1987, 1993 price update.

Black collectibles have gone through a number of collecting cycles in the past fifteen years. Popular among both white and black collectors, black memorabilia is likely to cycle several more times in the years ahead. Because of this, prices in any black collectibles book have to be taken with a grain of salt.

Gilbert, Ann. *40's and 50's Designs & Memorabilia: Identification and Price Guide* and *60's and 70's Designs & Memorabilia: Identification and Price Guide.* New York: Avon Books, 1993.

The plus of this two volume set is that it provides a chronological approach not found in other price guides. The negative is that the coverage is spotty. Hopefully, future editions will fill-in the gaps. Meanwhile, it offers a fresh organizational approach, one that is becoming increasing popular among collectors and interior decorators.

Giles, Cynthia. *The Official Identification and Price Guide to Vintage Clothing.* New York, NY: House of Collectibles, 1989, out of print.

While the vintage clothing market has stabilized outside the major metropolitan areas, it still thrives in the big cities. Post-World War II clothing is especially hot right now. Because the market is so large, any book on the subject is merely window dressing. An alternative selection is Maryanne Dolan's *Vintage Clothing: 1880 to 1960: Identification and Value Guide,* 2nd edition (Books Americana, 1987).

Hagan, Tere. *Silverplated Flatware,* revised 4th ed. Paducah, KY: Collector Books, 1990.

You do not see a great deal of sterling silver at flea markets because most dealers sell it for weight. Silver-plated items are in abundance. This book concentrates only on flatware, the most commonly found form. You can find information on silver-plated holloware in Jeri Schwartz's *The Official Identification and Price Guide to Silver and Silverplate,* 6th edition (House of Collectibles, 1989).

Hake, Ted. *Hake's Guide to . . .* series. Radnor, PA: Wallace-Homestead.

Over the past several years Ted Hake has authored a five-book priced picture-book series focusing on material sold in Hake's Americana Mail Auction. Each collecting category is introduced with a brief history, often containing information not readily available to the collector. The series consists of: *Hake's Guide to Advertising Collectibles: 100 Years of Advertising From 100 Famous Companies* (1992); *Hake's Guide to Comic Character Collectibles: An Illustrated Price Guide to 100 Years of Comic Strip Characters* (1993); *Hake's Guide to Cowboy Character Collectibles: An Illustrated Price Guide Covering 50 Years of Movie and TV Cowboy Heroes* (1994); *Hake's Guide to Presidential Campaign Collectibles: An Illustrated Price Guide to Artifacts from 1789–1988* (1992); and, *Hake's Guide to TV Collectibles: An Illustrated Price Guide* (1990).

Heacock, William. *The Encyclopedia of Victorian Colored Pattern Glass.* 9 volumes. Marietta, OH: Antique Publications

One of the major gaps in the antiques and collectibles literature is a general price guide for glass. On the surface, the subject appears overwhelming. Heacock's nine-volume set covers glass manufactured from the mid-nineteenth through the early twentieth centuries. Actually, , some volumes extended deep into the twentieth century. Book 1 on toothpicks, Book 2 on opalescent glass, and Book 9 on cranberry opalescent glass are among the most helpful.

Huxford, Bob. *Huxfords Old Book Value Guide,* 6th ed. Paducah, KY: Collector Books, 1994.

There are always piles of old books at any flea market. Most are valued in the 25 to 50¢ range. However, there are almost always sleepers in every pile. This book is a beginning. If you think that you have an expensive tome, check it out in the most recent edition of *American Book Prices Current,* published by Bancroft-Parkman.

Jones, Diane Carnevale. *Collectors' Information Bureau's Collectibles Market Guide and Price Index,* 12th ed. Radnor, PA: Wallace-Homestead, 1995.

The best thing about this book is that it covers a wide range of limited edition types, from bells to steins. It serves as a collector's checklist. The worst thing is that it is industry-driven. Important negatives and warnings about the limited edition market are missing. Field-test the prices before paying them.

Klug, Ray. *Antique Advertising Encyclopedia.* Volume 1 (1978, 1993 Value Update) and volume 2 (1985). Gas City, IN: L-W Book Sales.

Klug's is a classic. It is organized by advertising type and follows a priced picture format. It is by no means as encyclopedic as its title suggests. However, it serves as a checklist for many collectors and dealers. Make certain that you get the most up-to-date price list.

Kovel, Ralph and Terry. *The Kovels' Bottle Price List,* 9th ed. New York, NY: Crown Publishers, Inc., 1992.

This is another category where the best of the mundane wins the prize. The book is organized by bottle type and within each type alphabetically by manufacturer. The quality of pricing is spotty. Totally missing are bottles in the 10¢ to $4.00 range. This is precisely the range of most bottles found at flea markets. Jim Megura, bottle consultant at Skinner, has taken over authorship of the House of Collectibles bottle guide. Do not look for low-end bottles to appear in this book either.

Malloy, Alex. *Comics Values Annual 1994–1995: The Comic Books Price Guide.* Radnor, PA: Wallace-Homestead, 1994.

The king has fallen, long live the king. For decades, Robert M. Overstreet's *The Overstreet Comic Book Price Guide,* now in its twenty-fourth edition (New York: Avon Books, 1994) has dominated the comic book price guide market. Malloy offers more— more accurate listings and prices for modern comics (those you are most likely to find at flea markets), values for European, Pacific Rim, Underground, and Fanzine comics (missing from Overstreet), and quality state-of-the-market information. Try it. You'll like it.

Malloy, Roderick A. *Malloy's Sports Collectibles Value Guide: Up-to-Date Prices for Noncard Sports Memorabilia.* Radnor: Attic Books and Wallace-Homestead, 1993.

This book captures the growing interest in memorabilia associated with professional sports ranging from baseball to racing. It focuses on three types of objects—equipment, individual and team memorabilia, and generic material, e.g., games, magazines, etc. The basic introduction that has been long needed for this broad collecting category.

Martinus, Norman C., and Harry L. Rinker. *Warman's Paper.* Radnor, PA: Wallace-Homestead, 1994.

The paper market is hot and getting hotter. Paper is available and affordable. The market already has dozens of specialized shows. *Warman's Paper,* organized into seventy-five col-

lecting topics and over two hundred subject topics, is Dad's latest effort. Next to *Warman's Americana & Collectibles,* it is the finest thing he has done. I'm proud of the old man.

McNulty, Lyndi Stewart. *Wallace-Homestead Price Guide to Plastic Collectibles.* Radnor, PA: Wallace-Homestead, 1987, 1992 price update.

The problem with things made of plastic is that they tend to be collected within specialized categories such as kitchen collectibles, advertising, and so on. Plastic as a category has never really caught on. McNulty's book shows the potential. Opportunity awaits.

Miller, Herrice Simons. *The Official Identification and Price Guide to Costume Jewelry.* New York, NY: Avon Books, 1994.

My heart is breaking. In order to add this book to the list, I had to drop Arthur Buy Kaplan's *The Official Identification and Price Guide to Antique Jewelry,* sixth edition (House of Collectibles: 1990)—in my opinion, the best of the jewelry price guides. The only problem is that you rarely see antique jewelry at a flea market. On the other hand, costume jewelry exists in abundance.

Morykan, Dana Gehman, and Harry L. Rinker. *Warman's Country Antiques and Collectibles,* 2nd ed. Radnor, PA: Wallace-Homestead, 1994.

This is the general text-oriented price guide to Country that has long been needed. A special feature is the names and addresses of reproduction craftspersons and manufacturers. For those who still feel the need for a picture-oriented guide, check out Don and Carol Raycraft's *Wallace-Homestead Price Guide to American Country Antiques,* 13th edition (Radnor, PA: Wallace-Homestead, 1993).

O'Brien, Richard. *Collecting Toys: A Collectors Identification and Value Guide,* 6th ed. Florence, AL: Books Americana, 1993.

The reason that there are no specialized toy or game books on this list is that you have no need for them if you own a copy of O'Brien. The book dominates the field. It is not without its weaknesses, especially in the area of post-World War II toys. However, each edition brings improvement. O'Brien has enlisted the help of specialists to price many of the sections, an approach that greatly strengthens the presentation.

Schiffer, Nancy N. *Costume Jewelry: The Fun of Collecting.* Atalen, PA: Schiffer Publishing, 1988.

Costume jewelry dominates flea market offerings. The amount of material is so large that it is virtually impossible for one book to do justice to the subject. Nancy Schiffer's book comes the closest. It uses a picture format, something that is essential since word descriptions for jewelry tend to be terribly imprecise.

Shugart, Cooksey, and Richard Gilbert. *Complete Price Guide to Watches, No. 13.* Cleveland, TN: Cooksey Shugart Publications, 1993.

Although this book has been distributed by four different publishers during the past seven years, it has never failed to maintain its high quality. It is the best book available on pocket and wrist watches.

Sports Collectors Digest. *Baseball Card Price Guide,* 8th ed. Iola, WI: Krause Publications, 1994.

This is the new kid on the block that has become a superstar. It is more comprehensive and accurate than its competition. James Beckett's *Sports Americana Baseball Card Price Guide,* published by Edgewater Books, has been relegated to bench warmer.

Swedberg, Robert W. and Harriett. *Collector's Encyclopedia of American Furniture.* **3 Volumes: Volume 1—The Dark Woods of the Nineteenth Century: Cherry, Mahogany, Rosewood, and Walnut (1991); Volume 2—Furniture of the Twentieth Century (1992); and Volume 3—Country Furniture of the Eighteenth and Nineteenth Centuries (1994). Paducah, KY: Collector Books.**

The Swedbergs write about furniture. While their most recent work is done for Collector Books, Wallace-Homestead, their previous publisher, still keeps their series on Oak, Pine, Victorian, and Wicker furniture in print. It is worth a referral from time to time. Also do not ignore the Swedbergs' *Furniture of the Depression Era: Furniture & Accessories of the 1920's, 1930's & 1940's* (Collector Books, 1987, 1994 value update). All books utilize a priced-picture approach. Text information, including descriptions for individual pieces, is minimal. Sources are heavily Midwest. The plus factor is that the books feature pieces for sale in the field, not museum examples.

Tumbusch, T. N. *Space Adventure Collectibles.* **Radnor, PA: Wallace-Homestead, 1990.**

The TV and toy markets are becoming increasingly sophisticated, *Space Adventure Collectibles* is typical of the wide range of specialized books on toy types (e.g., action figures), individual cartoon characters (e.g., Dick Tracy), and manufacturers (e.g., Tootsietoy), that are entering the market. It also demonstrates a problem found in many of these books—the use of broad price ranges that often verge on being meaningless for individual objects.

Wellbaum, Bob, ed. *Tomart's Price Guide to Garage Sale Gold.* **Radnor, PA: Wallace-Homestead, 1992.**

I have included this book because it includes a number of hot contemporary and trendy collectible topics such as Dankin and Pez. However, a word of warning is necessary. The prices were provided by individuals with strong vested interests to prop up and support high market pricing. The information is good; use the prices cautiously.

General Sources

Hyman, H. A. *I'll Buy That Too!* **Claremont, CA: Treasure Hunt Publications, 1992.**

Tony Hyman is one of the most magnetic radio personalities that I have ever heard. He writes and compiles. Most importantly, he hustles what he has done. This is a list of people who buy things. One good contact pays for the cost of the book. It is also a great place to get your collecting interests listed.

Lehner, Lois. *Lehner's Encyclopedia of U.S. Marks on Pottery, Porcelain, and Clay.* **Paducah, KY: Collector Books, 1988.**

This is the best reference book for identifying the marks of United States pottery and porcelain manufacturers. It contains detailed company histories and all known marks and trade names used. Whenever possible, marks and trade names are dated.

Kovel, Ralph and Terry. *Kovels' Antiques & Collectibles Fix-It Source Book.* **New York, NY: Crown Publishers, 1990.**

Many flea market treasures have not withstood the test of time well. While they should probably be passed by, they all too often wind up in the hands of a collector. This book provides the options available to have these objects fixed.

Maloney, David, Jr. *1994–1995 Maloney's Antiques and Collectibles Resource Directory.* **Radnor, PA: Wallace-Homestead, 1993.**

This is the one reference book to buy if you are only going to buy one. It is a comprehensive directory to the antiques and collectibles field containing approximately 6,000 entries (names, addresses, telephone numbers, and a wealth of other information) in approximately 1,500 categories. It is fully cross-referenced. It covers buyers, sellers, appraisers, restorers, collectors' clubs, periodicals, museums and galleries, show promoters, shops and malls, and many other specialists.

Manston, Peter B. *Manston's Flea Markets Antique Fairs and Auctions of Britain.* **Travel Keys (PO Box 160691, Sacramento, CA 95816, 1987).**

When you are hooked on flea markets, they become part of your blood. Some of the greatest flea markets are in Europe. Peter Manston has written three flea market guides, one each for France, Germany, and Great Britain. Do not go to Europe without them.

Miner, Robert G. *The Flea Market Handbook.* **Radnor, PA: Wallace-Homestead, 1990.**

This book explains how to become a flea market dealer. Collectors should read it to understand the mind-set of the flea market dealer. Understanding the dealer makes doing business easier.

Rainwater, Dorothy T. *Encyclopedia of American Silver Manufacturers,* **3rd ed. Atglen, PA: Schiffer Publishing, 1986.**

This book focuses on handcrafted and mass-produced factory-manufactured silver and silver plate from the mid-nineteenth century to the present. It is organized alphabetically by company. Each detailed company history is accompanied by carefully drawn and dated marks. A glossary of trademarks is another welcome feature.

Rinker, Harry L. *Rinker on Collectibles.* **Radnor, PA: Wallace-Homestead, 1989. Out of print.**

This book is a compilation of the first sixty test columns from Dad's weekly column, "Rinker on Collectibles." Many are now classics. The book allows you to delve into the mind-set of the collector. It deserves textbook status.

Wanted to Buy, 4th ed. Paducah, KY: Collector Books, 1994.

This is another book listing individuals who want to buy things. If you are a serious collector, write to Collector Books and see if your name and interests can be included in subsequent editions. The book differs from *I'll Buy That Too!* because it contains several dozen listings and prices for most categories.

Werner, Kitty, ed. The Official Directory to U.S. Flea Markets, 4th ed. New York, NY: House of Collectibles, 1994.

My opinion of this book is clearly stated earlier. Nothing has changed in my mind since I wrote that section. (see Chapter 2)

Just for the Fun of It

Gash, Jonathan. The Sleepers of Erin. New York, NY: Viking Penguin, 1983.

If you are unfamiliar with Lovejoy the antiques dealer, it is time you make his acquaintance. You will not regret it. I had a hard time picking a favorite. I could just have easily chosen *The Judas Pair, Gold by Gemini, The Grail Tree, Spend Game, The Vatican Rip,* and *The Gondola Scam,* all in paperback from Viking Penguin. *The Tartan Sell, Moonspender,* and *Pearlhanger* are in hardcover from St. Martin's Press.

Rinker, Harry L. The Joy of Collecting with Craven Moore. Radnor, PA: Wallace-Homestead, 1985. Out of print.

Try never to become so serious about your collecting or dealing that you forget to laugh and have fun. Find out if you are Craven or Anita Moore or Howie and Constance Lee Bys. You are in *The Joy of Collecting with Craven Moore.* I guarantee it. Dad still sells copies. Send him $6.00 and he will send you one.

Warman's Encyclopedia of Antiques and Collectibles

Chilton Book Company, parent company of Wallace-Homestead, has launched a series of major antiques and collectibles reference books utilizing the Warman format. Dad is in the thick of things acting as series editor. He is rather possessive about the Warman format, and who can blame him. It is a proven winner.

A few of these titles appear among the fifty books listed previously. They are there for emphasis. Actually, you should own all these titles. I strongly recommend buying them.

Bagdade, Susan and Al. *Warman's American Pottery and Porcelain* (1994).

Bagdade, Susan and Al. *Warman's English and Continental Pottery and Porcelain,* second edition (1991).

Berman, Allen, and Alex G. Malloy. *Warman's Coins & Currency* (1994).

Martinus, Norman, and Harry L. Rinker. *Warman's Paper* (1994).

Mascarelli, Gloria and Robert. *Warman's Oriental Antiques* (1992).

Morykan, Dana Gehman, and Harry L. Rinker. *Warman's Country Antiques and Collectibles* 2nd edition (1994).

Rinker, Harry L., ed. *Warman's Americana and Collectibles,* seventh edition (1995).

Rinker, Harry L., ed. *Warman's Furniture* (1993).

Romero, Christie. *Warman's Jewelry* (1995).

Schroy, Ellen Tischbein. *Warman's Glass* (1992).

Antiques and Collectibles Trade Newspapers

National

American Collector
PO Box 686
Southfield, MI 48037
(313) 351-9910

American Collector's Journal
PO Box 407
Kewanee, IL 61443
(309) 852-2602

The Antique Trader Weekly
PO Box 1050
Dubuque, IA 52004
(319) 588-2073

Antique Week (Central and Eastern
  Edition)
27 North Jefferson Street
PO Box 90
Knightstown, IN 46148
1-800-876-5133

Antiques & the Arts Weekly
Bee Publishing Company
5 Church Hill Road
Newtown, CT 06470
(203) 426-3141

Collector News
506 Second Street
Grundy Center, IA 50638
(319) 824-6981

Maine Antique Digest
PO Box 645
Waldoboro, ME 04572
(207) 832-4888 or 832-7341

Regional

NEW ENGLAND

*Antiques & Collectibles and the Long
  Island Arts Review Magazine*
PO Box 33
Westbury, NY 11590
(516) 334-9650

Cape Cod Antiques & Arts
Register Newspaper
PO Box 400
Yarmouth Port, MA 02675
(508) 362-2111

The Hudson Valley Antiquer
PO Box 561
Rhinebeck, NY 12572
(914) 876-8766

MassBay Antiques
North Shores Weekly
9 Page Street
PO Box 293
Danvers, MA 01923
(508) 777-7070 or (617) 289-6961

New England Antiques Journal
4 Church Street
Ware, MA 01082
(413) 967-3505

Unravel The Gavel
PO Box 171, Rt. 126
Ctr. Barnstead, NH 03225
(603) 269-2012

MIDDLE ATLANTIC STATES

Antique Country
Ultra Graphics
PO Box 649
Berryville, VA 22611
(703) 955-4412

*Antiquer's Guide to the Susquehanna
  Region*
PO Box 388
Sidney, NY 13838
(607) 563-8339

Antiques & Auction News
PO Box 500
Mount Joy, PA 17552
(717) 653-9797

Eastern Seaboard Antique Monthly
3611 Autumn Glen Circle
Burtonsville, MD 20866
(301) 890-0214

*The New York Antique Almanac of Art,
  Antiques, Investments & Yesteryear*
The N.Y. Eye Publishing Company
PO Box 335
Lawrence, NY 11559
(516) 371-3300

New York–Pennsylvania Collector
Drawer C
Fishers, NY 14453
(716) 924-4040

Renninger's Antique Guide
PO Box 495
Lafayette Hill, PA 19444
(215) 828-4614 or 825-6392

Treasure Chest
253 West 72nd Street, #211A
New York, NY 10023
(212) 496-2234

SOUTH

The Antique Press
12403 North Florida Avenue
Tampa, FL 33612
(813) 935-7577

The Antique Shoppe
2311 63rd Avenue East, Suite F
Bradenton, FL 34203
(813) 753-8354

Antiques & Crafts Gazette
PO Box 181
Cumming, GA 30130
(404) 887-3563

Carolina Antique News
PO Box 241114
Charlotte, NC 28224

Cotton & Quail Antique Trail
205 East Washington Street
PO Box 326
Monticello, FL 32344
(904) 997-3880

The MidAtlantic Antiques Magazine
Henderson Daily Dispatch Company
304 South Chestnut Street
PO Box 908
Henderson, NC 27536
(919) 492-4001

*The Old News Is Good News Antiques
    Gazette*
4928 Government Street
PO Box 65292
Baton Rouge, LA 70896
(504) 923-0575 or 923-0576

Southern Antiques
PO Drawer 1107
Decatur, GA 30031
(404) 289-0054

MIDWEST

*The Antique Collector and Auction
    Guide*
Weekly Section of Farm and Dairy
PO Box 38
Salem, OH 44460
(216) 337-3419

Antique Gazette
6949 Charlotte Pike, Suite 106
Nashville, TN 37209
(615) 352-0941

Antique Review
12 East Stafford Street
PO Box 538
Worthington, OH 43085
(614) 885-9757

The Buckeye Marketeer
PO Box 954
Westerville, OH 43081
(614) 895-1663

Collectors Journal
1800 West D Street
PO Box 601
Vinton, IA 52349
(319) 472-4763

Indiana Antique Buyers News, Inc.
PO Box 213
Silver Lake, IN 46982
(219) 982-7074

Michigan Antiques Trading Post
132 South Putnam
Williamstown, MI 48895
(517) 655-5621

Midwest Illinois Antiques Gazette
4 South Hill Street
Winchester, IL 62694
(217) 742-3595

Old Times
4937 Xerxes Avenue, South
Minneapolis, MN 55410
(612) 925-2531

Yesteryear
PO Box 2
Princeton, WI 54968
(414) 787-4808

SOUTHWEST

Antique & Collector's Guide
8510 Frazier Drive
Beaumont, TX 77707
(409) 866-7224

The Antique Traveler
PO Box 656
Mineola, TX 75773
(903) 569-2487

*Arizona Antiques News and Southwest
    Antiques Journal*
PO Box 26536
Phoenix, AZ 85068
(602) 943-9137

ROCKY MOUNTAIN STATES

Mountain States Collector
PO Box 2525
Evergreen, CO 80439
(303) 987-3994

WEST COAST

Antique & Collectables
Californian Publishing Co.
1000 Pioneer Way
PO Box 1565
El Cajon, CA 92022
(619) 593-2925

Antique & Collectible Marketplace
Pacific West Publications
17301 Beach Blvd, Suite 6
Huntington Beach, CA 92647
(714) 847-8500

Antiques Today
Kruse-Arett Publishing
977 Lehigh Circle
Carson City, NV 89705
(702) 267-4600

Antiques West
3315 Sacramento St., #618
San Francisco, CA 94118
(415) 221-4645

Art, Antiques & Collectibles
PO Box 750895
Petaluma, CA 94975
(707) 769-9916

Collector
436 West 4th Street, #222
Pomona, CA 91766
(714) 620-9014

The Flea Market Shoppers Guide
PO Box 400
Maywood, CA 90270
(213) 587-5100

Old Stuff
PO Box 1084
McMinnville, OR 97128
(503) 434-5386

West Coast Peddler
PO Box 5134
Whittier, CA 90607
(213) 698-1718

International

CANADA
Antique Showcase
PO Box 260
Bala, Ontario P0C 1A0
Canada

ENGLAND
Antique Trade Gazette
17 Whitcomb Street
London WC2H 7PL
England

Index